TRAVELER

great britain

NATIONAL GEOGRAPHIC
TRAVELER

great britain

by Christopher Somerville
photography by Alison Wright

National Geographic
Washington, D.C.

CONTENTS

Pages 2–3: Milton Abbas, a charming, classic Dorset village
Opposite: The Highland bagpipe dates from the 15th century, possibly even earlier.

TRAVELING WITH EYES OPEN

Alert travelers go with a purpose and leave with a benefit. If you travel responsibly, you can help support wildlife conservation, historic preservation, and cultural enrichment in the places you visit. You can enrich your own travel experience as well.

To be a geo-savvy traveler:

- Recognize that your presence has an impact on the places you visit.

- Spend your time and money in ways that sustain local character. (Besides, it's more interesting that way.)

- Value the destination's natural and cultural heritage.

- Respect the local customs and traditions.

- Express appreciation to local people about things you find interesting and unique to the place: its nature and scenery, music and food, historic villages and buildings.

- Vote with your wallet: Support the people who support the place, patronizing businesses that make an effort to celebrate and protect what's special there. Seek out shops, local restaurants, inns, and tour operators who love their home—who love taking care of it and showing it off. Avoid businesses that detract from the character of the place.

- Enrich yourself, taking home memories and stories to tell, knowing that you have contributed to the preservation and enhancement of the destination.

That is the type of travel now called geotourism, defined as "tourism that sustains or enhances the geographical character of a place—its environment, culture, aesthetics, heritage, and the well-being of its residents." To learn more, visit National Geographic's Center for Sustainable Destinations at *www .nationalgeographic.com/travel/sustainable.*

great britain

ABOUT THE AUTHOR & THE PHOTOGRAPHER

Christopher Somerville spent his childhood in a remote village in rural Gloucestershire, where he reveled in the freedom to roam the woods, fields, and riverbanks. This upbringing gave him a lifelong love of walking in the open air and a taste for the quieter corners of the British countryside.

During the 15 years he spent as a schoolteacher, he wrote several books about walking and landscape. A lucky break gave him the chance to swap the rigors of the classroom for the pleasures and uncertainties of travel journalism. He has written some 40 books, including guidebooks, walking guides, and personal travel accounts. Somerville writes regularly for the *Times* (he is its Walking Correspondent) and other national publications about his travels, on foot and otherwise, in the hidden corners of Britain and Europe.

Island communities and their way of life fascinate him, particularly in the Celtic fringe of Scotland and Ireland.

Alison Wright, a New York–based documentary photographer, has spent a career capturing the universal human spirit through her photographs. For many of her editorial and commercial projects, Wright travels to all corners of the globe photographing endangered cultures and people while documenting issues concerning the human condition. Wright's photography is represented by the National Geographic Image collection and is published in a number of National Geographic books and publications.

She is a recipient of the Dorothea Lange Award in Documentary Photography and a two-time winner of the Lowell Thomas Travel Journalism Award. On January 2, 2000, Wright's life was nearly cut short in a bus accident on a remote jungle road in Laos. Her memoir, *Learning to Breathe: One Woman's Journey of Spirit and Survival,* chronicles her story of survival and years of rehabilitation, and her ongoing determination to recover and continue traveling the world as a photojournalist.

Charting Your Trip

"This precious stone set in the silver sea, ... This blessed plot, this earth, this realm, this England." Shakespeare's image from *King Richard II* names England, but it's the British mainland and its off-islands—green, neat, timeless—that these phrases bring vividly to the mind's eye. There is more variety of landscape, culture, history, and tradition in this "blessed plot"—for its modest size—than anywhere else on Earth.

Getting Around

Car rental in Great Britain can be expensive, so you are well advised, if possible, to rent as part of an overall vacation package. Traveling by train is generally a fast and worry-free way to get around, while air travel is really only worth considering over long distances in such a small archipelago—for instance from London to Edinburgh. There are numerous bus companies, for both short- and long-distance travel. Ferries ply to almost all the inhabited offshore islands. Caledonian MacBrayne is the company you'll need if you are visiting the Scottish islands. See Travelwise (pp. 336–337) for detailed information on getting around Britain.

How to Visit: If You Only Have a Week

This recommended loop covers some 500 to 600 miles and starts in London. On **Day 1,** take an early morning stroll around Westminster, Soho, or the City or walk along the Thames Path through historic London. A spin on the big observation wheel of the London Eye, opposite Big Ben and the Houses of Parliament, offers a wonderful overview. That evening, drive the 15 miles west down the M4 motorway to Windsor Castle, and spend the night in a cozy inn here or farther out along the River Thames.

On **Day 2,** set off early in the morning for the chalk downs of Salisbury Plain and Stonehenge (about 90 miles west of London), mightiest of Europe's prehistoric monuments, to catch the spirit of ancient Britain. Then nip northwest about an hour to the M4 and across the Severn Bridge to get a taste of the border country of Wales—the Wye Valley up to Monmouth, for example. In the evening, return into England and make for Bath, a Georgian masterpiece of silver-gold stone.

Spend the morning of **Day 3** exploring Bath, Jane Austen's favorite spa town, then slowly make your way northeast for 70 miles across the rolling Cotswold Hills with their golden stone villages to arrive in Oxford by teatime. Enjoy a leisurely evening walk among the university "dreaming spires," and a pint or two in a famous old pub—perhaps the Eagle and Child (aka the "Bird and Baby") in St. Giles.

Big Ben, iconic clock tower of the Houses of Parliament

On the morning of **Day 4,** an hour's drive northwest brings you to Stratford-upon-Avon and the gorgeous timber-framed houses that William Shakespeare lived and loved in. Get away north by lunchtime and you can be in Derbyshire's beautiful Peak District by midafternoon. Visit the Duke of Devonshire's magnificent country mansion, Chatsworth House, or take a walk up narrow Dovedale under overhanging spires of rock. Continue north a couple of hours on **Day 5** by way of Howarth and the moors that inspired authors Charlotte, Emily, and Anne Brontë. Still heading north, wend through the undulating green landscapes of the Yorkshire Dales, of which Wharfedale is the cream of the crop. About an hour northwest of here lie the fells (mini-mountains), lakes, and narrow valleys of the Lake District National Park, playground of the Romantics.

Spend the night among these magical hills, and most of **Day 6** exploring them. Climb 3,210-foot Scafell Pike, the highest hill in England, visit William Wordsworth's Dove Cottage in Grasmere, or just wander through the fabulous mountain scenery of Borrowdale. Then it's a long, beautiful evening drive north for 100 miles through the wild hills of the Scottish Borders to Edinburgh, Scotland's capital, 330 miles from London. While away **Day 7** with a visit to Edinburgh Castle and the historic Old and New Towns, before returning your rental car at Edinburgh airport and taking a 1.25-hour flight back south to London.

NOT TO BE MISSED:

The view of London from the London Eye big wheel **89**

Visiting Stonehenge, at dawn or sunset if possible **135, 138**

The 'Obby 'Oss in Padstow on Merrie May Morning **147**

Magnificent Caernarfon Castle, an Iron Ring fortress **170–171**

Take Simon Jenkins's *England's Thousand Best Churches* on an East Anglian church crawl **219**

Pennine views from the Settle & Carlisle Railway **258**

Walking the remarkable city walls of York **268–269**

The fun of a Scottish ceilidh **330**

If You Have More Time

You'll be able to do better justice to Shakespeare's blessed plot if you have more time to stay longer along the route above or venture farther afield.

London & the Home Counties: You could spend several additional days in London alone, visiting its many great museums and theaters, vibrant multicultural markets, and world-famous shops like Harrods. In the Home Counties (the countryside around London), make time for **Hever Castle** and **Penshurst Place,** and for a walk in the beechwoods of the **Chiltern Hills** to the northwest of London (vast bluebell carpets in spring).

Visitor Information

England, Scotland, and Wales each has its own tourist board. **Visit Britain** *(tel 020-8846 9000, www.visitbritain.com)* is the port of call for information concerning Great Britain as a whole. **Enjoy England** *(www.enjoyengland.com)* promotes England in particular. In Wales the national tourist authority is **Visit Wales** *(tel 08708-300 306, www.visitwales.co.uk).* Scotland's tourist authority is **Visit Scotland** *(tel 0131 332 2433, www.visitscotland.com).* See Travelwise (p. 340) for more information.

South Country & West Country: On the Sussex coast, an hour south of London by train, bustling, bohemian, self-consciously weird **Brighton** gives you the full-throttle English seaside experience. Moving west along the coast about 40 miles, you'll find Admiral Nelson's flagship Victory in **Portsmouth**'s Historic Dockyard, and farther on the Jurassic Coast of **Dorset** and **Devon,** whose multicolored, contorted cliffs are packed with 300 million years of fossils. At the southwesternmost tip of England lies **Cornwall,** with cream teas, sandy beaches, and the artists' haven of **St. Ives.**

East Anglia: The region north and east of London, East Anglia is famous for flatness and for its wonderful medieval wool towns of Thaxted, Saffron Walden, Kersey, and Lavenham. **Norfolk,** about 80 miles northeast of London, has the finest old churches in Britain, glorious celebrations of faith and of medieval wool wealth. And don't forget the architectural glories of **Cambridge University,** and farther north the windswept, empty beaches of the **Lincolnshire** coast. **Essex,** fringing East Anglia to the south, is often overlooked by visitors; there's fine rolling country in the north of the county, and a moody, gritty atmosphere along the Thames shore.

The Midlands: About 80 miles northwest of London in the Midlands counties, the waist of England, don't miss the "mountains-in-miniature" of the **Malvern Hills,** surrounded by the superb cathedrals of **Gloucester, Worcester,** and **Hereford.** Ten miles northeast of Stratford-upon-Avon, **Warwick Castle** is all you want a medieval fortress to be. Exploring the canals and curry houses of multicultural **Birmingham** is fun.

Wales: West of the Midlands run the hills of the **Welsh Borders,** leading to the lonely uplands, beautiful coasts, and mountains of Wales—the border is about 120 miles west of London. The **Big Pit Mining Museum** north of Cardiff in South Wales shows how much of the world's wealth was founded on Welsh coal; at the opposite (northwest) corner of the country, **Mount Snowdon,** ringed by spectacular mountains, challenges you to climb.

Edinburgh Castle perches high above the city atop the massive bulk of volcanic Castle Rock.

North Country: The north of England is a treat. The prime hiking country of **Derbyshire'**s White Peak (limestone) and Dark Peak (gritstone moors) gives way to the **Yorkshire Dales** with their green valleys, rugged moors, and stone-built walls and barns. The **North York Moors** roll in the east, moody and somber, and between the two is the lovely old city of **York** (200 miles north of London) with a huge minster church and intact medieval city walls. **Durham,** an hour north of York, is another compact, fascinating city, based around a towering Norman cathedral. A short drive north of here lies the greatest Roman monument in these islands—**Hadrian's Wall.**

Scotland: As for Scotland . . . it isn't all Edinburgh (see p. 9). Adventures abound—landing on **Bass Rock,** off the east coast, among 100,000 gannets; walking over wild country such as **Glen Coe** (80 miles north of Glasgow); climbing the **Highland Munros** peaks; or sailing and sea kayaking in the west coast's sea lochs. Golf fans should make for **St. Andrews** (30 miles northeast of Edinburgh) and the Royal and Ancient's hallowed fairways, while whisky connoisseurs should hit the Highlands distilleries of **Speyside'**s Whisky Trail. And if in search of peace and quiet, you need only lace up your boots and set off up any one of 10,000 beautiful hillsides. ∎

When to Go

Great Britain is temperate with generally mild springs and autumns, warm summers, and cool winters. Visit in spring (late March–May) for new leaves, fresh green colors, and wildflowers; summer (June–late Sept.) for the seaside and for outdoor festivals; autumn (Oct.–Nov.) for local fruit and spectacular tree colors; and winter (Dec.–March) for crisp, cold days, warm pubs, and the chance of frost and snow, especially in the Scottish Highlands.

History & Culture

The Union Flag, popularly called the Union Jack
Opposite: Timber-framed buildings, remnants of the Tudor era, line a street in Cambridge.

Great Britain Today

Great Britain—an archipelago nation made up of England, Scotland, and Wales—is quite small, measuring only 900-odd miles from top to bottom. Yet this little group of islands off Europe's northwest coast has influenced world culture as profoundly as any nation in history.

Visitors are coming in growing numbers to Britain—not just to enjoy the celebrated beauty of its green hills and meadows and its historic medieval towns and villages, nor simply to see where William Shakespeare was born, or where the Queen lives, or where the Beatles started out. Many come because they feel an empathy with these islands and their people, perhaps because of a shared

Opened in 2000, the London Eye has become a major landmark and tourist attraction.

language, perhaps because strands of so many cultures all over the world are closely interwoven with Britain's.

The British themselves—this motley mingling of Saxons, West Indians, Celts, Normans, Indians, Chinese, Africans, Danes, and others—stand at a cultural crossroads these days. They are justifiably proud of their history, of the great poets and writers, statesmen and thinkers, scientists and social reformers who have been nurtured in these small islands. They cherish the rich theater of pageantry bequeathed to them by history. They look with deep satisfaction on their ancient patchwork of farming landscapes, their half-timbered medieval houses, their remote mountain ranges. They take pride in their regional chauvinism, their strongly differentiated local accents, the subtle changes of flavor in beer or nuance of humor from one county to the next.

The British accept that their God-given right to a seat at the top table of world politics is no longer automatic.

Yet they see themselves at the same time as only one smallish society in a modern, competitive world. The British accept that their God-given right to a seat at the top table of world politics is no longer automatic. Their former certainties and sense of superiority are largely gone.

The political union among Scotland, England, and Wales—perhaps between these three and Northern Ireland, too—seems to be easing apart, not necessarily for the worse. The nation's hesitant, equivocal attitude toward closer links with Europe—a legal reality since 1973, but certainly not yet a political, social, economic, or emotional one—reflects this fairly general desire to preserve the historic status of the British as independent islanders while engaging positively with the wider world.

Meanwhile, that wider world continues to value the British for qualities which, with characteristic self-deprecation, they themselves would hardly admit to possessing: a sense of fun and fairness, a politeness and consideration for others developed of necessity by this multicultural society that lives cheek by jowl on an overcrowded island, dry humor laced copiously with irony, and a balanced way of dealing with each other and with strangers.

A decade into the third millennium, the British find themselves in a period of self-examination. In common with the rest of the developed world, the country took an enormous knock in the financial downturn of 2007–2010. Overexposure of the banking system; the fat-cat lifestyle of City brokers, bankers, and speculators; a shortage of credit and confidence—all these led to a good deal of national breast-beating and navel-gazing. Bankers were hauled over the coals; wage freezes were announced; and a general election in May 2010 ejected the long-serving Labour government (in power since 1997) in favor of a coalition between the historically uneasy bedfellows of the Conservative and Liberal Democrat parties. Government spending cuts, tax hikes, and decades of austerity were trailed before a somewhat skeptical public, which had heard this sort of thing before. In truth, Great Britain's continuing reluctance to adopt the European Union's official currency, the euro, proved to be a blessing, as the contagion of some member states' wobbly economies began to spread via Greece, Spain, Portugal, and Ireland. At the start of 2011, though the U.K. job market was weak and the governmental belt had been significantly tightened, things had steadied. Few of the British, however, wanted to hear champagne corks popping and limousines revving in the City yet a while.

> **At the start of 2011, though the U.K. job market was weak and the governmental belt had been significantly tightened, things had steadied.**

Who exactly are the British? That was the question rising again in the national consciousness during the late Noughties (as the 2000–2009 decade was dubbed). In 2009 net migration into the United Kingdom (more immigrants than emigrants) was 198,000, roughly the same figures as for the preceding four years. Of those, about two-thirds came from non-EU countries. How would these newcomers, many of them non-English speakers, fit in with the inhabitants of this already crowded archipelago? The answer, generally speaking, is what it has always been in this island nation with its ever changing demographic—with a bit of tolerance and give-and-take from both quarters, people get along as people tend to do. Seen in the round, the new Britons have contributed new ideas, customs, and traditions to the spicy stewpot of British culture, which is now undoubtedly one of the richest and most vibrant in the world.

Britons Rediscover Britain

One remarkable aspect of this recent (and ongoing) audit of themselves by the British has been a reengagement with a national asset they had all but forgotten— their own countryside. The causes may have ranged from an eco-aware disenchant- ment with long-distance flying to a sense that they had had enough of cheap wine and sunburn, but within the decade of the Noughties the holidaymaking British shortened their focus from an obsession with all things foreign, sun-drenched, and widescreen, and began to appreciate once more what was under their own noses. BBC-TV's surprise monster hit *Coast*, a series that revealed the coastline of Britain in all its beauty and complexity, was followed by a whole rash of programs about landscape, hiking, swimming, and outdoor survival. Books with the word "wild" in their title flew off the shelves, the finest of them Robert Macfarlane's *Wild Places*. Sports and active pursuits in the open air became all the rage. Walking in the coun- tryside—using a map, GPS, and Britain's unrivaled network of public footpaths—is now the nation's favorite leisure activity. And visitors to Britain have found them- selves the beneficiaries of a great increase of help, information, and infrastructure in enjoying the great outdoors. ■

EXPERIENCE: Join in the Fun of Multicultural Britain

Visitors from all over the world remark on one thing in particular when they first set foot in Great Britain: the multicultural society that thrives here. As a seafaring and sea-trading nation, Britain has always had a tradition of immigrants settling in its ports and major cities. Add to this a long-standing British tradition of welcoming refugees, and it's not surprising to find a tremendous mixture of creeds, beliefs, lifestyles, and ways of working and relaxing in these islands.

Notwithstanding the occasional clash and misunderstanding, the nation has been hugely enriched by multiculturalism—in general terms, by many different peoples learning to live, work, and play side by side; and in specific cultural ways, through a fertile cross-referencing of music, song, dance, cooking, humor, and especially celebration.

The street carnivals and public celebrations of many ethnic communities are one of the treasures of modern Britain. The Caribbean-flavored **Notting Hill Carnival** (www.thenottinghillcarni val.com) in central west London every August Bank Holiday is probably the best known, with dancers and musicians in fabulously elaborate costumes and headdresses sharing the streets with Caribbean food stalls, sideshows, sidewalk vendors, ear-splitting sound systems, and thousands of onlookers. Many former industrial towns and cities in Britain boast Afro-Caribbean communities, and several have spawned their own carnivals: Leeds (textiles), for example, holds its **West Indian Carnival** (www.leeds carnival.co.uk) in late August, and Luton (carmaking) stages its **Caribbean**

Skimpily clad dancers add color and bring the heat to London's Notting Hill Carnival, an annual fete of all things Caribbean.

Carnival (www.lutontoday.co .uk/carnival) on May Bank Holiday. Bristol, home of several genres of music with a Caribbean beat, puts on the splendid **St. Paul's Carnival** (www.stpaulscarnival.co.uk) on the first Saturday in July.

Britain's sizable Indian community celebrates **Diwali,** the Hindu festival of lights, at the end of October with fireworks, dancing, and street fun throughout the land. Among many venues are Trafalgar Square in central London (www.london.gov .uk/diwali), George Square in Glasgow, Birmingham (www .birmingham.gov.uk/diwali), and Leicester.

Chinese New Year in late January or February is marked with riotous festivities—complete with fireworks, dancing dragons, vigorous music, and tasty Chinese street food—in city Chinatown areas. Newcastle, Sheffield, Manchester (see sidebar p. 249), Liverpool, Birmingham, Cardiff, Belfast, Southampton, Brighton, and Plymouth offer great public shows (www.enjoyengland .com/attractions/events/ calendar/february/chinese-new-year.aspx), as does London's Trafalgar Square and Leicester Square area of Chinatown (www.londonchina town.org).

Land & Environment

Great Britain boasts mountains and moors, plains and bogs, arctic plateaus and parched pebble shores, nurturing a treasury of wild creatures, trees, and flowers—glories that are being cared for by a host dedicated organizations.

History of the Land

Mainland Britain has an astonishing variety of landscape, from rocky northern mountains nearly three billion years old to flat fields in East Anglia that were only reclaimed from the sea within the last century.

Dramatic basalt pinnacles point to the volcanic origins of Scotland's Isle of Skye.

Reading the landscape from the oldest to the newest means starting in the west: the volcanic rocks of the Scottish highlands and islands, the highest peaks of the Lake District in Cumbria and Snowdonia in Wales, and the granite heart of Dartmoor and Cornwall down in southwestern England. Some of these hard materials were formed of solidified molten rock—granite, basalt, gabbro, and dolerite. Some were transformed by immense heat and pressure—quartzite, gneiss, schist.

The carboniferous limestone of the Pennines, where flower-rich pastures grow, was formed from the shells of countless marine creatures.

Around 400 million years ago, upheavals exposed rocks around central and southern Scotland and the mountains of Wales. They formed gigantic mountain ranges, which were gradually worn away by wind and weather into the confused jumble of shales, slates, gritstones, and schists that now underlie some of Britain's most beautiful mountains and moorlands.

Looking at a geological map of Britain, you can see great snaking bands of limestone, gritstone, and old red sandstone. This sandstone underpins the cliff and coastal country of southwest Scotland and northwest England, parts of the Welsh Borders, and north Devon and Exmoor; it was formed of compressed sand from a vast red desert that filled the center of Britain 400 million years ago.

The gritstone that underlies the moors of southern Yorkshire and Lancashire is an amalgam of particles of sand and stone deposited by ancient rivers in prehistoric estuaries.

The carboniferous limestone of the Pennines, where flower-rich pastures grow, was formed from the shells of countless marine creatures. In parts of Lancashire, Yorkshire, Nottinghamshire, County Durham, and South Wales it contains layers of vegetation, compressed and hardened into coal.

Oolitic limestone forms a thick 300-mile belt that crosses the country from the North Yorkshire coast by way of the Lincolnshire Wolds, the eastern Midland uplands, and the Cotswold Hills, running down through Bath and Somerset into Dorset and on to the Devon coast. Formed some 200 million years ago from grains of sand surrounded by calcium carbonate, it is sometimes called "roestone," or "eggstone," because of its surface, which looks like a mass of close-packed fish eggs. Oolitic limestone varies in color from pale silver to deep honey-orange and enriches buildings in towns such as Stamford, Cirencester, and Bath.

Chalk, the foundation of much of southern England, is also formed from the shells of marine creatures—in this case minute organisms called foraminifera, which lived and died in the shallow waters of the Great Chalk Sea that drowned most of northern Europe about 100 million years ago. Unimaginable numbers of these minuscule shells accumulated on the bed of this sea—enough to have formed a layer which today, at Walbury Hill in Hampshire, extends down from the 1,000-foot hilltop to sea level, and on down beneath the water for a further 650 feet. The chalk blanket covered most of Britain after the sea receded; but subsequent weathering, along with a breaking up and sloughing off during subterranean upheavals, saw the erosion and disappearance of much of the layer. What remains of the chalk layer is especially impressive in the curves of the chalk downs, and in the rampart of cliffs along the south coast.

> **What remains of the chalk layer is especially impressive in the curves of the chalk downs, and in the rampart of cliffs along the south coast.**

Until the coming of the four great ice ages, rivers continued to drag clay, sand, and pebbles southeast toward the North Sea coasts of southern Britain. The ice ages themselves (about 600,000 B.C. to 12,000 B.C.) finished the shaping of Britain, as their glaciers gouged valleys through the hard rock of the mountains and smoothed out the softer rocks farther south. Meltwaters during the thaws brought down more silt and gravel, spreading a thick blanket of tilth and clay across East Anglia and the southeastern corner of the island that today—along with land reclaimed by man from the sea—provides Britain's most fertile arable soil.

Off the Beaten Track

Almost every visitor to Britain wants to see Big Ben, Shakespeare's birthplace, Edinburgh Castle, and the other main tourist attractions. But there is another Britain, one that most visitors never see. If you want a taste of that, you will need to slow down, take time for conversations, and penetrate odd corners of the country. Here are a few suggestions for quirky, stimulating sidesteps that will introduce you to Britain's unique countryside:

South Country Romney Marsh and Dungeness in southeast Kent.

West Country The Lizard Peninsula and Bodmin Moor in Cornwall.

Wales The Valleys north of Cardiff; the Wye Valley; the wild tip of the Lleyn Peninsula.

East Anglia The beautiful Deben estuary and bleakly haunting Orford Ness in Suffolk.

Northwest England Forest of Bowland moors and former mill towns; the little-visited coastline west of the Lake District.

Northeast England Out-of-this-world Spurn Head on the Yorkshire coast.

Scotland Unvisited southwest Galloway; the Moray Firth coast; any of the islands.

Climate

The archipelago of the British Isles lies alongside the warm flow of the North Atlantic Current, but is comparatively far north (London shares its latitude with Saskatoon, Canada, and Warsaw, Poland). Oceanic warmth, generally cold air, moisture-laden winds and a coastline of 20,000 miles have ensured these islands a temperate climate— mild wet springs, warm summers, mild autumns with a few storms, and winters that are cold enough for snow but not that cold.

Flora & Fauna

These various factors—the great variety of rocks and landforms, the wide assortment of soil types and their associated plants, and a temperate climate—assure a supply of food and shelter for an enviable diversity of wild-life, especially insects, plants, birds of passage, and resident birds.

Trouble in Paradise: The wildlife of Britain took a tremendous hammering in the mid- to late 20th century, due to postwar farming policies that set great store by production through intensive agricultural methods. More than 80 percent of all hedgerows, wildflower meadows, and wetlands were lost. Pesticides, herbicides, and fertilizers were sprayed whole-sale. Meanwhile, development of roads and housing destroyed farmland, meadows, and woods. Songbird, butterfly, insect, hawk, owl, and mammal numbers all dropped, and wild-flower diversity diminished drastically, too.

But legislative protection by European Union designation, by conservation groups, and by individual action is now, at last, on the increase. Recent changes in EU agricultural policy, too, mean that intensive agribusiness monoculture is less attractive than it was.

Red deer, Britain's largest mammal, range across open moors and hills as well as in forests.

There are still plenty of primrose banks and bluebell woods in spring; lane verges full of campion, wild garlic, cranesbill, and sweet cicely in summer; and hedgerows sheltering the nests of yellowhammers, dunnocks, and chaffinches. Up on the northern moors you can hear the haunting, bubbling call of curlew. In the Scottish mountains golden eagles, mountain hares, and pockets of relict post–Ice Age flowers are still there. Red kites in Wales and elsewhere have flourished, bringing the species back from the brink of extinction. And blue-legged, high-stepping avocets now breed on the marshy islets of the Suffolk coast, having returned after the war to a Britain in which they had been shot to extinction during the previous century. ■

Local Festivities

An aspect of British life that has resisted all attempts to stifle or dilute it is the nation's remarkable penchant for local customs, festivals, ceremonies, and other forms of more or less eccentric ritual. Some have deep traditional or religious roots and mysterious significance; others are bogus bits of invented hokum. All are good fun, and worth a look if you are in the area.

The midwinter Up Helly Aa in Shetland culminates with the burning of a full-size Viking longship.

January

1—New Year's Day.
25—Burns Night: Scotland's celebration of national poet Robert Burns.
Last Tuesday—Up Helly Aa: The Shetland islanders' vigorous celebration of midwinter (see sidebar p. 333).

February

Late January/February—Chinese New Year: Firecrackers and dragons, celebrated in London, Glasgow, Manchester (see p. 249), and other cities.

Mid-month—Viking Festival: Ceremonial boat-burning and reenactments of battles in York mark the founding of the Viking city, Jorvik.

March

17—St. Patrick's Day: Celebrations by Irish communities of their patron saint.
Shrove Tuesday—Pancake Day races; street soccer game at Corfe in Dorset.

April

Easter Monday—Hare Pie Scramble and Bottle Kicking at Hallaton, Leicestershire (see p. 197).

23—St. George's Day: Celebrations in many English towns and villages.

May

May Day—'Obby 'Oss, Padstow, Cornwall: Crazy capers (see sidebar p. 147).
8—Furry Dance, Helston, Cornwall: In and out of the houses in a floral dance.
Ascension Day (40 days after Easter)—Decking the wells with floral pictures in Tissington and other Derbyshire villages.
Last Monday in May—Spring Bank Holiday: Cheese-rolling and breakneck running down a precipitous slope at Cooper's Hill, near Brockworth, Gloucestershire.

June

Mid-month—Appleby Horse Fair, Cumbria: Gypsies and horse dealers assemble for the great annual travelers' get-together.
24—Druids welcome Midsummer Day dawn at Stonehenge.

July

Second Saturday—Durham Miners' Gala: Banners, speeches, and pit-related nostalgia.
Third week—Swan Upping at Cookham, Berkshire: Counting the Queen's and others' swans on the Thames.

August

First week—Royal National Eisteddfod: Welsh arts and music; changing venues.
Third Wednesday—Priddy Fair, Somerset: Sheep auctions and fairground hucksters on top of the Mendip Hills in a unique country fair, over 650 years old.

September

First Saturday—Braemar Gathering: Caber tossing and traditional sports in the presence of the Royal Family.

October

First Thursday–Saturday—Nottingham Goose Fair: One of Britain's most spectacular fairs.

In medieval times this was the largest hiring fair in the Midlands, where thousands came to find work. As for the geese—upward of 20,000 were sold in one weekend.
31—Halloween: Children hollow out pumpkins to make faces and dress up as witches.

November

Early in month—Bridgwater Guy Fawkes Carnival, Somerset: Britain's largest nighttime carnival, starting in Bridgwater and visiting small Somerset towns over ten days.
5—Bonfire Night/Guy Fawkes Night: Fires and fireworks mark the failed Gunpowder Plot of 1605. One of the largest events is at Lewes in East Sussex, with an effigy burning of Guy Fawkes.

December

26—Boxing Day: Traditionally, a day when the gentry gave presents to servants.
31—Allendale Tar Barrelers, Northumberland: Men parade with blazing headpieces.
31—Hogmanay: Traditional Scottish celebration of New Year (see sidebar p. 303).

Gypsy caravans, Appleby Horse Fair, Cumbria

History of Great Britain

The first hunters were active in Britain from the end of the first great ice age, around 250,000 B.C. Some probably ventured across the English Channel and North Sea land bridges during the warmer periods between the following ice ages, but it wasn't until after the last big freeze, around 10,000 B.C., that Paleolithic or early Stone Age hunter-gatherers arrived in any numbers.

They followed the northward creep of the tundra as the climate warmed up. By the time the Neolithic or late Stone Age farmers arrived from the Mediterranean region around 3700 B.C., a tribally owned, patchwork landscape was appearing. Britain was now an island cluster, thanks to rising sea levels. The newcomers brought skills of animal husbandry; they planted wheat and barley, and slashed and burned more forest, especially across the downs of southern England with their easily worked chalk soils.

The clever immigrants known as "Beaker Folk"—from the fine pottery vessels they buried with their dead—arrived about 2000 B.C. With them they brought the secret of bronze from the Iberian Peninsula and the Low Countries of Europe.

The dark-haired Celts who came across from France about 600 B.C. imported ironmaking and efficient plows. They were skilled warriors, builders of hill forts, druidical worshipers, jewelers and swordsmiths, singers and poets. On the outer and western fringes of Britain, such strains live on.

For 250 years, the Romans dominated life in Britain with their effective, practical methods.

Roman Occupation

The Romans' first attempt to invade Britain was tentative—Julius Caesar arrived in 54 B.C., met some resistance from the Britons, and departed. In A.D. 43, four legions landed, with orders from Emperor Claudius to stay put. By A.D. 50 they had captured Caractacus, chief of the Catuvellauni, and by A.D. 61 they had survived the hurricane rebellion by the Iceni under Queen Boudicca. By A.D. 84 Julius Agricola, working with small units of well-trained, efficient soldiers, had subdued all of England and as much as was thought necessary of Scotland and Wales. Between A.D. 122 and A.D. 128, Hadrian's Wall was built across the 73-mile neck of land between the Tyne and the Solway Firth—a solid northern boundary to the entire Roman Empire.

For 250 years, the Romans dominated life in Britain with their effective, practical methods. They laid down well-engineered highways such as Ermine Street from London to York and Hadrian's Wall, and Watling Street from London to Chester. They built a network of byways to open up the forested hinterland. They cultivated an extensive acreage of corn, and cleared pastureland. They drained fens and marshlands. They mined coal, silver, tin, lead, and gold. They built towns such as Verulamium (St. Albans), Glevum (Gloucester), Camulodunum (Colchester), and Eboracum (York). They laid out estates with beautiful villas and created wonderful mosaic floors, intricate gold ornaments, marble statues, and delicate glassware.

Ancient history still imprints Britain's landscape, including the Bronze Age Stonehenge.

Lasting Legacy

The Romans built to last and left their treasures scattered in the earth when their 400-year occupation came to an end. What they built can be seen most dramatically along the 73 miles of Hadrian's Wall (see pp. 284–285) in Northumberland, and in the foundations of the Roman baths (see p. 154) at Bath, the town of Verulamium (see p. 111) at St. Albans, the palace at Fishbourne (see p. 127) in Sussex, the villa at Chedworth (see p. 183) in Gloucestershire, and the foundations of Colchester Castle (see p. 213) in Essex. Their jewelry, statuary, and glass is shown in county museums up and down the country—most stunningly in the intact and beautiful silverware of the Mildenhall Treasure, found in Suffolk and now displayed in Room 49 of the British Museum (see pp. 71–73).

Yet they could not maintain their overstretched empire indefinitely. Shortly after A.D. 400, the last of the legions packed up and marched away.

Pastoralists & North Sea Wolves

There was a hiatus of perhaps 40 years, during which the works of the Romans began to crumble back into encroaching fen and forest. Then the blue-eyed, fair-haired Saxons came from the Low Countries in waves of immigration that lasted 200 years. King Arthur, often taken to be a mythical figure, may in fact have been a Romano-British chief whose battles against the new invaders passed into legend.

Taming the Land: These Anglo-Saxons established villages, usually near rivers, which offered them drink, transportation, and irrigation. Their laws were democratic, the rules being hammered out in council. They made huge inroads on Britain's remaining wildwood and cleared big swaths for agriculture, plowing with cooperatively owned ox teams. We read their settlement names in suffixes today: "-ton," a settlement by a river; "-ley," a clearing; "-ham," a flat pasture; "-wick," an animal farm. And we find their memorials all over Britain, from King Offa's great dike along the Welsh Borders to the gold and garnet treasures of the Sutton Hoo ship burial in Suffolk, now on display in the British Museum.

With a certain amount of fighting and feuding, the Saxons parceled part of Britain into a number of adjoining kingdoms—the chief ones being Wessex (southwest), Kent (southeast), Mercia (Midlands), East Anglia (east), and Northumbria (northeast). But the seafaring, warlike Danes (known as Vikings when raiding and plundering) had other ideas when they crossed the North Sea late in the eighth century and began three centuries of forcible settlement.

The monastic communities that had established themselves on the east-facing coasts were the first to suffer from the Danes' hunger for new land. The raids became a long-drawn-out immigration surge, violent and unstoppable. Some compromise and alliance-building became possible after Alfred the Great, King of Wessex (r. 871–899), defeated the Danes in 878. Some of the Norsemen settled the north of the country, as place-names on the map tell us—"beck," a stream; "-by," a farm; "thwaite," a meadow clearing. They themselves endured attacks from their former compatriots. It was not until after the next—and last—successful invasion of Britain that the North Sea wolves ceased to bite.

Northmen from France

Great castles symbolized the power of the Normans, and their will to stay and to dominate after they had defeated the Anglo-Saxon army under King Harold II (r. 1066) at Hastings on October 14, 1066. These Frenchified Norsemen were—like the Romans a thousand years before—efficient, ruthless, and highly effective. Under their dynamic king, William I (r. 1066–1087), they crushed resistance in the north. The Domesday Book survey (1085–86) showed the king exactly what he and every-one else owned, and what it was worth—a typically Norman achievement.

William the Conqueror's victory at the Battle of Hastings in 1066 ushered in Britain's Norman age.

Their Influence: The Normans changed the flavor of Britain. The Anglo-Saxon landlords were replaced by barons and bishops, whose power soon grew to challenge that of the king, and French and ecclesiastical Latin became the official languages for the next 150 years. With their close blood and trade links to the Continent, the Anglo-Normans invited French monastic orders to establish branches in Britain, bringing with them an increase in learning and culture.

Once the Norman succession had been resolved after the Civil War of 1135–1154, Henry II established the Plantagenet dynasty. It lasted through the 12th-century Crusades to the Holy Land; the Barons' Wars of 1215–1217 and 1263–1267, that saw the power of the barons reduced; and on to the end of the 14th century, by which time the Normans' successors were venturing back across the water to fight for the throne of France.

Norman Castles

The first castles, built shortly after the Norman Conquest, were of wood—a keep (stronghold) on a motte (mound), with a bailey (walled garrison enclosure) on an adjacent motte. None of these now remain.

Henry II (r. 1154–1189) ordered his turbulent barons to seek his permission before building a castle, and from then on building was in stone, with elaborate defenses—moat, portcullis, murder holes, offset entrances. Curtain walls were introduced early in the 13th century to divide the bailey into three wards (walled areas), and gatehouses and projecting barbicans (fortified courtyards) were added.

Castles were the focal point of warfare until the introduction of gunpowder and cannon, and a sharp reduction in the power of the barons, tipped them toward obsolescence.

Middle Ages

During the Middle Ages, wool-rich East Anglia became Britain's most populous and prosperous region. The feudal system, in which peasants worked their own strips of farmland and their lord's under allegiance and obligation to him, was in full swing. Monks drained many marshland areas, reclaiming the land for agriculture, and built sea banks. Houses began to be built unfortified as the barons' feuds subsided. Roads improved, towns grew apace, usually around castles, and their craftsmen organized themselves into powerful, self-protective guilds. The signing of the Magna Carta in 1215 underpinned the establishment of an independent legal system based on trial by jury, in which everyone had the right to be judged by his or her peers in a court uninfluenced by church, state, or monarch.

King Edward I (r. 1272–1307) was known as the Hammer of the Scots—though in fact he failed to subdue Scotland, but conquered Wales in 1284. He introduced a Model Parliament in 1295, in which representatives of rich townsmen and well-to-do country dwellers served as members.

End of an Era: Society was devastated by the outbreak of the Black Death in 1348, spread by fleas that had arrived on ships in the coats of black rats. About one in every three of Britain's four million population died. In the depopulated countryside labor was scarce, and the peasants became aware of the power they possessed to offer or refuse their labor. In this sellers' market a new relationship between landowner and worker began to emerge, one based on money rather than social obligation. It was the beginning of the end of the feudal system. The peasants had not escaped repression, however. When they raised a revolution in 1381 under their leaders, Wat Tyler and John Ball, and marched on London in protest against a poll tax levied to raise money for the Hundred Years' War, they were put down with measured savagery. More than 1,500 were hanged.

Ten years before the outbreak of the Black Death, the Hundred Years' War with France (1337–1453) had been initiated by King Edward III (r. 1327–1377) when he claimed the French throne. The conflict staggered on for well over a century, with cross-Channel expeditions culminating in battles such as Crécy (1346), Poitiers (1356), and Agincourt (1415) that were proving grounds for the British bowmen.

Hostilities lurched to a halt in 1453, by which date the French had recaptured all their national soil except the port of Calais, which was finally regained in 1558.

Deeply Divided: There had been trouble at home, meanwhile. In 1399 the direct Plantagenet line was broken when Henry Bolingbroke seized the throne from Richard II (r. 1377–1399) and set up the rule of the House of Lancaster. This is the stuff of William Shakespeare's plays *Henry IV Parts 1* and *2* and *Henry V*, sagas of plotting ending with bloody defeat at the Battle of Shrewsbury in 1403 for the rebel Earl of Northumberland, his tempestuous son, Henry "Hotspur" Percy, and the Welsh leader Owain Glyndwr.

> Once the Norman succession had been resolved after the Civil War of 1135–1154, Henry II established the Plantagenet dynasty.

In 1455, only two years after the end of the very expensive and draining war with France, civil strife broke out across England in what became known as the Wars of the Roses. Shakespeare chronicled this protracted struggle between the Houses of Lancaster (symbolized by a red rose) and York (white rose). For 30 bloody years the war went on, until Henry Tudor decisively won it for the Lancastrians in 1485 at the Battle of Bosworth. The victor himself married a Yorkist princess, ending the whole business and ushering in the Tudor era.

Medieval Church-building

Britain contains, mile for mile, one of the greatest collections of medieval ecclesiastical architecture in the world. There are many reasons for this extraordinary density, most of them to do with the trading prosperity of a country where top-quality wool grew naturally on the hoof. Church-building was not just an act of piety; it was a very visible benchmark of how well donors were doing, economically and socially.

Most sensitive of all about juggling their worldly and spiritual standing were the bishops, several of whom were as powerful as any baron. Where the latter built castles, the former built cathedrals, and continued to build them and add to them long after the castles had become all but redundant. Bishops and aristocrats keen to be floated to heaven on prayers and psalms would endow the building of chantry chapels within or at the side of cathedrals, where Masses could be said or sung for their souls.

The presence of a saint's relics, particularly those with miraculous powers of healing, would guarantee a flow of pilgrims through the shrine, each adding a contribution to the construction funds. The monastic communities, too—smooth-mannered sophisticates such as the Benedictines, farmers in remote sites like the Cistercians, or the more austere Augustinians—had far-flung estates and widespread commercial interests, and many could afford to build their abbeys and outbuildings in almost as much style as the grandest cathedrals.

Many grand cathedrals, such as at Exeter, are a legacy of church-building fervor in medieval times.

Evolving Styles: Many of the great cathedral buildings took centuries to build, and the often jerky march of architectural fashion can be traced in their fabric. The Norman or Romanesque style (ca 1050–1150) shows round-topped arches, often embellished with firmly incised dogtooth or chevron carving, square towers, and massive pillars—a solid, confident, "here-to-stay" style, as at Norwich and Durham.

Early English (ca 1150–1280) brought in pointed arches and tall, narrow lancet windows. Flying buttresses and rib vaulting, taking some of the roof weight off the walls, slimmed down the pillars and helped to make this a lighter style, as seen at Salisbury. Decorated (ca 1280–1380), exemplified in the chapter house of York Minster and Exeter Cathedral, offered an ornamented, flowery appearance, with elaborate tracery in the enlarged windows and plenty of richly detailed wood carving. Perpendicular, from 1350 to the 1530s, retreated from elaboration, flattening window and doorway arches and reintroducing uncluttered lines—though fan vaulting, as in Gloucester Cathedral and King's College Chapel, Cambridge, became ever more intricate and lacy.

At the Reformation (ca 1540), a violent revulsion against church privilege and decadence meant a virtual halt to development for the next hundred years.

Parish Churches: Humbler glories are found throughout Britain in thousands of beautiful medieval parish churches. Between the 13th and 16th centuries, many regions—for example, the Yorkshire Wolds, the broad East Anglian sheepwalks, the Cotswold Hills, and the close-turfed chalk downs of the South Country—grew prosperous on the quality of their wool and the (often imported) skill of their weavers.

When the medieval wool and cloth merchants became rich, many thought it fitting—or prudent—to thank God by paying for the creation of a new church, or the beautifying of an existing building. Most of these parish churches were built of materials available locally. Many are now kept locked, but inquiry at the nearest house (or information posted on a board in the porch) may produce the key. Inside, among the memorial tablets, the meticulously worked hassocks, and stained-glass windows with their tributes and dedications, you can read the story of any small community's continuing history.

Parish churches often contain signs from bygone masons and carvers—a wooden bench end of a fox stealing a goose, or a corbel head of a nun with toothache, or high on a roof boss the Green Man sprouting leaves from nostrils and mouth, a pagan guest invited by the mason to the Christian feast.

Ages of Discovery & Elegance

The House of Tudor was a very compact family affair, consisting of Henry VII (r. 1485–1509), his son Henry VIII (r. 1509–1547), and three grandchildren, Edward VI (r. 1547–1553), Mary I (r. 1553–1558), and Elizabeth I (r. 1558–1603). The two who began and ended this short-lived dynasty, the old man and his younger granddaughter, were chips off the same block—coolly competent people, bold yet crafty, not afraid to take a risk but prudently keeping one eye over their shoulder at the same time. Altogether the Tudors held power for just over a century. But what a century.

During its course, peace came to the troubled land and a whole new religious movement was founded in Britain. Adventurers sailed around the globe, established New World colonies, broke the power of Spain, and founded the British Empire in India. Britain's greatest dramatist was born and rose to literary glory. This, for Britain, was a time of renaissance, a golden age.

Catholics & Protestants: Henry VIII is famous forevermore for his six wives—Catherine of Aragon (divorced), Anne Boleyn (beheaded), Jane Seymour (died), Anne of Cleves (divorced), Catherine Howard (beheaded), and Catherine Parr (survived). Henry's virulent quarrels with the pope, and his abolition of Britain's monastic communities, stemmed from his inability to father a male heir with his first wife, Catherine of Aragon. Between 1533 and 1540 he divorced

Tudor Building

You see it everywhere, in timber church roofs and stained-glass windows, on pargeted walls, clipped into hedges, inset into brick terraces—the Tudor rose, symbol of the pride of the country's best-known ruling dynasty. Tudor construction was solid and self-confident, exemplified by the heavily carved timber frames of merchants' houses, by fine oak paneling, by superb guildhalls such as that at Lavenham in Suffolk (see p. 212), and by the great Elizabethan country mansions (Hampton Court Palace, see pp. 85–86; Burghley House, see p. 221; Hardwick Hall, see pp. 232–233), with their tall chimneys, acres of brickwork, and miles of glass.

Catherine, split with the pope, announced the formation of the Church of England and declared himself head of it, and oversaw the Dissolution, destruction, and selling off of the monasteries. Henry batted aside opposition. His son Edward—by his third wife, Jane Seymour—succeeded to the throne in 1547 at the age of nine, and was dead by 1553. Five years of mayhem followed, as Protestant churchmen and thinkers were hounded and burned by Roman Catholic Queen Mary.

Elizabeth succeeded in 1558, with civil and religious life in turmoil. But "Gloriana," a tough cookie when she needed to be, could also listen to advice. A self-confident national mood grew up. The sea captains Sir Francis Drake (1540–1596), Sir Walter Raleigh (1552–1618), Sir John Hawkins (1532–1595), and Sir Martin Frobisher (1535–1594) diminished Spanish power on the sea. Raleigh founded Virginia. The East India Company opened for business in India. When Elizabeth died in 1603, things were looking good for Britain.

In 1531 Henry VIII proclaimed himself the supreme head of the Church of England.

The throne passed to the Stuart dynasty, already well established in Scotland. James VI of Scotland now also became James I of England (r. 1603–1625). This twitchy but clever man survived the Catholic Gunpowder Plot of 1605 and tensions with his government; during his reign, the persecution of religious nonconformists persuaded the Pilgrim Fathers to follow their consciences to the New World.

James's son, Charles I (r. 1625–1649) abolished Parliament in 1629 and attempted autocratic rule until 1640 when he recalled it. A confrontation was inevitable, and it blew up in 1642 when royalist "Cavaliers" and parliamentarian "Roundheads" faced each other in another civil war. Seven years later, defeated and discredited, Charles went to the execution block. The Roundhead leader, the stern Puritan Oliver Cromwell (1599–1658), initiated 11 years of government by Parliament (1649–1660), a dour time during which merrymaking around maypoles and in theaters was banned, and war with the Dutch severely restricted trade and prosperity. This hiatus ended when Cromwell died and the not entirely reliable Merry Monarch, Charles II, returned from exile in 1660 to restore the monarchy.

The Restoration period may have given Britons some excellent stage comedies, but there were bad times, too, under the later Stuarts. A disastrous return of the plague in 1665, followed by the Great Fire of London in 1666, rocked the confidence of many. Charles II (r. 1660–1685) approved legislation that barred Roman Catholics from all official positions. His successor, James II of England (r. 1685–1688), made life difficult for himself by swinging the religious pendulum overenthusiastically toward Catholicism. In 1688, James was deposed in the so-called Glorious Revolution and, apart from a brief and unsuccessful comeback in Ireland in 1690, the Stuarts faded off the scene. Their return in 1715 (the uprising of the "Old Pretender," son of James II) and 1745 (of his son, Bonnie Prince Charlie) only confirmed their impotence.

The incoming monarchs, joint sovereigns William of Orange, who came over from Holland, and his English wife, Mary (the daughter of James II), were unimpeachably Protestant. There were still troubles on the Celtic fringes, notably the massacre of the Macdonalds at Glencoe in 1692, and further bloody repressions in Ireland. Under William and Mary (r. 1689–1702; William reigned alone after Mary's death in 1694), and then under Mary's younger sister, Queen Anne (r. 1702–1714), however, the troubled kingdom settled down, coalesced further by the 1707 Act of Union between the English and Scottish parliaments.

Georgian Era: After the death of Queen Anne, none of whose children had survived to maturity, the Elector of Hanover was invited across the North Sea to take the throne. So began the succession of the four Georges, a time of relative peace and prosperity. During the 18th century, the industrial revolution commenced along the fast-rushing rivers of the Midlands and the North, and soon made Britain the world's chief manufacturer. James Watt (1736–1819), a Scottish engineer and inventor, discovered steam power in 1781, and Sir Richard Arkwright (1732–1792), an English industrialist, harnessed it for the weaving industry. A great canal system came into being, forerunner of the world-telescoping railways.

> A disastrous return of the plague in 1665, followed by the Great Fire of London in 1666, rocked the confidence of many.

During the 60-year reign of George III (r. 1760–1820), the arts boomed and manufacturing prospered. Rich men built and landscaped dream environments for themselves, while the northern manufacturing towns sprouted slums and open sewers. America fought the old country and gained independence; the Scottish Highland clans disintegrated and all but disappeared. Napoleon Bonaparte was faced and beaten; desperate agricultural and industrial workers rioted near to revolution.

It was a period of paradox. Indigenous rural ways of life collapsed as a new, powerful bourgeoisie emerged. Rich landowners parceled up the landscape for pleasure and for profit in the form of the enclosures, whose demarcating hedges shaped what we now think of as the "traditional" landscape. The dispossessed rural working class flocked into the little hells of the factories.

Georgian Architecture

The distinctive architecture of the Stuart and Georgian Age of Elegance still seems stylish today. It was the early 17th-century "Grand Tour" of the Continent, undertaken by well-off youngsters, that opened British eyes to the ideals of the Italian designer Andrea Palladio (1508–1580)—a symmetrical and harmonious use of colonnades, pediments, porticoes, balustrades, and other classical features.

Palladian: This Palladian style, epitomizing perfection in simplicity and making the most of stone as opposed to the Tudor-era brick, inspired the great Inigo Jones (1573–1652) to produce masterpieces such as the Banqueting House in

EXPERIENCE: Attend the Highland Games

To see Scots physical prowess and competitiveness at its height, attend a Highland Games. The Games were adopted during the Georgian era as an expression of national identity after the smashing of the clans by Crown forces at the Battle of Culloden (see p. 323), which signaled the end of the traditional Highland way of life. Many Scots gentry, proclaiming themselves Jacobites (supporters of Scotland's exiled Stuart monarchy), became lost in a mist of nostalgic yearning. The Games gave the Scots something of their own to be proud of—an attitude still very evident today.

Among the singing, dancing, music, and animal exhibitions and contests, the heavy events retain their key position. It's hard to overstate the local prestige gained by victors in these categories, which include the following:

• tossing the caber—hurling a wooden pole, up to 30 feet long, end over end
• putting the stone—one-handed throwing of a stone up to 26.5 pounds in weight
• throwing the hammer (a 22-pound ball on a long handle)
• throwing a 55-pound weight, either for distance or over a bar
• tossing a sheaf of corn with a pitchfork

Highland Games take place all across Scotland between May and September. Some of the best known are at Blair Atholl, Forres, Inverness, Aberdeen, Aberlour, Edinburgh, Perth, Pitlochry—and Braemar, the Games attended by members of the Royal Family. Visit www.visitscotland.com/guide/see-and-do/events3/highlandgames for a complete listing of Highland Games.

London and his rebuilding of Wilton House near Salisbury. John Wood the Elder (1705–1754) and the Younger (1728–1781), who modeled most of Georgian Bath, and Robert Adam (1728–1792), one of whose achievements was the building of Edinburgh's New Town, further developed this pure Palladian style.

Baroque: Running simultaneously with the flowering of Palladianism was the far more exuberant and extravagant baroque style, which flourished from the mid-17th to the mid-18th century. Balance and symmetry were central to this style, too, but decoration was added with whimsical touches such as swags of drapery, luxuriant foliage, cherubim, and seraphim. At its best, as in the many London churches of Sir Christopher Wren (1632–1723) or in the solo works and collaborations of Nicholas Hawksmoor and Sir John Vanbrugh—for example, Blenheim Palace—the style took fantasy and wild imagination to splendid heights.

Regency: The Regency style, which was developing during the future George IV's long tenure as Regent for his periodically insane father, George III, is best shown at spa towns such as Brighton and Cheltenham, and in elegant suburbs like Clifton.

The design of gardens and grounds had been developing, meanwhile, from the 17th century's very formal geometric style to something much looser, epitomized in the landscapes of Capability Brown (1716–1783) and Humphry Repton (1752–1818).

Industrial Architecture

Scattered all across the country are examples of specialized forms of architecture that followed one another out of the womb of the industrial revolution. The succession can be clearly seen in Calderdale and Rossendale, where West Yorkshire meets east Lancashire. On the hill slopes are the weavers' cottages with their out-size upper-story windows to let in as much light as possible; beside the streams and rivers stand the water-powered mills that succeeded them; then, down in the valley floors, where roads and railroads ran, loom the great steam-driven textile mills with their multiple stories, long ranks of windows, and towering chimneys.

Ironbridge Gorge, just south of Telford in east Shropshire, was the cradle of the indus-trial revolution. Abraham Darby (1678–1717) pioneered the cheap smelting of iron with coke here in 1709; 70 years later his grandson, Abraham Darby (1750–1791), spanned the River Severn's gorge with the world's first cast-iron bridge (1779), which still stands.

Monuments to Wealth: Look to the great industrial cities of northern England such as Leeds, Manchester, Sheffield, and Bradford to see huge mills, factories, and cavernous warehouses—cathedrals of commerce, some of them lavishly decorated with glazed tiles, terra-cotta moldings, and elaborate door and window frames, to reflect the power and consequence of their owners. Around them, set in regulated ranks, are the redbrick walls and slated roofs of the workers' terraced houses.

Transport left its own architectural stamp on the landscape: lock gates, quays, warehouses, and highly ornate Victorian stations and multiarched viaducts along the railroads. In the valleys of South Wales and in the coal-mining northeast, a postindustrial landscape is emerging. Old pit heaps have been given new life as grassy hills, reservoirs as fishing lakes, and tramways as green countryside paths.

Victorian Heyday

The Victorian era has sunk deeply into the national psyche as a kind of Eden before the 20th-century fall. This image is a tribute to the Victorians' own mythmaking, based around the ideal of the Royal Family as a secular Holy Family, epitomizing goodness, stability, and the progress of enlightenment. The Great Exhibition of 1851—the brainchild of Prince Albert to celebrate Brit-ain's mid-19th-century preeminence as a world imperial power and industrial giant—drawing together threads of civilization from across the world, sums up what we think of the Victorians and what they thought of themselves.

> **The Victorian era has sunk deeply into the national psyche as a kind of Eden before the 20th-century fall.**

Massive Changes: Yet the 19th century, most of it spanned by the reign of Queen Victoria (r. 1837–1901), encompassed such social, economic, and spiritual depri-vation in rural and industrial areas of Britain as had never been known before.

Illumination of ordinary people's pleasures, hopes, and sufferings in the Victorian era is provided now—as it was then—by the novels of Charles Dickens (1812–1870). Many writers were appalled and fascinated by the effects of the industrial revolution as, given an infinitely greater boost by steam power, factories and mines, railroads and workers' slums spread out to cover much of the land. The resultant social change was on an epic scale. In 1800, about 70 percent of the population worked in agriculture; by 1900, it was about 10 percent.

Rebellion: The Factory Act limiting children's working hours to no more than 48 per week was not passed until 1833. Corruption in Parliament and the workingman's lack of a vote led to the Chartist Riots of 1838–39, with mass marches and demonstrations by tens of thousands of people.

Two dozen were killed by troops in Newport, South Wales, in August 1839. Agricultural and industrial workers laid off due to mechanization went on machine-smashing sorties. There was a desperate undercurrent to the triumphant surface that 19th-century Britain showed to the world.

New Frontiers: And there were triumphant times. The world's first passenger railroad (1830) introduced geographical and social mobility. Slavery was abolished throughout the empire in 1833, the same year that the Oxford Movement revived evangelical missionary Christianity. Anesthetics arrived in 1846, ending millennia of surgical horror. Charles Darwin's 1859 *Origin of Species* set minds off on hitherto unthinkable tracks. Compulsory education for all, up to age 11, was initiated in 1870. Electricity began to light and heat houses in the 1880s, and to supersede steam as a power source. Around this time, London's underground railway (the world's first, opened in 1863) swapped coal-burning locomotives for cleaner electric models.

20th Century

The 20th century brought enormous change to Britain. There was a brief golden Edwardian glow to open the century; then came World War I (1914–1918) with its million dead, its traumatized survivors, and its terrible, unanswerable questions. War memorials can be found in almost every village, carrying long lists of the local dead.

No society could escape fundamental change after such an ordeal. In 1918 the vote was granted to all men over 21 and all women over 30 (women's votes at 21 came in 1929). Primary education became free. The trade unions gained membership and power,

---

EXPERIENCE: Ride the Tube to the End of the Line

The London Underground—universally known as the Tube—opened in stages from 1863 onward; it was the world's first underground railway. Most visitors, and many Londoners, are aware of little beyond the central stations. Sloane Square, Oxford Circus, Piccadilly Circus, Knightsbridge—everyone gets to know these Tube stops. But what of Cockfosters or Epping? Give up half a day to the adventure: Ride the train until it emerges to run aboveground. And what will you discover there? Here are some of the treasures of the outer Tube:
Piccadilly line to Hounslow West (Hounslow Heath nature reserve) or to Cockfosters (Monken Hadley Common open space)
Central line to Perivale (Horsenden Hill open space), to West Ruislip (Mad Bess Wood, Ruislip Lido reservoir), or to Epping (ancient Epping Forest)
Metropolitan line to Chalfont & Latimer (Chess Valley, Chenies House) or to Amersham (charming old market town)
Northern line to High Barnet (London LOOP waymarked footpath)
District line to Upminster Bridge (Hornchurch Country Park, Ingrebourne Marshes), to Wimbledon Park (Wimbledon Common open space), or to Richmond (Thames Path)

leading to the General Strike of 1926 in support of miners' pay and conditions claims. The Great Depression of the 1930s put millions out of work; some, from the hard-hit northeast, walked 300 miles in the 1936 Jarrow March to protest in London. That year Edward VIII (r. 1936) succeeded his father George V (r. 1910–1936), fell in love with American divorcée Wallis Simpson, and abdicated his throne to marry her.

New Elizabethans: Six million Britons served during World War II (1939–1945), and 275,000 of them lost their lives. A further 58,000 died on home territory in bombing raids. Enormous pride in "winning the war" turned quickly into disillusion at "losing the peace," as rationing of commodities and austerity standards in clothing, cars, and buildings persisted well into the 1950s. At the time, locked into the uncertainties of the Cold War at the side of the United States, it seemed a tense and gray period. Looking back now, many Britons see it as a golden age when they were cradled by the welfare state and their children could explore the streets and countryside in safety.

Queen since 1952, Elizabeth II is one of Britain's longest reigning monarchs.

Queen Elizabeth II succeeded her father, George VI (r. 1936–1952), in 1952. During her reign the pace of change in Britain has accelerated. A multicultural society was initiated by immigrant workers from former colonies. The Royal Family, hitherto of demigod status, experienced a demotion to all-too-human standing in the eyes of press and public—a liberating shift of perception for all parties.

Striking a Balance: The 1970s were characterized by appalling labor relations, by an upsurge of trouble in Northern Ireland, by strikes and pickets, and by "winters of discontent." In 1973 Britain joined the European Community (now the European Union)—a commitment she is still dithering over. During the last two decades of the millennium, consumerism, selfishness, and greed often seemed to be staking a claim on the soul of the country. Britons hated seeing their landscape under threat from development, their towns and villages swollen and homogenized, their much-maligned, but now belatedly appreciated, welfare state dismantled. Yet overseas visitors continued to arrive in Britain, in search of deep roots of history and culture, and to enjoy seeing a country where change and tradition still exist side by side. ■

Food & Drink

Great Britain used to be renowned for its bad food—bland, suety, cold-weather stodge, cooked unimaginatively and served begrudgingly. That's all changed, thanks to exposure to foreign travel, an influx of immigrants and their native cooking, and the urgings of TV chefs to wake up and smell the international coffee.

The atmospheric British pub—a place to relax, socialize, and enjoy a pint of locally brewed beer

Great British Breakfast

Breakfast, as you experience it in hotels and bed-and-breakfast places, will probably be a variation on what is known as the Great British Breakfast—a mixed grill or fry of some combination of eggs, bacon, sausages, tomatoes, mushrooms, black and/or white pudding, and fried bread, followed by toast and marmalade, and washed down with tea.

British Pubs

These days pubs, formerly purely drinking establishments, almost all put on some kind of lunchtime menu. Many also offer evening meals, eaten either in the bar or in a separate restaurant area.

British food has greatly improved over the last 20 years and dishes have become more varied and innovative. But traditional dishes

British food has greatly improved over the last 20 years and dishes have become more varied and innovative. But traditional dishes are making a comeback.

Britain has a long tradition of cheesemaking, producing more than 700 distinct cheeses.

are making a comeback. Combinations are the name of the game: roast pheasant and bread sauce, roast beef and Yorkshire pudding with horseradish sauce, sausages and mashed potatoes with hot English mustard, steak and onions, steak and kidney pie, shepherd's pie with Worcestershire sauce, bread and cheese with pickled onions (known as a ploughman's lunch), fish and chips with salt and vinegar.

Desserts tend to be simple but effective: spotted dick (steamed pudding with raisins) or treacle tart with custard, strawberries and cream, steamed ginger pudding with ginger sauce, apple pie with custard, plum or rhubarb or gooseberry crumble with cream.

Rural pubs are places to sample the locally brewed beer, served without gas pressure from a hand pump or straight from the barrel, drunk a little cooler than room temperature, and savored for that elusive combination of the sweet richness of malt and the bitterness of hops that always tastes of beer and yet shifts and modulates in emphasis and balance almost from one town to the next. Once you have weaned yourself off the thin, cold, corporate blandness of lager and cottoned on to the many-layered, ever changing, subtly developing flavors to be found in a pint glass of beer—you'll be hooked for life.

Scottish & Welsh Specialties

In Scotland, try game (venison, grouse, wild salmon), kippers, Arbroath smokies (smoked haddock), Scotch broth, and the epic and iconic haggis, a savory concoction cooked traditionally in the lining of a sheep's stomach.

In Wales, cawl (mutton broth), lamb, freshly caught fish, crumbly white Caerphilly cheese, and the long and luscious leek—the national vegetable—can all be excellent.

These two countries come into their own at afternoon tea time. In Wales, try laverbread, made of seaweed and oatmeal, and a fruit bread called bara brith; in Scotland opt for shortbread, scones, and oatcakes.

EXPERIENCE:
Make Yourself a Cornish Cream Tea

An absolutely iconic British food experience is the cream tea. You can certainly buy one in any self-respecting tea shop in the southwest, the spiritual home of the cream tea; but it's also very easy to make for yourself. You need a bag of scones, a tub of clotted cream, and a jar of strawberry jam. Pile a lot of cream and jam onto your scone, and eat it on a sunny lawn with a cup of tea to wash it down. That's it—as simple as you like! It's greasy, sticky, crumby, cholesterol-rich . . . and heavenly.

The Arts

Britain's literary tradition supersedes all other artistic contributions it has made and continues to make to the arts; however, Britain is no lightweight in the fields of art, music, theater, and film, either.

Literature

Britain's contribution to world literature, from Geoffrey Chaucer's day up to the present, has been of the first importance. And Giraldus Cambrensis, the Norman-Welsh chronicler and ecclesiastic, predated Chaucer (ca 1345–1400) by 200 years when he wrote down his *Itinerarium,* a witty and gossipy account of his tour through Wales in 1188. Welsh, English, and Scottish bards and poets were creating an oral tradition of verse, song, and story for hundreds of years before the Dark Ages, when monks, traveling through Europe, brought back the notion of reading and writing. Education transferred the skills to the laity, and the great British literary tradition was founded.

> **Britain's contribution to world literature, from Geoffrey Chaucer's day up the present, has been of the first importance.**

Chaucer's *Canterbury Tales,* composed around 1387 to 1400, was a hugely ambitious project that death prevented him from finishing. A century would pass before William Caxton brought the craft of printing to the point where he could produce, in 1485, an edition of Sir Thomas Malory's *Le Morte d'Arthur,* an account of the life and death of the mythical "once and future king" that Malory had written 15 years before. And it would be another century before William Shakespeare began to create the plays and sonnets that would establish him as the greatest writer in history.

17th Century: The 17th-century preoccupation with the tensions between orthodox and nonconformist religion brought forth John Milton's (1608–1674) epic poem *Paradise Lost* (1667) and John Bunyan's (1628–1688) "spiritual travelogue," *The Pilgrim's Progress* (1678), written in Bedford Gaol where Bunyan was imprisoned for unlicensed preaching. Another classic is the witty diary kept for ten years by Samuel Pepys (1633–1703) beginning in January 1660; the book provides invaluable insight into 17th-century life and thought.

18th Century: During the 18th century, the English novel began to take shape. Daniel Defoe (1660–1731) led the way in 1719 with *Robinson Crusoe,* based on yarns he heard in a Bristol

tavern from rescued shipwreck victim Alexander Selkirk. In 1749, Henry Fielding (1707–1754) produced his full-blooded *Tom Jones*, and the novel was off and running.

Dr. Samuel Johnson (1709–1786) and James Boswell (1740–1795) took up the literary baton after their 1773 travels through Scotland, with Johnson's *A Journey to the Western Islands of Scotland* appearing in 1775 and Boswell's *Journal of a Tour to the Hebrides* in 1785. These splendidly characterful books set a standard few other travel writers could reach.

Two 18th-century poets who made an indelible mark were the Scottish national poet Robert Burns (1759–1796), whose short life blazed so brightly, and the visionary William Blake (1757–1827), with his *Songs of Innocence* (1789) and *The Marriage of Heaven and Hell* (1790–1793).

A woodcut used in a 15th-century printing of Chaucer's *Canterbury Tales*

19th Century: A tremendous literary flowering took place in Britain during the 19th century. The prolific talent of Charles Dickens (1812–1870) laid bare some of the worst aspects of the industrial revolution while creating some of the most memorable characters in fiction: Mr. Pickwick, Oliver Twist, Nicholas Nickleby, Little Dorrit, Ebenezer Scrooge, David Copperfield, Abel Magwitch, Pip, and Uriah Heep.

During the second decade of the century, the country parson's daughter Jane Austen (1775–1817) wrote *Sense and Sensibility* (1811), *Pride and Prejudice* (1813), *Mansfield Park* (1814), *Emma* (1816), *Northanger Abbey*, and *Persuasion* (the last two both 1817). Sir Walter Scott was turning out his "Waverley novels" among a great stream of historical romances—*Waverley* itself (1814), *The Antiquary* (1816), *Rob Roy* (1817), *The Heart of Midlothian* (1818), *Ivanhoe* (1819), *Kenilworth* (1821), and others—many of them written under frantic pressure to pay off creditors.

William Wordsworth (1770–1850) was most poetically active during this period, too, and his fellow poet and admirer John Keats (1795–1821) showed brilliant promise before his premature death. Quite another kind of writing was being produced around this time with the publication in 1830 of William Cobbett's *Rural Rides*, a stinging commentary and exposé of southern England's depressed agricultural scene and corrupt local politics.

The literary talents of the Brontë sisters shone during the 1840s. After a childhood spent writing about the imaginary realms of Gondal and Angria, in 1847 the three young women each produced a brilliant novel: Anne's *Agnes Grey*, Charlotte's masterpiece *Jane Eyre*, and Emily's demonic *Wuthering Heights*. Anne went on to write *The Tenant of Wildfell Hall* (1848), while Charlotte produced *Shirley* (1849) and *Villette* (1853). Within two years of their first work, Anne and Emily were dead, and Charlotte followed them in 1855.

Another writer to make her mark on the mid-19th century was Elizabeth Gaskell (1810–1865) with *Cranford* (1853) and *North and South* (1855); she also wrote the definitive *Life of Charlotte Brontë* (1857). Marian Evans (1819–1880), under the name of

EXPERIENCE: Hobnob with Literati at the Hay

With such a long and strong heritage of writers and poets, the British love their literary festivals. Just over the Welsh border in Powys, the small market town of Hay-on-Wye was famous for its dozens of secondhand bookshops long before it mounted the extremely popular **Hay Festival** *(box office tel 01497-822629, www .hayfestival.com)*, which takes place at the end of May/beginning of June. Hay is to literary festivals what Glastonbury is to music festivals—the one that everybody wants to go to—because this, the United Kingdom's flagship literary festival, is tremendous fun in a relaxed atmosphere and a lovely rural setting. Many of the events are free (reservations required), while others can cost up to £20 ($32) each. You're likely to spot international literary stars on any street corner during the festival, but it's Hay's generous support of homegrown British talent that gives it such an enviable reputation.

If you can't make it to Hay, choose from other literary festivals on the calendar *(www.britishcouncil.org/arts-literature-literary-festivals.htm)*. Heavy hitters include Britain's largest poetry festival, at Ledbury on the Welsh Borders, in July; the Edinburgh International Book Festival in August; and the prestigious Cheltenham Literature Festival, held in October.

George Eliot, produced such classics as *Adam Bede* (1859), *The Mill on the Floss* (1860), *Silas Marner* (1861), and *Middlemarch* (1871–1872). Later on came the romantic novels, short stories, and poems of Robert Louis Stevenson (1850–1894), the frail Scotsman with a wild Gothic imagination—*Treasure Island* (1883), *A Child's Garden of Verses* (1885), *The Strange Case of Dr. Jekyll and Mr. Hyde,* and *Kidnapped* (the last two both 1886), among a vast output. Sir Arthur Conan Doyle (1859–1930), another Edinburgh-born writer, introduced his detective hero Sherlock Holmes in *A Study in Scarlet* (1887), killed him off in *The Final Problem* (1893), and resurrected him ten years later through sheer pressure of public demand in *The Adventure of the Empty House* (1903). The Dorset-based writer Thomas Hardy (1840–1928) produced all his epic Wessex novels—*Far from the Madding Crowd, The Mayor of Casterbridge, Tess of the d'Urbervilles,* and the others—between 1874 and the turn of the century.

Literary treasures piled high. But of all the works of 19th-century British writers, the one that has had the most profound effect was published in 1859 by a middle-aged geologist and biologist and had the catchy title: *On the Origin of Species by Means of Natural Selection,* or *The Preservation of Favoured Races in the Struggle for Life* by Charles Darwin (1809–1882).

"J. K. Rowling," by Stuart Pearson Wright, 2005. Rowling is Britain's most successful author.

20th Century: In the 1920s, Virginia Woolf (1882–1941) and D. H. Lawrence (1885–1930) made their names. The interwar years saw Eric Arthur Blair (1903–1950), writing as George Orwell, produce *The Road to Wigan Pier* and *Down and Out in Paris and London,* which were followed by *Animal Farm* and *1984* just after World War II. Another key literary figure was novelist Graham Greene (1904–1991), with his piercing eye for downbeat atmosphere and characters caught between good and evil in such understated masterpieces as *Stamboul Train* (1932), *Brighton Rock* (1938), *The Power and the Glory* (1940), *The Heart of the Matter* (1948), *The End of the Affair* (1951), and *The Comedians* (1966).

Postwar writers included Kingsley Amis *(Lucky Jim),* Alan Sillitoe *(Saturday Night and Sunday Morning),* John Osborne *(Look Back in Anger),* and John Braine *(Room at the Top).* Iris Murdoch *(The Sea, the Sea),* Anita Brookner *(Hotel du Lac),* and John Fowles *(The French Lieutenant's Woman)* made big names for themselves. William Golding was awarded the Nobel Prize for literature in 1983; his *Lord of the Flies* (1954) opened a dark door into human behavior when all the rules of civilization are swept away. Salman Rushdie wrote the acclaimed *Midnight's Children,* about the birth of independence in his native India, and

"What's On" City Guides

Several cities publish print and/or online "What's On" guides, providing succinct, often enjoyably opinionated, information about local arts events, music, eating, drinking, entertainment, and much, much more.

London: *www.londononline.co.uk* and *www.londonnet.co.uk;* **Time Out** *(www.timeout.com/London)*

Birmingham: *www.birminghamonline. org.uk, www.viewbirmingham.co.uk,* and *www.mybrum.co.uk*

Bristol: *www.bristol.org.uk;* **Venue** *(www.venue.co.uk)*

Edinburgh: *www.edinburghonline.co.uk;* **The Skinny** *(www.theskinny.co.uk)*

Glasgow: *www.glasgowonline.co.uk;* **The Skinny** *(www.theskinny.co.uk)*

Cardiff: *www.cardiffonline.net;* **Buzz** *(www.buzzmag.co.uk)*

then went under sentence of death for offending orthodox Muslims with *The Satanic Verses*. Irvine Welsh carried the shock banner with his seamy dialect novels of drugs and crime in Edinburgh, notably *Trainspotting*. A new generation of dynamic 21st-century women novelists includes Zadie Smith, with her award-winning *White Teeth* (2000), and Monica Ali, whose *Brick Lane* (2003) explored the lives and frustrations of London's Bangladeshi community, while J. K. Rowling's *Harry Potter* saga (first book published 1997) made a world star of the boy wizard. David Mitchell's *Cloud Atlas* (2004) and Hilary Mantel's *Wolf Hall* (2009) hugely enhanced both authors' reputations. The biggest 20th-century success of all? J. R. R. Tolkien's epic *The Lord of the Rings* trilogy (1954–1955).

Poetry has continued to flourish. The front-line trenches of Flanders forged the romantic Wilfred Owen (1893–1918) into the Great War's finest and steeliest poet. Since then England has produced W. H. Auden (1907–1973), Ted Hughes (1930–1998), and Sir John Betjeman (1906–1984). Scotland discovered in Hugh MacDiarmid (1892–1978), Norman MacCaig (1910–1996), and Carol Ann Duffy (b. 1955) native poets fit to share the plinth with Robert Burns, and out of Wales have come the two great Thomases: Dylan (1914–1953) and R. S. (1913–2000).

Art

Britain's global influence in art, compared with its contribution to world literature, has been fairly modest. Each age has thrown up its singular genius, though, and there have been some British leaders in the varied fields of landscape painting and watercolor, satirical drawing, and innovative design.

The native art of Britain can be enjoyed in county and municipal museums; in private collections such as the Burrell Collection in Glasgow, and Sir John Soane's Museum and the Wallace Collection in London; and on the walls of dozens of country houses.

Outstanding examples of early jewelry and pottery have survived from the Stone Age onward. The rich hoard retrieved from the seventh-century Saxon ship burial at Sutton Hoo can be seen in the British Museum, and the interlaced patterns and glowing colors of the Lindisfarne Gospels' illuminations are in the British Library.

Churches and cathedrals are good places to look for Dark Ages and medieval art, from stained-glass windows and carved rood screens to statuary, frescoes, and treasures such as the Mappa Mundi in the New Library Building adjoining Hereford Cathedral and St. Cuthbert's painted coffin at Durham.

Post-Renaissance Britain gave rise to a broad range of artistic expression that covered the Elizabethan portrait painting of Nicholas Hilliard (1537–1619), the baroque woodcarving of Dutchman Grinling Gibbons (1648–1721) in late 17th-century churches and country houses, and the biting social and moral commentary of engraver and painter William Hogarth (1697–1764) in his serial conversation pieces "A Rake's Progress" and "The Election" and admonitory prints such as "Gin Lane."

The Georgian era was a golden age for British art and crafts. Thomas Gainsborough (1727–1788) and Richard Wilson (1714–1782) were turning out their light-filled landscapes, and Joshua Reynolds (1723–1792), George Romney (1732–1804), Sir Henry Raeburn (1756–1823), and Gainsborough himself were raising the art of portrait painting to new heights. Poet William Blake (1757–1827), meanwhile, was translating his apocalyptic visions into illustrations.

Thomas Sheraton (1751–1806), George Hepplewhite (d. 1786), and Thomas Chippendale (1718–1779) produced delicately carved and upholstered furniture for the landed gentry, who had their grounds landscaped by Capability Brown (1716–1783). Josiah Wedgwood (1730–1795), Thomas Minton (1765–1836), and Josiah Spode (1754–1827) created beautiful ceramics in the potteries of Staffordshire. And satirical, witty commentary was made on the life of the country by the celebrated caricaturists Thomas Rowlandson (1756–1827) and James Gillray (1757–1815).

John Constable (1776–1837) and J. M. W. Turner (1775–1851) were learning their craft as painters around this time. During the first half of the 19th century they would reach triumphant fruition—Constable with his meticulous depictions of East Anglian

Banksy's street art has captivated British and international audiences alike with its irreverence.

Elton John, singer-songwriter, composer, pianist

rural scenes, and Turner—also in landscapes—with a style increasingly impressionistic. Later in the Victorian era the Pre-Raphaelite brotherhood of painters tried to turn the clock back to the more lyrical and pastoral approach of the early Middle Ages. William Morris (1834–1896) became the most influential designer of the later 19th century with his back-to-traditional-basics arts and crafts movement, a vision that influenced the stylish art nouveau design work of Glaswegian Charles Rennie Mackintosh (1868–1928) around the turn of the 20th century.

The boundaries between art and craft—and art and almost anything else for that matter—have become blurred during the past century. The crowded religious paintings of Sir Stanley Spencer (1891–1959) and monumental, threatening landscapes of Paul Nash (1889–1946) have given way to far more expressive painting styles, from light and airy interiors by David Hockney (b. 1937) to the dark and obsessive portraits of Francis Bacon (1909–1992) and Lucian Freud (b. 1922). More recently enfant terrible Damien "half a cow in formaldehyde" Hirst (b. 1965), the anonymous street artist Banksy, and Tracey "unmade bed" Emin (b. 1963), along with ever more "challenging" entries for the annual Turner Prize (elephant dung, flashing lightbulbs), have posed the interesting question: What *is* art?

Sculpture moved into abstraction from Sir Jacob Epstein (1880–1959) through Barbara Hepworth (1903–1975) and Henry Moore (1898–1986). Caricature continued to be a British strongpoint, with stars of distortion such as Gerald Scarfe (b. 1936) and Ralph Steadman (b. 1936).

Music

Traditional British music and dance have roots that go far back in time. Such traditions have preserved a more vigorous life in the Celtic nations of Wales, Scotland, and Ireland. Here wild dance music is still played, and unaccompanied singing is enjoyed in pubs, village halls, barns, and back kitchens. The folk music of England—songs of rural life and labor, vigorous and (some might say) galumphing tunes to accompany country dancing—still keeps a toehold in folk clubs and a specialist record market, but has nothing like the social or musical cachet of its Celtic counterpart.

British religious and classical music ran a fairly straight course from the great choral works of Tudor composers such as William Byrd (1542–1623) and Thomas

Tallis (1505–1585), through Henry Purcell (1659–1695) and George Frederick Handel (1685–1759), into 19th- and 20th-century names such as Sir Edward Elgar (1857–1934), Frederick Delius (1862–1934), Ralph Vaughan-Williams (1872–1958), and Gustav Holst (1874–1934). Perhaps it is characteristic of British musical tastes that none of these serious composers finds quite such a niche in national affection as those Victorian spinners of sublime light opera, Sir William Schwenck Gilbert (1836–1911) and Sir Arthur Sullivan (1842–1900). This century has witnessed the flowering of Sir Michael Tippett, Sir William Walton (1902–1983), and Benjamin Britten (1913–1976), among others. Celebratory festivals of classical music such as those at Aldeburgh in Suffolk (Britten), Glyndebourne in Sussex (opera), and the Promenade Concerts performed in the Royal Albert Hall in London are always packed.

Pop and rock composers and musicians have been influential since the early 1960s. The Beatles, of course, took off like an express train in 1963 with their magical mix of R&B, rock and roll, balladry, country and western, music hall, schmaltz, and soul. Since then, new music styles—some taken from across the Atlantic, some genuinely home-grown—have continuously cropped up, keeping things fresh.

Sir Elton John (b. 1947) has become a world star, as has soft rock band Coldplay—while the ageless Rolling Stones have never stopped rolling. The musical heritages of Asia, the Caribbean, and Africa have all slotted into this multiethnic musical society.

Theater

In the world of British theater, William Shakespeare is as unassailable a benchmark as are the Beatles in pop music. More than 400 years after they were first written, his plays still pack theaters wherever they are produced.

The English theater was shut down during Puritan times, from 1640 to 1660, but apart from those dour decades, it has flourished.

After Charles II returned to the throne in 1660, audiences roared with laughter over Restoration comedies such as William Congreve's *Way of the World* and George Far-quhar's *Beaux' Stratagem*. Irishman Richard Sheridan's *School for Scandal* delighted Georgian audiences, while Victorians were amused by Irish writer Oscar Wilde's bitingly witty plays *Lady Windermere's Fan* (1892), *An Ideal Husband*, and *The Importance of Being Earnest* (the last two both 1895).

Today's crop of British playwrights includes names such as Tom Stoppard and Harold Pinter, while Sir Andrew Lloyd Webber *(Cats, Evita, Jesus Christ Superstar, Phantom of the Opera)* continues to dominate musicals. Far grittier and more shocking young playwrights include Sarah Kane (1971–1999), a genuinely confrontational and disturbing talent.

Twentieth-century stars of the stage form a roll call that features Dame Peggy Ashcroft, Paul Scofield, Sir Laurence Olivier, Sir John Gielgud, Richard Burton, Dame Judi Dench, Sir Anthony Hopkins, and Sir Ian McKellen. London's Royal National Theatre mounts innovative and challenging plays, while for Shakespeare the faithful flock to the Royal Shakespeare Company's theater at Stratford-upon-Avon, or—for an authentic Elizabethan playhouse atmosphere—to London's reconstructed Globe Theatre, in Southwark on the south bank of the Thames.

The boundaries between art and craft—and art and almost anything else for that matter—have become blurred during the past century.

Film & Television

Many stage players and writers have crossed over into film and television. British actors who have made big hits on film include Sir Ian McKellen (Scandal, X-Men, The Da Vinci Code, Lord of the Rings), Dame Judi Dench (A Room with a View, Pride & Prejudice), and youngsters Keira Knightley (Pirates of the Caribbean) and Orlando Bloom (Pirates of the Caribbean, Lord of the Rings). Two fields have always proved fruitful: costume dramas and comedy. Wry, quirky hits such as Four Weddings and a Funeral, The Full Monty, and Notting Hill grabbed audiences in the 1990s, while animator Nick Park and his Aardman studio flew the flag for little plasticine people with the much-loved Wallace & Gromit films.

Television's costume dramas (Pride & Prejudice, Sense and Sensibility) and comedy shows like Monty Python's Flying Circus, Fawlty Towers, Blackadder, The Office, and political screamathon The Thick of It have shone the lamp for Britain, as have David Attenborough's nature programs such as Life on Earth.

Good Locations: Dotted around the British towns and countryside, you will come across houses and landscapes that have been featured in classic cinema and television films.

In the south Midlands, Gloucester Cathedral was the setting for many scenes in Harry Potter and the Sorcerer's Stone and Harry Potter and the Chamber of Secrets. In the north Midlands, Sudbury Hall, west of Derby, was used for the Pride & Prejudice interior scenes, while exteriors were shot at Lyme Park, south of Stockport in Cheshire. Two popular TV series were filmed in Yorkshire—Last of the Summer Wine around Holmfirth, northwest of Sheffield, and the James Herriot country vet series, All Creatures Great and Small, farther north in the West Yorkshire dales of Swaledale and Wensleydale.

Scotland's spectacular castles, lochs, and glens have provided backdrops for many films. Castle Tioram on Loch Moidart in the west featured in Highlander (1986); Glen Nevis, south of Fort William, was in Kidnapped (1986) and Braveheart (1995); and Blackness Castle on the Firth of Forth, west of Edinburgh, and Dunnottar Castle, just south of Stonehaven on the northeast coast, were filmed for Franco Zeffirelli's Hamlet (1990). The freakish stone carving in Roslyn Chapel, just outside Edinburgh, was featured in The Da Vinci Code (2006). ■

EXPERIENCE: Laugh It Up in Glasgow

Aye, weel, yon wee wumman gangs intae a Glesca butchershop. Butcher's jes' came oot the freezer an' is staundin' haunds ahint him, wi' his back tae th' 'letric fire. Wee wumman peeps intae the chiller an asks: "Is that yer Ayrshire bacon?" "Naw," sez butcher. "It's jist ma haun's Ah'm heatin'."

Made you laugh? If so, you'll giggle yourself breathless over a thousand similar silly jokes at the **Glasgow International Comedy Festival** (box office tel 0844-395-4005, www.glasgowcomedyfestival.com, prices vary), mid-March through mid-April, staged in various venues across the city. And if not—it's time you went along and learned to understand some good broad "Glesca," to appreciate the humor you'll hear in every street and bar in the funniest and bawdiest city in Scotland.

Famous landmarks—St. Paul's Cathedral, Buckingham Palace,
Westminster Abbey—and intriguing byways and hidden corners

London

Entrance gate to Buckingham Palace

London

London is one of the world's great historic and contemporary cities. Here are the seat of government at Westminster, the great royal residence of Buckingham Palace, and the nation's premier art galleries, museums, theaters, and arts venues. This is the home of one Briton in seven, and of a great many folk born overseas who now call the city home.

An unmistakable landmark of London—the Houses of Parliament on the River Thames

This dense and rich human palimpsest has given London a self-confident, multicultural energy and buzz that other capital cities can only envy.

London is endlessly adaptable, having converted itself from a walled Roman fort and Dark Ages stronghold to a great medieval city, to a baroque phoenix literally risen from the ashes of the Great Fire of 1666, to a Georgian dream of elegance, to a Victorian powerhouse of empire incorporating extremes of wealth and poverty, to a faded and jaded interwar imperial shadow, to Swinging London of the 1960s, and to today's sprawling, cosmopolitan, money-centered ants' nest of a place—already looking forward to its next great occasion, the hosting of the 2012 Olympic Games.

You will find elements of each and all of these in Britain's capital city. There are the truly great tourist attractions that demand attention:

Westminster Abbey, St. Paul's Cathedral, the Tower of London, Buckingham Palace, the British Museum, the National Gallery, and Trafalgar Square, among many others. And there are hidden, tucked-away delights and pleasures: Sir John Soane's Museum in Lincoln's Inn Fields, for example, or the waterfront walk among the architectural extravaganzas of Docklands, or Chelsea Physic Garden, or the crispy-duck sellers beneath the dragon arch in Soho's Chinatown.

Consider spending a day or two on foot. London well repays a little extra time and attention, especially if you bring a broad-minded, good-humored attitude with you.

On Foot

London is a safe and pleasant place to walk around by day. Four walks are suggested in the following pages: Around the City of London and St. Paul's Cathedral; from Westminster and St. James's Park to Buckingham Palace and back by Trafalgar Square; through seedy but latterly "hip" Soho and lively Covent Garden; and from the smart shops of Knightsbridge to the famous museums of Kensington and into Hyde Park.

You can easily work out more walks for yourself; the bookshops of London are full of books of self-guided walks, the visitor information centers have leaflet guides to walks, and hundreds of walks are downloadable

---

NOT TO BE MISSED:

Climbing to the Golden Gallery of St. Paul's Cathedral **55**

The Changing of the Guard at Buckingham Palace, pageantry at its finest **61**

Wandering around the Victoria & Albert Museum **74–76**

A ride on a river boat from Westminster to Greenwich **87**

The view of London from the London Eye big wheel **89**

Walking on the Thames Path **89**

Seeing the Crown Jewels at the Tower of London **94**

Sir John Soane's Museum, Lincoln's Inn Fields—a quirky treasury of objects **95**

---

from the Internet. That's not to mention the three long-distance paths that will give you an unforgettable overview of one of the world's most historic and fascinating cities— the Thames Path through London along its river; the Capital Ring through the green spaces; and the London Loop that orbits the city's outlying countryside.

Do use the excellent Underground railway, better known as "the Tube," to discover for yourself more of this great and exciting city. ∎

Open-top Bus Rides

Because Buckingham Palace is such a magnet for visitors to London, it can be hard to find enough room to see properly through the crowds. There's no such problem, though, if you view London from on high, aboard one of the many open-top buses ($$$$$) that tour the city's main attractions. Companies that offer modern open-top buses include **Big Bus Tours** *(tel 020-7233 9533, www.bigbus*

tours.com) and the **London Tour Bus Company** *(tel 0844-879 7001, www.london tourbus.co.uk)*, both with hop-on/hop-off stops at dozens of locations; the tickets usually are valid for either 24 or 48 hours. **Premium Tours** *(tel 020-7713 1311, www .premiumtours.co.uk)* collects from nearly 200 hotels and takes you around on a vintage double-decker; the sightseeing tour lasts seven hours.

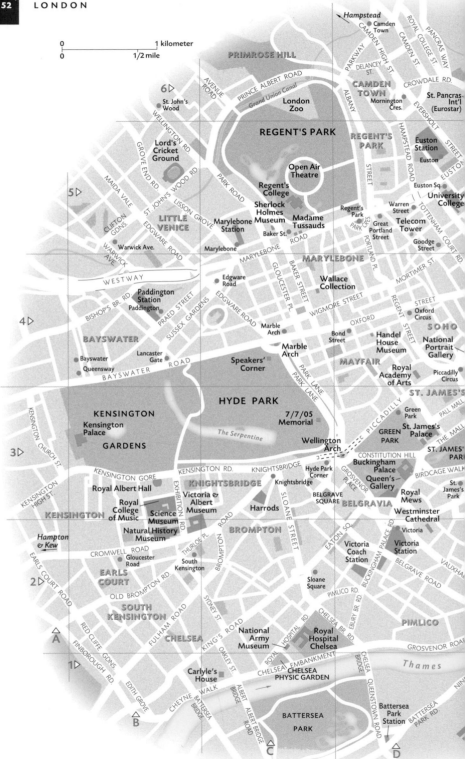

KING'S CROSS
COPENHAGEN STREET
King's Cross Station
YORK WAY
CALEDONIAN RD.
PENTON ST.
LIVERPOOL ST.
UPPER STREET
ISLINGTON
• Angel
King's Cross Thameslink
PENTONVILLE ROAD
CITY ROAD
PENTONVILLE
PANCRAS RD.
British Library
King's Cross St. Pancras
St. Pancras Station
ST. PANCRAS
GRAY'S INN ROAD
KING'S CROSS ROAD
ROSEBERY AVENUE
ST. JOHN STREET
GOSWELL ROAD
EAST RD.
Old St.
PITFIELD STREET
GREAT EASTERN ST.
Shoreditch
COMMERCIAL STREET
BRICK LANE
CLERKENWELL
ST. LUKE'S
WOBURN
Russell Square
BLOOMSBURY
FINSBURY
CLERKENWELL ROAD
FARRINGDON RD.
ALDERSGATE
CITY ROAD
OLD ST.
Liverpool Street Station
Dennis Severs's House
Univ. of London
Gray's Inn
SOUTHAMPTON ROW
GOWER ST.
Chancery Lane
Farringdon Station
Barbican Station
Moorgate Station
Moorgate
British Museum
HOLBORN
Farringdon
Barbican
Barbican Centre
LONDON WALL
BISHOPSGATE
Aldgate East
Tottenham Court Road
NEW OXFORD ST.
CHARING CROSS RD.
Sir John Soane's Mus.
Smithfield Market
Museum of London
Guildhall
Liverpool Street
Stock Exchange
Holborn
Lincoln's Inn
HOLBORN VIADUCT
ST. PAUL'S
CITY
Aldgate
ST. GILES
KINGSWAY
HIGH HOLBORN
Dr. Johnson's House
FLEET STREET
St. Paul's
St. Paul's Cathedral
Bank
Bank of England
Lloyd's
Royal Courts of Justice
Temple
CANNON STREET
Mansion House
FENCHURCH ST.
Fenchurch St. Station
Covent Garden
ALDWYCH
Blackfriars Sta.
QUEEN VICTORIA ST.
Tower Hill
Tower Gateway
STRAND
Temple
UPPER THAMES ST.
Cannon St.
Monument
TOWER HILL
Covent Garden
Leicester Square
Somerset House
EMBANKMENT
BLACKFRIARS BRIDGE
MILLENNIUM FOOTBRIDGE
Mansion House St.
Cannon Street Station
LONDON BRIDGE
Tower of London
St. Katharine Dock
National Gallery
VICTORIA
WATERLOO BRIDGE
Thames
National Theatre
NORTH SOUTHWARK
Tate Modern
Southwark Cathedral
H.M.S. Belfast
Charing Cross
TRAFALGAR SQUARE
Embankment
HUNGERFORD FOOTBRIDGE
Charing Cross Sta.
Royal Festival Hall
STAMFORD ST.
SOUTHWARK
Southwark
London Dungeon
London Br.
TOOLEY ST.
City Hall
TOWER BRIDGE
Greenwich
Horse Guards Parade
WHITEHALL
Banqueting House
London Eye
Waterloo
Shakespeare's Globe
Old Operating Theatre
London Bridge Sta.
H
Ministry of Defence
County Hall
Waterloo Station
Southwark
BLACKFRIARS RD.
Borough
ST. THOMAS ST.
Sea Life London Aquarium
WATERLOO RD.
BOROUGH HIGH ST.
GREAT DOVER STREET
LONG LANE
Westminster
WESTMINSTER BR.
Lambeth North
BOROUGH RD.
TOWER BRIDGE RD.
Westminster Abbey
Big Ben
WESTMINSTER BR. RD.
G
VICTORIA STREET
Houses of Parliament
LAMBETH PALACE RD.
ST. GEORGE'S RD.
SOUTHWARK
Lambeth Palace
NEW KENT ROAD
HORSEFERRY RD.
LAMBETH BRIDGE
LAMBETH
Imperial War Museum
Elephant & Castle
WESTMINSTER
MILLBANK
Tate Britain
ALBERT EMBANKMENT
NEWINGTON
BRIDGE RD.
Pimlico
KENNINGTON ROAD
KENNINGTON LANE
KENNINGTON PARK RD.
VAUXHALL
Kennington
VAUXHALL BRIDGE
SOUTH LAMBETH ROAD
Vauxhall Station
KENNINGTON
THE OVAL
OVAL
F
Vauxhall
Oval
WANDSWORTH ROAD
ELMS LANE
Covent Garden Flower Market
New Covent Garden Market
E

Area of map detail
London ★

The City

The City of London, or the "Square Mile," as the financial heart of the capital is known, is almost entirely given over to commerce, an exciting and sometimes jarring mishmash of solid Georgian and Victorian architecture alongside plate-glass modernism. It is a stimulating place to walk around—though the many very fine 17th-century churches provide havens of peace.

St. Paul's served as a onetime symbol of wartime resistance.

The Square Mile covers about the same area as the walled city of Londinium founded by the Romans on the Thames in A.D. 43. It was the farthest point that ships could reach at high tide, and the first feasible place upriver from the estuary mouth where a bridge could be built.

Londinium recovered quickly after being sacked in A.D. 60 by the rebel Iceni tribe under its warrior-queen Boudicca, and soon became the chief port and road junction of Roman Britain. The boundaries of the city did not expand outside the Roman walls until well after the Norman

Conquest; then they commenced a gradual creep westward.

Following the restoration of King Charles II, two disasters struck London. The Great Plague of 1665 killed a quarter of the capital's inhabitants, and the following year's Great Fire destroyed four out of every five houses. This was not an unmitigated tragedy, however, since it provided an opportunity to build a more modern city, mostly of stone, much of it heavily influenced by the baroque style.

St. Paul's Cathedral is the showpiece of the 17th-century rebirth of the City of London, but the City walk (see pp. 56–57) shows you many more post–Great Fire architectural treasures, as well as a number of medieval gems that have survived fire, wartime bombing, and modern developers.

St. Paul's Cathedral

One wartime photograph above all came to symbolize the resisting spirit of London during the 1940 Blitz—a shot of the dome of St. Paul's Cathedral silhouetted against a wall of flame and smoke, standing firm under attack. There was an irony to the image, too, for it was the Great Fire of London in 1666 that destroyed the city's medieval cathedral and enabled Sir Christopher Wren (1632–1723) to build the church that made his name and fortune. Wren dominated London's rebuilding after the fire, designing 52 churches, of which the great baroque Cathedral of St. Paul (1675–1710) was his masterpiece.

Huge, domed, swagged, and magnificent, bulky St. Paul's sits marooned in a green churchyard. Twin towers guard the west front, built in 1707—the northern tower houses the largest bell in England, the 17-ton "Great Paul." Inside, the saucer domes on the nave ceiling carry the eye forward to the crossing under the great dome (see sidebar this page).

Before climbing the 530 steps to the dome's topmost viewing gallery, stroll around the cathedral. Here, the beautiful wrought-iron choir screen was made by Jean Tijou, one of the Huguenot refugees who so greatly enhanced the cultural and artistic life of Britain. Another foreign settler, the Rotterdam master carver Grinling Gibbons (1648–1721), carved the choir stalls and organ casing to Wren's original decorative design.

Memorials: Wren wished that the cathedral be left uncluttered with memorials, but the cathedral's symbolic importance made this impossible. Indeed, much of the interest of St. Paul's lies in its many monuments. Immediately on entry, you pass on your left the Chapel of All Souls with its deathly white effigy of Lord Kitchener of Khartoum. A touching and seldom inspected pietà sits above the chapel's altar.

In the north aisle and north transept are memorials to famous men such as Dr. Samuel Johnson (see p. 57) and Field Marshal Lord Slim, as well as to forgotten heroes like Maj. Gen. Andrew Hay, who died "closing a military life marked by zeal, prompt decision, and signal intrepidity." Painter and sculptor Frederick, Lord Leighton (1830–1896) and the Duke of Wellington (1769–1852) both have remarkably hook-nosed effigies.

St. Paul's Cathedral

🅰 53 F4
✉ St. Paul's Churchyard, EC4
☎ 020-7236 4128
🕐 Closed Sun. except for services
💲 $$$$
🚇 Tube: St. Paul's
www.stpauls.co.uk

St. Paul's Dome

Wren's innovative genius was allowed full play in the construction of the dome, 364 feet high and second only in height to St. Peter's in Vatican City. It measures 157 feet from side to side of its famous Whispering Gallery, and it bears down with the weight of thousands of tons of stone and lead—the lantern alone weighs 850 tons.

Shallow wooden steps lead to a short flight of stone stairs and the entrance to the Whispering Gallery with its wall paintings and good view down into the nave.

From here, more spiral steps climb to the windy Stone Gallery, and there is a final flight of iron stairs to the little railed Golden Gallery, dizzyingly high, where you stand in the open 350 feet above the churchyard and look out over London.

Wellington himself lies buried in the crypt in a giant marble tomb surrounded by lions, while nearby are images of Florence Nightingale (1820–1910) tending a soldier, and the hero of Trafalgar, Admiral Lord Nelson (1758–1805), lying in a huge, black sarcophagus. His coffin was originally commissioned for Cardinal Wolsey in the 16th century, then seized by Henry VIII. It remained unused until 1805 when Nelson was buried within it. ■

A Walking Tour of the City

From the Monument pillar, this walk leads into the financial heart of the capital, with the Bank of England and the Stock Exchange, and on past three City churches and the great St. Paul's Cathedral to Fleet Street and the Inns of Court.

Set off from the 202-foot **Monument ❶** *(Monument St., EC3, tel 020-7626 2717, tube: Monument),* a column topped with a brilliant gold flame. It stands 202 feet from the site of the baker's shop in Pudding Lane where the Great Fire of London broke out on September 2, 1666. The fire raged for four days, consuming 13,200 houses and 89 churches.

Walk along Fish Street and turn right onto Eastcheap. Turn left on Philpot Lane, cross Fenchurch Street, and go along Lime Street; turn left onto Beehive Passage. **Leadenhall Market** on the left is a maze of curved, cobbled streets full of expensive food and gift shops, pubs, and chic restaurants. From Leadenhall Place view the boldly bizarre **Lloyd's Building ❷**, with

NOT TO BE MISSED:

Lloyd's Building • St. Paul's Cathedral • Sir John Soane's Museum

elevators scuttling up and down its gleaming metallic walls like robotic insects.

Turn left along Leadenhall Place to Gracechurch Street; turn right, cross Cornhill, then go west on Threadneedle Street to enter London's financial heart. On the right are the modern buildings of the Stock Exchange, then the impressive pillars of the grand Old Lady of Threadneedle Street, the **Bank of England ❸**, founded

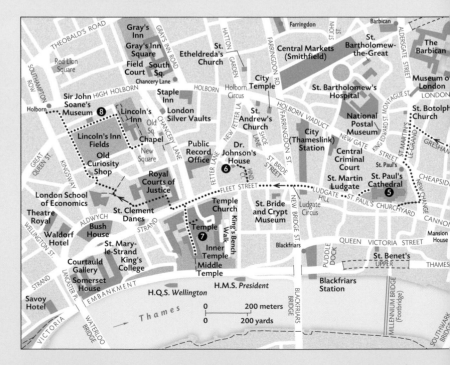

in 1694, with its **Bank of England Museum** *(Bartholomew Ln., EC2, tel 020-7601 5545, closed Sat.–Sun., tube: Bank).* Beyond on the left is narrow Lombard Street, hung with elaborate signs— a banking center since Norman times.

Cross the top of Lombard Street and take a left on Walbrook to **St. Stephen Walbrook** (1672–1679), an ornately domed stone church designed by Wren. Inside is a massive altar sculpted by Henry Moore (1898–1986).

Go along Bucklersbury, then turn left along Poultry; turn right and proceed north on King Street to Gresham Street. Here are the **Church of St. Lawrence Jewry,** with a stained-glass portrait of Wren, and the **Guildhall** ❹ *(Gresham St., EC2, tel 020-7332 1313, closed Sun. Oct.–April, tube: Bank, St. Paul's),* whose Great Hall holds monuments to William Pitt and Sir Winston Churchill.

From the Guildhall, go west on Gresham Street to the junction with Aldersgate Street. On the right is the Georgian **St. Botolph Church,** with a fine plaster ceiling and stained glass

showing John Wesley preaching. Walk south along St. Martin's-Le-Grand and New Change to **St. Paul's Cathedral** ❺ (see pp. 54–55).

West of St. Paul's

Walk west along Ludgate Hill, then Fleet Street; turn right along Hind Court to Gough Square. **Dr. Johnson's House** ❻ *(17 Gough Sq., EC2, tel 020-7353 3745, closed Sun., tube: Temple, Blackfriars),* is where Samuel Johnson (1709–1784) compiled his seminal *Dictionary of the English Language* (1755); cartoons and paintings by Johnson and his biographer, James Boswell (1740–1795), are shown.

Back on Fleet Street, cross and go right; past Cock Tavern, go left through Temple Bar gateway. In the early Middle Ages, the **Temple** ❼ *(Middle Temple Hall, Middle Temple Ln., EC4, tel 020-7427 4800, closed Sat.–Sun. & Aug., tube: Temple)* was headquarters of the Knights Templar. Here in a maze of lanes and courtyards are the Societies of the Middle and Inner Temples, where students train for the bar (law).

Back on Fleet Street again, cross and go left past the **Royal Courts of Justice,** then right to cut through to St. Clement's Lane. Cross Portugal Street and continue on St. Clement's; turn left into Portsmouth Street opposite the tiny **Old Curiosity Shop** (claiming to be Dickens's inspiration). At the top of the street is **Lincoln's Inn Fields,** where felons were executed.

Sir John Soane's Museum ❽ (see p. 95), a hidden jewel, sits on the square's north side. On the east side is **Lincoln's Inn** *(Chancery Ln., tel 020-7405 1393, closed Sat.–Sun., tube: Chancery Lane),* the oldest of the four Inns of Court. Enter to see the 17th-century houses and courtyards. From Lincoln's Inn Fields' northwest corner, turn right to reach Holborn tube station.

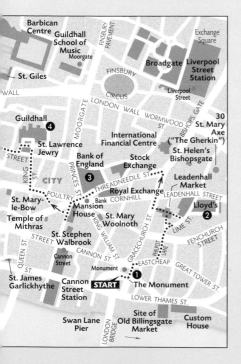

🅰	See area map p. 53
▶	Monument tube station
🕐	Half a day
↔	3.5 miles
▶	Holborn tube station

Westminster & the West End.

Westminster is undoubtedly the heart of visitors' London. This area of the capital lying west of the Thames contains the Houses of Parliament and Big Ben, Westminster Abbey and Buckingham Palace, Trafalgar Square and the National Gallery—all perennial attractions. Yet Westminster is also the constitutional, political, and royal heart of the nation. All the great ceremonial occasions, from the State Opening of Parliament to Trooping the Colour, take place here.

London's grand Westminster Abbey contains priceless treasures of medieval artwork.

Westminster is the London residence of the monarch, and kings and queens have been crowned, married, and buried here for a thousand years. The prime minister lives in Westminster; Parliament lays down the law here; and Big Ben strikes the national time signal.

The view across the Thames of the pinnacled Houses of Parliament and Big Ben's tower is the most photographed scene in the country, and the image most often associated with London.

The walk on pages 64–65 around the heart of the capital will show you the great sights of Westminster. It also will introduce you to some less familiar delights, such as the beautiful but often overlooked Church of St. Margaret, the Cabinet War Rooms where Winston Churchill and colleagues planned the conduct of World War II, and the touchingly overblown ceiling paintings of the Banqueting House that Charles I commissioned to celebrate the divinity of the Stuart dynasty.

Westminster Abbey

Filling the south side of Parliament Square, Westminster Abbey is not only the largest and loveliest Gothic church in London, but very evidently the point where the religious, political, and monarchical lives of the nation intersect. This site has been the scene of 38 coronations since that of William the Conqueror on Christmas Day 1066—all the monarchs save Edward V, murdered in 1483, and Edward VIII, who abdicated in 1936.

The present church was refounded in 1065 by Edward the Confessor just before the Norman Conquest, replacing a church of circa 960. Most of the abbey as it is today was begun in 1245, during the reign of Henry III. It was completed in leisurely medieval fashion; the nave, though in the same Gothic style, dates from the 14th century. The Lady Chapel at the east end brings us into the Tudor era, while the towers at the west end are the 18th-century work of Nicholas Hawksmoor (1661–1736) to a design by his mentor, Sir Christopher Wren.

Westminster Abbey is enormous, and a good impression of its bulk is gained from outside the mighty Victorian Great North Door, whose porch flaunts rank upon rank of offertory and musical angels, potentates, prelates, and saints. Inside, the immediate impression is of great height (the nave is 102 feet from floor to roof) and of narrowness, dramatically lit by huge chandeliers.

Interior: One of the church's chief attractions is its unrivaled collection of monuments to the great and good (and to the not so great or good).

After payment at the Great North Door, you can advance to see Statesmen's Aisle in the north transept. Here are some of the

Westminster Abbey

🅰 53 E3

✉ Parliament Sq., SW1

☎ 020-7222 5152

💲 Abbey $$, chapter house $–$$

Ⓜ Tube: Westminster, St. James's Park

www.westminster-abbey.org

EXPERIENCE: Watch Parliament in Action

Nothing could be more inspiring than to observe the Mother of Parliaments (commoners and lords enacting democratic laws since the 13th century) in action in the magnificent Houses of Parliament. The **House of Lords** is great on ceremony, but it works (generally) on a slower and more courteous basis than the rough-and-tumble **House of Commons.** That's where most visitors head, hoping to see lively debate with plenty of cut and thrust. You may be lucky and witness the sparks fly, or it may happen that some obscure local finance matter is being debated.

To see the prime minister challenged, sometimes bruisingly, by the opposition, you need to attend **Prime Minister's Question Time** (generally at 3 p.m.); tickets to the event are free, but only U.K. residents can book them (through their MP or lord), so it's a matter of luck and a short queue for spots not taken by ticket-holders. Attending a **debate** (Mon.–Thurs., some Fri.) is simpler—join the line outside the Cromwell Green Visitor Entrance, on St. Margaret Street, and eventually it will be your turn. No matter what the quality of the debate, the neo-Gothic masterpiece that is the main chamber of the House of Commons makes a superb backdrop. For more information, visit *www.parliament.uk/visiting/attend/.*

abbey's finest statues, including those of Benjamin Disraeli (1804–1881), William Gladstone (1809–1898), and Sir Robert Peel (1788–1850). William Pitt (1759–1806) has a 25-foot monument. On your right, the north choir aisle close to the organ is dedicated to musicians, with monuments to Henry Purcell, Sir Edward Elgar, and Benjamin Britten.

Royal Chapels: At the east end of the church are the chapels where the monarchs rest. Walking around the ambulatory you get glimpses of the carved stone shrine of Edward the Confessor (r. 1042–1066) and of the later medieval royal tombs erected close to it. At the foot of the stairs to Henry VIII's Chapel is the oak Coronation Chair, made in 1301 and used at every coronation since. The richly fan-vaulted Chapel of Henry VII conceals some splendidly heroic and humorous misericords under the choir stall seats. Here lies Henry himself (r. 1485–1509) in gilt bronze effigy. Below is the tomb of James I, far more modest than the overblown grandiosity of his adviser, the Duke of Buckingham (1592–1628), who lies surrounded by grieving bronze warriors. In the north aisle, Queen Elizabeth I looks coldly regal in marble; Mary, Queen of Scots, stares piously up at a display of gilt flowers in the canopy above her tomb in the south aisle.

Poets' Corner & the Chapter House: Poets' Corner, in the south aisle, holds monuments to William Shakespeare, John Dryden, Henry Wadsworth Longfellow, Lewis Carroll, W. H. Auden, Henry James, Alfred Lord Tennyson, D. H. Lawrence, Lord Byron, Robert Southey, Charles Dickens, and Sir Walter Scott. The 13th-century chapter house (reached from the east cloister) has superb stone carvings above a floor tiled in rich ocher and cream colors. The walls display mind-boggling 14th-century frescoes: St. John blissfully smiling in a vat of boiling oil, venerable saints casting down their golden crowns, a snub-nosed dromedary, a one-hump "Kameyl," and a fiery red depiction of a "reynder" hunt.

Nave: Toward the west end are floor slabs to politicians Stanley Baldwin (1867–1947), Clement Attlee (1883–1967), and David Lloyd George (1863–1945), among others, as well as to Sir Winston Churchill (1874–1965) and the symbolic Unknown Warrior of World War I. These contrast with monuments such as the one for Capt. Richard le Neve of the *Edgar*, killed in 1673 in a "sharp engagement with the Hollanders."

Buckingham Palace

The Royal Family does not particularly care for Buckingham Palace, it is said: They always appear happier at Windsor, Sandringham, or Balmoral. The original Buckingham House was built in 1703 for the Duke of Buckingham in what were then rural surroundings, but it has been greatly altered since.

The palace seen now was built in the early 1920s. It is the official London residence of the monarch, whose presence is signified by the flying of the Royal Standard.

King George III bought Buckingham House in 1762. John Nash carried out an enlargement in the early 1820s for George IV, but was "let go" when his plans proved too expensive. In 1837, at the threshold of Queen Victoria's reign, it became the sovereign's residence in preference to St. James's Palace.

Nineteen of the 661 rooms are open to the public each summer, originally to help pay for repairs to Windsor Castle (see pp. 102–105) after the 1992 fire there (renovations were completed in 1997). This arrangement will be reviewed in time but is likely to continue. You can view the red-and-gold Grand Hall, with Nash's curved staircase and glazed dome; the vaulted Picture Gallery, lined with a no-nonsense selection of Old Masters; the gold-ceilinged Throne Room; the sumptuous State Dining Room; and other ceremonial chambers.

Other, separate attractions are the **Royal Mews** *(tel 020-7766 7302, closed Sat.–Sun. late Sept.–July)* with its collection of extravagant state carriages and cars, and the Queen's art collection, presented as a series of changing exhibitions in the **Queen's Gallery** *(tel 020-7766 7301)*. One attraction that has never lost its appeal is the **Changing of the Guard** *(11:30 a.m. daily April–early July, alternate days early July–March)*, when red-jacketed guardsmen under tall black bearskin hats march in front of the palace.

Buckingham Palace

🅰 52 D3

✉ Buckingham Palace Rd., SW1

☎ 020-7766 7300

🕐 Closed Oct.–early Aug.

💲 $$$$

Ⓜ Tube: St. James's Park, Green Park

www.royalcollection .org.uk

Late in the morning crowds gather in front of Buckingham Palace to watch the Changing of the Guard.

National Gallery

 53 E4

✉ Trafalgar Sq.,
WC2

☎ 020-7747 2885

🕐 Late closing Fri.

$ Charge
for special
exhibitions

🚇 Tube: Charing
Cross, Leicester
Square

**www.national
gallery.org.uk**

National Gallery

With its great portico fronting
onto Trafalgar Square, the
National Gallery is London's
premier art gallery, displaying
one of the greatest collections of
Western European paintings in
the world. The four-wing layout
is user friendly: 1250–1500 in
the Sainsbury Wing; 1500–1600
in the West Wing; 1600–1700 in
the North Wing; and 1700–1900
in the East Wing.

angels with gull-like wings
surrounds the Virgin and Child.
Room 56 holds Van Eyck's
"Arnolfini Marriage."

In **Room 58** can be found
Botticelli's "Venus and Mars"
and in **Room 66** is the painting
"Baptism of Christ" by Piero
della Francesca (ca 1420–1492),
in which a glorious, sleepy-eyed
angelic choir sings hymns to
Mary with her beautiful, almond-
shaped face.

Arfully arranged, the National Gallery's collection entices visitors to linger over the artwork.

To make the most of your time
here, browse the gallery plan and
catalog, selecting about 30 paintings or artists you would really
like to see (a few star attractions
are suggested below). But along
the way you will stumble across
so much more, either familiar or
new to you.

Sainsbury Wing: Room 53

has the "Wilton Diptych," in
which a flock of blue-robed

West Wing: Room 2 contains
Leonardo da Vinci's famous
cartoon "The Virgin and Child
with St. John the Baptist and
St. Anne." Michelangelo's unfinished "Entombment," showing
a pale Christ held in a sling of
grave wrappings, is in **Room 8,**
as is Raphael's tiny, exquisite
"Madonna of the Pinks." **Room
9** has Veronese's "The Rape of
Europa" and a superb Tintoretto
of the seen-it-all face of Senator

Vincenzo Morosini in old age. There are several Titians here (you'll find his "Death of Actaeon," a savage composition in Titian's later, blurry style engendered by failing eyesight, in the Central Hall).

North Wing: In **Room 14** are a Pieter Bruegel the Elder "Adoration," with the Three Kings exhausted after their journey, and two ugly "Tax-Gatherers" by Marinus Van Reymerswaele. Jan Vermeer is in **Rooms 25 and 27** and Franz Hals in **Room 24.** Room 24 also contains several Rembrandts, as does **Room 23.** One shows the artist's wife, Saskia, in 1635, age 24, bursting with life and warmth; another is a beautifully affectionate portrait of Hendrickje Stoffels, nursemaid to Rembrandt's child after Saskia died, and later the painter's mistress.

In **Room 29** is "Samson and Delilah" by Rubens, with Samson collapsed in a stupor on Delilah's rich and sumptuous red dress. **Room 30** displays "The Toilet of Venus" (also known as "The Rokeby Venus"), painted by Diego Velázquez (1599–1660), celebrating the warm tints and curves of this narcissistic goddess.

East Wing: Room 34 is full of treasures: Works by J. M. W. Turner (1775–1851) include his early, storm-tossed "Dutch Boats in a Gale," as well as his later, poignant "The Fighting Temeraire" and tempestuous "Rain, Steam and Speed." Also here are superb landscapes by

John Constable (1776–1837), including "Salisbury Cathedral from the Meadows" and "Stratford Mill." His famous "Hay Wain" reveals many details on close inspection—haymakers in the distance, three red admiral butterflies in the foreground, a vase of red flowers in a window of Willy Lott's house.

Room 38 contains pictures of Venice by Canaletto, **Room 39** some nice dark Goya portraits, including a coldly efficient "Duke of Wellington."

Room 43 is packed with Impressionists—Manet, Monet, Morisot, Renoir's "A Nymph by a Stream," and Sisley's cold and watery "The Seine at Port-Marly." **Room 44** has studies for "La Grande Jatte" by Georges Seurat (1859–1891), along with several

INSIDER TIP:

The National Gallery is open until 9 p.m. every Friday. There is a range of activities, including talks, live music in Room 18, and a bar.

—ELOISE MAXWELL
Press Office Assistant,
National Gallery

beautiful calm scenes by Camille Pissarro. In **Room 45** are sunny Cézanne landscapes and his blue "Bather," plus several wild van Goghs, including the spiky "Wheatfield with Cypresses," painted in the St.-Rémy asylum, and one of his four "Sunflowers."
(continued on p. 66)

A Walking Tour of Westminster

From the Houses of Parliament, this walk leads to Westminster Abbey, then continues through St. James's Park to Buckingham Palace. From there it follows the Mall to Trafalgar Square before reaching Banqueting House.

From Westminster tube station cross the street to **Big Ben,** the great clock tower named after its 14-ton bell, which has tolled time for Britain since 1859. Turn right and continue around to the left into **Parliament Square,** with its statues of national heroes.

On your left rise the unmistakable **Houses of Parliament,** or more properly the **Palace of Westminster ❶** (*$$$, by guided tour only. Ticket office on Abingdon Green or call 0870-906 3773. See www.parliament.uk for hours*), a grand Gothic fantasy built between 1837 and 1860 by Sir Charles Barry (1812–1852) and Augustus Pugin (1795–1860) to accommodate the House of Lords and the House of Commons. The original palace was built here by Edward the Confessor in the 11th century. After the Reformation, the Commons were housed in what had been

INSIDER TIP:

The Supreme Court, across from Westminster Abbey, has a museum and courtyard café.

—MARY LAMBERTON
National Geographic contributor

the palace's chapel. When that was burned in 1834, Pugin and Barry were called in. The Speaker's Chair stands where the chapel's altar used to be. Beyond the House of Commons is the 11th-century **Westminster Hall,** built for William II, where Guy Fawkes was tried for treason in 1605, as was Charles I at the end of the Civil War. Charles II had Oliver Cromwell's head spiked on the roof in 1661, in revenge for his own father's execution.

Cross to **St. Margaret's Church,** used by the House of Commons since 1614, a late

---

NOT TO BE MISSED:

Palace of Westminster
• **Westminster Abbey** • **Cabinet War Rooms** • **National Gallery**

---

medieval gem with notable stained glass—at the west end, the blind poet John Milton dictating *Paradise Lost,* with scenes from the Fall all around him; at the east end, pain-wracked faces and bodies in a 16th-century Flemish Crucifixion; in the south aisle, daring modern spikes and slashes in gray, green, and yellow by John Piper.

Continue into **Westminster Abbey ❷** (see pp. 59–61). From the abbey, cross to the north side of Parliament Square. Go left along Great George Street to the edge of St. James's Park, then turn right to the **Cabinet War Rooms ❸** (*Clive Steps, King Charles St., SW1, tel 020-7930 6961, tube: Westminster, St. James's Park*).

In this complex of subterranean rooms, Winston Churchill and his staff planned the Allied conduct of World War II. The original maps, full of pin holes, are still stuck on the walls. Initially prepared as a small bunker in August 1939, the Cabinet War Rooms had by 1945 branched into 70 rooms, covering more than three acres underground. Some of Churchill's best known wartime speeches were broadcast from here. Audio guides lead you around the rather spooky chambers. There are giant radio sets and scramblers, telephone exchanges, typing pools, and bedrooms with functional iron bedsteads—a complete secret citadel under London's streets. Churchill's own workroom is on display, as is his bedroom (seldom slept in) containing an ash tin for the prime ministerial cigar, and a plain white chamber pot.

Back at street level cross into **St. James's Park ④** (see p. 79), London's oldest park, and walk through in a westerly direction to reach **Buckingham Palace ⑤** (see p. 61).

From the palace it is a little under a mile to Trafalgar Square along the ruler-straight, tree-lined Mall. En route you could detour to Stable Yard to view the great Tudor brick gatehouse of **St. James's Palace,** the monarch's residence until Buckingham Palace superseded it.

Trafalgar Square is a tourist magnet with its **Nelson's Column.** Admiral Horatio Nelson towers 185 feet above the fountains designed by Sir Edwin Lutyens (1869–1944) and the four famous lions, the work of Sir Edwin Landseer (1802–1873). Facing the square are the **National Gallery ⑥** (see pp. 62–63, 66), behind which is the **National Portrait Gallery ⑦** (see p. 66), and the early Georgian church of **St. Martin-in-the-Fields,** famous for sheltering the homeless and for its free, thrice-weekly lunchtime concerts.

Turn south on Whitehall to find the **Banqueting House ⑧** (*Whitehall, SW1, tel 020-3166*

6154/5, closed Sun. & for government functions, tube: Westminster, Charing Cross), remnant of the great Royal Palace of Whitehall that burned in 1698. Upstairs in the Great Hall, a Rubens ceiling celebrates the reign of Scottish King James VI, who in 1603 became James I of England. Charles I, who commissioned the paintings in 1629 to honor his father and to enshrine the divine status of the monarchy, was beheaded on January 30, 1649, on a scaffold built for the occasion against the wall of the Banqueting House.

Continue past the entrance to **Downing Street,** opposite, now gated to protect No. 10, the prime minister's residence. Pass the **Cenotaph,** Britain's national war memorial (also by Lutyens), to return to Westminster tube station.

▨	See area map pp. 52–53
▶	Westminster tube station
⊕	Half a day
⇄	2 miles
▶	Westminster tube station

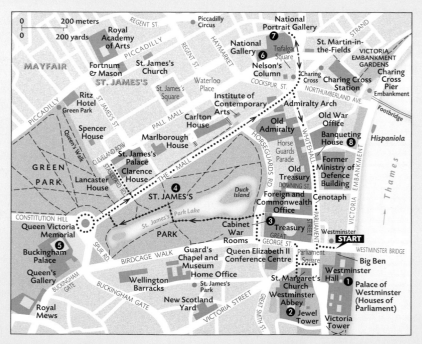

National Portrait Gallery

53 E4

St. Martin's Place, WC2

020-7306 0055. Recorded information: 020-7312 2463

Late closing Thurs.–Fri.

Charge for special exhibitions

Tube: Charing Cross, Leicester Square

www.npg.org.uk

Level O: Room C holds a darkly passionate "Agony in the Garden of Gethsemane" by El Greco, **Room E** Hieronymus Bosch's "Christ Mocked," full of brutal faces and spiked armor.

National Portrait Gallery

The National Portrait Gallery on St. Martin's Place contains some 9,000 portraits, drawings, photographs, and sculptures spanning more than 500 years. Many themes emerge. In old age William Wordsworth broods poetically, Charles II like a cynical satyr, and former Home Secretary Lord Whitelaw in gentle puzzlement, while poet Coventry Patmore stands dandyish and alert.

In all the flush of youthful beauty are actress Ellen Terry at 17; Emma Hamilton, Nelson's mistress, at 20; Christine Keeler, a call girl at the center of a 1960s government scandal, shown naked astride a trendy Arne Jacobsen chair; and poet Rupert Brooke.

Successful Figures: There are women accustomed to exerting power: a steely-haired Baroness Thatcher; Glenys Kinnock at ease over the teacups with politician husband Neil; a cold, implacable Queen Elizabeth I with hooded, unfathomable eyes; and a 1918 portrait by Augustus John of Lady Ottoline Morrell, socialite lover of several of the artists and sitters in this gallery, looking rapacious and rather mad in a huge black hat.

Then there is the self-confident power exuded by some of the most successful middle-aged men, exemplified in the portraits of architect Sir John Vanbrugh (1705) and royal painter Sir Peter Lely (1660).

Human Frailty: As for the eyes being the windows of the soul, they certainly open up the inner being in Sir Thomas Lawrence's unfinished 1828 presentation of reformer William Wilberforce in late middle age, George Romney's self-portrait of 1784 (unfinished), and Romney's 1792 depiction of poet William Cowper.

Hollow-faced poet Alexander Pope and piercing-eyed scientist Stephen Hawking, twisted up with amyotrophic lateral sclerosis and motor neuron disease, show the spirit's triumph over the flesh.

By contrast, we see the cigar-chomping Victorian engineering genius Isambard Kingdom Brunel (see sidebar p. 152), casually yet masterfully posed against giant chain links, and the saturnine media mogul Rupert Murdoch, alone and watchful in a deserted newsroom, icons of material success in their respective ages.

Money-saving Cards

These cards are well worth investing in— they'll save you a lot of money:

Oystercard: Reduced fares on buses, overground rail, the Underground, Docklands Light Railway, trams, and some mainline railway services. www.oystercard.com.

London Pass: Free entry, skip the queue, other benefits at dozens of attractions; reduces fares, too. www.londonpass.com.

Tastecard: Fifty percent off bill at nearly 4,000 restaurants. www.tastecard.co.uk.

A sleek, modern space in the National Portrait Gallery holds artwork from the 20th century.

Tate Britain/Tate Modern

Tate Britain (formerly the Tate Gallery), facing the Thames on Millbank, was a gift to the nation from Victorian sugar manufacturer Sir Henry Tate (1819–1899). It holds the best of British painting from Tudor times up to the 20th century. Downriver on the river's opposite bank is Tate Modern, housing an eclectic, often unconventional collection of modern painting and sculpture from around the world.

At **Tate Britain** the artwork is mostly on the ground floor, arranged in chronological order from the 16th century to the present day. Exhibits range from the richly tinted fashion of 17th-century portraiture through 18th- and 19th-century landscapes and society portraits to a wide-ranging collection of pre-Raphaelites, Impressionists, and 20th-century works by Pablo Picasso, Auguste Rodin, David Hockney, and others.

Tate Britain also holds the definitive collection of the works of J. M. W. Turner; letters, sketches, and a fascinating display of his working notebooks can also be seen.

Housed in a stunning transformation of the Victorian Bankside Power Station at Southwark, **Tate Modern** is one of the world's leading modern art galleries. It contains international art from the 20th century, including works by Matisse, Picasso, Pollock, and Warhol. The annually changing art installations in the enormous Turbine Hall—Anish Kapoor, Rachel Whiteread, Miroslav Balka—represent the forefront of postmodern art. Much more controversially, the annual award of the Turner Prize, lucrative and newsworthy, is guaranteed to stir up raging debate about the nature of art, with past entries having included a lightbulb going on and off, a voice singing in an empty room, and a dirty and crumpled bed. ■

Tate Britain
- 53 E2
- Millbank, SW1
- 020-7887 8888
- Charge for special exhibitions
- Tube: Pimlico

www.tate.org.uk

Tate Modern
- 53 F4
- Bankside, SE1
- 020-7887 8888
- Charge for special exhibitions
- Tube: Southwark, Blackfriars, London Bridge

www.tate.org.uk

Soho & Covent Garden Walk

This walk introduces you to two of the most colorful areas of central London, Soho and Covent Garden, both of which have seen great changes in the past couple of decades.

Emerging from the Piccadilly Circus tube station, you are confronted with the statue of **Eros** at the center of Piccadilly Circus. In fact, the delicately balanced winged figure represents the Angel of Christian Charity; it was put up in 1893 to honor the 7th Earl of Shaftesbury, a philanthropist who worked to abolish child labor in Victorian factories.

Head first for **Ripley's Believe It or Not! ❶** *(tel 020-3238 0022, tube: Piccadilly Circus),* in the London Pavilion, No. 1, Piccadilly Circus. In this emporium devoted to the amusement of the amazing, no one with a sense of humor and the ridiculous could fail to be enchanted by a statue of the Beatles made out of chewing gum, a genuine 16th-century Iron Maiden torture machine, a model of London's Tower Bridge made out of 264,345 matchsticks—and lots, lots more.

Next turn onto Shaftesbury Avenue, then left to Great Windmill Street into **Soho.** This region of narrow streets north of Piccadilly Circus was built as a pleasant residential area after the 1666 Great Fire. But eventually Soho became an immigrants' area where first Huguenot refugees and then Poles and Russians, Greeks and Italians set up house and shop. In Victorian times, Soho became a raffish night haunt for theatergoers and music hall devotees. By the 1950s it had declined into a seedy district of peepshows, strip joints, and sex parlors or—according to its many artistic and literary aficionados—a freewheeling refuge from bourgeois constraint. Both elements still exist, but some of the sordidness has waned in the face of a new wave of decent small restaurants and food-centered businesses, many owned by the area's Chinese.

East of Soho

Working your way north, you'll pass the **Hix Oyster and Chop House** *(tel 020-7292 3518),* a really good relaxed eating place. At

Berwick Street Market *(closed Sun.)* there are stalls piled with fruit, olives, and cheeses.

To the southeast, around Gerrard and Lisle Streets, is **Chinatown ❷** *(tube: Piccadilly Circus, Leicester Sq.),* marked by bilingual street names and a colorful ceremonial archway across Gerrard Street. During the Chinese New Year in late January or February, this district is alive with firecrackers and dragons. If you are hungry, try take-out crispy, aromatic duck and rice from any of two dozen restaurants.

North of Chinatown on Dean Street, above Leoni's **Quo Vadis** restaurant at No. 26, is a plaque recording the residence here of Karl Marx from 1851 to 1856, while he worked on *Das Kapital.* Across on the corner of Greek and Romilly Streets is the **Coach and Horses** pub (est. ca 1855), lined with cartoons and prints.

On Charing Cross Road make for Cambridge Circus, then go east along Earlham Street to **Seven Dials,** with its weird reconstruction of a 17th-century Doric pillar topped by sundials. Cross onto Shorts Gardens and turn left into **Neal's Yard ❸**, a little triangular oasis of New Age shops, "therapy rooms," alternative remedy emporia, and inexpensive eateries.

Covent Garden

From Shorts Gardens bear right on Neal Street, past crafts shops, kite sellers, cobblers, and vegetarian cafés. Cross Long Acre by the nice art deco tube station of Covent Garden to reach the former fruit and vegetable market itself in its big open square.

On your left is the **Royal Opera House** (see p. 390), one of the world's great opera venues, a splendid building recently overhauled. This is the home of both the Royal Ballet and Royal Opera companies. On the square's east side is the **London Transport Museum ④** (39 Wellington St., tel 020-7379 6344, www.ltmuseum.co.uk, tube: Covent Garden), whose collection of venerable old horse-drawn buses and trams, trolley buses, ancient underground steam locomotives, and vintage tube trains is housed in the old Victorian flower-market shed.

Just south on the Strand you'll find two adjacent theaters, old London favorites both—the **Vaudeville Theatre ⑤**, at No. 404 (tel 0844-412 4663), and the **Adelphi Theatre ⑥**, just along the street at No. 412–416 (tel 0844-412 4651). There's great theater history attached to these twins: genius actor Henry Irving got his first break at the Vaudeville in 1870, and many of Charles Dickens's early works received their stage premieres at the Adelphi.

Old Market Place: Centerpiece of the square is **Covent Garden Market ⑦** (tube: Covent Garden), a beautiful 1833 hall of iron and glass. Covent Garden was the Soho of

the 17th and 18th centuries, an unsavory mass of brothels and gambling dens that grew up around the market. The Victorians cleaned it up, and it remained the city's chief fruit-and-vegetable market until 1974, when business moved across the river. Today the old hall shelters very chic restaurants, cafés, craft stalls, and stores, with entertainment from street performers guaranteed.

On the west side of the square is **St. Paul's Church ⑧** (Bedford St., tel 020-7836 5221, www.actorschurch.org, tube: Covent Garden). It holds dozens of memorials to well-known stage stars, including Boris Karloff, Vivien Leigh, and Charlie Chaplin. To the left of the door is a glorious wreath carved in limewood by Grinling Gibbons—his own memorial.

Back on Long Acre turn left for Leicester Square tube station (one stop from Piccadilly Circus via the Piccadilly line).

- ⚑ See area map pp. 52–53
- ▶ Piccadilly Circus tube station
- 🕓 4 hours
- ↔ 1.5 miles
- ▶ Leicester Square tube station

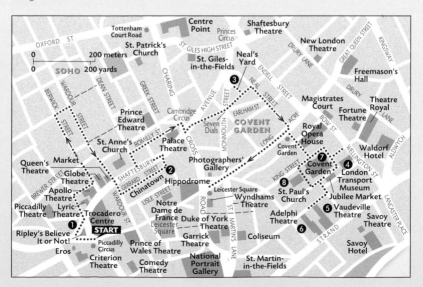

Bloomsbury

Bloomsbury lies northeast of Soho, north of New Oxford Street. The heart of the area is the British Museum, and around it lie the handsome garden squares laid out during London's 17th- and 18th-century shift west from the medieval city. A plaque in Bloomsbury Square pays tribute to the Bloomsbury Group, which was influential on early 20th-century thinking in the arts.

The roof that covers the British Museum's Great Court is made up of 3,312 glass panels.

Dickens House Museum

✉ 48 Doughty St., WC1

☎ 020-7405 2127

💲 $$

Ⓜ Tube: Russell Square

www.dickensmuseum.com

Sites particularly associated with literary figures are 46 Gordon Square, home to the Stephen family who founded the Bloomsbury Group (see sidebar opposite); Russell Square, where poet T. S. Eliot (1888–1965) worked for many years as an editor for the publisher Faber & Faber at No. 24; and Brunswick Square, north of Guildford Street, where Virginia Stephen (1882–1941) lived in 1911 at No. 28 with Leonard Woolf, whom she later married. The novelist E. M. Forster lived at 26 Brunswick Square from 1929 to 1939. Fitzroy Square (No. 29) was where Virginia and Adrian Stephen lived from 1907 to 1911; here they started Friday evening readings with Cambridge friends. Irish-born dramatist George Bernard Shaw wrote *Arms and the Man* and *Candida* (both 1894) at No. 39, during a stay of 11 years.

Charles Dickens, too, is strongly associated with Bloomsbury. On the eastern borders at 48 Doughty Street, now the excellent **Dickens House Museum,** he lived from 1837 to 1839 and

Bloomsbury Group

The Bloomsbury area is forever associated with the eponymous group, a coterie of avant-garde writers, designers, and artists who shared a bohemian lifestyle here and in the country before World War I and for a few years after. Centered around the Stephen brothers and sisters—Thoby, Adrian, Vanessa (later Bell), and Virginia (later Woolf)—and their home at 46 Gordon Square, the Bloomsbury Group included the pacifist socialist painter and critic Roger Fry; poet and novelist Vita Sackville-West; Virginia's publisher husband, Leonard Woolf; eminent writer on economics John Maynard Keynes; and biographer Lytton Strachey: a powerhouse of independent and willful intellect.

wrote *Oliver Twist* and *Nicholas Nickleby;* from 1851 to 1860 his home was Tavistock House in Tavistock Square, where he wrote *Bleak House, Hard Times, Little Dorrit,* and *A Tale of Two Cities* and started *Great Expectations.*

British Museum

The British Museum is one of the world's great museums. It was founded in 1753, when the government paid £20,000 ($33,000) on the death of Sir Hans Sloane (1660–1753), the royal physician, to secure his private collection of 79,000 objets d'art. The museum has grown ever since; current holdings total seven million items, from all over the world. In 1997 the British Library (see sidebar p. 73) moved from the museum to a new building at St. Pancras; its historic round Reading Room is now the Walter and Leonore Annenberg Centre and the Paul Hamlyn Library. The courtyard outside the Reading Room has been transformed into the Great Court, a 2-acre square spanned by a spectacular glass roof.

The museum is laid out on three floors with multiple levels—Rooms 1–24 and 26–35 on the main or ground floor, Rooms 36–73 and 90–94 on the upper floors, and Rooms 25 and 77–78 on the lower floor. It is impossible to see everything in the collection in one visit, so it's best to get a floor plan at the information desk and pick a few plum attractions.

Highlights: Room 18 contains the superb fifth-century B.C. relief frieze from the Parthenon's Temple of Athena, brought to London in 1801 by Lord Elgin, then British ambassador in Constantinople. In 1816 the British government paid him £35,000 ($58,000) for the marbles, and since then the Greek authorities have persistently asked to have them back—so far with no success. They are magical: an animated procession of horses and humans, among which agitated sacrificial heifers raise their muzzles to the sky. The Hellenistic theme occupies **Rooms 11–23,** where artifacts include a fine gold oak-leaf wreath decorated with tiny gold cicadas and a bee (ca 350–300 B.C.).

Enormous Assyrian friezes from the seventh century B.C. in

British Museum

🅰 53 E4–E5

✉ Great Russell St., WC1

☎ 020-7323 8299

💲 Donation. Charge for special exhibitions

🚇 Tube: Holborn, Tottenham Court Road, Russell Square

www.british museum.org

British Museum

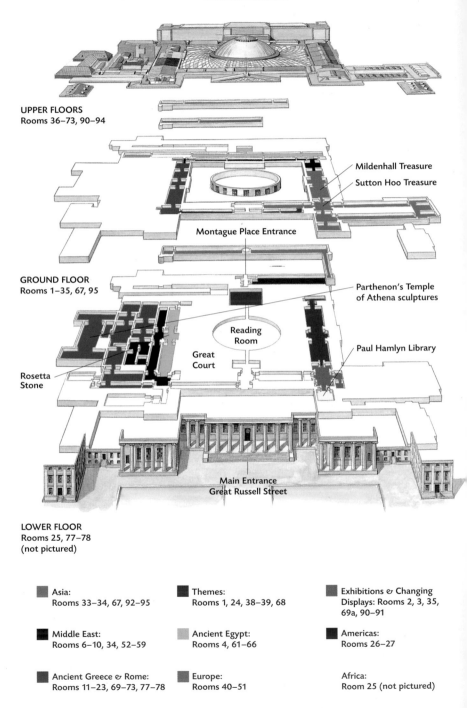

UPPER FLOORS
Rooms 36–73, 90–94

Mildenhall Treasure

Sutton Hoo Treasure

Montague Place Entrance

GROUND FLOOR
Rooms 1–35, 67, 95

Parthenon's Temple of Athena sculptures

Reading Room

Paul Hamlyn Library

Great Court

Rosetta Stone

Main Entrance
Great Russell Street

LOWER FLOOR
Rooms 25, 77–78
(not pictured)

Asia:
Rooms 33–34, 67, 92–95

Themes:
Rooms 1, 24, 38–39, 68

Exhibitions & Changing
Displays: Rooms 2, 3, 35,
69a, 90–91

Middle East:
Rooms 6–10, 34, 52–59

Ancient Egypt:
Rooms 4, 61–66

Americas:
Rooms 26–27

Ancient Greece & Rome:
Rooms 11–23, 69–73, 77–78

Europe:
Rooms 40–51

Africa:
Room 25 (not pictured)

Rooms 7–10 include the "Siege of Lachish," showing massed bowmen, spearmen, and slingers, as well as two unfortunate prisoners being flayed alive. The "Lion Hunt" friezes are even more striking, with snarling lions being stuck with arrows and speared as they try to board the royal chariot.

Room 4 has the Rosetta Stone, a big dark chunk of stone carved with three scripts—hieroglyphic, demotic, and Greek—each recording the same decree of a council of priests in 196 B.C. The stone's discovery enabled scholars to decipher Egyptian hieroglyphics for the first time.

Room 33 is laden with Oriental art, including Tibetan inlaid jewelry, 16th-century Vietnamese altar vases, 8th-century Indian carvings of gods and demons, Chinese jades and Tang tomb figures of horses and warriors, and fragile Ming bowls.

The Mexican Gallery in **Room 27** contains wonderfully colored, stylized, and vigorous Aztec and Maya mosaics and sculptures.

Room 68 holds the Money Gallery, exhibiting more than 2,000 years of British coinage, including pre-Roman gold coins. In **Room 41** is the stunning Sutton Hoo Treasure, excavated in 1939 from a Saxon chief's ship burial in Suffolk—a chased-iron sword blade, gold and garnet scabbard bosses, a whole-face helmet, worked gold-bronze shield fittings, a lyre, a huge bronze cauldron, a scepter crowned with a bronze stag, a gold and cloisonné purse.

Head for **Room 40** to see the Lewis Chessmen: 12th-century carved walrus-ivory chess pieces—broad-faced, bulgy-eyed warriors, bishops, kings, and queens—from the Isle of Lewis (see p. 331).

Next move on to **Room 49** to see the fourth-century Mildenhall Treasure, which was dug up in wartime Suffolk—beautiful, gleaming, masterfully worked Roman silver bowls and platters, and a great dish with relief scenes of the worship of Bacchus.

British Library

The highlight of the British Library's (96 Euston Rd., St. Pancras, tel 0843-208 1144, www.bl.uk, tube: King's Cross, St. Pancras, Euston) collection at St. Pancras is the Lindisfarne Gospels, a late seventh-century illuminated manuscript. It was exquisitely colored and illustrated with birds and foliage by monkish contemporaries of St. Cuthbert on the island of Lindisfarne (see p. 282). Other precious exhibits include two of the four remaining copies of the Magna Carta, the charter of liberty and political rights signed by King John at Runnymede in 1215 (see p. 101).

Rooms 62 and 63 are filled with ancient Egyptian mummies—cat, snake, ibis, crocodile, and falcon, as well as human—with elaborately painted cases. Adjacent rooms contain Egyptian jewelry and Coptic art.

Room 70 holds the Portland Vase. Dating from the first century A.D., this is a superb Roman work of art in cobalt blue, with a white glass relief depicting, it is thought, the marriage of Peleus and Thetis, and their offspring, Achilles. The vase was painstakingly rebuilt after being shattered into over 200 pieces by a drunken visitor. ■

Knightsbridge & Kensington

Knightsbridge and Kensington, the heavenly twins lying south of Hyde Park, are two of the smartest areas of London, where limousines pause on the Brompton Road or Sloane Street to decant expensive persons into elegant stores such as Harrods and Harvey Nichols, or into any one of several hundred top-flight boutiques.

Formal flower beds are but one highlight of the 275-acre Kensington Gardens.

This glossy image grew from the 1820s when the Buxton-born builder Thomas Cubitt (1788–1855) built the beautiful houses of Belgravia, and picked up more cachet after the 1851 Great Exhibition in Hyde Park, when South Kensington, to the west of Knightsbridge, suddenly became immensely fashionable.

Three of London's must-see museums are here—the Victoria & Albert Museum, the Science Museum, and the Natural History Museum—and the neighboring expanses of Hyde Park and Kensington Gardens border the area's northern edge, along with Kensington Palace, a royal residence since the late 17th century.

Victoria & Albert Museum

"Welcome to the world's greatest museum of decorative arts," says the map leaflet of the Victoria & Albert Museum, and that just about sums up the British institution known universally as the V&A. Somewhere along the 7 miles of galleries in this labyrinthine holdall of a museum, a representative sample probably exists of every form of fine and applied art known to man. It was Prince

Albert's vision for the 1851 Great Exhibition—of inspiring the ordinary British working-man and -woman with access to examples of excellence from all over the world—that generated the foundation of the V&A, one of the richest and most eclectic collections in the world.

The layout divides the collection into Art and Design, and Materials and Techniques. The former is mostly on levels A, Lower A, B, and C; the latter on C and D. There is also the Henry Cole Wing, with six floors of paintings, drawings, photographs, and prints, and the small Frank Lloyd Wright Gallery.

The V&A has revamped its entire British Galleries and has opened wonderful displays of ceramics, medieval artifacts, painting and sculpture, and the Jameel Gallery of Islamic art. Its Costume Collection is another must-see.

Level A: On the walls of a huge barrel-roofed gallery in **Room 48a** hang the enormous Raphael cartoons, templates for tapestries. These great colored pictures more than 20 feet long of scenes from the New Testament were commissioned by Pope Leo X for the Sistine Chapel in 1515. Especially striking is the "Miraculous Draught of Fishes," in which a flock of hungry cranes watches men straining at a bulging net, while a wild-haired Peter kneels before Christ in the bow of a small boat brimming with fish. In the same room is a Spanish retable of 1410, carved with scenes of

torture from the martyrdom of St. George.

Room 41 contains the Nehru Gallery of Indian Art, with dazzling jewelry, amazingly detailed 16th-century gouache paintings of battle, the gold throne of Maharaja Ranjit Singh, and the celebrated "Tippoo's Tiger," a three-quarter-life-size wooden tiger devouring a scarlet-jacketed official of the East India Company, while **Room 42** has beautiful Islamic tiles on themes of water and vegetation.

INSIDER TIP:

On the V&A's Exhibition Road side, about 200 yards up from Cromwell Road, you can see bomb damage from World War II, left as a memorial.

—LARRY PORGES
Editor, National Geographic Books

In **Room 43** is the Medieval Treasury, including the copper and enamel Becket Casket of circa 1180, which probably contained relics of the saint. Also here is the extraordinary English Romanesque 12th-century Gloucester Candlestick, writhing with entangled men, monkeys, evangelists, and dragons, and the late 12th-century Eltenberg Reliquary, shaped like a cruciform domed temple in enameled copper, ivory, and bronze gilt.

The Japanese Gallery in **Room 45** displays exquisite miniature workmanship in ornamentation

Victoria & Albert Museum

🅰 52 B2–C2
✉ Cromwell Rd., South Kensington, SW7
☎ 020-7942 2000
💲 $$ (free 4:30– 5:45 p.m.)
🚇 Tube: South Kensington

www.vam.ac.uk

Science Museum

📍 52 B3

✉ Exhibition Rd., South Kensington, SW7

☎ 0870-870 4868

🚇 Tube: South Kensington

www.science museum.org.uk

of dishes and cabinets, samurai swords 700 years old, and tiny netsuke figures—a lion; Futen, the god of wind; Hotei, the squat, obese god of prosperity.

Rooms 46A and B contain the Cast Courts, filled with plaster casts of medieval sculpture—Michelangelo's heroic "David" from Florence and his sensual "Dying Slave" and "Rebellious Slave," the shaft of Trajan's Column from Rome, and the entire Pórtico de la Gloria of 1188 from the Cathedral of Santiago de Compostela.

The **Gamble, Morris, and Poynter Rooms,** near the back of the building, were originally the museum tearooms and are decorated in arts and crafts style. They retain their Minton tilework, pre-Raphaelite panels, and stained glass.

Level Lower B: Rooms

52–58 form an L-shaped series of displays on Britain from 1500 to 1750—a Georgian music room, late 17th-century silverware, a Grinling Gibbons limewood carving of the stoning of St. Stephen, superb inlaid furniture, and the grotesque 10-foot Great Bed of Ware, made in 1590 by Jonas Fosbrook (who is said to haunt it).

Henry Cole Wing: This wing houses the Victoria & Albert Museum's superb collection of drawings, prints, and paintings, including many less well-known works by J. M. W. Turner, John Constable, and others. The wing contains nests of study rooms for closer examination of these treasures—for example, the **Prints and Drawings Study Room**—and special exhibitions are frequently mounted.

Science Museum

There are more than a thousand interactive displays among the hundreds of thousands of items in the National Museum of Science and Industry, better known as the Science Museum, making a visit here one that can be enjoyed by all. Exhibits and displays range over the long timescale of man's scientific inquiries, from pre-Christian medical technology to up-to-the-minute computing, nuclear physics, and microbiology. Forty topic areas are spread through

---

EXPERIENCE: Attend the Chelsea Flower Show

If you're in London toward the end of May—and you even very slightly have a liking for flowers, or gardens, or plants, or glamorous razzmatazz—then make sure you buy (or beg, borrow, or steal) a ticket to the **Royal Horticultural Society Chelsea Flower Show** (*www.rhs.org.uk/Shows-Events/RHS-Chelsea-Flower-Show, $$$$$*), held on the grounds of the Royal Hospital, Chelsea, south of Kensington. There are gardens traditional, outlandish, exotic, and ecologically friendly. Some of the rarest flowers in the world are on display, along with some of the biggest, brightest, smallest, deadliest, sweetest-smelling . . . Here are a host of ideas to try out in your own garden; hints, tips, and talks; the glitter of celebrity gardeners; hugely respected plant collectors—all against a backdrop of amazing color and mind-blowing scents. This is, simply, the greatest flower show on Earth.

seven floors. Some of the most intriguing are described here.

Ground Floor: The **Energy Hall** fascinates with the sheer weight and strength of early devices, from Newcomen's beam pumping-engine of 1791 to the gigantic mill engines built by Burnley Ironworks in 1903 and used until the 1970s.

From here you move into the **Exploring Space Gallery,** then on to **Making the Modern World,** an exhibition of 150 epoch-making objects, from George Stephenson's pioneering 1829 steam locomotive *Rocket* and the Apollo 10 space command module of 1969 to objects as mundane as an electric iron.

Level 3: There are some weird and wonderful early experiments in the **Flight Gallery**—the 1905 Weiss Glider based on the form of an albatross, or the Frost Ornithopter with its feathered wings flapped by a motorcycle engine. Hung from the roof of the gallery are various historic airplanes: Spitfire and Hurricane fighters from World War II, the Vickers Vimy that first flew the Atlantic in 1919, and Britain's first jet aircraft—the Gloster Whittle E28/39.

Level 4: The **Glimpses of Medical History** gallery makes a great introduction (for those with a strong stomach) to the vivid and often disturbing story of the slow, painful advance of medical science. Three-dimensional models give

The Science Museum has many interactive exhibits.

close-up insights into procedures that range from Stone Age brain operations (successful sometimes, apparently) to dissection of corpses by medieval men of science, and on through the horrors faced by wounded sailors of Nelson's day on a ship in the thick of battle, and the pain and danger of childbirth in Victorian times. Arriving at the diorama of a contemporary operation with its first-class anesthetics and highly skilled surgeons, you can only be grateful to be living in the modern medical era.

Natural History Museum

No longer does the Natural History Museum consist solely of rank upon rank of glass cases (though there are still plenty of these). Exhibitions have been brought up to date and feature a mix of hands-on areas and interactive technology.

(continued on p. 80)

Natural History Museum

🅰 52 B2

✉ Cromwell Rd., South Kensington, SW7

☎ 020-7942 5000

🚇 Tube: South Kensington

www.nhm.ac.uk

London's Parks & Gardens

London has many carefully preserved open spaces where everyone is welcome to wander at will. Some of this public parkland harks back to the 17th century, when the Stuart monarchs began to open up portions of hitherto private royal hunting forests. Other areas are remnants of common land, or leftovers from attempts to safeguard springs and wells, or the results of philanthropic endowment in Georgian and Victorian times.

A glorious view of Whitehall, as seen from the Blue Bridge, St. James's Park

Largest of the central parks north of the Thames are the neighboring **Hyde Park** *(map 52 C3–C4, tube: Hyde Park Corner; see p. 83)* and **Kensington Gardens** *(map 52 B3, tube: Lancaster Gate; see p. 83),* with fashionable Knightsbridge to the south. To the west, off Kensington High Street, rises hilly, wooded **Holland Park** *(tube: Holland Park),* opened in 1952 on the grounds of Holland House, which had been destroyed during World War II bombing. The park contains an open-air theater and a café and is surrounded by fine late Victorian houses.

In ultra-exclusive Mayfair, on the eastern border of Hyde Park, 200-year-old plane trees and sculptures stand at the heart of **Berkeley Square** *(tube: Green Park):*

> . . . there was magic abroad in the air;
> There were angels dining at the Ritz,
> And a nightingale sang in Berkeley Square.
> —Eric Maschwitz, "A Nightingale Sang in
> Berkeley Square" (1940)

Only the big traffic circle at Hyde Park Corner separates Hyde Park from **Green**

Park *(map 52 D3, tube: Green Park)*, a relatively uncrowded green space in spite of its proximity to Buckingham Palace. This was a noted dueling ground in Georgian times.

Just across the Mall is **St. James's Park** *(map 52 D3, tube: St. James's Park)*, London's oldest park; it was one of Henry VIII's deer parks. After the Restoration, Charles II opened it to the public. It was landscaped by John Nash (1752–1835) about 1828, a period when he was redesigning Buckingham Palace (see p. 61) and going through too much of George IV's money. From the beautiful bridge that nips in the waist of the park's lake, there is a good open view west to the Queen Victoria memorial on the traffic circle just in front of Buckingham Palace.

London's largest green space, Hyde Park provides a quiet retreat from the city noise.

North of Hyde Park is the roughly circular **Regent's Park** *(map 52 C5, tube: Regent's Park)*, also designed by Nash early in the 19th century to provide the Prince Regent with a place of recreation that could be reached from his residence in St. James's via a scenic drive. The terraced houses around the park are some of the finest in London. You can boat on the long lake here, and in summer there are performances in the open-air theater.

On the north side of the park is **London Zoo** *(tel 020-7722 3333, tube: Camden Town)*. Recent improvements have seen the zoo, in line with contemporary understanding, adopt more enlightened, conservation-minded policies to care for its collection of animals.

Just north across Prince Albert Road is **Primrose Hill** *(map 52 C6, tube: St. John's Wood)*, with splendid views over the city.

Less Famous Parks

A little east and south of Regent's Park, on the eastern borders of Bloomsbury, **Coram's Fields** *(Brunswick Sq., tube: Russell Sq.)* in the St. Pancras district incorporates a pets' corner in a calm playground shaded by plane trees. Only child-accompanied adults are admitted to these delightful gardens, which were once fields around a foundling hospital endowed in 1745 by a choleric but soft-hearted sailor, Capt. Thomas Coram.

Down in trendy Chelsea, just east of Albert Bridge, **Chelsea Physic Garden** *(66 Royal Hospital Rd., SW3, tel 020-7352 5646, call for hours, tube: Sloane Square)* on Swan Walk is an area of ancient plants and trees founded in 1673 by the Society of Apothecaries.

Speakers' Corner

Of the various Speakers' Corners in Britain, only one is truly iconic—the one in the northeast corner of central London's Hyde Park, where anyone may stand and say what's on their mind. No one really knows its origin— some say it sprang from the right of a condemned felon to make a speech from the gallows. During the politically turbulent 1850s and '60s there were big rallies in Hyde Park supporting the rights of the workingman—it was the nearest large open space to the Houses of Parliament—and the tradition grew from there. A legal ruling of 1999 asserted the right of speakers to be "irritating, contentious, eccentric, heretical, unwelcome and provocative." But hecklers have rights, too.

Kensington Palace State Apartments

- 52 B3
- Kensington Gardens
- 0844-482 7777
- $$$$$
- Tube: High St. Kensington, Queensway

www.hrp.org.uk

The museum is divided into four zones—Orange, Red, Green and Blue—with the **Darwin Centre** in the Orange Zone as the latest must-see. The Darwin Centre's self-guided **Cocoon Tour** is the best way possible to become absorbed in all that natural history really means—especially in the way of plants and insects. This walk (or wheelchair ride) from top to bottom of the Darwin Centre is peppered with big glass tables and wall-mounted cases full of beautifully illuminated specimens for close-up study, lots of hands-on and interactive experience ideal for youngsters, and plenty of opportunities to watch and question natural history scientists at work. Down at ground level is the **Attenborough Studio** with its events, shows, and films, and the interactive **Climate Change Wall** whose animated displays react to a

visitor's proximity, demonstrating humans' effect on their environment—and vice versa.

The museum's Red Zone contains the **Power Within** exhibition with its earthquake simulator and plenty of volcanoes, as well as the rocks and minerals in the **Earth Treasury.** In the Green Zone's **Central Hall** you'll find the famous *Diplodocus* skeleton and creepy-crawlies; while among the delights of the Blue Zone are the mammals—especially the vast blue whale—and the perennial favorites, dinosaurs. Coming soon is a **Treasures Gallery** showcasing an abundance of oddities and jaw-droppers.

Kensington Palace

Kensington Palace is well known around the world as the London home of Charles and Diana, Prince and Princess of Wales,

Harrods is known the world over for its opulent setting and the luxury goods it sells.

before their marriage broke up in 1991, and as Diana's home thereafter. The palace has become something of a shrine since the princess's death in 1997, with tributes of flowers often to be seen at the gates. Converted from a grand house into a palace between 1689 and 1696 by Sir Christopher Wren, the building has seen three centuries of royal history.

Until 1760 and George III's move to Buckingham Palace (see p. 61), this was the principal London residence of the sovereign. William III and Mary II ordered its conversion, and Wren gave the couple separate suites—and separate entrances.

Very grand State Apartments were added inside the building during the 18th century, with beautiful murals and painted ceilings by William Kent, a prime collection of royal portraiture, and a range of exquisite classic furniture. These form part of the visitors' tour that has become one of London's chief tourist draws; the other part consists of a collection of court dresses, costumes, and uniforms dating from the 1760s to the present day.

On June 20, 1837, the 18-year-old Princess Victoria was woken at the palace very early in the morning to be told that her uncle, William IV, had died, and that she was now sovereign. Outside Kensington Palace, facing the Round Pond, is a touching statue of her as a round-faced and innocent girl-queen.

You can stroll in part of the palace garden, then take tea in the nearby Orangery, which was designed by Wren's pupil Nicholas Hawksmoor and embellished by the Rotterdam-born master carver Grinling Gibbons.

INSIDER TIP:

At the Natural History Museum you can take a peek behind the scenes if you go on a Spirit Collection Tour.

—ESZTER DOBOS
Visit Planner,
Natural History Museum

Shopping Mecca

Other areas of London may come in and out of fashion, but the district of Knightsbridge takes the cake when it comes to top shopping. From Knightsbridge tube station, Sloane Street stretches south, lined with classic designer stores including Cartier, Armani, Chanel, Katharine Hamnett, and Christian Lacroix. Near the junction of Sloane Street and the Brompton Road, the Scotch House is tartan heaven for anyone with a dash of Celtic blood. Beauchamp Place (pronounced BEECH-am), off the Brompton Road, is another road full of fashionable and stylish little shops.

Harrods: All stores pale into insignificance beside the mighty Harrods, indisputably the reigning world monarch of style, elegance, opulence, and mercantile savoir faire. Charles

(continued on p. 84)

Harrods

🅰 52 C3
✉ 87–135 Brompton Rd., SW1
☎ 020-7730 1234
🚇 Tube: Knightsbridge

Knightsbridge & Kensington Walk

This walk includes three great museums, Harrods' store with all its seductive displays, Hyde Park and Kensington Gardens, and the royal residence of Kensington Palace. A good plan would be to allow a full day for the walk and to select just one of the three museums, leaving the other two for another day.

As you emerge from Knightsbridge tube station onto the Brompton Road, the **Harvey Nichols** store ❶ (see p. 84) is to your right. Turn left along the Brompton Road and in 300 yards on the left is the fairy-lit emporium of **Harrods** ❷ (see pp. 81, 84).

NOT TO BE MISSED:

Harrods • Victoria & Albert Museum • Science Museum

Leave the store by the main exit; turn left along the Brompton Road, window-shopping all the way, to the **Brompton Oratory** ❸ *(tel 020-7808 0900, tube: South Kensington)* on the right, its gray dome rising above a massive pillared portico. Inside, angels recline in elaborate drapery above the arches, while 12 beautiful 17th-century marble statues of the Apostles stand in the gloom, far from their original home in Siena's cathedral. The Oratory was opened in 1884, the dome and facade added in the 1890s. It was built in response to a great revival of English Catholicism during the Victorian era, which had been sparked during the 1840s by John Henry Newman, an influential Oxford academic, vicar, and theologian.

Bear right along Thurloe Place to reach the grandiose entrance to the **Victoria & Albert Museum** ❹ (see pp. 74–76) on Cromwell Road. If you ever extract yourself from its tangled mysteries, leave by the Exhibition Road exit to find, opposite, the entrance to the Earth Galleries section of the **Natural History Museum** ❺ (see pp. 77, 80). On the left, 200 yards north on Exhibition Road, is the **Science Museum** ❻ (see pp. 76–77).

After sampling one or more of these great museums, continue on Exhibition Road; turn left along Prince Consort Road, passing Imperial College (engraved "Royal School of Mines") and the **Royal College of Music** ❼. That college's

Cast court, Victoria & Albert Museum

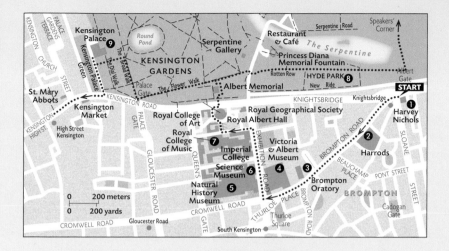

Museum of Instruments *(Prince Consort Rd.,
SW7, tel 020-7589 3643 ext. 4346, www.rcm
.ac.uk, open Tues.–Fri. during school term, tube:
South Kensington)* is full of strange creations:
a beautifully inlaid Parisian hurdy-gurdy, an
ophicleide (a primitive 1842 saxophone), and
a variety of fiddles, lutes, lyres, and guitars.

⛰	See area map p. 52
►	Knightsbridge tube station
🕐	Full day, with museum visits
⬌	2.5 miles
►	High Street Kensington tube station

INSIDER TIP:

**Sunday morning is a great
time to visit Speakers' Corner.
That's when a lot of people
come to air their opinions.**

—JANE SUNDERLAND
National Geographic contributor

Cross Prince Consort Road and climb
the steps past the **Great Exhibition Memorial.** This celebrates Prince Albert's instigation
of the "Great Exhibition of the Work and
Industry of All Nations," held in 1851 in Hyde
Park in a huge glass-and-iron hall called the
Crystal Palace. Pass the elliptical **Royal Albert
Hall** of 1871 with its frieze of scenes from
British history and everyday life, and cross Kensington Gore to reach the **Albert Memorial,**
erected in 1861.

Walk beyond the Albert Memorial to turn
left along Flower Walk, with beautiful flower
beds year-round. **Hyde Park ⑧** was part of
the land belonging to Westminster Abbey that
Henry VIII appropriated during the Reformation.
The Serpentine Lake—separating Hyde Park from
Kensington Gardens to the west—is a favorite
boating spot. On its south side is the oval water
feature unveiled in 2004 in memory of Diana,
Princess of Wales. A detour to the northeast corner of the park brings you to **Speakers' Corner**
(see sidebar p. 79), famous for soapbox orators.

Continue the walk from Hyde Park into
Kensington Gardens, home of the famous
statue of Peter Pan, and near the western end
of the parkland bear right along the Broad Walk
past the Round Pond to reach **Kensington
Palace ⑨** (see pp. 80–81).

From the palace walk along Palace Avenue
to leave Hyde Park on High Street Kensington,
then turn right to reach High Street Kensington
tube station.

Harvey Nichols

🅰 83

✉ 109–125
Knightsbridge,
SW1

☎ 020-7235 5000

Ⓣ Tube:
Knightsbridge

Henry Harrod opened his small family-run grocery store/tea merchant here in 1849, and the place has never looked back.

In the basement are the splendid marble halls of Harrods' own bank—Harrods Bank Ltd. On the ground floor, you could scour the Room of Luxury for a $5,000 Christian Dior crocodile handbag, a $17,000 set of Louis Vuitton luggage, or a perpetual motion wristwatch, as designed for the Pasha of Marrakesh, retailing at just $22,000. Most people don't. They drift through to the irresistible Food Halls with their lavish, sculptured ceilings and displays: arts and crafts tiles on walls and

INSIDER TIP:

Befitting the store's origin as a tea merchant, Harrods' Georgian Restaurant serves a classic afternoon tea. The teas are grown in the store's private tea gardens.

—LARRY PORGES
Editor, National Geographic Books

pillars; pigs and peacocks in flight above the charcuterie counter; a cupola full of hunters and shepherds; lovely mermaids above the iced fish display; and the aquarium at the oysters-and-champagne bar.

The rest rooms are stylish beyond belief: the gents' with marble automated basins and hushed attendants, the ladies' in Georgian splendor with original

tiles, woodwork, and marble, all with free scents and creams.

You could spend all day riding the Egyptian escalator with its sphinxes and acanthus capitals—up to the furniture department on the third floor to snap up a marble-topped cabinet at $42,000, or down to the basement barber shop with its padded red leather chairs and gleaming black-and-white walls.

Harvey Nichols: At the top of Sloane Street, where it meets Knightsbridge, is the famous department store of Harvey Nichols, London's best known retailer of high-fashion clothes. On the ground floor is every kind of celebrated perfume and accessory seller, from established favorites such as Yves Saint Laurent, Chanel, Versace, and Lancôme through Jean-Paul Gaultier to up-and-coming companies like Trish McEvoy. The first floor is given over to international women's fashion from Graeme Black, Couture Couture, and Alaia to Dries Van Noten's luxurious silks and brocades and Donna Karan's little black dresses.

Favorites in the designer collections on the second floor are Alexander McQueen's super-chic tailored look, Alexander Wang's clinging corset dresses, and pretty, girly frocks by Alice Temperley. Up on the fifth floor you can relax in the bright, clean restaurant where the chefs prepare everything out in the open. Alongside is Harvey Nichols's very upscale Food Hall. ∎

Following the Thames

Although not Britain's longest river, the Thames is its best known waterway, because of its association with London. It provides a really wonderful unrolling panorama of the capital when traveled either by boat or on foot. Walking the Thames has become possible since the 1996 opening of the Thames Path National Trail, while river cruises stopping off near the main attractions have always been a pleasure for Londoners and visitors alike.

Floodlights illuminate the fanciful Tower Bridge, opened in 1894 with great ceremony.

Downstream from Hampton Court

As it wends toward central London from Sunbury Lock, the River Thames takes a great southward and then northward loop, with **Hampton Court Palace** *(East Molesey, tel 0844-482 7777, www.hrp.org .uk, palace and formal gardens closed Dec. 25–26),* the finest and grandest Tudor building in Britain, on the left. This extraordinary riverside palace

was Cardinal Wolsey's before he gave it to Henry VIII in 1528 in vain hope of buying himself a return to royal favor.

Henry smothered the palace with the carved entwined initials of himself and his second wife, Anne Boleyn; after she had gone to the block, each of the following four was installed here in turn. The ghosts of gentle Jane Seymour and lecherous Catherine Howard still haunt the place. The closed court that Henry used for his

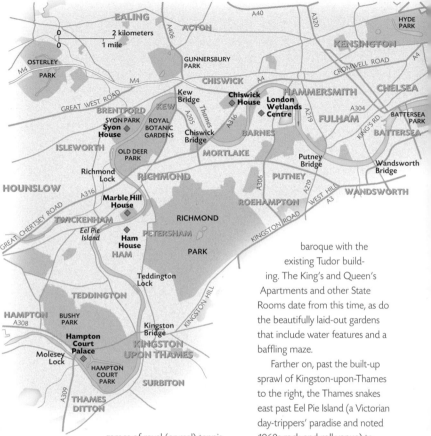

baroque with the existing Tudor building. The King's and Queen's Apartments and other State Rooms date from this time, as do the beautifully laid-out gardens that include water features and a baffling maze.

Farther on, past the built-up sprawl of Kingston-upon-Thames to the right, the Thames snakes east past Eel Pie Island (a Victorian day-trippers' paradise and noted 1960s rock-and-roll venue) to pass the green fields around **Ham House** (Ham St., Ham, Richmond-upon-Thames, tel 020-8940 1950, www.nationaltrust.org.uk, see website for hours, tube: Richmond, then bus 371). The house, built in 1610, has been beautifully restored. Lord Lauderdale was given the lease of the Ham Estate, and created 1st Earl of Dysart, as compensation for his rather painful childhood role as a "whipping boy," whose duty it was to receive any punishment beatings earned by the young prince who later became Charles I.

games of royal (or real) tennis is still in use. The king had the splendid hammerbeam roof installed in the Great Hall, and completed magnificently what Wolsey had started in the Chapel Royal.

From 1690 on, when the Dutch King William III and Queen Mary II felt themselves secure on the throne of England, they began to improve and extend Hampton Court. The work, overseen by Sir Christopher Wren and continued by Queen Anne, constituted a masterful blending of the

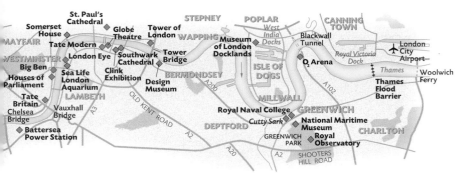

Parks & Gardens

Soon the Thames passes the edge of **Richmond Park** on the right, with Richmond Hill prominent—views down from the hilltop across the river are even better. Richmond Park was a royal hunting ground in the time of Charles I, and fallow deer still graze under its ancient oaks. On the left the river passes **Marble Hill House** (Richmond Rd., Twickenham, tel 020-8892 5115, www.english-heri tage.org.uk, see website for hours, tube: Richmond, then bus), a Palladian villa built in 1724–29 by Henrietta Howard, Countess of Suffolk, with £12,000 ($20,000) she received as a present from her young lover, the future George II.

Now the **Royal Botanic Gardens at Kew** (Kew Rd., Richmond, tel 020-8332 5655 for recorded information, tube: Kew Gardens) appear on the right. These are the yardstick by which all other botanical collections measure themselves. They were started in 1759 on 9 acres of ground; the

---

EXPERIENCE: Cruise the River Thames

If you're interested in seeing London by putting your feet up and letting someone else do all the work, take the classic route through the heart of the capital aboard a River Thames cruiser. You can step on board at several locations—Kew, Richmond, and Hampton Court in the west; the Tower of London, Greenwich, and the Thames Flood Barrier in the east; or Westminster in central London—and just enjoy the commentary and the passing spectacle of riverside scenery and buildings that range from historic to ultramodern.

Westminster to Greenwich is the classic cruise of this type. But why stop at that? There's an enormous range of specialist cruises to suit every taste and

pocket. How about a showboat cruise with live cabaret, or a jazz or summer disco cruise? Have a proper English afternoon tea (with Champagne, si vous voulez) or a Christmas dinner on the river. Or throw caution and dignity to the winds and strap yourself into a high-speed rib for a white-knuckle ride through London at 50 miles an hour.

Several companies operate cruises, including **River Thames Cruises** (tel 020-7237 3108, www.riverthamescruises .co.uk), **City Cruises** (tel 020-7740 0400, www.citycruises.com), and **Thames River Services** (tel 020-7930 4097, www.thames riverservices.co.uk). Prices vary by length and nature of cruise.

Chiswick House

- ✉ Burlington Ln., W4
- ☎ 020-8995 0508
- ⏱ See website for hours
- 💲 $$
- 🚇 Tube: Turnham Green, then bus E3; Hammersmith, then bus 190

www.english-heri tage.org.uk

Syon House

- ✉ Isleworth
- ☎ 020-8560 0882/0083
- ⏱ See website for hours
- 💲 $$$
- 🚇 Tube: Gunnersbury, then bus 237 or 267

www.syonpark.co.uk

orangery and the pagoda date from that era, when the great botanist and polymath, Joseph Banks, was appointed director and oversaw an enormous influx of exotic species collected from all over the world.

Today the gardens' staff continue their pioneering botanical research, while visitors stroll the site (expanded to fill 300 acres) and enjoy the two great Victorian conservatories (the Palm House with its rain forest species, and the Temperate House), to which the Princess of Wales Conservatory has been added with its display of plant adaptation across a spectrum of the climatic zones.

Coming up next on the left is **Syon House,** the residence of the Dukes of Northumberland ever since it was built on a nunnery site in Tudor times. Robert Adam remodeled the interior along Palladian lines in the 1760s. On the grounds, which were landscaped by Capability Brown, are a butterfly house and a collection of historic cars.

Chiswick House, also on the left, with its great colonnaded portico, was built in the 1720s by the 3rd Earl of Burlington as a country retreat in which to show off his art collection.

Heading into Town

From here downstream the houses begin to draw in closer to the leafy banks of the Thames. The river passes the pretty cottages of Chiswick, then the bird-haunted ponds of the **London Wetlands Centre** at Barnes *(Queen Elizabeth Walk, tel 020-8409 4400, tube: Hammersmith, BritRail station: Barnes),* and then the wharves, works, and reservoirs toward Putney Bridge—a stretch of the river rowed in the annual boat race between the crews of Oxford and Cambridge Universities.

The Thames slides past first Wandsworth, then the big pleasure-gardens complex of Battersea Park and the enormous chimneys of the landmark Battersea Power Station, to turn north for its passage through the heart of London. Here are the classic sites and views.

On the north bank **Tate Britain** (see p. 67) slips by, followed by the **Houses of Parliament** and **Big Ben** (see p. 64), the 3,500-year-old obelisk from Heliopolis known as **Cleopatra's Needle,** and the long eastward run of the Victoria Embankment below **Somerset House** *(Strand,*

Accorded royal status in the 12th century, the Thames's mute swans are counted annually.

*WC2, tel 020-7845 4600, www
.somersethouse.org.uk, tube: Temple,
Covent Garden, Holborn).* This
original headquarters of the Royal
Academy of Arts now houses the
Courtauld Gallery. The **Courtauld
Gallery** *(tel 020-7848 2526)*
contains a wide-ranging collection
from Italian Renaissance masters
to 20th-century British artists,
with an especially notable group
of French Impressionists that
includes work by Renoir, Cézanne,
van Gogh, Manet, and Degas.

Approaching Blackfriars Bridge,
the dome of **St. Paul's Cathedral**
(see pp. 54–55) is seen on the
north side.

INSIDER TIP:

I can't recommend the
Globe Theatre in the
summer highly enough.
It is only £5 ($8) for a
standing seat.

—MARY JO SLAZAK
*Manager, Subsidiary Rights,
National Geographic Books*

Downstream from Westminster

On the south bank beyond
Westminster Bridge, the river
passes the big florid County
Hall now containing the **Sea
Life London Aquarium,** one
of Europe's largest displays of
aquatic life. Next comes the
giant **London Eye** observation
wheel *(County Hall, booking tel
0870-990 8881 or www.london
eye.com, tube: Waterloo, Westminster),* then the **South Bank Centre** *(tel 020-7921 0600),* an arts

---

Thames Path

The London section of
the Thames Path National
Trail runs, clearly marked
on both banks, between
Hampton Court and the
Thames Barrier. This
London section is 38 miles
along the north bank,
36 miles along the south;
shorter sections can be
followed, of course. For
further details on walking
all or some of the Thames
Path, visit a tourist information center (see p. 341),
where you can pick up a
free brochure.

---

complex of gray concrete boxes
comprising the Hayward Gallery,
Royal Festival Hall, Purcell Room,
and Queen Elizabeth Hall; also
here is the **National Theatre**
(see p. 390).

Then comes Southwark, not
so long ago a red-light district.
That is what it was in William
Shakespeare's time, when he
part-owned the Globe Theatre in
an area of brothels, drinking dens,
and bear-baiting pits. The Globe
has been superbly reconstructed,
and **Shakespeare's Globe
Theatre** hosts Elizabethan plays in
its outdoor arena *(open May–Sept.,
tel 020-7401 9919).* An exhibition
tells the story of its re-creation.

Other attractions here are
the giant **Bankside Power Station,** reopened in 2000 as the
Tate Modern (see p. 67), an art
museum; the graceful bow of
the **Millennium Footbridge;** the
Clink Prison Museum *(1 Clink St.,*

**Sea Life London
Aquarium**

 53 E3

✉ County Hall,
Westminster
Bridge Rd., SE1

☎ 0871-663 1678

$ $$$

🚇 Tube: Waterloo,
Westminster

**www.visitsealife
.com/London**

**Shakespeare's
Globe Theatre**

 53 F4

✉ New Globe
Walk, Bankside,
SE1

☎ 020-7902 1400

🚇 Tube: London
Bridge, Mansion
House

**www.shakespeares-
globe.org**

Southwark Cathedral

- Montague Close, SE1
- ☎ 020-7367 6700
- ⏱ No tours during services
- 🚇 Tube: London Bridge

www.nmm.ac.uk

National Maritime Museum

- ✉ Romney Rd., SE10
- ☎ 020-8858 4422
- 🚇 DLR: Cutty Sark

www.nmm.ac.uk

Royal Observatory Greenwich

- ✉ Blackheath Ave., SE10
- ☎ Recorded information: 020-8312 6565
- 🚇 DLR: Cutty Sark

www.nmm.ac.uk

SE1, tel 020-7403 0900, www
.clink.co.uk, tube: London Bridge), an
atmospheric crawl through the
miseries of bygone prison life
and sexual misdemeanor;
and **Southwark Cathedral,**
which features a memorial to
Shakespeare and a very beautiful
fan-vaulted retrochoir.

Audio Tours

**Following the River
Thames through Rich-
mond and along the
Embankment, or saunter-
ing by the river through
Shakespeare's Bankside
or the pirate haunts of
Shadwell and Wapping,
there's no need to be con-
stantly wondering "What's
this?" and "I wonder
what happened there!"
Download an audio tour
(multiple MP3 files, maps
with numbered stopping
points) from Tourcaster
(www.tourcaster.com, $$$)
and be your own guide,
stopping and starting
wherever you fancy.**

Toward the Sea

Standing on the Thames's north
bank is the grim and mighty
Tower of London (see pp.
91–94), near the twin towers of
Tower Bridge (SE1, tel 020-7403
3761, tube: Tower Hill). This great
Gothic bridge began opening
for tall ships sailing up- and
downriver in 1894—an action still
carried out several times a week.

Now the Thames passes the
Design Museum (Shad Thames,

tel 0870-833 9955, tube: Tower
Hill), bends around the fantastic
postmodern architecture of Dock-
lands on the **Isle of Dogs,** and
passes **Greenwich** on the south,
where you will see the tall masts
of champion Victorian tea clipper
*Cutty Sark (King William Walk, tel
020-8858 2698, DLR: Cutty Sark),*
expected to reopen in 2011 after
a damaging fire.

Nearby, surrounding their
huge Grand Square, are the **Royal
Naval College** buildings *(King
William Walk, tel 020-8269 4747,
DLR: Cutty Sark),* founded by
King William and Queen Mary,
designed by John Webb, and
completed by Sir Christopher
Wren, Nicholas Hawksmoor, and
Sir John Vanbrugh. Behind lies the
National Maritime Museum,
recounting the history of man's
travels by water. The museum
is centered on the beautiful Pal-
ladian **Queen's House** *(separate
admission),* designed by Inigo
Jones in 1616.

Above rises **Greenwich Park,**
enclosing the **Royal Observatory
Greenwich,** founded in 1675 to
fix the exact position of longitude
worldwide. Daily at 1 p.m. the
Greenwich Mean Time ball
drops down its pole to precisely
measure time.

Moving downstream, the river
passes the futuristic "space tent"
shape of the **O2 Arena,** then
reaches the gleaming silver hoods
of the **Thames Barrier** *(Unity
Way, SE18, tel 020-8305 4188),*
opened in 1984 to prevent sea
surges from flooding London—
its monthly test-raising is a big
attraction. ∎

Tower of London

To nearly 30 generations of Britons the Tower of London was a grim instrument and symbol of harsh judgment, imprisonment, torture, and execution—undoubtedly the chief reasons for its position today as one of the country's top attractions. Add the scarlet-trimmed Beefeaters, the legendary ravens, and all the glamour and glitter of the Crown Jewels, and you can understand its enormous popularity.

The four turrets of the White Tower rise to form the centerpiece of the Tower of London.

The first wooden fortification was built at this site on the north bank of the Thames by William the Conqueror—almost as soon as he was established on the throne of England—to command the vital and vulnerable sea approach to London. The Tower of London (in fact a great stronghold incorporating 19 towers built over the centuries) was named after its first and greatest tower, the 90-foot **White Tower,** built in 1097 of stone and subsequently whitewashed in 1241.

The many hundreds of years of building on and adding to the Tower produced a roughly hexagonal moated stronghold with an enormously thick and high outer wall incorporating six towers and enclosing a narrow Outer Ward (patrolable space). Looking out onto the Outer Ward is an inner wall reinforced at regular intervals with cylindrical drum towers.

Tower of London
- 53 G4–H4
- Tower Hill, EC3
- Recorded information: 0807-756 6060. Reservations: 0807-756 7070
- $$$$
- Tube: Tower Hill

www.hrp.org.uk

Inside this inner wall is the Inner Ward, a broad enclosed area. Here, over the years, soldiers' quarters, houses, chapels, and other buildings have been incorporated, the ancient White Tower rising commandingly in the center to dominate all with its four onion-domed corner turrets.

Untimely Deaths

Over the course of 900 years, legend and history have woven themselves deep into the fabric of the Tower of London. In the south face of the Outer Wall is the foursquare **St. Thomas's Tower,** with the arched mouth

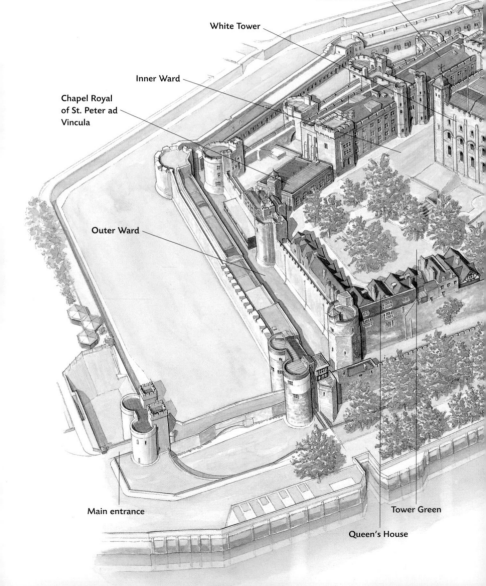

Waterloo Barracks

White Tower

Inner Ward

Chapel Royal of St. Peter ad Vincula

Outer Ward

Main entrance

Tower Green

Queen's House

of **Traitors' Gate** giving on to the Thames. Those enduring trial in Westminster Hall for high treason were brought by boat downriver in ceremonious ignominy to be taken into the Tower by this entrance.

Just behind Traitors' Gate in the inner wall, facing into the Inner Ward, is the **Bloody Tower.** Here the heir to the throne, Prince Edward, and his younger brother, Prince Richard, were brought in 1483 on the orders of their uncle, Richard, Duke of Gloucester, immediately after the death of their father, Edward IV. No one

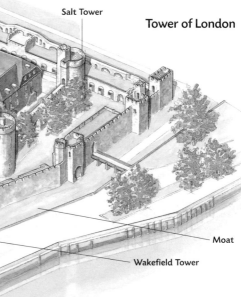

Martin Tower

Chapel of St. John's

Salt Tower

Tower of London

Moat

Wakefield Tower

St. Thomas's Tower

THAMES

Bloody Tower

Traitors' Gate

A re-creation of Edward I's portable bed, St. Thomas's Tower outside the Tower saw the boys again, and "Crookback Dick" was crowned Richard III before the year was out. In 1674 the skeletons of two boys were unearthed nearby, adding fuel to the general suspicion that the ambitious duke had had his nephews murdered. They were not the only royals to be done to death here; their father may well have ordered the killing of his mentally disturbed predecessor, Henry VI, who died in 1471 in **Wakefield Tower** next to the Bloody Tower.

Death, by execution or torture, is an integral part of the Tower of London's story. Traitors were executed in public on Tower Hill outside the fortress; but a "privileged" few were granted the privacy of decapitation on **Tower Green,** in front of the White Tower. These included two of the wives of Henry VIII: wild, six-fingered Anne Boleyn (No. 2), mother of Elizabeth I, beheaded by a French swordsman brought across to London for the job; and the injudicious, adulterous Catherine Howard (No. 5), executed with an ax like most other traitors.

The Guards

The Beefeaters—36 of them, properly called Yeoman Warders—look after the Tower and its 2.5 million visitors a year and pose for photographs in their Tudor uniforms of red and black. Each night they lock up ceremonially, an enjoyable ritual; the Ceremony of the Keys is at 9:35 p.m. *(to attend, write well in advance to the Constable's Office, Tower of London, EC3).* Other residents at the Tower are the ravens, whose continued presence guarantees the survival of the nation—so legend says.

You must line up to pass through the display hall in the **Waterloo Barracks** where the Crown Jewels are kept, but it is worth the wait. These glittering and gleaming baubles include rings, orbs, swords, and scepters; Elizabeth II's own crown with the famous Koh-i-noor diamond; and the Imperial State Crown made in 1837 for the coronation of Queen Victoria. This last incorporates the Star of Africa diamond and a sapphire that belonged to Edward the Confessor. ∎

A busby-clad soldier of the Queen's Guard stands watch at the Tower of London, still an official royal residence.

More Places to Visit in London

Chelsea

Trendy and fashionable Chelsea *(map 52 B2)*, on the north bank of the Thames, preserves a bohemian atmosphere and has attracted artists, writers, painters, and pub philosophers down the years. J. M. W. Turner, Henry James, T. S. Eliot, George Eliot, Mick Jagger, Mark Twain, and Oscar Wilde are just some of its famous and infamous residents, whose blue plaques can be seen on houses along riverside Cheyne Walk and elsewhere.

At the other end of the inhabitant spectrum are the 400 Chelsea Pensioners, old soldiers in long coats (blue "undress," red when out and about) who live in retirement in the Royal Hospital built by Sir Christopher Wren in 1682.

Hampstead

Up in the north of London, the hilly green acres of **Hampstead Heath** form a network of woods, meadows, open spaces, ponds, wetland, and grassland. Here you'll find an atmospheric old pub called Jack Straw's Castle and 17th-century **Kenwood House** *(Hampstead Ln., NW3, tel 020-8348 1286, tube: Archway, Hampstead, Golders Green)*, with paintings by Rembrandt, Reynolds, Van Dyck, Vermeer, and Gainsborough.

Marylebone

Two well-known attractions lie at the southwest corner of Regent's Park, in the district of Marylebone *(map 52 C5, tube: Baker Street)*. The theoretical personal belongings, furniture, and memorabilia of fiction's most famous private detective can be viewed at the **Sherlock Holmes Museum** *(221b Baker St., tel 020-7935 8866)*. Nearby is a perennial favorite—the world-famous waxworks **Madame Tussauds** *(Marylebone Rd., tel 0870-400 3000)*, where you can shudder at ghastly murderers, duet with your pop idols, and have your picture taken with the "Royal Family."

Museum of London

The Museum of London offers a fascinating insight into London's rich history. Permanent displays in seven galleries take you through Roman and Saxon London, the Middle Ages, and the Tudor, Stuart, Georgian, and Victorian eras, right up to the present day. Changing exhibits cover facets of the modern age.

INSIDER TIP:

Visit Brick Lane in the East End for some tasty (and authentic) Indian fare. The owners stand outside the doorways of their establishments telling you about their menus.

—MARY JO SLAZAK
Manager, Subsidiary Rights,
National Geographic Books

A little farther east, in the heart of the now revamped dock area of the city, you'll find the **Museum of London Docklands** *(No. 1 Warehouse, West India Quay, Hertsmere Rd., tel 020-7001 9844, tube: Canary Wharf; DLR: West India Quay)*, an outstation of the Museum of London, telling the rambunctious story of the docks and their late 20th-century re-creation as a showpiece business and residential area. For the kids there's a hands-on Children's Gallery.
🄰 53 F4 ✉ London Wall, EC2Y 5HN
☎ 020-7001 9844 🛱 $$ 🚇 Tube: Barbican, St. Paul's

Sir John Soane's Museum

John Soane was born in 1753, the son of a bricklayer. A brilliant architect (the Bank of England was one of his designs), he helped his fortunes along when he married the niece of a well-to-do builder. The museum consists of the many thousands of artifacts he crammed into the house where he lived.

Olympic Park

Britain is host nation of the 2012 Olympic Games, and all eyes are on London. The capital city is rising to the occasion by developing the superb Queen Elizabeth Olympic Park (www.london2012.com/games/olympic-park) on a semiderelict site in Stratford, East London. Where gutted factories and shuttered shops stood in the shadow of railway viaducts that cut up the area into compartments of neglect, new buildings are rising—stadia and athletes' facilities that include an aquatic center, residential apartments for 17,000 athletes and officials, restaurants, medical rooms, and a Village Plaza. Brand-new infrastructure and transport links will greatly improve access. Here is the framework for a stunningly successful Olympics. And what then?

Everything is being done in a commendable environmentally sound way, and that approach will continue after the Games when the park enters a new phase. The northern half will become a green space full of wildlife-friendly habitats, especially woodlands and wetlands, while the southern half will serve as a recreation and refreshment area with cafés, bars, waterside walks, gardens, and venues for theater, music, and other performance arts. At present it's a matter of "watch this space"—but those are the widescreen plans for revitalizing this hitherto under-the-radar quarter of East London.

In the **Dining Room** and **Library** are Sir Thomas Lawrence's 1828 portrait of Soane, the epitome of reflective sensitivity; Sir Joshua Reynold's "Love and Beauty," with the coquettish subject glancing playfully from behind her rounded white arm; and the Cawdor Vase, a late fourth-century B.C. Italian piece covered in warlike and sportive heroes and gods.

Delicately carved Roman marbles are in the **Dressing Room** and **Study,** with more on view from the window in the **Monument Court,** an internal light well, along with Hogarth's "Oratorio" and a Canaletto street scene.

There is an astonishing array of treasures in the **Picture Room,** featuring William Hogarth's original series of paintings, "A Rake's Progress" and "The Election." The walls are panels, cunningly hinged to fold out; behind the Hogarths are 18th-century monochromes of Doric temples by Piranesi and a Turner watercolor, "Kirkstall Abbey."

In the **Crypt** you'll find the Sepulchral Chamber, housing the enormous, bathlike alabaster sarcophagus of Pharaoh Seti I (d. 1279 B.C.), and the Catacombs stacked with decorative Roman funerary urns.

The **New Picture Room** has three Canaletto waterscapes, including the 1736 "View toward Santa Maria della Salute, Venice," which is considered one of his finest.

Hanging in the first-floor **Drawing Rooms** are poignant portraits Soane as a worried and prematurely old man, and of his two ne'er-do-well sons, George and John. 🔺 53 E4 ✉ 13 Lincoln's Inn Fields, WC2 ☎ 020-7405 2107 🕐 Closed Sun.–Tues. (but open first Tues. of month) 💲 Guided tours: $$ 🚇 Tube: Holborn

Wallace Collection

Displayed in 29 galleries in an Italianate mansion just south of Regent's Park, the Wallace Collection was bequeathed to the nation on condition it be kept intact. Four generations of the Seymour-Conway family, Marquesses of Hertford, assembled it during the late 18th and 19th centuries. Their legacy forms the richest private art collection in London. Most notable are the 18th-century French paintings and sculpture collected by the 4th Marquess and his son, Sir Richard Wallace (1818–1890). 🔺 52 C4 ✉ Hertford House, Manchester Sq., W1 ☎ 020-7563 9500 🚇 Tube: Bond Street

London's surrounding counties—neatly pretty and full of royal connections, great houses, and rolling countryside

Home Counties

Statue of Queen Victoria, Windsor Castle

Home Counties

The Home Counties is the name given to the counties that surround London. Setting aside Kent (more properly a part of the great chalk barrier that forms the South Country) and Essex (in atmosphere more closely aligned with East Anglia), they are Surrey to the south of London, Berkshire and Buckinghamshire out west, Bedfordshire and Hertfordshire to the north. The influence of London grows weaker the farther out you go.

Windsor Castle's soldiers come from active regiments of Foot Guards in the British Army.

Here are opulent country houses sealed away behind high walls and built by the wealthy for their proximity to London, charming villages, an astonishing amount of woodland, some of the prettiest British river scenery along the Thames in Berkshire and the Wey in Surrey, and everywhere a tangle of footpaths through beautiful countryside.

Surrey & Berkshire

Lying for the most part in Surrey is the chalk rampart of the North Downs, along which runs a bridlepath, the Pilgrim's Way. There are wonderful high views from this ancient track. Surrey also possesses plenty of scenic villages, and in the west some wide tracts of undeveloped heathland.

Royal Berkshire spreads lush meadows along the River Thames between Windsor and Henley-on-Thames and boasts the monarch's premier residence, Windsor Castle, as its chief landmark.

Bucks to Beds

"Leafy Bucks" has the glorious Chiltern Hills, a mecca for metropolitan riders and walkers, where old beechwoods smother rolling hills. It also has a great chalk escarpment that looks north and west over enormous plains stretching off into Oxfordshire and Bedfordshire. Here are some of the prettiest and most historic Home Counties villages—the perfect National Trust village of Hambleden near Henley; Chalfont St. Giles, where Milton finished *Paradise Lost;* and West Wycombe, home of the 18th-century Hellfire Club.

Hertfordshire has Hatfield House (the greatest Jacobean mansion in Great Britain), more excellent walking, and its own clutch of fascinating places such as picture-perfect Aldbury in the west, eccentric and irresistible Ayot St. Lawrence with the home of George Bernard Shaw, and Perry Green in the east, where Henry Moore's unfathomable and beautiful sculptures lie silhouetted on the skyline. ■

NOT TO BE MISSED:

London

Area of map detail

The Thames West of London

From the Oxfordshire lowlands south of Oxford, the River Thames flows by way of Pangbourne and Mapledurham through the outskirts of Reading before swinging north to reach Henley-on-Thames, one of this river's most agreeable little towns. Almost all of Henley's interest lies along its river frontage, for this is the venue of the world-renowned Henley Royal Regatta in the first week of July.

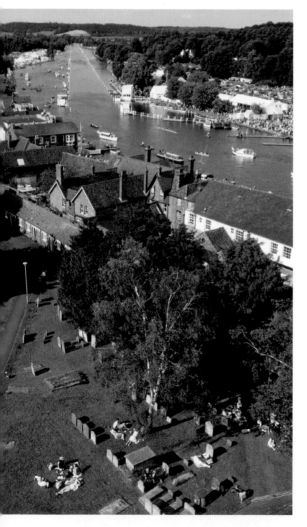

Henley-on-Thames hosts four annual rowing regattas; the five-day Henley Royal Regatta is the most prestigious.

Henley Week (*tel 01491-572153*) is one of those landmarks in the social calendar when the snobbish side of the English character is allowed full play—both on the part of the straw-boater-toting, blazer-wearing, champagne-swigging persons who fill the grandstands beside the River Thames, and of the chip-on-shoulder sourpusses who love to moan and complain about them.

The boat racing began in 1829 as a challenge between Oxford and Cambridge Universities. In 1839 it was instituted annually. When Prince Albert became patron in 1851, Henley Regatta received its royal imprimatur—and since then it has never looked back.

Marlow to Cookham

Hambleden village, just off the A4155, has enough charming flint-and-brick cottages edged with roses to satisfy any camera wielder. St. Mary's is a big cruciform church with some fine carving and a wonderful decorated tub font that probably predates the Normans' arrival in Britain. Beyond Hambleden, the Thames swings east to flow past the photogenic weir, mill, lock, and lockkeeper's cottage at **Marlow.** Soon the river is crossed by a fine 1836 suspension bridge. The

Compleat Angler Hotel (1653) has a stained-glass fish window to the memory of Izaak Walton (1593–1683), the London hardware dealer who fished all these waters and wrote a philosophical and piscatorial masterpiece, *The Compleat Angler*.

INSIDER TIP:

Henley's large and light-filled River & Rowing Museum will get you up to speed on all you need to know to watch the Henley Royal Regatta.

—ERIN MONRONEY
National Geographic contributor

Now the Thames skirts the meadows at Bourne End and reaches **Cookham,** where during the ceremonial "Swan Upping" each July Her Majesty's Swan Keeper counts the birds. Cookham High Street has the creaky old Bel and the Dragon Inn, and the **Stanley Spencer Gallery** *(High St., tel 01628-471885, closed Mon.–Fri. Nov.–Easter),* which displays many splendidly vigorous, individualistic paintings by local artist Sir Stanley Spencer (1891–1959).

Downstream to Windsor

Below Cookham, the Thames passes through the beechwoods of Cliveden Reach near the opulent **Cliveden House** (now a hotel, see Travelwise p. 347, but sympathetic to interested explorers), where the "Cliveden

Set" of 1920s and '30s politicians and glitterati gathered to chatter and arrange the world with Lord and Lady Astor.

Boulter's Lock and the handsome bridges at Maidenhead are next; then Bray and Monkey Island with its simian-themed hotel. Finally, the Thames slides by Eton and Windsor (see pp. 102–105) to reach the site of **Runnymede** just before passing under the M25 and approaching London proper.

At Runnymede there is a 1953 Commonwealth Air Forces Memorial to 20,000 unburied dead airmen of World War II, and a 1965 memorial to President John F. Kennedy on an acre of ground presented to the United States. Most pertinent to Britain's story, however, is a neoclassical temple donated in 1957 by the American Bar Association in memory of the signing at Runnymede of the Magna Carta. The world's first bill of civil rights was forced on a reluctant King John by his own barons in June 1215. ∎

Henley-on-Thames
🅰 99 B2
Visitor Information
✉ King's Arms Barn, King's Rd.
☎ 01491-578034

Marlow
🅰 99 B2
Visitor Information
✉ 31 High St.
☎ 01628-483597

River & Rowing Museum
✉ Mill Meadows, Henley-on-Thames
☎ 01491-415600
💲 $$$
www.rrm.co.uk

Riverside Walk

A lovely 6-mile walk goes downstream from Henley Bridge on the east bank of the Thames. It passes Temple Island midriver with its 18th-century James Wyatt folly, the starting point for the regatta crews on their 1-mile, 550-yard dash to Henley Bridge, and reaches Hambleden Lock and an exciting crossing of the river on a catwalk bridge to picturesque Hambleden Mill. From the lock, a path goes south to Aston and the delightful Flower Pot Hotel (characterful old bars and shady gardens), then southwest back to Henley by way of Remenham Woods.

Royal Windsor

Windsor is well known for its great castle, a royal residence for more than 900 years, but the town has highlights, too. The 1689 Guildhall on High Street was designed by Sir Christopher Wren, who installed its ornamental columns under protest. The crooked Market Cross House stands alongside. On Church Street is Burford House, where Charles II dallied with Nell Gwynne; also the Old King's Head Tavern, which bears a "Warrant to Execute Kinge Charles the First, A.D. 1648."

St. George's Chapel is the resting place of several British monarchs, including Henry VIII.

Windsor

⚑ 99 C2

Visitor Information

✉ 24 High St.

☎ 01753-743900

Windsor Castle

The castle's unmistakable shape is an icon to the British—in particular, the great Round Tower, from whose summit flies the Royal Standard when the monarch is in residence.

The first castle was built of wood shortly after the Norman Conquest, on a rise of ground commanding the Thames and only a day's march from William I's main residence in the Tower of London. Henry II was the first monarch to live at Windsor, rebuilding the castle in stone from around 1165. The **Round Tower,** centerpiece of the whole ensemble, was likewise converted from wood to stone construction around this time. The castle was laid out in three wards (walled

Make sure you see
the intricate Queen
Mary's Dolls' House
when on the tour of
Windsor Castle.

—ALISON WRIGHT
National Geographic photographer

areas), with the Round Tower
built in the Middle Ward. The
tower's upper works were added
from 1828 by George IV, in a
burst of full-blooded medieval-
izing. Nowadays it houses the
**Royal Archives and Photo-
graphic Collection.**

Upper Ward: This part of the
castle contains a 13th-century
court with the **Waterloo
Chamber,** a state apartment
built in 1832 to celebrate the
victory at the Battle of Waterloo. Also here is **St. George's
Hall,** built in 1362–1365. It
was very badly damaged in
a major fire in 1992, but has
since been restored. The **State
Apartments** are crammed
with treasures—Antonio Verrio frescoes on the ceilings,
Adam fireplaces, carvings by
Grinling Gibbons, paintings by
Canaletto, Van Dyck, Holbein,
Rembrandt, Rubens, Hogarth,
Gainsborough, and Constable.
It is a solid assemblage of the
masters of various branches
of art down the ages. One bit
of fun: Queen Mary's Dolls'
House, designed in 1923 by Sir
Edwin Lutyens to a meticulous
1:12 scale, with real miniature

books, pictures, electric lighting,
and running water.

Lower Ward: Most impressive of the castle's buildings is
the late Gothic **St. George's
Chapel,** a Tudor creation of
1475–1528 with delicate stone
carving, pride of place going to
the elaborate fan vaulting. The
Order of the Knights of the
Garter, founded by Edward III
in 1348, has 26 members, and
their tall, carved stalls stand in
the chapel under their individual
banners and crests. Ten monarchs are buried in St. George's—
they include Henry VIII and his
third wife, Jane Seymour; the
beheaded Charles I; George V;
and George VI.

The castle also contains the
13th-century **Albert Memorial
Chapel,** restored from 1861 in

Windsor Castle

 Windsor

Recorded
information:
020-7766 7304

Closed during
State visits
(call to check).
Chapels closed
Sun. except for
services

$$$$$

**www.royalcollection
.org.uk**

Shields bearing the coats of arms of the Garter Knights, some 980 in total, stud the ceiling of St. George's Hall.

memory of Queen Victoria's beloved Prince Consort. Here also are a number of grace-and-favor houses, and the 13th-century Curfew Tower.

Great Park & Eton

The 4,800 well-wooded acres of **Windsor Great Park** are interlaced with a network of footpaths. **Savill Garden** (*tel 01784-435544*) lies to

Albert Memorial Chapel

St. George's Chapel

Curfew Tower

the southeast of the park. Its 35 acres feature formal rose gardens, perennial borders, and glorious fall foliage.

North of the town a footbridge crosses the Thames to Eton, where you may see top-hatted and tailcoated boys from **Eton College** *(High St., tel 01753-671000, closed Oct.–March. & a.m. during school year),* Britain's most exclusive school, founded in 1440 and source (to date) of 18 prime ministers. ■

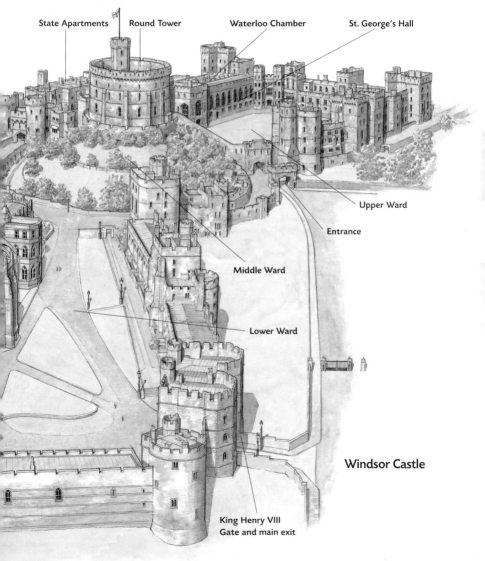

State Apartments   Round Tower   Waterloo Chamber   St. George's Hall

Upper Ward

Entrance

Middle Ward

Lower Ward

Windsor Castle

King Henry VIII
Gate and main exit

Woburn Abbey

Woburn Abbey, southwest of Milton Keynes, stands in a 3,000-acre park crisscrossed with beautiful tree-shaded walks. About 350 acres of Woburn land is used for the Woburn Safari Park, home to myriad exotic animal species. But Woburn's best known conservation work is with Chinese deer. The deer park was set up in 1900 by the 11th Duke of Bedford to nurture 18 Père David deer, the remnants of the last known herd of its type.

Woburn Abbey's Grotto, an early 17th-century folly

Woburn Abbey
- 🅜 99 C3
- ✉ Woburn
- ☎ 01525-290333
- 🕓 Closed Nov.–March
- 💲 $$$$

www.woburnabbey
.co.uk

Woburn Safari Park
- ✉ Woburn Park
- ☎ 01525-290407
- 🕓 Closed Nov.–early March & Mon.–Fri.
- 💲 $$$$$ (cheaper after 3 p.m.)

The Père Davids are contentedly at home in the park. The painstaking recovery program was so successful that in 1985 the Duke of Bedford was able to return a small herd to China, where they are now breeding successfully.

The Big House

Woburn Abbey itself is a splendid mid-18th-century house built for the Russell family, dukes of Bedford. There had been a Cistercian monastery here since 1145, but at the Dissolution it was handed to the Russells by Henry VIII. It took another hundred years for the family to move to Woburn from their Tudor house of Chenies in south Buckinghamshire, and they took their time modernizing and rebuilding their new Bedfordshire residence. Begun in 1747, it was completed around 1788.

The State Apartments are graced with superb gilded ceilings, and paintings by Reynolds, Gainsborough, and Canaletto (21 works). In the Long Gallery hang Tudor portraits.

Beyond the Park

The village of **Woburn,** just west of the abbey, was largely rebuilt at the same time as the house. You can spot various "B" monograms, capped with coronets, on walls and gables around the place. Some of the houses have no front doors: The doorlessness was ordered by a former Duke of Bedford, who was distressed to see his tenants standing gossiping at their front doors.

East of Woburn the lowlands of Bedfordshire sweep up toward the hills of northern Hertfordshire. The heights of this exhilarating escarpment are crossed by the 6,000-year-old track known as the **Icknield Way,** now a long-distance trail. An excellent section crosses the B655 just east of Pegsdon. You can walk it southwest over Telegraph Hill, site of one of the 18th-century semaphore stations set up by the Admiralty at 10-mile intervals to carry news between London and Great Yarmouth. ∎

EXPERIENCE:
Masterpieces of English Artificial Landscapes

When money and snobbery—a great catalyst for both good and ill in the story of Great Britain—were poured into the development of country estates, they allowed mountains, almost literally, to be moved. Colonial and industrial riches, allied to a human desire to keep up with the Joneses (and go one better if possible), created and landscaped estates all over the country.

Beginning in the 18th century, rich young sprigs coming back home after the Grand Tour of Europe were enthused by the classical architecture they had seen, and by the romantic and pastoral notions of landscape that were becoming all the rage in a nation whose own countryside was being ripped up and fouled by unrestricted mining, quarrying, and industrial waste. The last thing a gentleman wanted was to be associated with all that—most especially if he had made his money from it. The fashion for creating one's own artificial piece of pastoral heaven made the fame and fortune of notable landscapers of the 18th and 19th centuries, such as William Kent (1685–1748), Humphry Repton (1752–1818), and the greatest of them all, Lancelot "Capability" Brown (1716–1783).

The essential theme of landscaping was to make the view more and more "wild" the farther from the house you looked. Near at hand lay the thoroughly civilized and controlled formal gardens, from whose boundaries ran lawns and shrubberies; beyond stretched the park where cattle, sheep, and haymakers roamed charmingly; and beyond that rose hills where follies of temples or mock castles were piquantly set off by the wild woods that framed them. Such a setting hymned man's dominance over nature, while adding a little frisson of the wild as a moral corrective against delusions of omnipotence.

INSIDER TIP:

Enjoy simple splendor at Blenheim Palace with a picnic by the huge lake, created out of a canal in the undulating countryside.

—ERIN MONRONEY
National Geographic contributor

Those who poured out money on these landscapes knew they would not live to see them to fruition. Decades after Brown, Repton, or Kent had finished their work and been paid (or not—thereby hangs many another tale!), the landowner's woods would be half grown, the new hillsides muddy and sparsely grassed, the lakes still murky and bare.

The artificial landscapes created more than two centuries ago have now matured, each realizing its individual creator's vision. Many of them are open to the public. Walking around the grounds of these estates is like stepping into a painting. Try to visit one of the following masterpieces, which represent each of the landscape architects at his finest hour:

Rousham House Designed by William Kent, the unspoiled, classical gardens at Rousham epitomize the first design aesthetic of artificial landscapes. *Near Bicester, Oxfordshire, tel 01869-347110, www.rousham.org, $.*

Blenheim Palace Capability Brown superbly blended water, woods, follies, hills, and valleys to complement the palatial mansion. *Woodstock (8 miles NW of Oxford on A44 Evesham Rd.), tel 01993-811091, www.blenheimpalace.com, $$$ palace, park, & gardens, $$ park & gardens only.*

Sheringham Park This wonderful woodland garden and park was created by Humphry Repton and his son John; it was Repton's own favorite. *Wood Farm, Upper Sheringham, Norfolk, tel 01263-820550, www.nationaltrust.org.uk, $ parking.*

The Chilterns

The Chiltern Hills hold a very special place in the hearts of London and Home Counties countryside lovers. This great rise of chalk and flint, smothered with beechwoods and dotted with quiet open spaces and rough downland slopes, curves for 30 miles as it shadows the western perimeter of London. The Chilterns bend like a bow northeast from the Thames around to the meeting point of Buckinghamshire, Bedfordshire, and Hertfordshire near Ivinghoe Beacon.

The Chilterns
🗺 99 B2–B3
Visitor Information
✉ High Wycombe Library, 5 Eden Pl., High Wycombe
☎ 01494-421892
🕐 Closed Sun.

The range's outer rim, at the top of an impressive chalk escarpment, commands wonderful views. In the beechwoods and on the downland slopes thrive huge numbers of wildflowers—orchids, Chiltern gentian, rockrose, yellow-wort—along with yews, spindle bushes, wild service trees, and ancient holly. Butterflies, songbirds, and hawks thrive. This is some of the best walking territory within 30 miles of London, crisscrossed with footpaths and dotted with village pubs for en route refreshment.

Around Wycombe

In the slice of countryside between the M40 London–Oxford freeway and the M1 lies some of the most attractive Chiltern countryside, less frequented than the sometimes overcrowded region farther south around Henley-on-Thames and Hambleden (see p. 100). **West Wycombe,** just northwest of High Wycombe, is a delightful brick and timber village. Here are the **Hellfire Caves** (*tel 01494-533739, www.hellfirecaves.co.uk, closed Mon.–Fri. Nov.–March*), excavated in Georgian times by local squire Sir Francis Dashwood for stone to surface the roads. He put the caves to more notorious use as the setting for orgies held by his Hellfire Club, a band of wild pranksters that included many of the most eminent men of the day. On the hill above the village, **St. Lawrence's Church** (*West Wycombe, closed Sun. & some Sat.*) is topped with a big, hollow, golden globe; it served

Wycombe and many other towns in the Chiltern Hills have become bedroom communities for London.

EXPERIENCE:
Enjoy a Pub Lunch & a Stroll on the Ridgeway

Buckinghamshire is the classic rolling, wooded Chiltern county, and the very well waymarked 87-mile-long **Ridgeway National Trail** runs right through its most scenic parts. The **Plough** (Cadsden Rd., Princes Risborough, tel 01844-343302, www.ploughatcadsden.com), which dates from the 16th century, sits right on the walking trail and is a popular stopping point for trail walkers. Enjoy a typical pub lunch—perhaps a pint of their well-kept bitter and (appropriately) a ploughman's

lunch of bread, cheese, and pickled onions—either before or after stretching your legs on the Ridgeway. For a good walk, follow the white acorn waymarkers north and east from the pub for 3.5 miles, passing the handsome Elizabethan mansion of Chequers, the British prime minister's country retreat, to reach **Coombe Hill**—a stupendous view. You can also climb up Coombe Hill in half an hour from the pretty market town of **Wendover.**

as a bizarrely sited clubroom where Hellfire members could gamble and drink. Nearby is the hexagonal shell of a mausoleum built to house their hearts.

On the Northern Slopes

Farther east on the A413 is the very attractive valley of the River Misbourne, stretching between the Georgian market town of Amersham and the village of **Chalfont St. Giles.** Here the cottage in which the blind poet John Milton finished writing *Paradise Lost* in 1665–1666 has been turned into a small museum—**Milton's Cottage. St. Giles's Church** has beautiful 14th-century wall paintings, notably the Creation, the Cru-cifixion, and the beheading of John the Baptist.

Ten miles north, on the far side of the A41 and the Grand Union Canal, the Ashridge Estate's 4,000 acres of prime National Trust woodland occupies a long north–south ridge. Tucked under its western flank is **Aldbury,**

charmingly grouped around its duck pond, village green, and 16th-century manor house. The Pendley Chapel in St. John's Church holds the superbly carved 15th-century effigies of Sir Robert and Lady Whittingham.

A footpath climbs east up the ridge, then follows a sunken trackway north through the beech-woods to the 100-foot column of the **Bridgewater Monument.** It was erected in 1832 in honor of the 3rd Earl of Bridgewater, whose pioneering canal-building in 18th-century England hastened the coming of the industrial revolution. It also made him rich, and his descendants built the huge Gothic Ashridge House on the ridge opposite. Spiral steps lead to a spectacular view from the top of the monument, but an even better one can be had by follow-ing the path north for 2 miles to join the long-distance path called the **Ridgeway** (see sidebar this page). From the 755-foot brow of Ivinghoe Beacon you look out over 30 miles of countryside. ∎

Milton's Cottage
- Dean Way, Chalfont St. Giles
- ☎ 01494-872313
- 🕑 Closed Nov.– Feb. & Mon. March–Oct.

www.miltonscottage .org

Bridgewater Monument
- ☎ 01442-851227
- 🕑 Closed Nov.– March & Mon.– Fri. April–Oct. (except by appt.)

www.nationaltrust .org.uk

St. Albans Cathedral

The restoring zeal of Lord Grimthorpe in mid-Victorian times saved the St. Albans Cathedral in south Hertfordshire from being another pretty ruin left over from the Reformation. The great Norman abbey church had been steadily decaying since it was saved from destruction at the Dissolution, but the townsfolk rescued it by buying it for use as their own parish church.

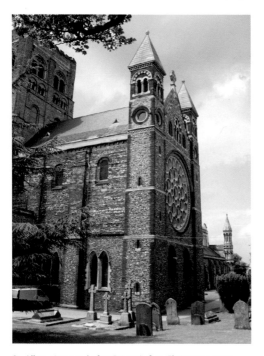

St. Albans is named after Britain's first Christian martyr.

St. Albans

🅐 99 C3

Visitor Information

✉ Town Hall, Market Pl.

☎ 01727-864511

St. Albans Cathedral

✉ Sumpter Yard

☎ 01727-860780

💲 Donation

www.stalbans cathedral.org

Whether the Victorian restoration was an aesthetic success has been vigorously questioned. The exterior of the cathedral (the church was consecrated a cathedral in 1877) certainly does not compare with Wells, Canterbury, York Minster, or the other soaring masterpieces of medieval church architecture in Britain. There is something crouched and bulky about it. The huge west window overshadows its spindly flanking turrets, and the tower is squat and plain. But inside there are some fine 13th- and 14th-century frescoes on the piers, one showing the Crucifixion, and several areas of beautifully fresh blue and red medieval glass.

Patron Saint

Here, too, is the 14th-century marble shrine of the church's patron saint, St. Alban, carved with scenes from his martyrdom. Alban himself was a Roman soldier-citizen who became Britain's first Christian martyr in A.D. 209, when he was beheaded for giving shelter to Amphibalus, the priest who had converted him to Christianity. He was canonized in 429, a time when the exhausted Roman Empire was crumbling in the face of barbarian vigor and appetite for conquest. Offa, the Mercian king who built a mighty dike along the border with Wales (see p. 174), founded St. Albans Abbey in 793 over the spot where the martyrdom was said to have taken place. When the Normans arrived, they quickly built a splendid church here, using many of the bricks that the Romans had made to build their town of Verulamium a thousand years before.

Early Beginnings

The Romans were not the first settlers in the valley of the River Ver. In **Prae Wood,** a couple of miles west of St. Albans, extensive earthworks show where the Belgae tribe of Britons had its stronghold. Verulamium was one of the most important towns in Britain, a social and economic center for the many Roman villas and estates scattered across the Chilterns. Roman and Celtic farmers came into town to have their corn ground at the water mills and to sell and barter produce. Standing at the crossing place of the two important Roman highways of Watling Street and Akerman Street, Verulamium had its

INSIDER TIP:

For some great Japanese food in St. Albans, check out Sukiyaki *(tel 01727-865009)* **at 6 Spencer Street.**

—ANJALI RAMCHANDANI
National Geographic contributor

interests and safety guaranteed by a legion that was garrisoned in the town.

On display in St. Albans' excellent **Verulamium Museum** is a variety of finds unearthed from the Roman town. There are some wonderfully intricate mosaics, particularly one based on a beautiful scallop shell. Embossed, heavily ornamented lead coffins show one mood of Roman culture; delicate and lively paintings of birds on plaster demonstrate another. There are extensive remains of an enormous theater (A.D. 140), big enough to seat up to 6,000 spectators, complete with its stage.

The Town

The town of St. Albans has been a trading center and staging post since Roman times, and its position on a hill has given it strategic importance, too. You can get an overview of the whole place by climbing the early 15th-century clock tower on High Street *(tel 01727-751810, closed Mon.–Fri. & mid-Sept.–Easter).*

The **Church of St. Michael** stands on Saxon foundations which are themselves bedded on the basilica and forum of the Roman town of Verulamium. In the nave, a fine Norman structure, a handsome tomb holds the remains of the Tudor statesman, philosopher, and writer Sir Francis Bacon (1561–1626), who lived at nearby Gorhambury.

St. Albans is full of old pubs with character; one of the best known is **Ye Olde Fighting Cocks** on Abbey Mill Lane. Parts of the building probably date back to Norman times (it started life as the dovecote of St. Albans Abbey); it is said locally to be the oldest pub in Britain. Its octagonal shape, pyramidal roof, and crooked chimneys are certainly striking. Another handsome old building worth looking at is the carefully restored 16th-century **Kingsbury Water Mill,** beside the River Ver. ■

Verulamium Museum

✉ St. Michael's St.
☎ 01727-751810
$ $$

www.stalbans museums.org.uk

Hatfield House

Robert Cecil, 1st Earl of Salisbury, was probably the most influential man in the kingdom when he started building Hatfield House in 1607. His father, William, 1st Lord Burghley, chief adviser to Elizabeth I, had died nine years before. Subsequently Robert had made himself invaluable to the Queen, and after her death in 1603 his was the voice in the ear of James I, who succeeded to the English throne.

Robert Cecil demolished most of the Old Palace at Hatfield to make way for this newer house.

Hatfield House

⊠ 99 C3

✉ Hatfield

☎ 01707-287010

🕐 Closed Oct.– Easter

💲 $$$, park only $

www.hatfield-house .co.uk

The house stands squarely on its raised and balustraded terrace, a dignified, E-shaped building of red brick dressed with white stone, its tall, stone-casemented windows topped by crown motifs—the most magnificent and impressive house of its day. The architect was Robert Lyminge, who went on to produce the wonderful Jacobean house Blickling Hall, near Norwich in Norfolk (see p. 219).

The Jacobean **gardens** at Hatfield House were laid out for Robert Cecil by, among others, John Tradescant the Elder and Salomon de Caus. These formal 17th-century knot and scented gardens are one of a few remaining examples.

A descendant of Cecil's, the present Marquess of Salisbury, still resides at Hatfield House today.

The Old House

Superb though the Jacobean mansion and its gardens are, there is as much history attached to the mellow old early Tudor building by way of which you approach Hatfield House itself.

This was Hatfield Palace (known today as the Old Palace), built before the turn of the 16th century. The original palace was far bigger than the single wing that survives, most of it having been dismantled by Robert Cecil while he was building his great house.

Queen Elizabeth I spent much of her rather lonely childhood in Hatfield Palace. Her father, Henry VIII, was not much interested in his second daughter, as he was desperate for a son to succeed him. He had her mother, Anne Boleyn, executed for treason and adultery before the princess was three years old. Elizabeth spent more time penned up out of the way at Hatfield after her half sister, Mary, came to the throne in 1553. It was in this house in 1558 that Elizabeth first heard of her accession to the throne.

Queen Elizabeth

Of the various mementoes of Elizabeth I at Hatfield House, the most amusing

INSIDER TIP:

The East Garden, including the formal parterres, is only open one day a week. Call ahead if you want to explore it.

—JANE SUNDERLAND
National Geographic contributor

is a family tree painstakingly concocted to show her descent from—among other more verifiable ancestors—Adam, Noah, and King Lear.

There are also several portraits of the Queen. The Isaac Oliver portrait, with its allegorical comparison of Elizabeth to a rainbow, and another by Nicholas Hilliard, suggesting all her intelligence and steeliness of character, show a woman marooned in the isolation of absolute power. William and Robert Cecil must have been a formidable pair to have steered the diamond-hard Virgin Queen the way they did. ■

William & Robert Cecil

Both Elizabeth I and her successor, James I, had cause to be grateful to the Cecils. It was the good advice and steadying influence of William Cecil (1520–1598), 1st Lord Burghley, and his son Robert (1563–1612), 1st Earl of Salisbury, that kept the country on an even keel through the turbulent waters of the Reformation. This period of unease was whipped up by the anti-Catholicism of Henry VIII and the fervent persecution of Protestants conducted by his Catholic

daughter, Queen Mary. In 1558 William Cecil was appointed adviser to Queen Elizabeth, a post that lasted for 40 years until his death in 1598; Robert followed suit, becoming secretary of state both to Elizabeth and to King James. The exceptional ability and subtlety of this father-and-son team was highlighted in retrospect by the shortsighted arrogance of Robert Cecil's successor as adviser, the high-handed and much disliked George Villiers, Duke of Buckingham.

More Places to Visit in the Home Counties

Ayot St. Lawrence

Ten miles north of St. Albans, in the quiet south Hertfordshire countryside, is the village of Ayot St. Lawrence, with its fine dark-beamed **Brocket Arms** pub *(off Hill Farm Ln.)* and its neoclassical **Church of St. Lawrence,** built in the 1770s in the Palladian style by rich tobacco merchant Sir Lionel Lyde. His tomb and that of his wife are set in pavilions on opposite sides of the church. Sir Lionel left orders that since the church had forced them to stay together in life, he would at least make sure it separated them in death.

Just along the road is **Shaw's Corner** *(Ayot St. Lawrence, tel 01438-820307, www.nation altrust.org.uk, closed Nov.–March & Mon.–Tues. April–Oct.),* a 1902 arts and crafts house where George Bernard Shaw, the often controversial Irish-born playwright, lived from 1906 to his death at age 94 in 1950. While living at Shaw's Corner he wrote, among other works, *Androcles and the Lion, Saint Joan,* and *Pygmalion* (the basis for the successful musical *My Fair Lady*). He was awarded the Nobel Prize for literature in 1925.

🄰 99 C3 **Visitor Information** ✉ Town Hall, Market Pl., St. Albans ☎ 01727-864511

Much Hadham

West of Bishop's Stortford in the east of Hertfordshire, the Church of St. Andrew at Much Hadham contains wonderful medieval carvings. Flanking the west doorway are two heads by modern sculptor Henry Moore (1898–1986), whose house and studio at **Perry Green** *(map 99 D3, tel 01279-843333, www.henry-moore.org, by appt. only, closed mid-Oct.–March)* are surrounded by his enigmatic, large-scale figures.

🄰 99 D3 **Visitor Information** ✉ Town Hall, Market Pl., St. Albans ☎ 01727-864511

Surrey

Immediately south of London is Surrey, a commuter county with beautiful and well-cared-for countryside. The heavily wooded country just east of Guildford contains villages with lots of character such as **Abinger Hammer** and **Friday Street,** sunk deep in the trees. **Leith Hill Tower** offers a splendid view, as does the Pilgrim's Way on the chalky escarpment of steep **Box Hill** *(map 99 C1).* Nearby **Shere** *(map 99 C1)* features on many "rural England" calendars; its Norman Church of St. James is full of treasures.

Stowe

The Dukes of Buckingham and Chandos were owners of the house at Stowe (now accommodating a public school) in the northwest of Buckinghamshire. But it is the **Stowe Landscape Gardens** *(map 99 B4, 2.5 miles NW of Buckingham, tel 01280-822850, www.nationaltrust.org.uk, closed Mon.–Tues. in summer, call for visiting times Nov.–April, $$)* that command attention. All the landscaping luminaries of the 18th and early 19th centuries worked on Stowe: Sir John Vanbrugh, James Gibbs, William Kent, Charles Bridgeman—and Capability Brown spent ten years as head gardener here before beginning a freelance career.

These grounds capture the transitional period between 17th-century formality and later 18th-century pastoral idyll. Classical ideals are in evidence throughout—Greek temples, Roman columns, a wonderful Palladian bridge over the lake, a "Grecian Valley" designed by Capability Brown (his maiden landscaping feat), and heroic monuments to British Worthies, to Concord, and to Victory.

A landscape of billowing chalk cliffs and downs, verdant meadows, and lively trout streams—and strewn with prehistoric monuments

The South Country

Detail of stained-glass window, Winchester Hall

The South Country

The South Country—a term coined by the poet and country writer Edward Thomas (1878–1917)—is not one of the portmanteau geographical labels universally used and understood by the British, as are the West Country or East Anglia or the Highlands. But it does suggest a cohesion in the great sweep of rolling countryside, characterized by open downs and lush green valley pasture, that runs west from Kent for 200 miles all the way to Dorset.

It is chalk that knits the South Country together—the smoothly undulating billows of the downs under grain or grass, and the bitten-off walls of the white cliffs that march from Kent into Sussex, decline to a flat sandy coast in Hampshire, and then rise again beyond Bournemouth for a final flourish around the Isle of Purbeck in Dorset.

South of London

Kent, so close to London and so conveniently placed for journeys to the Continent, boasts more than its share of impressive and historic great houses and smallish castles, and one of the world's great cathedrals at Canterbury, while to the north is the setting for some of Charles Dickens's best known novels.

Sussex has its South Downs that enfold charming flint-and-brick villages, and a

splendidly overblown seaside resort in Brighton. Hampshire is for trout fishing in clear chalk streams, and for reading Jane Austen—her house at Chawton is now a museum and her memorial stands in splendid Winchester Cathedral nearby.

To the West

The county of Wiltshire has two outstanding pieces of architecture as its chief claim to fame. One is the sublime 13th-century cathedral at Salisbury with its immense spire, the tallest in Britain. The other is around 3,000 years older: the enigmatic Bronze Age monument of Stonehenge. The downs and plains of Wiltshire are thickly dotted with prehistoric sites, especially around the mighty stone circle at Avebury.

Dorset is associated with Thomas Hardy, and here are most of the settings of his Wessex novels. The hills hide secret valleys, and the coast is spectacularly beautiful. ■

NOT TO BE MISSED:

Ightham Mote, a moated medieval manor house **119–120**

Northern Kent's marsh country, home to many of Dickens's settings for *Great Expectations* **124**

Wandering the gorgeous old hilltop town of Rye **125**

A day out in oddball Brighton—a quintessential seaside town **126**

Spectacular Salisbury Cathedral **132–134**

Visiting Stonehenge, at dawn or sunset if possible **135, 138**

Thomas Hardy's birthplace and the nearby settings for his Wessex novels **136–137**

Kent

East of Greater London, County Kent is home to several grand country houses open to visitors; Canterbury, a city that dates to medieval times and is famous for its cathedral; a wealth of towns and settings that served as inspiration for Charles Dickens; and charming seaside towns that beckon with bracing promenade walks and glorious Channel views.

Leeds Castle is superbly situated on two islands in a lake formed by the River Len.

Penshurst Place

🏛 117 F3

✉ Penshurst

☎ 01892-870307

🕓 Closed Nov.–
Feb. & Mon.–Fri.
March

💲 $$–$$$

**www.penshurst
place.com**

Great Houses of Kent

Considering the geographical position of the county—conveniently near London, yet far enough removed to be a separate entity, and placed ideally to form the gateway between the capital and the Continent—it is not surprising that so many rich and influential people should have settled here. Kent probably contains, acre for acre, more fine houses than any other county in Britain, some of them dating back to early medieval times or even further.

Penshurst Place: This is one of the greatest of Kent's great houses, on the western edge of the county. Penshurst is also one of England's oldest country houses, built for the rich London merchant Sir John de Pulteney in

1341. The Barons' Hall—64 feet long and almost as high—still survives with its roof of chestnut beams and its minstrels' gallery, along with the original solar, buttery, and pantry.

Sir Philip Sidney, the very flower of Renaissance manhood, who could fight and sing as well as he could rhyme and reason, was born at Penshurst Place in 1554, two years after his family came into possession of the estate. After his untimely death at the Battle of Zutphen in 1586, the house found a most hospitable owner in his younger brother, Robert. Many early 17th-century visitors commended Penshurst, and especially the beauty of its gardens. Dramatist Ben Jonson described the gardens this way:

> Then hath thy orchard fruit, thy
>   garden flowers,
> The early cherry with the
>   later plum,
> Fig, grape and quince, each in his
>   turn doth come;
> The blushing apricot and
>   woolly peach

> Hang on thy walls, that every
>   child may reach.

The pleasure Jonson took in the fishponds was almost as intense:

> Fat, aged carps, that runne into
>   thy net,
> And pikes, now weary their owne
>   kinde to eat;
> Bright eeles, that emulate them,
>   and leape on land
> Before the fisher, or into his hand.

The Penshurst Place gardens with their tall old beech trees, and the formal Italian gardens around the house itself, are open to all comers these days.

Ightham Mote: Ten miles north of Penshurst, the hills are blanketed in the oak, birch, and sweet chestnut of the northern Kentish Weald. Weald meant "woodland" to the Saxons, and much remains of the great forest they knew. Sunk among the trees lies Ightham Mote, a beautiful medieval manor house, moated as its name suggests.

Ightham Mote

- 117 F3
- Mote Rd., Ivy Hatch
- 01732-810378
- See website for hours
- $$

www.nationaltrust .org.uk

Garden of England

Kent is sometimes called the "Garden of England," a tribute to its long establishment as a fruit-growing county. Blossom time in the Kentish orchards is beautiful and memorable. In the tall, conical shapes of the old oast houses or hop-drying kilns that are common here, and in the hop fields themselves, you can trace Kent's enduring—and continuing—association with the sticky and odoriferous flower that gives beer its essential bitterness.

"After passing an afternoon with the drier in the kiln," enthused the Victorian rural writer Richard Jefferies, "seated close to a great heap of hops and inhaling the odour, I was in a condition of agreeable excitement. . . . I wanted music, and felt full of laughter. Like the half-fabled haschish, the golden bloom of the hops had entered the nervous system; intoxication without wine, without injurious after-effect, dream intoxication; they were wine for the nerves." Beware the power of Kentish hops!

Hever Castle

⚑ 117 F3
✉ Hever
☎ 01732-865224
🕐 Closed Dec.–late Feb.
$ Castle & gardens $$$$, gardens only $$$

www.hevercastle .co.uk

Chartwell

⚑ 117 F3
✉ Maple Rd., Westerham
☎ 01732-866368
🕐 Closed Nov.–March & Mon.–Tues. April–Oct. (open Tues. July–Aug.)
$ House, gardens, & studio $$$, gardens & studio only $$

www.nationaltrust .org.uk

Leeds Castle

⚑ 117 G3
✉ 4 miles E of Maidstone
☎ 01622-765400
$ $$$$

www.leeds-castle .com

Unlike Penshurst Place, Ightham is of modest size, but its history stretches back at least as far. A 14th-century Great Hall and chapel are hidden inside the Tudor exterior of local brick, timber, and ragstone, a harmonious mishmash of materials and architectural styles.

INSIDER TIP:

While visiting stunning Leeds Castle, don't forget to see the one-of-a-kind Dog Collar Museum in the gatehouse.

—PAULA KELLY
National Geographic contributor

Hever Castle: Hever Castle, in the rolling countryside just west of Penshurst Place, has a poignant place in the story of the six wives of Henry VIII. Anne Boleyn, the ill-starred second wife, grew up at Hever; and it was here that, as a bewitching young woman, she began to receive visits from the king. Later in Henry's marital saga his fourth wife, Anne of Cleves, was given Hever Castle as part of the divorce settlement, when the king divorced her less than a year after their marriage.

The moat and gatehouse at Hever date from around 1270. Within these walls a Tudor manor house was built for the Boleyn family. The interior was restored with notable Edwardian woodwork early in the 20th century, after the American owner of the *Times* newspaper, William Waldorf Astor (1848–1919), took a fancy to Hever Castle and bought it. For good measure he also built an entire neo-Tudor village behind the castle, for the servants and any overspill guests.

In the Inner Hall hangs a Hans Holbein portrait of Henry VIII, looking fat and ruthless. He certainly made his two Annes suffer. Anne Boleyn paid at the execution block for her failure to produce a male heir, and perhaps for sexual misdemeanors, too. But Anne of Cleves—"that Flanders mare," as Henry contemptuously called her—at least got out of it with her life.

Chartwell: Five miles north of Hever, Chartwell, a big Victorian house, is well known as the country home of Sir Winston Churchill from 1924 until his death in 1965. Here you can see a collection of Churchill memorabilia. The rooms are decorated as they were in Sir Winston and Lady Churchill's lifetime. The garden studio contains Sir Winston's easel and paintbox; he was a keen artist, and several of his paintings are on display here.

Leeds Castle: Four miles east of Maidstone, Leeds Castle—often named the most beautiful castle in England—rises dreamily above its own reflection in a lake under wooded hills. This Norman castle was given to Edward I in 1278 and remained a royal residence until Tudor times. The castle was a favorite of Henry VIII, who stayed here often. His first wife, Catherine of Aragon, was sent to live here after their divorce. The castle passed out of royal hands in 1552 when Henry gave it to Anthony St. Leger, his long-serving lord deputy in Ireland. Later, French prisoners were held here during the Napoleonic Wars.

History soaks the building, astutely marketed these days as a center for conferences and cultural and sporting events. Many are held in the Banqueting Hall, with its superb Tudor oak ceiling. Among attractions in the castle's 500 acres of parkland, landscaped by Capability Brown, are a huge maze, an aviary, herb gardens, and a golf course.

Sissinghurst Castle Garden: At Sissinghurst, 10 miles south of Maidstone, is Sissinghurst Castle Garden. Here beautifully designed areas are planted alongside others that grow in rough profusion. It was created in the 1930s in and around the ruin of a moated Elizabethan mansion by Vita Sackville-West and her husband, Sir Harold Nicolson, members of the Bloomsbury Group (see p. 71).

In Vita's study in the four-storied gate tower is the printing press used by Virginia and Leonard Woolf to run off the first volumes produced by their Hogarth Press—including, in 1922, T. S. Eliot's *Waste Land*.

Canterbury

Medieval city walls extend around three sides of Canterbury, enclosing streets lined with crooked, half-timbered buildings. The monks built in stone; their early 14th-century Fyndon Gateway stands in Monastery Street at an entrance to St. Augustine's Abbey, where the pioneer saint is buried. Charles I and his bride, Henrietta Maria, spent their wedding night in a chamber over the gateway. Of the original gates into the city, only the 1387 West Gate survives; it was once used as the city jail and holds a display of prison hardware (fetters, manacles, and the like), along with arms and armor.

In the former St. Margaret's Church in St. Margaret's Street there is audiovisual and olfactory fun with **The Canterbury Tales**

Sissinghurst Castle Garden

- 🅰 117 G3
- ✉ Biddenden Rd., near Cranbrook (10 miles S of Maidstone)
- ☎ 01580-710701
- 🕐 Closed Nov.– late March & Wed.–Thurs. late March–Oct. Due to limited capacity, visit early or late in the season to avoid disappointment. Timed ticket system operates.
- 💲 $$$

www.nationaltrust .org.uk

EXPERIENCE: Canterbury Cathedral— Behind the Scenes

For something out of the ordinary, go on one of Canterbury Cathedral's hugely popular "Behind the Scenes" tours ($$$). A great cathedral is like a miniature city or an ocean liner, with hundreds of specialists repairing, making, mending, and generally keeping it running. Here's your chance to see the cathedral team creating and rehearsing the great church's music, conserving the wonderful rare books in the library, or restoring and creating beautiful fittings such as carvings, vestments, and stained glass. Chat with these artists and craftspeople, and learn the 1,001 secrets of the "real" Canterbury Cathedral. Reserve well ahead (*e-mail: visits@canterbury-cathedral.org*).

Canterbury

🅰 117 G3

Visitor Information

✉ 12–13 Sun St.,
Buttermarket

☎ 01227-378100

🕐 Closed Sun.
Jan.–March

Canterbury Cathedral

✉ Buttermarket

☎ 01227-762862

💲 $$$

www.canterbury-cathedral.org

(tel 01227-479227), tableaus of some of Chaucer's fruitiest. **Eastbridge Hospital** on High Street (tel 01227-471688, closed Sun.), founded in 1190 to care for pilgrims to St. Thomas à Becket's shrine, has early 13th-century frescoes of Christ in Majesty.

The **Museum of Canterbury** on Stour Street (tel 01227-475202, closed Sun. Nov.–May), housed in a superb medieval building, offers a tour through 2,000 years of the city's history.

The Cathedral: Chief of the many treasures in the city of Canterbury is the cathedral, Mother Church of the Church of England and seat of its premier archbishop. The main

INSIDER TIP:

Be sure to stand directly below the central Bell Harry Tower and look up. The design and decoration of the vaulting is very beautiful.

—CAROLINE HICKEY
Editor, National Geographic Books

approach to the cathedral is through Christ Church Gate, ornate and brightly painted, with a lugubrious Christ looking gravely down from the center. The twin west towers and central 235-foot Bell Harry Tower are splendidly pinnacled.

The church was started in 1070, very shortly after the

Norman Conquest, on the site of an Anglo-Saxon cathedral destroyed by Danish marauders. St. Augustine had arrived on the pope's orders in 597 to begin converting the locals, and so Canterbury—a few miles inland from his landing place on the east Kent coast—became a place of pilgrimage well before the December 1170 murder of Thomas à Becket in the cathedral.

In the northwest transept is **The Martyrdom,** the spot where Becket—close friend turned critic of Henry II—was killed on his return from a period in exile by four knights after the king had uttered in hot blood the infamous exclamation: "Will no one rid me of this turbulent priest?" A 15th-century panel shows a reproachful Becket being cut down by his fiendish-looking assassins.

The murder was very swiftly declared a martyrdom (Becket was canonized only three years after his death), and his golden shrine became the object of one of the most popular medieval pilgrimages. A penitent Henry II was one of the first pilgrims, but the most famous are the fictional travelers—the Miller, the Wife of Bath, the Nun's Priest, and all the other companions—in Geoffrey Chaucer's wise and bawdy *Canterbury Tales,* written between 1387 and Chaucer's death in 1400.

In **Trinity Chapel,** at the east end of the cathedral, the Altar of Sword Point stands on the site of Becket's shrine, which was destroyed at the Reformation in 1538 on the orders of Henry VIII after a posthumous "trial" had

Canterbury's 13th-century nave is a magnificent example of English Perpendicular Gothic.

convicted Becket of high treason. Candles are kept burning in the chapel in memory of the saint, whose life and death are depicted in early medieval stained glass. The hollows in the steps were worn by the friction of countless millions of pilgrims' knees.

Other features at this east end of the church include the splendid brass effigy of the Black Prince (d. 1376), with reproductions of his armor hanging above, and the finely sculpted alabaster tomb of Henry IV and his queen, Joan of Navarre. The sky blue and leaf green of the stained glass here shows multiple biblical scenes—Abraham and Isaac with the ram caught in the thicket, Moses striking water out of the rock, ancient Methuselah in medieval robes and footwear.

Below in the crypt is a stone forest of Romanesque arches and pillars, their capitals carved with foliage and faces. There is 14th-century fan vaulting in the chapter house, and a fine early 15th-century stone screen shielding the choir.

Charles Dickens & Northern Kent

Charles Dickens (1812–1870) used north Kent as a setting in many of his novels, including *The Pickwick Papers* (1836–1837), *The Uncommercial Traveller* (1860), and the unfinished *Mystery of Edwin Drood* (1870). Dickens knew the county well; he spent several childhood years in Chatham and lived at **Gad's Hill Place** near Rochester from 1856 until his death. It was *Great Expectations* (1860–1861), written at Gad's Hill Place, that Dickens most fully imbued with the strange, moody presence of this mostly flat and estuarine landscape.

Gad's Hill Place

✉ S of Higham

☎ 01474-822366

🕐 Open only 1st Sun. of each month p.m. & Bank Holidays

 $$

Rochester

117 F3

Visitor Information

✉ 95 High St.

☎ 01634-843666

Rochester: Rochester is home to several venues from *Great Expectations.* Across from **Eastgate House** on the town's High Street stands the gabled and timbered building that was pompous Uncle Pumblechook's seed-and-corn shop. In the Bull Hotel (now the **Royal Victoria & Bull Hotel**), Pip had his meeting with Bentley Drummle. Dickens featured the curly gabled Restoration House on

white weatherboard cottage by the road was Joe Gargery's forge and Pip's adoptive home. Farther west, a mile north of Higham village, stands lonely **St. Mary's Church.** In the graveyard, the convict Magwitch jumped out at Pip and swung him upside down so that the steeple flew under his feet.

A footpath leads north for a mile to **Cliffe Fort,** a stark ruin facing the broad River Thames,

Rye's steep cobbled streets and red-tiled roofs and walls make it magnetically attractive to visitors.

Maidstone Road as the creepy Miss Havisham's house.

The town has a fine Norman cathedral and an impressive castle with a 125-foot keep—the tallest in England.

Great Expectations Country: The novel has many connections with the marsh country to the north of Rochester. In **Chalk** village, on the A226, the

where Pip ran through the fog on Christmas morning to bring "wittles" and a file to Magwitch.

Just east, in **Cooling churchyard,** are 13 small, lozenge-shaped children's tomb slabs. Dickens used them as the gravestones of Pip's brothers; Pip believed, from the shape of the slabs, that his brothers "had all been born on their backs with their hands in their trouser-pockets."

White Cliffs of Dover

Why do the British cherish the White Cliffs of Dover so greatly? A lot of the affection for these tall chalk ramparts was crystallized during World War II. They resembled strong teeth bared defiantly at the enemy; they delineated the boundary of home with a decisive white slash; they sheltered fugitives from German bombing in deep tunnels. In peacetime, seen from a cross-Channel steamer, their advancing shape, a porcelain wall in the sea, assured every Englishman that he was returning to his country and his comfort zone. And—ultimate accolade—William Shakespeare put them into *King Lear:* "There is a cliff whose high and bending head / Looks fearfully in the confined deep." It doesn't get more iconic than that.

Around the Kent Coast

Sea surrounds Kent on three sides, the coastline running clockwise from the creeks of the Medway estuary on the north coast to the wetlands of Romney Marsh, haunt of smugglers in the 18th century, on the south.

Chatham, at the mouth of the Medway estuary, has a wonderful maritime heritage attraction, the **Chatham Historic Dockyard and World Naval Base** on Dock Road. Under nearby **Fort Amherst** *(tel 01634-847747)* are nearly 6,000 feet of tunnels hacked out by Napoleonic prisoners-of-war.

At the estuary's eastern end, the **Isle of Sheppey** is a wildfowl-watcher's paradise. Here the tiny Norman Church of St. Thomas stands near the remote Ferry House Inn.

North Kent boasts three shoulder-to-shoulder resorts—cheap and cheerful **Margate;** slightly more attractive **Broadstairs,** where Charles Dickens wrote *David Copperfield* (1849–1850) and *Bleak House* (1852–1853) and where you can visit the **Dickens House Museum** *(tel 01843-861232, www .dickenshouse.co.uk);* and the faded elegance of **Ramsgate.**

Sandwich and **Deal,** farther south, are two historic old fishing and smuggling ports, rich in flint-and-brick architecture.

Around the curve of the South Foreland, the famous white chalk cliffs (see sidebar above) cradle the ferry port of **Dover,** with its enormous castle, and the Victorian seaside resort of **Folkestone,** since autumn 1994 the point of entry to the Channel tunnel railway link with France.

Beyond Folkestone lie the 80 square miles of beautiful **Romney Marsh,** a dead-flat apron of green fields and straight watercourses.

On the western edge, just across the border in East Sussex, the fascinating old red-roofed town of **Rye** perches on its hill, as pretty as a picture with its crooked, steep little streets, medieval Land Gate, Mermaid Inn (an old smugglers' haunt), and **Lamb House** *(West St., tel 01580-762334, www.national trust.org.uk, open Thurs. & Sat. only, April–Oct.),* where the American novelist Henry James (1843–1916) lived from 1898 until his death. Climb St. Mary's Church tower to get good views. ∎

Chatham
🗺 117 F3

Chatham Historic Dockyard and World Naval Base
✉ Dock Rd., Chatham
☎ 01634-830404
🕐 Closed mid-Dec.–mid-Feb.
💲 $$$

Rye
🗺 117 G2
Visitor Information
✉ Strand Quay
☎ 01797-226696

Sussex

Brighton and Chichester shine brightly in Sussex. Seaside Brighton has a wealth of Regency architecture, including the fanciful Royal Pavilion, recalling the town's grand years of the 19th century. Georgian architecture takes center stage at Chichester, but the nearby Fishbourne Roman Palace, dating to about A.D. 75, offers a glimpse of the Roman era.

Brighton Pier is one of several pleasure piers in Britain.

Brighton

- 117 E2
- **Visitor Information**
- 4–5 Pavilion Buildings, Royal Pavilion
- 01273-290337

Royal Pavilion

- Pavilion Parade, Brighton
- 01273-290900
- $$
- www.royalpavilion.org.uk

Brighton

Brighton is a paradox: an attractive conference center as well as a seaside resort for day-trippers, where superb elegance and glitzy raffishness sit happily side by side. As a vacation destination Brighton has suffered, like many of Britain's seaside resorts, from cheaper and sunnier foreign competition. But there are still enough aesthetically pleasing buildings here, and enough roguish twinkle, to reflect the town's former glory as "old Ocean's Bauble, glittering Brighton."

During the late 18th century, the tiny Sussex fishing village of Brighthelmstone swelled into a seawater spa. There are still reminders of the old Brighthelmstone in the area of narrow streets called **The Lanes,** just behind the seafront.

Inland spread the terraces and crescents of Regency architecture that proliferated when the Prince Regent, George IV-to-be, came to Brighton early in the 19th century to rule as the Prince of Pleasure. In 1815 he had a palace built for himself right in the heart of Brighton—the ostentatiously vulgar and delightful **Royal Pavilion,** an absolute must-see for any visitor, with its enormous onion domes, its minarets, its great ceiling-mounted dragons, and its tree-shaped chandeliers. Contemporary critics enjoyed themselves—"turnips and tulip bulbs" (William Cobbett); "one would think that St. Paul's Cathedral had come to Brighton and pupped" (Sidney Smith).

Down on the seafront are the **Brighton Pier** (1899) and the **Sea Life Centre** *(Marine Parade, tel 01273-604234),* where an underwater tunnel—the longest in Europe—allows you to view sharks and other marine animals at close quarters. Here you can ride in one of the little carriages of **Volks Electric Railway** *(tel 01273-292718, closed Oct.–Easter)* out east to Marina Station, or under your own power climb the hill to elegant **Kemp Town.** The town's designer, local wild boy (and MP) Thomas Read Kemp, died broke before his plans were realized in the 1850s, but his memorial is one of the finest Regency-style developments ever built.

Chichester

Although Brighton is the flashiest, biggest, and most prosperous town in Sussex, the county capital of West Sussex is the ancient cathedral city of Chichester, 30 miles west of Brighton along the coast. Its Roman street plan still radiates out from the finely carved Tudor market cross at the town's heart, though the buildings are mostly solid Georgian.

Begun in about 1075 but rebuilt at the end of the 12th century after a fire, **Chichester Cathedral** (tel 01243-782595) soars in pale, silvery limestone over its red-roofed Deanery. Its slim 277-foot spire is a landmark seen for many miles. Rare early 12th-century stone carvings on the south side of the choir show Lazarus being raised from the dead. At the other end of the age spectrum are Graham Sutherland paintings, a 1966 tapestry by John Piper, and a vivid 1978 stained-glass window by Marc Chagall, full of prancing and skipping figures on a bloodred background.

The **Chichester Festival Theatre** (tel 01243-781312) is a celebrated venue, with a main season between May and October that is generally booked solid.

Fishbourne Roman Palace

Just west of Chichester is Fishbourne Roman Palace, the largest Roman villa to be excavated to date in Britain. It was discovered in 1960 during ditch digging. The palace was built circa A.D 75, shortly after the Romans' arrival. More than a hundred rooms were set around a garden, and remnants include walls, baths, and a hypocaust heating system. Superb mosaic floors feature intricate geometrical designs; a really remarkable one depicts a winged god riding a cavorting dolphin. ∎

Chichester
▲ 116 D2
Visitor Information
✉ 29A South St.
☎ 01243-775888

Fishbourne Roman Palace
▲ 116 D2
✉ Salthill Rd., Fishbourne
☎ 01243-785859
🕓 Closed Mon.– Fri. mid-Dec.– early Feb.
💲 $$

Seaside Piers

Piers and promenades are integral to the English seaside experience. The fate of Brighton's sister piers sums up the glory and vulnerability of such structures: **West Pier** is a storm-battered wreck, but neighboring **Brighton Pier,** formerly known as Palace Pier, goes from strength to strength with plenty of visitor attractions for all—from side shows and merry-go-rounds to horse racing and stunt driving in the arcades to white-knuckle amusement rides. Meanwhile, Brighton's Promenade is a perfect place for a saunter, complete with cast-iron lamps and ornamental shelters.

The following towns also have great piers (www.piers.org.uk):
• Blackpool, Lancashire—a choice of three
• Southend-on-Sea, Essex—longest pier in the world at 1.341 miles
• Weston-Super-Mare, Somerset— superbly refurbished
• Cromer, Norfolk—open 24/7, traditional end-of-the-pier theater shows

Hampshire

The bucolic atmosphere of Hampshire entices nature lovers to wander the county's forests, fish in its rivers, and stroll along its coast, while Winchester, once an ancient seat of kings and the most important settlement in the area, has an air of mystery to it and an astounding medieval church. The county's delights may seem quiet, but they are not without appeal.

The Round Table in Winchester's Great Hall is, in fact, a resplendent medieval fake.

Winchester

The chief town in England one thousand years ago, capital of the ancient kingdom of Wessex, seat of the Anglo-Saxon kings from Alfred the Great until the Norman Conquest—Winchester is founded upon a deeply rooted rock of history. Twenty kings are buried here. The city is rich in myth, too, swirling around its association with King Arthur and the Knights of the Round Table. This is a place to walk around slowly, savoring the atmosphere.

Cathedral: At 556 feet, Winchester Cathedral (The Close, tel 01962-857200) is the world's longest medieval building, a truly mighty church. It was a long time in construction, started in 1079 and not finished until 1404. Saxon kings who died before the present church was begun are buried around its choir. Among them lies King William II (known as Rufus), son of the Conqueror, killed—probably accidentally—by an arrow while hunting in the New Forest (see p. 131). The choir stalls are beautifully carved with very early 14th-century misericords, the oldest in Britain.

At the east end of the cathedral is the shrine of St. Swithun, Bishop of Winchester from 852 to 862. Swithun, who once taught Alfred the Great, was very popular with medieval pilgrims—particularly those keen to negotiate a change in the weather, since superstition held that if it rained on St. Swithun's Day (July 15), it would continue to rain for 40 days and 40 nights.

The cathedral's 12th-century font is especially beautiful, its black marble carved with scenes from the life of the patron saint of seafarers, St. Nicholas. Three memorials stand out among the many. One in the north aisle is to Jane Austen, who died at 8 College Street, Winchester, in 1817 *(house not open to the public)*; another in the south transept honors Izaak Walton (1593–1683), hardware dealer and author of *The Compleat Angler* (1653), who died at 7 Cathedral Close. His memorial window shows him sitting reading by a river, his rod and creel by his side. "Study to be quiet" runs the legend. The third memorial, at the east end, is a statue of diver William Walker in his clumsy suit and boots. Between 1906 and 1911 he worked in cold, dark water under the cathedral's east wall, ramming over a million bricks and sacks of concrete into place to shore up the medieval masonry, which was threatening to collapse.

Outside the building, the **Pilgrims' Hall** in the cathedral close was built for devotees of St. Swithun; its beautiful hammer-beam roof of 1290 is the oldest in the country.

In the city, the **Great Hall** *(Castle Ave., tel 01962-846476)* of 1235 houses the 18-foot-diameter Round Table, like a giant dartboard in black-and-white segments, with a red-lipped and curly-bearded King Arthur seated at the top. Experts have dated it to the 13th century—but legend says that Merlin created it by magic for Arthur's court, so that every knight's place would have equal honor.

Jane Austen's House

Author Jane Austen (1775–1817) lived with her mother and sister in a simple redbrick house in Chawton, a small Hampshire village, from 1809 until 1817. Here she revised *Sense and Sensibility* (1811) and *Pride and Prejudice* (1813) and wrote *Mansfield Park* (1814), *Emma* (1816), *Persuasion*, and *Northanger Abbey* (the last two published posthumously in 1817). The house is full of mementos: first editions, manuscripts, her comb and portrait, and much more.

Through the Water Meadows: A lovely walk runs through the water meadows by the River Itchen, passing **Winchester College** *(Kingsgate St., tel 01962-621100, call for details of tours)*, Britain's oldest school, founded in 1382; the Norman ruins of **Wolvesey Castle** *(College St., tel 01962-854766, closed Oct.–March)*; and the nearby Stuart residence of the Bishop of

Winchester
116 D2
Visitor Information
Guildhall, Broadway
01962-840500
Closed Sun. Oct.–May

Jane Austen's House
Chawton, Alton
01420-83262
Closed Mon.–Fri. Jan.–Feb.
www.jane-austens-house-museum.org.uk

Portsmouth
 116 D2

Visitor Information

✉ The Hard

☎ 023-9282 6722

Portsmouth Historic Dockyard
✉ Victory Gate, College Rd.

☎ 023-9283 9766

$ Site free, each ship $$–$$$, or combined ticket for all 3 ships $$$$

www.historic dockyard.co.uk

Winchester, to reach the **Hospital of St. Cross** *(St. Cross Rd., tel 01962-851375, closed Sun.)*.

St. Cross was founded in 1132 to provide shelter for 13 paupers and sustenance for 100 more. Travelers can still knock on the hatchway in the Porter's Lodge of the Beaufort Tower here to claim "Wayfarer's Dole"—a horn cup of ale and a cube of bread. At St. Cross and around the city, you may still see the hospital's brethren (senior citizens) in their black-and-purple gowns marked with a silver cross.

Built to celebrate the new millennium, the Spinnaker Tower reflects Portsmouth's maritime heritage in its design.

Hampshire's Rivers & Coast

The soft landscape of Hampshire—water meadows and valley pastures threaded by fast-flowing chalk streams, crooked lanes, and straight-backed downs topped with beechwoods known as "hangers"—is the very heart and spirit of the South Country.

This is a county where fishing is taken seriously. Fly-fishing for trout in shallow rivers, particularly along the Rivers Itchen and Test, is a popular pastime.

The downs north of the Test between Overton and Whitchurch are where Richard Adams set his classic children's novel *Watership Down* (1972).

On Hampshire's south coast lies **Portsmouth,** the Royal Navy's home port during the centuries that Britain ruled the waves—a connection symbolized by the giant waterfront **Spinnaker Tower** *(tel 023-9285 7520)* with its viewing platforms 300 feet above ground. At the **Portsmouth Historic Dockyard** you can visit the *Mary Rose,* Henry VIII's flagship, which capsized in the Solent in 1545 and was raised in 1982, and the H.M.S. *Warrior,* a magnificently restored Victorian warship. Nearby is Lord Horatio Nelson's flagship H.M.S. *Victory,* on which he was killed on October 21, 1805, at the Battle of Trafalgar.

Other must-see sites are the **D-Day Museum** *(Clarence Esplanade, tel 023-9282 7261)* in Southsea, with its 272-foot Overlord Embroidery depicting the Allied landings in Normandy on June 6, 1944, and the **Charles**

Dickens Birthplace Museum *(tel 023-9282 7261, closed Oct.–April)* on Old Commercial Road.

New Forest National Park

East of Dorset's sprawling seaside resort of Bournemouth, just across the border into Hampshire, lies the New Forest, a real forest in the traditional sense of being an interrelated patchwork of woodland, farmland, common land, and small settlements. At nearly 150 square miles, this is one of the largest stretches of open, undeveloped country in England.

In spite of its name, the New Forest is the oldest of the royal hunting forests, planted well before the Norman Conquest. The second Norman king of England, William Rufus, was killed while hunting here on August 2, 1100, transfixed by an arrow fired by his companion, Walter Tyrrell.

Ancient Customs: The many quirky customs and laws of the New Forest have more to do with tradition these days than with the administration of justice. But they were serious enough back in the Middle Ages, when to disturb one of the king's deer carried a penalty of blinding, to shoot at one meant losing both hands, and to kill one condemned the poacher to death. In spite of the harsh consequences of crossing the king, the inhabitants or "commoners" of the forest applied ongoing pressure to be allowed to collect wood and graze their animals. A Verderers Court has

adjudicated on forest law for centuries, and still sits; its green-jacketed "agisters" (agents) patrol on horseback.

Within the mosaic of habitats that thrive across the New Forest are woodland, wetland, ponds and streams, heaths, and farmland. The commoners exercise their historic rights of turbary (peat cutting) and estover (firewood collecting), as well as the autumnal mast when pigs are permitted to forage for acorns and beechnuts.

Isle of Wight

The diamond-shaped Isle of Wight, separated from the mainland by the Solent Channel, is a small but distinct world apart. Chief attractions are **Osborne House** *(tel 01983-200022, closed Nov.–March, except by prebooked tour),* where Queen Victoria and Prince Albert relaxed; **Carisbrooke Castle** *(tel 01983-522107),* where Charles I was held from 1647 to 1648 after the Civil War; and the colored cliffs of **Alum Bay** and the tall chalk blades of **The Needles,** both out west.

Wildlife: The New Forest is a superb wildlife refuge for deer, foxes, birds, amphibians, and butterflies, as well as for the shaggy and appealing New Forest ponies (descended from Spanish horses shipwrecked from the 1588 Armada, some people claim). ■

New Forest National Park Museum & Visitor Centre

- 🅰 116 C2
- ✉ High St., Lyndhurst
- ☎ 023-8028 3914
- 💲 $$

Isle of Wight
- 🅰 116 C1–D1

Visitor Information
- ✉ Isle of Wight Tourism, 81–83 Union St., Ryde
- ☎ 01983-813818
- 🕐 Closed Sat.–Sun.

Wiltshire

Wiltshire's claims to fame are the stone circle of Stonehenge and the grand cathedral of Salisbury. How and why the ancient circle was built remains a mystery, and the site draws curious visitors by the thousands. No mystery surrounds Salisbury Cathedral, however: One of Britain's most stunning Gothic cathedrals, it stands in a market town that dates to medieval days. Interesting country houses and a few other ancient monuments round out Wiltshire's attractions.

The principal niches on Salisbury Cathedral's west facade—the topmost row—hold statues of angels.

Salisbury

Salisbury
116 C2

Visitor Information
✉ Fish Row
☎ 01722-334956

Set in a hollow among the hills, Salisbury is an excellent strolling and exploring town, centered on the pinnacled **Poultry Cross** on Silver Street and known far and wide for its spectacular cathedral. Medieval street names indicate former trades: Butcher Row, Fish Row, Salt Lane. Visit the upstairs display room in **Watsons** china shop on Queen Street to see wonderful 14th-century woodwork. Seek out **St. Thomas's Church** at

the turn of High Street, with its carved angel roofs of 1450 and medieval frescoes. Enjoy the creaky old **Haunch of Venison** pub on Minster Street, where in a barred recess they keep a grisly relic—the severed hand of an 18th-century gambler, and the playing cards it was holding when discovered.

Salisbury Cathedral: There is no mistaking Salisbury Cathedral; its spire, at 404 feet the tallest in Britain, dominates the medieval city. The views from the Eight Door Level at the base of the octagonal spire are lovely.

The cathedral, built in the Early English Gothic style, is a remarkably unified piece of building work. Unlike most of the great cathedrals, which took up to centuries to complete and incorporated many consecutive eras of architectural fashion, Salisbury Cathedral was finished in less than 40 years, in 1258.

Richard Poore, Bishop of Salisbury, founded it down in the water meadows by the River Avon after the Norman cathedral settlement on the heights of Old Sarum (see p. 134) had to be abandoned in 1220. The church was built of chalky limestone quarried nearby at Chilmark, which gives it a silvery sheen in sunlight and a ghostly paleness under cloud.

As for that enormously tall and sturdy-looking spire—it's actually two feet five inches out of true, for the cathedral foundations go down only four feet into the loose gravelly ground.

Ranks of saints adorn the **west facade** of the cathedral, approached across a tranquil close. Inside, the inverted boat shape of the **nave** is bathed in a dim pinkish green light. The dark Purbeck marble pillars look too slender for their job—as, in fact, they are. Standing at the crossing and looking up, you can see how their burden of 6,400 tons of stone roof, tower, and spire has bowed them out of the perpendicular.

In the **north aisle,** under the tattered and faded colors of the Wiltshire Regiment, the cogged wheels and rotor arm of an ancient clock turn with a solemn, heavy ticking. It was built in 1386 and is the oldest working clock mechanism in Britain. Farther along is the 16th-century chantry **chapel of Bishop Edmund Audley,** a delicate stone box with intricate fan vaulting. Victorian medallions in the choir roof show scenes of medieval rural labor—peasants chopping wood, sowing seeds, picking apples. In the **south aisle** is a 13th-century **Tree of Jesse window** (ca 1240).

A stroll through the **vaulted cloisters** (added 1263–1266) brings you to the octagonal 13th-century **chapter house**. A big umbrella of vaulting ribs springs from a slender central pillar. Around the walls are lively carvings of the Genesis and Exodus stories.

Salisbury Cathedral
- ✉ The Close
- ☎ 01722-555120
- 💲 $$

Open Days on Salisbury Plain

The vast open area of Salisbury Plain has been a military training ground since Victorian times, with limited public access and a continuous program of training and live firing. About 50 days a year, however, the Ministry of Defence (recorded visitor information tel 01980-674763) opens routes that are normally closed, disclosing a remarkable landscape of historic monuments, unspoiled chalk grassland, and wonderfully rich wildlife. The most popular of these hidden attractions is the village of **Imber,** evacuated in 1943 and never repopulated. Its empty manor house and pub, and its beautifully restored Church of St. Giles, make a poignant sight in their isolation on the great plain.

Mompesson House

⊠ The Close, Salisbury

☎ 01722-420980

🕐 Closed Thurs.–Fri. mid-March–Oct. & all Nov.–mid-March

💲 $$

www.nationaltrust.org.uk/

Rifles (Berkshire and Wiltshire) Museum

⊠ 58 The Close, Salisbury

☎ 01722-419419

🕐 Closed early Dec.–early Feb., Sun.–Mon. Feb. & Nov., & Sun. March & Oct.

💲 $

www.thewardrobe.org.uk

Old Sarum

🅰 116 C2

☎ 01722-335398

💲 $

Wilton House

🅰 116 C2

⊠ Wilton

☎ 01722-746714

🕐 Closed Fri.–Sat. & Sept.–Easter

💲 $$$$

www.wiltonhouse.com

Here is kept one of only a handful of original copies of the Magna Carta, the bill of rights reluctantly signed in 1215 by King John.

In the Close: The cathedral close is crammed with beautiful old buildings, including the little redbrick Matron's College, built in 1682 for the widows of clergy, and **Mompesson House** of 1701, with its carved staircase, glass collection, and garden laid out with perennial borders, all arranged to give the flavor of 18th-century life in the close. The patched and crooked brick and flint of the 13th-century Wardrobe houses the **Rifles (Berkshire and Wiltshire) Museum.** The Queen Anne facade on the 13th-century **Malmesbury House** and the **Bishop's Palace,** built at the same time as the cathedral, now housing the Cathedral School, are there, too.

Around Salisbury

The city of Salisbury lies in a hollow, with the Wiltshire countryside undulating in all directions. Tucked into this rolling, chalky landscape are fine country houses, charming small villages, and dozens of prehistoric monuments.

Old Sarum: Two miles north of Salisbury rises the flat-topped hill of Old Sarum, its sides corrugated with earthen ramparts. The hilltop is a wonderful spot to look down on Salisbury and its cathedral, established near the river when the former

hilltop settlement was abandoned around 1220.

Old Sarum, high above the surrounding country, was always a valuable lookout point. Iron Age tribesmen first fortified Old Sarum; then the Romans strengthened the ramparts of Sorviodunum and ran their Portway road to it from the settlement at Silchester, 40 miles to the northeast.

INSIDER TIP:

Take a tour out of Bath that encompasses both Stonehenge and the Cotswolds—it's a great way to link inaccessible sites if you don't have your own car.

—AMY KOLCZAK
National Geographic International Editions

The Saxons were here, too, calling it Searoburgh, or "dry town," for there was very little water at hand. A cramped, unsanitary township grew up around the cathedral that the Normans completed in 1092, but lack of water and space to expand drove the inhabitants down to the valley two centuries later, to start again.

Wilton House: Just west of Salisbury, Wilton House is a 17th-century Palladian mansion, adapted by Inigo Jones from a Tudor house that was itself a conversion of a convent dissolved at the Reformation. Pride of the house are the Single Cube

Room (30 feet in length, width, and height) and the Double Cube Room (same width and height, but 60 feet long) with their painted and gilded plaster-work ceilings, and fine furniture by Chippendale and William Kent (1685–1748).

Lacock: In the northwest of Wiltshire, Lacock is a perfectly preserved National Trust village of gray stone houses, where time has stopped in the 18th century. At **Lacock Abbey** you can see the oriel window from which William Henry Fox Talbot took the world's first photograph in 1835. Adjacent to the abbey a Tudor barn houses the **Fox Talbot Museum.**

Stonehenge

There are problems with Stonehenge—not just the age-old problems of interpreting Europe's best known ancient

site but also modern problems of security and overwhelming visitor numbers. Visitors must keep outside a fence that draws a wide circle around the monument (call for details on the limited out-of-hours access to the stones). There's an inadequate interpretive center, soon to be replaced, and the whole site is cut across by two fast, noisy roads. All these difficulties will be addressed, but, at present, the ambience is not ideal.

None of this, however, should dissuade you from making a pilgrimage to this astonishing structure, whose impact must strike anyone with an ounce of imagination. The doorway-like silhouettes of Stonehenge's great trilithons, outlined against the sky, are as challenging to the intellect as they have ever been, still provoking questions of when, how, and why.

(continued on p. 138)

**Lacock Abbey
& Fox Talbot
Museum**

 116 B3

✉ Lacock

☎ Abbey:
01249-730227.
Museum:
01249-730459

⏱ See website for hours

💲 $$$

www.nationaltrust
.org.uk/

Stonehenge

 116 C3

✉ 10 miles N of
Salisbury, 2 miles
W of Amesbury

☎ 0870-333 1181

💲 $$

www.english-
heritage.org.uk/

Mighty, enigmatic Stonehenge dates from the Bronze Age, erected for purposes still unknown.

Hardy's Dorset

In Dorset the figure of Thomas Hardy (1840–1928) casts a long shadow. What Sir Walter Scott is to the Scottish Lowlands, or William Wordsworth to the Lake District, Hardy is to Dorset. The area of southwest England that he immortalized in his "Wessex novels" covers parts of Hampshire, Berkshire, Oxfordshire, Wiltshire, Somerset, Devon, and Cornwall; but the heart of the region, called by Hardy "South Wessex," is his native county of Dorset.

The pretty cottage at Higher Bockhampton that was the birthplace of Thomas Hardy

Immortalized in Print

Many places in Dorset are central to Hardy's life and writing. He was born on June 2, 1840, in a thatched cottage—now called **Hardy's Cottage** *(tel 01305-262366, www .nationaltrust.org.uk, see website for hours)*—at Higher Bockhampton, a hamlet near the county town of Dorchester. While living at his birthplace, Hardy wrote *Under the Greenwood Tree* (1872) and *Far from the Madding Crowd* (1874). The house features as Tranter Dewy's house in *Under the Greenwood Tree*, in which Higher and Lower Bockhampton and neighboring Stinsford are amalgamated to form "Mellstock."

In Stinsford churchyard, Hardy's heart is buried in the grave of his first wife, Emma

Gifford (d. 1912), whom he mourned all the more bitterly for having drifted into a cold relationship with her in life. There is a stained-glass window memorial to Hardy in the church, of which he wrote:

> *On afternoons of drowsy calm*
> *We stood in the panelled pew*
> *Singing one-voiced a Tate-and-Brady psalm*
> *To the tune of "Cambridge New."*
> *We watched the elms, we watched the rooks,*
> *The clouds upon the breeze,*
> *Between the whiles of glancing at our books,*
> *And swaying like the trees.*

The heathland south of here, much of it nowadays planted with conifers, is Hardy's somber "Egdon Heath," the ruling feature of *The Return of the Native* (1878).

Three miles east along the A35 is Puddletown, where Hardy's grandfather would play his bass viol in the church orchestra and at village dances. Puddletown was "Weatherbury" in *Far from the Madding Crowd.* Bathsheba Everdene's farmhouse, "Weatherbury Farm," where Gabriel Oak had to endure the sight of Bathsheba married to Sergeant Troy, was probably modeled on handsome Tudor Waterstone Manor, on the B3142 west of Puddletown.

Bere Regis, 6 miles east of Puddletown, was "Kingsbere-sub-Greenhill" in *Tess of the D'Urbervilles* (1891). In its Saxon church you can see the Turberville tombs and their lion-rampant crest in a 15th-century window.

South of here the River Frome runs east through a lush valley, Tess's "Valley of the Great Dairies." Woolbridge Manor, in the village of Wool on the A352, was transformed by Hardy into "Wellbridge Manor house," where Tess and Angel Clare had their strange, lonely wedding night.

Cranborne Chase—"The Chase," where caddish Alec D'Urberville had his way with Tess—lies off the A354 about 15 miles northeast of Puddletown.

Other Attractions

A Dorset site not to miss is **Max Gate** *(Arlington Ave., tel 01297-489481, www .nationaltrust.org.uk, see website for hours)* in **Dorchester** *(visitor information, Antelope Walk, tel 01305-267992)*—Hardy's home from 1885 until his death, where he wrote all his great and late poetry.

Dorset has some wonderful walks among its chalk downs and wooded valleys, and some dramatic coastal scenery—particularly east of the Georgian resort of **Weymouth** *(visitor information, Kings Statue, The Esplanade, tel 01305-785747)*, where Lulworth Cove and the cliff-flanked promontory of St. Aldhelm's Head can be enjoyed from the Dorset Coast Path.

Other coast sites include **Lyme Regis** *(visitor information, Church St., tel 01297-442138)* with its fossil beach, ancient massive Cobb breakwater, and Undercliff wilderness (John Fowles's *French Lieutenant's Woman* was set here); the medieval **Swannery** *(New Barn Rd., tel 01305-871858, closed late Oct.–mid-March)* and the **Sub Tropical Gardens** *(Bullers Way, tel 01305-871387)* at **Abbotsbury**; and oddball **Swanage** *(visitor information, Shore Rd., tel 01929-422885)*, crammed with architectural rarities salvaged by local stonemason George Burt from the Victorian rebuilding of London.

EXPERIENCE: Stay on a Working Farm

The English countryside is full of farms, and in recent years—in part due to EU regulations and cheap foreign imports—times have been hard for them. Ever since people began to take their holidays in the countryside, certain farms have offered inexpensive accommodations; now a great many more are in the bed-and-breakfast business. For sheer earthiness and strong local flavor, little beats staying on a working farm, eating bacon and eggs produced right there, and learning directly from the farmer about the farm and about farming in general—and sometimes taking part, too.

A word to the wise, though. Plenty of accommodations advertised as "farm" or "farmhouse" don't actually have any farming activity associated with them. So if your rural dream is to fall asleep to the sound of lambs on the hillside, and wake to the sound of moos and baas outside the window, make sure it's a working farm before you book. Dorset is home to many such farms, which you can find out about at *www.ruraldorset.co.uk* or at *www.farmstay .co.uk/dorset-bed-and-breakfast.dot*. For information on farm stays in other parts of Great Britain, visit *www.farmstay.co.uk*.

Wiltshire's Ancient Monuments

Two ancient, long-distance tracks cross Wiltshire. The well-marked **Ridgeway** starts on Overton Hill a mile east of Avebury and goes 85 miles northeast to the Icknield Way (see p. 106) on Ivinghoe Beacon. The **Harroway**—possibly more than 6,000 years old—passes Stonehenge.

A notable group of monuments lies around **Avebury** *(tel 01672-539250),* north of Salisbury Plain. From the early Bronze Age stone circle, made up of around a hundred sarsen stones, a ceremonial avenue of standing stones leads to Overton Hill.

Just south of Avebury are **West Kennet Long Barrow,** England's largest chambered communal tomb, built circa 3250 B.C., and the puzzling flat-topped **Silbury Hill,** 130 feet high and 200 yards around the base, built circa 2600 B.C. As much as can be explained is superbly done so in Avebury's **Alexander Keiller Museum** *(tel 01672-529203, www.english-heritage.org.uk).*

Avebury

116 C3

Visitor Information

✉ Avebury Chapel Centre, Green St.

☎ 01672-539179

The "when" of Stonehenge has been reasonably accurately pinned down. About 2950 B.C. a circular bank was constructed, and around 400 years later a double circle of 80 bluestones—dolerite stones from the Preseli Hills in southwest Wales, some of them up to 10 feet high—was erected inside the bank. Later the bluestones were rearranged, and sarsen ("saracen" or alien) stones from the Marlborough Downs were put up instead, much as they stand today, in the form of trilithons—pairs of upright stones 14 feet high, joined together by a third laid on top like the lintel of a doorway and held in place with a mortise-and-tenon joint. An outer ring of 25 of these was set up, enclosing an inner horseshoe shape of five more trilithons. Later on, some of the dismantled bluestones were erected again between the outer and inner trilithons, and the largest bluestone—these days known as the Altar Stone—was placed at the center of the horseshoe. After about 1600 B.C., no further alterations were made.

As for how Bronze Age men managed to transport, shape, and erect such enormous stones—in particular the bluestones, which traveled 200 miles—tremendous organization and disposition of manpower would have been needed. But if the imperative was strong enough, Bronze Age leaders did wield enough authority, and the necessary technology of rafts, rollers, and levers was advanced enough to carry out what must have been decades' worth of planning and effort.

Which begs the question—why? Once all the New Age theories have been set aside, all that is known for sure is that on Midsummer's Day (June 21), the sun, when viewed from the Altar Stone in the center of the structure, is seen to rise directly over the Heel Stone, 256 feet away at the far end of what now remains of an earthwork avenue. Stonehenge may have been some kind of observatory for seasonal timekeeping; but whether that was its only function, no one can say. ■

An intriguing mix of lush cider orchards, cattle pastures, thatched cottages, and quintessential English seascapes

The West Country

Whitewashed seaside cottage, Clovelly, Devon

The West Country

The long peninsula that forms the southwestern corner of Britain is a land of dairy pastures, moors, woodlands, and gentle hills. The coasts of these West Country counties of Somerset, Devon, and Cornwall grow sharper teeth the farther south and west you venture. Down in the western toe tip of Cornwall there are craggy headlands and storm-carved cliffs to rival anything elsewhere in England.

This area is a vacation playground, fringed with fine, clean, sandy beaches and one lovely view after another, from the chocolate-box prettiness of thatched Devon villages to the huddles of weatherbeaten fishermen's cottages that spill down the sides of Cornish coves.

Rounding the southernmost tip of England, now comes the far bleaker north coast of Cornwall, a 100-mile stretch of granite cliffs and sand-floored, rocky coves relieved by appealing little towns such as St. Ives, Padstow, and Tintagel. Inland is a sparsely populated environment of windswept uplands dotted with ancient

Devon to Cornwall

As you enter from Thomas Hardy's Wessex, the red earth and green hills of southeast Devon surround the county's capital city of Exeter, with its great medieval cathedral. West along the coast are the small, steeply sloped fields and woods of the South Hams, and then the city of Plymouth, from which the Pilgrims set out for the New World in 1620.

Next you cross the River Tamar, the boundary of the civilized world for all right-thinking Cornishmen. The south coast of Cornwall, all high headlands and sandy bays, leads west to the wild and little-frequented Lizard Peninsula, and finally to the rock stacks of Land's End.

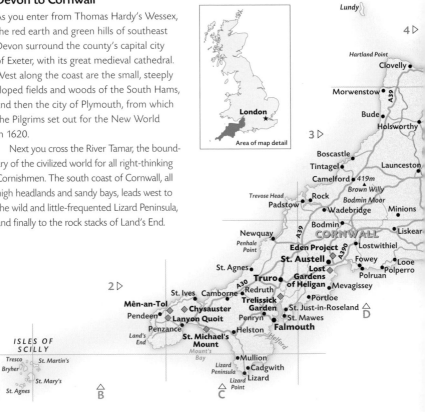

stone monuments and with the shafts and pumping houses of the county's now defunct tin-mining industry.

Somerset & Avon

Three great moors (open expanses of rolling infertile land) lie at the heart of the southwest peninsula—Bodmin, Dartmoor, and Exmoor. From Exmoor you enter Somerset, the county of cider drinkers and dairy farmers, moving north to the West Country's great maritime city of Bristol, and finally to the onetime Roman spa town of Bath with its graceful Georgian buildings of cream-colored stone. ■

Devon

Sandwiched between two bodies of water—Lyme Bay and Bristol Channel—County Devon offers seaside escapes and upland adventures in wild moors. Notable towns include Exeter, known for its Norman-style cathedral begun in the 1100s, and Plymouth, a port that often played a pivotal role in Britain's history.

In Exeter, heavily bombed in World War II, troops honor the 70th anniversary of the Battle of Britain.

Exeter

🗺 141 F3

Visitor Information

✉ Civic Centre, Paris St.

☎ 01392-265700

🕐 Closed Sun. in winter

Exeter Cathedral

✉ The Close

☎ 01392-285983

💲 Donation

Exeter & Around

Although best known for its cathedral, the city of Exeter has some nice surprises tucked away. Exeter Cathedral, one of Britain's great church buildings, dominates the close at the heart of the city.

Exeter Cathedral: The massive bulk of the cathedral is crowned by two stubby, square Norman towers on the transepts—instead of a central tower—while flying buttresses spring out and down to the ground like slender legs. The cathedral was begun by the Normans between 1112 and 1206, but most of it was built from around 1270 until the mid-14th century. Of this era are the seated statues, ranked in their hundreds in three tiers, that decorate the pale stone west front: monarchs and prelates, saints and sages, with Christ and his Apostles taking pride of place in the center.

Inside, the eye is drawn immediately up the length of the Purbeck marble pillars to possibly the world's longest continuous stretch of Gothic vaulting, a run of over 300 feet that covers both nave and choir. Carved bosses, picked out in gold and bright colors, stud the vaulting.

A big 15th-century astronomical clock in the north transept traces the cycles of the sun and moon. A great screen, from 1325, guards the choir with its battered but still vigorous early medieval misericords and its great Bishop's Throne, almost 60 feet high and carved of oak in 1312. Near the entrance to the Lady Chapel is a beautiful fresco of the Coronation of the Virgin Mary, painted in early Tudor times, about 40 years before the Reformation.

City Sights: The Benedictine **St. Nicholas Priory** in the Mint has a Norman undercroft and kitchens, a Great Hall from about 1400 with a fine timber roof, and some striking plasterwork ceilings.

Medieval wool paid for the handsome sandstone **Tuckers Hall** (Fore St., tel 01392-412348, call for hours) in the 15th century for the newly founded Guild of Weavers, Fullers, and Shearmen.

An even older **Guildhall** (High St., tel 01392-665500, call for hours) stands on the pedestrianized High Street: This magnificent building has a Tudor upper story propped on granite pillars; but the oldest part dates from 1330, and the chamber where the council meets is at least 600 years old. For a look back into Exeter's distant history, sections of a third-century Roman city wall are found on the west side of Southernhay, in Northernhay, and in Rougemont Gardens.

Down on the Quay is a collection of warehouses and industrial buildings dating from the 17th and 19th centuries, now used to house antiques centers, craft shops, offices, and excellent pubs and restaurants.

Out of Town: Seventeen miles along the A30 is **Honiton,** famous for producing delicate lace. On the Georgian High Street is the **Allhallows Museum** (tel 01404-44966, closed Sun. & late Oct.–March), where lacemaking is occasionally demonstrated, and the **Honiton Lace Shop** (44 High St., tel 01404-42416), where you can buy lace made locally.

Another enjoyable venue worth visiting close to Exeter is the highly eccentric, 16-sided house called **A La Ronde.** It was built in 1796 by cousins Jane and Mary Parminter and contains rooms decorated with seashells, feathers, and seaweed.

South, on the coast, the small Regency resort of **Sidmouth** hosts a celebrated International Festival of Folk Arts in early August.

St. Nicholas Priory

- ✉ The Mint, off Fore St., Exeter
- ☎ 01392-665858
- 🕐 Closed Sun. Nov.–Feb. & Sun.–Fri. during school terms

A La Ronde

- 🗺 141 F3
- ✉ Summer Ln., Exmouth
- ☎ 01395-265514
- 🕐 See website for hours

www.nationaltrust.org.uk

Sidmouth

- 🗺 141 F3
- **Visitor Information**
- ✉ Ham Ln.
- ☎ 01395-516441
- 🕐 Closed Sun. Nov.–Feb.

Exeter's Close

In the cathedral close is a number of fine buildings. The most striking of these is the late Tudor Mol's Coffee House, dated 1596 on its lion-and-dragon coat of arms of Elizabeth I. Mol's is a handsome timber-framed house with curly gables and a railed gallery high on the third story. A great bay window checkered with panes fills the whole width of the first floor.

EXPERIENCE: Water Sports in the West Country

Vigorous Atlantic tides, rugged scenery, and a laid-back party lifestyle make the West Country coast a mecca for water sports enthusiasts.

Sailors haunt the more sheltered southern or English Channel coast of Devon (especially Poole Harbour, and farther west in the Salcombe Estuary); the wilder and more exposed north Devon coast pulls in extreme performers who like rough stuff with their seaside fun.

Experienced surfers will love Croyde Bay (the surfer's surf beach), or Woolacombe just to the north; beginners should head to Saunton Sands, south of Croyde. The beach and surrounding coast at Westward Ho! are excellent for sea kayaking, kite surfing—for lessons, consider **North Devon Kitesurfing** (tel 01271-815032, www.northdevonkitesurfing.co.uk)—wake boarding, and kite buggying.

Swimmers flock to plenty of safe but exciting beaches, including Tunnels Beach, Ilfracombe; Woolacombe Sands; Putsborough, just south of Woolacombe Sands; and the sand and pebbles at Combe Martin and Woody Bay, along the Bristol Channel.

Porlock

◪ 141 F4

Visitor Information

✉ West End, High St.

☎ 01643-863150

Lynton

◪ 141 E4

Visitor Information

✉ Town Hall, Lee Rd.

☎ 01598-752225

Barnstaple

◪ 141 E4

Visitor Information

✉ Museum of North Devon, The Square

☎ 01271-375000

Bideford

◪ 141 E4

Visitor Information

✉ The Quay

☎ 01237-477676

North Devon Coast

The cliffs of the north Devon coast are beautifully rounded, presenting to the ever widening Bristol Channel. At their feet are pebbly beaches, which become sandier and better for swimming the farther west you go.

Dunster and **Porlock** are, in fact, in Somerset, but these two highly attractive villages, each set a little way inland, belong in character and spirit to this region. Dunster has a Norman castle, home of the Luttrell family from 1376 until the late 1990s, and its octagonal **Yarn Market** of 1609, where local cloth was once sold, is the centerpiece of its sloping main street. Porlock's thatched houses huddle under steep hills.

Beyond here, notoriously steep roads switchback westward to **Lynton,** perched on a plateau 500 feet above its sister village of **Lynmouth.** A rattly but safe cliff railway, installed in 1890 and worked by the weight of water, connects the two. Lynton contains the eccentric, cramped **Lyn and Exmoor Museum** (Market St., tel 01598-752225, closed Sat.) and the **Exmoor National Park Visitor Centre** (Esplanade, tel 01598-752509, closed Nov.–March), where an exhibit tells the story of an epic overland lifeboat launch. A beautiful, well-marked cliff walk runs west from Lynton for a couple of miles through the Valley of Rocks.

West of Lynton: Farther west on a sandy beach lies the Victorian seaside resort of **Ilfracombe** (visitor information, The Promenade, tel 01271-863001). Then the coast turns a sharp corner and runs south, by way of superb sands at **Woolacombe** and a famous surfing bay at **Croyde,** to pass the sand dune nature reserve of **Braunton Burrows** before reaching the great twin estuary of the Rivers Taw and Torridge.

Here stand the neighboring towns of **Barnstaple** and **Bideford,** with their ancient bridges and narrow byways. Beyond lies **Clovelly,** picturesquely packed around a precipitous cobbled street descending the cliffs; cars are not allowed.

Plymouth & Around

Much of Britain's long and distinguished seafaring story is wrapped up in the historic seaport of Plymouth. Among other ventures, Capt. James Cook set sail from here in 1772 for his three-year voyage of discovery of the South Seas.

On July 31, 1588, sea captains Drake, Frobisher, and Hawkins sailed from here to challenge the ships of the Spanish Armada. Along **Plymouth Hoe,** a broad park with a raised promenade for strolling, is Sir Francis Drake's statue; the green where, although the Spanish galleons had already been sighted, he insisted on finishing his game of bowls; and the leonine Armada monument.

The harbor is guarded by the grand **Royal Citadel** *(Plymouth Tourist Information Centre, tel 01752-306330)*, built between 1666 and 1670 on the orders of Charles II. In the eastern part of the harbor is the excellent **National Marine Aquarium** *(Rope Walk, Coxside, tel 01752-600301, open daily)*.

Opposite the aquarium you'll find the **Mayflower Steps,** a simple arch monument honoring the Pilgrims. After abandoning the *Speedwell* due to storm damage, the Puritan adventurers successfully set sail for the New World from Sutton Pool, Plymouth, on September 6—102 souls all packed into one ship, the tiny *Mayflower.*

Nearby Attractions: These include the hands-on industrial museum at **Morwellham Quay** *(tel 01822-832766)*, north off the A390; **Buckland Abbey,** just north of Plymouth, Drake's home from 1581 to 1596; the cobbled quays and tight streets of **Dartmouth** *(visitor information, Mayors Ave., tel 01803-834224)* east of the city via the A3, the A385, and Totnes; and the preposterous but delightful art deco **Burgh Island Hotel** *(tel 01548-810514)* enjoyed by Noël Coward, Agatha Christie, and the Duke of Windsor—on tidal Burgh Island, off Bigbury-on-Sea near Kingsbridge. ∎

Plymouth
- ▲ 141 E2

Visitor Information
- ✉ 3–5 The Barbican
- ☎ 01752-306330

Buckland Abbey
- ▲ 141 E2
- ✉ 0.25 mile S of Yelverton
- ☎ 01822-853607
- ⏱ Closed Thurs. April–Oct. & Mon.–Fri. Nov.–March
- 💲 Abbey & grounds $$, grounds only $

Smeaton's Tower is the third Eddystone lighthouse to have been built. It was reassembled on Plymouth Hoe in the 1880s.

Cornwall

Geographically isolated from the rest of the country at the wildest end of the westernmost peninsula, the self-contained Celts of Cornwall nurtured their own language until 200 years ago, their working tradition of mineral mining until 1998, and their livelihood through sea fishing up through the present day.

St. Ives has been a popular holiday destination for Britons since the late 19th century.

Trelissick Garden
- 🅰 140 C2
- ✉ Feock
- ☎ 01872-862090
- 💲 $$

St. Michael's Mount
- 🅰 140 C2
- ✉ Marazion
- ☎ 01736-710507
- 🕐 Closed Sat. & Nov.–late March (open some days in winter for tours; see website for details)
- 💲 $$

www.stmichaels mount.co.uk

Visitors return year after year to enjoy Cornwall's clean seas and beaches, cave-burrowed cliffs, spectacularly sited fishing villages, and narrow flowery lanes.

Fishing Villages

Thirty miles west of Plymouth lies **Polperro,** a classic Cornish fishing village of steep narrow streets; from the harbor, footpaths lead west over 400-foot cliffs to superb, lonely beaches. Narrow roads shadow the paths to **Fowey** (*visitor information, 5 South St., tel 01726-833616*), a charming little gray-stone town set on a winding estuary; take the foot-ferry across to Bodinnick

and wander along the cliffs, returning by ferry from Polruan.

To the west is St. Austell, surrounded by the "Cornish Alps," white mountains of china-clay waste. From the B3272 St. Austell–Mevagissey road, signs direct you to the **Lost Gardens of Heligan** (*Pentewan, tel 01726-845100*). Since 1991 the gardens developed by the Tremayne family over 300 years, then overgrown and forgotten, have been wonderfully restored. Equally striking and ambitious is the nearby **Eden Project** (*Bodelva, signed from main roads, tel 01726-811911*), where exotic climates and vegetation are reproduced inside enormous "biomes" in an old slate quarry.

Down to Land's End

South of **Truro** (visitor information, Boscawen St., tel 01872-274555), capital of Cornwall, the A3078 approaches **St. Just-in-Roseland,** where the little Norman church looks across the wooded Fal Estuary. Cross by the King Harry Ferry to Feock to visit **Trelissick Garden,** where flowers crowd tree-shaded paths by the river. Pendennis and St. Mawes Castles, on either side of the estuary, were built by Henry VIII against the threat of French invasion.

Now comes the **Lizard Peninsula.** At **Helston** (visitor information, 79 Meneage St., tel 01326-565431, closed Sun.), in early May, the famous Furry Dance winds in and out of the houses. Visit **Lizard Village** on the peninsula's tip to buy polished green, red, and white serpentine rock, and walk out to **Kynance Cove** to see the colored rock in the cliffs.

St. Michael's Mount, a rocky isle in the sea crowned by a Norman abbey, a fort, and a grand house, is reached from Marazion by causeway across the sands at low tide, and by boat (summer only) at high water.

Out at **Land's End,** follow the scenic coastal footpath to enjoy the stirring views.

North Coast

Cornwall's north coast is rugged and exposed. On the moors at this western end are ancient relics to make you gasp: **Chysauster Ancient Village;** the Bronze Age burial chamber of **Lanyon Quoit;** and the holed stone of **Mên-an-Tol** near Morvah.

Busy **St. Ives** (visitor information, Guildhall, Street-an-Pol, tel 01736-796297) has superb galleries and museums: Sculptor Dame Barbara Hepworth (1903–1975) lived on Barnoon Hill; her home forms the **Barbara Hepworth Museum and Sculpture Garden.** Bernard Leach's (1887–1979) pottery (closed Sun.) is on the western edge of town in Higher Stennack; and a branch of the **Tate Gallery** (tel 01736-796226, closed Mon. Nov.– March) is on Porthmeor Beach.

Padstow is famous for its 'Obby 'Oss festival (see sidebar this page). Commercialized **Tintagel** (visitor information, Bossiney Rd., tel 01840-250010), higher up the coast, claims its romantic castle is King Arthur's birthplace. **Boscastle,** 5 miles north, is a lovely village in a narrow cleft of the cliffs. ∎

Chysauster Ancient Village

 140 C2

✉ 2.5 miles NW of Gulval, off B3311

☎ 01831-757934

🕐 Closed Nov.– March

💲 $

Barbara Hepworth Museum and Sculpture Garden

✉ Barnoon Hill, St. Ives

☎ 01736-796226

🕐 Closed Mon. Sept.–May

💲 $$

Padstow

 140 D3

Visitor Information

✉ North Quay

☎ 01841-533449

EXPERIENCE: Revel with the 'Obby 'Osses

It's rare to see local traditions celebrated so loudly and vigorously as they are at Padstow's **'Obby 'Oss festival** (www.blueribbon oss.org.uk). Pack into the town's narrow streets early on May Day (May 1) to see the 'Osses and accompanying dancers and musicians come whirling by. The 'Osses are dancers caped and dressed in the form of demonic-looking creatures, more like beasts from a nightmare than "hobby horses," symbolizing the death of sterile winter and the coming of spring and fertility. Everyone sings the chorus of the May Day song:

Unite and unite and let us all unite,
For summer is acome unto day,
And whither we are going we will all unite
In the merry morning of May.

West Country Moorland

At the heart of the West Country lie three extensive tracts of moorland. Cornwall's Bodmin Moor is known to few. Devon possesses warm sandstone Exmoor in the north, while in the south of the county broods grim, granite-bedded Dartmoor, famous for fogs and wild legends.

Dartmoor features many newtakes—enclosed areas of moorland, usually bounded by drystone walls.

Bodmin Moor

Of the three great West Country moors, Bodmin (map 140 D3, Bodmin tourist information, Shire House, Mount Folly Sq., tel 01208-76616), some 15 miles in diameter, is certainly the least well known, although it is sliced in two by the busy A30, traveled every year by millions of vacationers.

Closely associated with the moor is Dame Daphne du Maurier's smuggling romance, Jamaica Inn, published in 1936. Du Maurier (1907–1989) was inspired by yarns spun to her when she stayed on Bodmin Moor in 1930 at the pub called Jamaica Inn—no longer lonely and evocative in its location above the roaring A30 but still worth a stop for its grim, slate-hung aspect and atmospheric interior. From here, it's a short walk south to the allegedly bottomless Dozmary Pool, into which Sir Bedevere flung Excalibur after taking the sword from the mortally wounded King Arthur. Five miles east of Dozmary Pool stand the Hurlers, three stone circles dating from 2200–1400 B.C., which, stories say, are impious locals turned to stone for playing hurling games on the Sabbath. Nearby is the Cheesewring, a granite tor 30 feet high made of slabs of rock undercut by wind and rain. A couple of miles south is Trethevy Quoit, an ancient burial chamber with a giant capstone poised on massive stones.

Signposted off the A39 along the northern edge of Bodmin Moor, just north of Camelford, is the highest point of the moor and Cornwall, the 1,377-foot hummock of Brown Willy. A mile-long footpath connects the peak with neighboring Rough Tor (1,311 feet).

Dartmoor

Dartmoor National Park *(map 141 E3, High Moorland Visitor Centre, Princetown, Yelverton, tel 01822-890414),* covering more than 300 square miles of granite tors, heathery cleaves (valleys), and lonely bogs, lies in a great ragged oval to the northeast of Plymouth.

From Postbridge on the B3212, you can walk north along the River East Dart to find the stone circles called the Grey Wethers.

Farther east, at Manaton, there are beautiful walks along the wooded cleft of the River Bovey, while on the western fringe of the moor a dramatic footpath winds deep down in the bottom of Lydford Gorge.

Exmoor

Devon's light and airy **Exmoor National Park** *(map 141 E4, 7–9 Fore St., Dulverton, Somerset, tel 01398-323841, www.exmoor-na tionalpark.gov.uk),* has none of Dartmoor's oppressive grimness. The warmth of the underlying sandstone seems to pervade the moor, and the combes (wooded valleys) cut

INSIDER TIP:

When covered with thick, swirling mist, the moors fulfill your every expectation, but drive slowly—wildlife can suddenly appear out of the gloom.

—MEREDITH WILCOX
*Administrative Director, Illustrations,
National Geographic Books*

deep grooves in the upland flanks. England's largest herd of wild red deer (see sidebar this page) roams freely here. The B3223 and B3224 cut across Exmoor, and from these there are a number of well-marked walks.

Other celebrated Exmoor locations are scattered around the edges of the moor: **Arlington Court** *(7 miles NE of Barnstaple, tel 01271-850296, www.nationaltrust.org.uk, see website for hours)* in the west, with walks through lovely wooded grounds; Dunkery Hill in the north, Exmoor's highest point at 1,703 feet; and the medieval clapper bridge of Tarr Steps, northwest of Dulverton.

R. D. Blackmore's (1825–1900) romantic novel *Lorna Doone* (1869) is set between Watersmeet and Dunkery. Here is Doone Valley itself (Lank Combe off Badgworthy Water) and St. Mary's Church at Oare, where the jealous Carver Doone shot Lorna at her wedding.

Red Deer of Exmoor

The three moors of the West Country have a number of wild creatures in common—notably buzzards, otters, and semiwild Exmoor ponies—but one animal that is peculiar to Exmoor is the red deer. This animal is Great Britain's largest and most striking native animal, especially during the rutting or mating season in October/November, when the stags, as big as racehorses and crowned with magnificent, many-branched antlers, come down into the lower woods and fields to gather and defend a harem of females. Exmoor boasts a free-ranging herd of perhaps 5,000 red deer, but their russet coats are surprisingly hard to spot against the red and brown bracken and heather.

Exmoor National Park *(see visitor information this page)* offers red deer spotting expeditions ($–$$) led by an experienced ranger. These treks across the moor with a knowledgeable guide are a great way to improve your chances of getting close these striking creatures.

Somerset & Around

Somerset County is home to moorlands, dairy farms, and the small city of Wells, which is dominated by a spectacular Gothic cathedral. Bordering the county to the north are the inland seaport of Bristol and the famous spa of Bath; although near to each other, the two towns couldn't be more different, but each offers myriad delights.

Legends of King Arthur and other heroes cluster around the strange hummock of Glastonbury Tor.

Glastonbury

  141 G4

Visitor Information

✉ The Tribunal,
9 High St.

☎ 01458-832954/
832949

Somerset Rural Life Museum

✉ Chilkwell St.,
Glastonbury

☎ 01458-831197

🕐 Closed Mon.,
& Sun. Nov.–
Easter

Glastonbury & the Somerset Levels

The Somerset Levels—500 square miles of flatland between the Quantock and Mendip Hills—were marshy sea washes until medieval monks built flood defenses and reclaimed them. Straight, narrow roads are lined with pollarded willows, fields are bounded by watercourses called rhynes (pronounced REENS), and little knolls protrude from the peat tableland.

Glastonbury Tor, just outside Glastonbury, is the best known

Levels knoll. Legend, myth, and history cluster thickly around this sleeping-dragon shape, topped by its 14th-century church tower. Some say that King Arthur and his knights lie sleeping under the tor; others assert that the "once and future king" and his tragic, star-crossed queen Guinevere are buried in the sparse but beautiful ruins of **Glastonbury Abbey** *(Magdalene St., tel 01458-832267).*

Saxon monarchs were buried here, two Edmunds and an Edgar, for Glastonbury is the earliest Christian foundation in England.

There is a lovely late Norman Lady Chapel on the site of a wattle-and-daub church (burned down in 1184), said to have been built by Joseph of Arimathea.

Nearby is the 14th-century **Abbot's Kitchen** with its octagonal roof, and the **Somerset Rural Life Museum** is housed in the 14th-century Abbey Barn.

Wells

Wells is England's smallest city, though with more an air of a small market town. It lies at the foot of the Mendip Hills, its medieval streets dominated by its great Gothic cathedral. The limestone hills offer several attractions west of the city—the **caves at Wookey Hole and Cheddar,** and the West Mendip Way footpath along the spine of the hills.

Wells Cathedral: Approaching Wells Cathedral *(tel 01749-674483)* either through Penniless Porch from the Market Place or through the medieval gateway in Sadler Street known as the "Dean's Eye," you are confronted by what many reckon is the finest west front of any cathedral in Europe. Between the square-topped twin towers sit six tiers of 13th-century statues of priests, kings, and saints—300 figures in all.

Entering, you are immediately struck by the futuristic yet entirely harmonious appearance of the huge scissor-arches with their spectacle holes, installed between 1338 and 1348 to shore up the unsteady central tower. The cathedral, begun in 1180, is rich in treasures of medieval carving and architecture; particularly noteworthy are the animated astronomical clock of 1392 in the north transept, on which jousting knights knock each other flat every hour, and the early 14th-century chapter house at the top of its flight of wide steps, where 32 ribs of fan vaulting spring with supreme grace from a slender central column.

Wells
🅰 141 G4
Visitor Information
✉ Town Hall, Market Pl.
☎ 01749-672552

Wookey Hole Caves
🅰 141 G4
✉ Wookey Hole, 2 miles NW of Wells
☎ 01749-672243
🆂 $$$

Cheddar Caves & Gorge
🅰 141 G4
✉ Cheddar, 8 miles NW of Wells
☎ 01934-742343
🆂 $$$

EXPERIENCE: Visit a Rural Cidermaker

There is sweet, clear, fizzy cider for the commercial market, and then there is scrumpy. The national drink of Somerset is cloudy, sharp, and extraordinarily heady. Ask in a pub or farmyard the whereabouts of the local scrumpy shed; then go and watch apple juice being squeezed by ancient screw presses out of a "cheese" of straw and pomace. Confused? Don't fret—enjoy the matured result of the cidermaker's labor, and lay the rest of the day in the lap of the apple god.

The Somerset Levels with their many orchards are one of the strongholds of cidermaking, and here Roger Wilkins is king. In his old-fashioned cider shed at Mudgley, on a hillside overlooking the moors, this rubicund farmer dispenses his West Country nectar from traditional barrels—a drop of sweet from one, a drop of dry from the other, until the mixture tickles the customer's palate to perfection. There's tasty local cheese and pickles, too. Everything is calm, quiet, sweet scented, and timeless at Roger's place. No wonder it's called **Land's End** *(Land's End Farm, Mudgley, Wedmore, Somerset, tel 01934-712385, http://wilkinscider.com).*

Bristol

◩ 141 G5

Visitor Information

✉ 1 Canons Rd., Harbourside

☎ 0333-321 0101

At Bristol

✉ Harbourside, Bristol

☎ 0845-345 1235

www.at-bristol .org.uk

S.S. Great Britain

✉ Great Western Doc, Gas Ferry Rd., Bristol

☎ 0117-926 0680

The moated **Bishop's Palace** (tel 01749-988111, closed Nov.–March), the 14th-century **Vicars' Close** (the oldest complete medieval street in Europe), and the excellent **Wells Museum** (8 Cathedral Green, tel 01749-673477) are all one minute's walk from the cathedral.

Bristol

Bristol is an anomaly—a famous seaport that is not actually on the sea, although the 4-mile Avon Gorge connects the city with the Bristol Channel. Atlantic-facing Bristol enjoyed seaborne prosperity for centuries, through trade with the United States and the West Indies. John Cabot, a Genoese-born navigator, sailed from the city in 1497 to "discover" Newfoundland and mainland America; his statue sits on Narrow Quay.

Around the waterfront in the city's center are the shops and cafés of cobbled Narrow Quay; the Explore hands-on science center and Blue Reef Aquarium at **At Bristol;** atmospheric old King Street with the **Theatre Royal** of 1766 and the half-timbered 17th-century **Llandoger Trow;**

and above all the superbly graceful 14th-century **Church of St. Mary Redcliffe,** with its tall spire and elaborately carved north porch.

Little yellow-painted water taxis buzz around all these attractions and down the harbor to the **S.S. Great Britain.** They'll also transport you to **Temple Meads Station,** where you'll find the castle-style frontage of the 1840 terminus of the Great Western Railway, built by Isambard Kingdom Brunel (see sidebar this page).

Wander around the Regency terraces and crescents of elegant **Clifton,** northwest of the center, before crossing the dizzyingly high suspension bridge (see sidebar this page) to enjoy a stroll through Leigh Woods, above the gorge.

INSIDER TIP:

Before visiting Bath's Roman Baths, count the angels climbing a stairway to heaven on the facade of Abbey Church.

—PAULA KELLY
National Geographic contributor

Isambard Kingdom Brunel (1806–1859)

This man with the big name epitomized all the swagger, confidence, and inventiveness of the Victorian engineer. He developed steamships, built bridges and docks, and dreamed up a railway that ran on air suction. Bristol displays many of his brilliant works, including the 1840 Bristol Old Railway Station (now Temple Meads Station), the oldest terminus in the world and the end of Brunel's Great Western Railway; the S.S. *Great Britain* (launched in 1843), the world's first oceangoing steamship with screw propulsion; and the Clifton Suspension Bridge (1836–1864) across the Avon Gorge, Bristol's symbol and Brunel's chief monument.

Bath

As England's showpiece of harmonious Georgian architecture, Bath is an absolute must for any traveler through Britain. And the beautiful, if often overcrowded, city is one of the

The Romans built and dedicated a temple to Sulis Minerva, the Romano-Celtic goddess of healing, together with baths and other fine buildings. The extensive remains of most of these lay unexcavated until the 1880s.

The Roman Great Bath, once covered by a roof, is now exposed to the elements.

most enjoyable and rewarding in Europe for strolling around (see pp. 154–155).

Britain's premier inland spa town, unmatched for elegance and sophistication during the 18th-century height of its fame, started in a humble way around 850 B.C. when (according to legend) King Bladud became an outcast swineherd after he contracted leprosy. Seeing his itchy-skinned pigs wallowing in the warm muddy springs of these limestone hills, Bladud followed suit and found his complaint cured.

When the Romans arrived around A.D. 44 they found the locals already using the springs.

Fashionable Spa: After the Romans left the town, sufferers continued to use the healing waters at Bath, but Bath was primarily a market town throughout the medieval ages. The town became really fashionable after 1704, when Richard "Beau" Nash (1674–1762) was elected Master of Ceremonies—a taste and style arbiter whose word was absolute law. Balls, parties, card sessions, and visits were arranged, and Bath became the most fashionable meeting, greeting, flirting, and marriage-marketing place in Britain.

(continued on p. 156)

Bath

▲ 141 G4

Visitor Information

✉ Abbey Chambers, Abbey Church Yard

☎ 01225-477746

A Walk Around Bath

This walk takes you on a tour of the highlights of Bath—from the superbly preserved Roman Baths of the first century to the parks, terraces, squares, and Royal Crescent, the epitome of Georgian elegance.

A sculpture of a Roman goddess, unearthed in 1790 when the Pump Room was being built

Begin at the visitor information center on Abbey Church Yard. Here you can pick up a Trail Guide entitling you to a reduced entrance fee at many of the museums along the way.

Outside are the **Roman Baths ❶** (Stall St., tel 01225-477785), built about A.D. 65–75. The green waters of the adjacent hot spring feed the baths, at a constant temperature of 115.7°F. In the Baths Museum is a model of the whole bath/temple complex, along with fascinating artifacts unearthed here, most striking of which are a superb bronze head of Sulis Minerva and a giant, staring god's head carved in stone, with knotted and writhing hair and beard.

Above is the elegant 18th-century **Pump Room,** where you can take tea or dare to drink a glass of the health-giving water—tasting faintly of eggs, soap, and metal.

NOT TO BE MISSED:

Roman Baths • Abbey Church • Royal Crescent

Outside the baths stands **Bath Abbey ❷** (tel 01225-422462), a church begun by Bishop Oliver King in 1499, on whose west front a host of angels climbs up and tumbles down ladders. Inside is much delicate fan vaulting and a clutter of effigies and monuments.

Leaving the street performance artists in **Abbey Church Yard,** go between the pillars across Stall Street and along Bath Street to the very elegant **Cross Bath ❸,** where James II's wife erected a cross in 1688 in gratitude for having at last become pregnant after bathing in this spring. **Thermae** (tel 01255-331234), just next door, is an extremely popular contemporary spa bath center.

Turn right into Saw Close to Barton Street to pass the **Theatre Royal ❹** (Saw Close, tel 01225-448844, tours at 11 a.m. 1st Wed. & Sat. of month), carefully restored and maintained, plush and ornate. Continue on Barton Street into Queen Square, around which John Wood the Elder displayed the Bath stone to best advantage.

From the top left corner of Queen Square, ascend to the lion-guarded entrance into **Royal Victoria Park,** and take the raised gravel walk on the right, which curves around to meet the classic sweep of **Royal Crescent.** The harmonious frontages were built in the 1760s and '70s by John Wood the Younger, and speculators ran up the houses behind as they pleased. **No. 1 Royal Crescent ❺** (tel 01225-428126, closed Dec.–Jan. & Mon. Feb.–Nov.) is done up complete with sedan chair in the hall, port and pipes in the study, and a big cheerful kitchen to re-create a mid-Georgian atmosphere.

Continue along Brock Street to the **Circus** ❻, John Wood the Elder's masterpiece of circular building, with a weird frieze of masks, foliage, magical symbols, musical instruments, and wildlife running all the way around.

Just beyond, turning right off Bennett Street, are the **Assembly Rooms** ❼ *(tel 01225-477789)* of 1772: A long ballroom lit by 18th-century chandeliers, an octagonal card room with a musicians' gallery, and a pillared and curtained tearoom. Here the fashionable Bathonians of Jane Austen's day would gather to gamble, flirt, and dance. In the basement is Bath's **Fashion Museum** *(tel 01225-477173)*, featuring modes of dress from Elizabethan

blackwork embroidery to ultramodern fashion.

Bartlett Street and Broad Street bring you to Robert Adam's beautiful **Pulteney Bridge** ❽ of 1769–1774, just above a broad weir across the River Avon. Grand Parade, the circular Orange Grove, and elegant Terrace Walk land you close to your starting point in North Parade Passage, where you can relax over a cup of tea and one of Bath's enormous and justly celebrated buns in **Sally Lunn's House.**

🗺 See area map p. 141
▶ Visitor information center
🕐 Half a day
⟷ 1.5 miles
▶ North Parade Passage

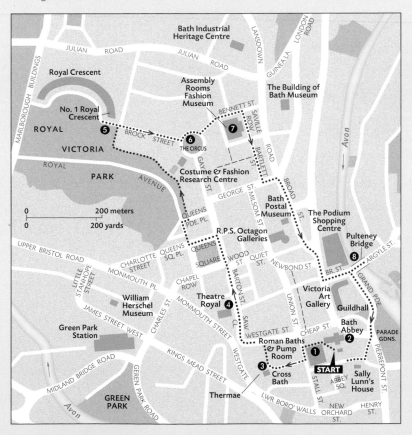

Bradford-on-Avon

East of Bath, where Somerset gives way to Wiltshire, is the charming stone-built wool town of Bradford-on-Avon *(map 141 G4, visitor information, The Greenhouse, 50 St. Margaret's St., tel 01225-865797)*. Bradford, like Bath, has many fine houses of Stuart and Georgian wool merchants, but it has a few other architectural gems as well. Perhaps its most important building is a rare pre-Norman church, which stood for centuries unrecognized; it is one of the most complete Saxon buildings still in existence. Along the riverside path can be found another medieval treasure, a great tithe barn built in the 14th century. The most curious structure in Bradford, however, is probably the grim little jail on the bridge, built in the 18th century to house drunks or other troublemakers overnight.

Dyrham Park

⚑ 141 G5

☎ 0117-937 2501

🕐 See website for hours

💲 House & gardens $$$, gardens only $$, park & domestic rooms $$, park only $

www.nationaltrust
.org.uk

American Museum in Britain

⚑ 141 G4

✉ 2.5 miles SE of Bath

☎ 01225-460503

🕐 Closed Nov.–March (Christmas opening late Nov.–mid-Dec.) & Mon. April–Oct.

💲 $$

www.american
museum.org

Ralph Allen opened his quarries in Combe Down, south of the little spa, and the golden Bath stone was fashioned by the two John Woods, father and son, into the incomparably elegant squares, circuses, terraces, and crescents you see today.

Around Bath: Just north of the A431, 4 miles west of the city, the tiny hillside village of North Stoke is the starting point for a lovely, if often extremely muddy, walk to the beech clump on the top of Kelston Round Hill. On a clear day, views from here extend 50 miles from Wiltshire through Somerset and Gloucestershire to the Severn Estuary and the Welsh hills.

Farther north, off the A46, 8 miles north of Bath, the 17th-century mansion of **Dyrham Park** sits at the foot of a great landscaped slope in a park where deer roam. South of Bath is a ridge by Beechen Cliff, giving views over the city.

Two miles out of town to the southeast is **Prior Park** *(tel 01225-833422, www.nationaltrust .org.uk, see website for hours)*, the big house built for Ralph Allen by John Wood the Elder from 1735 to 1750. The house is not open to the public, but you can stroll in the landscaped grounds *(no parking on grounds)* and admire one of the finest Palladian bridges in existence.

Nearby is the **American Museum in Britain** at Claverton Manor, which takes you on a journey through American domestic life from colonial days to the end of the 19th century. It has the simplicity of early pioneer furnishings, the quiet elegance of the 18th century, and the heavy elaborations of the 19th century— all offset by quilting and rugmaking, Navajo art, and Shaker furniture in its pristine severity. You can snack on Connecticut snickerdoodles, baked the way Grandma made them.

South again are secret valleys, where pleasing villages such as **Englishcombe, Wellow,** and **Priston** wait to be discovered.

Great Country Houses

The architecture of south Somerset is dominated by the glorious, honey-colored hamstone quarried from Ham Hill. Hereabouts the cool chalk of the South Country gives way to the warmth of the West Country limestone and sandstone.

Montacute House: Montacute *(tel 01935-823289, www .nationaltrust.org.uk, closed Nov.– March & Tues. April–Oct., garden open year-round, $$$, garden only $$)* lies just off the A3088, 4 miles west of Yeovil in south Somerset. This Tudor Gothic mansion, started during the year of the Spanish Armada, was built of honey-colored hamstone for Sir Edward Phelips, Speaker of the House of Commons.

Under the house's balustraded roofline, sculptured figures stand guard in their niches, looking over formal terraced gardens with trimmed old yew hedges—contorted into a maze-like pattern—and Tudor rose bushes. Inside are 16th- and 17th-century portraits, Jacobean tapestries and samplers, and huge Elizabethan fireplaces.

Longleat House: Just across the northeastern border of Somerset into Wiltshire, between Frome and Warminster on the A362, stands Longleat House, a grand Elizabethan mansion. It was built between 1559 and 1580 by Sir John Thynne, who, in 1541, had snapped up the local priory after the Dissolution of the Monasteries, together with 900 acres of prime land, at the bargain price of £53 (about $90).

Inside the symmetrically square-sided house are the original Great Hall with its dark hammerbeam ceiling, a fine collection of Old Master paintings, and nearly 50,000 books housed in seven library rooms.

In 1948, the 6th Marquess of Bath opened Longleat to the public. The park now contains a safari park, a big maze, adventure playgrounds, a narrow-gauge railway, an adventure play castle, and many other delights.

INSIDER TIP:

There's great biking outside of Bath along old rail trails and bucolic countryside.

—AMY KOLCZAK
National Geographic International Editions

Stourhead: This big Palladian house was built between 1721 and 1724 for a rich banker, Henry Hoare, and contains furniture by Chippendale and romantic landscape paintings by Poussin and Claude. These French artists were a great influence on Hoare and his son, "Henry the Magnificent," when they were laying out Stourhead's superbly landscaped grounds. Grottoes, rotundas, and temples stand by the lake and among fabulously varied trees.

Two miles away, but still on the estate, stands a Hoare folly, the 160-foot **King Alfred's Tower** *(tel 01747-841152, closed Nov.– March, $)*—climb its 206 steps for a 50-mile view. ∎

Longleat House

141 G4
Just off A362 bet. Frome & Warminster
01985-844400
Safari park & attractions: closed Nov.– mid-Feb.
House & grounds $$$, safari & adventure park $$$$$

www.longleat.co.uk

Stourhead
141 G4
Stourton
01747-841152
See website for hours
House & gardens $$$$, house or gardens only $$

www.nationaltrust .org.uk

More Places to Visit in the West Country

A stone maze sits on the coast of Bryher, the smallest of the Isles of Scilly.

Isles of Scilly

Off the southwestern extremity of Britain lies a scattering of small islands. Remotest of all are the Isles of Scilly, visible from Land's End on a clear day. Of the five inhabited islands, **St. Mary's** is the biggest. Daffodils grow in tiny walled fields, and the twisty lanes are uncrowded. **Tresco** is a subtropical paradise, planted with exotic species. Roads here, as on all the other islands except St. Mary's, are car free. Neighboring **Bryher** is rugged and tiny; **St. Martin's** is long and spiky-backed, with beautiful beaches. Lonely little **St. Agnes**, the southernmost island, faces the Western Rocks in Cornwall.

⚠ 140 A1–B1 **Visitor Information** ✉ Old Wesleyan Chapel, Well Ln., Hugh Town, St. Mary's ☎ 01720-422536; ✈ Isles of Scilly Skybus ☎ 0845-710 5555 ✈ British International Helicopter Services ☎ 01736-363871 ⛴ Isles of Scilly Steamship Company ☎ 0845-710 5555

Lundy

Off the northwestern corner of Devon rises Lundy, 11 miles out into the widening mouth of the Bristol Channel. Three miles long, half a mile wide, isolated and beautiful, the island has a spectacularly indented cliff coastline to flank its rounded back. About 20 people live here year-round, running the Marisco Tavern, a shop, and a small number of vacation cottages for the Landmark Trust, which owns the island.

⚠ 140 D4 ⛴ From Bideford, Ilfracombe, and Clovelly ☎ 01271-863636

Steep Holm & Flat Holm

Farther up the Bristol Channel are the hump of Steep Holm and the low-lying pancake of Flat Holm, two island bird sanctuaries well worth a day's exploration.

Steep Holm ⚠ 141 F4 ⛴ Tel 01934-522125; **Flat Holm** ⚠ 141 F4 ⛴ Tel 029-2035 3917

A land of steep borderlands in the east and splendid mountains in the west, studded with castles and bounded by a dramatic coastline

Wales

The Welsh flag—Y Ddraig Goch (the Red Dragon)—flying atop Caernarfon

Wales

Wales is strikingly attractive, with dramatic mountains in the north, a hilly interior, a coastline of fishing villages among long stretches of cliffs and sandy beaches, and rolling hills and valleys punctuated with castles. The country looks with pride on its artistic heritage of legend, song, and poetry, and on its contribution to British society of so many politicians, thinkers, orators, and social activists.

Llangollen Canal, a popular, scenic canal

In 1997 the Welsh voted to establish their own Assembly, a decision that reflects the country's mood of self-confidence and its strength of national identity. It has not always been so. Like their fellow Celts in Scotland and Ireland, the Welsh came off second-best in confrontations with the Saxon and Norman English. In the eighth century, Offa, King of Mercia, built an 80-mile defensive bank and ditch along the border. After the Norman Conquest the barons known as the Lords Marcher (Lords of the Border) ruled from their castles like kings.

There were plenty of Welsh uprisings, notably under Prince Llewelyn the Great (1173–1240) and his grandson, Llewelyn the

Last (d. 1282), but Edward I crushed Welsh autonomy during two decisive campaigns in 1277 and again in 1282–1284. One last great confrontation took place around 1400, when the charismatic Prince Owain Glyndwr set the Borders on fire. After he was defeated, the English dominance of Wales was complete.

Still Its Own Country

England and Wales were unified under Henry VIII from 1536 to 1543. Evidence of the previous 400 years of occupation and resistance lies all across Wales in the shape of great castles, fortified manor houses, defensive earthworks, and churches built as grimly as fortresses.

Recently there has been a resurgence in Welsh language and culture. Welsh showbiz names have come to the fore—actor Catherine Zeta Jones, rock bands Manic Street Preachers and Stereophonics, singers Tom Jones, Duffy, and Charlotte Church. It all points to a strengthening of the "Welshness" of Wales. ■

London ★

Area of map detail

1. RHONDDA CYNONTAFF
2. MERTHYR TYDFIL
3. BLAENAU GWENT
4. TORFAEN

0   50 kilometers
0   25 miles

Wye Valley

For visitors crossing the Severn estuary from Bristol by way of the twin bridges, the Wye Valley is their first glimpse of Wales. This heavily wooded, deeply cut valley, with England on its eastern bank and Wales on its west, makes a beautiful introduction to the principality.

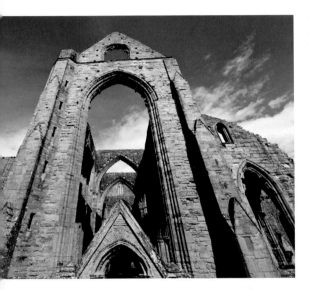

Wordsworth revered Tintern Abbey, honoring it in verse.

Wye Valley

🗺 161 D2

Visitor Information

✉ Chepstow Castle Car Park, Bridge St., Chepstow

☎ 01291-623772

Chepstow Castle

✉ Bridge St., Chepstow

☎ 01291-624065

💲 $$

Tintern Abbey

✉ 5 miles N of Chepstow

☎ 01291-689251

💲 $

It is 18 miles from **Chepstow** at the mouth of the muddy tidal River Wye to Monmouth at the head of the valley, a stretch of country where you can walk on the ancient rampart of **Offa's Dyke** (see p. 174) high up on the English bank, looking down through beech and hazel woods to the snakelike river hundreds of feet below. Alternatively, you can drive along the floor of the valley on the winding, often crowded A466.

Chepstow Castle, the earliest stone-built Norman castle in Britain, sprawls along its narrow ledge above the sheer limestone cliffs

of the Wye. From here the valley curls north through St. Arvans to Tintern, where the tall gray stone ruins of **Tintern Abbey,** as fine and delicate as lacework, stand on their leveled ground by the river. Three of the abbey's soaring windows still remain intact.

Tintern village itself is an unrepentant tourist trap, but a little farther up the valley you can cross the Wye to eat and drink in the friendly old **Brockweir Inn** (tel 01291-689548) without having your elbow jogged. Here, in the old days, goods from Bristol were transferred from vessels into trows (flat-bottomed barges), to be pulled to Monmouth over the Wye's weirs by teams of men known as "bow-haulers," whose leather chest-harnesses were attached to the trows by ropes.

North of Brockweir the valley road passes beneath the hanging white houses of Llandogo, then crosses the river to the English bank for its final run up to **Monmouth** (visitor information, Shire Hall, Agincourt Sq., tel 01600-713899). By the time you reach the town, the pale limestone river cliffs have given way to gentler slopes of red sandstone. With its cobbled square and 13th-century gatehouse on the bridge, Monmouth is a typical Welsh Borders market town, self-contained and easy paced. ∎

Cardiff & the Valleys

Cardiff, now the capital city of Wales, was a modest coastal town until the Marquess of Bute developed its docks at the dawn of the railway era in the 1830s. Within a hundred years it had become the busiest coal port in the world, a conduit for the mighty flood of coal pouring out of the mines in the valleys just to the north.

Cardiff City

The mines are closed now, and Cardiff Bay has been reborn as a leisure area of bars, restaurants, stores, and upscale housing.

Cardiff Castle is an extravagant fantasy, assembled in 1867–1875 by the 3rd Marquess of Bute around the nucleus of a Norman keep. Enjoy the galleried Summer Smoking Room; the hand-painted nursery-rhyme tiles in the Nursery; and the Arab Room with Islamic designs created in marble, lapis lazuli, and gold.

Other city sites worth seeing are the impressively pompous **City Hall** in Cathays Park, with a dragon perched atop its 200-foot dome, and the nearby **National Museum and Gallery,** with its superbly displayed prehistoric collection and its comprehensive coverage of Impressionist art. On the city's outskirts, at St. Fagans, is the **Museum of Welsh Life** *(tel 029-2057 3500)*, which focuses on old Welsh customs and lifestyles.

In the Valleys

North of Cardiff stretch the Valleys, roughly parallel slashes in the landscape where coal and iron were dug and metal ores smelted until the 1980s. To understand the miners' toilings, visit the mine workings at the **Big Pit Mining Museum** (see sidebar this page), 27 miles north of Cardiff.

Rewarding walks can be had from the long, narrow industrial villages on the valley floors, up along old tracks onto the high, windy tops of the hills. ■

Cardiff
- 🗺 161 C1

Visitor Information
- ✉ The Old Library, The Hayes
- ☎ 029-2087 3573

Cardiff Castle
- ✉ Castle St.
- ☎ 029-2087 8100
- 💲 $$

National Museum and Gallery
- ✉ Cathays Park
- ☎ 029-2039 7951
- 🕐 Closed Mon.

EXPERIENCE: Go Underground with an Ex-miner

When Blaenafon's Big Pit closed in 1980, the miners and engineers turned adversity into good fortune by making their colliery into a visitor attraction, the **Big Pit Mining Museum** *(Blaenafon, Torfaen, tel 01495-790311, www.museumwales.ac.uk/en/bigpit)*. After looking at a fascinating exhibition on the miner's life and work, you can don helmet and headlamp to descend in a miner's cage for an authentic tour of the workings, in the company of a blackly humorous and friendly ex-miner guide.

You crouch and stumble along iron-braced galleries 300 feet below ground, at times standing in pitch-black silence to better imagine the plight of the eight-year-old children employed until the 1840s to open the compartment doors for the coal trams. The guide also shows you hewn coalfaces, their polished cut coal gleaming in the lamplight, and tells of the half-blind pit ponies' joy when they were taken to the surface for their annual weeklong holiday in the fresh air. It's a unique experience.

Pembrokeshire Coast & Gower Peninsula

The Pembrokeshire Coast National Park comprises the wild and storm-sculptured tip of Wales's extreme southwest. Out at the westernmost point of Pembrokeshire's rough and rugged peninsula sits St. David's, the smallest city in the United Kingdom and one of the most appealing. Its glory and pride is the great cathedral of St. David's, which was begun in 1180 on the site of a monastery founded by the saint himself about 550.

Pembrokeshire's coastline features such delights as the Green Bridge, a natural arch near Bosherston.

St. David's

🗺 161 A2

Visitor Information

✉ The Grove

☎ 01437-720392

St. David's Cathedral

Graced with a 125-foot central tower, the cathedral has at its west end a big rose window, at its east end a 14th-century rood screen, and in the nave a finely carved early 16th-century oak roof. Fresh flowers always stand at the cathedral's crossing to decorate the shrine of St. David, a 1275 replacement of the stolen pre-Norman original. In the choir one stall is always reserved for the British monarch. Lift the seats to enjoy 15th-century misericords, which feature scenes of shipbuilding and hunting.

Next door is the grand ruin of the **Bishop's Palace,** with its superb Great Hall rose window, and the private chapel of the bishops of St. David's. Stories say that Bishop Barlow, the first Protestant bishop to be enthroned here at the Reformation in 1536, had the lead roofs stripped for sale, so that he could provide dowries for his five daughters.

Coastal Walks & Island Sanctuaries

Of the many glorious coastal walks in Pembrokeshire and the **Pembrokeshire Coast National Park,** the 4-mile round-trip from Whitesands Bay around **St. David's Head** (3 miles beyond St. David's) is one of the best—it takes in Iron Age and Stone Age relics and the beach from which St. Patrick set off early in the fifth century to convert the Irish.

Another 4-mile walk, picked up in **Bosherston** (some 20 miles southeast of St. David's), leads around **St. Govan's Head,** visiting along the way the village's beautiful lily ponds and the tiny Chapel of St. Govan, which is built wedged into a crack in the cliffs.

Twenty miles northeast of St. David's is **Dinas Head,** a blunt-nosed promontory with a very enjoyable 3-mile walk around its craggy perimeter.

Offshore islands include **Ramsey Island, Skokholm Island,** and **Skomer Island,** bird and wildlife

INSIDER TIP:

My favorite place in the Gower is Rhossili Bay. At the southern end is a small tidal island called Worms Head, accessible at low tide only.

—ALED GREVILLE
Director, Inventory & Operations, National Geographic Books

sanctuaries of beauty and isolation. An overnight stay here is a never-to-be-forgotten experience, but one that should be planned well in advance. For details contact the St. David's visitor center (see p. 164).

Gower Peninsula

Some of the most unspoiled and beautiful scenery in South Wales can be found farther east on the Gower Peninsula, just 18 miles long by 5 miles wide. Its cliffs and beaches are considered to be among the finest in Britain. ∎

St. David's Cathedral
- ✉ The Close
- ☎ 01437-720202
- 🅂 Donation. Tours $$

St. David's Bishop's Palace
- ✉ The Close
- ☎ 01437-720517
- 🅂 $

Pembrokeshire Coast National Park
- 🄰 161 A2
- ✉ Llannion Park Pembroke Dock
- ☎ 0854-345 7275

Gower Peninsula
- 🄰 161 B1–B2
- **Visitor Information**
- ✉ Plymouth St., Swansea
- ☎ 01792-468321

Dylan Thomas

Dylan Thomas (1914–1953), Wales's national poet, used language as no one else has. His mellifluous voice, reciting one of his poems or reading such rich, dense prose as *A Child's Christmas in Wales,* became well known through his BBC broadcasts. It is his play for voices, *Under Milk Wood,* published posthumously in 1954, by which he is best known. Thomas's last home, known as the **Dylan Thomas Boathouse** *(Dylan's Walk, tel 01994-427420),* stands on a rough track beside the Taf Estuary at Laugharne, off the A40 10 miles west of Carmarthen. The

living room with its wonderful estuary view is preserved, as are the writing table and materials in the garage shed in the lane, where *Under Milk Wood* and many other poems and stories were written.

In November 1953, the poet, whose drinking habits were out of control, died of a "massive insult to the brain" while on a lecture tour of the United States. His grave is in the churchyard at Laugharne.

The **Dylan Thomas Centre** *(Somerset Pl., tel 01792-463980, www.dylanthomas .com)* in Swansea gives a good overview of the life and death of this flawed genius.

Central Wales

The central highlands of Wales are wild and lonely—superb walking country with the highest mountains in Britain south of Snowdonia. Towns and villages—ancient settlements quietly brooding in a landscape of standing stones and hill forts—are few and far between.

Brecon Beacons National Park

 161 C2

✉ Plas y Ffynnon, Cambrian Way, Brecon

☎ 01874-624437

www.brecon beacons.org

Brecon Beacons

The Brecon Beacons range lies north of the Valleys, forming the heart of the **Brecon Beacons National Park.** The high hills are crisscrossed with horseback riding routes as well as paths leading to and around the two main summits of Pen-y-Fan (2,907 feet) and nearby Corn Du (2,863 feet). These sandstone peaks look north over impressive sheer cliffs; the A470 Merthyr Tydfil–Brecon road near Storey Arms is a good starting place, and the path is clearly marked.

Black Mountains

The Black Mountains, rising northeast of the Brecon Beacons, form a parallel series of four northwest–southeast sandstone ridges with straight, horizontal backs above deep valleys. Take at least a day to explore them, winding up and down the narrow valley roads to find the elegant, soaring 12th-century arches of the ruined **Llanthony Priory** in the Vale of Ewyas. Also worth a visit are the churches at Michaelchurch Escley and Partrishow, decorated with macabre medieval murals. Don't miss **Hay-on-Wye,** north of the mountains, where there is a huge number of secondhand bookshops.

Old Radnor

Just off the A44, 12 miles north of Hay-on-Wye, Old Radnor consists of a few houses, a big church containing a rough, round, eighth-century font that some think might have once been a Bronze Age altar stone, and the dark-beamed old Harp Inn across from the church.

Open moorland edged by a clear stream, Brecon Beacons

Powis Castle

Farther north and 1 mile south of Welshpool off the A483, Powis Castle is one of the country's finest mansions, built up around a 13th-century fortress in Tudor and Stuart times. The Long Gallery and State Bedrooms are gloriously ornate, and the castle's Italianate gardens, landscaped between 1688 and 1722, are Britain's sole remaining design of this type.

Aberystwyth & Around

The seaside town of Aberystwyth stands on the A487 halfway up the enormous curve of the Cardigan Bay coastline. The town itself, with its University College of Wales, National Library of Wales, and Welsh Language Society headquarters, is uncompromisingly Welsh.

In Aberystwyth's stores and pubs more Welsh than English is spoken. Pro-Welsh sentiment is as strong here, given a prominent voice by the presence of so many bastions of Welsh nationalism and cultural identity. Yet the look of the town, particularly the seafront with its pier and ranks of tall hotels, is of an English Victorian seaside resort—a legacy of the expansion that followed the arrival of the railroad in 1864.

A good overview of this lively, self-possessed town is had from the **Great Aberystwyth Camera Obscura** (*tel 01970-617642, closed Nov.–March*) on Constitution Hill to the north, reached by the little wooden carriages of the **Aberystwyth Electric Cliff Railway** (*tel 01970-617642, closed Nov.–March*)

that rises slowly up the bushy face of a 380-foot cliff. From here a path runs for 6 steep and exhilarating miles north to Borth, from which you can journey back to Aberystwyth by train.

INSIDER TIP:

Trek along Glyndwr's Way, a less-traveled national path in mid-Wales that crosses barren moors and rolling hills with patches of dense forest.

—ERIN MONRONEY
National Geographic contributor

Twelve miles inland along the A4120—or half an hour's ride on the **Vale of Rheidol Steam Railway**—is **Devil's Bridge,** a spectacular spot where the Afon Mynach (Monk's River) leaps 300 feet downward beneath a triple bridge. The lowest span is Norman; it is said to have been created in a magical flash by the devil, who was trying to outsmart an old Welsh woman. Needless to say, she came off best.

North of Aberystwyth is the wide estuary of the River Dyfi (Dovey), and north of that rises the 2,927-foot peak of Cader Idris, one of Wales's most satisfying mountains to climb.

The steepish path, starting 3 miles southwest of Dolgellau, is clear all the way to the stony cairn at the top. Sleep here, legend claims, and you will awaken either a poet or a madman. ∎

Hay-on-Wye
🗺 161 D2
Visitor Information
✉ Craft Centre
☎ 01497-820144

Old Radnor
🗺 161 D3

Powis Castle
🗺 161 C3
✉ 1 mile S of Welshpool, off the A483
☎ 01938-551929
🕐 See website for hours
💲 House & garden $$$, garden only $$
www.nationaltrust.org.uk

Aberystwyth
🗺 161 B3
Visitor Information
✉ Terrace Rd.
☎ 01970-612125
🕐 Closed Sun.

Vale of Rheidol Steam Railway
🗺 161 C3
✉ Park Ave., Aberystwyth
☎ 01970-625819
www.rheidolrailway.co.uk

Glyndwr's Way
www.nationaltrail.co.uk/glyndwrsway

A Drive from Dolgellau to Conwy

In the streets of Dolgellau you will hear plenty of Welsh spoken, for the northwest corner of Wales is the heartland of the national language. Slate and gold were both dug from the surrounding hills, of which there are fine views as you drive west to Barmouth, where a great railway viaduct strides across enormous sands on 114 spindly legs.

From **Dolgellau** *(visitor information, Ty Meirion, Eldon Sq., tel 01341-422888)*, take the A496 10 miles west and north to **Harlech Castle** ❶ *(Castle Sq., tel 01766-780552)*, one of the Iron Ring fortresses (see p. 170) established by Edward I. Harlech was built between 1283 and 1289 of dark gritstone, perched on a crag to exude impregnability with its great gatehouse, 40-foot walls, and corner towers.

From Harlech, the A496 crosses the Dwyryd estuary at Maentwrog. Turn left here onto the A487, passing the little steam trains and stations of the **Ffestiniog Railway** ❷ *(Blaenau Ffestiniog, tel 01766-516000, limited service early Nov.–late March)*. The line once carried slate quarried in the hills at Blaenau Ffestiniog 13.5 miles to the harbor at **Porthmadog** *(visitor information, High St., tel 01766-512981)*. It closed in 1946, but enthusiasts later reopened it for passengers. The steam trains of the very scenic **Welsh Highland Railway** *(tel 01766-516024)* now journey the 25 miles from Caernarfon to Porthmadog to link up with the Ffestiniog Railway.

At Porthmadog bear right on the A498, up over the steep and spectacular pass of Aberglaslyn, to reach **Beddgelert** ❸. Here you can visit **Gelert's Grave** (see sidebar p. 171) by the River Glaslyn, where lies (or so it is said) Llewelyn the Great's faithful hound.

Over to Anglesey & Back

The A4085 snakes its way to **Caernarfon** ❹ and the mightiest of the Welsh castles (see pp. 170–171). Here you rejoin the A487 and skirt the Menai Strait, a narrow channel of water with fierce currents spanned by twin bridges, which separates the Welsh mainland

NOT TO BE MISSED:

Harlech Castle • Ffestiniog Railway • Caernarfon Castle • Penrhyn Castle

from the **Isle of Anglesey.** If you decide to explore this intensely Welsh island, wander the back roads across the rolling interior. Make time to see **Beaumaris Castle** ❺ *(Castle St., tel 01248-810361)*, the last of Edward I's castles to be built.

Just beside the more westerly of the Menai bridges is **Llanfairpwllgwyngyllgogerychwyrndrobwllllantysiliogogogoch** *(visitor information, Holyhead Rd., tel 01248-713177)*, or "Church of St. Mary in the hollow of the white hazel near a rapid whirlpool and St. Tysilio near the red cave"—the longest place-name in Britain, generally shortened to Llanfair PG.

Back on the mainland, the A55 coast road leads east, skirting Bangor and passing **Penrhyn Castle** ❻ *(Llandegai, 1 mile E of Bangor, tel 01248-353084, closed early Nov.–late March & Tues. April–Oct.)*, a fascinating 19th-century extravaganza built around the shell of a Norman castle by local slate baron George Dawkins-Pennant. The A55 leads north to reach **Conwy** ❼ *(visitor information, Cadw Visitor Centre, Castle Entrance, tel 01492-592248)*, a delightful small town ringed by medieval walls. Walk a circuit of these before exploring the huge, adjoining **castle** *(Castle St., tel 01492-592358)*, another Iron Ring fortress, which crouches magnificently over the Conwy Estuary.

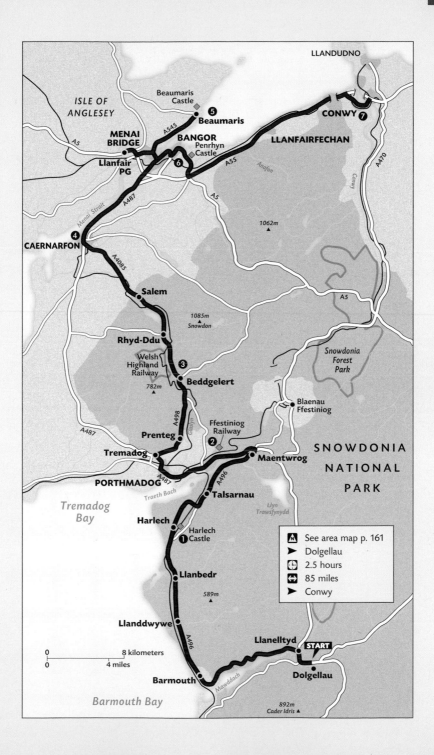

LLANDUDNO

Beaumaris Castle

⑤ Beaumaris

ISLE OF ANGLESEY

A545

CONWY ⑦

MENAI BRIDGE

BANGOR

LLANFAIRFECHAN

Penrhyn Castle

A55

Llanfair PG

⑥

A55

Afon

A5

CAERNARFON ④

1062m

A4085

A5

Salem

A470

1085m
Snowdon

Rhyd-Ddu

Snowdonia Forest Park

Welsh Highland Railway

③

782m

Beddgelert

A498

Blaenau Ffestiniog

Glaslyn

Ffestiniog Railway

②

Prenteg

A487

SNOWDONIA

Tremadog

Maentwrog

NATIONAL

PORTHMADOG

A487

A496

PARK

Traeth Bach

Tremadog Bay

Talsarnau

Llyn Trawsfynydd

Harlech

Harlech Castle

①

	See area map p. 161
▶	Dolgellau
🕐	2.5 hours
↔	85 miles
▶	Conwy

Llanbedr

589m

A496

Llanddwywe

Llanelltyd

START

0   8 kilometers
0   4 miles

Barmouth

Mawddach

Dolgellau

Barmouth Bay

892m
Cader Idris ▲

Caernarfon Castle

Caernarfon Castle, said Daniel Defoe, was "built by Edward I to curb and reduce the wild people of the mountains"—a very succinct summation of the reason for this mighty fortress on the Menai Strait. This is the most famous and impressive castle in Wales, though by no means the most picturesquely sited. Dourly glowering over the water, it conveys exactly the message of formidable strength that Edward I intended the Welsh to read in its massive walls and towers.

Caernarfon's massive crenellated walls represent the statement of authority intended by Edward I.

The Iron Ring

Caernarfon was begun in 1283 as the strongest link in the Iron Ring, a loop of eight castles placed around the perimeter of the northern half of Wales. Flint, Rhuddlan, Conwy, Beaumaris, Caernarfon, and Harlech formed a defensive chain hemming in the mountains of Snowdonia, each castle a day's march from the next. Aberystwyth and Builth Wells stood farther south.

In his bid to regain lost land and establish Welsh autonomy, the charismatic Llewelyn ap Gruffydd, "Llewelyn the Last," the last truly Welsh Prince of Wales, provoked Edward I of England into his decisive all-out drive to crush the Welsh for once and all time (see p. 160). Victorious by 1284, Edward set about stamping his authority on the troublesome mountain people in the form of impregnable-looking castles.

Structure

The designer of Caernarfon Castle was James of St. George d'Espéranche, master stone-mason and foremost military architect of the late 13th century. His instructions were to combine in one building the strongest defenses and the most civilized and comfortable accommodations.

The great walls of the castle were built in bands of dark sandstone and light limestone. The bands give the walls an oddly unmilitary, exotic look, compared with those of Conwy, Beaumaris, and Harlech; the same is true of the octagonal shape chosen for the towers, which are topped by slender, castellated turrets.

The **King's Gate** makes a most impressive entry, with five distinct gateways and six portcullises, sniper slits for bowmen, and murder holes for the pouring of boiling oil, all impeding any attack. Of the towers, the most interesting to explore are the **Eagle Tower** at the western end, with its weathered eagle sculptures, and the **Queen's Tower** on the south, which contains a museum that gives an enjoyable run-through of the history of the Royal Welch Fusiliers since Stuart times.

You can walk between the towers, either through connecting passages built into the walls or along the tops of the walls.

History

In 1282, Edward I defeated the Welsh and had Llewelyn the Last beheaded. For the sake of security it was essential for him to install an English Prince of Wales. According to the (likely apocryphal) story, he let it be known that the chosen one had been born in Wales and spoke no English. The unsuspecting Welsh agreed to accept the king's nominee sight unseen, believing that one of their native leaders had been appointed. The wiliness of the king was revealed when he produced the new Prince of Wales—his son Edward, who had just been born in Caernarfon Castle.

In the early 1400s the nationalist leader Owain Glyndwr made two unsuccessful attempts to capture the castle; a measure of its strength is that a garrison of just 28 men kept him at bay. In the Civil War of the 1640s, the castle changed hands three times before finally coming under the control of Parliament.

Caernarfon Castle

🅐 161 B4
✉ Castle Ditch
☎ 01286-677617
💲 $$
www.caernarfon.com

Gelert's Grave

Llewelyn the Great left his dog Gelert to guard his baby son. On returning he found the cradle overturned and Gelert covered in blood. Thinking the dog had killed his son, Llewelyn slew Gelert. Only after he found his son safe, along with the body of a wolf, did he realize that Gelert had in fact saved the baby. The dog's grave is in Beddgelert (see p. 168).

During the 20th century Caernarfon Castle, seat of government for North Wales and the official Welsh residence of the monarch, saw two investitures of a prince of Wales: Prince Edward (later Edward VIII) in 1911, and Prince Charles in 1969. ∎

Snowdonia

Snowdonia National Park covers nearly 840 square miles of northwest Wales and includes some of the most impressive mountains and moorlands in Britain. This is walkers', climbers', and outdoor enthusiasts' country, a genuine mountain landscape that tops out on Snowdon, the highest mountain in Wales.

Snowdonia National Park

▲ 161 C4

✉ Information Section, Snowdonia National Park Authority, Penrhyndeudraeth, Gwynedd LL48 6LS

☎ 01766-770274

www.eryri-npa.gov.uk

Blaenau Ffestiniog

▲ 161 C4

Visitor Information

✉ Isallt, High St.

☎ 01766-830360

🕐 Closed Oct.– March

Betws-y-Coed

▲ 161 C4

Visitor Information

✉ Royal Oak Stables

☎ 01690-710426

Royal St. David's Golf Club

✉ Harlech

www.royalstdavids.co.uk

Nefyn and District Golf Club

✉ Near Pwllheli

www.nefyn-golf-club.co.uk

There is one exclusion zone, the "Hole in the Park," which contains the slate-producing village of **Blaenau Ffestiniog**—an important industrial landscape considered insufficiently attractive to be included in the park. The **Llechwedd Slate Caverns** (tel 01766-830306) here offer a fascinating tour as well as demonstrations of the specialized skills of slate-splitting—which you can try for yourself.

Eleven miles north is **Betws-y-Coed,** a favorite village with hill walkers. A whole network of paths into the surrounding mountains starts from here.

Capel Curig, 5 miles west of Betws-y-Coed, is another great hiking and climbing center, looking

Mountain Walk with a Warden

Both Snowdonia National Park and the Snowdonia Society (www.snowdonia-society.org.uk, donation if nonmember) offer warden-guided walks into Snowdonia's mountains, which are a happy hunting ground for experienced climbers and hill walkers, but can look pretty formidable to a beginner—so set off in confidence with a knowledgeable warden.

north and west to the jagged and rugged Glyders and Carneddau ranges, and southwest into the **Nant Gwryd Valley** toward Snowdon. Information can be obtained from the Snowdonia National Park Authority.

The jewel in the crown is 3,560-foot **Snowdon**—Yr Wyddfa to the Welsh, meaning "tomb": This is the burial place of the giant Rhita Gawr, who wore a cloak woven of the beards of kings he had killed. This monster was killed here by the hero King Arthur.

Climb Snowdon from Pen-y-Pass Youth Hostel (tel 01286-870428) on the A4086, midway between Capel Curig and Llanberis (an 8-mile circuit, steep in places, allow five to six hours), or go up on the **Snowdon Mountain Railway** (tel 01286-870223, closed Nov.–mid-March & in bad weather) from Llanberis. From the summit, in clear weather, you can see Wales, England, Scotland, and Ireland in a 250-mile circle. ■

Portmeirion & the Lleyn Peninsula

The fantasy "village" of Portmeirion, set on a private peninsula to the southeast of Porthmadog, is a must-see for any visitor to North Wales. This bizarre confection, a theatrical and exuberantly overblown Italianate village, was assembled here between 1925 and 1972 by Welsh architect Sir Clough Williams-Ellis (1883–1978).

Williams-Ellis grabbed pieces of endangered buildings from everywhere—statues of gods from Hindu temples, a mock-classical colonnade from Bristol, an Italian campanile shaped like an extended telescope.

Entering Portmeirion through the Triumphal Arch, you find buildings scattered around a central piazza, with more on the slopes and shores around—a castle, a lighthouse, an Indian hotel bar, and a Town Hall with a 17th-century fresco of Hercules on its ceiling. Little color-washed cottages with red roofs are dotted about. Eucalyptus and cypress trees grow in the landscaped gardens. The widely known Portmeirion pottery, decorated with flowers and butterflies, is sold from a shop with a curlicued facade. Visitors may stay overnight in the lavish Portmeirion Hotel or in one of the vacation cottages.

Portmeirion appealed to Noël Coward: He wrote his play *Blithe Spirit* (1941) while staying at Fountain Cottage.

Lleyn Peninsula

Portmeirion lies at the root of the 30-mile-long Lleyn Peninsula, a narrowing finger drooping southwest from Snowdonia. The peninsula is flanked by cliffs and

In Portmeirion, examples of architecture from around the world and across the ages rub shoulders.

indented with sandy bays. Its south coast claims the three seaside resorts of Criccieth, Pwllheli, and Abersoch. The north coast is quieter, with superb bicycling and walking.

Out toward the tip, the south side is torn by the 3-mile gash of **Hell's Mouth** (Porth Neigwl), a bay notorious for shipwrecks. Beyond lies the rugged little village of **Aberdaron,** and off the very tip of Lleyn the humped shape of **Bardsey Island.** You can visit the lonely island by boat from Pwllheli or Aberdaron, tide and weather permitting, and even stay on it; details from the Bardsey Island Trust *(tel 01758-760667).* ∎

Portmeirion
- 🅰 161 B4
- ✉ 2 miles SE of Porthmadog
- ☎ 01766-770000
- 💲 $$

Lleyn Peninsula
- 🅰 161 B4

Welsh Borders

The Welsh Borders are a land apart, knitted together as one entity by the great 80-mile earth rampart of Offa's Dyke. Although the political border between England and Wales runs nearby, it is the defensive bank built between 778 and 796 by Offa, King of Mercia, that truly marks the boundary. The Offa's Dyke footpath runs more than twice as far (168 miles), crossing and following the ancient earthwork from Chepstow in the south to Prestatyn in the north.

Offa's Dyke
- 161 D3–D4

Offa's Dyke Association
- ✉ West St., Knighton
- ☎ 01547-528753
- ⏰ Closed Sat.–Sun. Nov.–Easter

Plas Newydd
- ✉ Hill St., Llangollen
- ☎ 01978-861314
- ⏰ Closed Nov.–March
- 💲 $–$$

Forest of Dean
- 161 D2

As you make your way south from the North Wales coast along the Welsh Borders, the **Vale of Clwyd** is well worth a look. Offa's Dyke runs right along the spine of the Clwydian Range on the east (a beautiful walk in its own right), while down in the broad vale are the county town of Denbigh, in the shadow of a ruined castle, and **Ruthin** *(visitor information, Ruthin Craft Centre, Park Rd., tel 01824-703992)*, with its medieval St. Peter's Square and collegiate Church of St. Peter with a very fine, carved Tudor roof.

At the southern end of the Clwydian Range is **Llangollen** *(visitor information, Town Hall, Castle St., tel 01978-860828)*, a trim little town on the A5 with craggy hills all around. Enjoy diesel-driven canalboat rides over the Pontcysyllte aqueduct nearby, and visit black-and-white **Plas Newydd,** once the home of the eccentric bluestocking "Ladies of Llangollen," crammed full of fantastic oak carvings and tooled-leather fittings.

There is more good, non-specialist walking southwest of Llangollen in the **Berwyn Mountains,** where at Tan-y-Pistyll (4 miles northwest of Llanrhaeadr-ym-Mochnant) the tremendous **Pistyll Rhaeadr** waterfall (the highest in England and Wales) plunges 240 feet in two mighty leaps as the Afon Disgynfa tumbles off a cliff.

One more area of the borders not to be missed is the **Forest of Dean,** some 24,000 acres of lovely, tangled woodland on the eastern (English) flank of the Wye Valley, way down south. "Foresters" are not like other folk, and their tree-smothered kingdom is unlike anyplace else in Great Britain. Explore its many beautiful footpaths from the ancient **Speech House Hotel** on the B4226, in the very center of the forest. ■

Horseshoe Pass, near Llangollen

The rolling uplands of the Cotswolds, Shakespeare's haunts, a university town, and vibrant cities where many cultures mix and match

South Midlands

Queen's Hotel, Cheltenham, built circa 1840 to cater to spa-goers

South Midlands

The Midlands are England's heartland, a circle of mostly low-lying land between what northerners would call the "soft South," and what southerners consider the "hard North." Their character combines elements of both: the gentleness of oolitic limestone and red sandstone landscapes of fields and woods, and the severity of a clutch of traditionally hardworking cities now facing a future shorn of many of their manufacturing industries.

Oxford's origins date from Saxon times.

Too often it is these great conurbations—especially Birmingham, sprawling untidily around its tangle of highways—that people picture when they think of the South Midlands. Yet most of this region is pastoral, peaceful countryside, dotted with some of the most appealing cathedral cities, market towns, and villages to be found anywhere in Britain.

Three Cathedrals

The western boundary is marked by the Welsh Borders, where the celebrated "Three Cathedrals" of Gloucester, Worcester, and Hereford lie around the ancient Malvern Hills. Farther east, the Cotswold Hills—archetypal English countryside in all its beauty—roll from Gloucestershire away into Oxfordshire. The beautiful villages built of silvery or creamy limestone, the richness of the medieval churches, and the gentleness of the landscape draw visitors by the hundreds of thousands to the Cotswolds.

Midland Towns

Even more popular is Stratford-upon-Avon, birthplace of William Shakespeare and biggest attraction of the county of Warwickshire, though mighty Warwick Castle comes close. North from here again you will find three Midland towns: Coventry, with its showpiece postwar cathedral crammed with modern works of art; Leicester, with a vibrant Asian culture; and much maligned Birmingham—no beauty, but a friendly and lively city of mixed ethnic groups.

Oxford & Great Houses

Southeast is Oxford, a world away from all of this, where you can stroll around a superb collection of medieval colleges and their churches, halls, and quads—unparalleled, except perhaps by Cambridge. Blenheim Palace, all pomp and glory, lies just north, and out to the east is Althorp House, where Diana, Princess of Wales, lies buried on a lake island on its grounds. ∎

NOT TO BE MISSED:

Deerhurst's Saxon church and chapel **179**

The revelry of the Cheltenham Gold Cup **181**

Seeing a Shakespeare play performed by the RSC in Stratford-upon-Avon **186**

A Warwick Castle joust **187**

The art in Coventry Cathedral **190**

Walking around the Oxford colleges **192–194**

Strolling the superbly landscaped park of Blenheim Palace **196**

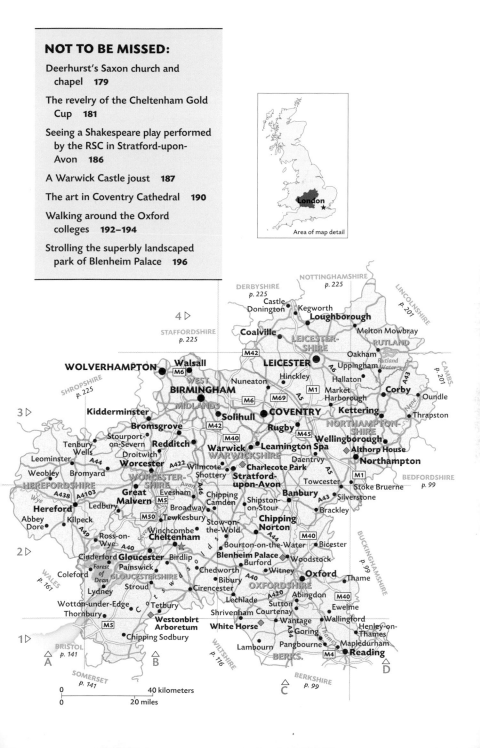

Area of map detail

London ★

Three Cathedral Cities

The three cathedral cities and county capitals of Gloucester, Hereford, and Worcester form a triangle in the southwest region of the South Midlands, a triangle that encloses the distinctive upthrust spine of the Malvern Hills. This is cattle-grazing and fruit-growing country of red earth and green meadows, well provided with orchards of apples for eating and cidermaking.

Gloucester Cathedral's 14th-century cloisters are England's earliest surviving fan vaults.

Gloucester

🅰 177 B2

Visitor Information

✉ 28 Southgate St.

☎ 01452-396572

Gloucester Cathedral

✉ College Green

☎ 01452-528095

Gloucester

The southernmost of the three cities, Gloucester boasts one of the most glorious cathedrals in Britain. Marked by its beautiful 225-foot tower, **Gloucester Cathedral** stands in a green close secluded from the city's streets. It was started in 1089 and finished within 20 years; the dogtooth decoration of the rounded arches in the nave shows these early Norman origins. In 1216 Henry III was crowned in this church.

The death of Edward II—killed in nearby Berkeley Castle on the orders of his wife Isabella—and his burial in Gloucester Cathedral in 1327 sparked a whole new phase in the life of the building. A sympathetic popular cult of pilgrimage to his alabaster tomb in the cathedral brought riches that

---

EXPERIENCE: Watch a Cricket Match in Worcester

Even though football has become the national sport of Britain (see sidebar p. 251), there's no doubt that English County Championship cricket catches—in its subtle, long-view, and rather unemphatic way—something of the peculiarly English character. Modern versions of the game (played with a severe time limit and featuring lots of action and razzmatazz) offer a Technicolor thrill that's generally lacking in the County Championship, but the longer contests—up to four days—between rival teams are to the limited matches what a gourmet meal is to a burger.

Many county cricket grounds have beautiful settings, but perhaps the peachiest of the lot is the ground of the **Worcestershire County Cricket Club** *(New Road, Worcester, box office tel 01905-337921, www.wccc.co.uk, $$$$–$$$$$),* lapped by a big curve of the River Severn, lined with trees and overlooked by the graceful bulk of Worcester's ancient cathedral. Settle down there on a summer's afternoon with a cup of tea or a pint of beer, listening to the distant shouts of the players and the click of willow bat on leather ball. No matter if you don't know your googly from your silly mid-off . . . this is pure lazy midsummer magic. If you can't make it in summer, don't worry: The cricket season runs spring through fall.

---

were used to rebuild and beautify the church.

From this era dates the huge east window of 1352, showing the Coronation of the Virgin Mary and the coats of arms of nobles who had fought at the great defeat of the French at the Battle of Crécy in 1346. Measuring 80 feet by 38 feet, this is an enormous area of medieval stained glass. The Great Cloister was beautifully fan vaulted between 1370 and 1410. It provided a suitably Gothic setting for several scenes in the first of the *Harry Potter* films.

Outside in College Court is the crooked little house, now a museum, that featured in Beatrix Potter's (1866–1943) *Tailor of Gloucester.* Down at the docks in Llanthony Warehouse is a big collection of boats in the **National Waterways Museum** *(tel 01452-318200).* Off the A38/B4213, 8 miles north of Gloucester, is the

beautiful Saxon church at **Deerhurst.** Two miles on, **Tewkesbury** *(visitor information, 100 Church St., tel 01684-855040)* has one of Britain's finest abbey churches and some extravagant woodcarving on its medieval houses.

Hereford

Northwest of Gloucester stands Hereford and its cathedral. **Hereford Cathedral** is a marvelous Romanesque building of pink-gray sandstone, full of memorably decorated tombs such as those of the fully armored Sir Peter de Grandison (1358) and St. Thomas of Hereford (1320) with his guard-of-honor of sorrowing Knights Templar.

Attached to the 15th-century Southwest Cloister, the **New Library Building** (1996) houses the Mappa Mundi, or map of the world. Drawn in 1289 by Richard of Haldingham, who jammed in

Hereford
 177 A2
Visitor Information
✉ 1 King St.
☎ 01432-268430
🕐 Closed Sun. Oct.–Easter

Hereford Cathedral
✉ Cathedral Close
☎ 01432-374200
🕐 Mappa Mundi & Chained Library exhibition closed Sun. Oct.–Easter
💲 Cathedral donation, exhibition $$

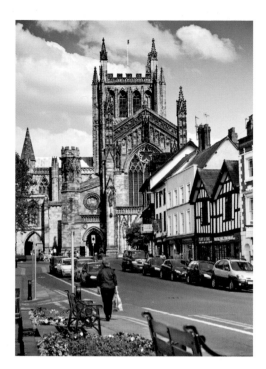

Hereford's imposing cathedral dates from the 12th century.

English king lies buried here, too—King John, whose final resting place in 1216, at his own command, was between the two saints Wulstan and Oswald.

A big Norman crypt of 1084 underlies the church. There is also a superb ten-sided chapter house of about 1120 and a 14th-century 200-foot-tall tower. The cathedral shows many traces of its restoration in Victorian times at the hands of George Gilbert Scott (1811–1878), notably the black-and-white marble nave floor and stained glass.

In town, the **Royal Worcester Porcelain Company** (Severn St., tel 01905-746000) has produced beautiful china since 1751. The on-site **Worcester Porcelain Museum** (tel 01905-21247) welcomes visitors.

INSIDER TIP:

You can see a fragment of Worcester's long-gone 12th-century city wall from City Walls Road.

—CAROLINE HICKEY
Editor, National Geographic Books

Worcester

⚠ 177 B3

Visitor Information

✉ Guildhall, High St.

☎ 01905-726311

Worcester Cathedral

✉ College Green

☎ 01905-732900

🕐 Tower, call for hours

💲 Donation

every known fact or fantasy about the medieval world, it presents a vivid and moving glimpse into the educated medieval mind. In the same building is the finest **Chained Library** in Britain—1,500 books chained to their original 17th-century book presses, full of exquisitely decorated Dark Ages and medieval monkish work.

Worcester

Worcester, to the northeast, possesses the third of these fine churches. **Worcester Cathedral** occupies a splendid position, with its great east window overlooking the county cricket ground (see sidebar p. 179) and the looping River Severn. An

Southwest of Worcester are the **Malvern Hills** (visitor information, 21 Church St., Malvern, tel 01684-892289), a 9-mile succession of ridges and peaks of ancient granite with a high-level footpath running their length. You can see seven counties and the three cathedrals from the 1,394-foot summit of Worcestershire Beacon. ∎

Two Cotswolds Drives

The Cotswold Hills, with their gently rounded pastures and hanging beech and oak woods, their secret little valleys, and, above all, their small towns, villages, churches, and field walls made of silvery limestone, are quintessential rural England. These two drives, both based on Cheltenham, show off the region's chief attractions.

Cheltenham *(visitor information, 77 Promenade, tel 01242-522878)* has been a spa town since the early 18th century and contains some of Britain's best Regency architecture. From the green-roofed Rotunda and the extravagantly curlicued wrought-iron trellises and balconies of **Montpellier,** descend to the town's broad central Promenade, lined with flower beds, trees, a splendid Neptune fountain, and a parade of exclusive stores. The domed **Pittville Pump Room** (1825–1830) in Pittville Park, built for balls, galas, and social intercourse, and now a museum *(tel 01242-523852, closed Tues.),* still contains its fountain of mineral-rich spa water. The Cheltenham Gold Cup (see sidebar this page), one of Britain's premier horse races, is held each March at the Prestbury Park racecourse, east of the town. A large and lively Irish contingent usually attends.

NOT TO BE MISSED:

Cheltenham • Chedworth Roman Villa • Chipping Campden • Sudeley Castle

South Cotswolds

From **Cheltenham ❶**, take the A46 south to **Painswick ❷** *(visitor information, Library, Stroud Rd., tel 01452-813552),* a pretty ridge-top village with a celebrated churchyard containing 99 yew trees and many ornate 18th-century table tombs.

Continue to **Stroud** *(visitor information, Subscription Rooms, George St., tel 01453-760960),* where huge old textile mills line the wooded Golden Valley. The A46 continues south, up over the Cotswolds with wide views all around.

EXPERIENCE: Attend the Cheltenham Gold Cup

Horse racing is big news and big business in Britain. There are famous horse-racing festivals held up and down the country and throughout the year. Three of the best known are the Grand National at Aintree, Liverpool, in early April; the Derby at Epsom in early June; and the Royal Ascot (celebrated for outrageous hats), also in June. But the **Cheltenham Festival** *(Prestbury Park, Cheltenham, box office tel 08445-793003, www.cheltenham festival.net, $$$$$),* held in March, is something unique. And not just because the Cheltenham Gold Cup, the culmination of the four-day festival, is for many

people the most prestigious horse race in the world.

A lot of the festival's exuberance and buzz is due to a strong Irish flavor. The festival usually coincides with St. Patrick's weekend (nearest to St. Patrick's Day, March 17, the Irish national holiday), and huge contingents of Irish punters invariably turn up in Cheltenham in search of the fabled "craic"—fun, laughter, loud chatter, drink, dancing, leg-pulling, betting, and all sorts of celebration. If you have any feeling for our long-faced four-legged friends, or for fun and games in general, this festival is for you.

A left turn 4 miles south of Nailsworth leads to the 600-acre **Westonbirt Arboretum** ③ (*3 miles S of Tetbury, tel 01666-880220*), one of the world's largest collections of trees, glorious in autumn with blazing maples and other delights.

From the arboretum turn left onto the A433, then right through Shipton Moyne

to **Malmesbury** ④ (*visitor information, Town Hall, Market Ln., tel 01666-823748*). The town is built on several levels high above the Avon. Its Norman abbey has a wonderfully carved south porch and a stained-glass window depicting Elmer the Monk, who tried to fly from the tower in 1005 (he broke both legs). Follow

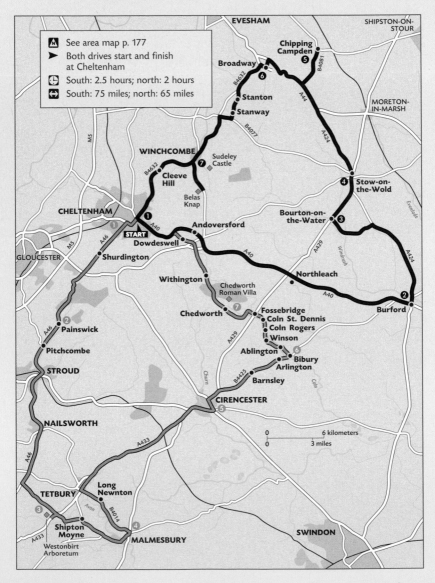

See area map p. 177

Both drives start and finish at Cheltenham

South: 2.5 hours; north: 2 hours

South: 75 miles; north: 65 miles

the B4014, which leads northwest to **Tetbury** *(visitor information, 33 Church St., tel 01666-503552),* another charming small town with a Georgian church.

From Tetbury, follow the A433 northeast for 10 miles to **Cirencester** ❺ *(visitor information, Corn Hall, Market Pl., tel 01285-654180),* capital of the south Cotswolds. The late medieval parish church of St. John the Baptist, built of golden stone, has a beautiful fan-vaulted south porch. The **Corinium Museum** *(tel 01285-655611, closed Nov.–March)* on Park Street contains Roman mosaics unearthed nearby.

The B4425 goes northeast to **Bibury** ❻, where you can see charming Arlington Row with its 17th-century weavers' cottages, then take the pretty Coln Valley minor road north-west to cross the A429 and reach the superbly preserved **Chedworth Roman Villa** ❼ *(Yanworth, tel 01242-890256, www.nationaltrust.org.uk, closed Nov.–Feb. & Mon.–Tues. March–Oct.).*

Continue northwest through Withington to Dowdeswell. Pick up the A40 here and turn left to reach Cheltenham.

Drystone walls are a quintessential feature of the Cotswolds landscape.

North Cotswolds

From **Cheltenham** ❶, head east on the A40 to **Burford** ❷ *(visitor information, The Brewery, Sheep St., tel 01993-823558),* a delightful, small stone-built town with a strong Georgian feel, then take the A424 toward Stow-on-the-Wold. After 6 miles turn left to **Bourton-on-the-Water** ❸ *(visitor information, Victoria St., tel 01451-820211),* the "Venice of the Cotswolds," with its tiny footbridges spanning the River Windrush.

The A429 leads north to **Stow-on-the-Wold** ❹ *(visitor information, Hollis House, The Square, tel 01451-831082),* high and windswept, with its huge marketplace where sheep are still sold. From here the A424 runs northwest toward Broadway; after 8 miles turn right onto the B4081 to **Chipping Campden** ❺, the Cotswolds' best-preserved town. In the 15th-century Church of St. James, a splendid Doomsday painting broods over the chancel arch. See

the Woolstaplers' Hall, where medieval experts assessed the quality of fleeces.

South of elegant **Broadway** ❻ *(visitor information, 1 Cotswold Ct., tel 01386-852937, closed Jan. & Sun. early March–Oct.)* lie **Stanton** and **Stanway,** two lovely Tudor/Jacobean villages.

In **Winchcombe** *(visitor information, Town Hall, High St., tel 01242-602925, closed Mon.–Fri. Nov.–March),* 4 miles south, fabulously grotesque 15th-century gargoyles surround the church where Saxon carvings from the former Benedictine abbey are preserved.

From here, walk a mile up the well-marked **Cotswold Way** trail to **Sudeley Castle** ❼ *(tel 01242-602308, closed Fri.–Sat. Mar–mid-April & Sept.–mid-Oct. & Nov.–Feb.),* with its Elizabethan knot garden and fine paintings; then on to **Belas Knap,** a gigantic neolithic, 5,000-year-old chambered cairn. Return to Winchcombe, and descend into Cheltenham.

Stratford-upon-Avon & Warwick Castle

Stratford-upon-Avon, on the River Avon, is England's premier cultural visitor destination outside London, thanks to the genius of celebrated playwright/poet William Shakespeare, born here in 1564. Warwick Castle, one of Britain's finest stately homes, stands just 7 miles northeast.

Classic black-and-white half-timbered Tudor buildings make up Stratford-upon-Avon's historic core.

Stratford-upon-Avon

⚑ 177 C3

Visitor Information

✉ 62 Henley St.

☎ 01789-264293

Stratford-upon-Avon

The town is best avoided on summer holiday weekends. To get the most out of a visit, focus on a few sites and take time to enjoy them. Luckily, the center of the town, where the chief locations stand close together, is small enough to stroll around in a couple of hours.

Family Homes: Shakespeare's Birthplace on Henley Street is where the Bard (see pp. 188–189) was born. A Tudor half-timbered building, the birthplace was for many years divided into two houses, but is now one. In 1847, after years of use as a pub, the building was bought for the nation, reconstructed, and refurbished. The room styled the "birthroom" may not be the one in which William was born; it was selected extempore by actor David Garrick in 1769. Names of famous people connected with the literary and theatrical

worlds—Thomas Carlyle, Henry Irving, Isaac Watts, Ellen Terry, Walter Scott—can be seen scratched into the glass of the window. Outside, the gardens are filled with flowers, herbs, and trees mentioned in various works of Shakespeare.

At the foot of Henley Street make a right turn onto High Street. Here on the corner stands **Judith Shakespeare's House** (once Stratford's town prison, long before William was born), where his daughter Judith lived; it is now a shop and tearoom.

Outside the Town Hall is a fine statue of Shakespeare, donated to the town in 1769 by Garrick, who was instrumental in reviving interest in the national playwright.

Also on High Street is **Harvard House** (closed at time of writing; call 01789-204016 for information), a timber-framed house of 1596, where John Harvard's mother was born. Harvard, an early settler in America, bequeathed his estate in 1638 to what later became known as Harvard University. In 1909 the house's then owner, novelist Marie Corelli, presented the house to the university.

High Street becomes Chapel Street, where **Nash's House** (tel 01789-204016), now a museum of local history, stands on the site of New Place, to which Shakespeare retired in 1610 and where he died in 1616. There is an Elizabethan-style knot garden with low-trimmed box hedges where New Place itself stood; it was demolished in 1759 on the orders of its owner, the Reverend Francis

Gatrell, who had had enough of uninvited Shakespeare devotees, inspired by Garrick's enthusiasm, knocking on his door.

Other Landmarks: Farther along, where Chapel Street turns into Church Street, is **King Edward VI Grammar School.** Shakespeare may have studied here as a boy, in the timber-roofed room above the **Guildhall.**

On the chancel wall of the adjacent **Guild Chapel,** which dates from the 13th to 15th centuries, is a threatening Doomsday scene, painted over shortly before Shakespeare was born.

INSIDER TIP:

In Stratford, rent a boat and row the River Avon, where other boaters pass by and weeping willows dip into the water.

—ERIN MONRONEY
National Geographic contributor

Church Street bears left into Old Town, where stands **Hall's Croft** (tel 01789-204016) with its oversailing upper story. Shakespeare's daughter Susanna lived here with her doctor husband, John Hall; the house contains an exhibition on the medical practices of his era.

At the bottom of Old Town is the golden-gray **Holy Trinity Church** (Trinity St., tel 01789-266316), above the River Avon.

Shakespeare's Birthplace
✉ Henley St.
☎ 01789-204016
💲 $$$
www.shakespeare.org.uk

Royal Shakespeare Theatre

✉ Waterside, Stratford-upon-Avon

☎ 01789-403409/403437. Recorded information: 01789-403404

www.rsc.org.uk

Inside the altar rail lies the body of Shakespeare, flanked by his wife, daughter, and son-in-law. You can obtain a copy of the parish register entries of his birth and death and admire the 19th-century stained-glass window that depicts the Seven Ages of Man from *As You Like It*.

From the church a riverside footpath leads back to the red bulk of the **Royal Shakespeare Theatre,** opened in 1932, where the Royal Shakespeare Company performs the Bard's plays. Turn left on the bridge beyond the theater to get back to Stratford's center.

Warwick's grim external appearance belies its lavish interior.

Warwick Castle

Warwick is 7 miles northeast of Stratford-upon-Avon, just beyond the point where the northern Cotswolds run down into the fertile Vale of Evesham and the great plains of the central Midlands. This was one of the natural gateways between northern and southern England. In 1068, only two years after invading Britain, the Normans began building a castle here—the remains of which still stand on the landscaped hillock called the Mound.

In 1264, during the Barons' Rebellion against Henry III, the rebels' leader Simon de Montfort captured and destroyed the Norman castle. Between 1350 and 1501 it was largely rebuilt, much as it stands today. The great ramparted outer walls and gray turrets of Warwick Castle dominate a curve of the River Avon, reflecting the power and consequence of the incumbent Earls of Warwick.

Crown Property: After the end of the Wars of the Roses the castle was appropriated by the Crown and spent more than a century as the property of the sovereign, until in 1604 the newly enthroned James I gave it to Sir Fulke Greville, one of his allies. Greville, a great friend of Sir Philip Sidney, met a bizarre end in 1628; he was murdered by a servant who thought he had been cut out of his master's will. The murder victim allegedly still walks the castle's Watergate Ghost Tower.

With the final ebbing away of the military power of the nobility, the Earls of Warwick turned their attention over the next 200 years to creating a residence that would reflect their social standing. The Great Hall was remodeled, State Rooms were paneled and furnished with Adam fireplaces and Old Master paintings, and the grounds were landscaped—most strikingly in 1750 by Capability Brown himself. Much of the castle had to be refurbished after a fire in 1871.

INSIDER TIP:

For a good scare, visit Warwick's Castle Dungeon attraction. The waxwork and live-action tableaus are truly ghoulish.

—JANE SUNDERLAND
National Geographic contributor

Today's Attractions: The castle's aspect of a classically grim medieval fortress makes it one of Britain's most popular visitor attractions and one of the country's finest stately homes. It was taken over in 1978 by the Tussaud Group, which introduced some top-quality waxwork tableaus.

The enormous **gatehouse,** built in the 1350s, has its original portcullis and cleverly concealed murder holes.

The castle's **Armory** is lined with complete sets and individual pieces of historic armor, including

---

Warwick the Kingmaker

The most influential of all the Earls of Warwick was Richard Neville, "Warwick the Kingmaker," whose machinations during the Wars of the Roses engineered Edward IV's deposition of Henry VI in 1461.

Then the Kingmaker, having fallen out with the king he had installed, changed camps and oversaw the brief and doomed return of Henry in 1470, before being killed at the Battle of Barnet the following year when Edward staged his own successful comeback.

---

the severe peaked helmet of Oliver Cromwell, complete with cheek and neck guards. There are more suits of armor and weapons on display in the **Great Hall,** with its red-and-white marble tiled floor.

Outside, the grounds are split up into various types of gardens, including the famous and beautiful **Victorian Rose Gardens.** Rather more dramatic is the 60-foot-tall replica trebuchet or medieval siege catapult, operated daily—in trials, it broke the world record by throwing a 29-pound ball a distance of 817 feet at a fantastic speed of 160 miles an hour.

On some summer weekends there may be jousting tournaments; these are always hugely popular and draw big crowds. ■

Warwick Castle

- 177 C3
- Castle Hill, Warwick
- 01926-495421 / 406600
- $$$$, extra for Castle Dungeon

**www.warwick-castle
.co.uk**

William Shakespeare

There was nothing particularly special about the family into which history's most richly talented wordsmith was born. William Shakespeare's father, John Shakespeare, married somewhat above himself; he was the son of a humble yeoman from the village of Snitterfield, not far from Stratford-upon-Avon, and the playwright's mother, Mary Arden, was the daughter of a well-to-do gentleman farmer at Wilmcote.

Shakespeare and his wife, Anne, lived for five years in the house where he was born.

On her father's death in 1556, Mary found herself well provided for, with a good house and land. Within a year John Shakespeare had married her and embarked on a steady livelihood as a glover and wool merchant, and a climb up the social ladder that would eventually make him a prosperous, middle-class alderman and high bailiff of Stratford.

William was the third of eight children born to the couple. His actual birth date is unknown, but since he was baptized (as Gulielmus Shakspere) on April 26, 1564, it has become customary to celebrate his birthday on April 23,

feast day of St. George, England's patron saint; it is also the date on which he died, in 1616. Almost nothing is known of William's childhood, although it is assumed that he attended the grammar school on Church Street, and that he was bitten by the stage bug through seeing performances of plays by one of the traveling acting companies.

A Prolific Writer

In 1582, at the age of 18, Shakespeare married Anne Hathaway, daughter of a yeoman farmer who lived at Shottery, a mile away from Stratford. The couple had a son and two daughters. Sometime between 1585 and 1592 William Shakespeare left Stratford (possibly with a troupe of strolling players) to make his way in London as an actor, director, manager, and playwright. He made quick progress; by 1597 he was joint owner of the Globe Theatre (see p. 89) on the south bank of the Thames, in the seedy but vibrant red-light district of Southwark. Six years later, already well known and underwritten by patronage, Shakespeare himself became patron of the royal theater troupe, the King's Men.

INSIDER TIP:

Buy a Great British Heritage Pass for free entry to more than 400 of Great Britain's popular heritage sites. It saves a lot of money in the long run and waiting in long lines.

—ALISON WRIGHT
National Geographic photographer

Meanwhile, the plays poured out of him, 37 in all, from *Love's Labour's Lost* (about 1590) to *Henry VIII* (about 1611)—poems, too, from scores of pungent and brilliant sonnets to a handful of rambling historico-classical epics written to please patrons.

By 1610, Shakespeare had had enough. He sold his share in the Globe Theatre and moved back to Stratford-upon-Avon, where he died six years later. At this time his reputation had probably not spread far beyond the world of the theater, and it was not until 1623 that his collected plays were published in a folio edition. For more than a century after that there was little general appetite for Shakespeare, until in the mid-18th century actor David Garrick spearheaded a revival of interest in the life and work of the finest playwright the world has ever seen.

John Taylor's 1610 portrait of Shakespeare

Other Shakespeare Sites

Mary Arden's House *(tel 01789-293455)*, at Wilmcote, off the A3400, 4 miles north of Stratford, is the Tudor farmhouse where Shakespeare's mother was born. Displays of country crafts and pursuits, inside and out, make up the Shakespeare Country Museum.

Anne Hathaway's Cottage *(tel 01789-292100)*, in the hamlet of Shottery on the northwestern outskirts of town, is a thatched farmhouse of some size, timber-framed and brick-built, whose low-ceilinged rooms are filled with Tudor furniture. The lovely garden outside is planted with a representative of each species of tree mentioned in the works of Shakespeare.

Off the B4086, 4 miles east of Stratford, is **Charlecote Park** *(tel 01789-470277, www.nationaltrust.org.uk, see website for hours)*, an Elizabethan mansion in whose park—tradition says—Shakespeare was caught in his youth poaching deer by Sir Thomas Lucy, the owner, and flogged. Shakespeare took revenge by circulating some rude doggerel about Sir Thomas, and fled to London to escape the landlord's wrath. The fact that Charlecote did not have a deer park in Tudor times has not diminished this story's popularity.

Cities of the South Midlands

Ask most Britons to name the attractions of the three neighboring cities of Birmingham, Coventry, and Leicester, and you'll get a blank stare. "Ugly" and "boring" are the adjectives you are most likely to hear in relation to these former powerhouses of Midlands industry. But times have changed, and it would be a pity to miss out on their lively, multicultural buzz.

Birmingham

▲ 177 B3

Visitor Information

✉ The Rotunda, 150 New St.

☎ 0121-205 5115

Coventry

▲ 177 C3

Visitor Information

✉ Cathedral Ruins, Priory St.

☎ 024-7622 5616

Leicester

▲ 177 C3

Visitor Information

✉ 7–9 Every St., Town Hall Sq.

☎ 01162-998888

Birmingham

Birmingham is loud, energetic, brazen, and enormous fun. The gay quarter, south of New Street Station, stays sharp and trendy till the early hours. Farther south is the "Balti Triangle" (see sidebar below) with excellent, inexpensive Asian restaurants—bring your own drink. Nearby Cannon Hill Park is a green, leafy oasis.

Around **Centenary Square** in the city center, skyscrapers dwarf the Georgian humpbacked bridges and clustered canal boats of **Gas Street Basin.** (Birmingham has more canals than Venice.) On Curzon Street you'll find **Thinktank** (tel 0121-202 2222), a museum celebrating the city's great industrial heritage. The superb **Birmingham Museum and Art Gallery** (tel 0121-303 2834) on Chamberlain Square is rich in pre-Raphaelite art.

Coventry

East of Birmingham is Coventry, horrifically bombed in 1940. The shell of the medieval cathedral, burned out in the raid, stands next to **Coventry Cathedral** (tel 024-7652 1200), Britain's most remarkable postwar church, designed by Sir Basil Spence. Take note of Sir Jacob Epstein's sculpture "St. Michael Subduing the Devil" and the giant west wall of glass etched with angelic figures. Benjamin Britten composed his War Requiem for the dedication of the church on May 30, 1962.

Leicester

Leicester, 17 miles northeast of Coventry, has a very successful and distinctive Asian community. Visit the Sikh temple and **Guru Nanak Sikh Museum** (tel 0116-262 8606, open Thurs. p.m.) in the Holy Bones area, and the intricately decorated **Jain Temple** on Oxford Street; stroll down Belgrave Road to shop for filigree jewelry, silks, and Indian cooking ingredients and to eat in one of the restaurants. ■

EXPERIENCE: Eat at a Balti Triangle Curry House

The balti, a most delicious style of thick spicy Indian curry cooked and served in a cast-iron bowl, has its British stronghold in the "Balti Triangle," an area of more than 50 curry houses centered on the Balsall Heath, Sparkbrook, and Sparkhill neighborhoods to the south of Birmingham's city center. Go there to appreciate fine British-Asian cooking—you've plenty of choices. Stroll around looking at the various traditional curry houses, or plan ahead by looking at the restaurant guide found online at www.baltitriangle.com.

Oxford & Around

Oxford is all about ambience: a mellow, beautiful mixture of medieval architecture, church spires rising above ancient centers of learning, neat lawns and gardens surrounded by arcaded or gabled quadrangles, and always in the background the sight or sound of a river. Matthew Arnold's "sweet city with her dreaming spires"—though surrounded by all the drab ordinariness of highways and housing developments—still lives on at the heart of Oxford.

Much of Oxford University is made up of colleges formed around a series of interlinked quadrangles.

Of course, if it were not for **Oxford University** (see pp. 192–194), the "sweet city" would be nothing. This, Britain's oldest seat of learning, was probably already a monastic center of education before 1167, when English scholars ejected from the university at Paris settled here under the protection of a royal residence of Henry II.

The first colleges were founded by religious organizations during the following centuries. They were laid out to a monastic pattern: A chapel and a refectory or dining hall forming part of a quadrangle, with the graduates' rooms around

it like monks' cells. Undergraduate students lived out in hostels or lodgings until Tudor times.

These medieval students were far from monkish. Their drunkenness, rowdiness, and frequent runins with locals became a byword. But their collective influence was remarkable, with a very high proportion of the most powerful positions in the Church, the City of London, politics, the judiciary, and intellectual life filled by Oxford (and Cambridge) graduates. Much the same situation holds true today, though an "Oxbridge" degree is no longer the meal ticket and social imprimatur that it was.

Oxford

🅰 177 C2

Visitor Information

✉ 15–16 Broad St.

☎ 01865-252200

🕐 Closed Sun. in winter

A Walking Tour of Oxford

In all Europe there is nothing comparable to the richness of Oxford's concentration of religio-academic architecture. This walk lets you taste the cream of it. It can be done at a leisurely pace in a single day, but you might prefer to take a couple of days and divide it up into two sections, one south and the other north of High Street, known as the High.

Set between Turl and Cornmarket Streets, the Oxford Covered Market is a Victorian-era building.

South of the High

Carfax is the center of Oxford, the point where the four main roads meet. From the top of **Carfax Tower** ❶ *(tel 01865-792653)*, a remnant of the 14th-century Church of St. Martin, there is a superb panoramic view over the whole university and central city.

From Carfax, walk south down St. Aldate's past the Victorian **Town Hall** housing the **Museum of Oxford** *(tel 01865-252761)*, a good overview of the city's history from Roman times.

Continue past **Christ Church College** ❷ *(tel 01865-276492/276150)*, otherwise known as "the House," founded in 1525 by Cardinal Wolsey. The college chapel is Oxford's city cathedral, a Saxon foundation with a Norman nave and choir and 15th-century vaulting. The

NOT TO BE MISSED:

Botanic Garden • Sheldonian Theatre • Ashmolean Museum

main quadrangle is the arcaded **Tom Quad.** One of its gateways is Sir Christopher Wren's Tom Tower, from which the Great Tom bell still rings evening curfew for Christ Church undergraduates at 9:05 p.m.—although they ignore it these days.

Turn left along Broad Walk beside Christ Church Meadow to reach the River Cherwell. Bear left up Rose Lane to the High (main street). Turn right here for the **University Botanic Garden** ❸ *(tel 01865-286690)*, founded in 1621. It was the first garden in Britain dedicated to the scientific study of plants and is always beautiful with its herbaceous borders, Jacobean formal flower beds, and big greenhouses.

Via Magdalen & Merton

Beyond the garden is **Magdalen Bridge** ❹, where you can rent punts (boats) in summer, and across the road is **Magdalen College** *(tel 01865-276000),* pronounced MAUD-lin, founded in 1458 and rich in grotesque gargoyles. The choir here sings a hymn from the top of the Tudor bell tower at dawn on May Day.

Return up the High past Rose Lane, and turn left along cobbled Merton Street past **Merton College** *(tel 01865-276310),* founded in 1264 by the lord chancellor of England. Within is the 14th-century **Mob Quad,** which contains the oldest library in England still in use: It holds, among other treasures, Geoffrey Chaucer's own astrolabe (star-measurer).

From here bear right onto Oriel Square, then left past Oriel College along Bear Lane; take the first right to reach the High. Turn left if you want to return to Carfax.

North of the High

To continue the walk, turn right along the High, passing on the left the medieval **Church of St. Mary the Virgin,** the official church of the university. Continue past **University College** ❺ *(tel 01865-276602),* from which the poet Percy Bysshe Shelley (1792–1822) was rusticated (sent home) in 1811 for subversive pamphleteering. U.S. President Bill Clinton was a Rhodes scholar

🅜	See area map p. 177
➤	Carfax
🕒	6 hours
↔	2.5 miles
➤	Carfax

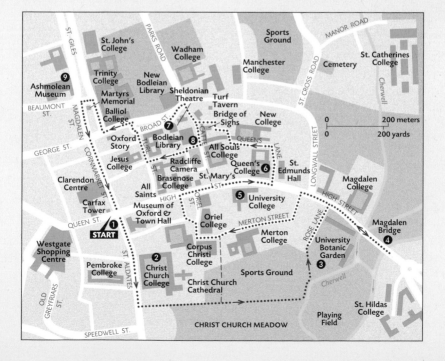

here. Now turn left up Queen's Lane, looking up to enjoy the extravagant stone gargoyles, with **Queen's College** ❻ *(tel 01865-279120)* on your left (mostly Nicholas Hawksmoor's work, though Sir Christopher Wren designed the chapel), and on along New College Lane with **New College** *(tel 01865-279500)* on your right. Founded in 1379 by the Bishop of Winchester to turn out educated priests after their numbers

INSIDER TIP:

The small, atmospheric Turf Tavern (4–5 Bath Pl.), popular with students and dons, is a great place to get a pint.

—PAT DANIELS
National Geographic contributor

had been decimated by the Black Death, the college has a beautiful quadrangle and gardens, and a chapel with a Nativity by Sir Joshua Reynolds, "St. James" by El Greco, and Sir Jacob Epstein's modern "Lazarus" rising powerfully from the dead.

Pass under the **Bridge of Sighs,** a 20th-century reproduction of Venice's famous bridge, to reach Catte Street. Bear right onto Broad Street, where the curved rear of the **Sheldonian Theatre** ❼ *(tel 01865-277299, closed Sun.)* fills the corner. It was built by Wren in 1669, his first design. Balustraded and green-domed, it is used for degree ceremonies and concerts. The painted ceiling shows Art and Science banishing Ignorance and Jealousy, two chubby miscreants looking suitably downcast.

Return south on Catte Street to reach **All Souls College** *(tel 01865-279379),* founded by Henry VI in 1438 to commemorate the dead of the Battle of Agincourt. There are no undergraduates here, only fellows. Opposite All Souls, cross the street to walk between the Bodleian Library and the Radcliffe Camera.

The **Bodleian Library** ❽ *(Broad St., tel 01865-277216, closed Sat. p.m. & Sun.)* receives a copy of every book published in the U.K. Rarities among its eight million books and manuscripts are on display in the fan-vaulted, 15th-century Divinity School—the university's oldest lecture room. The **Radcliffe Camera** *(closed to the public),* just across the way, was built between 1737 and 1749: An eccentric circular building, Italianate in spirit, domed and port-holed, it is used as a university reading room.

Trinity to the Ashmolean

Keep straight on Brasenose Lane, and turn right onto Turl Street. **Trinity College** *(tel 01865-279900)* sits opposite at the junction with Broad Street. Founded in 1555, Trinity has Grinling Gibbons carvings in its chapel and a beautiful Lime Walk in its gardens.

Turn left along Broad Street, then go north on Magdalen Street, with **Balliol College** *(tel 01865-277777)* on your right; it was founded in the 13th century by a Scotsman, John Balliol, as penance for insulting the Bishop of Durham.

Where the street broadens into St. Giles, pass the **Martyrs' Memorial,** designed in 1843 by Sir George Gilbert Scott to honor the Reformation martyrdoms of the Protestant bishops Latimer, Ridley, and Cranmer.

Beyond the memorial is the splendid **Ashmolean Museum** ❾ *(Beaumont St., tel 01865-553823, closed Sun. a.m. & Mon.),* Britain's oldest museum and art gallery (founded 1683), with eclectic contents from the collection of explorer John Tradescant (1570–ca 1638). Here are Michelangelo's "Crucifixion" and King Alfred's ninth-century jewel, Egyptian mummies and Turner landscapes, Guy Fawkes's conspiracy lantern and Oliver Cromwell's death mask.

Reel back along Magdalen Street and Cornmarket Street to return to Carfax.

NOTE: Some of the colleges may charge entrance fees, and any of them may be closed to the public at any time—particularly in term time and in May and June during undergraduate examinations.

Around Oxford

Thames riverside footpaths offer beautiful walks on both sides of Oxford. A particularly enjoyable upstream walk starts on the western edge of the city at the black-beamed old Trout Inn by Godstow Bridge. You can then follow the river from the pale stone ruin of Godstow Nunnery up to the graceful old toll bridge at Swinford, and on to the Ferryman Inn at Bablockhythe.

South from Oxford, downstream along the Thames, there is a whole string of attractive and interesting little places to explore. **Sutton Courtenay** is a typical English village around a green; writer Eric Arthur Blair (pseudonym George Orwell, 1903–1950) is buried in its churchyard.

Ewelme is another lovely village, where the 15th-century church, school, and almshouses make a highly photogenic group. Jerome K. Jerome (1859–1927), who wrote the ultimate comic novel about boating on the River Thames, *Three Men in a Boat* (1889), is buried here.

Mapledurham House is the big Elizabethan mansion built for the Blount family; also in the village is another waterside grouping of lock, mill, and weir, which inspired Ernest Shepherd while he was composing his illustrations for Kenneth Grahame's 1908 children's classic, *The Wind in the Willows*. Grahame himself, born in 1859, lived in Church Cottage at **Pangbourne,** just upriver from Mapledurham, from 1924 until his death in 1932.

Berkshire Downs: Some 20 miles southwest of Oxford lies **Lambourn,** a famous racehorse-training center on the Berkshire Downs. From here take either the B4000 Ashbury or the B4001 Childrey road to bisect the course of the ancient **Ridgeway** track along the crest of the Downs.

On the Ridgeway, between the two crossing points, lies the famous **White Horse,** its outline cut into the chalk in the Bronze Age, and the vast Neolithic burial chamber of **Wayland's Smithy.**

Blenheim Palace

At the edge of Woodstock, 8 miles north of Oxford, stands a marvel of baroque architecture, Blenheim Palace, home of the Duke of Marlborough.

When the Royal Manor of Woodstock, which included Woodstock Park, was granted to John Churchill, 1st Duke of Marlborough, in the beginning of

Mapledurham House
- 🅰 177 C1
- ✉ 5 miles NW of Reading, off A4074
- ☎ 0118-972 3350
- 🕐 Closed Oct.– Easter & Mon.– Fri. Easter–Sept.
- 💲 House & mill $$, house only $$, mill only $

www.mapledurham .co.uk

Blenheim Palace, the grandest baroque house in Britain

Blenheim Palace

▲ 177 C2

✉ On the A44 at Woodstock, 8 miles N of Oxford

☎ Recorded information: 0870-849 6500

🕐 Closed (except park) mid-Dec.–mid-Feb. & Mon.–Tues. Nov.–mid-Dec.

💲 $$$, park only $$–$$$ per car or $ per person

Visitor Information

✉ Oxfordshire Museum, Park St., Woodstock

☎ 01993-811456

www.bleinheim palace.com

the 18th century, there were only a few traces left of the old royal hunting lodge, where Henry II and his mistress "Fair Rosamund" Clifford dallied and were discovered by Queen Eleanor. The land at Woodstock was the nation's gift to the Duke, a thanksgiving for leading Queen Anne's troops to victory over the French at the Battle of Blenheim in 1704. Parliament also voted the hero an enormous sum of money—in the end it came to £240,000 ($450,000)—to build himself a palatial mansion that would properly reflect the scale of the nation's gratitude.

As the building of this house gradually progressed—it took almost 20 years, from 1705 until 1724—the project became ever more expensive and troublesome, and Parliament proved reluctant to come up with the necessary funds. The Duke of Marlborough died in 1722, and his widow, Sarah, had to finish off the enormous baroque structure.

Grand Plans: This really is a palace, the only nonroyal one in the country. The designer was Sir John Vanbrugh (1664–1726), essentially a self-taught architect, and he planned on the grandest of scales with the help of Sir Christopher Wren's star pupil, Nicholas Hawksmoor. There are said to be more than 200 rooms in the palace, whose entrance portico is impressively colonnaded. From the central block, wings stretch forward to flank the Great Court. The impression one gets—as was intended—is of viewing a national monument as well as the dwelling of a successful general.

Of the many very splendid rooms, the 183-foot **Long Library** is particularly impressive with its arched ends, richly stuccoed ceiling, and collection of paintings. The **Great Hall**'s painted ceiling shows the Duke of Marlborough explaining his plans for the Battle of Blenheim to Britannia. In other **State Rooms** are elaborate murals by Louis Laguerre and tapestries depicting the duke's military triumphs in his campaigns. His heroic marble monument, sculpted in 1733 by Michael Rysbrack, stands in the **chapel** in the West Wing.

Sir Winston Churchill, a descendant of the 1st Duke of Marlborough, was born in the palace on November 30, 1874—several rooms are given over to a display about him. Churchill died in 1965 and lies buried in the churchyard at **Bladon** on the southern edge of the park. ∎

Blenheim's Landscaping

Near the house are superb rose gardens, a formal Italian garden, and a water terrace garden with sinuous ponds, fountains, and statues. Farther out in the 2,100-acre park, landscaped by Capability Brown between 1764 and 1774, are a beautiful Temple of Diana, a great posthumous Victory Column topped by the duke dressed as a Roman general, and a Grand Bridge with a 100-foot span. Brown planted trees that are now in their full pomp, and he dammed the River Glyme to create a lake on which today's visitors can idle in a rented boat.

EXPERIENCE: Hallaton Bottle Kicking & Other Eccentric Games

Hallaton is a beautiful village, all thatched roofs and golden walls, set in the rolling wolds of Leicestershire, some 15 miles southeast of Leicester. But there's more to Hallaton than meets the uninformed eye. Arrive in the village bright and early on Easter Monday to witness something truly unique: the village's annual ritual Hare Pie Scramble and Bottle Kicking.

A morning procession precedes Hallaton's annual bottle kicking.

In the morning, crowds of people, many in medieval dress, parade to the gates of St. Michael's Church for the ceremonial cutting of a giant hare pie, the gentler half of the day's celebration. Later, the dismembered pie is sent flying into the crowd at the Hare Pie Bank—if you don't like rough play, beer drinking, and large muddy men, stand clear. The crowds then venture to Hare Pie Hill for good views of the coming action.

First the "Master of the Stowe" launches a painted wooden cylinder, or bottle, into the air, then hundreds of men and one or two women hurl themselves on top of it, and battle commences. The rough aim is for Hallaton to score by getting the 12-pound bottle—actually a wooden keg filled with beer—across to their bank of the Medbourne brook through fair means or foul, while the neighboring and rival villagers of Medbourne do their damnedest to force it across to their side. Best of three bottles wins. And that's it. Unlimited numbers can take part, with no time limit and no rules. The participants act as a large, disorganized scrum, moving this way and that way at will.

Everyone ends up plastered with mud, covered with bruises, full of ale and hilarity. Bragging rights and glory are all the victors gain.

There are reasons—myths of origin, rather—for this revelry. Some say that two ladies who'd escaped being tossed by a bull bequeathed a hare pie and plenty of ale to the village annually as a mark of gratitude. Others think it's a very ancient male springtime ritual of fertility and initiation. What's certain is that both Hallaton and Medbourne are immensely proud of their particular show of true British eccentricity, and would rather cease to exist themselves than let it peter out.

They're not the only ones. Consider these other eccentric celebrations, too— some ancient, some modern: **Haxey Hood** Dressing up, scrummaging in the mud, and drinking ale, with a leather tube (the Hood) at the center of the mayhem. Haxey, Lincolnshire (Jan. 6). **Cheese Rolling** A breakneck chase after cheeses rolling down a steep hill. Cooper's Hill, Brockworth, Gloucestershire (May Bank Holiday). *www.cheese-rolling.co.uk*. **World Bog-Snorkelling Championship** Fancy dress swimming in a filthy peat ditch. Waen Rhydd Bog, Llanwrtyd Wells, mid-Wales (August Bank Holiday). *www.green-events.co.uk*.

Northamptonshire

Northamptonshire, a long and narrow county on the eastern edge of the South Midlands, is often overlooked by visitors, perhaps because of the unremarkable character of Northampton as a county town. However, there is plenty to explore here.

The house at the center of the beautiful Althorp estate conceals a Tudor core well worth seeing.

Althorp House
- 🏛 177 C3
- ✉ Off the A428, 6 miles NW of Northampton
- ☎ Recorded information: 01604-770107
- 🕐 Closed Oct.–June
- 💲 $$$–$$$$

www.althorp.com

Oundle
- 🏛 177 D3

Visitor Information
- ✉ 14 West St.
- ☎ 01832-274333

Stoke Bruerne
- 🏛 177 D3

Althorp House

The county's best-known house is undoubtedly the Spencer family's seat of **Althorp,** on whose grounds Diana, Princess of Wales, lies buried on an island in a lake. The house itself, an 18th-century remodeling of a Tudor country house, contains fine furniture and portraits (Van Dyck, Gainsborough, Reynolds).

Oundle

Oundle is a very handsome old town built of pale limestone. The 13th-century **Church of St. Peter** is worth inspection. Its 203-foot spire was climbed in 1880 by a boy from Oundle School; when he reached the ground again his headmaster thrashed him soundly for insubordination, and gave him a golden sovereign for his daring.

A beautiful 3-mile walk by the River Nene starts from the church by way of Market Place, South Road, and Bassett Ford Road. The path loops from south to north to reach pretty Ashton Mill, before returning to town. Beside the Nene just north of Oundle stands the mound of **Fotheringhay Castle,** where Mary, Queen of Scots, was imprisoned and executed.

Stoke Bruerne

Northamptonshire is bisected by the **Grand Union Canal,** connecting London with Birmingham. There is a good walk along the towpath. At Stoke Bruerne the whole community is focused on the canal, its brightly painted narrowboats, shops, and the delightful waterside **Boat Inn** where impromptu singalongs can occur. ∎

A great treasure of beautiful old churches, handsome Elizabethan country houses, and medieval villages, skirted by uncrowded coasts

East Anglia & Lincolnshire

Medieval houses, Saffron Walden

East Anglia & Lincolnshire

East Anglia is another of those nebulous areas of Britain whose exact boundaries remain unfixed. The counties of Suffolk and Norfolk are its heartland; Essex fringes it to the south, Cambridgeshire to the west, Lincolnshire to the north. Its chief characteristic is a lack of dramatic hills, though the East Anglian landscape is not all as flat as its reputation would have you believe.

During the Middle Ages, between the 13th and 15th centuries, East Anglia was the wealthiest and most populous part of Britain, thanks to the quality of its woolen textiles and the skills of Flemish weavers who settled here when religious persecution drove them across the Channel from their own countries.

Since those high days, East Anglia has been out of the mainstream of British commerce and fashion, a region with no main through-roads and (apart from Cambridge) only one significant city, Norwich. Agriculture has been its mainstay: grain grown on heavy clay lands, and vegetables on superb silty coastal soil.

Recently East Anglia has been "discovered" by escapees from city pressures who have moved out from London to live the good life here, attracted by the moderate pace of life.

Hidden Gems

The county of Essex is often overlooked, but its coasts contain hidden marshlands and creeks ideal for bird-watching, while in Saffron Walden and Thaxted in the northwest are some of East Anglia's finest medieval buildings. Suffolk and Norfolk are the real architectural treasure-houses of the region; the medieval wool merchants spent their riches building elaborately carved timber-frame houses and the finest collection of parish churches in Britain, while 16th- and 17th-century landowners built themselves magnificent redbrick mansions.

Cambridgeshire, of course, is famous for the beauty of its great university city. North of Cambridge the countryside smooths out into the dead-flat spaces of Fenland—rich farmland cut by straight watercourses, where church spires and pylons spear into huge skies. Beyond here rise the Lincolnshire Wolds, a limestone upland that stretches north to the old cathedral city of Lincoln. ∎

St. Benets Level wind pump, built, as many others were, to help drain the Norfolk Broads

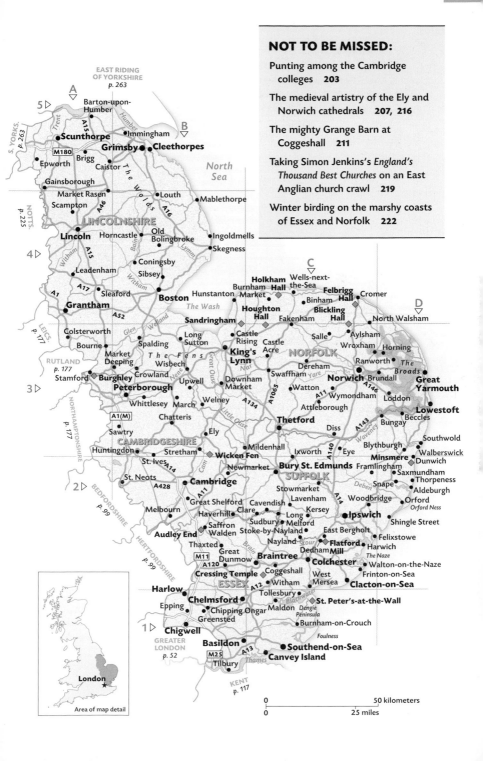

NOT TO BE MISSED:

Punting among the Cambridge colleges **203**

The medieval artistry of the Ely and Norwich cathedrals **207, 216**

The mighty Grange Barn at Coggeshall **211**

Taking Simon Jenkins's *England's Thousand Best Churches* on an East Anglian church crawl **219**

Winter birding on the marshy coasts of Essex and Norfolk **222**

EAST RIDING OF YORKSHIRE
p. 263

S. YORKS. p. 263

Barton-upon-Humber

Scunthorpe Immingham
M180
Grimsby Cleethorpes
Epworth Brigg
Caistor
Gainsborough
Market Rasen
Scampton

North Sea

NOTTS. p. 225

LINCOLNSHIRE

Louth Mablethorpe
Lincoln Horncastle Old Bolingbroke Ingoldmells
Skegness
Coningsby
Leadenham Sibsey
Sleaford

Grantham
A52

LEICS. p. 177

Colsterworth Glen Welland
Bourne
Market Deeping Spalding
Wisbech
RUTLAND p. 177
Stamford Burghley Crowland
Peterborough Upwell

Holkham Wells-next-the-Sea
Burnham Hall Felbrigg Hall Cromer
Hunstanton Market Binham Blickling Hall North Walsham
Houghton Hall Fakenham
Sandringham Castle Rising Castle Acre Salle Aylsham
King's Lynn NORFOLK Wroxham Horning
Swaffham Dereham Ranworth The Broads
Downham Market Watton Norwich Brundall Great Yarmouth
Welney Attleborough Wymondham Loddon
Lowestoft
Thetford Diss Bungay Beccles
Southwold
Blythburgh Walberswick
Mildenhall Ixworth Eye Minsmere Dunwich
Newmarket Bury St. Edmunds Framlingham Saxmundham
Thorpeness
Stowmarket Snape Aldeburgh
Lavenham Woodbridge Orford
Orford Ness

The Wash
The Fens Great Ouse Nar
Nene
A1(M)
Whittlesey March Welney
Chatteris
Sawtry
Huntingdon Stretham Wicken Fen
St. Ives
St. Neots A14
A428 Cambridge
Melbourn

NORTHAMPTONSHIRE p. 177

CAMBRIDGESHIRE

Ely Cam

SUFFOLK Deben

BEDFORDSHIRE p. 99

Great Shelford Cavendish Kersey Ipswich Shingle Street
Haverhill Clare Long Melford East Bergholt Felixstowe
Saffron Walden Sudbury Nayland Flatford Mill Harwich
Thaxted Stoke-by-Nayland Dedham The Naze
Great Dunmow Braintree Colchester Walton-on-the-Naze
Audley End
M11
A120 Cressing Temple Coggeshall West Mersea Frinton-on-Sea
HERTFORDSHIRE p. 99
Harlow ESSEX A12 Witham Clacton-on-Sea
Tollesbury St. Peter's-at-the-Wall
Chelmsford Maldon Dengie Peninsula
Epping Chipping Ongar Burnham-on-Crouch
Greensted
Chigwell Foulness
GREATER LONDON p. 52
Basildon Southend-on-Sea
M25 A13
Tilbury Canvey Island
Thames
KENT p. 117

London
Area of map detail

0   50 kilometers
0   25 miles

Cambridge

Cambridge is just as beautiful as Oxford—some think it more so, because it has not been built up and urbanized in the way that Oxford has. The beauty of Cambridge is of a subtle and dreamy order. There is often a misty thickening of the air here on the borders of Fenland, which softens the towers and pinnacles.

Punting on the River Cam at Cambridge is a timeworn ritual for undergraduates and visitors alike.

History of the University

Cambridge was a flourishing small town and a seat of regional importance, complete with monastic houses and seats of learning along the River Cam hereabouts, when lay scholars arrived from Oxford about 1209. Religious disagreements and a certain amount of trouble between the scholars and the Oxford townsfolk had prompted them to move here and thus found the second oldest university in Britain.

At first the Cambridge scholars—in many cases only in their early teens—lived out in the town, each selecting his own tutor. In 1284 Peterhouse (see p. 206), the oldest and smallest Cambridge college, was founded to bring tutors and pupils together in one community. Dozens of colleges were endowed over the following centuries by academics, religious orders, rich men hoping to pay for a ticket to heaven, and trade unions or guilds. The layout of the Cambridge colleges was the same as at Oxford, with cloisters, dining hall or refectory, chapel, and accommodations laid out around an open square after the general monastic pattern.

Over the years, there were the usual "town-and-gown" confrontations as privilege and poverty

INSIDER TIP:

After a stroll through the Backs, quaff a pint at the Anchor pub in Cambridge while you relax and watch the punts drift on the River Cam.

—PAULA KELLY
National Geographic contributor

lived side by side. When riots broke out in Cambridge during the Peasants' Revolt of 1381 (see pp. 28–29), some of the colleges were plundered and there were several arson attempts. After the dust settled, five locals were hanged for their impudence.

In the 16th century, at the Reformation, the University of Cambridge became one of the hotbeds of Protestant thought. Archbishop Cranmer (Jesus College) and Bishops Latimer (Clare) and Ridley (Pembroke) were all educated here. A century later Oliver Cromwell (Sidney Sussex) became Member of Parliament for Cambridge. The university continued to have a radical edge and has maintained its position as a spearhead of learning and research. In the 20th century, James Watson and Francis Crick discovered the structure of the DNA double helix here, and Ernest Rutherford split the atom in the Cavendish Laboratory. ∎

Cambridge
🅰 201 B2
Visitor Information
✉ Old Library, Wheeler St.
☎ 01223-322640

The Anchor
✉ Silver St.
☎ 01223-353554

EXPERIENCE: Punting Among the Colleges

No one seems quite sure how or why punting became so popular in and around the city of Cambridge. But it is pretty certain that these rectangular, flat-bottomed craft were imported into Cambridge for leisure boating shortly before World War I from the marshy, watery Fen district just to the north, where they were used to transport cut reeds, hay, livestock, and people around the maze of rivers and waterways. Shallow of draft and propelled by pushing a long pole into the riverbed to lever the punt forward, they are simple boats, simply operated, and perfectly suited to the kind of

timeless atmosphere that hangs around the Backs, the green lawns that line the River Cam behind the medieval colleges.

Scudamore's Punting Company *(Mill Ln., tel 01223-359750, www.scudamores .com, $$$$$)* has a fleet of punts for rent by the hour. A quick lesson and you're off along the Backs—or in the opposite direction toward Grantchester Meadows. Be prepared to splash yourself a bit at first, but you'll acquire the art of polemanship quickly enough. Or consult the "Punting Technique" page of their website beforehand and turn up as an "expert."

A Walk Around Cambridge

This walk around the compact center of Cambridge can easily be done in a day, or it can be split into north and south Cambridge, with a day allotted to each to allow thorough exploration of one of the finest assemblies of medieval buildings in Europe. Some colleges now charge admission fees. Any of them may be closed to the public at any time, especially during May/June examinations. Telephone first to avoid disappointment.

A quiet street near Trinity College

North Cambridge

Leave the visitor information center on Wheeler Street and turn right to reach King's Parade. Bear right to find **Great St. Mary's Church ❶** on your right. Climb the tower of this 15th-century church for superb views over the city. Farther along on the left is **Gonville & Caius College** (pronounced KEYS), founded in 1348, with its Gates of Humility, Virtue, and Honour representing stages on the path to academic fulfillment.

NOT TO BE MISSED:

Trinity College • The Backs • King's College Chapel • Queens' College • Fitzwilliam Museum

Trinity to the Round Church

Keep straight on Trinity Street, with **Trinity College ❷** (tel 01223-338400) on your left. It was founded in 1546; witness the statue of Henry VIII over the gateway. He holds a chair leg, substituted for his scepter in the 19th century either by a student prankster or by a college porter tired of replacing the oft-pilfered symbol of sovereignty. Trinity's two courts—Cambridge's equivalents of Oxford's quads—are famous. **Great Court** is the scene of a well-known race in which undergraduates try to run around its perimeter while the clock is striking 12, a scene immortalized in David Putnam's 1981 movie, *Chariots of Fire*. In the other court, **Nevile's Court,** Isaac Newton (1642–1727) calculated the speed of sound by stamping and timing the echo.

Trinity Street becomes St. John's Street, leading to Bridge Street, where the **Round Church (Church of the Holy Sepulchre) ❸**, with its fine Norman doorway, stands at the intersection. Its circular nave was built in imitation of Jerusalem's church of the same name.

Magdalene to St. John's

Bear left along Bridge Street and cross Magdalene Bridge, where punts can be rented, to find the tall brickwork walls and chimneys of **Magdalene College ❹** (tel 01223-332100)

on the right. In Second Court the 17th-century **Pepys Building** contains Samuel Pepys's library, including his famous diary written in his own shorthand. It took 19th-century scholars three years to decode, after which they discovered Pepys's key lying unnoticed among the books.

Retrace your steps down St. John's Street and turn right into **St. John's College** ❺ *(tel 01223-338600)*, a Tudor foundation, through the turreted gateway. This was William

Wordsworth's college (1787–1790). He wrote of Cambridge in *The Prelude*: "Gowns grave or gaudy, doctors, students, streets / Courts, cloisters, flocks of churches, gateways, towers."

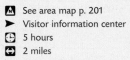

- ▲ See area map p. 201
- ► Visitor information center
- 🕒 5 hours
- ⬌ 2 miles
- ► Visitor information center

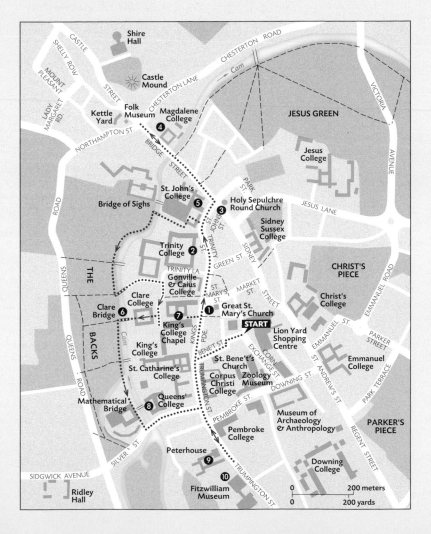

Along the Backs to King's

Walk through St. John's to cross the River Cam by Kitchen Bridge; look downstream to see the **Bridge of Sighs,** a covered bridge, pinnacled and crenellated, built in 1831. Across the Cam, bear left along the **Backs,** Cambridge's famous riverside green spaces.

At Garret Hostel Lane recross the Cam, noting upstream the lovely balustraded **Clare Bridge ❻** of 1639, the oldest bridge in Cambridge.

Continue ahead to turn right along Trinity Lane to the buttresses and turreted white stone walls of **King's College Chapel ❼**, one of the best known churches in the world thanks to its annual radio and television broadcast of the Christmas service of Nine Lessons and Carols. Probably Britain's finest example of perpendicular Gothic architecture, the chapel was begun in 1446 and finished in 1515. The fan-vaulted nave, the vivid Tudor glass, the huge baroque organ, and the Rubens altarpiece all lend grandeur and fascination to this wonderful church.

King's College (tel 01223-331100) faces onto King's Parade, from where you can return to the visitor information center.

INSIDER TIP:

At 5:30 p.m. daily (except Mon.) in King's College Chapel, enjoy the red-cassocked choir's celestial singing at Evensong.

—CHRISTOPHER SOMERVILLE
National Geographic author

South Cambridge

From King's College Chapel return to Trinity Lane, bearing left through the Jacobean courts of **Clare College** (tel 01223-333200) to recross the Cam by Clare Bridge. Turn left and follow the path along the Backs (behind King's College), bearing left along Silver Street down the side of beautiful **Queens' College ❽** (tel 01223-335511),

with wonderful Tudor courts and the half-timbered **President's Lodge.** Recross the river over Silver Street Bridge, from where you can see the **Mathematical Bridge,** built using coach screws in 1749 by James Essex the Younger and rebuilt in 1866 and 1905.

Continue up Silver Street and then turn right onto Trumpington Street. **Peterhouse ❾** (tel 01223-338200), founded in 1284, is on the right, the oldest and smallest college, retaining its 13th-century hall. The poet Thomas Gray, a fellow here in the 1740s, was terrified of fire and had iron bars (still there) fixed to his window to support an escape ladder. Unsympathetic students roused him one night by shouting "Fire!" and watched him drop in his nightshirt into a tub of water they had placed under his window. Mortally offended, Gray quit Peterhouse forthwith.

Back via the Fitzwilliam

Beyond Peterhouse are the granite and marble halls of the **Fitzwilliam Museum ❿** (Trumpington St., tel 01223-332900, closed Mon.), one of Europe's best museums. The Lower Galleries hold a classical collection; the ceramics and English pottery are well known; and there are many illuminated medieval and Dark Ages manuscripts. The Upper Galleries' art collection is breathtaking, from Titian and Hans Hals through English masters to pre-Raphaelites, Impressionists, and 20th-century stars including Modigliani and Picasso.

Return along Trumpington Street, passing **Pembroke College** (tel 01223-338100). Beyond Silver Street is **Corpus Christi College** (tel 01223-338000), on the right. Corpus Christi was founded in 1352 to give gifted men of humble birth the chance of a decent education. On the north side a gallery links the college to St. Bene't's Church, whose Saxon tower is the oldest structure in this ancient town.

Continue along King's Parade, and turn right up Bene't Street to return to the visitor information center.

Ely & Newmarket

North and east of Cambridge stand the towns of Ely and Newmarket, both noteworthy for very different reasons. Ely boasts a crowning achievement in the form of the octagon atop its Norman cathedral, while Newmarket is the British epicenter of horseflesh and horse racing.

Ely Cathedral's jewel-like lantern is supported by a wooden superstructure painted to resemble stone.

Ely

Fifteen miles north of Cambridge, on the edge of the great flat region of Fenland, the small city of Ely stands on a low rise. In 1083 building began on **Ely Cathedral** *(tel 01353-667735)*; it was completed in 1189. In 1322, after the original Norman tower had collapsed, a great octagon of wood weighing 400 tons was raised to a central position over the building, topped off in 1348 with a graceful 62-foot lantern held in place by enormous trunks of oak. This crownlike structure, together with the 217-foot tower at the west end of the church, gives Ely Cathedral an unmistakable and dominant profile in the level landscape.

Inside, the wooden roof of the nave was painted during Queen Victoria's reign with scenes from the Bible. At the east end are two elaborately carved Tudor chantry chapels, and in the roofs of the two transepts the medieval carvers left wonderful bosses—best seen with a pair of binoculars.

Examples of the glass painter's skill, dating back through the

Ely

🅰 201 B3

Visitor Information

✉ Oliver Cromwell's House, 29 St. Mary's St.

☎ 01353-662062

Newmarket

🔺 201 B2

Visitor Information

✉ Palace House, Palace St.

☎ 01638-667200

NOTE: In Newmarket, Musk's sausages are sold at **Eric Tennant Butcher** *(11 The Guineas, Fred Archer Way, tel 01638-661530).* The sausages may also be found in delicatessens and fine food stores around the country.

centuries to 1240, are displayed in the **Stained Glass Museum** *(South Triforium, tel 01353-660347)* in the cathedral.

Newmarket

In the mid-18th century the Jockey Club was founded in Newmarket to regulate the unbridled and dissolute sport of horse racing. Since then, Newmarket has been the very heart of British racing, training, and bloodstock breeding. In the flattish, open country around the town are some 50 stud farms, several dozen training stables ranging from world-famous names with

INSIDER TIP:

On race days, people come to Newmarket to stock up with Musk's sausages. Musk's holds a royal warrant from the Queen.

—ANJALI RAMCHANDANI
National Geographic contributor

hundreds of horses to unknown hopefuls with a handful of also-rans, and nearly 50 miles of gallops on which the horses can be seen exercising year-round.

The trim little town of Newmarket lies 13 miles east of Cambridge off the A45. On High Street, a handsome avenue of Georgian and Victorian buildings, is the **National Horse Racing Museum** *(tel 01638-667333, closed Nov.–Easter),* with many fascinating trophies and racing exhibits.

Nearby is the headquarters of the **Jockey Club** *(visits possible on tours organized by National Horse Racing Museum),* where racing's rules are reviewed and errant jockeys and owners are hauled over the coals.

Along the Avenue, just below the museum, is **Tattersalls** *(www .tattersalls.com, tel 01638-665931, call for dates of sales),* Britain's most famous venue for bloodstock sales. Nearby are the buildings of the **National Stud** *(tel 01638-663464, www.nationalstud.co.uk, closed Nov.–Jan., tours by appt. only).* ∎

Sport of Kings

Newmarket has been a favorite with horse-racing enthusiasts ever since James I stopped on his way through to enjoy a little hare-coursing on the great sandy heaths around the town.

In 1622 the first recorded horse race was run, and within 50 years King James's grandson had made Newmarket one of the most fashionable places in the land.

The Merry Monarch, Charles II, not only shifted his whole court each spring and summer to a palace he had built for himself in Newmarket, he

once risked his own neck riding in the 4-mile Newmarket Town Plate race—and came in first. At night Charles would go adventuring incognito under the name of his favorite stallion, Old Rowley.

Nowadays the sport is influenced by immensely rich Arab owners, but still takes place in much the same way as of old—public days out in summer on the July Course, and a more serious form in spring (e.g., the two Classics, 1,000 and 2,000 Guineas) and fall (the Champion Stakes) on the Rowley Mile nearby.

Saffron Walden & Around

"The best-looking small town in East Anglia" is the boast of Saffron Walden. Around Gold Street, High Street, Church Street, and King Street, the half-timbered, color-washed houses crowd the sidewalks of this beautifully preserved town in the northwest corner of Essex. The town derives its name from the mauve saffron crocus flower that—used in the manufacture of yellow dye—gave the town its prosperity from the late Tudor times onward.

Saffron Walden is one of Essex's most appealing small towns, its streets lined with medieval buildings.

The visitor information center has an excellent Town Trail leaflet (downloadable from the website) and sells bulbs of the mauve saffron crocus flower. (Leave your name with the visitor center and they'll let you know when the much-sought-after bulbs are in stock—generally only in August.)

There are effigies of the crocus on Saffron Walden's coat of arms, in an aisle carving opposite its church's south door, and on the sides of its old houses in the form of pargetting—the art of ornamental plasterwork. Pargetting reaches its apogee on the walls of the 14th-century **Sun Inn** (now an antique shop) on Church Street, where, tangled up in a riot of foliage and wildlife, some strange symbols are seen, among them a stockinged foot and the Giant

Saffron Walden
🅜 201 B2
Visitor Information
✉ 1 Market Pl.
☎ 01799-510444
www.saffronwalden
.gov.uk

Audley End

 201 B2

✉ 1 mile W of
Saffron Walden

☎ 01799-522399

🕐 Closed Oct.–
March & Mon.–
Tues. April–Sept.

💲 $$$

www.english-heritage
.org.uk

Thaxted

201 B2

Visitor Information

✉ On the B184,
6 miles SE of
Saffron Walden

☎ 01371-831641

🕐 Closed Nov.–Feb.
& Mon.–Wed.
March–Oct.

of Wisbech doing battle with local hero Tom Hickathrift. Across Church Street and up Museum Street, under a 193-foot spire, stands the big **Parish Church of St. Mary;** angels support its medieval roof, and the organ has a phenomenally loud extra set of pipes known as a *trompeta real.*

Parallel with Church Street is Castle Street, with the remains of Walden Castle and the excellent **Saffron Walden Museum** *(Museum St., tel 01799-510333)* at its northern end. Across from St. Mary's on Castle Street is the narrow entrance to **Bridge End Gardens** *(tel 01799-510444)*—some formal, some informal, all grown around with roses; the key to the garden's Victorian maze is available at the town's tourist information center. **Bridge Street,**

at the foot of Castle Street, is an attractive huddle of medieval houses looking west into open country, while **Myddylton Place** off the High Street is crammed with lovely old buildings. Perhaps the best view of the town, showing the dominance of St. Mary's clerestory windows and spire, is from **Gold Street.**

East Street leads out to Saffron Walden's big open common, into which someone cut a circular **turf maze** (see sidebar opposite) some 800 years ago.

Audley End

A mile west of Saffron Walden, Audley End is a monument to the pride and ambition of Thomas Howard, 1st Earl of Suffolk and lord treasurer to James I, who spent a quarter of

Vast pastoral parklands surround Audley End, a grand Jacobean mansion with ornate interiors.

a million pounds building this superb mansion between 1605 and 1614. What you see today is only one-third of the original house; the rest was demolished in the 1720s under the direction of Sir John Vanbrugh to make it more habitable. During the 18th century Robert Adam redesigned the drawing and dining rooms and Capability Brown landscaped the grounds.

Thaxted

Six miles southeast of Saffron Walden on the B184 is Thaxted, another town that became rich

INSIDER TIP:

Thaxted's church is stunning and is the setting for a classical and jazz music festival on weekends in June and July.

—ALEX GOATMAN
National Geographic contributor

on the medieval wool trade, and also on the manufacture of cutlery—quite a novel concept in pre-Tudor times. This wealth paid for the slow building, during the 14th and 15th centuries, of the big **Parish Church of St. John the Baptist,** with its 181-foot spire. Gustav Holst (1874–1934) composed parts of his suite "The Planets" while he was organist here.

In the town's marketplace stands a 14th-century **Guildhall** *(tel 01371-831281, closed Oct.–Easter*

EXPERIENCE:
Walk a Medieval Maze

The origin of mazes is obscure, but there's something curiously pleasing about their convoluted ways and the ingenuity of their construction. If you follow Rose & Crown Walk from Saffron Walden's Market Place, you will reach the Common, where lies a turf maze, which is actually a labyrinth. The maze could be 800 years old or even older: No one knows. Stories say that the monks of Walden Abbey constructed it so that they could make long penitential journeys on their knees. There's no need to be so rigorous, though; it's hard enough following the maze on foot, with more than a mile of fiendish windings to negotiate until you finally reach the central mound. You're scarcely in danger of losing your way, however: The labyrinth is simply a long, winding path on open ground. For more information, contact the Saffron Walden visitor center (see p. 209).

& Mon.–Sat. Easter–Sept.); its three stories overhang the sidewalk. Along Mill Lane, **John Webb's Windmill** *(tel 01371-830285, call for visiting hours)* houses a rural museum.

Coggeshall

Coggeshall is a notable town boasting more than 200 medieval buildings. The **Woolpack Inn** near the church is gorgeous; so is the elaborately carved **Paycocke's House,** a merchant's house built circa 1500. **Coggeshall Grange Barn** *(Grange Hill, tel 01376-562226, www.national trust.org.uk, see website for hours),* a reputedly haunted cathedral of the harvest, dates back to 1140, making it one of the oldest barns in Europe. ∎

Coggeshall
🄰 201 C2

Paycocke's House
✉ 25 West St., Coggeshall
☎ 01376-561305
🕐 See website for hours

www.nationaltrust.org.uk

Suffolk's Wool Towns

The gently rolling valleys of south Suffolk are particularly rich in small towns beautified by wealth from the medieval wool trade. The River Stour forms the boundary between Suffolk and Essex, and along the Stour Valley lies a string of these wool towns.

Lavenham is noted for its half-timbered medieval houses.

for hours) and **Kentwell Hall** *(tel 01787-310207, closed Jan., by appt. only Feb.–March & Nov.–Dec., call for summer hours)*, a long main street lined with picturesque half-timbered houses and a super-abundance of antiques shops.

To the south lies **Sudbury,** dotted with more medieval houses; **Gainsborough's House** *(46 Gainsborough St., tel 01787-372958)*, the birthplace of the artist, is now a museum of his work.

Southeast again are **Nayland** in the valley and **Stoke-by-Nay-land,** with its striking church tower on the ridge.

North of Stoke is half-hidden **Kersey** in its dip of ground, a tumble of medieval houses.

Lavenham

Farther north of Kersey is the showpiece wool town of Suffolk, Lavenham. It features the superb **Guildhall of Corpus Christi** *(Market Pl., tel 01787-247646, www.nationaltrust.org .uk, see website for hours)*, now a local history museum; the 15th-century **Little Hall** *(Market Pl., tel 01787-247019, closed Nov.–Easter)*; the Angel Hotel, with 14th-century murals; the great church (1480–1520) buttressed by a big tower; and the crazily half-timbered **Swan Inn** with the medieval Wool Hall swallowed up inside. ■

Sudbury
🅰 201 C2
Visitor Information
✉ Town Hall, Market Hill
☎ 01787-881320

Lavenham
🅰 201 C2
Visitor Information
✉ Lady St.
☎ 01787-248207
🕓 Closed Jan.–Easter, & Mon.–Fri. Nov.–Dec.

Clare and **Cavendish** are twin towns to the northwest of Sudbury. Clare has a number of half-timbered houses and the active Nethergate Brewery; Cavendish is all pink-faced charm around a broad green.

Farther downstream, **Long Melford** has one of East Anglia's most splendid parish churches in Holy Trinity, two fine Elizabethan mansions in **Melford Hall** *(tel 01787-376395, www .nationaltrust.org.uk, see website*

Essex Coast

Essex has a ragged, indented coast sliced into marshy creeks and tidal mudflats. Three well-known seaside resorts lie shoulder to shoulder along its northern reach: Clacton-on-Sea (brash and commercial), Frinton-on-Sea (clean and upscale), and Walton-on-the-Naze (quirky and old-fashioned). But there are subtler pleasures to be enjoyed.

Around the Dengie Peninsula

Northeast of London the Rivers Crouch and Blackwater fringe the lonely **Dengie Peninsula;** out on its northeast tip is **St. Peter's-at-the-Wall,** the oldest Saxon church (A.D. 654) in use in Britain. On the Blackwater lies **Maldon,** an atmospheric little port where sea salt is processed and red-sailed veteran barges lie up at the Hythe. North of the Blackwater is **Tollesbury,** with wooden sail-drying lofts and a big red lightship moored in the salt marshes; **Mersea Island,** where you can eat oysters caught locally; and **Old Hall Marshes bird reserve,** wardened by the Royal Society for the Protection of Birds, superb for watching wildfowl.

INSIDER TIP:

Walton-on-the-Naze has a great sandy beach and a good walk out to the Naze.

—ALEX GOATMAN
National Geographic contributor

The Naze & Harwich

Northward again are the crumbling red cliffs of the **Naze,** yielding prehistoric sharks' teeth, and, sheltered behind them, **Hamford Water** (also known as Walton Backwaters), a tidal inland sea where a few people live on little marsh islands.

Finally, where Essex looks at Suffolk across the estuary of the River Stour, stands **Harwich,** a medieval port packed on a headland that contains lighthouse museums, one of the oldest cinemas in the country, the house where the *Mayflower*'s captain lived, and the Redoubt fort built by French prisoners-of-war to keep their own Napoleon Bonaparte at bay. ∎

Colchester

The Colchester Town Trail leaflet, available from the tourist information center, shows you Britain's oldest recorded town in a two-hour stroll. Highlights include the Roman city wall; the Norman St. Botolph's Priory; the Saxon tower of Holy Trinity Church (now a museum); the Roman Balkerne Gate; Jumbo, the Victorian water tower; medieval weavers' houses in the Dutch Quarter; and the Colchester Castle Museum (*tel* 01206-282939).

Maldon
△ 201 C1
Visitor Information
✉ Coach Ln.
☎ 01621-856503

Harwich
△ 201 C2
Visitor Information
✉ Iconfield Park, Parkeston
☎ 01255-506139
⏱ Closed Sun. Oct.–March

Colchester
△ 201 C2
Visitor Information
✉ 1 Queen St.
☎ 01206-282920

Constable Country

Following the River Stour for a couple of miles through the lush meadows of John Constable's Dedham Vale, this 3-mile walk presents you with one famous view after another from Constable's best known landscapes. Remarkably little has changed here in the century and a half since the painter died.

"Hay Wain," Constable's 1821 depiction of Willy Lott's House, facing the pool of Flatford Mill

John Constable was born in 1776 at East Bergholt, 2 miles northeast of Dedham where your walk begins at the river bridge. For a time the young painter was apprenticed to his father, Golding Constable, a well-to-do miller who owned the water mill at **Flatford** *(visitor information, Flatford Ln., tel 01206-299460, closed Nov.–mid-Dec., Mon.–Fri. Jan.–Feb., & Mon.–Tues. March),* a mile or so downriver, and also the mill here at Dedham. "Dedham Lock and Mill," painted in 1820, shows the old brick-built mill (later replaced by the present one), its mill pond and sluice, and the lock that admitted barges to the upper reaches of the Stour. Dedham's late 15th-century church and wide, tree-lined High Street of half-timbered medieval houses make a typically East Anglian ensemble.

Along the River

From Dedham's bridge walk toward the village along the B1029, turning left past the mill by a redbrick house onto a lane to reach a little ford. Go over the stile on the right and pass through the grounds of elegant **Dedham Hall.** Bear left at the top of the drive onto a footpath, dropping diagonally down through fields and trees to reach the southern bank of the Stour, where you bear right along the river. The broad stretch of river between here and Flatford is, in fact, a canal, cut when the Stour was being altered to take barge traffic early in the 18th century. Its original course is marked by a narrow channel that wriggles through the fields on your right-hand side.

Famous Landscapes

Handsome trees shade these broad meadows
where sheep and cows graze. The path winds
beside the river among gnarled old willows
to reach Flatford by a bridge. Compare the
view with the one painted by John Constable
in "Flatford Mill" (1817). The impatient lad
whom the artist placed astride a huge, placid
barge horse has his present-day counterpart
in the local boys who wait by the bridge
with baited lines and bated breath. This is
the same tranquil scene of water, trees, and
mellow old buildings that Constable painted.
There is a superb photogenic view of the
mill, seen across the mill pond, from a point
a few yards down the south bank. To reach

Willy Lott's House, oft painted by Constable

the mill, cross the bridge and turn right
down the lane by the thatched, 16th-century
Bridge Cottage *(tel 01206-298260, www
.nationaltrust.org.uk, see website for hours),* with
teas, boat rental, a Constable exhibition, a
shop, and guided walks. Just beyond is the

dry dock depicted in "Boat-building near
Flatford Mill" (1815), rediscovered a few
years ago along with the skeleton of one of
the Constable family's barges.

At the end of the land stands Golding Constable's Mill, given to the National Trust in 1943
and now a field studies center. Across the mill
pond is Willy Lott's House, which overlooks
the carters, horses, and laden wagon depicted
in the "Hay Wain" of 1821, the most famous
Constable landscape of all.

More Classic Views

From Flatford Mill, retrace your steps up
the lane past Bridge Cottage to the top of
the large parking lot on the hillside above,
and turn left onto a narrow lane (busy on
summer weekends). This climbs in half a
mile to a right-angle bend. A stile on the
left here brings you onto a path descending
a field slope, from which you can enjoy the
wonderful view that Constable celebrated in
"The Valley of the Stour, with Dedham in the
Distance" (1805).

Continue down to the bottom of the slope
then turn left to cross a wooden footbridge
and continue to the River Stour. On reaching
the river, bear right and follow the north bank
which returns you to the Dedham bridge.

Medieval Church Murals of Dedham Vale

John Constable may be the most
famous painter of the Suffolk/Essex
border country, but tucked away in
this low-rolling landscape you'll find
remarkable work by his anonymous
medieval predecessors, the church
mural painters. The mural work in
two churches is worth seeking out. In
Wissington, the Norman church of **St.
Mary** *(Nayland–Bures road, off A134 Colchester–Sudbury)* has red ocher frescoes
dating from around 1280, including
one of a huge, snarling dragon. At Bel-
champ Walter, a few miles northwest,
St. Mary's Church *(off A131 Sudbury–
Halstead)* contains murals of St. Edmund
being shot to death by outsize Danish
arrows, and a very tender Virgin Mary
suckling the infant Jesus. These works
of art are every bit as arresting as
those of the Flatford miller's son.

Norwich

Norwich, capital of East Anglia, is a beautiful medieval city of manageable size. Twelfth-century Flemish settlers brought it prosperity as a weaving center; the industrial revolution of the 18th and 19th centuries largely sidelined it. Here life runs at an agreeably relaxed pace.

Norwich's 1899 Royal Arcade, a covered shopping avenue

Norwich

🅰 201 C3

Visitor Information

✉ The Forum, Millennium Plain

☎ 01603-213999

🕐 Closed Sun.

Norwich Castle

☎ 01603-493625. Recorded information: 01603-493648

Norwich Cathedral

By far the most striking building in the city is its magnificent Norman cathedral *(tel 01603-218321)* of pale Caen limestone, the nave's height enhanced by superb 15th-century fan vaulting and more than 700 individually carved roof bosses (which can be inspected with the help of special wheeled mirrors). A slender spire soars 315 feet into the sky—only Salisbury's is

taller (see pp. 132–133)—and delicate flying buttresses soar off the east end of the building. Chapels bulge from this end, their interiors decorated with 14th-century frescoes.

Around the Close

Tudor buildings, made of stone from the demolished monastery, surround the cathedral green, which is entered by the tall and imposing **Erpingham Gate,** built in 1420 by Sir Thomas Erpingham. The knight, whose effigy adorns the gateway, directed the archers' deadly arrow fire at the Battle of Agincourt in 1415.

The River Wensum encloses the cathedral, and footpaths run along its bank to the east and north past attractive **Pull's Ferry,** the cathedral's 15th-century watergate, or riverport, and the bottom of Wensum Street.

Southwest of the cathedral is the busy **Market Place.** Here stands the beautiful 15th-century **Church of St. Peter Mancroft,** with a roof of carved angels and an east window showing biblical scenes in the stained glass.

Above is **Norwich Castle,** its Norman keep now a museum notable for its early 19th-century East Anglian landscapes by the Norwich school and its huge collection of teapots. ∎

Norfolk Broads

There are nearly 50 of the shallow lakes known as the Norfolk Broads. They spread out in a great arc to the north and east of Norwich between the city and the Norfolk coast. This area is threaded by wriggling, snakelike rivers—the Yare, Bure, Waveney, Ant, and Thurne—and bedded on peat.

It was the peat that brought the Norfolk Broads into being, for the broads are flooded pits that were excavated by peat-diggers during medieval times, the peat used as fuel in the quickly expanding city of Norwich. The Norfolk marshmen dug channels to join up the water-filled pits; reeds and sedges were cut for thatching from shallow boats; and wild ducks and fish were trapped and netted.

This entire landscape of broads, fen, reeds, carr woodland, pasture, and watercourses is known as Broadland, nowadays a playground for amateur sailors and motorboaters, fishermen, and vacationers. The area was designated a national park in 1989.

Broadland, in its healthy and properly managed state, is a delicately balanced jigsaw in which each element contributes to the whole. It is a spellbinding place, particularly away from the main tourist area around Hoveton, Horning, and Wroxham. Sailing (see sidebar this page) is the best way to enjoy the Norfolk Broads, with walking the duckboard trails of such nature reserves as Hickling Broad and Ranworth Broad a close second. The **Broadland Conservation Centre** is at Ranworth.

Wildlife includes reed buntings and marsh tits, grasshopper warblers and spotted flycatchers, and, among the reed beds, the shy booming bittern and the dramatic yellow swallowtail butterfly. ∎

Norfolk Broads

 201 D3

Broadland Conservation Centre

🅜 201 D3

✉ Ranworth, off the B1140, 4 miles SE of Wroxham

☎ 01603-625540

🕐 Closed Nov.– March

EXPERIENCE: Sailing in the Norfolk Broads

The nature of the Norfolk Broads means that you can't hope to see more than a small fraction of this magical landscape unless you take to the water. There is a wide choice of craft, from narrowboats (barges) and motor cruisers to small sailing dinghies, antique sailing barges, and full-blown sail yachts. Any of these will suffice, but competent sailors who are used to inland cruising in light airs will relish the challenge of touring a unique, timeless part of England under sail.

Wroxham and Hoveton are great places for hiring motorboats, but if you want to hire a proper sailing craft—whether a dinghy or a yacht—try one of these companies: **Martham Boats** (Valley Works, Cess Rd., Martham, tel 01493-740249, www.marthamboats.com), **Norfolk Broads Yachting Company** (Lower St., Horning, tel 01692-631330, www.norfolk-broads.com), **Hunter's Yard** (Horsefen Rd., Ludham, tel 01692-678263, www.huntersyard.co.uk), or **Whispering Reeds Boats** (Staithe Rd., Hickling, Norwich, tel 01692-598314, www.whisperingreeds.net).

Beginners can learn to sail on Barton Broad near Wroxham with the **Norfolk Broads Yacht Training Centre** (tel 01603-782897, www.trysailing.com).

North Norfolk

The gently rolling flint, chalk, and clay landscape of north Norfolk, thickly wooded and wonderfully peaceful, is remarkably well endowed with notable buildings, signposting a thousand years of history. Ecclesiastical architecture of the Middle Ages, which reached its English rural apogee in East Anglia, is also well represented.

Sandringham
- 201 B3
- 01485-545408
- Closed Nov.– Easter & one week in July
- $$

www.sandringham-estate.co.uk

Castle Rising & Castle Acre

Over in the westernmost part of the region at **Castle Rising,** 4 miles northeast of King's Lynn, stands a splendid late Norman **castle** *(tel 01533-631330, closed Mon.–Tues. Nov.–March)* built inside Roman ramparts by William d'Albini in 1138, its great stone staircase losing itself in a warren of vaulted rooms and galleries.

Fifteen miles east is **Castle Acre,** where a tree-lined village street of great charm runs from the ruined walls and massive earthworks of the castle to the impressive remains of an early Norman Cluniac **priory** *(tel 01760-755394, closed Tues.–Wed. Nov.–March),* founded around 1090. The arcaded west front with its expressive grotesques is striking, as is the all-but-intact Prior's Lodging.

Binham & Salle

Another very fine Norman priory church of the same date survives at **Binham,** off the A148 8 miles northeast of Fakenham. The west front with its round window is a very early example of Early English architecture.

Perhaps the finest example among literally hundreds of lovely and memorable parish churches in north Norfolk is that of **St. Peter and St. Paul** at **Salle,** a tiny hamlet off the B1145, 12 miles northwest of Norwich. The church's great 111-foot tower dwarfs the houses in its shadow. There are strangely feathered angels swinging censers over the west door, ragged wild men (woodwoses) guarding the north porch with clubs, and, inside the church, a great deal of remarkable work from memorial brasses to woodcarving. But it is the supreme dignity and harmony of the interior, the sense of great space flooded with clear light, that gives Salle its preeminence among north Norfolk churches.

Sandringham, one of the Royal Family's country homes

Tips for Visiting Country Houses & Churches

East Anglia, like much of Great Britain, has a wealth of country houses and churches. Plan ahead to make the most of your visit:

• Join conservation entities for discounted (or free) entry to their holdings: **National Trust** (England and Wales; *www.nationaltrust.org.uk*), **National Trust for Scotland** *(www.nts.org.uk)*, **English Heritage** *(www.english-heritage.org.uk)*, **CADW** *(www.cadw.wales.gov.uk)*, and **Historic Scotland** *(www.historic-scotland.gov.uk)*.

• Pick up the superb guides by Simon Jenkins, *England's Thousand Best Churches* and *England's Thousand Best Houses* (Allen Lane/Penguin).
• Take binoculars to appreciate a building's high-up details.
• Find beautiful deconsecrated churches via **Churches Conservation Trust** (England; *www.visitchurches.org.uk*) and **Scottish Redundant Churches Trust** *(www.srct.org.uk)*.

Sandringham

Of the great country houses that are the glory of north Norfolk, Sandringham, 10 miles north of King's Lynn, is the best known by virtue of its use since 1862 by the Royal Family as their East Anglian vacation hideaway.

There is a museum of field sports and a collection of vintage royal vehicles, but the attraction of looking around this Georgian house is the opportunity to touch (figuratively) the hem of the robe of the House of Windsor.

Houghton & Holkham

Before purchasing Sandringham in 1862 for her son Edward, Prince of Wales, Queen Victoria had considered buying, but turned down, **Houghton Hall,** 7 miles to the east, a splendid Palladian pile built in the 1730s for England's first prime minister, Sir Robert Walpole (1676–1745). The William Kent–designed State Rooms and Stone Hall qualify Houghton as one of England's most impressive country houses.

The same also can be said of **Holkham Hall** *(map 201 C4, tel 01328-710227, closed Oct.–May, except Bank Holiday weekends, & Tues.–Wed. June–Sept.)*, another Kent design, with grounds designed by Capability Brown, 8 miles north of Fakenham. Huge and sprawling, its State Rooms contain paintings by English and Dutch masters and classical Roman sculpture.

Blickling & Felbrigg

The north Norfolk house best known on its own merit is **Blickling Hall**, 15 miles north of Norwich. This wonderful redbrick Tudor mansion with its curly Dutch-style gables, where Anne Boleyn lived as a child, was largely redesigned in Jacobean times. Plasterwork ceilings ornamented with allegorical figures and splendid tapestries are among the attractions here.

As an antidote to grandeur, visit **Felbrigg Hall,** 2 miles southwest of Cromer, a 17th-century gentleman's residence with an orangery and a fine walled garden. ∎

Houghton Hall
🅰 201 C4
☎ 01485-528569
🕐 Hall closed late Sept.–Easter & Mon.–Wed. & Fri.–Sat. Easter–late Sept. Park, garden, museum, shop open year-round.
🅂 $$–$$$
www.houghtonhall.com

Blickling Hall
🅰 201 C4
☎ 01263-738030
🕐 See website for hours
🅂 $$$
www.nationaltrust.org.uk

Felbrigg Hall
🅰 201 C4
☎ 01263-837444
🕐 See website for hours
🅂 $$$
www.nationaltrust.org.uk

Fenland

Fenland is a man-made landscape, a huge 700-square-mile saucer of peat and silt bounded by the uplands of Lincolnshire, Cambridgeshire, Suffolk, and Norfolk. Most of it lies flat, at or below sea level, drained of its water during the 17th century, protected by sea walls and levees, and converted from waterlogged marsh and fen to some of the richest farmland in the world.

Cows are a familiar sight on the rich farmland of Fenland.

The Fens

🗺 201 B3

Wicken Fen

✉ Lode Ln.,
Wicken

☎ 01353-720274

💲 $$

www.nationaltrust
.org.uk

King's Lynn

🗺 201 B3

Visitor Information

✉ The Custom
House, Purfleet
Quay

☎ 01553-763044

Wicken Fen & Stretham

A taste of old predrainage Fenland can be had at **Wicken Fen,** 17 miles northeast of Cambridge, where 600 acres of undrained, unimproved fen is traditionally managed with sedge- and reed-cutting for the benefit of dragonflies, butterflies, owls, songbirds, and waterbirds such as the great crested grebe.

At **Stretham,** 3 miles away off the A10 Ely road, a huge 1831 steam-driven beam pumping engine powers a 37-foot wheel to show how water was lifted into drainage channels from the fields, which are still sinking as their underlying peat dries and shrinks.

Up to the Wash

To the west run the twin Bedford Rivers, cut in the 17th century; halfway up their 20-mile, dead-straight course is the **Welney Wetland Centre** *(tel 01353-860711),* the Wildfowl and Wetlands Trust's bird reserve, where you can see dramatic flights of wildfowl in winter.

The A1101 runs north from Welney to **Upwell,** a pretty village with curly-gabled houses along the banks of the Old River Nene.

Five miles north of Upwell on the A1101, the New (straightened) Nene divides the town of

INSIDER TIP:

The daily winter swan feeds at Welney are amazing, drawing hundreds of wild swans up close for you to see.

—JANE SUNDERLAND
National Geographic contributor

Wisbech, set among fields of strawberries, daffodils, and roses. The Georgian houses of North and South Brinks shadow the river. The Nene runs north into the great estuary of **the Wash.** Here stands **King's Lynn,** another dignified old port with medieval churches and guildhalls. ∎

Lincolnshire

In the extreme southwest of little-visited Lincolnshire lies Stamford, one of England's most attractive Georgian towns. Barn Hill gives the best overall view of the town's winding medieval street plan and its cluster of church spires.

Burghley House

Just south of Stamford is Burghley House *(tel 01780-752451, closed Nov.–March)*, a giant Elizabethan mansion built between 1565 and 1587 for Queen Elizabeth I's favorite and counselor, William Cecil, 1st Lord Burghley (1520–1598), and altered and improved during the following century. Pepperpot cupolas, chimney stacks like runs of classical colonnading, side towers, and buttresses are all dominated by the great central gatehouse.

Inside are 240 rooms: Star sights are the fantastic double Hell Staircase, whose ceiling by Antonio Verrio (1639–1707) shows sinners being devoured by a demonic cat, and the equally exaggerated Heaven Room, with its frolicking Verrio nymphs and gods. Burghley's splendid deer park was landscaped about 1766 by Capability Brown.

Boston

Northeast of Stamford is Boston, whence came the religious dissenters who sailed from Southampton in 1630 to found Boston in America. Boston's beautiful 14th-century **Church of St. Botolph** is crowned by the Boston Stump, a 272-foot tower that commands a vast prospect over Lincolnshire.

Lincoln

The city of Lincoln, 35 miles northwest of Boston, was one of Britain's wealthiest medieval towns, with cloth and wool the basis of its economy. It has medieval streets, a Norman castle, and a superb triple-

Lincolnshire Wolds

The Lincolnshire Wolds are a 40-mile-long range of unfrequented, rolling limestone hills, rising between Lincoln and the coast. Prettiest among the villages they shelter is Old Bolingbroke in the south, where Henry IV was born in 1367. Louth, to the east, is an attractive Georgian market town with a tall church steeple.

towered **Norman cathedral** *(Minster Yard)* high above the River Witham, visible from miles away. Especially notable are the 13th-century rose windows with original stained glass, the rood screen carvings and 14th-century choir stall misericords, the ten-sided chapter house, and the angels of 1280 supporting the choir roof, with the mischievous little Lincoln Imp (the city's emblem) among them. ∎

Stamford
🄰 201 A3
Visitor Information
✉ Stamford Arts Centre, 29 St. Mary's St.
☎ 01780-755611

Boston
🄰 201 B4
Visitor Information
✉ Market Pl.
☎ 01205-356656

Lincoln
🄰 201 A4
Visitor Information
✉ 9 Castle Hill
☎ 01522-545458

More Places to Visit in East Anglia & Lincolnshire

Bury St. Edmunds

This is Suffolk's spiritual capital, where a shrine holds the body of St. Edmund (martyred in 870). Medieval houses are incorporated into the striking west front of the 11th-century abbey ruins. The **Cathedral of St. James** (begun 1438, completed 2004 with a new tower) stands next door in lovely gardens. Charles Dickens had Mr. Pickwick staying at **The Angel** on Angel Hill, reached from the abbey via a 14th-century gateway.
🅰 201 C2 **Visitor Information** ✉ 6 Angel Hill ☎ 01284-764667

Cressing Temple

At Cressing Temple are two enormous, early medieval barns *(tel 01376-584903, buildings only Nov.–March & Sat.),* beautifully restored.
🅰 201 C2

Ipswich

Ipswich is an old port on the River Orwell. Worth seeing here are the extravagantly pargetted **Ancient House** in the Buttermarket; the local landscape paintings, including some Constables, in **Christchurch Mansion Museum and Art Gallery** *(Soane St., tel 01473-433554);* and the copies of the Sutton Hoo treasure, superb funerary paraphernalia excavated in 1939 from a nearby Anglo-Saxon ship burial—in **Ipswich Museum** *(High St., tel 01473-433550, closed Sun.–Mon.).*
🅰 201 C2 **Visitor Information**
✉ St. Stephen's Church, St. Stephen's Ln.
☎ 01473-258070

Suffolk Coast

The lonely Suffolk coast, a crumbling, shingle-lined shore, stretches north from the Stour estuary across from **Harwich** (see p. 213). Between Stour and Orwell lies the Shotley Peninsula; the Butt *&* Oyster, on its north shore at Pin Mill, is a superb sailing pub.

Other coastal pleasures include the Napoleonic Martello Tower at **Shingle Street;** the little port of **Orford;** Benjamin Britten's grand concert hall at **Snape;** the eccentric House in the Clouds at **Thorpeness;** the **Minsmere bird reserve** *(tel 01728-648281, $$);* and the resort of **Southwold,** where Adnams brews its beer.

EXPERIENCE: Bird-watching in East Anglia

East Anglia offers some of Britain's best bird-watching territory, with fens, marshes, estuaries, and mud flats for shelter and year-round feeding. Its easterly and northerly aspect and long coastline make it a haven for wintering wildfowl from lands as far north as the Arctic Circle—pink-footed and brent geese, teal and pintail ducks, waders such as dunlin and knot.

The **Royal Society for the Protection of Birds** *(www.rspb.org.uk)* runs several reserves in the area, including West Canvey Marshes, Canvey Island, Essex; Minsmere, Suffolk; Titchwell Marsh, Norfolk; Frampton Marsh, Lincolnshire; and Nene Washes, Cambridgeshire. To get the most out of your visit to one of them, go on a bird-watching tour offered by one of the following organizations: **Norfolk Birding** *(Norfolk; www.norfolkbirding.com),* **Bird ID Company** *(Norfolk and Suffolk; www.birdtour.co.uk),* **Essex Birdwatching Society** *(www.essexbirdwatchsoc.co.uk),* **Local Birding Tours** *(Essex and Suffolk; www.localbirdingtours.co.uk),* or **Suffolk Birdwatching Breaks** *(Suffolk; www.suffolk birdwatchingbreaks.co.uk).*

If you're looking for something more casual, check out **Birdingpal** *(www.birding pal.org/unitedkingdom),* which offers contacts with local birding volunteers willing to take you out.

A region of contrasts, from historic Nottingham and border towns to the limestone dales of Derbyshire, where great houses stand

North Midlands

Chester's Eastgate clock, which honors Queen Victoria's Diamond Jubilee

North Midlands

The North Midlands region completes the upper half of the great ragged circle, of which the South Midlands is the lower segment, that lies at the heart of England. Nottinghamshire, in the east, is a true Midlands county, rural in the east where it slopes to the River Trent, industrial in the west where the city of Nottingham lies south of the remnants of Robin Hood's Sherwood Forest and a wide scatter of coal mines and pit villages.

A statue of Robin Hood stands at Nottingham Castle, to which his legend is firmly tied.

Peak District

West of Nottinghamshire is Derbyshire, again a county of contrasts, with an industrial southern belt around the county town of Derby. North and west lies one of Britain's best loved and most frequented national parks, the Peak District. This is high, exciting country. In the south—known as the White Peak—are deep, water-cut limestone gorges and small villages of dove gray stone. Farther north the pale limestone gives way to sparkling, dark gritstone, the grass to heather moorland, and the light White Peak atmosphere to the brooding moodiness of the Dark Peak. Both White and Dark Peaks are superb walking country.

Derbyshire contains two of England's grandest and most enjoyable country houses,

NOT TO BE MISSED:

A cruise on the River Trent **228**

Wandering the trails through Robin Hood's Sherwood Forest **228**

Southwell Minster's medieval carvings **229**

The grandness of Chatsworth house **230–231**

A slice of Bakewell pudding **234**

Walking in the White Peak **234**

Seeing the ceramicmaker's art in Stoke-on-Trent **236–237**

Market day in Ludlow **238**

Long Mynd views **240**

Chatsworth and Hardwick Hall, both of which are bound up with the story of the imperious, egocentric, dynamic Elizabethan woman Bess of Hardwick.

Cheshire & Shropshire

The Peak District spills over into Cheshire, a broad county of plains and low hills. Its ancient capital city of Chester, full of medieval, Tudor, and Stuart buildings, lies on the eastern border near the wide Dee Estuary. Staffordshire, neighbor of southwest

Derbyshire, also catches some of the best limestone fringes of the Peak District, and has a fascinating industrial history to explore around Stoke-on-Trent, home of the world's finest china for 200 years.

The western flank of the North Midlands is shaped by the long, whaleback heights of Shropshire's great hill ranges—Wenlock Edge, the Long Mynd, the Clee Hills—all wonderful for walkers and back-road explorers. Jewel of the Welsh border country is black-and-white Ludlow, on its ridge. ∎

Nottingham & Around

Nottingham comes as a very pleasant surprise to visitors. It lies well to the northeast of the industrial heartland sprawl of Birmingham and Coventry, with the M1 expressway on its western flank and the looping River Trent to the east. Notwithstanding patches of modern blight, the result of planning decisions made in the 1950s and '60s, Nottingham is definitely the North Midlands' prime city for historical interest and visitor attractions.

The 17th-century Ye Olde Trip to Jerusalem inn sits on the site of an inn founded during the days of the crusaders.

Castle Area

Nottingham Castle has a history packed with drama. It stands on a high rock honeycombed with caves and passages. The Norman castle was twice destroyed and rebuilt during the 1135–1154 civil war between King Stephen and his cousin Matilda. In October 1330, so stories say, Edward III and his men sneaked in through a tunnel more than 300 feet long to capture his mother, Isabella, and her lover Roger Mortimer, who had ordered the murder of his father Edward II three years before. You can inspect the underground passages in the Castle Rock as part of the **Castle Caves Tour** *(tel 01159-153676, no tour Sun.)*.

It was from Nottingham Castle that Charles I rode out in August 1642 to set up his standard and signal the opening of the English Civil War. After the war was over, the castle was partly destroyed by Parliament. From 1674 to 1679 the Duke of Newcastle converted the grand shell into an even grander Italianate residence; this was torched in 1831 by rioting factory workers. Forty years later, the castle was restored once more; now it houses **Nottingham**

Castle Museum and Art Gallery

(tel 0115-915 3700), with some fine pre-Raphaelite and modern paintings, and a display of late medieval alabaster sculpture.

Robin Hood

Outside the 13th-century gatehouse is a statue of Robin Hood, a folk outlaw hero. Who exactly the legendary Robin Hood was, or if he even existed, is questionable, but the tales of his incarcerations and escapes, and his besting of the wicked Sheriff of Nottingham in archery contests held at the castle, are irresistible. For a long, exciting weekend in October each year, the "Merrie England" of Robin Hood springs back to life during the Robin Hood Pageant, held on the grounds of Nottingham Castle, with archery contests, knights on horseback, and fair ladies in medieval dress.

City of Attractions

An area worth exploring is the **Lace Market,** a district beyond the Broadmarsh Shopping Centre that derives its name from the once thriving lace industry of this area. Victorian warehouses stand along narrow little roadways around the 15th-century St. Mary's Church. Here you'll find the **Galleries of Justice, Nottingham** (Lace Market, tel 0115-952 0555), one of Nottingham's most popular attractions. There are exhibits on crime and punishment, tours among thieves and murderers, ghost suppers, and plenty of opportunity for young and

old to dress up and play judges and felons.

Below the castle, **Ye Olde Trip to Jerusalem** inn (Brewhouse Yard, tel 0115-947 3171) is tucked into the rock, backed up against caves that serve as natural cellars. This 17th-century building is founded on an inn built in 1189 where crusaders setting off for the Holy Land would toast for their success.

A 15-minute walk east of the city center stands the **Green's Mill and Science Centre** (tel 0115-915-6878), a 19th-century windmill with working sails. Its child-friendly Science Centre celebrates the Nottingham baker and mathematical genius George Green (1793–1841).

INSIDER TIP:

Despite its bland-sounding name, the World Service Restaurant, a short walk from Nottingham Castle, serves fine food in charming surroundings.

—PAT DANIELS
National Geographic contributor

Another notable attraction is the redbrick Elizabethan mansion of **Wollaton Hall** (Wollaton Rd., tel 0115-915 3900), sitting atop a hill some 3 miles from the city center. In addition to the hall, the 500-acre estate has on its grounds a natural history museum and an industrial museum, as well as a beautiful deer park.

Nottingham
🔼 225 D3

Visitor Information
✉ 1–4 Smithy Row
☎ 08444-775678

World Service Restaurant
✉ Newdigate House, Castlegate
☎ 0115-847 5587

**Sherwood Forest
Country Park**

225 D3

Edwinstowe

01623-824490

Park open year-
round. Visitor
center open
seasonally.

$ (parking)

Eastwood

225 C3

Sherwood Forest

The ancient royal hunting
forest where Robin Hood
and his Merry Men had their
hideout, Sherwood Forest once
covered a vast area of the east
Midlands. At the time when
Robin Hood may actually have
lived, around the 12th century,
the forest stretched nearly 30
miles north of Nottingham.
But foresting, coal mining,
agriculture, industrialization,
and the expansion of towns
have decimated Sherwood.

The most atmospheric
remnant of the forest lies around
the village of **Edwinstowe** (where
Robin married Maid Marian in
St. Mary's Church), about 20
miles north of Nottingham on
the A6075, and all the woodland
northward, to the west of the
A614. Here is the entrance to the
Sherwood Forest Country Park,
near the ancient Major Oak, with
its 33-foot girth. Footpaths lead
off among the oaks and bracken.

Eastwood

The coal-mining village of
Eastwood, 7 miles northwest of
Nottingham, was the birthplace
of the controversial novelist,
poet, playwright, and essayist
D. H. Lawrence (1885–1930).

Lawrence, fourth son of a
miner, was born in a "two-up,
two-down" (four-room) row
house at 8A Victoria Street, now
the **D. H. Lawrence Birthplace
Museum** *(tel 01773-717353).*
Its cramped little rooms have
been evocatively furnished in the
sparse manner of any miner's
house in 1885. The **Durban
House Heritage Center** *(Mansfield Rd., tel 01773-717353)* depicts
the origins of Eastwood itself
and its links with Lawrence. ∎

EXPERIENCE: Riverboat in the Heart of England

At 170 miles long, the River Trent is one of
Britain's lengthiest rivers, winding gradually
east through the Peak District of Staffordshire and Derbyshire before swinging north
through Nottinghamshire on its way to the
Humber Estuary. A great way to experience
the River Trent is on a theme cruise aboard
one of the lively river cruise boats (*$$$$$*).
Themes include costume party, floodlit
cruising, cabaret, Sunday lunch, disco, jazz,
and more, if you're in the mood—or a
simple sit-back-and-enjoy-it cruise. Cruising
companies include **Princess River Cruises**
*(Trent Ln. South, Colwick, tel 01159-100400,
www.princessrivercruises.co.uk)* and **Trent
River Cruises** *(Trent Ln. South, Colwick, tel
01159-100507, www.trentcruising.com)*, both
on the outskirts of Nottingham, or **Newark**

Line River Cruises *(Cuckstool Wharf, Castle
Gate, tel 01636-706479, www.newarkline
.co.uk)* in Newark.

If you fancy steering your own
narrowboat (barge), you could follow the
Leicestershire Ring, a weeklong (at least)
cruise on canals and rivers through parts of
Leicestershire, Derbyshire, Staffordshire,
and Warwickshire. The route features
tunnels, locks, riverside pubs, and lovely
scenery. Try **Hire a Canalboat** *(Sawley
Marina, tel 01707-655649, www.hireaca
nalboat.co.uk)*, just outside Nottingham,
or splurge on a luxuriously appointed narrowboat from **Excellence Afloat at Valley
Cruises** *(Springwood Haven Marina, Mancet-
ter Rd., Nuneaton, tel 02476-393333, www
.valleycruises.co.uk)* in Warwickshire.

Southwell Minster

"By my blude," exclaimed James I when he first saw Southwell Minster, "this Kirk shall justle with York or Durham, or any other kirk in Christendom!" The king's enthusiasm was understandable, for the great Norman church at Southwell (pronounced SUTH-ll) has a rare beauty.

The minster's medieval brass eagle lectern was given to the church by Archdeacon Kaye in 1805.

The minster shows the twin towers of its west end to the approach path, while the inside is flooded with dusky light reflected from old, pale pink sandstone. The 18th-century **chapter house** is decorated with superb stone carving: a riot of foliage, out of whose leaves peep pigs, hounds, a hare, and a Green Man. The 14th-century chancel screen is wonderfully carved, too, with nearly 300 figures. Far older carving decorates a door lintel.

On the south wall of the minster is a fragmented fresco of Cupid and attendant fish, reassembled from the bathroom wall of a Roman villa excavated just beyond the church's east end.

In the great east window are scenes from the stained-glass workshops of Flemish artists, full of lively, expressive faces under extravagant medieval headgear.

The brass **eagle lectern** nearby was dredged from a pond where it had been thrown during the Dissolution of the Monasteries (1536–1541). Inside the lectern were the deeds to Newstead Abbey, still in place where the monks had hidden them 300 years before. ■

Southwell Minster

🅰 225 D3
✉ Church St., Southwell
☎ 01636-812649
💲 Donation

Peak District

To the west of Nottinghamshire lies Derbyshire, whose northwestern area contains the beautiful and very varied Peak District National Park (see pp. 234–235), a landscape of moody moorlands, swaths of woodlands, and sweeping dales designated Britain's first national park in 1951. Of the many fine country houses within and without the national park, the best known and most impressive are Chatsworth and Hardwick Hall.

Peak District National Park encompasses vast swaths of rural agricultural lands.

Chatsworth

The home of the Duke and Duchess of Devonshire, Chatsworth sits some 35 miles northwest of Nottingham. A thorough exploration of the house and gardens makes a very full day's excursion.

Driving through the deer park toward the house, you are struck by the tremendous orderliness of the grounds, and by the symmetry of the enormous mansion of honey-colored sandstone that stands squarely on the far side of a gently landscaped valley. This must be one of Britain's best approaches to a historic house,

and the carefully planned message of grandeur and condescension is still conveyed effectively.

Chatsworth is a country palace, a baroque mansion with a harmonious Palladian facade, built from 1687 to 1707 for the immensely rich 1st Duke of Devonshire. The duke had a solid foundation to build on, for the house that his Chatsworth replaced was a splendid mansion built by his imperious and egocentric great-great-grandmother, Bess of Hardwick (see pp. 232–233).

Mary, Queen of Scots, stayed here several times on the orders of Queen Elizabeth I, under more or less stringent house arrest as the "guest" of Bess of Hardwick's fourth husband, the Earl of Shrewsbury. Bess, suspecting that the earl and the still alluring Mary were getting on a little too well, soon walked out on him.

Treasures Within: In the entrance hall hangs Sir Edwin Landseer's painting of Bolton Abbey. Marble is used to great effect on the ornate floors and short flights of stairs. The **State Rooms** have beautifully painted ceilings by Verrio and Louis Laguerre. In the **Music Room** you see what you will swear is a real violin hanging up behind a door, but it is a trompe l'œil painting, a little joke by Jan Van der Vaart (1651–1727).

Pictures vary from formal Van Dyck and Rembrandt portraits to a charming painting of the schoolgirls who were billeted here during World War II. The **chapel** (1693), tall and subdued, contains a giant, elaborate altarpiece. The **Great Dining Room** is immaculately and formally laid out as it was for the 1933 visit of George V and Queen Mary.

By contrast, the **Oak Room,** with its baroque wooden sculptures and bizarre twisty columns recalling those above the shrine of St. Peter in the Vatican City, is a freakishly oppressive and eccentric kind of bachelor smoking room.

Tall vases of highly polished Blue John, or fluorspar, a mineral retrieved from nearby caves in the limestone, glitter and wink from pedestals as you wander through Chatsworth and out

by way of the cold white marble beasts and human figures in the **Sculpture Gallery.**

Park & Gardens: Chatsworth is set in a vast park of 1,000 acres. The garden near the house was created with an orangery and wonderful rose gardens from 1826 onward by Joseph Paxton, who later modeled the Crystal Palace, built in London to house the Great Exhibition of 1851, on his since-demolished Great Conservatory at Chatsworth. But the garden designer's **Conservative Wall** of glass still climbs the slope to the east of the house.

INSIDER TIP:

Have a picnic by Chatsworth's turreted Hunting Tower (closed to the public), built on an escarpment overlooking the house.

—JANE SUNDERLAND
National Geographic contributor

Capability Brown landscaped Chatsworth's park in the 1760s. The park is rich in grottoes, summerhouses, vistas across shallow valleys, and walks through the rhododendron groves.

To the southeast of the house a grand cascade of 1696 tumbles from a domed temple down a flight of spillway steps; while the south front itself looks out over the long, narrow Canal Pond, where Paxton's **Emperor Fountain** spurts 100 feet into the air—only a third of its original height.

Peak District National Park
◩ 225 C3–C4
Visitor Information
✉ Old Market Hall, Bridge St., Bakewell
☎ 01629-816558
www.peakdistrict .gov.uk

Chatsworth
◩ 225 C3
✉ 8 miles N of Matlock, off the B6012
☎ 01246-565300
🕐 Closed mid-Dec.–mid-March
💲 $$$, garden only $$
www.chatsworth.org

EXPERIENCE: Solve a Murder Mystery

The British love a good detective—Sherlock Holmes, Miss Marple, Inspector Morse, and their fictional ilk. The British also love to dress up and swagger around a stately home. Put the two together, and . . . bingo! A murder mystery weekend! Pack your finest deerstalker and meerschaum pipe and prepare for thrills, spills (of "blood"), and lots of schlock horror and laughs, as well as a little exercise of the gray matter. In Derbyshire **Hardwick Hall** (*see contact information below*), near Chesterfield, stages occasional murder mysteries (*$$$$$*), where you dress up in period costume and play murder detective while putting away a three-course dinner. There's also the annual Murder Most Foul, held in April, at the Georgian manor house of **Ringwood Hall Hotel** (*Brimington, tel 01246-280077, www.ringwoodhallhotel.com, $$$$$*), also near Chesterfield, with corpses, murderers, shrieks, and plot twists enough to satisfy the most blasé amateur Hercule Poirot.

A listing of more murder mystery fun and games, nationwide, can be found online at *www.killinggame.co.uk* or *www.murdermostfoul.co.uk*.

Hardwick Hall

[M] 225 C3

[✉] Doe Lea, 9 miles SE of Chesterfield

[☎] 01246-850430

[🕐] See website for hours

[$] Hall & Old Hall $$$, garden only $$

www.nationaltrust.org.uk

Hardwick Hall

The other great house built by Bess of Hardwick lies in the extreme east of Derbyshire, only a mile across the county border from the coal-mining area of western Nottinghamshire. Coming west, you pass from grim pit villages into rolling parkland near junction 29 of the M1 expressway. As you follow the long approach drive and get your first good look at Hardwick Hall, you see the monumental letters "ES" carved repeatedly along the gold stone balustrades, and realize that Elizabeth, Countess of Shrewsbury, was the possessor of a healthy—not to say rampant—ego.

Bess of Hardwick: "Hardwick Hall, more glass than wall," ran the jingle, and the most striking aspect of the exterior of Hardwick Hall is the high proportion of glass to stone or brick in its walls. Hardwick's lattice-paned windows are enormous, inserted regardless of cost at a time when windows tended to be built small because of the exorbitant expense of glass. This display was a sign that Bess of Hardwick had plenty of money. Bess was canny, however; it was her own glassworks, and her own quarry that supplied the raw materials.

The appearance and atmosphere of Hardwick Hall is entirely bound up with the hard, flamboyant, practical, and egocentric character of the woman who built it. Four centuries have softened and mellowed the house, but not the memory of the firebrand Bess.

She was born in 1527. Her father, John Hardwick, was a modest gentleman farmer; Bess, however, grew up ambitious. She married four husbands, each time raising herself a notch on the social scale. There were six offspring of these marriages, three sons and three daughters. Contemporary likenesses (no shortage of these in the house) show her red haired, dark eyed, and hawk faced—as purposeful and implacable as that other Tudor Bess, her sovereign.

When she left her last husband, the Earl of Shrewsbury (see p. 231), Bess was in her mid-50s. She bought Hardwick Old Hall from her brother and began to refurbish it. The extensive ruins of the nearby **Old Hall** (owned by English Heritage) contain ornate plasterwork and other additions ordered by Bess during the 1580s.

Then, in 1590, the Earl of Shrewsbury died, and Bess set out to spend his money on mirroring her own pride and consequence in the stone and glass of her brand-new Hardwick Hall. The housebuilder herself died in 1608, in her 81st year. The self-referential portraits, the carved initials, the broken marriages all speak of an appalling arrogance allied to an appealing insecurity—part of Bess's enduring fascination.

A Grand House: Hardwick was never really intended to be a home; it was more of a grand reception center in the country, a place to entertain royalty and the aristocracy—hence, perhaps, its poignant air of coolness, of empty grandeur.

The walls of most rooms are smothered with tapestries, which are only allowed a few hours of light each day for fear of fading. These fragile hangings, their original bright colors dimming, make for a claustrophobic atmosphere in many of the rooms. Intricate needlework applied to soft furnishings is on display, mostly the work of Bess and her servants, men included. Everyone was expected to chip in some sewing time. Their obscure lives are brought a little closer by the 1601 inventory of the hall's contents, which reveals many of the original furnishings—an inlaid wooden table, beds, and painted hangings—still present.

A Tour of the Hall: The tour begins in the **Main Entrance Hall** and winds through to the **Great Hall.** A strikingly wide Tudor staircase rises to the **High Great Chamber** with its painted frieze.

In the **Long Gallery** hangs an impish portrait of Mary, Queen of Scots—catalyst, innocent or otherwise, of the break up of Bess's fourth marriage. The tour ends in the cavernous **kitchens.** ■

Hardwick lifts on high its crowning motifs, the initials "ES."

A Drive Around the Peak District

Crossing the wild moorland and rolling limestone dales of the Peak District National Park, this drive passes through the charming Georgian towns of Buxton, Ashbourne, and Matlock and visits two of the Peak District's great country houses, medieval Haddon Hall and stately Chatsworth.

A stone-built house typical of the Peak District

Best of the sights in **Buxton** ❶ *(visitor information, The Crescent, tel 01298-25106)* are the elegant sandstone **Crescent** of 1780–1790, modeled on Bath's Royal Crescent (see p. 154); the **Edwardian Opera House** (the Theatre in the Hills) with its rich golden interior; the **Victorian Pavilion** of iron and glass in its beautiful gardens; the great dome on the Duke of Devonshire's palatial stables, now the **Devonshire Royal Hospital;** and the **Old Baths.** Across from the baths, **St. Ann's Well** still pours a stream of mineral water at 82.4°F, collectible for free.

Buxton to Ilam

From Buxton, take the A54 west for 10 miles, then bear left on a minor road through the village of Wincle. Continue southward from the bridge below the Ship Inn to the town of **Leek** ❷ *(visitor information, 1 Market Pl., tel 01538-483741),* with **Brindley Mill,** a 1752 water mill devised by the famous engineering genius James Brindley. Now bear east across

NOT TO BE MISSED:

Leek • Matlock • Haddon Hall • Chatsworth • Bakewell

high, lonely moors, through Warslow and Alstonefield to **Ilam,** whose 19th-century hall is now a youth hostel. The village churchyard contains the decorated shafts of two Saxon crosses.

 Ashbourne ❸ *(visitor information, 13 Market Pl., tel 01335-343666, closed Sun. Oct.–Feb.),* just south of Ilam, is a Georgian town and a good base for exploring the **White Peak.** The 13-mile **Tissington Trail** starts here, running north along a disused railroad line and joining

Bakewell Pudding

Raspberry jam and eggs and sugar, a lot of melted butter, and plenty of ground almonds . . . that's what goes into a Bakewell pudding, the culinary pride and joy of Derbyshire. The story goes that a careless kitchen apprentice in Bakewell created the pudding by pure luck when he poured the eggs and sugar into the bottom of the pan instead of adding them to the pastry. Whether that's true or not, you can taste the finest pudding in the whole wide world, bar none (so every true-born Derbyshire man and woman will tell you), at the **Old Original Bakewell Pudding Shop** *(The Square, tel 01629-812193, www.bakewellpuddingshop.co.uk)* in Bakewell.

up at Parsley Hay with the **High Peak Trail,** another railroad path of 17 miles.

To Alton Towers & Back

A detour of 20 miles round-trip (signposted) takes you out of Ashbourne along the A52 Stoke-on-Trent road, then left on the B5032 at Mayfield, to reach **Alton Towers ④** *(Alton, tel 08705-204060),* a brash, white-knuckle-ride theme park.

On to Bakewell

From Ashbourne, the B5035 runs through Kniveton and on to Wirksworth and Matlock Bath, picturesquely tucked down in the bottom of Derwent Gorge.

  Matlock ⑤ *(visitor information, Crown Sq., tel 01629-583388),* just beyond, along the A6, is a late Georgian spa with a mammoth 1853 hydro-health-center on the hill above. The

B5057 and B5056 run west and north in beautiful upland country through Winster to the A6, passing **Haddon Hall ⑥** *(tel 01629-812855, www.haddonhall.co.uk, see website for hours, $$$),* a fortified medieval manor with a Tudor Long Gallery and a 14th-century Great Hall.

  Turn right on the A6 to Rowsley, then left on the B6012 to **Chatsworth ⑦** (see pp. 230–231). After visiting the grand house, continue on to **Bakewell** *(visitor information, Old Market Hall, tel 01629-813227),* where you can sample the local delicacy, Bakewell pudding (see sidebar opposite). From here the A6 leads west for 12 miles back to Buxton.

▲	See area map p. 225
▶	Buxton
⊕	2.5 hours
⬌	80 miles
▶	Buxton

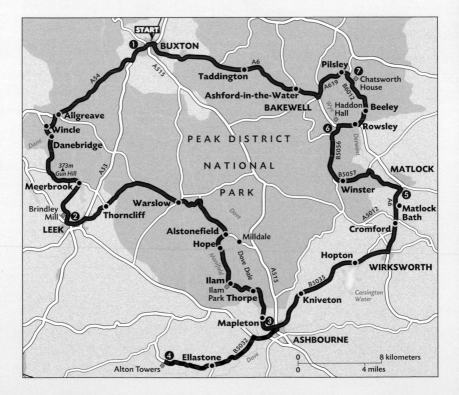

Wedgwood & the Potteries

During the 1960s, the North Midlands conurbation of Stoke-on-Trent *(visitor information, Victoria Hall, Bagnall St., Hanley, tel 01782-236000)*, up in the northwesternmost corner of Staffordshire, had a greater proportion of derelict land than any city in Europe: more marl holes per square mile, more slag banks, scraff heaps, pit heads, and kiln yards. Stoke was one of the most polluted places in the world.

Since then there has been a green revolution. Industrial excavation holes have been turned into athletics stadiums, coal-mine spoil hills converted to grassy uplands, flooded clay pits metamorphosed into fishing lakes. It has been a remarkable turnaround in the fortunes of postindustrial Stoke-on-Trent, comprising the "Six Towns"—Burslem, Tunstall, Hanley, Stoke, Fenton, and Longton—whose foundations, prosperity, and traditions were all bedded for centuries on the coal and clay that underlie the region. Stoke City Football Club mirroring the change in the city's fortunes, has become a successful English Premier League team.

Classic Wedgwood: white figures on blue

The pottery that was made in and around the area from Neolithic times onward was plain, utilitarian stuff. Most of what has been unearthed is workaday earthenware in brown or red. Then, in Stuart times, ships began to bring tea back to Britain. Tea drinking became de rigueur at fashionable gatherings. The gentry desired fine and fancy crockery for the tea ceremony, and stoneware was developed to meet the demand—it was hard, nonporous, and translucent. But fine tableware could only be produced for local consumption. The rough surfaces of the roads and the jolting suffered by goods being transported in horse-drawn goods wagons meant that delicate ceramics could not travel far.

Wedgwood & Others

Josiah Wedgwood (1730–1795), destined to become one of Britain's most successful and celebrated pottery manufacturers, was born in Burslem. He learned his trade and opened his first factory there in 1759. Two years later, the Duke of Bridgewater's pioneering canal opened near Manchester, and a new transport age had dawned.

When the Trent & Mersey Canal opened in 1777, the products of the potteries could be transported smoothly and safely to the coast, from where ships could take them anywhere in the world. China-clay and other raw materials could be brought into the potteries in bulk. It meant a huge expansion in business for Wedgwood, as for the other Six Towns potters: Josiah Spode (1754–1827), with his willow-patterned bone china; the transfer-printed earthenware of Thomas Minton (1765–1836); Toby jugs made by Ralph Wood of Burslem; and, later in the railway age, the Parian ware statuettes from Copeland of Stoke, and Henry Doulton's superb Doulton ware (to become Royal Doulton in 1901).

Etruria—a New Town

By 1769 Wedgwood was in business at Etruria nearer Hanley, based in a newly built factory. He had bolstered his reputation with the production of cream-colored tableware that the Queen adored, and which by royal assent became known as Queen's Ware. He had also begun to produce his trademark "Jasper," fine stoneware items in blue, green, lavender, black, and yellow, with a white design, often a classical scene, applied in relief.

The new factory and its attendant workers' cottages formed a sizable industrial township. There was excitement at that time over the excavations at Herculaneum and Pompeii in Italy, and the exquisite quality of the highly decorated Etruscan vases that were being unearthed. Wedgwood named his new town Etruria in homage and began producing his own "basalt" vases of black stoneware with classical designs. But he, like the other master potters of the Potteries, also turned out mass-produced tableware.

Visit the Potteries

Etruria Industrial Museum

Lower Bedford St., Etruria, Stoke-on-Trent, tel 01782-233144, closed Thurs.–Fri., & Sat.–Sun. Jan.–March, www.stokemuseums .org.uk/eim

Factory Tours

www.visitstoke.co.uk/see-do.aspx

Wedgwood Visitor Centre & Museum

Barlaston, Stoke-on-Trent, tel 01782-282986 (visitor center) or 01782-371919 (museum), www.wedgwoodvisitorcentre.com or www.wedg woodmuseum.org.uk

Visitors can watch skilled potters at work in the Wedgwood Visitor Centre at Barlaston.

Ludlow

Just southwest of Stoke-on-Trent you slip over the boundary, by way of the A53, from industrial Staffordshire into Shropshire, one of the most rural, green, and pleasant counties in England. Shropshire runs cheek by jowl with Wales along its entire western border, and here there are round-backed hills with hidden valleys. Farther south and east the hills become rougher in profile, the Clee Hills in particular, under whose southwestern spurs sits Ludlow.

Ludlow
🗺 225 A1
Visitor Information
✉ Castle St.
☎ 01584-875053
🕐 Closed Sun. Oct.–Feb.

Ludlow Castle
✉ Castle Sq.
☎ 01584-873355
🕐 Closed Mon.–Fri. Jan.
💲 $$
www.ludlowcastle
.com

Ludlow is one of those small country towns that people fall instantly in love with. It perches on a long spine of high ground, cradled in the arms of the Rivers Corve and Teme. The walls of **Ludlow Castle** stand high at the western end of the crest, enclosing Norman fortified buildings and later additions. Edward IV's two young sons, Edward and Richard, were held here until their father died in 1483; then they were taken to the Tower of London and murdered (see p. 93).

A market (Mon., Fri.–Sat., & Wed. Easter–Sept.) under striped awnings takes place in Castle Square. **St. Laurence's Church** (to the left of the square), built high and mighty during the 14th and 15th centuries by rich Ludlow wool merchants, contains beautiful stained glass, and the church's misericords are among the finest in central England. In the churchyard lie the ashes of A. E. Housman (1859–1936), whose slim book of poems A Shropshire Lad is on sale in the town's bookshops. The poems reveal Worcestershire-reared Housman's sentimental yearning for neighboring Shropshire.

There are many finely carved, half-timbered old buildings in Ludlow. Showiest among them is the 17th-century **Feathers Hotel,** its black-and-white frontage crawling with faces, foliage, and checkerboard and diamond timber patterns.

Bridgnorth (visitor information, The Library, Listley St., tel 01746-763257, closed Sun. Oct.–Feb.), 20 miles northeast across the Clee Hills by the B4364, is a historic town on the River Severn. It is well worth exploring for its old houses and pubs, steep river-steps, Norman castle, and little cliff railway. ∎

EXPERIENCE:
See Morris Dancing

There's no more potent symbol of earthy rural fun and games than a Morris side (dancing troupe) in full flow outside a country pub, all dressed in white with flowers in hats and sticks in hand, bells strapped to legs, twirling in intricate steps to the wheeze of a squeeze-box. The sides go under many names—a couple of Shropshire examples are the Shrewsbury Bull and Pump Morris Men and the Shrewsbury Clog. Look for Morris dancing at pubs, their natural home, and leave time to enjoy the inevitable pub sing-along that follows.

Morris sides dance at events all over Britain. Ask at visitor centers, or visit www.themorrisring.org for news of what's on.

Shrewsbury & Around

The oldest part of Shrewsbury, county town of Shropshire, sits on a bulbous peninsula in a tight loop of the River Severn, toward the northwestern corner of the county.

Shrewsbury grew up at the crossroads of two trading routes, the River Severn and Watling Street.

Shrewsbury

Blood and conquest are inextricably bound up with the story of Shrewsbury, plugging as it does one of the important river gaps in the border between England and Wales. The town changed hands many times during the three centuries of fighting between the two countries. Prince Dafydd, brother of Llewelyn the Last, was hanged, drawn, and quartered at Shrewsbury's High Cross in 1283. Harry "Hotspur" Percy was killed at the Battle of Shrewsbury in 1403, having thrown in his lot with the Welsh rebel leader Owain Glyndwr against Henry IV. Hotspur's body was displayed at the High Cross and pieces of it dispatched around the country.

Early Norman **Shrewsbury Castle,** built on the narrow neck of the peninsula, was added to over the centuries; much of what stands today (housing the **Shropshire Regimental Museum**) dates from the years of Edward I's great offensive against the Welsh at the turn of the 13th century.

On nearby St. Mary's Street, the beautiful medieval **Church of St. Mary** (*tel 01743-357006, closed some Sun.*) contains the finest display of medieval stained glass anywhere along the Welsh Borders. Among many treasures, the entire east window is filled with a vivid 14th-century Tree of Jesse, and there is a wonderfully

Shrewsbury
A 225 A2

Visitor Information
- Rowley's House, Barker St.
- 01743-281200
- Closed Oct.–April

Shrewsbury Castle & Shropshire Regimental Museum
- Castle St.
- 01743-361196
- Call for winter hours
- Museum $

www.shrewsbury
museums.com/castle

Church Stretton

▲ 225 A2

Visitor Information

✉ Church St.

☎ 01694-723133

🕐 Closed Oct.–
Feb. & Sun.

Stokesay Castle

▲ 225 A1

✉ 1 mile S of
Craven Arms,
off the A49

☎ 01588-672544

🕐 Call for winter
hours

💲 $$

www.english-heri
tage.org.uk

compassionate Crucifixion scene of roughly the same date in the south aisle.

Elsewhere, Alkmond's Square is surrounded by narrow streets lined with medieval buildings. **Ireland's Mansion** (1575) and **Owen's Mansion** (1592) are a pair of magnificent timber-framed Tudor houses on High Street. There are good walks beside the River Severn all around the town.

South of Shrewsbury

The hilly country south of Shrewsbury, bisected by the A49 road to Ludlow (see p. 238), contains some nooks and corners well worth seeking out. To the east rises the 16-mile-long

INSIDER TIP:

You'll want to rent a car in order to best appreciate the English border countryside in and around Shrewsbury.

—CAROLINE HICKEY
Editor, National Geographic Books

double ridge of Wenlock Edge, a green wooded barrier with a hollow heart. Tucked away between the two spines of the Edge is the hidden valley of Hopedale, where stands the supposedly haunted Wilderhope Manor, now a youth hostel.

The Long Mynd: To the west of the A49 looms the rounded, rolling whaleback of the Long Mynd, a grassy limestone

upland whose flanks are cut by steep stream valleys known as "batches" on the south and east, and "beaches" on the north and west of the range. **Church Stretton** lies on the A49 at the feet of the Long Mynd, a neat, orderly, small town full of cozy tea shops. At the Burway Bookshop on Beaumont Road you can buy a paperback edition of *A Night in the Snow* by the Reverend Donald Carr, before climbing up the beautiful **Cardingmill Valley** (signposted) and its tributary batch of Lightspout Hollow to the top of the Long Mynd. Here, on January 29, 1865, Carr survived an epic night wandering in a ferocious blizzard. The account he wrote of his terrifying and almost fatal ordeal reads as snappily as any thriller.

From Church Stretton a narrow moor road snakes west over the Long Mynd, by way of Ratling-hope, to the quartzite outcrops of the **Stiperstones,** weird shapes against the sky with demonic reputations and the Devil's Chair itself in their midst. A path connects the five chief outcrops.

Stokesay Castle: Seven miles north of Ludlow is Stokesay Castle, England's oldest and finest moated manor house, founded in Norman times and fortified against the Welsh in 1296 on the order of Edward I. Beyond the half-timbered, stone-roofed gatehouse stands the Great Hall with its timbered roof and original upper chamber. A beautiful garden, colorful in spring, follows the moat. ■

Chester

Chester is the county town of Cheshire on the border with North Wales. The Romans arrived in A.D. 79 and established a fortress—Castle Deva by the River Dee, a natural deepwater harbor. During the 19th century, the early Norman castle above the river was rebuilt in grand style.

Chester, a walled city, is famous for the black-and-white half-timbered buildings lining its streets.

A 2-mile walk around the city's red sandstone walls—the best preserved and most complete medieval city walls in Britain—leads to the castle, and also to the partly unearthed first-century **Roman Amphitheatre,** the largest in Britain, on Little John Street. From the **King Charles Tower,** in the northeast corner of the walls, Charles I watched his beaten army straggle into Chester after their defeat on Rowton Moor in September 1645. It was the death knell of the Royalist cause in the English Civil War.

The four main streets of Chester converge at the 15th-century **High Cross,** from which the stentorian town crier shouts the news at noon Tuesday to Saturday, May through August. Along these streets are Chester's famous **Rows,** covered galleries of shops built at second-floor level during the 13th and 14th centuries. Above the Rows are mock-medieval frontages, all Victorian reproductions. But there are dozens of genuinely Stuart, Tudor, and older buildings around, too. **Bishop Lloyd's House** is on Watergate Street, as is the splendid Tudor **Stanley Palace,** and there are more half-timbered houses beyond the ornate Victorian Jubilee archway and clock in Eastgate.

In **Chester Cathedral** *(tel 01244-324756),* on St. Werburgh Street, there is fine Norman stonework, rich 14th-century carving in the choir stalls and pew ends, and some good grotesque-beast misericords under the seats. ■

Chester
- 225 A3

Visitor Information
- ✉ Town Hall, Northgate St.
- ☎ 01244-402111

King Charles Tower
- ☎ 01244-402111
- 🕓 Closed Nov.– March

More Places to Visit in the North Midlands

Castleton

The great attraction here is the numerous caves. The half-mile-long **Peak Cavern** *(tel 01433-620285, closed Mon.–Fri. Nov.–March)*, with its 100-foot opening, lies just southwest of the village; all the others are northwest under the "shivering mountain," Mam Tor. Here are **Speedwell Cavern** *(Winnats Pass, tel 01433-620512)* with stalactites, boat trips, and a bottomless pit; **Blue John Cavern** *(Buxton Rd.)*; and **Treak Cliff Cavern** *(tel 01433-620571)*, where fluorspar was retrieved—some used for decoration at Chatsworth (see pp. 230–231).
 225 C3 **Peak District National Park Information Centre** ✉ Buxton Rd. ☎ 01629-816572

Eyam

The village of Eyam (pronounced EEM) in Derbyshire, just north of the A623, is famous for its self-sacrifice during the 1665 Great Plague. The bubonic plague arrived in Eyam on September 7, 1665, via infected fleas in cloth brought from London by tailor George Viccars. The rector, William Mompesson, ordered self-imposed quarantine for Eyam. Food was left at the parish boundaries and paid for with coins left in bowls of disinfectant vinegar. The disease claimed the lives of 250 of the 350 inhabitants.

The Eyam History Trail map from the church guides you around Mompesson's Well, his grave, plague-struck sites, and the Riley graves where, in August 1666, a mother buried three sons, three daughters, and her husband within eight days.
225 C3

Ironbridge

Ironbridge *(visitor information, tel 01952-884391)*, on the River Severn 5 miles south of Telford, was the cradle of the industrial revolution. A range of fascinating museums tells the story, and from a number of footpaths you can view the graceful, semicircular bridge of 1779, the world's first cast-iron bridge. 225 B2

During the plague of 1665–1666, Eyam's church was shuttered and services were held outdoors.

Classic northern cities—Liverpool and Manchester—and the lakes and mountains of William Wordsworth's beloved Lake District

Northwest England

A celebrated Liverpool nightclub, onetime haunt of the Beatles

Northwest England

Northwest England contains one outstanding jewel of landscape—the Lake District, far famed thanks to William Wordsworth and the Romantic poets, writers, and painters. Yet there is much more to this region, whose character derives largely from the massive industrial complexes that weigh down its southerly border from Liverpool to Manchester, and from the great bleak uplands of the Pennine Hills, which fill most of its northern width.

Relics of the 19th century, steam trains still chug through the Lake District.

the great overblown Victorian temples of Mammon—warehouses, spinning mills, dockside offices, factories—that made the prosperity of these great and still lively commercial cities.

The once grimy industrial towns of east Lancashire—Rawtenstall, Bacup, Todmorden, Blackburn, and others—have also lost their palls of smoke since the virtual shutdown of the northwest's textile industry. Here, too, the architecture reflects Victorian prosperity. Today these towns make good bases for exploring the packhorse trails and green lanes across the high moors that surround them.

Cumbria

Compressed into the westward bulge of the county of Cumbria are the glories of the

The mill hands and factory workers of Sheffield, Manchester, Bradford, and the Lancashire cotton-spinning towns have always looked to the high, bare Pennine moors for their leisure time, walking and cycling. These enormous vistas of rolling moors and deep-cut valleys are lent extra drama by the tightly huddled towns with their black houses, factories, chapels, and public buildings made of gritstone (hard crystalline rock) that lie below the hillsides.

The cities of Liverpool and Manchester are well worth exploring. Each has suffered economic decline, Liverpool in its 7-mile stretch of docks, Manchester in its vast textile industry. Both have fought back by sensitively restoring once derelict areas. Their streets are filled with

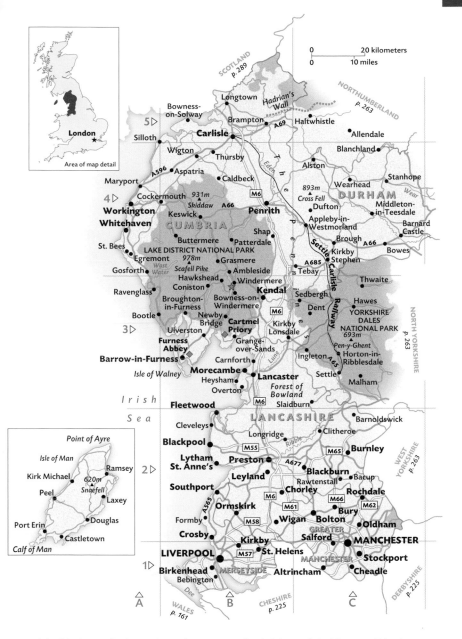

Lake District—endlessly exciting and inspirational, however many times you may have admired and walked along these rounded or sharp-edged mountains that enfold a spatter of bright little lakes. The area was designated a national park in 1951. It's worth exploring

Cumbria beyond the lakes, too: Take time for a railway ride all around the forgotten Cumbrian coastline to the historic city of Carlisle and leave a day or two to walk those moody, starkly beautiful Pennines around Weardale and Teesdale. ■

Liverpool

Liverpool—the British Empire's second most important port after London—got its first dock in 1715 and thrived on transatlantic trade; soon the wharves stretched 7 miles along the Mersey. During the 19th century, transatlantic liners and emigrant ships brought rich and poor alike to the city. A cosmopolitan population formed—Irish, Scots, Indians, Chinese, Americans, and Eastern Europeans—who, for one reason or another, never got any farther than the great port.

Liverpool's Cavern Club is famous for being where the hometown Beatles made their reputation.

Liverpool

⚑ 245 B1

Visitor Information

✉ Albert Dock

☎ 0151-233 2008

These days Liverpool can be a poignant place. Grand 19th-century waterfront buildings rise eerily above a silent river shore. The wharves and warehouses along the River Mersey are being redeveloped for housing and leisure activities.

Down on the waterfront, at the Pier Head, the Mersey Ferries embark passengers for Birkenhead across the water and run several excellent theme cruises (tel 0870-608 2608). These are enjoyable rides, worth taking for the view back to Liverpool's

grand Merseyside threesome: the domed **Port of Liverpool Building,** the great bulk of the **Cunard Building,** and the soaring clock towers of the **Royal Liver Building** with their spread-winged twin Liver Birds.

Generically known as Scousers, the Liverpudlians have developed an instant wit and skill in repartee that makes any conversation here an enjoyable entertainment.

Albert Dock, near the Pier Head, is the city's contemporary showpiece, an innovative conversion of early Victorian warehouses into a variety of museums, shops, and cafés. The **Merseyside Maritime Museum** (tel 0151-478 4499) tells the story of Liverpool's shipyards and ocean liners and its earlier prosperity on the back of the slave trade, as well as outlining its key role during the World War II Battle of the Atlantic. This is not to be missed. Likewise, the contemporary art in Tate Britain's northern outstation, **Tate Gallery Liverpool,** is well worth a visit.

Beatles fans will enjoy the **Beatles Story** in the Albert Dock's Britannia Vaults (tel 0151-709 1963) and can get some mild kicks at 8–10 Mathew Street, site of the **Cavern Club** (tel 0151-236 1965), where the Beatles made their reputation in 1961–62. The original "Cellarful of Noise" was thoughtlessly destroyed in the 1970s; but a faithful reproduction exists, a venue for live music and much nostalgia. The Beatles phenomenon is better celebrated on a guided tour of Beatles sites, on foot or by bus, organized by

INSIDER TIP:

Don't miss Anthony Gormley's "Another Place," a hundred cast-iron, life-size figures set in the Merseyside sands of Crosby Beach.

—TIM JEPSON
National Geographic author

Cavern City Tours (tel 0151-236 9091), or on a minibus visit to the National Trust–owned childhood homes of John Lennon (Mendips, 251 Menlove Ave.) and Paul McCartney (20 Forthlin Rd., tel 0151-427 7231, a.m. reservations tel 0151-233 2457).

Elsewhere in the city, the **Walker Art Gallery** ranges from very early Italian Renaissance painting up to David Hockney, by way of Bellini, Rembrandt, Constable, and Matisse. Liverpool's two modern cathedrals, both worth a visit, are built on high ground overlooking the city. ■

Tate Gallery Liverpool
- The Colonnades
- 0151-702 7400
- Closed Mon. except Bank Holidays

Walker Art Gallery
- William Brown St.
- 0151-478 4199

Crosby Beach
- Waterloo, Liverpool, Merseyside. Beach is 15 min. walk from Waterloo train station via South Rd.

EXPERIENCE: International Beatle Week Festival

You don't need to have been there in the 1960s (and if you were, you probably wouldn't remember, so they say) to admire, adore, and treasure the Beatles—their music, their personalities, and their incredible working-class-nobodies-to-world-conquering-everybodies story. Now that their catalogue is available on iTunes, the world has been conquered all over again. In their hometown, of course, the Beatles have never been anything less than kings. Beatles fans from the four corners of the Earth come to worship at the various shrines beside the River Mersey—Paul's

home, John's home, the Cavern Club, Penny Lane, the Casbah—and to pour out their Big Love at the **International Beatle Week Festival,** held in late August. Bands, exhibitions, events, guest speakers, parties, shows, Merseybeat heroes, appearances by participants in the multicolored masque that was the Beatles—all come together here in Liverpool for a week that true Beatles people wouldn't miss. Package deals (tickets and accommodations) are available, or you can buy individual tickets ($$$–$$$$$) to events. Check online at www.beatlesfestival.co.uk for more information.

Manchester

A century ago, Manchester was Britain's premier textile city. Richard Arkwright's spinning machines, steam power, and proximity to the coalfields and to the port of Liverpool had all made the city's cotton trade huge business. Georgian cotton barons, and later Victorian traders and merchants, grew rich and built warehouses and offices. They endowed art galleries, public parks, and civic buildings. Meanwhile, the mill hands lived in desperate and unsanitary conditions.

Manchester

⩕ 245 C1

Visitor Information

✉ 45–50 Piccadilly Plaza, Portland St.

☎ 0871-222 8223

From the Ashes

Cheap textiles from the colonies and world recessions put the skids under Manchester's business in the 20th century. World War II bombing tore big holes in the city, then postwar clearance of slums and derelict sites opened up the face of Manchester. Civic buildings were cleaned of grime as the Clean Air Act took a grip. These days, with Manchester United established as one of the world's top soccer teams, and a very active and trendy nightclub scene (the rave revolution of the late 1980s was rooted here), there is a new confidence about Manchester.

Booklets and maps, available from the Manchester Tourist Information Centre, steer you around most of the sights in a day. You can also get a good vivid impression of this great redbrick and terra-cotta industrial city from one of the Metrolink trams that ply the streets.

Victorian Magnificence

Behind the visitor center is Albert Square, dominated by the giant Gothic **Town Hall** with its 280-foot clock tower. The first-floor Great Hall has pre-Raphaelite murals by Ford Madox Brown.

On the corner of Peter Street, across from the circular Central Library and Theatre, is the florid purple **Midland Hotel** (officially the Crowne Plaza Manchester—The Midland), excellent for taking English afternoon tea on the terrace.

Canals, Clubs, & Chinatown

The **G-Mex Centre** (tel 0161-834 2700) is on Watson Street, housed under the soaring, arched

Albert Square honors Prince Albert, Queen Victoria's consort.

iron-and-glass roof of the former Central Station. The G-Mex metro station is just beyond; cross the tracks and bear left down a ramp and steps to the Rochdale Canal. Opposite, on the corner of Whitworth Street West, its curved wall stuck with blue- and red-glazed tiles, was the **Hacienda Club,** seedbed of the rave scene.

Follow the canal towpath west to **Castlefield Urban Heritage Park** *(Liverpool Rd., Castlefield, tel 0161-834 4026),* a mix of canals and boats, heavy Victorian bridges and architecture. The excellent **Museum of Science & Industry in Manchester** *(tel 0161-832 2244)* on Liverpool Road, Castlefield, has hot oil and hissing engines in the Power Hall, ramshackle early gliders, and huge reconnaissance planes in the Air and Space Gallery.

Where Liverpool Road meets Deansgate, turn left. Off Deansgate to the right is Brazenose Street with its Abraham Lincoln statue and nearby **St. Mary's Church,** with its stained-glass cupola and swirly marble pillars.

Farther up Deansgate is St. Ann's Street and Square (off to the right), with dignified **St. Ann's Church** (1712). Nearer the Victorian cathedral, the eye-catching pale green glass Urbis building rides the pedestrian traffic like a beautiful ocean liner—it houses the **National Football Museum** *(tel 0161-870 9275).*

Other enjoyable sites are **Chinatown,** between Princess and York Streets, with its ornamental archway, Ho's Bakery, excellent

EXPERIENCE:
Celebrate Chinese New Year in Manchester

If you're in England around early February, try to catch the Chinese community enacting one of their loud, lively, and friendly celebrations of the Chinese New Year. These take place in the Chinatown areas in most of the United Kingdom's large cities, but Manchester, with a Chinese population of around 20,000—second only to London among U.K. cities—has an especially joyous and colorful celebration. In Albert Square and all through neighboring Chinatown the celebrants take over the streets with madly dancing dragons, gong orchestras, and enough firecrackers to kill off a million demons. Visit *www.manchester.gov.uk/events* for more information.

restaurants, and the lively **Gay Village** around Princess and Sackville Streets. Also visit the **City Art Galleries** *(tel 0161-235 8888)* on Mosley Street at Princess Street, with its collections of early medieval religious paintings, Canalettos and Gainsboroughs, pre-Raphaelites, and L. S. Lowry's "matchstick men" depictions of Manchester folk walking bowed in the shadow of oppressive factories.

In Lowry's birthplace of Salford *(visitor information, Salford Quays, tel 0161-848 8601),* near Manchester United football club's famous **Old Trafford** stadium, the **Salford Quays** complex offers bars, theaters, galleries, and two main attractions—the **Imperial War Museum North** *(tel 0161-836 4000)* and **The Lowry** *(tel 0161-876 2000),* which holds the world's largest collection of works by Lowry. ∎

Lancashire Moorlands

Between Manchester and the Lake District lie the remote Lancashire moorlands of the Forest of Rossendale and Forest of Bowland, with a superb network of walks on old packhorse trails, high above the valleys dotted with former textile towns.

Treeless, rugged moorlands, such as these near Blackburn, are part of the Lancashire landscape.

Lancaster
🏰 245 B3
Visitor Information
✉ Meeting House Ln.
☎ 01524-582394

Rawtenstall

This mill town has been the region's most successful at sprucing itself up for visitors. The **Weaver's Cottage** loom shop in Fall Barn Fold introduces you to preindustrial textile manufacture.

East of here along the A681, through Bacup to Todmorden, a whole run of huge mill buildings, terraced houses, factory chimneys, and Methodist chapels under precipitous hillsides recalls the gritty nature of life in these communities until the decline of the textile industry in the 1950s and '60s.

Forest of Bowland

North of Burnley, narrow roads straggle north and west over the empty moorland of the Forest of Bowland, Lancashire's wildest region. **Slaidburn,** on the B6478 in the middle of the moors, has several ancient stone houses, the cheerful Hark to Bounty Inn, and some fine footpaths leading onto the moorlands.

Lancaster

The Trough of Bowland road leads northwest through Dunsop Bridge and Abbeystead to Lancaster, a handsome old river port built in black-and-pink sandstone, full of narrow medieval lanes and solid Georgian merchants' houses. A grim battlemented castle crowns the knoll above the city, and the restored quays and warehouses below, along the tidal River Lune, are Georgian industrial architecture at its most dignified.

The **Maritime Museum** *(tel 01524-382264)* in the Custom House on St. George's Quay tells the tale of Lancaster's seaborne prosperity.

South of this is **Sunderland Point,** a huddle of houses on a windswept point cut off at high tides, where the first bale of cotton from the New World was landed.

Across the point (signposted) lies the grave of Sambo, a West Indian serving man who died here in 1736 of a broken heart at leaving his homeland. ∎

EXPERIENCE: Football—The Real National Game

Cricket might be the "official" national game of England. But throughout the British Isles the national sport is actually the game that the British call football and Americans know as soccer. No visit to Great Britain is complete without experiencing this most British of occasions.

Britain's islanders were playing the sport almost a thousand years ago, in sometimes deadly melees in which masses of men and boys hurled themselves after a ball regardless of life or limb. By Tudor times footballers were using only their feet to strike the ball, and soon the idea of goals, set limits for the field, and some rules became the norm. In 1863 the Football Association drew up proper rules, and from then on the popularity of the sport grew enormously with the establishment of thousands of clubs, great and small—particularly in the working-class mill and factory towns of the north of England and southern Scotland, where football became the working man's obsession, love affair, and means of escape.

The English Premier League is the best known and most widely followed football league in the world, with highly skilled footballers from around the globe earning a king's ransom by showing off their footwork in front of huge audiences in thoroughly modern stadia—the largest, Old Trafford (home of Manchester United), accommodates up to 76,212 fans. Attending a Premier League game is a big thrill—go online at *www.premierleague.com* for how-to details.

For a more gritty and authentic atmosphere, look farther down the scale, at matches between clubs in the Football League, which has three levels of play: Championship (the top level), or even less exalted games in Leagues One and Two (the next levels of play down, respectively). They will be easier to get tickets for, and you'll stand more of a chance of catching U.K. football's traditional blood-and-thunder ("thud-and-blunder," some term it) approach.

Occupying the lower echelons of the Football League at the time of writing are the Lancashire mill towns of Bury, Accrington, Bradford, Oldham, Rochdale, and Burnley; Bradford (wool), Barnsley, and Doncaster (coal) in Yorkshire; the Lincolnshire steel town of Scunthorpe; and many more. Any of these football grounds would give you a true-to-life experience of the sport. Information on attending a Football League match can be found online at *www.football-league.co.uk.*

A few things to know before attending any match:
• You will hear an awful lot of "robust" language.
• Ask for tickets for the "home" section—and avoid wearing the colors of the opposing team!
• The offside rule—don't worry, no one understands it any better than you.
• Try one of the hot pies on sale. Gourmet they ain't—warming and filling they certainly are.

Manchester United star Ryan Giggs, in red, chases the ball.

Lake District

The Lake District holds a special place in English hearts, for it is here that cultivation and wilderness—landscape features much prized in this orderly yet individualistic country—are best seen in juxtaposition, the one in the green, fertile valley bottoms, the other around the upper regions of the fells (hills).

**Lake District
National Park**
🅰 245 B3–B4
Visitor Information
✉ Brockhole,
   Windermere
☎ 015394-46601
🕐 Closed Nov.–
   March
**www.lakedistrict
.gov.uk**

Cockermouth
🅰 245 B4
Visitor Information
✉ Town Hall,
   Market St.
☎ 01900-822634
🕐 Closed Sun.
   Oct.–Feb.

Lake District National Park

The 900-square-mile Lake District National Park, set up in 1951, includes 16 natural lakes and several reservoirs, and 180 fells over 2,000 feet high—four of them over 3,000 feet. Scafell Pike is the highest mountain in England at 3,210 feet.

These statistics say nothing of the glorious beauty of England's best loved, most jealously guarded, and most frequented piece of landscape, nor of the overcrowding in the little towns, erosion of fell paths, and noise pollution of lakes that such popularity inevitably brings. Yet you can easily avoid these annoyances, for the vast majority of visitors stick to the main roads; the well-known beauty spots; the towns of Windermere, Bowness, Grasmere, and Keswick; the low-level trails; and the summer and bank (public) holidays. The fells out on the fringes of the Lake District are still uncrowded. Exercise sensible caution, though, when you fell-walk, and check the weather forecast *(tel 017687-75757)* beforehand.

In the southwest corner of Lakeland there are several excellent walks from the stations of the **Ravenglass & Eskdale Railway** *(tel 01229-717171),* whose miniature steam and diesel locomotives draw the tiny carriages up from Ravenglass on the coast to the foot of the hills at Dalegarth.

Wast Water: This is a wonderful spot for lovers of unadorned, uncompromising lake and fell scenery. Wast Water is the darkest, deepest, and moodiest of the lakes, its southeast slopes one long curtain of loose scree. The little church and inn at Wasdale Head lie tucked down under the slopes, backed by the hunched, pyramid shape of Great Gable.

Cockermouth: This market town was where the Wordsworths were born—William

Beautiful Wast Water never fails to impress visitors.

EXPERIENCE: Climb a Fell with Alfred Wainwright

The supreme achievement of guidebook writer and walker Alfred Wainwright (1907–1991) was to demystify the fells. The maps and notes in his series of Lake District walkers' guides, *A Pictorial Guide to the Lakeland Fells*, give you confidence; his beautiful, meticulous pen-and-ink drawings entice you; and his words of wisdom tell you that it's quite all right to do it your way.

Wear what's comfortable. Go alone if you want to. The only advice you need is to watch where you put your feet. He assures you, "Fellwalking isn't dicing with death, it is a glorious enjoyment of life." So pick up one of Wainwright's volumes (all widely available in the Lake District) and the relevant Ordnance Survey 1:25,000 Explorer map (invaluable for exploring on your own), and make for the fells.

The books are: Book 1, *The Eastern Fells;* Book 2, *The Far Eastern Fells;* Book 3, *The Central Fells;* Book 4, *The Southern Fells;* Book 5, *The Northern Fells;* Book 6, *The North Western Fells;* Book 7, *The Western Fells;* and Book 8, *The Outlying Fells of Lakeland.* The last book contains easier walks "for old age pensioners and others who can no longer climb high fells."

on April 7, 1770, Dorothy on Christmas Eve 1771—in what is now called **Wordsworth House.** Their father, John, is buried in the shady little churchyard.

Southern Lakeland & the Coast

To enjoy a corner of the Lake District that is not inundated with visitors, make for the three broad peninsulas that push south from the coastal fringe of Lakeland into Morecambe Bay's vast 117-square-mile saucer of tidal sands.

This beautiful, wide-open coastline holds many attractions: **Furness Abbey** and **Cartmel Priory Gatehouse;** seals, orchids, hen harriers, and natterjack toads in the nature reserves on the **Isle of Walney** *(tel 01229-471066);* and a guided Sands Crossing over **Morecambe Bay** *(Grange-over-Sands Tourist Information Centre, Victoria Hall, Main St., tel 015395-34026),* through rivers and swaths of sand—a most unusual expedition.

Built by the old Furness Railway Company to carry iron ore out of the hills, the Cumbrian coast railroad snakes and loops on skeletal viaduct legs across the three great estuaries of the Rivers Kent, Leven, and Duddon. It is over 100 miles by this rattling coastal railroad from Carnforth right around to Carlisle.

Whitehaven *(visitor information, Market Hall, Market Pl., tel 01946-852939, closed Sun. Oct.–Feb.),* halfway up, is a planned Georgian town refurbishing itself after decades of decay. **St. Bee's Abbey** is a fine example of Norman architecture. **Carlisle** *(visitor information, Old Town Hall, Green Market, tel 01228-625600, closed Sun. Oct.–Feb.),* at the end of the journey, is a solidly handsome city with a grim and massive sandstone castle. The Norman cathedral contains medieval stained glass, wood carving, and sandstone sculpture. ∎

Wordsworth House

- ✉ Main St., Cockermouth
- ☎ 01900-824805
- 🕐 Closed Nov.–March & Sun. April–Oct.
- 💲 $$
- www.nationaltrust.org.uk

Furness Abbey

- ✉ Barrow-in-Furness
- ☎ 01229-823420
- 🕐 Closed Mon.–Tues. Oct.–Easter
- 💲 $$

Cartmel Priory Gatehouse

- ✉ Cavendish St., Cartmel
- ☎ 01524-701178
- 🕐 Closed Mon.–Fri. Nov.–March & Mon.–Tues. April–Oct.
- 💲 Self-guided tour $
- www.nationaltrust.org.uk

A Drive Around the Central Lakes

This drive starts at Windermere, the Lake District's chief visitor center, and heads north via the Kirkstone Pass up to Keswick. The southern return goes through Borrowdale and Newlands Valley to Grasmere, passing Buttermere and Crummock Water along the way.

The A592 leaves Windermere and Bowness, two towns given over to tourism, and runs south along **Windermere ❶** *(visitor information, Victoria St., tel 015394-46499)* to Newby Bridge. Cross the River Leven and turn right onto the minor road up the lake's heavily wooded western shore. The steam-powered **Lakeside & Haverthwaite Railway** *(tel 015395-31594, closed Nov.–Easter)* makes short trips along here.

At Near Sawrey is **Hill Top ❷** *(tel 015394-36269, www.nationaltrust.org.uk, closed late Dec.–mid-Feb. & Fri.)*, the gray stone, 17th-century farmhouse where Beatrix Potter lived from 1905 to 1913 and wrote her beloved children's tales.

In Sawrey village turn left on the B5285 beside Esthwaite Water to reach **Hawkshead ❸** *(visitor information, tel 015394-36525, closed Mon.–Fri. Nov.–Feb.)*. Here are the grammar school that Wordsworth attended from 1779 to 1787 (he carved his name on his desk lid),

INSIDER TIP:

Go to the Grasmere Gingerbread Shop, in the churchyard of St. Oswald's Church, for the best gingerbread in the world.

—ALISON WRIGHT
National Geographic photographer

and the **Beatrix Potter Gallery** *(Main St., tel 015394-36355, www.nationaltrust.org.uk, closed late Oct.–early April & Thurs.–Fri. early April–late Oct.)* in the former office of the writer's lawyer husband. The road continues to **Ambleside** *(visitor information, Central Buildings, Market Cross, tel 015394-32582)*, a place of dark-stone houses with gables and bargeboards.

NOT TO BE MISSED:

Hill Top • Hawkshead • Derwent Water • Dove Cottage

Over the Fells

Follow the A591 Grasmere and Keswick signs out of town; in 0.25 mile take the steep road on the right signed "Kirkstone 3." Turn left onto the A592 as the road snakes over 1,489-foot Kirkstone Pass, the highest in the Lake District. The view into Patterdale is breathtaking, down between the sweeping arms of the fells to Little Brother Water and the crinkled humps of Angletarn Pikes and Place Fell.

Beyond Glenridding, the A591 turns left for Troutbeck. Just past the junction, on the A592, a signed path goes left above beautiful Ullswater to the fine 70-foot waterfall of **Aira Force ❹**. Beyond Troutbeck turn left on the A66 for busy **Keswick,** through a broad green valley with first Blencathra and then the rounded slate shoulder of 3,054-foot Skiddaw to the north.

Keswick & Back

From Keswick the B5289 runs south into dark and rugged Borrowdale, alongside the beautiful oval of **Derwent Water ❺**. From the road a signed path climbs to **Lodore Falls.**

The steep, brackeny road climbs at a 1:4 gradient from Seatoller over the Honister Pass, then plunges down to **Buttermere** and **Crummock Water,** twin lakes under the slopes of Red Pike and High Stile, and the bulky block of Haystacks. Just before the Bridge Hotel, turn right up a narrow mountain road, over the spectacular pass of **Newlands Hause,** and down into the Newlands Valley.

The A591 leads back to Windermere through **Grasmere,** a must-see for Wordsworth fans. Here is **Dove Cottage** ❻ *(tel 015394-35544),* Wordsworth's home from 1799 to 1808; the **Jerwood Collection Centre,** which houses over 50,000 Wordsworth documents; and, farther along the A591, **Rydal Mount** ❼ *(tel 015394-33002, closed Mon.–Tues. Nov.–Feb. & all Jan.),* where Wordsworth settled from 1813 on. His grave is in St. Oswald's churchyard.

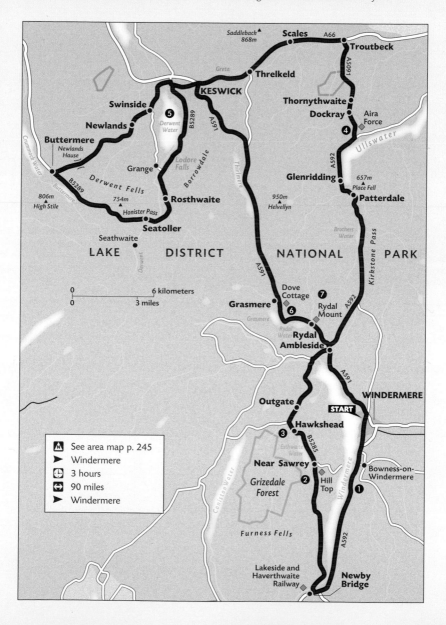

0 ___ 6 kilometers
0 ___ 3 miles

See area map p. 245
▶ Windermere
🕐 3 hours
↔ 90 miles
▶ Windermere

Wordsworth & the Romantics

William Wordsworth (1770–1850) is not the only poet to have extolled the drama and beauty of England's Lake District, but it was he who first focused and expressed the feelings of awe, delight, and magnetic fascination that these 900 square miles of mountain, moor, and lake spark in almost everyone who comes to see them.

The Wordsworth family plot in St. Oswald's churchyard in Grasmere

Wordsworth celebrated the attractions of Lakeland, but he also wrote of how the fells could inspire fear, as in this incident on Esthwaite Water:

> . . . I struck and struck again,
> And growing still in stature the grim shape
> Towered up between me and the stars,
>   and still,
> For so it seemed, with purpose of its own
> And measured motion like a living thing,
> Strode after me. With trembling oars I turned,
> And through the silent water stole my way . . .
> —The Prelude, Book I

Early Visitors

Before the late 18th-century picturesque movement "discovered" the area, the big, bare fells (hills) were generally seen as an abomination. In 1698, Celia Fiennes rode through and spared only a brief, disapproving glance for "those inaccessible high rocky barren hills which hangs over ones head in some places and appear very terrible." In the 1720s Daniel Defoe thought Lakeland "a country eminent only for being the wildest, most barren and frightful of any that I have passed over . . . frightful appearances to the right and left . . . this terrible aspect of the hills. . . ." It was poet Thomas Gray

(1716–1771) with his *Journal* (1775) who suggested that the fells and lakes might be worth looking at, rather than hiding from (though Gray himself would pull down his carriage blind to shut out the sight of particularly terrifying hills).

Thomas West's *Guide to the Lakes* (1778) recommended "viewing stations" and gave road directions, while employing the purplest of prose to encourage visitors. The waterfall above Ambleside "is precipitated with a horrid rushing noise into a dark gulph, unfathomable to the eye. . . . It is dashed with a thundering noise headlong down a steep craggy channel . . . this scene is highly awful and picturesque."

Tourism Begins

A number of factors combined to set up the Lake District as an earthly paradise for early 19th-century visitors. The disfiguring effects of the industrial revolution upon the countryside were sharpening people's appreciation of "unspoiled" landscape, at the same time that revolution in France and the Napoleonic Wars had shut off access to the Continent for the customary horizon-expanding Grand Tour.

Thomas Gainsborough came to paint the fells and lakes in 1783, John Constable in 1806. Turner was a frequent visitor. The Lake District, around the time that Wordsworth began writing about it, was established by the Romantics as the "English Switzerland."

The Lake District homes in and near Grasmere (see p. 255) that Wordsworth shared with his sister, Dorothy, and later with his wife, Mary Hutchinson, and their children, became magnets for visiting and resident poets and men of letters. Samuel Taylor Coleridge (1772–1834) came to Keswick in 1800, the year after William and Dorothy had taken up their life of "plain living and high thinking" at Dove Cottage. Robert Southey arrived in 1802, Thomas De Quincey in 1808. Dorothy brilliantly details all the comings and goings at Dove Cottage in the years 1799–1808 in her journal, published as *Home at Grasmere*. Wordsworth himself became a Romantic tourist attraction. His curiously undetailed *A Description of the Scenery of the Lakes in the North of England*, published in 1810, was a roaring success. By the time he died in 1850—poet laureate, and full of honors—the Lake District was on the railroad, and well and truly on the vacationer's map.

Over the Hills

In the ensuing century, unguided walking over the Lakeland fells (with an eye on the weather) became the norm. Far and away the best companion on the hills has proved to be Alfred Wainwright, with his quirky, hand-drawn, eight-volume *Pictorial Guide to the Lakeland Fells* (see sidebar p. 253). Wainwright was another Romantic admirer of the fells, his bluff style only a thin veneer over a true Lakeland lover's heart.

Isle of Man

Wordsworth also waxed poetic about the Isle of Man, which can be reached by ferry (3.5 hours) from Heysham or by Seacat (2 hours) from Liverpool. The humpbacked island in the Irish Sea, 30 miles long and 10 wide, possesses its own parliament, customs, and special atmosphere.

The best way to see the island is to walk the 25-mile Millennium Way footpath, which runs from Ramsey to Castletown down the hilly spine of Man. The best view is from atop 2,036-foot Snaefell (also reachable by mountain railway).

Each year the island plays host to the leather-clad bikers of the world during its famous Tourist Trophy (or T.T.) Races.

The visitor information center is in the Sea Terminal Building *(Douglas, tel 01624-686766, www.gov.im/tourism, closed Sat.–Sun. Oct.–Feb.).*

The Pennines

The Pennine Hills, backbone of England, run from the north Midlands through the great industrial collection around Manchester, Sheffield, and Leeds, and on northward for another 100 miles to Hadrian's Wall and the Scottish border. The Derbyshire Dales surround their southern extremity, the Yorkshire Dales penetrate their eastern flanks, and the Lake District outlies them on the west; but the more northerly Pennines have a character all to themselves.

Historic structures dot the Pennines.

These are high, bleak uplands, dark gritstone in the south and lighter limestone and sandstone farther north, with extensive stretches of peat moorland and huge swaths of high grassland— really exhilarating walking country, under skies that can deliver rain, hail, mist, and sunshine within the space of an hour.

You can appreciate this lonely grandeur from the 70-mile **Settle & Carlisle Railway** line, whose best known feature, the 24-arch Ribblehead Viaduct, is regularly cited as too expensive to maintain.

Settle, Brough, Appleby, and **Penrith** are northern country towns on or just off the railroad line—solid, stone-built, windswept places, often cut off by winter snow.

As for road routes, the M6 freeway cuts up the western flank of the range, closely shadowed by the far more atmospheric A6 it superseded. The A6 over Shap Fell in winter is still a snowy, slippery, and adventurous journey.

Other, quieter roads to give you a taste of Pennine wildness are the A684 (Sedbergh–Hawes), the A683 (Sedbergh–Kirkby Stephen), and the A686 (Penrith–Alston).

Alfred Wainwright (see sidebar p. 253) devised a west–east **Coast-to-Coast Walk** from the Cumbrian to the North Yorkshire coast. The

Ice Age Flora of the Upper Teesdale

In April and May, the hay meadows along the River Tees are blanketed with glorious wildflowers, but the flowers found higher up on the sides of the dale are perhaps more interesting: smaller, more delicate, and far rarer flowers—relic arctic-alpine flora. The species have successfully clung on (thanks to the cold, wet conditions that repel rival species) since the end of the last glacial period 10,000 years ago. Here thrive mountain pansies, boldly colored purple flowers with a broad lower lip of yellow striped with black; tiny Teesdale violets; bird's-eye primroses, delicate and deep pink, with an intense yellow eye glowing at the heart of each flower; and the symbol of Teesdale, the trumpet-shaped spring gentians of a celestial royal blue, vibrating in the wind as if blowing a silent paean to spring.

Contact the **Moor House National Nature Reserve** (tel 01833-622374, www .ecn.ac.uk/sites/moorh.thml) for guided walks with an expert.

35-mile section between Bampton Grange, northeast of Haweswater, and Keld on the Pennine Way offers some very fine northern upland walking.

From strung-out Shap, a wide-built village on the old A6, the path crosses the fells by ancient settlements and reedy ponds, mine-scarred fellsides, and stone-walled green pastures—all beautiful, harsh, and lonely.

Northeast Pennines

A less well known section of the Pennine Hills is where northwest County Durham meets Northumberland, around Weardale and Allendale. This is an uncrowded corner of England, with its own harsh beauty. The wild moors of Weardale show signs of past lead- and iron-mining. The A689 runs up the length of the valley, with several intriguing detours.

Barnard Castle: Just beyond Stanhope, the B6278 runs south across remote moors into Teesdale, where Barnard Castle makes an enjoyable stopping place. In 1838 Charles Dickens stayed at the King's Head Hotel while researching his setting for Dotheboys Hall in *Nicholas Nickleby*. Steep streets run below the big ruined Norman **Barnard Castle** (tel 01833-638212, closed Mon.– Tues. Nov.–March). Outside town is the **Bowes Museum,** a splendid French château built in 1869 as a museum by local coal-owner John Bowes and his wife, Josephine. Artworks include paintings by Canaletto, Goya, and El Greco; porcelain; silver; and tapestries.

Around Weardale: From Westgate in Weardale a steep side road zigzags north to **Blanchland** in the Derwent Valley, an ancient village with remnants of a medieval monastic settlement, including a superb 15th-century gatehouse and the Abbot's Lodge (now the Lord Crewe Arms Hotel), where there is a bar in the vaulted undercroft, a priest's hiding hole, and huge medieval fireplaces.

Another good side road is the B6295, which leaves Weardale at Cowshill and runs north for 10

Barnard Castle

🅰 245 C4

Visitor Information

✉ Woodleigh, Flatts Rd.

☎ 01833-690909

Bowes Museum

✉ Newgate, Barnard Castle

☎ 01833-690606

💲 $$

www.thebowes museum.org.uk

Pennine Way

www.nationaltrail
.co.uk/PennineWay

wild miles beside the River East Allen to the small market town of **Allendale.** Every New Year's Eve the "tar-barrelers" take over its streets, carrying blazing containers of tar on their heads. Trails lead off across the moors in all directions from the town.

Pennine Way

The 259-mile **Pennine Way National Trail,** one of Britain's longest and toughest long-distance paths, takes about three weeks to complete at a reasonable pace. There are all kinds of circular detours off the main route.

INSIDER TIP:

Not all moors are created equal, as you'll find out if you hike a lengthy section of the Pennine Way. Some are wild, some tame.

—JANE SUNDERLAND
National Geographic contributor

If you want to sample a couple of days—say Malham to Hawes, or Middleton-in-Teesdale to Dufton—remember that the Pennine Way is extremely popular, and in high summer accommodations en route may be full. Weather can be wet, cold, windy, and misty, so take suitable hiking clothing and equipment. For all its eccentricity and occasional inaccuracy, and the fact that it was written nearly 40 years ago, Alfred Wainwright's *Pennine Way Companion* (revised edition)

is still the best guidebook. When soaked and lost in failing light, you can always get comfort and a laugh from the author's acerbic little comments on dreary or tricky sections of the way: "A wet and weary trudge," "Mostly muck and manure," and even "You will question your own sanity."

Heading Northward: The southernmost portion of the way, from Edale in Derbyshire's Peak District to Hebden Bridge in Yorkshire's Calder Valley, is mostly a heavy upland slog through sodden peat. Then come the Brontë moors (see p. 272), **Malham's** spectacular limestone cove, and superb hills and dales in open, breezy country, descending to the charming small towns of **Hawes, Horton-in-Ribblesdale,** and **Middleton-in-Teesdale.**

North of Middleton lies the **Upper Teesdale** with its rich flora, including royal blue spring gentians and other fragile survivals from post–Ice Age Britain (see sidebar p. 259). The Pennine Way passes **High Force,** a thunderous fall of water over the lip of the Whin Sill, and then climbs to more open moorland.

From peaceful little Dufton you hurdle the 2,930-foot summit of **Cross Fell,** highest point of the trail, then descend through the South Tyne Valley to Hadrian's Wall (see pp. 284–285). Last come the Northumbrian forestry plantations and very wild and lonely moors to journey's end at Kirk Yetholm, just across the Scottish border. ∎

A treasure-house of lovely cities, fine cathedrals, misty moors, and the memorable Hadrian's Wall, a Roman monument

Northeast England

Mansion House, the official residence of the lord mayor of York

Northeast England

The three counties of Yorkshire, Durham, and Northumberland contain some of the most beautiful pastoral countryside in England, some of the wildest and bleakest moorland, and nearly 200 miles of cliff-edged coastline. Where pockets of the northeast once were strong in textiles, coal mining, steelmaking, mineral extraction, and shipbuilding, many disused industrial areas are now landscaped or turned into factory or office developments.

A typical Yorkshire dale scene

Yorkshire

Yorkshire, as all its true-born sons and daughters will loudly tell you, has more and better of everything. There are three national parks in England's biggest county: the Yorkshire Dales, with their wide gritstone and limestone valleys and pretty villages; the North York Moors, with a superabundance of unfrequented peat moors and a splendid craggy coastline dotted with fishing villages; and the Peak District, whose northern tip encroaches into Yorkshire.

Pride of all Yorkshire is York itself, the city that gave its name to the whole county, snug and appealing under the eye of its great minster inside a tight ring of medieval walls. To the south are the great manufacturing centers of Sheffield, Leeds, and Bradford, thinning out westward into revitalized and cleaned-up textile towns that shelter under the moors where the Brontë sisters lived and received their inspiration.

Durham & Northumberland

County Durham, farther north, has its share of former mining villages and industrial towns stripped of their raison d'être. But the western moors are wonderfully wild, and the great cathedral city of Durham is a magnet for any visitor. Here, perched dramatically on a river peninsula, is the castle of the medieval prince bishops, sharing the ridge with Durham's crowning glory, the finest Norman cathedral in Britain.

The northernmost county in England, Northumberland fills a triangular space bounded by the Scottish border and the beautiful, brisk Northumbrian coast. In the southeastern corner is the county capital of Newcastle upon Tyne, sharp and lively by day or night. England's

NOT TO BE MISSED:

The stone-carved musicians of Beverley Minster 267, 270

Walking the remarkable city walls of York 268–269

Drinking a pint of Theakston's Old Peculier—strong and tasty beer 274

Eating a Whitby-smoked kipper in Whitby 276

Cruising among the seabirds and seals of the Farne Islands 282

Magical Holy Island 282–283

Walking from Sewingshields to Housesteads Fort along the Hadrian's Wall Path 285

wildest national park, Northumberland, fills the interior with hills blanketed in forests or covered in moor grass and heather. Along the Scottish border roll the high Cheviot Hills, a walker's paradise. ■

0 _____ 50 kilometers
0 _____ 25 miles

SCOTLAND p. 289

6 ▷   **Berwick-upon-Tweed**
       Northumberland Coast
       Holy Island
       Lindisfarne Castle
       Beal   **Bamburgh** *Farne Islands*
       Wooler   • Seahouses
       816m   A1   **Dunstanburgh**
       The Cheviot   **Castle**
5 ▷   Alwinton   • Craster
       Alnwick   • Alnmouth
       NORTHUMBERLAND Rothbury **Warkworth**
       NATIONAL PARK   **Castle**
       Otterburn   • Longframlington
       NORTHUMBERLAND
       Kielder Water   Morpeth   **Blyth**
       Housesteads   *N Tyne*
       Fort   A696
       Birdoswald Hadrian's Wall
       Fort   *Tyne*   **Chesters Fort**
       Greenhead   **Vindolanda** Corbridge
       Haltwhistle Hexham   **Newcastle upon Tyne**
       Bowness-   **Sunderland**
       on-Solway   **Stanley** **Washington**
       TYNE & WEAR
4 ▷   **Consett** **Beamish**   *North*
                    Durham   **Peterlee**   *Sea*
       Stanhope *Wear*   **Hartlepool**
       DURHAM   A1(M)
       Middleton-in-   Sedgefield
       Teesdale   **Bishop**
       Barnard   **Auckland**   **Middlesbrough**
       Castle   A66   **Stockton-** A171 Staithes
       Bowes   **Darlington** **on-Tees** Guisborough **NORTH YORK** Whitby
                    Scotch   Stokesley **MOORS N.P.**
       Keld   Corner   Grosmont   **Robin Hood's Bay**
3 ▷   Thwaite   Reeth Richmond   Goathland   Ravenscar
       Swaledale   Ellerbeck Rosedale Abbey **North Yorkshire**
       Wensleydale Leyburn Northallerton Hutton- **Moors Railway**
       YORKSHIRE DALES Bedale **Rievaulx** le-Hole Lastingham
       NATIONAL PARK Aysgarth *Ure* **Abbey**   **Scarborough**
       693m Buckden **NORTH** Thornton
       Pen-y-Ghent 704m Masham **YORKSHIRE** le Dale • Filey
       Ingleton Arncliffe *Great* Studley Thirsk Helmsley Pickering   *Flamborough*
       Settle   Grassington Royal Easingwold *Rye* *Derwent*   *Head*
       Malham Bolton **Brimham** Ripon **Fountains Abbey** **Castle** Flamborough
       Skipton Abbey **Rocks** Ripley A1(M) **Howard**   **Bridlington**
       Ilkley   Knaresborough A64 Driffield Skipsea
2 ▷   **Keighley**   Tadcaster **Harrogate** **York** **EAST RIDING** Hornsea
       Bingley   Wetherby   **OF YORKSHIRE**
       Haworth *Wharfe*   Market Beverley A165
       Bradford Tadcaster Selby Weighton   **Hull** Hedon
       Hebden Bridge **Halifax** **LEEDS** A63   **Goole** Withernsea
       Todmorden   **WEST** M62   Easington
       Huddersfield **YORKSHIRE** **Wakefield**   *Humber* Spurn Head
       Holmfirth   M1 **Barnsley** **LINCOLNSHIRE**
1 ▷   **GREATER** **SOUTH** A1(M) M18 p. 201
       MANCHESTER **YORKSHIRE** **Doncaster** C   D
       p. 245   **PEAK**
       A   **DISTRICT** **Rotherham**
       NATIONAL
       B **PARK** **SHEFFIELD**
       DERBYSHIRE   *NOTTINGHAMSHIRE*
       p. 225   p. 225

London ★

Area of map detail

Yorkshire

A land of sweeping vistas dotted with farmlands and former mill towns that serve up a healthy dollop of charm, Yorkshire has something for everyone. History buffs—and anyone who loves a good Viking tale—will thrill to the sights of medieval York and its magnificent minster, while nature lovers will delight in the undulating wilds of the Yorkshire Dales.

Once a street of butcher shops, Little Shambles is now lined with various shops and cafés.

York

⬛ 263 C2

Visitor Information

✉ Exhibition Square

☎ 01904-621756

✉ 20 George Hudson St.

☎ 01904-554488

York

York is the finest small city in the north of England. Other places have ancient town walls, narrow old streets, good museums, and fine big churches, but none has them in quite such a concentration of excellence as does York.

The circular walk around the walls of York (see pp. 268–269) is the best of its kind in Britain. The tangle of medieval streets (called "gates" in York, a corruption of the Viking word *gata*, which means "street") and alleyways inside those walls draws you in and along, from one oversailing, timbered, or stonework corner to the next, down Gillygate and Davygate; Fossgate and Goodramgate; Stonegate, where a skinny red printer's devil sits chained by the waist high over the crowds; and narrow little Whip-ma-whop-ma-gate, whose name has never quite been satisfactorily translated. The Shambles, once the medieval butchers' quarter, is now stuffed with bookshops and knickknackeries, but with the original meat hooks still jutting out where they were driven in above the ground-floor windows.

Fine Museums: The main focus of interest in York, of course, is the magnificent **York Minster,** but there are also a number of excellent museums worth seeing.

The **Yorkshire Museum** in the Museum Gardens and the **York Castle Museum** (both tel 01904-687687) on the Eye of York, an oval green, are two further attractions, with superb treasures from Roman times to the present day.

The ever popular **Jorvik Viking Centre** (tel 01904-54302, www.jorvik-viking-centre.co.uk, $$$) in Coppergate, with its time machine travel and "authentic" sounds and smells, shows Viking York (Jorvik) and its excavations in a way you would not otherwise see. Vikings controlled the city from 866 to 954.

The **York Dungeon** on Clifford Street (tel 01904-632599) takes you on a spine-chilling tour around the plague-infested streets of 14th-century York. You can follow highwayman Dick Turpin to the gallows for horse theft and be introduced to ghostly reincarnations of Roman legionnaires.

The **National Railway Museum** on Leeman Road, outside the city walls, holds a host of gleaming behemoths of the rails, from the early 19th century to the present day, including the beautiful *Duchess of Hamilton,* a 1930s art deco locomotive.

York Minster: Begun in 1220 and finished in 1472, York Minster is the largest medieval church in northern Europe, a great storehouse of fine artistic treasures—chief among them being the 120-odd stained-glass windows. Its official title is the Cathedral and Metropolitan Church of St. Peter in York.

The enormous **west window,** 54 feet high, is filled with 14th-century glass, its fine traceried stonework formed in the shape of a heart. The **nave** (1291–1360), with its slender pillars, soars almost 100 feet to a rib-vaulted roof studded with gilt bosses. One shows the Virgin Mary feeding Jesus with a bottle—a Victorian bowdlerization of the more natural medieval original. Halfway along on the north side notice a curious golden dragon—a pivoted crane most likely used to lift a font cover—sticking out of the clerestory.

National Railway Museum

- ✉ Leeman Rd.
- ☎ 01904-621261

www.nrm.org.uk

York Minster

- ✉ Deangate
- ☎ 01844-939 0011
- 🕐 Closed Sun. a.m.
- 💲 Foundations $, treasury $, chapter house $$, central tower & crypt $

www.yorkminster .org

EXPERIENCE:
Explore York with a Blue Badge Guide

Discerning visitors to York will choose a Blue Badge guide to show them around the city. The Blue Badge guides are the gold standard, all across Great Britain. Registered, reliable, and professional, they are renowned for their friendly personalities, intelligence, quick wits, and lively minds. Training and examination weed out all but the best. They know their specialist area like the back of their hand, and they throw in lots of quirky and up-to-date local tidbits, too. You can book a Blue Badge guide through a city's tourist office or you can search online at *www.uk-tourist-guides.com.*

The **north transept** contains an **astronomical clock** and the spectacular five-lancet **Five Sisters window** of 1250, filled with more than 100,000 pieces of grisaille (gray) glass—get up close to appreciate its muted beauty. Off this transept, leading to the chapter house, is an area lined with wonderful examples of stonework.

The octagonal late 13th-century **chapter house** (1260–1307) is edged with stone carvings—a monkey making a face, a cat

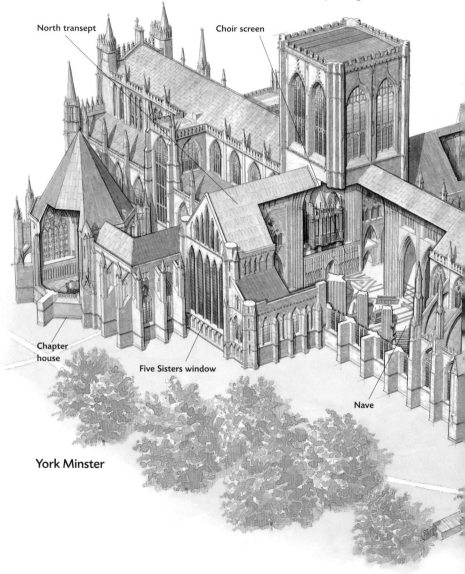

North transept

Choir screen

Chapter house

Five Sisters window

Nave

York Minster

and a ram, a falconer—and some splendid irreverent grotesques of priests and prelates.

There are more finely carved bosses in the roof of the crossing, and some wildly coiffed and bearded kings in the 1461 **choir screen**. Across in the south transept is the minster's famous **rose window,** filled kaleidoscopically with Tudor glass. Below, in the **crypt,** are pillars from the original Norman church.

South transept

Rose window

Main entrance

West window

At the east end rises the great **east window,** as big as a modern tennis court, the largest area of medieval stained glass in the world. Creation and Doomsday are its themes, best admired with binoculars to savor their glorious color and detail.

Around York

Although the city of York itself is the chief jewel in the crown of this region, there are many other delights in the Vale of York, as well as farther to the west where the land begins to rise toward the Yorkshire Dales. And the flat, green farming country out east toward the fast-crumbling coast of southeast Yorkshire—an area known as Holderness, with Beverley at its heart—is too often overlooked by visitors.

Beverley: Thirty miles east of York lies Beverley, whose chief glory is its 13th-century **minster** *(Minster Yard, tel 01482-868540).* King Athelstan (r. 924–939) gave the minster the Saxon "frith," or sanctuary stool, kept beside the altar, as a thank-you
(continued on p. 270)

Beverley
263 C2
Visitor Information
34 Butcher Row
01482-867430
Closed Sun. Sept.–June

A Walk on York's City Walls

Unlike many other British cities whose medieval city walls survive only in half-eroded bits and pieces, York has an almost complete ring of about 3 miles of sturdy wall—15 or 20 feet high in most places. An excellent booklet, *Walking the Walls,* is available from the tourist information center (see p. 264).

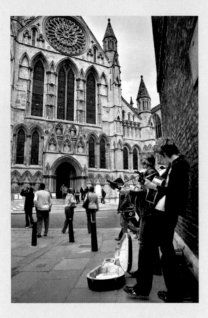

Street performers are common in York.

From the footway you enjoy good views across the tight-packed roofs of the city to the great towers of York Minster, and also of the streets and parks that have grown over the centuries outside of the medieval city.

The Roman city of Eboracum was defended by a stout wall, earth banks, and ditches, but by the Norman Conquest these had almost disappeared. The medieval strengthening and rebuilding was of a different order: a full moated defensive wall with strong towers, its entrance gates (called "bars") guarded by barbicans—gateways with out-thrusting fortified courtyards. All the barbicans save the one at Walmgate Bar were pulled down in the 1820s and '30s, in spite of protests. One protester was

---

NOT TO BE MISSED:

Clifford's Tower • Museum Gardens • York Minster

Sir Walter Scott, who offered in vain to walk from Edinburgh to York if the city's corporation would agree to spare Micklegate Barbican.

What is striking about the walls is how much has survived nearly 800 years of assault by siege and aerial bombardment (York was the target of a "Baedeker raid" in 1942), as well as the ravages of neglect and the rapacity of developers.

Bridges & Bars

Starting from the castle parking lot, you pass the bulging stone walls of **Clifford's Tower ❶** *(Tower St., tel 01904-646940).* It was completed in 1313 to replace a wooden keep in which 150 Jews killed themselves during a pogrom in 1190 rather than fall into the hands of the rioting mob outside.

Skeldergate Bridge takes you across the River Ouse, up and down steps and along the walls to reach **Micklegate Bar,** where medieval traitors' heads were impaled on spikes as a public warning.

Beyond the bar the wall starts to bend and snake north to recross the Ouse by **Lendal Bridge ❷,** with a good view over to the minster. Across the river the wall disappears at **Lendal Tower;** you continue through the lovely **Museum Gardens ❸,** beside the ruins of St. Mary's Abbey and the Roman masonry of the big **Multangular Tower,** to the squat and solid medieval gateway of **Bootham Bar,** which straddles the Roman road into Eboracum.

Now **York Minster** ❹ (see pp. 265–267) looms close alongside, dwarfing the trees, flowers, and vegetable patches in the Deanery gardens below the wall.

The next gateway is **Monk Bar,** tall and grim, topped by stone statues making threatening gestures toward the outside world. Beyond here, just outside the walls, is the domed brick roof of the city's circa 1800 **Ice House** ❺. Ice was collected from ponds each winter and stored here in straw until needed for cooling and refrigeration purposes the next summer.

The route leads to a break in the defenses caused by the creation of a fish pool during William the Conqueror's reign. You walk beside the River Foss along Foss Islands Road to the stumpy Tudor brick lookout post called the **Red Tower.** Here the wall reappears and brings you to **Walmgate Bar** ❻, with its jutting, castellated, and turreted barbican, the only complete example left in England. The spiked portcullis hangs in its slot above the gateway, and the great oaken doors still stand, pierced with a tiny wicket gate. There are bullet and cannonball scars in the stonework, inflicted during the Civil War siege of York in 1644. Curiously, given its military purpose, the barbican softens and lessens the grim effect of the gateway behind it, which is so noticeable at York's other bars.

Beyond Walmgate Bar comes the tall outlook tower of **Fishergate Postern,** just before the circuit ends at the castle.

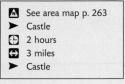

> 🗺 See area map p. 263
> ▶ Castle
> 🕒 2 hours
> ⟷ 3 miles
> ▶ Castle

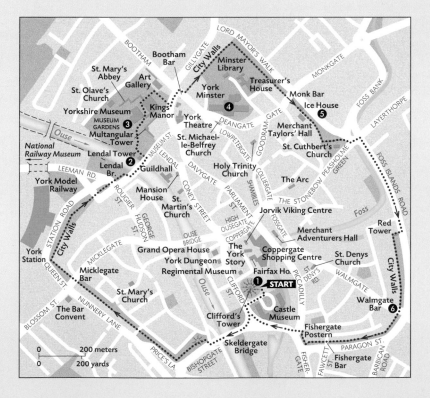

Castle Howard

🅰 263 C3

✉ 6 miles SW of Malton

☎ 01653-648333

🕐 See website for hours

💲 $$$$

www.castlehoward .co.uk

Knaresborough

🅰 263 B2

Visitor Information

✉ 9 Castle Courtyard

☎ 0845-389 0177

🕐 Closed Nov.– Easter

to St. John of Beverley for answering his prayers by helping him to beat the Scots.

There are some enjoyable grotesque medieval carvings of musicians in the north aisle, including a madly grinning lute player, puff-cheeked woodwind blowers, and a hurdy-gurdy man with a Zapata moustache.

Beverley has one fortified gateway, **North Bar,** and plenty of cobbled medieval streets and lanes to explore. **St. Mary's Church** is a good place to wield your binoculars on the bright chancel ceiling paintings of kings, and on the finely carved nave roof bosses. There are chubby-cheeked Tudor minstrels on a nave pillar, and at the entrance to the **Chapel of St. Michael,** a cartoonish sculpture of a rabbit with a pilgrim's scrip slung across one shoulder, which is said to have inspired illustrator Sir John Tenniel in his famous depiction

of the White Rabbit in Lewis Carroll's *Alice's Adventures in Wonderland* (1865).

Castle Howard: Northeast of York is Castle Howard, the Palladian mansion used in the television adaptation of Evelyn Waugh's snobbery-and-decadence novel *Brideshead Revisited.* Designs for a great palace of a house were commissioned from Sir John Vanbrugh in 1692 by the 3rd Earl of Carlisle, Charles Howard. Vanbrugh, only 28 and with no track record as an architect, was delighted. He took seven years to finish the plans, and Sir Christopher Wren's pupil Nicholas Hawksmoor oversaw the building of the house, which was largely completed by 1712.

The big cupola above the enormous north-facing facade shelters a Great Hall with a vast acreage of tiled floor. Other state

The houses of Knaresborough make a picturesque ensemble on the cliff above the River Nidd.

rooms include the Long Gallery, with portraits by Van Dyck and Holbein, among others. There is a fine collection of historical costumes, too.

Two-thirds of the house is currently open to the public, with the remaining third, the East Wing, occupied by the Howard family.

Outside in the castle grounds are follies, towers, and obelisks to enhance the views. Here stands a beautifully balanced **Temple of the Four Winds,** with its dome and porticos. This was Vanbrugh's last throw—he died shortly after the temple was completed in 1726.

Knaresborough: West of York is picturesque Knaresborough, above the gorge of the River Nidd, with the castle ruins rising above all. Chief attraction is **Mother Shipton's Cave** (*Prophesy House, tel 01423-864600*), where you can learn the story of local seer Ursula Sontheil, born in 1488 in a riverside cave. She predicted all manner of events and discoveries such as the launch and defeat of the Spanish Armada and the invention of cars and airplanes.

In the nearby well, everyday objects hang under streams of limestone-filtered water, slowly "turning to stone"—that is, becoming coated with a thick calcified layer.

Harrogate: Just down the road is elegant, gray stone Harrogate. Between the late Victorian era and World War I, sufferers and society-seekers

would come to drink the sulfurous water under the dome of the octagonal **Royal Pump Room** (*Crown Pl., tel 01423-556188*), nowadays mostly given over to a museum. Its stained-glass window shows a pre-Raphaelite angel rising in a puff of steam from the town's healing springs, which were discovered in 1571 on the Stray, a grassy common area south of town.

INSIDER TIP:

Several caves underlie the dales. You can tour White Scar Cave, which has one of the largest underground chambers in Britain.

—LARRY PORGES
Editor, National Geographic Books

Stroll in Valley Gardens to the west of the town center, where "temples" stand over wells, and try a genuine Victorian Turkish bath at the 1897 **Royal Baths Assembly Rooms** (*Crescent Rd., tel 01423-556746*).

Yorkshire Dales

North of Keighley and west of Harrogate stretches **Yorkshire Dales National Park,** hundreds of square miles of wild upland moors, grasslands, and hills, cut by broad valleys with shallow rushing rivers where some of the lushest pasture in Britain makes everything green. Dales (continued on p. 274)

Harrogate

🅰 263 B2

Visitor Information

✉ Royal Baths Assembly Rooms, Crescent Rd.

☎ 0845-389 3223

🕐 Closed Sun. Oct.–March

White Scar Cave

✉ Ingleton

☎ 01524-241244

🕐 Closed Mon.– Fri. Nov.–Jan.

💲 $$$

www.whitescarcave .co.uk

Yorkshire Dales National Park

🅰 265 A3–B3

Visitor Information

✉ Colvend, Hebden Rd., Grassington, Skipton

☎ 01756-751690

🕐 Closed Mon.– Thurs.

www.yorkshiredales .org.uk

A Drive in the West Riding

The industrial southwest of Yorkshire might strike anyone not in the know as a surprising area to visit. All mill towns, textile factories, and bleak moors—that has been the reputation of what was known as the West Riding of Yorkshire. But here today, as in so much of postindustrial Britain, it is all changing.

The textile trade has disappeared, and the small industrial towns have rediscovered the lovely silvery stone that has been hidden for more than a century under coats of sooty grime and skins of oxidized black. The wholesale demolition of mills, factories, and row houses that went on in the 1960s and '70s has slowed, if not halted, as their significance to Britain's industrial and social heritage is being recognized.

Up on the Moors

As for the moors—bleak they certainly can be in dour weather. But they are also beautiful, striped with gritstone walls, rising steeply above the manufacturing towns that huddle in the depths of the valleys. Methodist and Baptist chapels are scattered everywhere: The West Riding was one of the most fertile seedbeds for John Wesley, William Darney, and other founding fathers of militant nonconformist religion.

The West Riding moors are lonely, moody places, often swept by wind and rain. In the 19th-century, the Brontë sisters—Charlotte, Emily, and Anne—lived and wrote in the hilltop village of Haworth, and the landscape seems full of their spirit—particularly the wild, brooding spirit of Emily Brontë, who set her masterpiece *Wuthering Heights* here.

Haworth to Hebden Bridge

Start at **Haworth** *(visitor information, tel 01535-642329)*. The **Brontë Parsonage Museum** ❶ *(Church St., tel 01535-642323, closed Jan.)* is at the top of the village street, a sandstone Georgian house in whose dining room the Brontë sisters wrote their

---

NOT TO BE MISSED:

Brontë Parsonage Museum
• Piece Hall

---

astonishing novels. Study, dining room, kitchen, bedrooms—all are spotless, quiet, and sober, unlikely ground for the growth of such vivid, self-assertive minds.

A 7-mile round-trip walk from Haworth takes you across **Haworth Moor,** passing the Brontë Waterfalls and the rock called the "Brontë Chair," and along the Pennine Way (see p. 260) to the ruin of **Top Withens farmhouse**—Emily's model for Heathcliff's house, Wuthering Heights. A walk booklet can be bought at the Haworth visitor information center.

From Haworth, the A629 leads south for 10 miles into **Halifax** *(visitor information, tel 01422-368725)*, a northern textile town to the bone and one that is unjustifiably overlooked by many visitors. **Shibden Hall** ❷ *(Lister's Rd., tel 01422-352246)*, a 15th-century timber-framed manor house turned folk museum, demonstrates rural traditions and crafts. The **Piece Hall** ❸ of 1779, on Blackledge, is a massive monument to Georgian wool trading—it contains over 300 merchants' rooms around a vast cobbled, arcaded, Italianate courtyard. A visitor information center is also sited here. In a splendid Victorian millowner's house, **Bankfield Museum** *(Akroyd Park, Boothtown Rd., tel 01422-354823/352334, closed Mon.)* is a cornucopia of textile history that frequently changes exhibitions.

Two detours worth taking are to Bradford (M26, Jct. 26), where the **1853 Gallery** *(tel 01274-531163)* in Salt's Mill, Saltaire, houses Europe's largest collection of works by Bradford-born artist David Hockney; and to Wakefield (M26, Jct. 29 or 30) with its splendid **National Coal Mining Museum** *(tel 01924-848806).*

Cut west along the A58 and A646 to the market town of **Hebden Bridge ④** *(visitor information, tel 01422-843831)* to see how beautiful cleaned-up gritstone mills and terraces can be.

The A6033 from Hebden Bridge leads you across the Wadsworth Moors to Haworth.

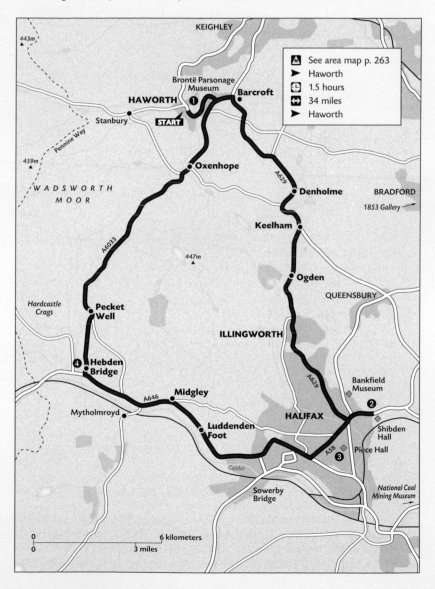

Ripley Castle

- ✉ Ripley
- ☎ 01423-770152
- 💲 $$$, gardens only $$

www.ripleycastle
.co.uk

Fountains Abbey & Studley Royal

- 🅰 263 B3
- ✉ Fountains, Ripon
- ☎ 01765-608888
- 🕐 Closed Fri. Nov.–Jan. (deer park open year-round)
- 💲 $$$

www.nationaltrust
.org.uk

folk are extremely proud of their small, neat villages, cozy little pubs, green fields seamed with drystone walls, and far-ranging views.

Wharfedale: Wharfedale runs northwest from the lower edge of the Yorkshire Dales, with the village of Bolton Abbey at the entry to the national park. **Bolton Priory** *(tel 01756-718009)* was built in the

---

Theakston Brewery

Yorkshire has a reputation for making quality beers. At Masham, 10 miles northwest of Ripon, is the Theakston Brewery *(Red Ln., Masham, tel 01765-680000, www.theakstons .co.uk)*, established in 1827. The brewery offers tours *($$)* of its 1875 "tower-style" brewery, designed to use gravity to advantage, and will introduce you to its pale and potent bitter and to the celebrated Old Peculier ale—treacle dark and very strong.

---

mid-12th century; the great east window still stands flanked by tall arches, while the nave is used as the parish church. Two miles north at **the Strid,** the River Wharfe crashes in white water between narrow rocky jaws. Many have drowned attempting to jump across.

The B6160 runs up Wharfe-dale to **Grassington** *(Yorkshire Dales National Park information*

center, Colvend, Hebden Rd., tel 01756-751690, closed Mon.–Thurs.), the dale's chief village, where the **Upper Wharfedale Folk Museum** *(6 The Square, tel 01756-752469, seasonal)* gives a good idea of the area and its history. Four miles north, a side road to the left leads up Littondale to **Arncliffe,** where the **Falcon Inn** is unspoiled and serves an excellent pint of beer.

Back in Wharfedale, the B6160 continues through pretty Kettlewell and Buckden to **Hubberholme** and its striking grouping of George Inn, humpbacked bridge, and little church, which contains a rare Tudor rood loft.

Nidderdale & Around: Strictly speaking located outside the national park, **Ripley,** on the eastern edge, is an Alsatian village re-created around a cobbled square. It was built in the 1820s by one of the Ingilby family, who have lived at **Ripley Castle** for seven centuries (28 generations and counting). The churchyard has a remarkable "kneeling cross," with hollows scooped out by penitents' knees. **Nidderdale** goes northwest from here—though strung with reservoirs, it is still lovely.

The B6265 leaves to the right of the dale road, passing the bizarrely shaped gritstone outcrops of **Brimham Rocks** on its way over to **Fountains Abbey,** set in a lovely wooded valley. Founded by Benedictines in 1132 and taken over by Cistercians three years later, within a generation Fountains was the richest abbey in Britain through wool, lead, quarrying, and agricultural interests. The refectory, infirmary, abbot's house, dormitory, cloister, chapter house, and giant vaulted undercroft (300 feet long) remain. In 1720, John Aislabie bought the ruins and land. He and his son William created **Studley Royal** water garden and 1,800 acres of landscaped grounds—grottoes, cascades, temples, lakes, bowers and alcoves, deer parks, woods, and wide open spaces—a treat not to be missed.

Two miles east, **Ripon** *(visitor information, Minster Rd., tel 01423-537300)* has the late Norman **Cathedral of Sts. Peter and Wilfrid,** showing a beautiful 13th-century west front with twin towers, but concealing a seventh-century Saxon crypt. In the Market Square, at 9 p.m., the Wakeman in his scarlet-trimmed coat and black hat blows curfew on a great curved horn—the original, of Saxon date, is in the Town Hall.

Wensleydale: The A6108 and A684 travel west beside the River Ure along Wensleydale, famous for its cheese and pastoral beauty. At **Aysgarth** *(map 263 B3, Aysgarth Falls National Park Centre, tel 01969-662910)* the river tumbles spectacularly in two long falls over limestone steps.

Swaledale: North of Wensleydale runs Swaledale, the most northerly and most rugged of the Yorkshire Dales (save

Arkengarthdale, which swings off northwest). Keld, Thwaite, Muker, and Gunnerside are hamlets under the moors. **Richmond** *(visitor information, Friary Gardens, Victoria Rd., tel 01748-828742),* at the eastern foot of the dale, has a massive Norman castle perched on a knoll, its great curtain walls enclosing a 100-foot-high keep with walls 11 feet thick. Scolland's Hall, inside, dates from 1080 and may be the oldest domestic building in Britain.

The town itself has the biggest cobbled marketplace in Britain, steeply sloping with many narrow, medieval alleys leading off it. ∎

EXPERIENCE: Attend a Yorkshire Sheep Sale

Sheep farmers and their practices have brought the characteristic landscape of the Yorkshire Dales into being—stone walls, stone barns, and stone farmhouses in the green "in-bye" pastures low down, the rougher grazing higher up, and the open moor on top. Watch these tough, humorous, resilient men and women bidding for sheep (and cattle) at the local auction marts (markets) held year-round, responding with imperceptible nods and winks to the auctioneer's singsong patter. Be sure to wander around the holding pens, where you can admire the livestock up close and personal. Three noted venues are **Craven Cattle Marts** *(Gargave Rd., Skipton, tel 01756-792375, www.ccmauctions.com),* **Kirkby Stephen Auction Mart** *(Faraday Rd., Kirkby Stephen, tel 01768-371385, www.kirkby-stephen.com/farming-animals/auction-mart.html),* and **Hawes Auction Mart** *(Burtersett Rd., Hawes, tel 01969-667207, www.hawesmart.co.uk).*

North York Moors Drive

North York Moors National Park holds harshly beautiful moorland, lonely hills, and spectacular coastal cliffs. This is an area of country with little of the soft green pastorality of the Yorkshire Dales, but with its own wild and exciting character.

North York Moors at sunset

Begin at **Pickering** ❶ *(visitor information, tel 01751-473791).* Situated near the southern edge of the national park at the junction of the A170 and the A169, it makes a good base. It is a compact town, whose Parish Church of Sts. Peter and Paul contains 15th-century frescoes, including Thomas à Becket at the moment of his martyrdom, and St. George dealing with a rather weedy dragon.

Running 18 miles from Pickering north to Grosmont, the **North Yorkshire Moors Railway** *(Pickering Station, Park St., tel 01751-472508, call for schedule)* gives superb views throughout the journey. The line closed in 1965, but since 1973 it has operated as a steam railway. There are good walks from the intermediate stations; one from the moorland village of **Goathland** descends to Mallyan Spout, a 70-foot waterfall.

Just west of Goathland you can explore **Wade's Causeway,** a remarkable paved road dating from the later stages of the Roman occupation, although modern researchers suggest it may predate the Romans altogether.

From Pickering to the Coast

Take the A170 east to Thornton Dale, then a side road on the left to reach the **Dalby Forest Drive** ❷, looping and winding for 9 miles from one viewpoint to the next, emerging at Hackness.

Continue east to **Scarborough** *(visitor information, tel 01723-383636),* Yorkshire's premier seaside resort. North Bay beyond the castle-topped headland is quieter than the central South Bay.

The A165 or the A171 leads north to Cloughton, where the coast road switchbacks north to Staintondale and Ravenscar. From Ravenscar you can follow on foot the abandoned railway track or the cliff-top path to reach Robin Hood's Bay, 3 miles north.

Take the A171 north from Ravenscar, and a short, steep right turn down a minor road (B1447) will bring you to **Robin Hood's Bay** ❸ *(information from Whitby visitor center),* a red-roofed fishing village very picturesquely piled in its narrow cleft.

The B1447 and A171 continue north to **Whitby** ❹ *(visitor information, tel 01723-383636),* charm encapsulated, with its 13th-century abbey ruins on the cliff. At the top of the 199 Church Stairs stands the Norman Church of St. Mary, its interior woodwork reputedly the creation of ships' carpenters. Bram Stoker set part of *Dracula* (1897) in the graveyard. Explorer James Cook (1728–1779) lodged as an apprentice on Grape Lane—the house is now the **Captain Cook Memorial Museum** *(tel 01947-601900, closed Nov.–Jan.).* From Whitby the A174 leads in 10 miles to **Staithes** ❺, a pretty cliff village where Cook served as assistant to a grocer until,

NOT TO BE MISSED:

Robin Hood's Bay • Whitby • Rievaulx Abbey

legend says, he stole a shilling from his master and ran away to Whitby.

Over the Moors

Continue to Easington on the A174. Take a side road on the left to turn right onto the A171. In a mile turn left on minor roads through Danby, Castleton, and Westerdale. South of Westerdale pass **Ralph Cross,** where medieval travelers left coins for "those less fortunate"; then bear left past Fat Betty, or White Cross, to Rosedale Abbey.

Side roads connect Rosedale Abbey with **Hutton-le-Hole ❻** (*Pickering visitor information, The Ropery, tel 01751-473791*), a very popular

village with a collection of restored local buildings in the **Ryedale Folk Museum** (*tel 01751-417367, closed Dec.–late Jan.*).

Two miles east is **Lastingham ❼**, where St. Mary's Church shelters a Norman crypt full of earlier stonework. On the A170, south of Hutton-le-Hole, turn right for the market town of **Helmsley** and nearby **Rievaulx Abbey ❽** (*Rievaulx, tel 01439-798228*). This 12th-century Cistercian building had to be orientated north–south rather than the conventional east–west because of its constricted site. The A170 returns you to Pickering.

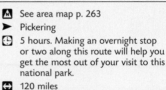

Ⓐ	See area map p. 263
▶	Pickering
⏱	5 hours. Making an overnight stop or two along this route will help you get the most out of your visit to this national park.
↔	120 miles
▶	Pickering

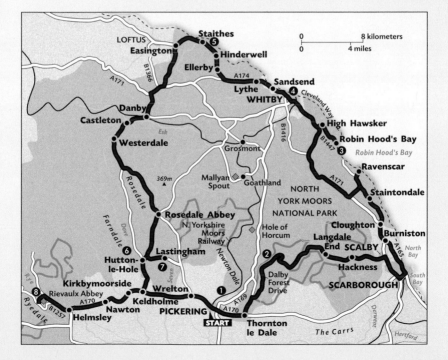

Durham

Durham has come a long way since the 1950s, when coal mines all around this university city gave it a gritty, working-class aura. Now the pits are all closed, and the place has been spruced up. The medieval quarter of Durham is a compact area of not much more than half a mile, squeezed into a narrow, southward-pointing peninsula formed by a tight loop of the River Wear. Though a tour around this city center on foot is short on distance, it is long on interest.

The Normans started building Durham Castle, which now forms part of Durham University, in 1072.

Durham

🅰 263 B4

Visitor Information

✉ 2 Millennium Pl.

☎ 0191-384 3720

🕐 Closed Sun. Oct.–Feb.

A good place to start exploring the city of Durham is the pedestrianized **Market Place,** with its 1861 equestrian statue of Charles William Vane Stewart, 3rd Marquis of Londonderry and Lord Lieutenant of Durham, a splendid figure in a frogged uniform and plumed shako astride a proudly pawing stallion.

From here, curving Silver Street leads across the 14th-century **Framwellgate Bridge,** from where you can enjoy the first of a succession of wonderful views across the river to the castle walls and twin cathedral towers rising above the wooded banks of the sinuous Wear.

Along the Riverbank

At the far end of the bridge, steps to the left lead down to the riverside path. Soon a slanting weir—a favorite spot for white-water canoeists—crosses the river to Jesus Mill (mostly 18th-century, but on medieval foundations) on the far bank. The profits of this former fulling mill (where cloth was beaten and thickened) were used to build the cathedral's altar—hence the name. Nowadays the building houses the excellent **Durham University Museum of Archaeology.** This view of weir, mill, castle walls, and cathedral towers is a photographers' favorite.

On the other side of the River Wear, across the three slender arches of Prebend's Bridge (built in 1776 to replace a timber bridge washed away in floods), the path turns right to continue around the inner curve of the peninsula.

A short way along the bank, half hidden under the trees, is a curious little stone structure like a summerhouse. Its entrance is flanked by fluted pillars. They once formed part of a house built on this spot for one of Durham's most celebrated citizens, the Polish émigré Count Boruwlaski. The count settled in Durham early in the 19th century, and died here in 1837, at the age of 97. His fame came from his diminutive size, for he was just 3 feet 3 inches tall—a wise and generous man, according to reputation. The tiny count loved to stroll the riverbank with his friend, the outsize man-mountain actor Stephen Kemble.

Farther on, the riverside footpath passes under modern Kingsgate Bridge, with Durham University's students' union building and some lecture rooms along the far bank. Soon the narrow, pointed arches of 12th-century **Elvet Bridge**—Durham's oldest

bridge—appear ahead. Beyond lies **Brown's Boathouse,** where in summer you can rent a boat.

Up to the Castle & Back

Just before the bridge, the narrow steps of Drury Lane Vennel climb away on the left to emerge through a low archway on the spine of the promontory in North Bailey. To the left, cobbled Owengate leads right to Palace Green, surrounded by 17th-century buildings, with **Durham Cathedral** (see pp. 280–281) ahead and the **castle** (see p. 280) on your right.

INSIDER TIP:

Guided walks with Durham on Foot are a great idea. You can choose from one of their set walks or customize one to suit your interests.

—CHRISTOPHER SOMERVILLE
National Geographic author

After visiting the cathedral, leave it via the entrance near the Treasury to reach South Bailey. This winding street leads down past the university colleges of St. John's, St. Chad's, and St. Cuthbert's Society. The roadway then passes through the 1778 Watergate arch. Before Prebend's Bridge, a path bearing right leads along the east bank of the River Wear past Jesus Mill to return to Framwellgate Bridge, Silver Street, and the market square.

Durham University Museum of Archaeology

✉ Old Fulling Mill, The Banks

☎ 0191-334 1823

🕓 Closed Tues.– Thurs. Nov.– March

💲 $

www.dur.ac.uk/ fulling.mill

Durham on Foot

☎ 01913-847895

💲 $$$$$

www.durhamon foot.com

St. Cuthbert, Hermit Saint

Cuthbert preferred to live alone with the seals and seabirds on the windswept and rocky Farne Islands (see p. 282), but his restless fate, wisdom, and skill as an orator led him into high office and responsibility.

He died in 687, but he had no peace in death. To preserve his body from the attacking Vikings, the Lindisfarne monks removed it from the island in 875. They wandered with it for more than a hundred years, until in 995 a vision told them to lay Cuthbert to rest at Dun Holme—now Durham. Legend says that William I ordered the tomb to be opened so that he could see for himself if the saint's body was, as the monks insisted, perfectly preserved. Whatever the Conqueror saw scared him so badly that he ran for his horse and galloped off, never drawing rein until he had crossed the Tees, 20 miles away.

In 1104, Cuthbert's body was buried behind Durham Cathedral's easternmost altar. His shrine, focus of medieval pilgrimages, was broken up at the Reformation, and his bones reburied. In 1827 he was exhumed yet again, a skeleton in a silken shroud with a jeweled pectoral cross on its breast.

Durham Castle
- ✉ Palace Green
- ☎ 0191-334 3800
- 🕐 Guided tours only; call for details
- 💲 $$

www.dur.ac.uk/university.college

Durham Cathedral
- ✉ The College
- ☎ 0191-386 4266
- 🕐 Tower closed Sun.
- 💲 Donation for cathedral. Monk's Dormitory $, tower $, treasury $

www.durhamcathedral.co.uk

Durham Castle & Cathedral

The medieval Prince Bishops of Durham ruled the northeast of England as the authorized delegates of the king. Mandated as they were by the crown to use any and every means to keep the Scots at bay and the rule of law secure, they possessed power, wealth, and influence of an order unimaginable today. They had their own army, their own mint, and their own courts of law. Their palace at Durham was a fully fortified castle, and the cathedral where their spiritual influence was centered, sharing its narrow eminence above the River Wear with the castle, was—and still is—reckoned to be the finest and most spectacularly sited church that the Normans built in Britain.

Durham Castle: Begun in 1072, the castle retains some older features—notably a Tudor chapel with some beautiful misericords, and a 15th-century kitchen. Most of it, though, is an 18th-century Gothic rebuild for the bishops of Durham, who remained in residence until 1836 when the castle was given to the university (founded in 1832 by Bishop van Mildert).

Durham Cathedral: From the center of the great railroad viaduct that spans the northern half of the city, you are struck with the impression of castle and cathedral as a single temporal and spiritual stronghold. Close up, the size of the cathedral makes an unforgettable impact when viewed from Palace Green. This is building to a grand design, an impression reinforced as you step past the replica lion's head sanctuary knocker on the north door and enter the dusky interior.

Durham's Romanesque cathedral was started in 1093 and completed in 1274, but almost all of it is high Norman, 12th-century work—solid, bulky, everything on the massive scale. The cylindrical piers, and both round and pointed arches in the **nave,** are geometrically carved with dogtooth, chevron, and lozenge patterns, a Byzantine or perhaps Moorish effect as a reminder that experiences on Crusade had expanded many 12th-century minds in England. The 11th- to 12th-century **choir** soars high; its aisle roofs are seamed with stone rib vaulting installed some time shortly after the Conquest.

The beautiful **Galilee Chapel** at the west end, built in the 1170s, echoes the Moorish influence seen in the nave; but here everything is done with a light, delicate touch. Slender Purbeck marble columns support the roof over the simple **tomb** of the Venerable Bede. The monkish scribe from Jarrow on the River Tyne, who died in 735, was a historian of the early Christian Church in England and biographer of the north of England's favorite saint, Cuthbert, the shepherd and Bishop of Lindisfarne (see sidebar opposite).

St. Cuthbert himself lies under a plain slab marked "Cuthbertus" at the cathedral's eastern end in the **Chapel of the Nine Altars.** The chapel was built from 1242 to 1280 so that dozens of monks in the Durham community could all receive communion more or less simultaneously. St. Cuthbert's cross and his wooden coffin, carved with the images of the apostles, along with treasures of the cathedral of Durham, can be seen in the cathedral **Treasury,** where you can also view a copy of the fabulously illustrated seventh-century Lindisfarne Gospels. ■

Durham Cathedral reigns as Britain's finest Norman cathedral.

Newcastle & the Northumbrian Coast

Newcastle upon Tyne, former capital city of England's northernmost county of Northumberland, is a vibrant, lively place. It has seen its shipbuilding and heavy engineering fade away, but the Geordies (Newcastle natives) have lost neither their strong local accent nor their quick-fire wit in the city's recent scramble for a consumerist good-time image.

Perched atop Beblowe Crag on Holy Island's south side, Lindisfarne Castle was built in the 1550s.

Newcastle upon Tyne

🅰 263 B4

Visitor Information

✉ 132 Grainger St.

☎ 0191-277 8000

🕐 Closed Sun.

Warkworth Castle

✉ Warkworth

☎ 01665-711423

🕐 Closed Tues.–Fri. Nov.–March

💲 $$

www.english-heritage.org.uk

Don't miss the bridges across the River Tyne, especially the graceful bow-girder **Tyne Bridge** of 1928 and its ingeniously opening neighbor, the so-called **Blinking Eye.** Nearby on the south, or Gateshead, bank of the Tyne stand **BALTIC, the Centre for Contemporary Art** (tel 0191-478 1810) and the futuristic-looking music center **Sage Gateshead** (tel 0191-443 4666). On the outskirts of Gateshead looms Antony Gormley's gigantic "Angel of the North" sculpture.

Northumbrian Coast

From Newcastle the Northumbrian coastline stretches 70 miles north to the Scottish border. Only a cold climate keeps the crowds from this superb run of low rocky cliffs and sandy bays.

Heading north along the coast from Newcastle, you come first to the 12th- to 14th-century **Warkworth Castle,** a setting in Shakespeare's *Henry IV Part I.* Next comes **Alnmouth,** a handsome little red- and gray-roofed coastal town behind extensive sandbanks, and at **Craster** you can eat locally smoked herring and walk the cliffs for 1.5 miles to the impressive ruins of **Dunstanburgh Castle** (tel 01665-576231, winter hours vary, call for details).

The wonderful **Alnwick Garden** (tel 01665-511350) near **Alnwick Castle** features a Grand Water Display, tree house, Poison Garden, Bamboo Labyrinth, and much more. **Bamburgh Castle** frowns out from its shoreline crag toward the 28 low rock ledges of the **Farne Islands.** Boats from nearby **Seahouses** (visitor information, car park, Seafield Rd., tel 01665-720884, closed Nov.–March) visit the islands to see the seals and birds, and the monastic ruins on Inner Farne.

At Beal, drive over the causeway (check the tide times) to **Lindisfarne** to visit Holy Island village, the church and priory (founded A.D. 635), and the castle. Beyond Beal is **Berwick-upon-Tweed,** an ancient border town often bloodily disputed between England and Scotland.

Northumberland

Northumberland National Park (tel 01434-605555) is the wildest, remotest, and least visited of the national parks. Much of its bare, peat-bedded upland area has been planted with woodland, especially around **Kielder Water reservoir**—there are 250 square miles of close-packed conifers here. Yet Kielder has its own beauty, around the lake and along the footpaths of the peaceful, endlessly wind-stirred forest.

Off the Beaten Track

Fast cross-border roads streak northwest through this landscape between Newcastle and Edinburgh, but to catch a more intimate flavor of Northumbrian forest and hill farmland, take the side road east from Saughtree (on the B6357 Carlisle–Jedburgh road) for 30 miles, through the heart of the Kielder Forest and north by Lanehead to Otterburn.

An alternative approach to the heart of Northumberland is from its eastern flank at Longframlington (on the A697 Morpeth–Edinburgh road), coming west through **Rothbury** with its old fortified defensive tower, and on up the B6341 through the villages of Thropton, Sharperton, and Harbottle to Alwinton.

This is wonderful empty country, deep in the flanks of the rolling Cheviot Hills, with a cul-de-sac road winding on for a dozen miles past lonely hill farms. Take your pick of a number of green lanes here—challenging or easy walking routes across the hills, following ancient tracks such as Salter's Road and Clennell Street, or stick to the well-beaten Pennine Way (see pp. 258–259). ∎

Craster

 263 B5

Visitor Information

☎ 01665-576007

🕐 Closed Mon.–Fri. Oct.–Feb.

Bamburgh Castle

✉ Bamburgh

☎ 01668-214515

🕐 Closed Nov.–late March (unless by appt.)

💲 $$

Berwick-upon-Tweed

🔺 263 B6

Visitor Information

✉ 106 Marygate

☎ 01289-330733

🕐 Closed Sun. Oct.–Feb.

Lindisfarne Castle

✉ Lindisfarne

☎ 01289-389244

🕐 Winter hours vary; call for details

💲 $$

EXPERIENCE: Learn to Play the Smallpipes

The native music of Northumberland—jigs, reels, hornpipes and the like—is best appreciated when played on the region's own instrument, the Northumbrian smallpipes. Their keening, skirling tone and stuttering tempo bring this wild music to life. You can hear it played at the **Rothbury Traditional Music Festival** in July (www.rothbury-tradition-music.co.uk), which showcases some of the finest pipers (including local heroine Kathryn Tickell). Informal music sessions also take place year-round at the **Queen's Head Inn** (Townfoot, Rothbury, tel 01669-620470,

www.queensheadrothbury.com).

If you're inspired to pick up the smallpipes—or any other instruments of the folk tradition—contact **Folkworks** (tel 0191-443 4666, www.thesagegateshead .org/folkworks/folkworks_participation .aspx). This magnificent organization offers learning workshops for all abilities (including total beginners), summer schools, dances, concerts, and more—many of them at the **Sage Gateshead** (St. Mary's Sq., Gateshead Quays, www .thesagegateshead.org), a music center in Gateshead, Newcastle upon Tyne.

Hadrian's Wall

Hadrian's Wall is far and away the most important relic of Roman rule in Britain. Its sheer size (73 miles in length) means that huge numbers of archaeologically priceless items have been excavated on, under, or near it. Its unbroken westward run from Wallsend in Newcastle upon Tyne to Bowness on the Solway Firth gives it a coherence and solidity that helps bring the 400 years of Roman occupation alive across two millennia.

Hadrian's Wall, astonishingly complete and nowadays well maintained, stretches 73 miles across the top of England.

Though tumbledown in places, the impact of the wall is stunning—particularly where it rides the rim of the great dolerite cliffs of the Whin Sill like the crest of an enormous, northward-breaking wave.

About 50 years after the Romans arrived in Britain, the northern limit of their presence—and the northern boundary of their entire empire—was the ground between the Tyne and the Solway. North of here was barbarian land, the country of the Caledonians. In A.D. 120 Emperor Hadrian ordered a wall be built, both as a defensive position in case of barbarian attack and as a physical expression of the boundaries of Roman law and order. Hadrian visited the wall in 122.

As it finally stood, Hadrian's Wall was stone-built, 8 feet thick and 15 feet high, with 6-foot battlements on top. Every Roman mile (1,620 yards) there was a milecastle, garrisoned by troops; between each milecastle stood two signal and observation turrets. Every 5 miles was a fort, like a barracks. A deep ditch ran along the front, except where there were natural defenses such as cliffs. The garrison soldiers were mostly recruits from outlying Roman provinces.

INSIDER TIP:

If you can, visit the stretch of wall near Newcastle upon Tyne. It's the best.

—ALISON WRIGHT
National Geographic photographer

By the early fifth century, Hadrian's Wall had been abandoned. Much of the stonework was taken by locals over the ensuing centuries, and sharp eyes may spot the shaped blocks, some inscribed, in the walls of farm buildings, houses, and churches all over the area.

What Remains

Running west from Newcastle upon Tyne, there is a stretch of wall and remains of a turret at **Low Brunton.** The cavalry fort at **Chesters,** in parkland in the Tyne Valley, has a museum full of inscriptions and sculpture, and a well-preserved regimental bathhouse layout with steam rooms and chilling-out chambers. The best section of the wall begins here and runs for 20 miles to Greenhead.

Best known of all the wall sites is **Housesteads Fort,** very well preserved and complete, set in a superbly dramatic position right on the edge of the Whin Sill cliffs with a marvelous view north. The on-site museum is small and rather disappointing, but the fort makes up for it with its gate thresholds worn down by the soldiers' feet, the north gate cornerstones scarred with the scraping of wagons, and a commanding officer's house with black slag still lumped around the bathroom's furnace hearth. There are also communal latrines, cheerless barrack blocks, and a chilly stone-built hospital—and plenty of poignancy and despair.

At **Vindolanda,** just west, extensive military and civilian settlement remains are on show, along with a helpful reconstruction of a stone turret, a length of wall, and a timber milecastle gate. The museum at Vindolanda is excellent.

Hadrian's Wall Path

The Hadrian's Wall Path National Trail stretches 84 miles from Wallsend to Bowness-on-Solway, running for the most part next to the wall. It passes through outstanding scenery and takes in all the Roman forts, museums, and existing sections of the wall. The *Hadrian's Wall Path National Trail Guide* by Anthony Burton (Aurum Press) is the official guide.

Beyond, at **Cawfields,** is a clear section of wall ribboning up and down the undulating landscape. At Walltown Crags are more spectacular views and a good **Roman Army Museum,** next to Magnis Roman fort. At **Birdoswald,** just a little farther west, you'll find another well-preserved fort and bridge abutment worth visiting. ∎

Hadrian's Wall
 263 A4–B4

Chesters Fort
✉ 1.5 miles W of Chollerford
☎ 01434-681379
💲 $$

Housesteads Fort
✉ 2.75 miles NE of Bardon Mill
☎ 01434-344363
💲 $$
www.nationaltrust.org.uk

Vindolanda
✉ 1.25 miles SE of Twice Brewed
☎ 01434-344277
🕐 Winter hours vary; call for details
💲 $$
www.vindolanda.com

Roman Army Museum
✉ Near Greenhead
☎ 01697-747485
🕐 Closed mid-Nov.–mid-Feb.
💲 $$

Birdoswald Fort
✉ Gilsland
☎ 01697-747602
🕐 Interior closed Dec.–Feb.
💲 $–$$

Hadrian's Wall Path National Trail

www.nationaltrail.co.uk/hadrianswall

More Places to Visit in Northeast England

Beamish, the North of England Open Air Museum

To get a flavor of what the northeast was like before the coal mines closed, visit this open-air museum in northern County Durham. Here, set in 300 acres, is a reconstructed pit village complete with pithead buildings, chapel, school, a mine with underground tours guided by ex-miners, and a row of pit cottages with their own vegetable plots (allotment gardens).

A tram ride away is "The Town," complete with cooperative store, candy factory, working pub, dentist's surgery, and its own railroad station. There is also a working farm and Pockerley Manor and gardens, which re-creates life in the early 1800s and 1900s.

A crypt lies underneath Hexham Abbey.

◾ 263 B4 ☎ 0191-370 4000 ⊕ Closed Mon. & Fri. Winter times vary ⑤ $$$

Corbridge

Corbridge is a handsome little place with the fine **Corbridge Roman Fort Museum** *(tel 01434-632349, closed Mon.–Fri. Nov.–March, $$)* just outside town. Here is the outline of a garrison town, and a museum with pottery, weaponry, and superb Roman stonemasonry, including the famous Corbridge Lion crouched over a deer, grinning through his curly beard.

◾ 263 B4 **Visitor Information** ✉ Hill St. ☎ 01434-632815 ⊕ Closed Oct.–Feb.

Hexham

Three miles along the valley by road or train is Hexham, another old town close to the wall that has seen plenty of bloodshed and strife. In **Hexham Abbey,** perched high above the river, are fascinating historical relics, including the elaborately carved pagan memorial slab of Flavinus, a standard-bearer in a Roman cavalry regiment. Ask a steward to be taken down into the dark, cold crypt; here are inscribed stones from Hadrian's Wall and pagan altar slabs.

◾ 263 B4 **Visitor Information** ✉ Wentworth Car Park ☎ 01434-652220 ⊕ Closed Sun. Oct.–Feb.

Hull

The old fishing port on the River Humber in southeast Yorkshire is a fascinating place often bypassed by visitors. It's a town with a strong flavor—and aroma, when the wind blows from the docks! You can pick up walking guide leaflets to Hull's **Fish Trail** and **Ale Trail** at the tourist office. Well worth visiting is **The Deep** aquarium and sea museum *(tel 01482-381000).*

◾ 263 D2 **Visitor Information** ✉ 1 Paragon St. ☎ 01482-223559

Diversity and beauty combined—tumbled lands, Border abbeys and castles, lively Glasgow, and dignified Edinburgh

Scottish Lowlands

A dress sporran, a kilt's equivalent of a pocket

Scottish Lowlands

Published in Sir Walter Scott's compilation of folk ballads, *The Minstrelsy of the Scottish Border* (1802–1803), the "Lads of Wamphray" celebrates a 16th-century skirmish between two Scottish families: "Out through the Crichtons Willie he ran, / And dang them down baith horse and man; / O but the Johnstones were wondrous rude, / When the Biddesburn ran three days blood!" But it was not just the Crichtons and the Johnstones who fought, feuded, and raided across the rolling landscape of the Scottish Borders.

Border Strife

During medieval times these rounded hill ranges, which form the southernmost region of Scotland, were savagely disputed between neighbor and neighbor. Cattle-thieving, raiding, and opportunistic killing were a way of life. As for cross-border relations, a Scots defeat by the English army of Edward I at the Battle of Dunbar in 1299, and another by the army of Henry VIII at Flodden Field in 1513, bookended more than two centuries of international warfare and bloodshed throughout the region. Incursion and counterthrust went on until the mid-17th century, and a more settled—though not entirely happy—atmosphere only really descended after the 1707 Act of Union between the two countries.

Various Strongholds

Four great Border abbeys were founded within a short distance of each other during the reign of the Scots king David I (*r.* 1124–1153), partly bankrolled by the king as a statement of his would-be authority among these lawless hills: Kelso, Melrose, and Dryburgh along the Tweed Valley southeast of Edinburgh, and Jedburgh 10 miles farther south.

The most powerful local lords, who actually wielded the influence that counted hereabouts, built themselves castles and fortified towerfortresses such as the Douglases' 15th-century Tantallon Castle on the East Lothian coast and the 16th-century Smailholm Tower near Kelso, where Sir Walter Scott spent boyhood vacations, or less celebrated strongholds such

Sir Walter Scott

Sir Walter Scott (1771–1832), though rarely read nowadays, is undoubtedly Scotland's best known and most influential novelist. As a delicate and imaginative boy, he became passionately attached to Jacobite, Highland, and Border history and legend.

Scott's 1802–1803 poetical collection *The Border Minstrelsy* sparked tremendous interest in the bloody Border feuds, and his Waverley series of novels (produced at yearly intervals from 1814 on—*Waverley, Ivanhoe, Rob Roy, The Heart of Midlothian*, and others) romanticized and popularized Scottish legend as history,

especially the Jacobite Rebellions of 1715 and 1745. The great 19th-century revival of interest in tartans, kilts, and Scottish music and dance was largely due to Scott's influence.

In spite of his enormous fame and success, Scott's finances were always in poor shape because of unlucky business moves and overspending on his beloved house of Abbotsford (see p. 291). He wrote his great novels under pressure, to stave off debt, and ruined his health with overwork. This son of the Borders, who did so much to restore the pride of Scotland, lies buried in Dryburgh Abbey (see p. 290).

NOT TO BE MISSED:

A visit to national poet Robert Burns's birthplace **293**

Climbing up Ben Lomond, the "everyman's Munro" **296**

Glasgow's eclectic Burrell Collection **296**

Playing a round of golf at the Royal & Ancient **301**

Exploring Edinburgh's Old and New Towns **304–307**

A boat trip to the gannet-haunted Bass Rock **308**

as the 14th-century Neidpath Castle and the 15th-century Barns Tower on the River Tweed, near Peebles.

For all the area's grim history, this is one of Scotland's most beautiful regions. Among the hills are small characterful market towns, each a center for walking, horseback riding, and exploring the great houses of the Borders, from Scott's Abbotsford and the old Maxwell Stuart seat of Traquair to the 18th-century Floors and Culzean Castles. And around Alloway lie the birthplace and haunts of Scotland's national poet, Robert Burns. ■

Scottish Borders

Put aside a couple days at least to explore the country between England and Scotland. Here are great pine forests and heather moors, giving way as you go north to a greener and more pastoral landscape along the valley floors and around the little Scottish Border towns. And don't forget to venture south and west, to discover the hills and coasts of Galloway.

The Border lands offer beautiful vistas of rolling hills dotted with small towns.

Jedburgh Abbey
- ⚑ 289 D2
- ☎ 01835-863925
- 💲 $$

Dryburgh Abbey
- ⚑ 289 D2
- ✉ 5 miles SE of Melrose on B6404
- ☎ 01835-822381
- 💲 $–$$

Kelso Abbey
- ⚑ 289 D3
- 🕐 Closed Sun. a.m.

Jedburgh Abbey

Heading north from Hadrian's Wall (see pp. 284–285), the first of the four great 12th-century Border abbeys is Jedburgh (1138). The garth (monk's garden) at the abbey is evocatively complete behind its cloister wall, and there are some ornate tombs of medieval bishops and abbots as well.

The abbey museum contains early Christian carvings and a 12th-century walrus-tusk comb with both fine and coarse teeth.

Dryburgh Abbey

North of Jedburgh, in the wide valley of the River Tweed, is Dryburgh Abbey (1150), whose monastic buildings are in excellent condition, including the vaulted chapter house and the refectory with its rose window. The abbey's north transept holds the tombs of two famous Scots: Field Marshal Earl Haig, architect of many of Britain's World War I triumphs and disasters, and poet and novelist Sir Walter Scott (see sidebar p. 288).

Kelso Abbey

At Kelso, east of Dryburgh, not much remains of the Benedictine abbey (1128), but the north transept's beautifully carved facade is worth the detour.

Just outside the town is **Floors Castle** (tel 01573-223333, closed late Oct.–Easter), a huge castle-style mansion designed by William Adam in the early 1720s.

Melrose Abbey

Melrose Abbey (1136), the area's fourth abbey, is charmingly sited below the Eildon Hills just north of Dryburgh. Arches set the keynote here, among them soaring window arches (Robert the Bruce's heart is said to be buried below the great east window) and the arches of the cloisters and monastic quarters.

Two miles west on the bank of the River Tweed is **Abbotsford House** (tel 01896-752043, closed Nov.–mid-March), built by Sir Walter Scott between 1811 and 1822. Inside, you can see the desk at which Scott wrote the Waverley novels, the chair he sat in, the bed he died in, and a collection of memorabilia celebrating his life.

Traquair House

West again is Innerleithen and Traquair House, the oldest continuously inhabited house in Scotland. Traquair looks every inch the dwelling of an ancient Border family. The ups and downs of that family through the centuries are touchingly apparent in the assortment of Jacobite mementoes, Tudor relics, and secret holes and corners where priests, villains, and heroes hid in various states of extremity.

Dumfries

To the southwest is the town of Dumfries, where poet Robert Burns (see pp. 292–293) died in 1796. You can visit **Burns House** (Burns St., tel 01387-255297, closed Sun.–Mon. Oct.–March), where he died, now a museum; the **Burns Mausoleum,** where he lies in St. Michael's Churchyard; the **Burns Statue** by Greyfriars Church; and the **Robert Burns Centre** (Mill Rd., tel 01387-264808, closed Sun.–Mon. Oct.–March), which tells of his life here.

The north coast of the Solway Firth offers superb bird-watching, especially at the **Wildfowl and Wetlands Trust Centre** (Caerlaverock, tel 01387-770200). Nearby is moated **Caerlaverock Castle** (tel 01387-770244). ■

Melrose Abbey

- 🅐 289 C3
- ☎ 01896-822562
- 🕐 Closed Sun. a.m. Oct.–March
- 💲 $$

Traquair House

- 🅐 289 C3
- ✉ Innerleithen
- ☎ 01896-830323
- 🕐 Closed Nov.–Easter
- 💲 $$$
- **www.traquair.co.uk**

Dumfries

- 🅐 289 B2
- **Visitor Information**
- ✉ 64 Whitesands
- ☎ 01387-253862

EXPERIENCE: Explore the Border Hills

The delectable, rolling, easily manageable Border hills and valleys beckon you to explore the excellent **Southern Upland Way** (SUW; www.southernuplandway.gov.uk). This waymarked footpath runs 212 miles from Portpatrick in the extreme southwest of Galloway, right across the Border wilds to Cockburnspath on the east coast. It crosses some tough and rugged country of wonderful beauty. There are also plenty of opportunities to do short loop walks from the SUW; local rangers have prepared a guide to more than 50 such excursions on the eastern section of the SUW, downloadable at www.scotborders.gov.uk/pdf/4986.pdf.

Burns Country

Robert Burns (1759–1796), the "heaven-taught ploughman," is a towering figure in the national psyche of Scotland. Born in a poor clay cottage, sketchily educated, with a deep-rooted aversion to authority and the high-and-mighty, and fond of high jinks in bed and bar, Burns lived fast (by the standards of a small-time rural Scots farmer) and died comparatively young.

Brig o'Doon in Alloway, the setting for one of Burns's most famous poems, "Tam O'Shanter"

Alloway

🏛 289 A2

Ayr

🏛 289 A2

Visitor Information

✉ 22 Sandgate

☎ 01292-290300

🕐 Closed Sun.
Nov.–Feb.

Robert Burns used his quick-witted poetic gift to excoriate the rich and wellborn, satirize politicians, glorify the nation's heroes, and make epic comic verse out of the drunken adventures of his friends.

Burns Night suppers are celebrated with haggis, turnips, whisky, and a kilted piper on January 25, the poet's birthday, not only in Scotland itself but in every corner of the world where members of the Scottish diaspora are found.

Early Years

Burns was brought up in a plain-living household among rural-dialect speakers, and that earthy atmosphere informs all his

best poetry. The family moved about from farm to farm around the Ayr district until Burns's father, William, died in 1784. Two years later Burns produced his first volume, *Poems Chiefly in the Scottish Dialect*, which was an immediate hit with Scots of all classes. A head-turning winter in Edinburgh followed, with the young farmer often camouflaging his awkwardness by playing up his lack of polish and sophistication.

The next few years saw Burns's best work: a comic masterpiece in "Tam O'Shanter," a socialist polemic in *A Man's a Man for a' That*, and a flood of songs still passionately sung by Scots today, including "Auld Lang Syne," "Green

Grow the Rashes-O," "Scots Wha Hae wi Wallace Bled," and dozens more. Toward the end of his life Burns achieved financial stability with a job as an exciseman. But he had burned himself out and died of rheumatic fever in Dumfries at age 37, his future status as a Scottish icon assured.

Alloway

The very heart of Burns Country is undoubtedly Alloway, just to the south of Ayr. On the main road through the village is **Robert Burns Birthplace,** the house where Burns was born on January 25, 1759.

Nearby are the heroic **Burns Monument** of 1823, and two places featured in Burns's comic epic poem "Tam O'Shanter"—the roofless shell of **Alloway Old Kirk** (burial place of the poet's father), where drunken Tam saw the devil playing bagpipes for a wild witches' and warlocks' dance, and below it the early medieval **Brig o'Doon,** the bridge across which Tam's mare, Meg, "brought off her master hale / But left behind her ain grey tail."

Ayr & Around

In Ayr town stands the 13th-century **Auld Brig,** Burns's "poor narrow footpath of a street / Where two wheelbarrows tremble when they meet." The **Tam O'Shanter pub** on High Street is decorated with quotations from the poet.

Five miles northeast of Ayr is **Tarbolton** village, with the thatched house, now a National Trust for Scotland museum, where

Burns learned to dance, became a Freemason, and formed a Bachelors' Club. Burns lived at nearby **Lochlea Farm** (signposted) from 1777 until his father's death.

East at **Mauchline** are **Burns House Museum,** where in February 1788 the poet rented a room for his mistress Jean Armour; **Gavin Hamilton's House** (private residence), next to Mauchline Tower, where he married her; **Poosie Nansie's Tavern,** one of his haunts; and **Mauchline Church** (closed Sept.– May & Thurs.–Mon. June–Aug.), since rebuilt, where Burns had to do public penance for fornication, and in whose churchyard four of his children are buried.

INSIDER TIP:

Dunure, 6 miles southwest of Ayr, is a classic fishing village, pretty and low key, with the ruins of a castle nearby.

—JANE SUNDERLAND
National Geographic contributor

Twelve miles south of Ayr, Kirkoswald has a Burns museum in **Souter Johnnie's Cottage** (Main Rd., tel 0844-493 2147, closed Oct.–March), the thatched house of "souter" (cobbler) John Davidson. Burns featured him in "Tam O'Shanter" as the "ancient, trusty, drouthy cronie" of the poem's hero, Tam, who was also based on a local man, Douglas Graham of nearby Shanter Farm. ∎

Robert Burns Birthplace

- ✉ Burns National Heritage Park, Murdoch's Ln., Alloway
- ☎ 0844-493 2601
- 💲 $$

www.burnsmuseum.org.uk

Burns House Museum

- ✉ Castle St., Mauchline
- ☎ 01290-550045
- 🕐 Closed Nov.–Easter & Sun.–Mon. Easter–Oct.

Glasgow & Around

Glasgow's recent shedding of a long-established grim image has been something of a modern miracle. The city has been selected to host the 2014 Commonwealth Games; yet only 30 years ago Glasgow was notorious for unemployment, violence, and slum housing. But the city owes much to its prosperous industrial heritage, not least the superb art collections donated to the city over the years by the sons of Glasgow, such as Sir William Burrell, who made it big.

The late Victorian bulk of the City Chambers towers above George Square.

Glasgow

◪ 289 B3

Visitor Information

✉ 11 George Sq.

☎ 0141-204 4400

In the 18th century Glasgow merchants, enriched by transatlantic trade, established a city of fine dwellings, grand offices, and warehouses. Victorian bankers and insurance brokers built handsome squares and terraces.

During the 19th century, the city's population grew tenfold. Shipyards lined the River Clyde, and iron foundries and heavy engineering works proliferated. Some of the worst city slums in Europe developed, persisting until long after World War II. It has taken some typically bold and aggressive self-promotion, a very Glaswegian attitude, to turn things around.

George Square

Grand civic buildings dominate George Square, chiefly the enormous 1888 City Chambers. St. Vincent Street leads west, lined with elaborate Victorian pomp-and-circumstance: unicorns above the Old Post Office Building door, Ionic columns on the Old Bank of Scotland (now a pub), and the towering pink sandstone Royal Chambers and Liverpool & London & Globe Insurance buildings. Compare these sonorous temples of commerce with the modern lines of the Prudential offices or the adventurousness of Nos. 151 to 155.

North of Vincent Street, and parallel to it, runs famous Sauchiehall Street, once the rowdiest thoroughfare in the city. North again, at 145 Buccleuch Street, the **Tenement House** is a Glasgow apartment block built in 1892. The upstairs is crammed with the possessions of Miss Agnes Toward, a typist who lived here from 1911 until 1965.

Glasgow School of Art

At the corner of Scott and Renfrew Streets is the Glasgow School of Art, an architectural masterpiece by pioneering art nouveau designer Charles Rennie Mackintosh (1868–1928). It still functions as an art school, but guided tours introduce visitors to Mackintosh's novel ideas—maximizing space; simple, dark wood paneling to emphasize light from above; bold bow shapes in ceiling joists; and the use of worked metal and stained glass.

St. Mungo's Cathedral

The interior of the medieval St. Mungo's Cathedral (tel 0141-552 6891) descends from the tall west end by steps to the much lower east end, which is the cathedral's crypt. In the crypt's vaulted chapel lies the tomb of St. Mungo, who founded a chapel here in the sixth century.

Nearby in Castle Street is the **St. Mungo Museum of Religious Life and Art** (tel 0141-276 1629), an intriguing mishmash that includes Hindu gods, Taoist chinaware, animist fetishes, Islamic prayer rugs, Egyptian mummies, and Christian stained-glass images.

Across the road stands the tall **Provand's Lordship** (tel 0141-552 8819), Glasgow's oldest house, built in 1471 for one of the canons of St. Mungo's. Later, the house became—among other things—a common tavern, as an exhibit points out. Outside is a garden, planted with medicinal herbs.

Kelvingrove Park

In Glasgow's leafy West End a few good galleries and museums cluster around beautiful Kelvingrove Park. The **Art Gallery and Museum,** in a vast sandstone pseudo-castle of 1901, contains collections of British and Continental paintings; these feature a gallery of Scottish works

INSIDER TIP:

Take tea in style in the Willow Rooms, a 1903 Mackintosh creation with tall ladderbacked chairs and his characteristic stained-glass windows.

—CHRISTOPHER SOMERVILLE
National Geographic author

(the Glencoes by McCulloch and Hamilton are noteworthy), Constable's "Hampstead Heath," Turner's "Modern Italy," and some beautiful Flemish landscapes and French works.

On the other side of the park are the dour Victorian buildings of Glasgow University; here is the **Hunterian Art Gallery** (82 Hillhead St., tel 0141-330 5431, closed

Glasgow
 289 B3
Visitor Information
✉ 11 George Sq.
☎ 0141-204 4400

Tenement House
✉ 145 Buccleuch St., Garnethill
☎ 0844-493 2197
🕐 Closed Nov.–Feb.
💲 $$
www.nts.org.uk/ Property/59

Glasgow School of Art
✉ 167 Renfrew St.
☎ 0141-353 4500
🕐 Closed Sun. Sept.–June

Art Gallery and Museum
✉ Aryle St., Kelvingrove
☎ 0141-276 9541
www.glasgowlife.org .uk/museums

Willow Rooms
✉ 217 Sauchiehall St.
☎ 0141-223 0521

EXPERIENCE: Climb Ben Lomond

Ben Lomond is a proper mountain, a 3,192-foot Munro (a 3,000-foot-plus peak) that rears magnificently from the eastern shore of Loch Lomond. A very well beaten track leads west from the National Trust for Scotland parking lot just beyond Rowardennan Hotel *(6 miles N of Balmaha)*, before swinging north on a long but straightforward climb to the summit. This is a climb for fit people on a day of good weather. On average, allow six hours. Ben Lomond makes a splendid challenge, with a 100-mile view from the summit. Bring a packed lunch and plenty of hot drinks, and keep an eye

on the time and weather—with tired legs it takes as long to come down as it does to go up. The reward is not only the view but also the unbeatable sense of achievement—something that can light the fuse on a long love affair with the Scottish mountains.

You can also tackle this "everyman's Munro" by a less used path from Rowardennan up the western flank, with fabulous views over Loch Lomond. For either climb, refer to the map "OS Explorer 364" *(www .ordnancesurvey.co.uk)*. Visit the website of Loch Lomond and the Trossachs National Park (see p. 297) for more information.

Burrell Collection

✉ 2060 Pollokshaws Rd., Pollok Country Park

☎ 0141-287 2550

www.glasgowlife.org .uk/museums

Riverside Museum

✉ Pointhouse Quay, Yorkhill

☎ 0141-287 2720

www.glasgowlife.org .uk/museums

Sun.), with paintings, drawings, and prints by such artists as Pissarro and Corot, Rembrandt and Whistler, as well as a reconstruction of principal rooms from the town house of art nouveau design genius Mackintosh. The **Hunterian Museum** *(University Ave., tel 0141-330 4221, closed Sun.),* whose zoological and archaeological displays are the longest established in Scotland (since 1807), is also here.

Farther north, at 870 Garscube Road, **Queens Cross Church** is the only example of a complete Mackintosh-designed church, a curious-looking sandstone construction, tapered outside and full of images of light and dark within. The church is the headquarters of the **Charles Rennie Mackintosh Society** *(closed Sat.);* ring the bell to be admitted or call 0141-946 6600.

Burrell Collection

Three miles southwest of the center of Glasgow is Scotland's finest individual collection of art and artifacts—the delight

and obsession of Glaswegian shipowner Sir William Burrell (1861–1958), who gave it to his native city in 1944 and then continued to add to it.

Housed in a modern building within the leafy acres of Pollok Country Park, the collection is superbly laid out. Elaborately carved medieval doorways lead from Rodin bronzes to Etruscan mirrors, Persian carpets, Tang dynasty tomb guardians, suits of armor, and 16th-century German religious carvings in limewood. Hogarth, Rembrandt, Reynolds, Romney, and Sir Henry Raeburn are among the portrait painters; Lucas Cranach the Elder's "Judith" (1530) shows the biblical heroine smiling over her bloody sword at the severed head of Holofernes; Millet, Sisley, Cézanne, Degas, and Manet represent the French Impressionists.

Around Glasgow

The **Riverside Museum** at Pointhouse Quay, Yorkhill, is the new site and name of the former Museum of Transport. It displays huge steam locomotives, a tall sailing ship, vintage cars, trams, and much more transport treasure to gladden any child's heart.

South of Glasgow you'll find the tall cotton mills of **New Lanark,** a workplace that in the 19th century became a model of good practice, humane treatment, and education, and now a UNESCO World Heritage site. Take the New Millennium Experience ride and walk the path to the spectacular Falls of Clyde.

North of the city are the **Campsie Fells,** the nearest piece of upland walking country for Glaswegians. The Campsies rise to 1,800 feet, a hummock of moorland, farmland, and rolling hills with deeply scored sides.

Loch Lomond: By far the best known countryside recreation area north of Glasgow is Loch Lomond, still—despite the fame of its "bonny, bonny banks"—enjoyable at all times of the year except crowded summer weekends. In 2002 the whole area of Loch Lomond and the neighboring Trossach Hills was designated **Loch Lomond and the Trossachs National Park,** Scotland's first national park.

The A82, narrow and winding, shadows the west bank of the loch and gives the best views; the even narrower and far less frequented east bank road is too often among the trees for consistently good views, but takes you north for 6 miles from Balmaha to the Rowardennan Hotel. Climb Ben Lomond (see sidebar p. 296) from here.

You can continue all the way up the loch on the West Highland Way footpath. Or, if you're feeling lazy, take a boat trip among Loch Lomond's islands from Balloch at the south end, but get there early to avoid the lines. ■

New Lanark
- 289 B3
- ✉ 25 miles SE of Glasgow via the A73
- ☎ 01555-661345
- $ $$ (visitor center)

www.newlanark.org

Campsie Fells
- 289 B3

Loch Lomond and the Trossachs National Park
- 289 A3–A4

www.lochlomond-trossachs.org

The beauty of Loch Lomond draws countless visitors to its shores.

A Drive from Glasgow to St. Andrews

This pleasant drive takes you north from central Glasgow, passing the rolling Camspie Fells, to Stirling with its magnificent castle. From here, you follow a rural route south of the Ochil Hills before reaching St. Andrews, the home of golf.

From junction 17 of the M8 motorway in Glasgow (see pp. 294–297), follow the A82 Dumbarton road, then turn right onto the A81, heading north. Ten miles north of Strathblane, turn right onto the A811 to descend the wide Forth Valley to Stirling.

The town of **Stirling** ❶ *(visitor information, tel 08707-200620)* rises up the spine of a long volcanic crag, culminating in the famous castle perched dramatically at the 250-foot summit.

Among the attractions along the cobbled streets are the 15th-century **Church of the Holy Rude** (Rood), where James VI (later James I of England), the 13-month-old son of Mary, Queen of Scots, was crowned in 1567 as successor to his deposed mother; a 1632 town house, residence for the Dukes of Argyll,

known as **Argyll's Lodging** *(tel 01786-431319)*; and the ornate 16th-century facade of **Mar's Wark,** a grand residence planned but not completed by the 1st Earl of Mar, hereditary Keeper of Stirling Castle and regent of Scotland during James VI's infancy.

Pride of the town, though, is **Stirling Castle** ❷ *(tel 01786-450000),* used by Scottish monarchs James IV (r. 1488–1513), James V (r. 1513–1542), Mary, Queen of Scots (r. 1542–1567), and James VI (r. 1567–1625) as their Royal Court.

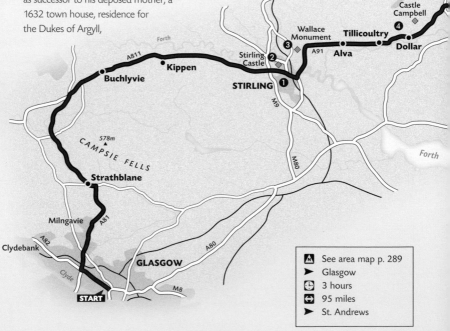

See area map p. 289
▶ Glasgow
🕓 3 hours
↔ 95 miles
▶ St. Andrews

Inside are spacious State Rooms; most of them are empty, but one contains the Stirling Heads—56 beautifully carved oak medallions commissioned by James V when he converted the grim fortress into a comfortable dwelling. The Chapel Royal contains a 17th-century frieze and a trompe l'oeil west window; and the sumptuous Great Hall echoes all the kingly pride of James IV, its creator. In the higher part of the castle

NOT TO BE MISSED:

Mar's Wark • Stirling Castle • Castle Campbell • St. Andrews castle

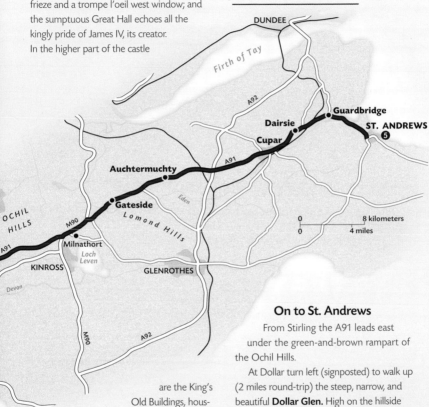

are the King's Old Buildings, housing the excellent **Regimental Museum** of the Argyll and Sutherland Highlanders, with ceremonial dress, mementoes from the regiment's service around the world, and remarkable photographs of the Crimean War.

Two miles north of the town stands the **National Wallace Monument** ❸ (*Abbey Craig, tel 01786-472140*), erected to the Scots hero Sir William Wallace executed by the English in 1305. There are superb views from the top.

On to St. Andrews

From Stirling the A91 leads east under the green-and-brown rampart of the Ochil Hills.

At Dollar turn left (signposted) to walk up (2 miles round-trip) the steep, narrow, and beautiful **Dollar Glen.** High on the hillside at the top is the stark, atmospheric ruin of **Castle Campbell** ❹ (*tel 01259-742408, closed Thurs.–Fri. Oct–March*).

The A91 continues into the flatter farming country of Fife, eventually reaching **St. Andrews** ❺ (*visitor information, tel 01334-472021*), a charming town set above broad sands and rocky bays, and a mecca for golfers (see pp. 300–301). Visit the cathedral ruins on a headland, the castle with its 16th-century mine tunnels, and the two university college quadrangles of St. Salvator and St. Mary's.

The Game of Golf

The worldwide fame of St. Andrews rests squarely on its status as the home of golf. It was here, on the flat grass that covers the St. Andrews sand dunes, that medieval Scots began banging a ball about with a stick. Three Scots kings in succession—James II in 1457, James III in 1471, and James IV in 1491—banned the "unprofitable sporte of golfe," which was distracting young men from going to church and from practicing their archery.

Keen players enjoy a round of golf on the course at St. Andrews's Royal and Ancient Golf Club.

James IV must have thought better of his decree—or maybe he was himself bitten by the bug—because in 1502 he legitimized the game. By 1567, the year that Mary, Queen of Scots, played golf at St. Andrews, the sport had become the ruling passion of Scots from all walks of life.

Royal Approval

In 1754 a group of "22 noblemen and gentlemen of Fife" established the Society of St. Andrews Golfers in order to run an annual competition. The seal of royal approval was granted in 1834 when William IV accepted the patronage of the society, which renamed itself the Royal and Ancient Golf Club (R&A). Twenty years later the R&A built itself a handsome stone clubhouse, which still stands in its superb position overlooking the Old Course and the wide West Sands. In 1873 the British Open Championship took place here for the first time, and since then it has regularly been held at St. Andrews.

Great Golfers

Most of the greatest names in the history of golf have had strong connections with St. Andrews, and revolutionary developments in the equipment, rules, and conduct of the game have emanated down the years from this small Fife seaside town.

In 1845 the first gutta-percha ball was made here, replacing the old-style ball with its core of feathers. Allan Robertson (1815–1859), a ballmaker now recognized as one of the world's first professional golfers, won a championship match here with a feathery ball in 1842, and another with a gutta-percha ball in 1858. Robertson was so good at the game that after his feather-ball triumph, he was banned from caddy contests by his brother caddies, "it being their impression that they would have no chance in any competition in which Allan took part."

Another great character was Old Tom Morris (1821–1908), who became the Royal and

Swilcan Bridge connects the 1st and 18th fairways and has become a cultural icon in golf.

Ancient Golf Club's first professional golfer in 1865. He won the Open in 1861, 1862, 1864, and 1867 and laid out the New Course, which was opened in 1895.

Tom's son, Young Tom Morris (1851–1875), was a golfer as redoubtable as his father, winning the Open in 1868, 1869, 1870, and 1872. Young and Old Tom, along with Robertson and a dozen more golfing greats, lie in the precincts of St. Andrews Cathedral burial ground; a leaflet *(available from St. Andrews visitor center, 70 Market St., tel 01334-472021)* shows the location of their graves.

INSIDER TIP:

You can walk the Old Course for free on Sundays, when it is closed to golf. Another great walk is the beach below.

—LARRY PORGES
Editor, National Geographic Books

EXPERIENCE: A Round or Two at the R&A

Each year tens of thousands of golfers come to St. Andrews with the intention of playing a ceremonial round on the R&A's celebrated **Old Course.** If you want to do the same, make a reservation months ahead *(tel 01334-466666, www .saintandrews.org.uk, $$$$$)*, bone up on the rules *(www.randa.org)*, turn up well in advance of your tee time, and allow four or five hours to complete the 6,566-yard course (par 72).

Bunkers with names such as Pulpit, Principal's Nose, Cat's Trap, Lion's Mouth, and Hell lie in wait for the unwary. Deacon Sime's Bunker contains the ashes of the eponymous cleric; he declared that since he'd spent half his life in the bunker, he should spend eternity there, too.

Other courses in St. Andrews are New (par 71), Jubilee (par 72), Bronze (par 69), Eden (par 70), Strathtyrum (par 69), and the nine-hole Balgrove (par 30).

Edinburgh

Solid, dignified, complacent: traditional Edinburgh as it appears through its monumental architecture and superb location on and among rugged volcanic crags. Lively, outgoing, unstuffy: modern Edinburgh, as its citizens think of it. In spite of Glasgow's pretensions, Edinburgh is unquestionably the capital city of the Scots.

Edinburgh Castle became Scotland's primary royal castle during the Middle Ages.

Edinburgh

▲ 289 C3

Visitor Information

✉ 3 Princes St.

☎ 0845-225 5121

Edinburgh is an outstanding city. The dark courts and cobbled streets of the medieval Old Town contrast with the grand Georgian squares, circuses, and crescents of the New Town, planned in the 18th century. These areas are explored in the walks on pages 300–303, starting with **Edinburgh Castle,** with which the city's history is closely bound.

Perched high atop Castle Rock, an extinct volcano, the castle gives views over nearly 100 miles of Lowland Scotland. This high point

has been a strategically used for centuries, with records indicating that a fortress, Din Eidyn, appeared circa A.D. 600. The first major castle was erected around 1130; it was rebuilt in 1356 and then again in 1574–1578, becoming at that point very much the castle that exists today.

Within the castle's walls are dank cells and dungeons for both military and civilian prisoners; the great siege cannon Mons Meg, forged in 1457; military museums exploring more than 400 years of military history; and the shrine of the **Scottish National War Memorial,** which commemorates Scottish casualties in both World Wars and ensuing military campaigns. The royal palace of

INSIDER TIP:

Make time to enjoy an Edinburgh Literary Pub Tour. Tours begin at the Beehive Inn at 7:30 p.m. Bring your thirst for Robert Burns, Sir Walter Scott, and others (and good ales, of course)!

—MARY JO SLAZAK
*Manager, Subsidiary Rights,
National Geographic Books*

the Scottish monarchs contains a lineup of its incumbents' portraits, among which the dour, dark Stuarts stand out in sulky pride.

Also here are displayed the ancient regalia (Ceremonial Honours of Scotland)—jeweled sword, scepter, and crown—which were discovered in 1818 as the result of a search initiated by Sir Walter Scott, sealed in the Crown Room where they had lain forgotten for over a century. Alongside lies the Stone of Destiny (sometimes called the Stone of Scone, after Scone Palace where it was kept from 838 onward), on which all Scots kings were crowned from the sixth century until the English king Edward I took it south to Westminster Abbey in 1296. The stone was ceremoniously returned to Scotland in November 1996. ∎

Edinburgh Castle
- ✉ Castle Hill
- ☎ 0131-225 9846
- 💲 $$$
- **www.edinburgh
castle.gov.uk**

**Edinburgh
Literary Pub
Tour**
- ✉ Beehive Inn, 18–20 Grassmarket
- 💲 $$$
- **www.edinburgh
literarypubtour.co.uk**

EXPERIENCE: Hogmanay in Edinburgh

The biggest, loudest, proudest Scottish national celebration of the year takes place on New Year's Eve. This seeing-out of the last night of the old year is known to all Scots as Hogmanay. Are the origins of the word French (*homme est né,* man is born), Anglo-Saxon (*halege monath,* holy month), Flemish (*hoog min dag,* big love day), or Gaelic (*oge maiden,* young morning)? No one knows—and no one cares, once the whisky is poured and the ceilidh is under way.

Hogmanay is to the Scots what St. Patrick's Day is to the Irish and Thanksgiving is to U.S. citizens—a chance to express national solidarity and pride with one's compatriots, preferably on home soil. Expatriate Scots come home from far and wide for the Hogmanay celebrations, and the venue for the biggest party of them all is, naturally, Edinburgh.

Torchlit procession, fireworks display, bands, lights, music, and dancing—it's all here, and it's all intense. Don't plan to start for home at midnight-plus-one—you won't be able to, and you won't want to. All you'll need is a bottle to share, lots of stamina, and the words of Robert Burns's classic all-together-now song of solidarity, "Auld Lang Syne":

*Should auld acquaintance be forgot,
and never brought to mind?
Should auld acquaintance be forgot,
and auld lang syne?*

CHORUS:
*For auld lang syne, my jo,
for auld lang syne,
we'll tak a cup o' kindness yet,
for auld lang syne.*

Two Edinburgh Walks

Two very distinct Edinburghs stand side by side—Old Town and New Town. Allow at least a day to walk slowly about each. The Edinburgh and Scotland Information Centre (see visitor information p. 302) provides all kinds of background and arranges walking tours of the city with themes ranging from architecture to ghosts and crime.

Old Town Walk

Many of Edinburgh's oldest and most interesting buildings have survived and are still in use. "Auld Reekie," the stinking and smoky old city crammed upon a ridge, lives on (though it is now more salubrious) along the flanks of the Royal Mile, the sloping road that connects the grim military castle on its high crag and the Palace of Holyroodhouse at the foot of the hill. **Edinburgh Castle** (see p. 302) commands the city from its height and is the place to start your walk.

From the esplanade in front of the castle, the **Royal Mile** descends as Castlehill, Lawnmarket, High Street, and then Canongate between the tall houses of the **Old Town.** The Royal Mile is packed with whisky sellers, kiltmakers, Highland crafts shops and weavers, excellent museums, and other attractions. Chief among these, in order of encounter walking down from the castle, are the self-explanatory **Scotch Whisky Heritage Centre ❶** (354 Castlehill, tel 0131-220 0441); **Gladstone's Land ❷** (477b Lawnmarket, tel 0131-226 5856, closed Nov.–March), a restored six-story land (tenement house) built for an Edinburgh merchant in 1620 and featuring colorful painted ceilings and astonishingly cramped accommodations; the **Writers' Museum ❸** (Lady Stair's Close, Lawnmarket, tel 0131-529 4901,

---

NOT TO BE MISSED IN OLD TOWN:

Gladstone's Land • Palace of Holyroodhouse

---

closed Sun.), dedicated to Scott, Stevenson, and Burns, housed in the turreted and elaborately carved Lady Stair's House, built in 1622; **St. Giles' Cathedral,** below the Lawnmarket, the High Kirk of Edinburgh where John Knox was minister (1559–1572); and **John Knox's House ❹** (43–45 High St., tel 0131-556 9579, closed Sun. Oct.–June), elbowing into High Street, a beautifully carved and painted 16th-century town

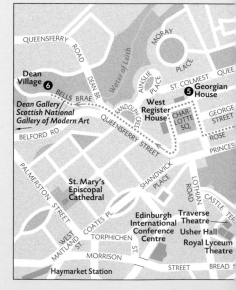

Old Town Walk

- ⬛ See area map p. 289
- ► Castle Esplanade
- 🕐 6 hours
- ↔ 2 miles
- ► Palace of Holyroodhouse

house where the fiery preacher and spearhead of the Scottish Reformation lived toward the end of his life.

Below this are the **People's Story Museum** *(tel 0131-529 4057, closed Sun.),* housed in the old Tolbooth (city jail) on the left of Canongate, which explores the work, fights, fun, and suffering of the city's citizens through the centuries, and the **Museum of Edinburgh** **⑤** *(142 Canongate, tel 0131-529 4143, closed Sun.)* on the right, housed in three 16th-century houses and full of the city's history—a contemporary copy of the original 1638 National Covenant is here.

Taverns & Kirks: Along the Royal Mile are numerous wynds (narrow alleys) and closes (enclosed courts), hemmed in by tall lands built ever higher during the cramped Middle Ages. The 17th-century **Milne's Court,** on the left above Gladstone's Land, gives a good idea of a close.

There are many characterful pubs to enjoy as well. In **Deacon Brodie's Tavern** on the Lawnmarket, mural paintings tell the story of William Brodie. This respectable Edinburgh councillor by day and burglar by night designed the gallows on which he was himself hanged in 1788. Robert Louis Stevenson is believed to have based his novel *The Strange Case of Dr. Jekyll and Mr. Hyde* (1886) on the double life of Deacon Brodie.

Across from Deacon Brodie's Tavern, George IV Bridge leads off to the right. A five-minute walk along here leads to **Greyfriars Kirk,** in whose graveyard dissenting Presbyterians signed the National Covenant in 1638—some in their own blood. Under pink granite headstones lie "Auld Jock" Gray (1858) and his faithful terrier Bobby (1872). The dog mourned by his master's grave for 14 years and became an international celebrity. A memorial drinking fountain, topped with a statue of Greyfriars Bobby, stands outside the churchyard.

New Town Walk

- 🅜 See area map p. 289
- ➤ The Mound, Princes Street
- 🕐 6 hours
- ⬌ 2.5 miles
- ➤ Dean Village

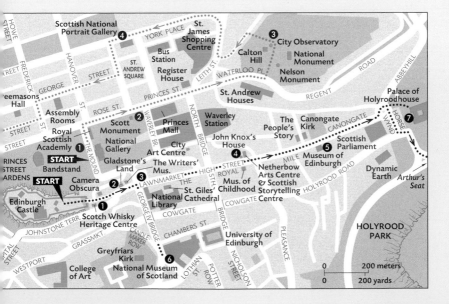

On Chambers Street, just opposite the Greyfriars Bobby memorial, the history of Scotland unrolls in the fortress-like modern **National Museum of Scotland** ❻ (tel 0300-123 6789).

A Royal Palace: At the bottom of Canongate stands the Scottish Parliament's new Holyrood building. Its stunningly bold design has been a talking-point since it was opened by the Queen in 2004. Beyond, behind its gates of intricate ironwork and a splendid overblown fountain, is the handsome **Palace of Holyroodhouse** ❼ (www .royalcollection.org.uk, tel 0131-556 5100, closed when the Queen is in residence), the British monarch's official residence when staying in Edinburgh. Holyrood Abbey was founded here in 1128 by David I of Scotland; from about 1500 on, James IV and James V built a royal palace around the abbot's guest quarters. Burned in the mid-16th century, it was rebuilt more than once. In the 1670s, the old

to grotesque purpose in the Great Picture Gallery, where 89 portraits depict a Stuart lineage retreating 2,000 years into the mists of time.

A darker note is struck when you reach the Historical Apartments and climb the twisting staircase from Lord Darnley's rooms to those of his wife, Mary, Queen of Scots—as the jealous Darnley and his henchmen did on March 9, 1566. They dragged Mary's Italian secretary and close adviser David Rizzio from the little cabinet room off the Queen's bedroom and stabbed him 56 times. Rizzio bled to death under the window in Mary's bedroom.

South of Holyroodhouse hangs the long gray curtain of **Salisbury Crags,** the buttress of Edinburgh's own mini-mountain **Arthur's Seat** (822 feet). An enjoyable walk leads counterclockwise along Queen's Drive into **Holyrood Park's** green acres.

Set against the breathtaking backdrop of Salisbury Crags and opposite the Palace of Holyroodhouse is **Dynamic Earth** (tel 0131-550

Edinburgh Festivals

The **Edinburgh International Festival** (tel 0131-473 2000) takes over the city the last two weeks in August and the first week in September; it comprises theater, classical music, opera, and dance. An epic **Military Tattoo** (tel 0870-225 1188) takes place at night in front of the castle for three weeks in August. Complementing the official

festival is the **Edinburgh Festival Fringe** (tel 0131-226 0026), where artists from jugglers to comedians perform. Simultaneous events are the **International Film Festival,** the **International Jazz and Blues Festival,** and the **International Book Festival.** For information on all the festivals, visit www.edinburghfestivals.co.uk.

---

northwest tower was incorporated into the present palace.

Tours move fairly briskly up the Grand Stair, through the Household Dining Room with its portrait of Bonnie Prince Charlie, and then through the State Apartments—a drawing room and bedrooms with fabulous, elaborate 17th-century ceilings. Jacob de Wet the Younger was extensively employed to great effect with his painted ceilings ("Hercules Gaining Entry to Heaven" in the King's Bedroom is superb), and

7800, closed Mon.–Tues. Nov.–March), which tells the story of the planet using state-of-the-art interactives and dramatic effects.

New Town Walk

Edinburgh's New Town was planned in 1767 to relieve the congestion and unsanitary conditions of Auld Reekie. It is one of the most complete—certainly the most spacious and dignified—Georgian townscapes in Britain.

The Scott Monument honors Sir Walter Scott.

NOT TO BE MISSED IN NEW TOWN:

National Gallery of Scotland
• Georgian House • Dean Village

Begin across from the **Mound** adjoining **Princes Street,** Edinburgh's famous chief thoroughfare, bordered on the south by a steep drop to gardens. Here stands the imposing **National Gallery of Scotland ❶** (*off Princes St., tel 0131-624 6200*), with works from the 15th to the 19th centuries by most of the major European artists from Raphael and Veronese to Turner and Constable. Next door is the heavily pillared frontage of the **Royal Scottish Academy** (built 1823–1836).

Turn east to pass the dramatic Gothic spire of the **Scott Monument ❷** (1840–1844), which commemorates novelist Sir Walter Scott (see sidebar p. 288), and then **Waverley Station** under the huge clock tower of the Balmoral Hotel. At the top of the street, climb the steps up **Calton Hill ❸** to enjoy its clutch of bizarre neoclassical monuments: the fluted columns of the never finished **National Monument** (begun in 1822, it is also known as "Edinburgh's Disgrace"); the **City Observatory;** obscure philosophy don **Dugald Stewart's Monument** of 1837; the Corinthian temple of a memorial to Burns (1830); and the extended-spyglass-on-end that is the **Nelson Monument** (1807–1815). Climb this last for another splendid city, sea, and mountain prospect.

City of Contrasts: A footpath northward around the hill leads via Royal Terrace onto **York Place.** Here is celebrated Georgian painter Sir Henry Raeburn's house, No. 32, with a palette-shaped plaque. The excellent **Scottish National Portrait Gallery ❹** (*1 Queen St., tel 0131-624 6200*) is farther along.

George Street runs parallel with Queen Street, wide and dignified; Rose Street, between George and Princes Streets, is packed with Victorian pubs—try the Abbotsford at No. 3 or the Rose Street Brewery.

Charlotte Square, at the western end of George Street, is the New Town's finest square, designed in 1791 by architect Robert Adam. No. 7, the 1796 **Georgian House ❺** (*tel 0131-225 2160, closed Jan.–Feb.*), reproduces a town house of the era with period furnishings, china, silverware, and art.

A ten-minute walk westward via Queensferry Street brings you steeply down Bell's Brae into **Dean Village ❻,** a hidden area of restored cottages, mills, and warehouses crammed into the secluded wooded valley of the Water of Leith in the heart of the city—one of Edinburgh's best kept secrets. Just above Dean Village the **Dean Gallery** and the **Scottish National Gallery of Modern Art** (*tel 0131-624 6200*) face each other across Belford Road.

More Places to Visit in the Scottish Lowlands

East Neuk of Fife

On the north shore of the Firth of Forth, along the A917 east of Kirkcaldy, the East Neuk (eastern "corner") of Fife has a string of attractive small fishing harbors, notably **Anstruther** *(map 289 C4)*. Here you'll find the excellent **Scottish Fisheries Museum,** which tells the story of Scotland's long relationship with the sea; exhibits include costumes, equipment, paintings, and historic

---

EXPERIENCE:
Bird-watching at the Bass Rock

The **Scottish Seabird Centre** *(The Harbour, North Berwick, tel 01620-890202, www.seabird.org, $$)* at **North Berwick** offers an enthralling experience with its webcams, displays, and boat trips *(March–Oct., weather permitting, $$$$$)* to see the hundreds of thousands of seabirds that cluster round the rocky islands in the Firth of Forth. Best by far is the very popular 5.5-hour landing trip to the Bass Rock *(April–Sept.),* which puts you right next to vast numbers of gannets (estimates vary wildly, and from year to year, but there could be 100,000), observing their private lives from extremely close quarters. Be prepared for a mighty noise and stink, and for one of the most extraordinary wildlife experiences in Britain. Don't forget your binoculars!

---

boats among the displayed objects. Four miles east of Anstruther lies tiny, picturesque **Crail.** And at **St. Monans,** about 4 miles west of Anstruther, stands a late 18th-century windmill that was used to pump seawater to once nearby saltpans.

Scottish Fisheries Museum ✉ St. Ayles, Harbour Head, Anstruther ☎ 01333-310628

Firth of Forth

From Edinburgh take the train or follow the A198 along the coast to **North Berwick** *(map 289 C3, visitor information, Quality St., tel 0845-225 5121, closed Sun. Oct.–Feb.),* where you can climb the 613-foot cone of **Berwick Law** to the whale's jawbone-arch at the top. Boats from the harbor visit the **Bass Rock,** in the Firth of Forth, a lump of volcanic rock smothered with 50,000 gannets; for a thrilling experience, take one of the Scottish Seabird Centre's bird-watching trips (see sidebar this page). **Tantallon Castle,** a 600-year-old Douglas fortress spectacularly sited on the cliffs, stands 3 miles east.

To visit gull-haunted **Inchcolm Island** and its magnificent 13th-century **St. Colm's Abbey,** take a boat *(tel 0131-331 4857, not sailing mid-Oct.–March)* from South Queensferry, west of Edinburgh.

Tantallon Castle 🔺 289 D3 ☎ 01620-892727 🕐 Closed Thurs.–Fri. Oct.–March

South of Edinburgh

Scene of the dramatic denouement of Dan Brown's blockbusting historical thriller *The Da Vinci Code,* **Roslyn Chapel** (sometimes spelled "Rosslyn" or "Roslin") is a richly carved 15th-century chapel crammed with myths and creepy stories, situated off A701. The **Pentland Hills,** just south of the city, are threaded with wonderful footpaths that offer the chance for communing with nature. In the rolling Border country farther south, the romantic ruin of 13th-century **Neidpath Castle** stands beside the River Tweed near Peebles. To the southwest, 5 miles north of Moffat, the A701 runs along the lip of the **Devil's Beef Tub,** a cavernous hollow. In *Redgauntlet,* Sir Walter Scott had a character roll into the Beef Tub to escape from soldiers—as a real-life Jacobite did in 1746.

Neidpath Castle 🔺 289 C3 ☎ 01721-720333 🕐 Closed Sept.–mid-June

A breathtaking landscape of lochs, glens, great mountain ranges, rugged coastline, and far-flung islands—all steeped in history

Highlands & Islands

A highland cow, or kyloe, a cattle breed developed in the Highlands

Highlands & Islands

No one can say for sure exactly where the Highlands of Scotland start, but everyone knows when they have reached them. The landscape lifts, loses its lowland roll, and gains a High-land roughness and cragginess. The air smells sharper, water tastes sweeter, and evenings and mornings are mistier and chillier. Rural houses become small and white; accents soften and begin to dance. The Highlands, like Scotland itself, are partly a state of mind.

As for the islands, each is a world apart, where time and perceptions tend to run differently from the way they do on the mainland.

Argyll & Inverness

The power of Atlantic wind and waves has clawed deep rips in the southwestern flank of the Highlands. Narrow, winding sea inlets such as Loch Fyne, Loch Linnhe, and Loch Sunart penetrate far into the Argyll and Inverness coasts. Lonely peninsulas have been left isolated between the sea lochs of Kintyre, Morvern, Ardnamurchan, Moidart, Morar, and Knoydart. These are remote, hilly places where roads are few and narrow, walking and boating are superb, and the coastal bays and hidden beaches warmed by the North Atlantic Current seem to stretch forever. They are also the cradle of Scottish culture, for it was here that Irish Celts settled during the first few centuries A.D. In early medieval times the Macdonalds were hugely powerful in the region, but they lost power to their bitter rivals, the Campbells.

North & South of the Grampians

It was a Campbell who led the massacre of Macdonalds in 1692 at Glencoe, the savage glen bordering wild Rannoch Moor and the approaches to Angus and Perthshire.

Below these are the Trossachs. This range of hills and lakes is Rob Roy country, with a romantic skein to it that Sir Walter Scott wove into several of his books.

Farther northeast the long and beautiful glens of Angus—Glen Esk, Glen Clova, Glen Doll, and Glen Isla—push up into the southern flanks of the Grampians, topped by the many high peaks of the central Cairngorm range at over 4,000 feet. This is classic skiing and mountain sporting country.

Running in from the "granite city" of Aberdeen on the east coast is the handsome valley of the River Dee, Royal Deeside, so beloved of the Royal Family.

North again, bounding the southern shores of the Moray Firth, is a region often overlooked by visitors, a gentle farming countryside edged by a dramatically rough coastline dotted with sturdy, granite-built fishing villages.

Northern Highlands & Islands

To the north and west of Inverness and the Great Glen are the Highlands proper, where the clan system survived and flourished for a thousand years.

NOT TO BE MISSED:

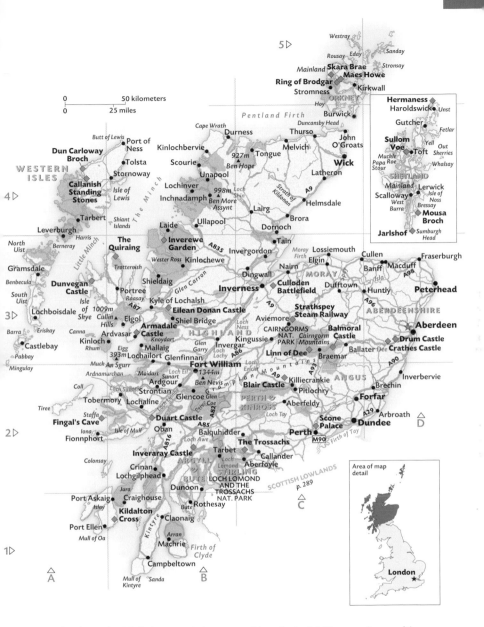

p. 289

After the Battle of Culloden in 1746, the clan way of life began to disappear. By the end of the 19th century, much of the Highlands had been forcibly cleared of people to make way for sheep farming. Hence the emptiness of the superbly beautiful and awe-inspiring mountains and glens of Wester Ross and Sutherland, the wild peatlands of Caithness, and many of the Hebridean islands.

North Sea oil has brought an economic boom to Shetland in recent years; most of the other islands—enormously hospitable and magical—still struggle against depopulation. Beauty and sadness, hand in hand. ■

Southwestern Highlands

From Tarbet on Loch Lomond, the A83 leads westward to Inveraray, a planned town built on Loch Fyne in 1745 by the Duke of Argyll. He built Inveraray Castle at the same time. Victorian additions have made it a Gothic dream of candlesnuffer roofs and turrets.

Inveraray
🗺 311 B2
Visitor information
✉ Front St.
☎ 0870-720 0616

Inveraray Castle
☎ 01499-302203
✉ Inveraray
🕐 Closed Nov.–
   March & Fri.
   April–May &
   Oct.
💲 $$

From here you can continue south on the A83 for nearly 100 miles down the Kintyre Peninsula to the **Mull of Kintyre** (fine views of the Antrim Mountains in Northern Ireland), or turn north on the A819 and A85 to **Oban** (33 miles), then on north via the A828 and A82 to **Invergarry** (75 miles), where the A87 runs west to **Kyle of Lochalsh** (50 miles). West of these long roads lie the lonely, underpopulated peninsulas that make up the beautiful southwestern coast of the Highlands. To reach them, head west from Fort William on the A830, along Loch Eil to Glenfinnan.

Glenfinnan

At Glenfinnan a Highlander stands in monumental statue form against the mountains of Lochaber, commemorating the raising of Bonnie Prince Charlie's standard here on August 19, 1745. Prince Charles Edward Stuart (1720–1788)—the Young Pretender, grandson of the exiled James VII of Scotland (James II of England)—had been in Scotland for a month after landing from France, in the hope of raising enough Highland support to march on London, overthrow George II, and have his father James Stuart—the Old Pretender—crowned king. Donald Cameron of Lochiel threw in his lot with the prince, and others soon followed. It was all the encouragement Charles needed to proclaim his father King James VIII and to start the doomed Jacobite uprising that would end so disastrously at Culloden eight months later.

From Lochailort, 10 miles west of Glenfinnan, the A861 snakes south on a 70-mile circuit of **Moidart, Sunart,** and **Ardgour.**

A bridge leads to Eilean Donan ("island of Donan") Castle.

At Salen (22 miles), the B8007 strikes off west into the heart of **Ardnamurchan,** a long finger of hills, cliffs, and sandy coves.

Just beyond Strontian (33 miles), the A884 threads through bleak and beautiful **Morvern.** But these southerly peninsulas, wild as they are, are tame compared with the northern face of **Morar** and the whole of **Knoydart.**

Inverie on Loch Nevis in South Knoydart can be reached by boat from Mallaig; Barrisdale on the northern side, on Loch Hourn, from Arnisdale, itself a tiny settlement on the nearly-as-remote peninsula of Glenelg.

Kyle of Lochalsh, at the end of the A87, was the ferry port for the Isle of Skye until the expensive and not altogether popular toll bridge was opened in 1995. Here the spectacular Kyle railway line from Inverness (see p. 324) comes to an end.

Eilean Donan Castle

The drive toward Glasgow along the A87 (8 miles) brings you to Eilean Donan Castle, picturesquely perched on a rock where lochs Duich, Aish, and Long all meet. Built in 1230 as a defense against Viking raids, it was blown up by a Hanoverian frigate in 1719 after Jacobite Spaniards had occupied it in support of the Old Pretender's last and futile uprising. Later restored, it has become a prime local attraction.

Fort William

The A87 runs east through spectacular mountain scenery to Invergarry. From here the A82

leads in 25 miles to Fort William, an unprepossessing town from which Glen Nevis curves southeast under the bulky, shapeless mass of **Ben Nevis,** at 4,406 feet the highest mountain in Britain. Rangers at **Glen Nevis Visitor Centre** (Glen Nevis Rd., tel 01397-705922) can advise on mountain climbs and on walks in the glen.

Glen Coe

Eighty miles north of Glasgow, the A82 passes Glencoe village, where nearby on February 13, 1692, Campbell of Glenlyon and his soldiers notoriously massacred 38 of the local Macdonalds. The road climbs through the truly dramatic and dark pass of **Glen Coe,** overhung with upswept rocky slopes.

From Altnafeadh the **Devil's Staircase,** a zigzag 17th-century track built by soldiers, climbs to cross the moors to the village of Kinlochleven. ∎

Traditional Scottish Music

There is music for war: stirring marches played on the bagpipes to summon clans to gatherings, battles, and mourning. There is music for peace: leaping strathspeys, tearing reels, and tender slow airs played on the fiddle and accordion for dancing, celebrating, and lovemaking. You can hear it at formal gatherings and competitions, in the massed accordion and fiddle clubs, in bars at informal sessions where anyone can join in, at village dances in remote rural community halls, and on city street corners from lone pipers with a hat out on the ground for public donations. Visit *www .musicscotland.com* for gig news.

Glenfinnan
- 311 B3

Kyle of Lochalsh
- 311 B3
- **Visitor Information**
- Car park
- 01845-2255 121
- Closed Nov.–March

Eilean Donan Castle
- 311 B3
- Dornie
- 01599-555202
- Closed Nov.–March
- $$

Fort William
- 311 B2
- **Visitor Information**
- Cameron Sq.
- 0845-225 5121

Glen Coe
- 311 B2

Central Scotland

The A81 leads northward from Glasgow to the Trossach Hills, which rise on the southernmost fringe of the Scottish Highlands. Aptly nicknamed "Highlands in Miniature," the Trossachs form part of Loch Lomond and the Trossachs National Park, Scotland's first national park.

Numerous treasures fill the drawing room of Blair Castle, ancient seat of the dukes of Atholl.

Aberfoyle

◪ 311 C2

Visitor Information

✉ Main St.

☎ 0870-720 0604

🕘 Closed Mon.–
Fri. Nov.–March

Queen Elizabeth Forest Park

Visitor Information

✉ 1 mile N of
Aberfoyle on
the A821

☎ 01877-382258

🕘 Call for hours

💲 $ (parking)

Around Aberfoyle

Aberfoyle lies at the heart of the Trossachs and is surrounded by beautiful sights. The **Lake of Menteith** (*5 miles E on the A81*) shelters the wooded **Inchmahome Island,** reached by boat from just beyond the Lake of Menteith Hotel. Here are the striking ruins of a 1238 **priory** (*tel 01877-385294, closed Oct.–March*), where five-year-old Mary, Queen of Scots, was hidden from the English in 1547 before being spirited away to France.

North of Aberfoyle the A821 winds through wild, thickly forested mountains to the 50,000-acre **Queen Elizabeth Forest Park Visitor Centre,** which has details of superb walks and forest drives—in particular the **Achray Forest Drive** (*A821, 3 miles N of Aberfoyle*).

Loch Achray

At Loch Achray follow the sign a half mile to the parking lot at the eastern end of **Loch Katrine,** the lake made famous by Sir Walter Scott in *The Lady of the Lake*. Ellen's Isle can be seen near the landing stage (in real life the MacGregor clan grazed stolen cattle on the island), and the antique steam cruiser *Sir Walter Scott* (*Trossachs Pier, tel 01877-376316, no sailings Nov.–March, $$*) will take you and a rented bicycle up the lake to Stronachlachar, from where you can walk or ride back along the quiet and pretty north bank track.

Back beside Loch Achray, the A821 continues east to the popular holiday town of **Callander.**

Balquhidder

The churchyard at Balquhidder, 12 miles north of Callander on the A84, holds the **grave** of Scott hero Rob Roy MacGregor (1671–1734). Rob Roy (Red Robert) made a reasonably honest living as a cattle dealer until his chief drover absconded with money that belonged to MacGregor's patron, the Duke of Montrose. The duke impoverished Rob Roy, who turned to plundering his former boss. Whether the outlaw ever performed the Robin Hood–type deeds postulated by Scott in *Rob Roy* (1817) is unclear. He surrendered in 1722, was pardoned in 1727, and returned to Balquhidder for the last seven years of his life.

Perth

The A85 runs east through fine Highland scenery. The A827 diverges at Killin along the north bank of Loch Tay, giving access to **Ben Lawers** (see sidebar this page). Perth, the Fair City, set by the River Tay, is full of interesting old buildings. On North Inch, 60 warriors of Clan Chattan and Clan Quhale (Kay) fought in 1396 a bloody combat to decide who should have pride of place in battle. Scott tells the tale in *The Fair Maid of Perth* (1828).

Two miles north is the medieval sandstone **Scone Palace,** where the Stone of Destiny (see p. 303) stayed from 838 until 1296.

Pitlochry

Pitlochry sits nestled among the hills north of Perth. Here the renowned **Festival Theatre** *(tel 01796-484626)* puts on a season of drama and music between late July and late October. At the foot of nearby Loch Faskally is a **salmon pass,** where people watch the fish climb the ladder.

Above Pitlochry the hills press in to form the very dramatic Pass of Killiecrankie, where the deposed James II's Highlanders under Graham of Claverhouse charged and defeated King William's troops on July 27, 1689. The **Killiecrankie Visitor Centre** recounts the story.

Beyond the pass is **Blair Castle,** a striking white edifice—turreted and gabled—dating from 1296. ∎

Callander
311 C2
Visitor Information
Ancaster Sq.
0870-720 06280
Call for winter hours

Perth
311 C2
Visitor Information
Lower City Mills
01738-450600
Closed Sun. Oct.–Feb.

Pitlochry
311 C2
Visitor Information
22 Atholl Rd.
01796-484626

Killiecrankie Visitor Centre
3 miles N of Pitlochry, off the B8079
01796-473233
Closed Nov.–March
$ (parking)

Blair Castle
Blair Atholl
01796-481207
Call for hours
$$–$$$

EXPERIENCE: Explore the Blooms of Ben Lawers

Ben Lawers is a mountain richly blessed with arctic-alpine and other delicate upland flowers. A short nature trail starts from behind the **Ben Lawers National Nature Reserve visitor center** *(A827, on the north bank of Loch Tay, about 70 miles SW of Ben Nevis, www.nts.org.uk/property/94).* The path winds through some of these treasures in all their glory—yellow saxifrage, alpine gentian, rock speedwell, eyebright, mountain pansy, lemon-scented fern, and more. Blooming starts as early as March on the lower slopes and continues through August higher up. Visit www.walkhighlands.co.uk/Perthshire/lawers-nature-trail.shtml for more information on the trail.

A Drive Through Royal Deeside

This meandering drive takes you west from Aberdeen for 60 miles to reach Braemar beyond Balmoral Castle, and in that distance the landscape alters entirely from the low pastoral meadows and cornlands of the Aberdeenshire coast to the full rugged splendor of the Cairngorm Mountains.

Royal Deeside has everything—woodlands, a noble river, high mountains, castles, small neat villages. No wonder Queen Victoria fell in love with this "chocolate-box" valley and persuaded Prince Albert to buy the Balmoral Estate in 1852.

The 195-foot steeple of St. Nicholas's Kirk dominates the pale granite buildings of **Aberdeen ❶** *(visitor information, tel 01224-288828, closed Oct.–Feb.),* a town that sparkles and shimmers on a sunny day. Aberdeen is a good place to explore on foot, with the turreted and many-windowed 16th-century **Provost Skene's House** *(tel 01224-641086)* the chief attraction—if you can spot it cowering in Guestrow under the monstrous, modern multistory block of St. Nicholas House—along with the superb **Mercat Cross** (1686) on Castle Gate, decorated with likenesses of ten Stuart monarchs.

Ten miles west of Aberdeen along the A93 stands **Drum Castle ❷** *(tel 01330-811204,*

NOT TO BE MISSED:

Provost Skene's House • Drum Castle • Crathes Castle • Balmoral Castle • Linn of Dee

closed Oct.–March), followed shortly by **Crathes Castle ❸** *(tel 01330-844525, closed Mon.–Wed. Nov.–March).* These are two wonderful twins— Drum, a 13th-century keep with a 1619 mansion tacked on, and Crathes, a late 16th-century tower house (altered later) with several turrets jutting from a solid base.

The road goes through Banchory and Aboyne to reach snug **Ballater ❹** *(visitor information, tel 013397-55306, closed Oct.–Feb.)* among its rounded, conifer-clad hills. Ballater came into being when the water from a local well was found to cure scrofula, and it became a popular spa resort.

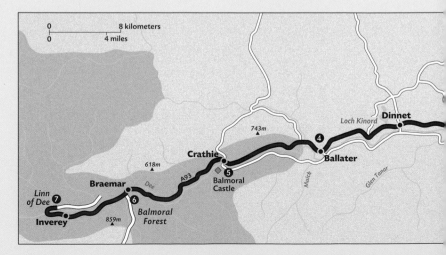

Tartans

The House of Windsor, so often seen and photographed in tartan kilts around Royal Deeside, has done a lot to popularize this traditional Highland cloth.

Plaids of tartan have been worn by Scots since Roman times, their checkered patterns (setts) referred to by visiting or invading commentators time and again down the years. At first only chiefs had tartans vegetable dyed with multicolored grid patterns; then ordinary people began to sport setts that distinguished their home district, and then their clan—very handy in the confusion of a raid or skirmish.

Until Jacobite times, plaids contained up to 16 yards of tartan and doubled as sleeping blankets. Then the short philibeg (knee-length kilt) became popular. The tartan kilt was adopted throughout Scotland as a Jacobite symbol, and as such was stringently outlawed after the Battle of Culloden.

The ban was lifted in 1782, and with Sir Walter Scott's enthusiastic promotion tartan became high fashion during the 19th century. The sett patterns became prescribed and fixed.

Nowadays there are setts for individual clan bigwigs, for families, for regions, and for units of the armed services. Huge sentiment attaches to these post-Culloden tartans, but somewhere along the line the essential beauty of the sett's original aptness has been obscured.

Next comes the royal bit of Royal Deeside. The simple **Parish Church of Crathie** *(tel 013397-42208, closed Nov.–March)*, on the right, is used for worship by the Royal Family when they are staying at **Balmoral Castle** ❺ *(tel 013397-42534, closed Aug.–early April, $$$)*. The big Scottish baronial castle, glimpsed through trees from the A93, still is largely what Queen Victoria and Prince Albert built after they purchased the estate in 1848. The grounds are open for walks, and some rooms are occasionally shown.

In 8 miles is **Braemar** ❻ *(visitor information, tel 013397-41600)*, whose annual Highland Gathering (see sidebar p. 34) sees strong men toss cabers and hurl hammers.

From Braemar, follow "Linn of Dee" signs for 6 miles on a narrow back road to the **Linn of Dee** ❼, where the River Dee foams through a rocky defile.

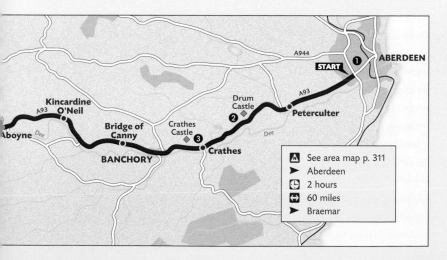

See area map p. 311
► Aberdeen
🕐 2 hours
↔ 60 miles
► Braemar

Grampians & Cairngorms

The Grampian Range of mountains forms the central spine of Scotland—a spine with curvature, a bent bow springing from southwest Argyll, curving northeast until it dips toward the North Sea coast near Aberdeen. The beautiful glens of Angus furrow the southern flank of the Grampians at this eastern end.

The River Spey—one of the best salmon-fishing rivers in Scotland—is wide, shallow, and fast flowing.

Banff
⚑ 311 D3
Visitor Information
✉ Collie Lodge
☎ 01261-812419
🕓 Closed Sun.
   Oct.–Feb.

Aviemore
⚑ 311 C3
Visitor Information
✉ Grampian Rd.
☎ 0845-225 5121
🕓 Closed Sun.
   Oct.–Feb.

Abutting the great Grampian massif on the north are the gray granite Cairngorm Mountains (designated Scotland's second national park in 2003), six of the craggy peaks rising over 4,000 feet—their central platform the highest, wildest, and coldest place in Great Britain. Ptarmigan, mountain hare, wild cat, red deer, golden eagle, and a wealth of other wildlife are all present, particularly in the 100 square miles of the **Cairngorms National Nature Reserve** (*Glenmore Forest Park Visitor*

Centre, Glenmore, Aviemore, tel 01479-861220).
    Any excursion on the A93 road from Ballater to Spittal of Glenshee, the A939 from Ballater to Tomintoul, and the B970 from Aviemore to Feshiebridge and on up Glen Tromie to Gaick Lodge will give an excellent idea of the mountains' grandeur.

Coastal Hinterland

Northeast of the Cairngorms, a rocky, rough coast curves west between Aberdeen and Inverness along the Moray Firth.

The twin towns of **Banff**, with its fine Georgian domestic architecture and splendid William Adam–designed baroque **Duff House** (tel 01261-818181), and **Macduff**, with its small lively fish market, are worth exploring. **Cullen**, west along the coast, is a delightful small town dominated by a handsome old railroad viaduct. It is possible to walk along the former track.

Spey Valley

The western flank of the Cairngorm Mountains is defined by the wide and extremely beautiful Spey Valley. **Aviemore** is its "capital"; **Kingussie**, 12 miles southwest, is lower key, older, and better looking. The **Strathspey Steam Railway** puffs the 8 miles from Aviemore to Broomhill, and a mile away is the **Loch Garten Nature Reserve** (8 miles NE of Aviemore, off the B970, tel 01479-831694), where you can observe ospreys feeding and

INSIDER TIP:

Perhaps the most classic-looking distillery in Scotland is Strathisla, with pot stills a couple of centuries old tucked snug into the old wooden still house. The tour is extremely well done.

—JIM RICHARDSON
National Geographic photographer

nesting from April to August. The seven distilleries and one cooperage that comprise the **Malt Whisky Trail** (brochure at any visitor center) are strung out along the Spey, one of the best fly-fishing rivers in Britain (permit information available at Aviemore visitor center). The **Speyside Way** gives 84 miles of superb walking from Buckie to Aviemore, with a spur to Tomintoul. ■

Kingussie
- 🅰 311 C3

Visitor Information
- ✉ King St.
- ☎ 08452-255121
- 🕐 Closed Oct.–April

Strathspey Steam Railway
- ✉ Aviemore Station, Dalfaber Rd., Aviemore
- ☎ 01479-810725
- 🕐 Diesel service only Nov.–March
- 💲 $$–$$$

Speyside Way Ranger Service
- ✉ Boat o'Fiddich, Craigellachie
- ☎ 01340-881266

Strathisla
- ✉ Seafield Ave., Keith
- ☎ 01542-783044
- 💲 $
- **www.maltwhisky distilleries.com**

Scottish Whisky

Uisge beatha, the Water of Life—inspiration for dancing and musicmaking, greetings and farewells, solo evenings and the communal visits called ceilidh.

Most whisky is now a blend of malted spirit (made in a pot still from malted barley) and grain spirit (made from a mixture of malted and unmalted barley and grain). Soft water from a burn (brook) and a good yeast are other essentials. Single malt or unblended whisky is the connoisseur's choice—either a lighter and sweeter Speyside variety such as Glenlivet or Glenfiddich or the oily whiskies of the islands (such as the Islay-distilled

Laphroaig and Lagavulin), whose malt is smoked over peat to produce a rich, tarry, and smoky tang.

The golden color develops gradually over years of maturing in oak casks—often bought secondhand for flavor from American bourbon distilleries. Up to 30 percent of the whisky can be lost through evaporation during this aging process, and this upward-drifting and invisible spirit is known as the "angels' share."

Almost any distillery, given a little notice, will be happy to let you look around and sample the Water of Life.

Outdoor Scotland

Scotland's scenery, from the rolling Border hills, through the Lowlands and up to the dramatic Highlands and islands, is as varied as it is beautiful. Snowcapped mountains, heather moorland, fast-flowing rivers, sparkling lochs, desolate beaches, and endless tidal estuaries each hold their own particular charm and offer numerous outdoor pursuits, as well as some of the most wonderful opportunities for observing the country's wildlife.

Mountain Walking & Climbing

Mountain walking and climbing is extremely popular in Scotland, with locals and visitors alike. You can walk and climb anywhere within reason, although it is always wise to ask permission if you meet a private landowner—especially during the deer-stalking season (mid-Aug.–mid-Oct.), when stray bullets may be flying. The best known and most challenging walking areas are the Cairngorms, the mountains in the West Highlands, and the formidable Cuillin Hills on the Isle of Skye. But always walk and climb with care.

In 1992–1993, a particularly bad year, more than 50 people died in the Scottish mountains, most of them through ignorance and poor preparation. Every year hundreds have to be rescued by volunteers risking their own lives. The Scottish mountains are small stuff compared with the world's great ranges, but they can be extremely dangerous if not treated with proper respect.

The Basic Rules:

- Seek local advice; find out the local weather forecast.
- Be realistic about your fitness and experience, and go in parties of three or more.
- Be suitably equipped—boots, bad-weather gear, food and drink, a cell phone (note: reception is uncertain), an emergency whistle, and a survival bag if going high or far.
- Take a large-scale map, GPS, and a compass, and know how to use them.
- If things look bad, be prepared to call off the expedition, or turn around.
- Tell someone where you are going, and

EXPERIENCE: Spend a Night in a Snow Hole

The Cairngorm Mountains rise more than 4,000 feet above sea level, and their high plateau is subject to prolonged weather of arctic severity in winter. This landscape under snow is breathtaking and can give rise to some truly astounding moments in a walker's life. If you're fit and looking for an intense Cairngorm winter experience, sign up for the Snow Hole Expedition offered by **Mountain Innovations** (Fraoch Lodge, Deshar Rd., Boat of Garten, Inverness-shire, tel 01479-831331, www.scotmountain.co.uk), in which a small group ventures into the wilds to spend a night in a self-dug snow hole.

After a day's crash course in winter skills (ice axe, crampons, snow step cutting), you climb into the high Cairngorm plateau—an inhospitable place of thick snow and cutting wind, but you're snugly kitted out. Once at the chosen snow hole spot, you set to as a team and cut your own accommodation out of a solid snow bank. It's hard work for tired bodies. You saw great blocks of snow, shovel debris, sweat and curse, dig and giggle, and end up with a split-level, wonky-roofed series of interconnected chambers. It feels like home, and heaven, however, by the time you're snug in your sleeping bag with a belly full of hot food. And stepping outside next morning into a silent world of pristine whiteness is an experience you'll never forget.

Trails at Aonach Mor, near Ben Nevis in the Grampian Mountains, lead to spectacular views.

what time and where you intend to finish. Keep to your planned route and report in when you reach your destination.

- If bad weather or darkness threatens on the hills, get down fast.
- If things do go wrong, stay calm. If someone is hurt or exhausted, one person stays with the casualty, others go for help. Keep warm, dry, and optimistic.

Other Outdoor Activities

For skiing and other snow sports, try the **Nevis Range** (tel 01397-705825), near Fort William; **Cairngorm Chairlift Company** (tel 01479-861261), near Aviemore; or **The Lecht** (tel 01975-651440), near Tomintoul. The **Ice Factor** (tel 01855-831100), at Kinlochleven, near Glencoe village, offers ice, rock, and boulder climbing and many more activities.

Coarse fishing thrives in the Lowlands and is generally organized through local clubs; the Highlands are likely to offer game fishing for salmon (expensive) or trout (reasonable). Sea fishing is available all around the coast.

Golf is a democratic game in Scotland and public golf courses are plentiful and inexpensive. You'll need your handicap certificate to play at the best known courses, which include **St. Andrews** (tel 01334-466666; see pp. 300–301); **Carnoustie** (tel 01241-802270), near Dundee; **Gleneagles** (tel 01764-662231), near Auchterarder; **Royal Dornoch** (tel 01862-810219), north of Inverness; and **Turnberry** (tel 01655-334032), south of Glasgow.

Flora & Fauna

In the south, the Solway Firth is a vast natural larder of tidal muds and merses (salt marshes) lying between the Cumbrian and Galloway coasts. Here the entire population of barnacle geese from Spitzbergen in the Arctic Circle (about 20,000 birds) spends the winter, a truly memorable sight and sound, best appreciated from the Wildfowl and Wetlands Trust Centre, Caerlaverock (see p. 291).

The farther north, and the higher the landscape, the better your chances of seeing the wildlife so typical of the Scottish Highlands. On the lower slopes, especially around pine woods, you may see pine marten, red deer, black grouse, wildcat (extremely wary), the still declining red squirrel, and, if you are lucky, the turkey-size capercaillie flouncing away among the trees. On the moors you'll find the ubiquitous red grouse, preserved for sport.

INSIDER TIP:

In the waters off Arisaig, between the mainland and the isles of Mull and Eigg, you can often see minke whales and basking sharks. One ferry, the M.V. _Shearwater_, stops if any are seen.

—RUS HOELZEL
National Geographic grantee

In remote places such as Wester Ross are the noble, red-trunked, native Scots pines. Deer and wildcat are still present high up, and in the Cairngorms you may spot the herd of reintroduced reindeer. Mountain hare and ptarmigan turn white for camouflage in the winter snows here, and ravens are often seen doing aerial acrobatics. The greatest wildlife thrill for most visitors, however, is to catch sight of a golden eagle in soaring flight. Speyside Wildlife (tel 01479-812498) offers wonderful wildlife expeditions.

The islands provide refuge for the reintroduced white-tailed sea eagle (Rhum), whimbrel, red-necked phalarope (Fetlar in Shetland), corncrakes (Coll and the Western Isles), and many other threatened species. Sandy machair—a grassy sward built up on lime-rich shell sand, rich in orchids, lady's bedstraw, bird's-foot trefoil, and huge clovers—is a distinctive feature.

Mountain biking is a popular sport in Scotland, with a growing network of trails in the Highlands.

Inverness & the North

The Great Glen, running northeast from Fort William for 70 almost straight miles to Inverness, in effect slices Scotland in two with a string of long, narrow stretches of water—Loch Linnhe, Loch Lochy, and Loch Ness. The A82 follows the glen all the way. Whether Nessie, the Loch Ness monster, really exists is all down to speculation based on old legends, dubious photographs, and sighting claims.

A medical hut on the Culloden Battlefield, where several thousand Highlanders lost their lives in 1746.

Inverness, known as the Capital of the Highlands, is just the right size for exploring on foot. Behind the tourist office is **Inverness Museum and Art Gallery,** with carved Pictish stones, Celtic jewelry, Jacobite relics, and much more.

Across the river from the gallery is **St. Andrew's Cathedral,** its polished pillars made of speckled Peterhead granite, with a beautiful angel font and unexpectedly subtle Victorian stained glass.

Church Street, across from the tourist office, has many interesting old buildings; on the left is the **High Church,** in whose yard is a gravestone with a notch said to have been used by marksmen shooting Jacobite prisoners after the Battle of Culloden.

Culloden Battlefield

The battlefield lies 5 miles east of Inverness on the B9006. On its exposed, heathery moorland, well marked, are the positions where 5,000 Highlanders lined up on April 16, 1746, to charge nearly twice as many English soldiers. They were slaughtered on the battlefield, and butchered in scores in the surrounding countryside by dragoons for days afterward.

Inverness
- 🅰 311 C3

Visitor Information
- ✉ Castle Wynd
- ☎ 0146-234353
- 🕐 Closed Sun. Oct.–Feb.

Inverness Museum and Art Gallery
- ✉ Castle Wynd
- ☎ 01463-237114
- 🕐 Closed Sun.

Culloden Battlefield
- ✉ Culloden Moor
- ☎ 0844-493 2159
- 💲 $$ (visitor center)

The Fate of Scotland's Clans

From the first centuries A.D., a clan system ruled in the Highlands. Members of a Scottish clan, by and large, shared a name, an allegiance to a chief, and a way of life dominated by farming, cattle raiding, and interclan feuding. It was a style of life, however, that could not survive the introduction of alien notions of law and order, property, and the value of things.

Increasing demands by monarchs, at first Scots and then English, for loyalty that overrode clan allegiance culminated at the Battle of Culloden, just east of Inverness, in 1746, the last warlike gathering of the clans under Bonnie Prince Charlie. The clans were smashed, their way of life deliberately and ruthlessly demolished by force and by statute, and the vast majority of their people cleared from the land during the late 18th and the whole of the 19th century by incoming landlords—or by the clan chiefs themselves—to make way for lucrative sheep farming.

Ullapool

◪ 311 B4

Visitor Information

✉ Argyle St.

☎ 0845-225 5121

🕐 Closed Oct.–Feb.

John O'Groats

◪ 311 C4

Visitor Information

✉ County Rd.

☎ 08452-255121

🕐 Closed Oct.–Feb.

Bonnie Prince Charlie escaped and soon exiled himself on the Continent, never to return. The clans he left behind sadly lost their coherence, leadership, and way of life (see sidebar this page).

Across to the West

ScotRail's spectacular **Kyle railway line** (tel 01599-534824) runs from Inverness to Kyle of Lochalsh on the west coast, down savagely beautiful Glen Carron—a good way to enjoy the scenery of Wester Ross.

From here the A832 loops around the necks of remote western peninsulas to **Ullapool** (ferry to Stornoway on Lewis), on the way passing **Inverewe Garden** (tel 01445-781200), with its acres of lush subtropical plants.

It is 80 long, mountainous, and extremely lonely but beautiful miles north from Ullapool to **Cape Wrath,** the granite headland over 500 feet tall at Britain's northwestern extremity. At **Inchnadamph,** on the A837 (25 miles), a footpath runs east from the Inchnadamph Hotel toward the striking 3,273-foot Ben More Assynt, through remote **Glen Dubh,** notable for wildflowers of both peat bog and limestone.

In 2 miles you reach a number of sinkholes, through which the river can be seen and heard rushing underground.

Up the Eastern Coast

Back on the east coast, 90 miles northeast of Inverness on the A9, the **Strath of Kildonan** is good, wild, walking country. The A897 follows the strath (valley), then leads through the bleak and beautiful **Flow Country** (a million acres of peat, loch, and mountain) to reach the north coast in 40 miles.

The A9 runs from **Helmsdale** along the dramatic Caithness coast for 55 miles to **John O'Groats,** touted as the "northernmost point" of mainland Britain. The town is 876 miles as the crow flies from Land's End at the southern tip of Britain. Visit the **Last House Museum** for a history of the area.

Duncansby Head, 2 miles east, offers good views of Orkney. ■

Scottish Islands

The offshore islands of Scotland are generally divided into three main groups: the Inner Hebrides, a loose scatter of islands just off the west coast, whose largest and best known component is beautiful Skye; the Outer Hebrides, or Western Isles, a ragged island chain 130 miles long that lies farther west and roughly parallel; and the sister archipelagoes of Orkney and Shetland, known as the Northern Isles, that stretch northward from the John O'Groats coast.

A Way of Life

History lies thickly on the islands' stones, prehistoric settlements, Pictish brochs (defensive stone towers), burial chambers, corrugated cultivation ridges called "lazybeds," and villages left abandoned during the Highland Clearances. And many island practices and traditions—nonmechanical cultivation of hayfields in the Western Isles, for example, or the ceilidhing and dancing of the Northern Isles—closely echo the customs of past generations.

Yet the islands are not static museums to the distant past, nor self-conscious theme parks portraying some idyllic way of life. Making a living on the islands, in the face of wind, frequently harsh weather, and isolation is still hard, requiring considerable determination and adaptability.

Winds of Change

In recent years there have been big changes. North Sea oil has brought economic benefits and social upheaval to Shetland. There has been a measure of self-government for the Western Isles through the Comhairle nan Eilean (Council of the Islands) and the Co-Chomunn (island cooperatives).

The basalt formation that characterizes tiny Staffa appears even more magical in the island's Fingal's Cave.

Isle of Skye

⚑ 311 A3–B3

Visitor Information

✉ Bayfield House, Bayfield Rd., Portree, Skye

☎ 0845-225 5121

🕑 Closed Sun. Oct.–Feb.

Isle of Skye Trekking Centre

✉ Suladale, Skye

☎ 01470-582419

💲 $$$$$

www.theisleofskye trekkingcentre.co.uk

Skye Museum of Island Life

✉ Hungladder, Kilmuir, Skye

☎ 01470-552206

🕑 Closed Nov.–March

💲 $

Museum of the Isles

✉ Clan Donald Centre, Armadale Castle, Sleat, Skye

☎ 01472-844305

🕑 Closed Nov.–March

💲 $$

The islands as a whole have benefited from European Union grants and other subsidies. Newcomers have begun to settle in ever increasing numbers, bringing change to the social structure of the islands, some of it for the better, some not.

The islands remain magical: There is no better word for the spell they cast on visitors. Except in extreme weather conditions, they are readily accessible. Don't make too many plans, though: If the weather does not slow you down, then the hospitality, the beauty, and the dreaminess of the islands certainly will.

Isle of Skye

No Scottish island perhaps is as well known as Skye. One of the Inner Hebrides (see pp. 327, 330), Skye is famous for its spectacular mountain scenery and beautiful transitions of rain, cloud, sun, and mist. **Portree,** the capital town, is strung around its bay, 35 miles from the mainland bridge at Kyleakin. Just south, on the A850, the **Aros Experience** (*Viewfield Rd., Portree, tel 01478-613649, $$*) displays the island's history.

(see pp. 327, 330)

INSIDER TIP:

Try to make time for a pony trek on Skye. Rides with the Isle of Skye Trekking Centre include a visit to the pretty horseshoe-shaped bay at Uig.

—LARRY PORGES
Editor, National Geographic Books

To fully appreciate Skye, you need to penetrate the hidden corners of its five far-flung peninsulas: Counterclockwise from Portree, these are Trotternish, Vaternish, Duirinish, Strathaird, and Sleat.

Northern Skye: The spine of **Trotternish** is a dramatic curtain of basalt cliffs 30 miles long, with superb walking around the **Quiraing** outcrops at 1,700 feet. **Flora Macdonald's house** (see sidebar this page) now forms part of the Flodigarry Hotel below the Quiraing. Her grave lies near the **Skye Museum of Island Life** at Kilmuir in western Trotternish.

In the northwest of Skye, where Vaternish and Duirinish

Flora Macdonald

Flora Macdonald was only 23 years old when, in June 1746, two months after the Battle of Culloden, she escorted the fugitive Bonnie Prince Charlie—disguised as her maid—from her native South Uist in the Outer Hebrides, "over the sea to Skye" in an 18-foot rowing boat. Charles managed to escape, but Flora wasn't as

lucky. She was captured and imprisoned for a year in the Tower of London.

In 1750, Flora married a Skye man, Allan Macdonald. In 1774 the family emigrated to America, but Flora returned with her seven children six years later after her husband was captured in the Revolutionary War. She died in 1790.

meet, is **Dunvegan Castle** *(tel 01470-521206)*, ancient and grim stronghold of the Macleods. Here is kept the famous Fairy Flag, which guarantees the Macleods' victory in battle.

Southern Skye: From **Elgol**, in south-facing **Strathaird**, a spectacular footpath leads to Camasunary Bay and superb mountain views.

Inner Hebrides

The Inner Hebrides lie in a jumble off the west coast. Skye (see pp. 326–327), Arran, Bute, and Mull are well known to visitors, the others less so—and all the more rewarding and seductive for that.

Arran, in the Firth of Clyde, is spectacularly mountainous in the north, with wonderful walking around 2,866-foot Goatfell, and

Arran
🅰 311 B1
Visitor Information
✉ The Pier, Brodick
☎ 01770-303774/6
🕐 Closed Sun. Oct.–Feb.

The Isle of Skye is a magnet for pleasure boaters, who can cruise around the entire island.

The **Museum of the Isles** at Armadale Castle in Sleat gives real insight into the history and heritage of clans.

Skye's landscape is dominated by the centrally placed **Cuillin Hills,** formed from volcanic rock; 20 of their crests top 3,000 feet. Their wilder heights provide climbing for experts; for lower and less hazardous walking, contact the Portree information center.

more pastoral toward the south end. There are ancient stone circles and burial chambers around Machrie in the west.

Bute, northeast of Arran, is a soft green island for gentle walks and golfing.

Islay lies isolated at the south end of the Hebridean chain. Its chief treasure is Kildalton High Cross, carved about A.D. 800 and *(continued on p. 330)*

Bute
🅰 311 B1
Visitor Information
✉ 15 Victoria St., Rothesay
☎ 0870-720 0619
🕐 Closed Sat.–Sun. Oct.–Feb.

Islanders

Although every island has its own landscape, character, and history, Scottish islanders have more in common with each other than they do with mainlanders. What first strikes every visitor is the tremendous island hospitality—a polite greeting on the road, the offer of a lift, an invitation to a ceilidh (social gathering), a courteous switch from Gaelic to English if a nonspeaker joins the conversation, and help given in any difficulty or emergency.

In the Shetlands, fishing plays a central role in the livelihood of many islanders.

This habit of hospitality and good manners, so deeply ingrained, is born—like most island characteristics—out of the hard reality of life in a small, isolated community and the absolute necessity not to tread on your neighbor's toes, but to give him the space you hope to be given. Together with the hospitality, and for the same good practical reason, goes a modesty and reserve that hold back intimacy.

Treading Carefully

Newcomers can easily misinterpret both hospitality and reserve, especially when they have witnessed another prominent side of the island character: wild abandon in celebration, at dances in village halls or late-night musical sessions in bars. It is tempting to trespass too far on the islanders' good nature or to take their hospitality for granted; equally, their reserve can be mistaken for indifference, even hostility.

By far the best way to appreciate the islanders, is to be yourself, but to be sensitive—carefully measure your level of familiarity against theirs. Don't be frightened to accept an invitation, though, to join in wholeheartedly with fun and celebrations, to go to church and the pub and the village dance. And leave yourself plenty of lazy, unplanned days for unexpected but invariably welcome opportunities.

A Workaday Place

Island life is demanding. Weather is harsher, soil poorer, communications more uncertain, everything more costly and more time-consuming than on the mainland. Some islanders hide from these challenges behind the bottle, or cocoon themselves in laissez-faire. But most are hard workers who have learned to be adaptable. The man who pulls your pint at the pub also drives the bus and trawls for lobsters. The woman running the shop also organizes the island dances and raises sheep.

These are practical people, whose houses more often than not stand in seas of flotsam and jetsam—fish boxes, lobster creels, lengths of wire, plastic tubs, fence stakes, tractor tires—things they may never need but are squirreling away in case they do. Their business is not to make their community as pretty as a picture, but to make it work and last.

New Ways

In recent years newcomers—generally known to the natives as "white settlers"—have abandoned mainland life in increasing numbers to settle in the islands. Strangely, these new faces have often been instrumental in preserving aspects of traditional island life—good neighborliness, visiting the elderly, communal care of children—which were

INSIDER TIP:

Don't pass up the long ferry ride to Shetland. It's a great way to meet locals.

—JANE SUNDERLAND
National Geographic contributor

dying out as young native islanders gradually left for the mainland's bright lights and the island population began to age.

The "blow-ins" have pushed for things that born-and-bred islanders never got around to demanding—reliable electricity supplies, decent health care, improved shops, better ferry and plane services, better schools, better political representation.

These new brooms have sometimes generated resentment, however, through their breezy clean sweeping. They are vocal, in a way that native islanders seldom allow themselves to be, about the very many delights that island life has to offer—the unpolluted air, the absence of crime and violence, and the freedom from nine-to-five stress.

The islands are there to enjoy for all these things, and for their fabulous, unspoiled beauty. The islanders, once befriended, will remain friends for life—take your time among them; you are sure to return.

EXPERIENCE: Learn to Speak Gaelic

The Gaelic language came from Ireland around A.D. 400, was almost extinguished after the Battle of Culloden, and is in fair shape today. It is widely spoken in the Western Isles—a lovely, mellifluous language. You can get by with a few phrases:
- *Kim-ma a hah-shiv?* — How are you?
- *Hag-ger ma, tar-pa lay-eve.* – Very well, thanks.
- *Slahn-cher vor ack-'t!* — Cheers!
- *Marsh-er oor tool-eh* — Please
- *Tar-plaht* — Thank you

- *Marshin lay-eve 'n drahs-ter.* — Goodbye, see you soon.

For anything more complex, sign up for a course in Gaelic. Learn online at *www.smo.uhi.ac.uk/gaidhlig/ionnsachadh*, or enjoy a course offered by **Clì Gàidhlig** (*www.iletec.co.uk/clinew/coursespe.asp*)— everything from a one-hour taster to a residential course. Fees range from £1.50 ($2.50) for a two-hour conversation session to around £200 ($327) for a six-day course (excluding board and lodging).

EXPERIENCE: Join in a Scottish Ceilidh

The islanders of both the Inner and Outer Hebrides are famous for their hospitality—it's an essential part of the give-and-take that makes life not only bearable but enjoyable in such remote and facility-poor locations. Hospitality comes in many forms, of which the most vigorous and communal is the ceilidh. "Ceilidh" used to signify a social gathering, anything from a fireside chat with neighbors to a full-blown dance. These days it's mostly about the dance.

Don't pass up an invitation to a ceilidh—it's brilliant fun, generally held in the community hall, and involves a lot of set dancing (reels, two-steps, quadrilles, or whatever happens along), a huge amount of eating and drinking (could be tea and coffee, could be beer and whisky), and talking the hind leg off a donkey in between whiles. People may stand up and do their party pieces, too—singing, playing, reciting. Don't feel out of it if you don't know the steps; just tell someone, and they'll gladly show you. It doesn't matter if the ceilidh turns toward individual performances and you can't or don't care to join in—though you'll delight everyone if you do. Just lay back, be cool, and enjoy it all. Everyone else is.

To find a ceilidh, inquire at a local pub, shop, or post office—or consult notices at the community hall. Everyone will know if there's a ceilidh planned. All are welcome; entrance fees are small.

Mull

 311 B2

Visitor Information

✉ The Pier, Craignure

☎ 01680-812377

miraculously preserved. The bird-watching is notable, likewise the famous peaty Islay whiskies.

Jura, just east of Islay, is wild and empty. George Orwell lived at Barnhill from 1946 to 1949 and wrote *1984* there. On this isle you can climb the 2,000-foot Paps of Jura, watch the 5,000-strong herd of red deer, and enjoy the peace and quiet.

Colonsay, north of Islay, is tiny, remote, and tranquil.

Mull boasts superb sea coasts on its three west-facing peninsulas. Enjoy a morning's exploration of 13th-century **Duart Castle** *(tel 01680-812309, closed early Oct.– March & Fri.–Sat. April),* and an evening's drama at the tiny **Mull Little Theatre** *(tel 01688-302828).*

From Fionnphort a foot ferry crosses to **Iona,** cradle of the Celtic church in Scotland; here, in sublimely peaceful surround-ings, are the restored abbey and chapels, and the gravestones of ancient kings. Boats sail from Fionnphort and Iona to **Staffa,** whose magical Fingal's Cave (227 feet by 66 feet) inspired Felix Mendelssohn's *Hebridean Overture.*

The so-called Cocktail Isles include wedge-shaped **Eigg** (climb the 1,292-foot Sgurr, walk Cleadale's inland cliffs, and discover the Massacre Cave), tiny round **Muck,** mountainous **Rhum** (Scottish Natural Heritage looks after the red deer, sea eagles, mountains, and eccentric Kinloch Castle), and low, green, peaceful **Canna.**

Coll and Tiree, farthest west, possess wonderful windy beaches. **Coll** has a Royal Society for the Protection of Birds (RSPB) corncrake sanctuary at Totronald *(tel 01879-230301),* its western end, while **Tiree** offers glorious flowery machair (see p. 322) and exciting windsurfing.

Outer Hebrides (Western Isles)

If you are looking for wonderfully wild and beautiful scenery, and people who retain hospitality and courtesy as second nature, the remote Western Isles will provide a few days you will never forget.

Barra's airstrip is a white cockleshell beach. Compton Mackenzie, author of the famous Western Isles romp *Whisky Galore,* is buried at Eoligarry. At Castlebay, Kisimul Castle (mostly dating from the 11th century) stands dramatically out in the bay. Here you can get a boat (inquire locally) to off-islands **Pabbay** (Pictish, Celtic stones) and romantic **Mingulay.**

Flora Macdonald's birthplace (see sidebar p. 326) is at Milton, toward the middle of **South Uist,** marked by a memorial. There is a museum and heritage center at Kildonan, and good hill-walking and climbing up to Ben Mhor (2,033 feet).

Take the passenger ferry from Ludag in the south to **Eriskay,** the island where the freighter *Politician* was wrecked in 1941 with 20,000 cases of whisky (Mackenzie's inspiration for *Whisky Galore*). Bonnie Prince Charlie's first landing was here on July 23, 1745.

Benbecula is flat, watery, and windswept.

North Uist has stone circles, cairns, fine western beaches, a Georgian folly (Scolpaig Tower), and excellent loch fishing, as well as bird-watching at Balranald reserve out west and the Uist Animal Visitor Centre in Bayhead.

Harris has superb beaches in the west and superb mountains in the north. Harris Tweed manufacture is coordinated by the Harris Tweed Association.

A passenger ferry from Leverburgh runs to **Berneray,** whose west coast is one long beach.

Lewis is the largest and most northerly of the Western Isles. In summer, the 12th-century walrus-ivory Uig chessmen are occasionally displayed in Stornaway's **Museum nan Eilean** *(tel 01851-709266).*

Across on the west is **Carloway Broch,** 70 feet high and 2,000 years old, the most complete Hebridean broch (stone tower). Here, too, are the famous **Callanish Standing Stones,** an impressive array of circles, rows, and other Neolithic megaliths beside a bleak and beautiful loch.

INSIDER TIP:

If the tide is low enough, make sure you walk out to North Uist's Scolpaig Tower. This open-to-the-elements folly is worth the effort.

—LEON GRAY
National Geographic contributor

Orkney

The Orkney archipelago is founded on warm sandstone, which gives these islets a pastoral, green fertility. Here you will find some of Scotland's most awe-inspiring prehistoric monuments.

Western Isles
◪ 311 A3–A4, B4

Visitor Information
✉ 26 Cromwell St., Stornoway, Lewis
☎ 01851-703088
🕐 Closed Sun. year-round & Sat. Oct.–Feb.

Barra
◪ 311 A3

South Uist
◪ 311 A3

North Uist
◪ 311 A3

Harris
◪ 311 A3–A4

Lewis
◪ 311 A4–B4

Orkney

△ 311 C5

Visitor Information

✉ 6 Broad St.,
Kirkwall

☎ 01856-872856

🕐 Closed Sun.
Oct.–Feb.

Mainland is the chief island, and **Kirkwall** the capital. Eight centuries have blurred and smoothed the sandstone of the magnificent St. Magnus's Cathedral; the nearby Earl's Palace (1600–1607) is encrusted with turrets.

Stromness in the west is a close-built little seaport, hosting a lively folk festival in May. In this area are four astonishing prehistoric sites: the grassy mound of **Maes Howe** burial chamber, the finest in Britain; the neighboring **Standing Stones of Stenness** and **Ring of Brodgar;** and the buried Stone Age settlement of **Skara Brae.**

To the south **Hoy'**s 1,000-foot cliffs play host to peregrine falcons and a host of seabirds, including arctic skuas, while offshore rises the famous Old Man of Hoy, a sandstone rock stack 450 feet high.

The A961 runs south from Mainland between **Lamb Holm, Burray,** and **South Ronaldsay** on wartime causeways built by Italian prisoners, who also created the poignant **Nissen Hut Chapel** on Lamb Holm.

Shapinsay has the baronial **Balfour Castle** *(tel 01856-711282, tours Sun., Wed. 2:15 p.m., May–Sept., reservations at Kirkwall Tourist Information Centre, tel 01856-872856)* and **Rousay,** the Great Ship of Death, a Stone Age chambered cairn where 24 seated skeletons were discovered in 1932.

On **Egilsay** is the round-towered, 12th-century St. Magnus's Church; on **Wyre,** Cubbie Roo's Castle, stronghold of 12th-century Norse warlord Kolbein Hruga; and on **Eday,** the 15-foot Stone of Setter.

There are remote early Christian hermit cells off **Stronsay,** a

Skara Brae, a Neolithic settlement, lay preserved in Orkney's sand dunes until uncovered in 1850.

big chambered cairn 5,000 years old at Quoyness on **Sanday,** old churches and a Jacobite cave on **Westray,** and on **Papa Westray** prehistoric farmhouses at the Knap of Howar.

North Ronaldsay, the island farthest north, has beautiful, empty beaches and a wonderfully tranquil feel.

To travel to Orkney by boat, contact P&O Scottish Ferries *(tel 01856-850655)* or John O'Groats Ferries *(tel 01955-611353);* to travel by air, contact Loganair *(tel 0870-850 9850).*

INSIDER TIP:

Take the marked path up Shetland's Staney Hill, just behind Lerwick, for a wide panorama of the myriad fishing and commercial boats clustered in Bressay Sound.

—JANE SUNDERLAND
National Geographic contributor

Shetland

The Shetland chain of islands, Britain's remotest and most northerly, is a ragged archipelago 70 miles long, windswept, and almost treeless. Here are harsh beauty, tremendous hospitality, and the most energetic music anywhere in the British Isles.

The capital of Shetland is Norse-flavored **Lerwick,** on **Mainland,** one of the three main islands. This harbor town hosts a folk festival in April. Off the

---

Up Helly Aa

On the last Tuesday in January each year, more than 40 bearded Vikings in full battle dress stamp and roar their way through the streets of Lerwick under command of their chief, the Guizer Jarl. With them they drag a full-size longship, which they have spent the whole previous year preparing. The Guizer Jarl, Lord of Misrule during this ceremony of Up Helly Aa, a celebration of midwinter, officiates during the evening's spectacular torchlit procession, which culminates when the longship, piled high with blazing torches, burns to ashes.

---

southeast coast, **Mousa Broch** on Mousa Island *(for ferries call 01950-431367)* is a 45-foot high broch (stone tower). At **Jarlshof Prehistoric and Norse Settlement** *(tel 01950-460112, closed Oct.–March),* on Sumburgh Head, five periods of occupation covering about 3,000 years are represented.

The east coast of windy **Yell** is moodily attractive. The Fishermen's Memorial at Gloup in the north commemorates 58 locals lost in a storm on July 20, 1881—a grim reminder of the reality of Shetland weather. **Fetlar** is for bird-watching; red-necked phalaropes are among the rarities on the **RSPB reserve** *(tel 01597-733246).*

Unst, bare and beautiful, has the wildly windblown headland seabird reserve of Hermaness *(tel 01595-693345),* looking down on Britain's most northerly point.

More Shetland Islands to

Visit: **Bressay** *(map 311 D4, car ferry from Lerwick)* lies just across the water from the Shetland

---

Shetland

⬛ 311 D4

Visitor Information

✉ Market Cross, Lerwick

☎ 01595-693434

🕐 Closed Sat.–Sun. Oct.–Feb.

Every spring, puffins flock to Scotland's coast. These birds landed at Fair Isle.

Fair Isle

🄼 off map 311 D5

🛳 Passenger ferry from Sunburgh/ Lerwick; air service from Tingwall

capital, Lerwick, its 380 people mostly involved in fish processing. On the east side, reached by inflatable boat, is the national nature reserve of **Noss Island,** with enormous cliffs topping 590 feet high at the Noup, where tens of thousands of seabirds breed.

Fair Isle is owned by the National Trust for Scotland. The bird observatory is world famous; so is the Fair Isle knitwear still produced by the 70-odd inhabitants—some newcomers and some Fair Isle families established for many generations.

Twenty miles south of Mainland, the same distance north of Orkney, Fair Isle is the most isolated island community in Britain. That does not stop the islanders from having fun; the Fair Isle dances, with music by the island band, are irresistible all-join-in affairs.

With a population of around 75, **Out Skerries** (map 311 D4, car ferry from Lerwick/Vidlin; air service

from Tingwall) is a group of three islands northeast of Whalsay, with a sheltered communal harbor.

Papa Stour (map 311 D4, boats from West Burrafirth; air service from Tingwall), lying off the northwest Mainland coast, has about 25 inhabitants. The coast of this Great Island of the Priests, a pilgrimage center during the Middle Ages, is spectacularly sea-cut into stacks, caves, and arches.

Off the northeast coast of Mainland, **Whalsay** (map 311 D4, car ferry from Laxo/Symbiste) has a population of around 1,030, doing well through fishing and fish processing. The 17th-century Bremen Böd on the quay at Symbister is a store built during the later days of the Hanseatic League, when all kinds of outlanders came to fish and trade in Shetland.

To travel to Shetland by boat, contact P&O Scottish Ferries (tel 01856-850655); to travel by air, contact Loganair (tel 0870-850 9850). ∎

Travelwise

A sightseeing ship on the River
Thames, London

TRAVELWISE

PLANNING YOUR TRIP

Climate

Britain is a temperate country, warmed by ocean currents and by a southwestern airflow, cooled by its northerly latitude. Winter and spring are mostly mild, though it gets noticeably colder the farther north you go, and in winter there can be significant snowfall on the hills of northern England and in the mountains of Wales and Scotland. A temperature below freezing is reckoned a cold snap. In summer, anything above 80°F is described as a heat wave. Recent years have seen a general rise in temperature.

What to Take

Pack warm and waterproof clothing at any time of year, just in case the British climate springs one of its surprises. If visiting in winter, you will need a heavy coat. A folding umbrella is also a good idea at all times. Jeans are acceptable in most establishments (even the theater now), though most nightclubs stipulate "no jeans." More formal attire (jacket and tie; dress or skirt and blouse) is the norm if dining out in better-class restaurants and for an evening at the opera, ballet, or classical concert. Also bring some sturdy, but comfortable, shoes—even if only visiting London, as you will be doing a lot of walking to see the sights—as well as one pair of more formal footwear. If visiting a church, dress respectfully (a scarf or shirt is a useful cover-up) and remove your hat on entering. See also sidebar p. 10.

HOW TO GET TO BRITAIN

Passports

For European Union, citizens a valid passport or national identity card is required to enter the United Kingdom. Nationals of other countries, including the United States, Canada, Australia, and New Zealand, can also enter on only a passport (no visa is required).

Air

Scheduled services on all the world's major airlines fly into one of London's two main airports—Heathrow, just west of the capital, tel 0870-0000 123, or Gatwick, just south, tel 0870-0002 468. These are connected to central London by tube (Heathrow), rail (Gatwick), and bus services, as is the third and smallest of London's airports at Stansted, tel 0870-0000 303, in Essex. Journey times from these airports to central London are between 30 and 75 minutes.

British Airways is the national airline. For reservations in the U.K., call 0870-850 9850; in the U.S., call 800/403-0882.

Most sizable cities in Britain have their own regional airport not far away, with adequate transportation into town—often by taxi.

Sea

It is still possible to cruise from the United States to Britain aboard a luxury liner. Most sea passengers arriving in Great Britain, however, do so from the Continent—chiefly France, Belgium, and Holland, with some service from Spain, Germany, and Scandinavia—at Plymouth, Poole, Southampton, Portsmouth, Newhaven, Folkestone, or Dover on the south coast. Services also run to Harwich (Essex) from the Hook of Holland.

Rail

Trains run through the Channel Tunnel: Le Shuttle, tel 08705-353535, takes cars and passengers between Calais (France) and Folkestone (Kent) in 35 minutes, while the fast Eurostar passenger service, tel 08705-186186, connects Paris (2 hours 15 minutes), Lille (1 hour 20 minutes), and Brussels (1 hours 50 minutes) with London's St. Pancras Station.

GETTING AROUND

Traveling Around Britain

By Car

Renting a Car

Car rental in Britain can be on the expensive side, so you are well advised, if possible, to rent as part of an overall vacation package. To drive in Britain, you need a current national driver's license, held for a minimum of one year. Many car-rental firms insist on a minimum driver age of 21.

The major international car-rental firms are all represented in Britain, with desks at the main airports and the biggest rail stations:

Reservations
Avis, tel 01344-426644
Budget, tel 0800-181181 (toll-free)
Europcar, tel 08713-849847
Hertz, tel 0207-365 3340/3338
Holiday Autos, tel 01483-909056
Thrifty, tel 0800-252897 (toll-free)

Motoring Information
Driving is on the left side of the road. Remember to yield at

roundabouts (traffic circles) to traffic coming from your right.

Breakdown Assistance: 24-hour breakdown coverage is offered by the Automobile Association (AA), tel 0800-887766, and the Royal Automobile Club (RAC), tel 0800-828282. You might consider joining either—their reasonably modest annual fee is a small price to pay for peace of mind while driving in Britain. Check first with your own motoring organization, as both AA and RAC have reciprocal agreements with many other organizations throughout the world. For advice on what to do in a traffic accident, see p. 341.

Drinking and Driving: Driving after drinking is frowned upon both legally and socially, and the penalties for driving while over the limit are severe. The limit is currently 80mg of alcohol to 100 ml of blood (about 1.5 pints of medium-strength beer, one measure of spirits, or two glasses of wine), but it's best to avoid alcohol entirely if you are driving.

Parking: In Britain's crowded city centers, parking is a problem. Where a "Park & Ride" plan has been established, you will have a more enjoyable and less anxious visit if you use it. This involves leaving your car in a parking lot on the outskirts of the town and taking a cheap, frequent bus service into the center. If you do take your own car into a major city, park in a designated parking lot; it's better to pay a small charge than risk having your car broken into, having to pay a fine, or being booted or even having your vehicle towed away if you park illegally. Double yellow lines at the side of the road forbid parking; single yellow lines restrict parking (see the notice displayed nearby for specific times of prohibition).

Peak Periods: In cities and larger towns, the peak rush hours (between 8 and 9:30 a.m. and 5 and 6:30 p.m. on weekdays) are best avoided.

Road Types: For getting around, a good touring map is essential. On route maps, B roads are secondary roads, A roads (often two-lane) are main routes, and M roads are motorways (freeways); other small, unclassified roads crisscross rural areas.

Seat Belts: Front seat belts, and rear belts if they are fitted to the car, must be worn.

Speed Limits

Speed limits (increasingly enforced by speed cameras) are 30 mph in built-up areas, 60 mph on highways, and 70 mph on two- to four-lane highways and freeways.

Motorcyclists

Motorcyclists must wear a helmet.

By Train

Now privatized into separate companies, the railroads are a worry-free and fast way to get around. There are two classes of travel: standard class and first class, which costs about one-third more. Generally round-trip (particularly same-day round-trip) fares are cheaper than two one-way tickets. Many saver tickets are available—the further ahead you book, the cheaper they are. Travel is cheaper after 9:30 a.m. Mon.–Fri. Ask about discounts for the young, elderly, or travelers with disabilities, as well as full-time students.

Telephone 08457-484950 for all train information. A BritRail Pass saves money if you are traveling extensively, but can only be bought by non-Europeans in their own country. See the British Tourist Authority's website, VisitBritain (*www.visitBritain.com*), for details.

By Bus

Travel by long-distance express bus is half the cost of rail travel, but can take up to twice as long on busy routes (especially into and out of London).

National Express, tel 08705-808080, is the national company.

There are also literally hundreds of small, private bus companies running vehicles all over Britain. Ask at the local visitor information center for details. Traveline (*www.traveline.info*) is an all-purpose travel website offering regional information. The *Scenic Britain by Bus* booklet, downloadable at *www.scenicbritainbybus.com*, provides information on bus services available in holiday locations.

By Taxi

Taxis will take you from provincial towns out to any obscure corner of the land. Expect to pay a little over £1 (approx. $1.85) per mile, and double it for the taxi's empty journey back home after dropping you off. For journeys of more than about 20 miles, you can negotiate a fare. Don't forget the obligatory 10 percent tip.

By Air

Britain's size means that internal air travel is only worth considering over longish distances, for example, from London to Scotland, or for easier access to many of the offshore islands. British Airways, tel 0800-727800, and several smaller airlines compete for business between regional airports—for example, Birmingham, Bristol, Cardiff, Edinburgh, Glasgow, Inverness, Liverpool, Manchester, and Newcastle. Small planes serve the numerous Scottish islands that possess an airstrip. Always shop around for the best ticket deal, as the cheapest can be several times cheaper than the most expensive.

Organized Tours & Sightseeing

Organized tours around the chief visitor attractions do not do justice to a country as small and diverse as Britain, where it is the odd corners that contain the most memorable sights. Better to explore for yourself, by car or public transportation. But you might consider joining one of the guided walks that visitor centers organize around their historic town centers.

Walking

Britain is superb walking territory. There are several national trails that introduce you to wide tracts of country—these include the 256-mile Pennine Way up the spine of northern England, the South West Coast Path that runs approximately 600 miles around the toe-tip of Britain, the 110-mile Cleveland Way around North Yorkshire's moors and coasts, the Thames Path that follows the River Thames for 175 miles from source to mouth, the Offa's Dyke Path running 168 miles along the beautiful Welsh Borders, and the 95-mile West Highland Way from Milngavie, near Glasgow, north into the Scottish mountains. In addition, there are scores of less well marked trails and hundreds of thousands of miles of walking on designated rights of way.

Recommended Books

Bookstores countrywide stock a huge array of walking guidebooks. The most comprehensive selections can be found at:
Stanfords 12–14 Long Acre, Covent Garden, London WC2E, tel 020-7836 1321
Ramblers' Association 2nd Floor, Camelford House, 87–90 Albert Embankment, London SE1, tel 020-7339 8500. This association provides comprehensive information and advice on walking in Britain.

A recommended selection of guidebooks includes:
Country Walks near London by Christopher Somerville (Simon & Schuster)
Discovering Walks in the Cotswolds by Ronald Kershaw and Brian Robson (Shire)
The Thames Path by David Sharp (Aurum Press)
Walks in the Country near London by Christopher Somerville (New Holland)

Getting Around London

Forget driving a car around London—you would be quicker walking. The famous black taxicabs and red buses, allied to the very comprehensive underground rail network known as "the Tube," will get you everywhere you want to go. Each tube station is clearly identified by its distinctive circular red-and-blue logo. The 12 tube lines are color-coded, and maps are posted at every station. The system is divided into nine zones (zone 1 is central London). Fares depend on how many zones you cross and can be expensive. Good value if you have several journeys to make is a One Day Travelcard offering unlimited travel after 9:30 a.m. Mon.–Fri. and all day weekends and public holidays on bus, train, and tube services within chosen zones. It can be bought at tube stations, National Rail stations in the London area, information centers, and newsstands. For information on times, fares, and journey planning of bus, tube, train and riverboat services, call 020-7222 1234 (24 hours). Arm yourself with the *London A–Z* street map guidebook, widely available from newsstands.

PRACTICAL ADVICE
Communications
Post Offices

Open 9 a.m.–5:30 p.m. Mon.–Fri. and 9 a.m.–1 p.m. Sat. In villages, they are often operated on the same premises as a general store. Buy postage stamps here. One price sends a letter to all European destinations outside of the United Kingdom. Rates to the United States are a little more. Within Britain, first class arrives the next day, second class takes two or three days.

Mailboxes

Mailboxes are red and may be freestanding or attached to a wall. Details of collection times are displayed on the mailbox.

Telephones

Calls are relatively cheap, and cheaper still between 6 p.m. and 8 a.m. and on weekends. Phone booths may be old scarlet beauties or new plastic uglies. Coin phones take 10p, 20p, 50p, and £1 coins (60p is the minimum to make a call). Unused coins will be refunded, though if you insert a large-value coin and do not use up the money, you will not get any money back—for this reason it is better to have several smaller denomination coins at hand and keep "feeding" the phone. Many phones are now equipped for phonecards (buy them from post offices or stores displaying a green "Phonecard" sign). Avoid the hotel room telephone: The markup is ludicrously high.

Useful Telephone Numbers
U.K. Operator 100
International Operator 155
U.K. Directory Inquiries 118500 (free from public phone booths)
International Directory Inquiries 118866 (free from public phone booths)

Using the Telephone

To telephone the United Kingdom from the United States: Dial 011, the U.K. country code 44, then drop the first 0 of the area code, followed by the number.

To telephone abroad from the United Kingdom: Dial the international code 00, then the national code (1 for the U.S. and Canada; 61 for Australia; 64 for New Zealand), then the area code (minus any initial 0), followed by the number.

Numbers prefixed by 0800 and 0808 are free calls. Other 08 number prefixes may indicate expensive calls (the situation varies)—these include 0845 and 0870. Numbers prefixed by 09 are certain to be expensive. Online, the excellent website *saynoto870.com* gives local rate alternatives.

Conversions

Britain, though officially metricated with the rest of Europe, has many imperial measures still in common use. Road distances, for example, are in miles, and beer is sold by the pint (the imperial pint is 20 percent larger than the U.S. measure). Gas is now sold in liters (1 liter = 0.2624 U.S. gallon), and loose food is sold by the kilogram (2.2 pounds). Size conversions are as follows:

Women's Clothing

U.S.	6	8	10	12	14	16
U.K.	8	10	12	14	16	18

Men's Clothing

U.S.	36	38	40	42	44	46
U.K.	36	38	40	42	44	46

Women's Shoes

U.S.	6	6½	7	7½	8	8½
U.K.	4½	5	5½	6	6½	7

Men's Shoes

U.S.	8	8½	9½	10½	11½	12
U.K.	7	7½	8½	9½	10½	11

Electricity

Britain's electrical current is 240V, 50-cycle AC. U.S. appliances require a voltage transformer (unless dual-voltage capable) and an adapter.

Gay & Lesbian Travelers

The British are generally open-minded and tolerant, and gay lifestyles and issues have become mainstream in the past few years. That said, you can still encounter prejudice, more particularly in small towns and villages—so a discreet public profile is wise.

London is the gay capital of Europe, and the other big cities have thriving gay scenes, too. For good advice on what's on where, try these websites:

London
www.timeout.com/london/gay/
Bristol and the West
www.pridewest.co.uk
Manchester
www.manchester2002-uk.com/gay/gay-vill2.html
Newcastle and Northeast
www.negayscene.co.uk
Glasgow
http://glasgow.gaycities.com
Edinburgh
www.edinburghgayscene.com
Cardiff
http://cardiff.gaycities.com

Media

Newspapers

Daily tabloid papers are small, cheap, and scandal rich. Low-level options are the *Sun*, the *Mirror*, the *Daily Star*, and the *Sport*. In the middle ground are the tabloids *Daily Mail* and *Daily Express*. Broadsheets contain weightier matter: the *Daily Telegraph*, the *Guardian*, the *Times*, and the *Independent* (the latter two now tabloid in size but broadsheet in content).

Radio

The BBC leads the field with Radio 1 (pop music on 97.6–99.8 MHz FM), Radio 2 (easy listening on 88–91 MHz FM), Radio 3 (classical music and serious talks on 90.2–92.4 MHz FM), Radio 4 (features, conversation, discussion, plays, and news on 92.4–94.6 MHz FM, 198 kHz LW, and 909 kHz MW), and Radio 5 (light news and sports on 693 and 909 kHz MW). Many commercial and local stations are on the air, too.

Television

Britain now offers hundreds of channels of all sorts—terrestrial, digital, free, and subscription. The BBC continues to lead the field in quality. Look for documentaries, news and current affairs, wildlife programs, costume drama and modern plays, and alternative comedy.

Money Matters

British currency is figured in pounds sterling (£) and pence (p): £1 = 100p. Coins come in denominations of 1 and 2 pence (bronze); 5, 10, 20, and 50 pence (silver); and 1 and 2 pounds and the rare 5 pounds (gold-colored). Banknotes are in amounts of 1 (Scotland only), 5, 10, 20, and 50 pounds. Scotland's banknotes differ from those of England and Wales, but they are legal tender throughout the United Kingdom; still, avoid any chance of difficulties by changing these before you cross the border coming south.

Most major credit cards are accepted in main centers, but always carry some cash with you, especially in the more remote areas and smaller towns. Cashpoints (ATMs) are installed in the outer walls as well as the inside of most banks and building societies.

Traveler's checks are the safest alternative to carrying around large amounts of cash. They can be exchanged at most banks, bureaux de change, and larger travel agencies such as American Express and Thomas Cook. If you have traveler's checks in pounds sterling, they can also be used like cash at most hotels, restaurants, and large stores.

Rates of exchange are posted in all banks and main post offices (for general opening times, see below), and at bureaux de change, which are at airports, major railroad stations, good travel agents, and the bigger hotels.

National Holidays
Also known as Public or Bank Holidays—on these days banks, offices, and most shops, restaurants, museums, and attractions close:
January 1 (New Year's Day)
January 2 (Scotland only)
Good Friday
Easter Monday (not Scotland)
May Bank Holiday (1st Mon. in May)
Spring Bank Holiday (last Mon. in May)
Summer Bank Holiday—Scotland (1st Mon. in Aug.)
Summer Bank Holiday—England and Wales (last Mon. in Aug.)
December 25 (Christmas Day)
December 26 (Boxing Day)

Other Days of National Celebration
On these days, places do not close:
Britain November 5 (Guy Fawkes Day, or Bonfire Night)
England April 23 (St. George's Day, patron saint)
Scotland January 25 (Burns Night); November 30 (St. Andrew's Day, patron saint)
Wales March 1 (St. David's Day, patron saint)

National Tourist Boards
Britain and England VisitBritain, Thames Tower, Black's Rd.,
Hammersmith, London W6 9EL, tel 020-8846 9000, www.visit britain.com
Also try the Britain and London Visitor Centre, 1 Regent St., London SW1Y 4XT (no telephone inquiries)
Scotland VisitScotland, 23 Ravelston Terrace, Edinburgh EH4 3TP, tel 0131-332 2433, www .visitscotland.com
Wales VisitWales, Brunel House, 2 Fitzalan Rd., Cardiff (mailing address: Dept. GE1, P.O. Box 1, Cardiff CF24 2XN), tel 0870-121 1251, www.visitwales.com

VisitBritain produces a map guide with the location, address, and telephone number of every local visitor information center in Britain.

National Trust
Many of Britain's historic buildings, parks, gardens, and expanses of countryside and coastline are administered by the National Trust (NT, *www.nationaltrust.org .uk*) or the National Trust for Scotland (NTS, *www.nts.org.uk*). Many NT and NTS properties have special architectural or historical interest and are protected from alteration or demolition.

If you expect to visit many NT or NTS properties, do the math and consider becoming a member. You might save money in the long run, as members get to park and enter for free at most properties.

Opening Times
Business hours may vary from place to place, but a general indication is given below:
Stores 9 or 10 a.m.–5:30 or 6 p.m. Mon.–Sat., 10 a.m.–4 p.m. Sun.
Large supermarkets 8 a.m.–8 p.m. Mon.–Sat.; 10 a.m.–4 p.m. Sun.
Pubs Generally 11 a.m.–11 p.m. Mon.–Sat. (some close 3 p.m.–
5:30 p.m. or stay open past 11:00 p.m.); noon–3 p.m. and 7 p.m.–10:30 p.m. Sun. (some open noon–10:30 p.m.); in Scotland, 12:30 p.m.–2:30 p.m. and 6:30 p.m.–11 p.m.
Post offices 9 a.m.–5:30 p.m. Mon.–Fri.; 9 a.m.–1 p.m. Sat.
Banks 9:30 a.m.–3:30 p.m. Mon.–Fri.; some also 9:30 a.m.–12:30 p.m. Sat., and Mon.–Fri. until 4:30 or 5:30 p.m. in bigger towns.
Gas stations Most big cities have at least one 24-hour station; most motorway service stations are open 24 hours.
Parish churches Places of worship are often kept locked to guard against theft.

The Pet Scheme
The PETS (Pet Travel Scheme) allows owners of cats and dogs from certain countries (including most European countries, the USA, Canada, Australia, New Zealand, and others) to bring their pets into the United Kingdom without quarantine, provided they have been microchipped, vaccinated, blood-tested, treated against tapeworms and ticks, and issued official documentation. Pets must enter the United Kingdom from another PETS country by an authorized route and with an approved transport company.

Full details of the scheme are available on the PETS help line, tel 0870-241 1710, or online at *ww2 .defra.gov.uk/wildlife-pets.*

Places of Worship
The Church of England and the Church of Scotland (equating to the American Episcopalian and Presbyterian churches, respectively) have historically been the predominant religions in Britain—essentially Protestant. In today's multicultural society, religious observance is probably

stricter and keener among other groups. Inquire at the local visitor information center to find which denominations are represented in the area and for times of services.

Rest Rooms

Rest rooms can be found in train stations, on main streets of towns, and in big stores, hotels, and all pubs and restaurants. Standards are usually good. (Ten or 20 pence entrance may be charged.)

Time Differences

Greenwich mean time (GMT) operates from the last Sunday in October to the last Sunday in March, British Summer Time (BST)—for which the clocks are put forward by one hour—for the rest of the year.

Tipping

Add 10 percent to the bill in restaurants, if a service charge has not already been added. Taxi drivers expect a 10 percent tip. Do not tip bar staff in a pub, although the offer of a drink instead is appreciated. Hairdressers should be tipped 10 percent and luggage porters 50p to £1. Do not tip theater or movie ushers. See also sidebar p. 10.

Travelers with Disabilities

In general, modern buildings, taxis, trains, and buses (post-1985) are wheelchair friendly. Many historic attractions such as castles and stately houses present problems to wheelchair users. There are reserved seats for travelers with disabilities on buses, tube trains, and rail cars; there is also reserved parking near the entrance of most supermarkets and many public buildings and visitor attractions.

Hearing-impaired travelers will find audioloop facilities in banks, telephone booths, and other places where the ear logo is displayed.

Reduced fares on public transportation are available. For advice on all matters connected with vacationing in Britain, contact **RADAR** (Royal Association for Disability and Rehabilitation), 12 City Forum, 250 City Rd., London EC1V 8AF, tel 020-7250 3222. Visitor information centers can advise on local conditions. Online, Tourism for All *(www .tourismforall.gov.uk)* has lots of information.

EMERGENCIES

Crime & Police

Britain is a safe place to visit, given the precautions that travelers anywhere need to take against being alone in isolated places after dark. Pickpockets and car thieves are the chief problem, and the remedies are obvious: Guard your wallet and open bags in crowded places, and don't leave valuables in your car. The police in their characteristic dark blue helmets (policewomen in caps) are unarmed and helpful with any inquiry.

Emergency Phone Numbers

999 for police, ambulance, fire, and coast guard

What to Do in a Traffic Accident

If you are involved in a road traffic accident with another vehicle in which no one has been injured, simply exchange names, telephone numbers, and insurance details. If you are driving a rented vehicle, phone the rental company and explain what has happened.

In the event of an accident that involves injury, call the police (tel 999) immediately.

Lost Property

Report any lost property to the nearest police station (don't forget to obtain a report signed by the duty officer if you intend to make a claim on your insurance company) or to the appropriate company if the loss occurs on public transportation.

Lost or Stolen Credit Cards

You should cancel any lost or stolen credit cards by calling the following emergency numbers: **American Express,** tel 01273-696933 **Diners Club,** tel 0800-460800 (toll-free) **MasterCard/Eurocard,** tel 0800-964767 (toll-free) **Visa,** tel 0800-895082 (toll-free)

Health

Valid travel and health insurance is advised. No vaccinations are needed for entry to Britain. National Health Service (N.H.S.) health care is free to all European Union (EU) nationals, and N.H.S. care is available to all in an emergency. A qualifying form (available from health departments of EU countries) enables EU nationals to claim back their expense. Other nationals should take out insurance to cover medical expenses. Emergency dental treatment may be chargeable—some dentists are N.H.S., most are not.

Tap water is safe to drink everywhere.

Pharmacies

Known as chemists, pharmacies stock standard remedies and dispense doctors' prescriptions; pharmacists can give advice. In larger towns, chemists operate a late-evening roster system.

Hotels & Restaurants

Accommodations in Britain come in all shapes and sizes to suit every taste, from mansion hotels to tiny cottages with only a few rooms; facilities and standards are reflected in the prices. During the last 20 years or so, food in Britain has improved enormously, and wherever you go you will find a wide variety of restaurants, particularly in the cities, where the choice is far more cosmopolitan. Many hotels have their own restaurants, and some restaurants also have rooms to rent.

The following is a recommended selection of the most comfortable, interesting, and welcoming places in which to stay and eat in Britain, from a luxury hotel in London to a country inn in the Lake District, and from foie gras to fish-and-chips

HOTELS

Many hotels offer "half-board" accommodations, which includes breakfast and dinner, while "full board" includes lunch as well. Wherever possible, the hotels chosen are both individual and typical. Always try to reserve in advance, particularly in high season; you may be asked for a deposit or credit card. Several hotels listed in this guide are graded according to the Automobile Association (AA) rating system.
★★ May be group or proprietor owned. Rooms are small to medium in size, and at least half the bedrooms will have a private bath/shower. There may also be a telephone and television.
★★★ Usually more spacious rooms with a greater range of facilities and services, including full reception facilities as well as a more formal restaurant and bar. All bedrooms have private bathrooms.
★★★★ Accommodations are more spacious still, offering high standards of comfort and food. All bedrooms have private facilities (both bath and shower).
★★★★★ Large luxury hotels offering the highest international standards.

Red stars (★), ranging from one to five, are awarded to hotels recognized for excellence within their star rating for consistent, outstanding levels of hospitality, service, food, and comfort.
Please note that, **unless otherwise stated:**
1. Breakfast is included in the price.
2. The hotel has a restaurant.
3. All rooms have a telephone and television.
4. Room prices are given only for guidance and do not take into account seasonal variations.

B&B's

Bed-and-breakfasts are a specialty in Britain. They are usually small, informal establishments, generally inexpensive and well run, and may also suit travelers who want to get more of a feel of local life. As the name suggests, prices include a room and breakfast (served in a communal room at a fixed time in the morning).

RESTAURANTS

The following selection recommends good regional restaurants offering typical local dishes, as well those featuring inventive fare reflecting foreign influences. Most restaurants offer a fixed-price menu, sometimes including wine. Otherwise (and usually more expensively), you order separate items à la carte.
Restaurants are awarded from one to five rosettes, according to the AA rating system, for the standard of cuisine:

❀ Chefs produce good quality meals using fresh ingredients.
❀❀ Dishes reflect technical skill, ability in balancing ingredients, and make use of seasonal produce.
❀❀❀ Cuisine is of the highest standard, imaginative, accurately cooked, demonstrating well-developed technical skills and flair.
❀❀❀❀ The cooking is innovative, highly accomplished, and achieves noteworthy standards of consistency, accuracy, and flair.
❀❀❀❀❀ Superb standards of cuisine at an international level. Faultlessly presented dishes cooked to perfection with intense, exotic flavors and using

luxurious ingredients (with imaginative flair of experienced and accomplished chefs).

Credit Cards

Most hotels, restaurants, and bed-and-breakfast establishments accept all major credit cards; if they don't, they will almost certainly say so when you make a reservation.

Dining Hours in Britain

Lunch usually starts around noon and continues until 2 p.m. Dinner may be eaten any time between 7 p.m. and 9 p.m. In peak season, reservations are recommended.

Smoking

Smoking is banned in hotels, restaurants, and pubs, although many have outdoor smoking areas.

Tipping

In a restaurant or hotel, a service charge is normally included in the bill. Where it is not, you are expected to leave a tip of between 10 and 15 percent, although this is at your own discretion and depends on the quality of service.

Travelers with Disabilities

Facilities for visitors with special needs can vary considerably. If you have special requirements, it is always best to check by telephoning in advance.

LISTINGS

Hotels and restaurants are organized by chapter, then by price, then in alphabetical order, with hotels listed first.

Please note that awards and ratings may change during the currency of this guide.

L = lunch, D = dinner

■ LONDON

THE CITY

🏨 MALMAISON CHARTERHOUSE SQUARE

$$$ ★★★ ✿✿
18–21 CHARTERHOUSE SQ.,
CLERKENWELL
EC1M 6AH
TEL 020-7012 3700
FAX 020-7012 3702
www.malmaison-london.com
A fine, comfortable hotel in a refurbished, elegant old building on a quiet square.
🛏 97 🚇 Barbican 🔄 🅂 🎽

🍴 BLEEDING HEART

$$$ ✿
19 GREVILLE ST.
BLEEDING HEART YARD
EC1N 8SQ
TEL 020-7242 2056
www.bleedingheart.co.uk
This ancient tavern offers superb but approachable French cuisine. You can breakfast here in style, quaff ale in the wonderful old bar, or descend in a rollicking party to the Crypt, where King Henry VIII once feasted upon swans. No children under age seven.
🍴 110 🚇 Farringdon Station 🕐 Closed Sat.–Sun., Christmas–New Year (10 days) 🅂

WESTMINSTER & THE WEST END

🏨 BROWN'S

$$$$$ ★★★★★ ✿✿
ALBEMARLE ST., MAYFAIR
W1S 4BP
TEL 020-7493 6020
FAX 020-7493 9381
www.brownshotel.com
Exclusive English elegance in the heart of London's Mayfair, with a traditional country-house feeling. Restaurant offers innovative menus using the best seasonal ingredients.
🛏 118 🍴 70 🚇 Green Park 🔄

🏨 DORCHESTER

$$$$$ ★★★★★ ✿✿
PARK LN.
W1A 2HJ
TEL 020-7629 8888
FAX 020-7629 8080
www.thedorchester.com
One of the world's finest hotels, sumptuously furnished. Traditional British food in the Grill, exotic Cantonese dishes in the Oriental. Discreet, friendly management and staff provide exceptional service.
🛏 250 🍴 81 (Grill) 🍴 51 (Oriental) 🅿 13 🚇 Hyde Park Corner 🔄 🅂 🎽

🏨 GORING

$$$$$ ★★★★★ ✿✿
BEESTON PL.
GROSVENOR GARDENS
SW1W 0JW
TEL 020-7396 9000
FAX 020-7834 4393
www.goringhotel.com
Personal hospitality and service by the Goring family, owners since 1910. Comfortable bedrooms with modern facilities. The restaurant features well-loved traditional British dishes such as grilled Dover sole, lobster thermidor, skate with capers, roast rump of lamb, and steak and kidney pie.
🛏 71 🍴 60 🅿 8 🚇 Victoria 🔄 🅂

🏨 HALKIN

$$$$$ ★★★★ ✿✿✿
5–6 HALKIN ST., BELGRAVIA
SW1X 7DJ
TEL 020-7333 1000
FAX 020-7333 1100
www.halkin.como.bz
Individualistic hotel with classically influenced, modern Italian design. Bedrooms are designed with the principles of feng shui foremost. Attentive and professional service in a relaxed atmosphere.
🛏 41 🍴 45 🚇 Hyde Park Corner 🔄 🅂 🎽

🔄 Elevator 🅂 Air-conditioning 🏊 Indoor Pool 🏊 Outdoor Pool 🎽 Health Club

🏨 **LE MERIDIEN**
🍽 **PICCADILLY**
$$$$$ ★★★★★ ❀❀
21 PICCADILLY
W1J 0BH
TEL 0870-400 8400
FAX 020-7437 3574
www.starwoodhotels.com/
lemeridien
Well-established, French-influenced hotel close to the center of the action near Piccadilly Circus. Splendid food in the Oak Room lounge and in the modern Terrace Restaurant.
ℹ 267 🛏 80 🚇 Piccadilly Circus ⊜ 🕒 🚭 📺

🏨 **RITZ**
🍽 **$$$$$ ★★★★★ ❀❀**
150 PICCADILLY
W1J 9BR
TEL 020-7493 8181
FAX 020-7493 2687
www.theritzlondon.com
A legend among great hotels with magnificent decor. This hotel has one of the most romantic dining rooms in the country—murals of swooning maidens, gilt ornamentation everywhere, waiters gliding to music from the grand piano. Fixed-price L.
ℹ 133 🛏 120 🚇 Green Park ⊜ 🕒 📺

SOMETHING SPECIAL

🏨 **SAVOY**
🍽 **$$$$$ ★★★★★ ❀❀❀**
STRAND
WC2R 0EU
TEL 020-7836 4343
FAX 020-7240 6040
www.fairmont.com/savoy
High standards of comfort and quality; famous art deco design features. The bathrooms at the Savoy are wondrous to behold in gleaming marble and white, dazzling chrome—even better to use, with their huge tubs and famous thunderstorm showers. Renowned Grill Restaurant with superchef

Marcus Wareing; afternoon tea a highlight for both hotel residents and visitors. Breakfast overlooking the river.
ℹ 263 🛏 150 🅿 65 🚇 Charing Cross ⊜ 🕒 🚭 📺

🏨 **SHERATON PARK**
🍽 **TOWER**
$$$$$ ★★★★★ ❀❀❀
101 KNIGHTSBRIDGE
SW1X 7RN
TEL 020-7235 8050
FAX 020-7235 8231
www.sheratonparktower.com
Unique circular modern hotel with splendid London views. In return for a (considerable) supplement, you can enjoy the luxury of full butler service. Cuisine de mer by chef Pascal Proyart at 101 restaurant. Health facilities at affiliated club.
ℹ 280 🛏 64 🅿 67 🚇 Knightsbridge ⊜ 🕒

🏨 **STRAND PALACE**
$$$$$ ★★★
STRAND
WC2R 0JJ
TEL 020-7836 8080
FAX 020-7836 2077
www.strandpalacehotel.co.uk
Well placed for theaters and the City. Club-floor bedrooms have added luxuries and use of an exclusive lounge. Bars and restaurants include Italian bistro and café-bar, also 372 The Strand (international menu).
ℹ 786 🚇 Charing Cross / Covent Garden ⊜

🏨 **WASHINGTON**
MAYFAIR
$$$$$ ★★★★
5–7 CURZON ST., MAYFAIR
W1J 5HE
TEL 020-7499 7000
FAX 020-7495 6172
www.worldhotels.com
Classy hotel, attractively furnished in burred oak, marble, and wood paneling.
ℹ 173 🚇 Green Park ⊜ 🕒

🏨 **LANCASTER LONDON**
🍽 **$$$$ ★★★★ ❀**
LANCASTER TERRACE
W2 2TY
TEL 020-7262 6737
FAX 020-7724 3191
www.lancasterlondon.com
Smart, stylish hotel with stunning views across London. Highly regarded Nipa Thai restaurant has been awarded a rosette.
ℹ 416 🚇 Lancaster Gate ⊜

🏨 **RUBENS AT THE PALACE**
$$$$ ★★★★ ❀
BUCKINGHAM PALACE RD.
SW1W 0PS
TEL 020-7834 6600
FAX 020-7233 6037
www.rubenshotel.com
Enviable location overlooking the Royal Mews behind Buckingham Palace. Well appointed, comfortable hotel. Two restaurants, extensive lounge menu.
ℹ 161 🚇 Victoria ⊜ 🕒

🍽 LE GAVROCHE
$$$$$ ❀❀❀
43 UPPER BROOK ST.
W1K 7QR
TEL 020-7408 0881 OR
020-7499 1826
www.le-gavroche.co.uk
Michel le Roux, Jr., maintains
the highest standards at this
classic French restaurant. Opulent setting, formal service,
and excellent food.
🍴 60 🚇 Marble Arch
🕐 Closed Sat. L, Sun., Christmas–New Year

🍽 TOM AIKENS
$$$$$ ❀❀❀❀❀
43 ELYSTAN ST.
SW3 3NT
TEL 020-77584 2003
www.tomaikens.co.uk
Tom Aiken continues to
delight discerning diners with
his modern French cuisine
served in his stylish, minimalist
Chelsea restaurant.
🍴 60 🚇 South Kensington
🕐 Closed L Sat.–Sun., 2 weeks
Christmas–New Year 🔊

🍽 CORRIGAN'S MAYFAIR
$$$$ ❀❀❀
28 UPPER GROSVENOR ST.
W1K 7EH
TEL 020-7499 9943
www.corrigansmayfair.com
Fabulous melding of down-
to-earth Irish and British influences by top Irish chef Richard
Corrigan.
🍴 85 🚇 Marble Arch 🕐
Closed Sat. L, Christmas

🍽 THE IVY
$$$$ ❀❀
1 WEST ST., COVENT GARDEN
WC2H 9NQ
TEL 020-7836 4751
www.the-ivy.co.uk
Immaculate service, unpretentious, with a lively atmosphere. The cooking, influenced
by French brasserie style,
reveals a welcome directness

and includes English favorites
among other global dishes.
Fixed-price L.
🍴 100 🚇 Covent Garden/
Leicester Square 🕐 Closed
Dec. 24–26, Jan. 1 🔊

🍽 LA PORTE DES INDES
$$$$ ❀❀
32 BRYANSTON ST.
W1H 7EG
TEL 020-7224 0055
www.laportedesindes.com
A beautiful, extravagantly
decorated restaurant serving
high quality Indian cuisine. Set
on two magnificent floors, it
features a 40-foot-high marble
waterfall cascading down
between carved stone balustrades. Fixed-price L & D.
🍴 300 🚇 Marble Arch
🕐 Closed Sat. L, 4 days over
Christmas 🔊

🍽 THE SQUARE
$$$$ ❀❀❀
6–10 BRUTON ST., MAYFAIR
W1J 6PU
TEL 020-7495 7100
www.squarerestaurant.com
Exciting cooking—short but
well-balanced modern French
menu. Luxury ingredients, and
all produce is of exceptional
quality. Fixed-price D.
🍴 75 🚇 Green Park 🕐 Closed
L Sat.–Sun., Dec. 24–26 🔊

🍽 NOBU
$$$–$$$$ ❀❀
15 BERKELEY ST.
W1J 8DY
TEL 020-7290 9222
www.noburestaurants.com
Fashionable restaurant serving
a range of Japanese food from
Nobu classic dishes (some of
which are cooked in a Japanese
wood-burning oven) to a six-
course tasting menu.
🍴 120 🚇 Green Park
🕐 Closed Sun. L, Mon., Bank
Holidays, Dec. 25

BLOOMSBURY

🏨 THE LANGHAM, LONDON
$$$ ★★★★★
PORTLAND PL.
W1B 1JA
TEL 020-7636 1000
FAX 020-7323 2340
www.london.langhamhotels
.co.uk
This grand, historic building
dating back to 1865 offers
luxurious contemporary accommodation and good facilities
close to theaters and London's
central shopping area.
🛏 380 🚇 Oxford Circus
🛗 🔊 🏊 🏋

🍽 HAKKASAN
$$$$$ ❀❀❀
8 HANWAY PL.
W1T 9DH
TEL 020-7929 7000
Ignore its exterior; inside it is
stylish and very chic. Try a perfect cocktail before a Chinese
meal of rare delicacy.
🍴 225 🚇 Tottenham Court
Road

KNIGHTSBRIDGE & KENSINGTON

🏨 MILLENNIUM
🍽 HOTEL LONDON KNIGHTSBRIDGE
$$$$$ ★★★★ ❀❀❀
17 SLOANE ST., KNIGHTSBRIDGE
SW1X 9NU
TEL 020-7235 4377
FAX 020-7235 3705
www.millenniumhotels.com
Near world-famous Harrods
and Harvey Nichols stores.
The restaurant serves modern,
cleverly crafted dishes.
🛏 222 🍴 100 🅿 7
🚇 Knightsbridge 🛗 🔊

🏨 ROYAL GARDEN HOTEL
🍽 **$$$$$** ★★★★★ ❀❀❀
2–24 KENSINGTON HIGH ST.
W8 4PT

🛗 Elevator 🔊 Air-conditioning 🏊 Indoor Pool 🌊 Outdoor Pool 🏋 Health Club

TEL 020-7937 8000
FAX 020-7361 1991
www.royalgdn.co.uk
This modern hotel, with views over Kensington Gardens and Hyde Park, offers very high levels of service and comfort. The bright, contemporary restaurant serves a menu of international cuisine.
🛈 398 🛏 100 🅿 160
🚇 Kensington High Street
🔄 ⛔ 🍷

🏨 CRANLEY HOTEL
$$$$ ★★★★
10 BINA GARDENS
SOUTH KENSINGTON
SW5 OLA
TEL 020-7373 0123
FAX 020-7373 9497
www.thecranley.com
In the soothing backwaters of South Kensington, you're assured of a welcome at this beautiful, elegantly furnished town house hotel.
🛈 39 🚇 Gloucester Rd.
🔄 ⛔

🏨 THE GAINSBOROUGH
$$–$$$
7–11 QUEENSBERRY PL.
SOUTH KENSINGTON
SW7 2DL
TEL 020-7957 0000
FAX 020-7970 1805
www.eeh.co.uk
Pleasant Georgian house in a quiet street near South Kensington's museums.
🛈 48 🚇 South Kensington 🔄

🍴 BIBENDUM
$$$$$ ✹✹
MICHELIN HOUSE, 81 FULHAM RD.
SW3 6RD
TEL 020-7581 5817
www.bibendum.co.uk
The best brasserie food of its kind in the capital. The atmosphere fizzes with life, tables are often turned three times in a session, and you need to make reservations weeks ahead. Fixed-price L.
🛏 72 🚇 South Kensington ⛔

🍴 THE CAPITAL
$$$$$ ✹✹✹✹✹
22 BASIL ST., KNIGHTSBRIDGE
SW3 1AT
TEL 020-7589 5171
FAX 020-7225 0011
www.capital-london.net/capital
Discreet and elegant restaurant, styled by Nina Campbell and Lord Linley. Dishes are eye-catching, imaginative, and display a vibrant freshness and clarity of flavor. Service is professional and friendly. Now expanded to include hotel accommodations.
🛈 49 🛏 34 🅿 10 🚇 Knightsbridge 🔄 ⛔

🍴 FOXTROT OSCAR
$$–$$$$ ✹
79 ROYAL HOSPITAL RD.
SW3 4HN
TEL 020-7352 4448
www.gordonramsay.com/foxtrotoscar
One from Gordon Ramsay's ever increasing stable of eateries. Its tongue-in-cheek name gives a clue to the food, too—basic, good value, fun.
🛏 46 🚇 Sloane Square
🕐 Closed Mon.–Tues., L Wed.–Thurs., 1 week at Christmas

ALONG THE THAMES

🏨 THE WYNDHAM
$$$$$ ★★★★★
CHELSEA HARBOUR
SW10 0XG
TEL 020-7823 3000
FAX 020-7351 6525
www.wyndham.com
Overlooking a small marina at Chelsea Harbour; the modern accommodations are full suites only, most with furnished balconies. A harborside terrace completes the waterfront feel. Exceptionally well-appointed meeting and function rooms.
🛈 160 🅿 200 🚇 Fulham Broadway 🔄 ⛔ ⛔ 🍴 🍷

🏨 IBIS HOTEL
$$
30 STOCKWELL ST.
SE10 9JN
TEL 020-8305 1177
FAX 020-8858 7139
www.ibishotel.com
A modern hotel in the heart of Greenwich. Public areas are limited to snack facilities, but a brasserie restaurant provides a self-service breakfast.
🛈 82 🅿 40 🚇 Greenwich ⛔

🍴 WAPPING FOOD
$$$–$$$$ ✹
WAPPING HYDRAULIC POWER STATION, WAPPING WALL
E1W 3SG
TEL 020-7680 2080
Part art gallery, part restaurant. Expect unconventional chic urban decor with delicious international food.
🛏 150 🚇 DLR: Shadwell
🕐 Closed Sun. D, Dec. 24–Jan. 3, Bank Holidays

■ HOME COUNTIES

AMERSHAM

🍴 GILBEY'S
$$$ ✹
1 MARKET SQUARE
HP7 0DF
TEL 01494-727242
www.gilbeygroup.com
Situated in the beautiful 17th-century former grammar school building in the heart of the historic Chiltern market town, Gilbey's is open every day for lunch, tea, and dinner.
🛏 50 🕐 Closed Dec. 24–29, Jan. 1

ASPLEY GUISE

🏨 MOORE PLACE
$$$–$$$$ ★★★
THE SQUARE, WOBURN
MK17 8DW
TEL 01908-282000
FAX 01908-281888
www.mooreplace.co.uk

A Georgian mansion on its own grounds with rooms. The Victorian-style conservatory restaurant offers English as well as French cuisine. Friendly and efficient service.

🛈 37 (27 annex) 🅿 70

AYLESBURY

🏨 HARTWELL HOUSE
$$$$$ ★★★★ ❀❀❀
OXFORD RD.
HP17 8NL
TEL 01296-747444
FAX 01296-747450
www.hartwell-house.com
Elegant building on a 90-acre estate dates from 1600. Features include delicate ceiling plasterwork and a Jacobean great staircase. Characterful bedrooms, some located in a converted stable block. Tennis courts, fishing, and croquet lawn. No children under eight.

🛈 30 (16 annex) 🅿 91
❁ 🖾 🖾 🖬

BRAY

🍴 WATERSIDE INN
$$$$$ ❀❀❀❀
FERRY RD.
SL6 2AT
TEL 01628-620691
www.waterside-inn.co.uk
Long windows overlooking the Thames, the perfect setting for dinner on a summer evening, oozing quality in the most relaxed kind of way. The service is highly polished, discreet, and unfailingly helpful. The cooking is French to the core. Fixed-price L & D.

🍽 75 🕐 Closing days vary; call ahead

🍴 HINDS HEAD
$$$$–$$$$$
HIGH ST.
SL6 2AB
TEL 01628-626151
www.thehindsheadhotel.com
The prize-winning Hinds Head has been an atmospheric

village pub for more than 400 years. It offers traditional pub food cooked with exceptional skill.

🍽 100 🕐 Closed Dec. 25–26

FLITWICK

🍴 MENZIES FLITWICK MANOR
$$$$ ❀
CHURCH RD.
MK45 1AE
TEL 01525-712242
www.bookmenzies.com
Elegantly decorated in gracious, classical style, with windows overlooking the grounds. Menus are complex, founded on classic tradition, yet experiment with oriental seasoning and Mediterranean flavors. Fixed-price L.

🍽 55 🅿 55

HASLEMERE

🏨 LYTHE HILL
🍴 $$$$ ★★★★ ❀❀
PETWORTH RD.
GU27 3BQ
TEL 01428-651251
FAX 01428-644131
www.lythehill.co.uk
Historic buildings on 20 acres of grounds. Bluebell wood, several lakes. Central courtyard garden. Some separate garden suites; some rooms in the original 15th-century black-and-white timbered house. Henry VIII Suite features four-poster bed dating from 1614. Oak-paneled Auberge de France Restaurant, and another restaurant in the main building. Tennis, fishing, and croquet lawn.

🛈 41 🅿 202

HORLEY

🏨 LANGSHOTT MANOR
🍴 $$$$ ❀❀
LANGSHOTT LA HORLEY
RH6 9LN
TEL 01293-786680

FAX 01293-783905
www.alexanderhotels.co.uk
Spirited modern cuisine enjoyed in a half-timbered Tudor house that's only a few minutes from Gatwick airport.

🛈 22 🍽 42 🅿 25

MAIDENHEAD

SOMETHING SPECIAL

🏨 CLIVEDEN
🍴 $$$$$ ★★★★★ ❀❀❀
TAPLOW
SL6 0JF
TEL 01628-668561
FAX 01628-661837
www.clivedenhouse.co.uk
One of England's great country houses, set on a 376-acre National Trust estate. Cliveden was the most famous political house in England between the wars, when Nancy Astor (1879–1964), Britain's first female M.P., held court here for all the star politicians and major names in finance and the arts. Superb view across the formal garden from the Terrace Restaurant; or try Waldo's for serious dining in discreet, well-upholstered luxury. Tennis, fishing, squash, snooker, Canadian hot bath, river cruises. Fixed-price L & D.

🛈 38 (& Spring Cottage)
🍽 Waldo's 24, Terrace 100
🅿 60 ❁ 🖾 🖾 🖬

🏨 FREDRICK'S
$$$$$ ★★★★ ❀❀
SHOPPENHANGERS RD.
SL6 2PZ
TEL 01628-581000
FAX 01628-771054
www.fredricks-hotel.co.uk
Family-run hotel and acclaimed restaurant where the emphasis is on exceptionally high standards of food, comfort, service, and hospitality. Quiet location, close to Heathrow.

🛈 37 🅿 90 🕐 Closed Christmas

🏨 ELVA LODGE
$$

CASTLE HILL
SL6 4AD
TEL 01628-622948
FAX 01628-778954
www.elvalodgehotel.co.uk
Family-run hotel offers a
warm welcome and friendly
service. The Lions Brasserie is a
popular rendezvous.
ⓘ 26 🅿 32 🕒 Closed
Christmas

MARLOW

🍴 DANESFIELD HOUSE
$$$$ ★★★★ ❁❁❁❁

HENLEY RD.
SL7 2EY
TEL 01628-891010
www.danesfieldhouse.co.uk
Formal dining in the grand
Oak Room with its ornate
plaster ceiling and oak panel-
ing. Menus follow the seasons,
blending classical French and
traditional English dishes. The
wine list is excellent. Bar food.
Fixed-price L & D.
🪑 45 🕒 Closed L Tues.–
Thurs., Sun.–Mon., 2 weeks
Aug., 2 weeks Christmas

REIGATE

🏨 BEST WESTERN
REIGATE MANOR
$$ ★★★

REIGATE HILL
RH2 9PF
TEL 01737-240125
FAX 01737-223883
www.reigatemanor.co.uk
On the slopes of Reigate Hill,
the hotel is ideally located for
access to the town, motorway
links, and Gatwick airport.
ⓘ 50 🅿 130

ST. ALBANS

🏨🍴 SOPWELL HOUSE
$$$$ ★★★★ ❁❁

COTTONMILL LN.
SOPWELL

AL1 2HQ
TEL 01727-864477
FAX 01727-844741
www.sopwellhouse.co.uk
Many bedrooms have four-
poster beds. Drinks in the
Library Lounge, followed
by dinner in the Magnolia
Conservatory Restaurant
where the cooking is techni-
cally polished, confident, and
imaginative. The original
magnolia tree grows through
the conservatory. Less formal
dining in the brasserie. Bar
food. Fixed-price L & D.
ⓘ 122 (16 annex) 🅿 360
🍴🖥🍸

SHERE

🍴 KINGHAMS
$$$ ❁

GOMSHALL LN.
GU5 9HE
TEL 01483-202168
**www.kinghams-restaurant
.co.uk**
A relaxed and cheerful
atmosphere in this charming
17th-century cottage restau-
rant. The menu is interesting,
the cooking modern British in
style. Fixed-price L & D.
🪑 48 🕒 Closed Sun. D, Mon.,
Dec. 25–Jan. 4

SONNING

🍴 FRENCH HORN
$$$$ ❁❁

SONNING
RG4 6TN
TEL 0118-969 2204
www.thefrenchhorn.co.uk
This long-established restau-
rant is superbly located on
the bank of the River Thames.
Guests can enjoy the classical
French cuisine, fine river views,
and lovely village setting. The
signature dish is half a duck,
spit roasted in front of the fire
in the bar and carved at the
table. Fixed-price L & D. No
children under three.
🪑 60 🕒 Closed Good Friday,
New Year's Day

PRICES

HOTELS
An indication of the cost of
a double room in the high
season is given by **$** signs.

$$$$$	Over $350
$$$$	$250–350
$$$	$180–250
$$	$120–180
$	Under $120

RESTAURANTS
An indication of the cost of
a three-course meal without
drinks is given by **$** signs.

$$$$$	Over $80
$$$$	$50–80
$$$	$35–50
$$	$20–35
$	Under $20

SULHAMSTEAD

🏨 OLD MANOR
$$

WHITEHOUSE GREEN
RG7 4EA
TEL 0118-983 2423
The owners treat everyone
as their personal guests. Four-
poster bed and spa bath in one
of the bedrooms. No children
under eight.
ⓘ 3 🅿 8 🕒 Closed Christmas

WARE

🏨 MARRIOTT
HANBURY MANOR
$$$$ ★★★★★ ❁❁

WARE
SG12 0SD
TEL 01920-487722
FAX 01920-487692
www.marriott.co.uk
Marriott group's U.K. flagship,
a Jacobean-style mansion on
200 acres of grounds and gar-
dens. Wood paneling, crystal

🏨 Hotel 🍴 Restaurant ⓘ No. of Guest Rooms 🪑 No. of Seats 🅿 Parking 🚇 Tube 🕒 Closed

chandeliers, antiques, wood fires. Bedrooms comfortably furnished in country-house style. Zodiac and Oakes restaurants serve modern French dishes of the highest standard. Vardons Bar offers bar food. Golf, tennis, and snooker. Fixed-price L & D.

🛈 161 🅿 200 ⬙ ⬚ 🛡

YATTENDON

🏨 ROYAL OAK
🍴 $$$$ ★★ ❀❀
THE SQUARE
RG18 0UG
TEL 01635-201325
FAX 01635-201926
www.royaloakattendon.co.uk
Wisteria-clad country inn with an Anglo-French feel. Carefully prepared dishes are cooked with style and confidence and served in the pretty restaurant. The wine list is extensive and desirable, with some wines by the glass. Old beams, comfortable furnishings, and a pretty garden all complete the country-house feel. Rooms are richly furnished and guests are well looked after.

🛈 5 ⚏ 24 🅿 20

■ SOUTH COUNTRY

AMBERLEY

SOMETHING SPECIAL

🏨 AMBERLEY CASTLE
$$$$ ★★★★ ❀❀❀❀
AMBERLEY
BN18 9LT
TEL 01798-831992
FAX 01798-831998
www.amberleycastle.co.uk
Eleventh-century castle complete with gatehouse, working portcullis, high curtain walls, gardens, and peacocks. The ancient walls also conceal an oubliette where enemies would be sealed in and forgotten. The Queen's Room restaurant offers several menus, including Castle Cuisine, based on old English recipes. No children under 12.

🛈 15 (5 annex) 🅿 50

ASHFORD

🏨 EASTWELL MANOR
🍴 $$$$$ ★★★★ ❀
EASTWELL PARK, BOUGHTON LEES
TN25 4HR
TEL 01233-213000
FAX 01233-635530
www.eastwell.co.uk
From the moment guests enter the magnificently paneled reception, they are promised "quality without compromise." The dining room is dominated by a baronial fireplace and overlooks immaculate gardens. The menu is classically inspired, the wine list excellent.

🛈 62 ⚏ 80

BOURNEMOUTH

🏨 DE VERE ROYAL BATH
$$$$ ★★★★★★ ❀❀
BATH RD.
BH1 2EW
TEL 01202-555555
FAX 01202-554158
www.devere.co.uk
Large Victorian hotel with fine views out to sea. Health club in a pavilion on the grounds. Choice of restaurants—either the Garden Restaurant or the celebrated Oscars.

🛈 140 🅿 70 ⬙ ⬚ 🛡

BRIDPORT

🍴 RIVERSIDE
$$$ ❀❀
WEST BAY
DT6 4EZ
TEL 01308-422011
Lively restaurant specializing in fresh local seafood. The kitchen relies on the day's catch for its repertoire.

⚏ 80 🕐 Closed Sun. D, Mon., Dec.–Feb.

BRIGHTON

🏨 DE VERE GRAND BRIGHTON
$$$$$ ★★★★★
KINGS RD.
BN1 2FW
TEL 01273-224300
FAX 01273-224321
www.devere.co.uk
Traditional luxury hotel, a well-known landmark on Brighton seafront. Leisure center, beautician, conservatory with sea views, weekend nightclub.

🛈 200 🅿 65 ⬙ ⬚ 🛡

CANTERBURY

🏨 FALSTAFF
$$$ ★★★
8–10 ST. DUNSTANS ST., WESTGATE
CT2 8AF
TEL 01227-462138
FAX 01227-463525
www.falstaffcanterbury.com
Sixteenth-century inn next to the Westgate Tower. Attractive restaurant serving English and French cuisine.

🛈 26 (22 annex) 🅿 41

🍴 THE GOODS SHED
$$$
STATION ROAD WEST
CT2 8AN
TEL 01227-459153
A quirky Victorian former railway shed turned farmers market and restaurant, serving rustic, unfussy British dishes.

⚏ 80 🕐 Closed Sun. D, Mon., Dec. 25

CASTLE COMBE

🏨 MANOR HOUSE
🍴 $$$$ ★★★★ ❀
CASTLE COMBE
SN14 7HR
TEL 01249-782206
FAX 01249-782159
www.exclusivehotels.co.uk
Fourteenth-century house on 26 acres of gardens and

parkland. Accommodations in the main house and cottage bedrooms. Log fires and floral arrangements in lounges. There is flair and imagination in the menu as well as a range of classic dishes. Golf, tennis, and fishing are available. Fixed-price L & D.

ⓘ 21 (24 annex) 🍴 75 🅿 100 🏊

CHICHESTER

🏨 MILLSTREAM
$$$ ★★★ ✿
BOSHAM LN., BOSHAM
PO18 8HL
TEL 01243-573234
FAX 01243-573459
www.millstream-hotel.co.uk
Attractive village hotel and restaurant. Cocktail bar opens out onto the garden. Candlelit restaurant offers fresh local produce and impressive wine list. Bar food. Fixed-price L & D.

ⓘ 33 🅿 44

🍴 THE FISH HOUSE
$$$ ✿✿
CHILGROVE
PO18 9HX
TEL 01243-519444
www.thefishhouse.co.uk
New restaurant with rooms that gets excellent reviews.

🍴 80

COWES

🏨 BEST WESTERN NEW HOLMWOOD
$$ ★★★
QUEENS RD., EGYPT POINT, ISLE OF WIGHT
PO31 8BW
TEL 01983-292508
FAX 01983-292050
www.newholmwoodhotel.co.uk
A very comfortable and stylish hotel with superb views enjoyed from its position at the water's edge.

ⓘ 26 🅿 20

DORCHESTER

🍴 YALBURY COTTAGE
$$$ ✿✿
LOWER BOCKHAMPTON
DT2 8PZ
TEL 01305-262382
www.yalburycottage.com
Thatched cottage restaurant with oak beams, inglenook fireplaces, and the original bread ovens. Thoughtful and reasonably priced wine list. Fixed-price D.

🍴 24 🕐 Closed 2 weeks in Jan.

DOVER

🍴 WALLETT'S COURT
$$$ ✿✿
WEST CLIFFE
ST. MARGARETS-AT-CLIFFE
CT15 6EW
TEL 01304-852424
www.wallettscourt.com
Based on a classic, traditional approach and built around bold flavors, the dishes are individual, created from the finest ingredients. No children under eight.

🍴 60 ⓘ 15

EVERSHOT

🏨🍴 SUMMER LODGE
$$$$$ ★★★★ ✿✿✿
EVERSHOT
DT2 0JR
TEL 01935-482000
FAX 01935-482040
www.summerlodgehotel.co.uk
Country-house hotel in charming walled gardens, personally owned and run. Tennis. An imaginative, daily set menu, as well as a seasonal menu strong on the modern repertoire. Fixed-price L & D.

ⓘ 10 (14 annex) 🍴 42 🅿 40 🏊

FAVERSHAM

🍴 READ'S
$$$$ ✿✿✿
MACKNADE MANOR,
CANTERBURY RD.
ME13 8XE
TEL 01795-535344
www.reads.com
One of the best restaurants in Kent. Refined cooking style is carefully considered, fresh local produce well found. Fixed-price L & D.

🍴 40 🕐 Closed Sun.–Mon.

FOREST ROW

SOMETHING SPECIAL

🏨 ASHDOWN PARK
$$$$–$$$$$ ★★★★ ✿✿
WYCH CROSS
RH18 5JR
TEL 01342-824988
FAX 01342-826206
www.ashdownpark.com
Very well run hotel with an extremely willing and friendly staff. Splendid, sprawling building was once home to a community of nuns. Features include a chapel with fine stained-glass windows and a working organ. Bedrooms decorated in a comfortable "homey" style. Restaurant offers classical dishes with modern influences. Golf, tennis, snooker.

ⓘ 107 🅿 200 🔧 🖥 📺

HORSHAM

🏨🍴 SOUTH LODGE
$$$$ ★★★★★ ✿✿
BRIGHTON RD., LOWER BEEDING
RH13 6PS
TEL 01403-891711
FAX 01403-891766
www.exclusivehotels.co.uk
Splendid restored Victorian mansion featuring the Camellia Restaurant, with its views of the South Downs. The restaurant serves enthusiastic cooking and makes use of

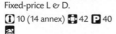

both local game and some fine organic beef to create a menu that is a convincing blend of both traditional and modern cuisine. Bar food also available. Fixed-price L & D.

ⓘ 89 🛏 40 🅿 200 🔽

LACOCK

🏨 AT THE SIGN OF THE ANGEL

$$$

6 CHURCH ST.
SN15 2LB
TEL 01249-730230
FAX 01249-730527
www.lacock.co.uk

A characterful 15th-century former wool merchant's house situated in a National Trust village. Good home-cooked traditional food is served in the lovely beamed dining rooms that are warmed by open fires.

ⓘ 6 (4 annex) 🅿 1 🕐 Closed Christmas

LEWES

🍴 SHELLEYS

$$$ ✿

HIGH ST.
BN7 1XS
TEL 01273-472361
www.shelleys-hotel.com

Elegant yet relaxed, a selection of seasonal specialties is offered to supplement the fixed-price menu. There is a serious attitude to the food, which does not stray too far from recognized combinations. Bar food is also available. Fixed-price D.

🛏 30

LITTLEHAMPTON

SOMETHING SPECIAL

🏨 BAILIFFSCOURT

$$$$–$$$$$ ★★★ ✿✿

CLIMPING
BN17 5RW
TEL 01903-723511

FAX 01903-723107
www.hshotels.co.uk

Hotel built in the 1930s using materials salvaged from redundant medieval buildings, with old stone windows, heavy iron-studded doors, and ancient arches. Bedrooms equipped with antique oak furniture and embroidered fabrics. Soundly cooked dishes in the beamed restaurant. Tennis.

ⓘ 9 (30 annex) 🅿 60 🏊

LYMINGTON

🏨 THE MILL AT GORDLETON

$$$ ★★

SILVER ST., HORDLE
SO41 6DJ
TEL 01590-682219
FAX 01590-683073
www.themillatgordleton.co.uk

A 300-year-old converted watermill complete with its original sluice gates and weir, a lily pond, and water gardens. Good range of dishes at lunch and dinner. Attractive bedrooms and bathrooms featuring whirlpool baths. No children under eight.

ⓘ 9 🅿 60

MAIDSTONE

🏨 MARRIOTT TUDOR PARK HOTEL & COUNTRY CLUB

$$$ ★★★★

ASHFORD RD., BEARSTED
ME14 4NQ
TEL 01622-734334
FAX 01622-735360
www.marriott.co.uk

In the heart of Kent, this is a country hotel with friendly and helpful staff and a good restaurant that always serves well-prepared and flavored meals. Golf and tennis facilities are also available.

ⓘ 120 🅿 250 ⬆ 🏊 🔽

MIDHURST

🍴 ANGEL HOTEL

$$$ ✿

NORTH ST.
GU29 9DN
TEL 01730-812421
www.theangelhotel.co.uk

A mellow atmosphere at this old inn with Tudor origins and Georgian additions. Dinner in the Cowdray Room emphasizes light sauces, maximizing full flavors without the need for overpowering garnishes.

🛏 60 🅿 35

MILFORD ON SEA

🍴 WESTOVER HALL

$$$ ✿✿

PARK LN.
SO41 0PT
TEL 01590-643044
www.westoverhallhotel.com

An elegant and sophisticated Victorian hotel dining room, featuring Jacobean ceiling molds and pre-Raphaelite stained-glass windows. Dishes range from country-house style to modern; all make good use of locally sourced produce. Bar food. Fixed-price L & D. No children under seven.

🛏 40 🕐 Closed Mon.–Wed. D in winter

NEWBURY

🍴 DEW POND

$$$ ✿

OLD BURGHCLERE
RG20 9LH
TEL 01635-278408
www.dewpond.co.uk

The whole place is imbued with a charm one expects from good English hospitality. Modern English and French dishes come from a classic repertoire based on fine ingredients and clear flavors. Fixed-price D. No children under five.

🛏 45 🕐 Closed L, Sun.–Mon., Christmas, New Year's

🔼 Elevator 🔵 Air-conditioning 🏊 Indoor Pool 🏊 Outdoor Pool 🔽 Health Club

NEW MILTON

🏨 **CHEWTON GLEN**
🍽 **$$$$$** ★★★★★ ✿✿✿
CHRISTCHURCH RD.
BH25 5QS
TEL 01425-275341
FAX 01425-272310
www.chewtonglen.com
A luxurious and hospitable
retreat with many thoughtful
touches and excellent house-
keeping. Maintains impeccable
cooking using the finest ingredients; impressive wine list.
Golf and tennis.
ⓘ 53 (2 annex) 🍴 120 🅿 100
🏊 ⛵ 🎾

RINGWOOD

🏨 **THE HOMESTEAD**
$
3 COXSTONE LN.
BH24 1DS
TEL 07990-572748
A 300-year-old thatched
cottage of great charm, convenient for exploring the New
Forest, which is right on the
doorstep. Crooked old nooks,
crannies, beams in abundance.
ⓘ 2

ROYAL TUNBRIDGE WELLS

🍽 **THACKERAYS**
$$$ ✿✿✿
85 LONDON RD.
TN1 1EA
TEL 01892-511921
www.thackerays-restaurant
.co.uk
Clever but delicious modern
French cuisine, particularly
good with fish and seafood.
🍴 54 🕐 Closed Sun. D, Mon.

RYE

🏨 **MERMAID**
$$$ ★★★ ✿
MERMAID ST.
TN31 7EY
TEL 01797-223065

FAX 01797-225069
www.mermaidinn.com
Famous medieval smugglers'
inn, full of character with
ancient beamed ceilings,
linen-fold paneling, huge old
fireplaces. The restaurant
serves classic Anglo-French
dishes; friendly staff. Bar food.
Fixed-price L & D.
ⓘ 31 🅿 25

🏨 **JEAKE'S HOUSE**
$$–$$$ ★★★★★
MERMAID ST.
TN31 7ET
TEL 01797-222828
FAX 01797-222623
www.jeakeshouse.com
This 16th-century house on
a pretty cobbled street was
formerly a wool store, Friends
meeting house, and Baptist
chapel. Shelves full of books,
parlor with piano, galleried
breakfast room. Vegetarian
breakfast available. No children
under age 12.
ⓘ 11 🅿 20

SALISBURY

🏨 **LEGACY ROSE AND CROWN HOTEL**
$ ★★★★
HARNHAM RD., HARNHAM
SP2 8JQ
TEL 0844-4119046
FAX 0844-4119047
Set on the banks of the River
Avon, with fine views of the
cathedral. Pavilions Restaurant
is virtually on the water's edge.
Fishing available. Bar meals.
Fixed-price L & D.
ⓘ 29 🅿 60

🍽 **ANOKAA**
$$ ✿
60 FISHERTON ST.
SP2 7RB
TEL 01722-414142
www.anokaa.com
Contemporary Indian food in
an exciting modern environ-
ment. Imaginative and tasty
dishes served by waiters

PRICES

HOTELS
An indication of the cost of
a double room in the high
season is given by **$** signs.

$$$$$	Over $350
$$$$	$250–$350
$$$	$180–$250
$$	$120–$180
$	Under $120

RESTAURANTS
An indication of the cost of
a three-course meal without
drinks is given by **$** signs.

$$$$$	Over $80
$$$$	$50–$80
$$$	$35–$50
$$	$20–$35
$	Under $20

dressed in traditional outfits.
No children under five.
🍴 80

🍽 **OLD MILL**
$$
TOWN PATH, WEST HARNHAM
SP2 8EU
TEL 01722-327517
www.simonandsteve.com
A reliable restaurant built in
a historic former papermill
with a cascading mill race, set
on the peaceful River Nadder.
Careful cooking and a range of
bar meals. Fixed-price D.
🍴 50

SHAFTESBURY

🍽 **LA FLEUR DE LYS**
$$$ ✿✿
BLEKE ST.
SP7 8AW
TEL 01747-853717
www.lafleurdelys.co.uk
Modern cooking *avec* a twist
of French—crab and samphire,

🏨 Hotel 🍽 Restaurant ⓘ No. of Guest Rooms 🍴 No. of Seats 🅿 Parking 🚇 Tube 🕐 Closed

venison with Armagnac sauce.
🍴 45 🕐 Closed Sun. D, Mon.–
Tues. L, 3 weeks in Jan.

STEYNING

🏨 **SPRINGWELLS HOTEL**
$$
9 HIGH ST.
BN44 3GG
TEL 01903-812446
FAX 01903-879823
www.springwells.co.uk
A creeper-hung Georgian
house, set in beautiful
gardens—a very comfortable
stopover under the Sussex
Downs.
ℹ️ 11 🅿️ 6 🕐 Closed Christ-
mas, New Year's

STOCKBRIDGE

🍴 **THE GREYHOUND**
$$$ ✿✿
HIGH STREET
SO20 6EY
TEL 01264-810833
Wooden tables and a general
air of comfortable informality
complement the fine cooking
in this delightful village pub.
Admire the trout in the River
Test as it slides by the garden.
🍴 52 🕐 Closed Jan. 1

SWAY

🏨 **NURSE'S COTTAGE**
$$$
STATION RD.
SO41 6BA
TEL/FAX 01590-683402
www.nursescottage.co.uk
Former district nurse's cottage.
Fresh fruit, flowers, chocolates,
and fridge in guest rooms.
Home-cooking in the attrac-
tive Garden Room restaurant.
Respectable wine list. No
children under ten.
ℹ️ 5 🅿️ 8 🕐 Closed 3 weeks in
March, 3 weeks in Nov.

WARMINSTER

🏨 **BISHOPSTROW HOUSE**
$$$$ ★★★★ ✿✿
WARMINSTER
BA12 9HH
TEL 01985-212312
FAX 01985-216769
www.bishopstrow.co.uk
Georgian house furnished with
English antiques and 19th-
century paintings. Four-poster
room; several suites with
whirlpool baths. The Mulberry
Restaurant and the Wilton
Room have traditional English
fare. Tennis, fishing, archery,
cycling, and croquet lawn.
ℹ️ 32 🅿️ 100 🏊🏊🏋️

WINCHESTER

🏨 **WINCHESTER ROYAL**
🍴 **$$** ★★★ ✿
ST. PETER ST.
SO23 8BS
TEL 01962-840840
FAX 01962-841582
www.thewinchesterroyal
hotel.co.uk
Popular hotel on a quiet street
within easy reach of historic
city center. Conservatory
dining room has an interesting
menu of well-prepared modern British dishes. In summer,
guests can enjoy a barbecue
lunch in the walled garden. Bar
meals. Fixed-price D.
ℹ️ 75 🅿️ 50

🏨 **HOTEL DU VIN**
🍴 **& BISTRO**
$$$ ★★★★ ✿✿
14 SOUTHGATE ST.
SO23 9EF
TEL 01962-841414
FAX 01962-842458
www.hotelduvin.com
Centrally located bistro and
18th-century town house.
The bistro is stylishly informal
with Mediterranean menu.
Bedrooms are comfortable,
each sponsored by a different
wine house.
ℹ️ 23 🍴 65 🅿️ 35

🍴 **CHESIL RECTORY**
$$$ ✿✿
1 CHESIL ST.
SO23 0HU
TEL 01962-851555
www.chesilrectory.co.uk
A classy, understated restaurant in Winchester's oldest
house. Great, unfussy cooking.
🍴 75 🕐 Closed 1 week in
Aug., 1 week at Christmas

▪ WEST COUNTRY

ASH MILL

🏨 **KERSCOTT FARM**
$
ASH MILL, SOUTH MOLTON
EX36 4QG
TEL 01769-550262
www.devon-bandb-kerscott
.co.uk
Working farm in beautiful
Devon countryside. The house
has exposed beams, flagstone
floor, inglenook fireplaces.
Home-cooking includes crusty
bread and hearty soups. No
children under 14.
ℹ️ 3 🅿️ 4 🕐 Closed Nov.–Jan.

BATH

🏨 **APSLEY HOUSE**
$$$ ★★★★★
NEWBRIDGE HILL
BA1 3PT
TEL 01225-336966
FAX 01225-425462
www.apsley-house.co.uk
Friendly hotel on the edge of
showpiece Georgian city.
ℹ️ 11 🅿️ 10 🕐 Closed
Christmas

🍴 **OLIVE TREE**
$$$$ ✿✿✿
QUEENSBERRY HOTEL, RUSSEL ST.
BA1 2QF
TEL 01225-447928
www.thequeensberry.co.uk
Bold European food in the
stylish basement restaurant of
a very smart city center hotel.
Fixed-price L & D.
🍴 60 🕐 Closed Mon. L

MOODY GOOSE AT THE OLD PRIORY

$$$ ❀❀

CHURCH SQUARE, MIDSOMER
NORTON
BA3 2HX
TEL 01761-416784
www.moodygoose.co.uk
A 12th-century manor house
with flagstone floors and
fireplaces capable of holding
a Yule log or three. The menu
tends to follow the seasons,
ensuring that you enjoy at its
freshest the very best of local
produce.

🛏 36 🕒 Closed Sun., Jan. 1,
Bank Holidays (except Good
Friday)

BRISTOL

SOMETHING SPECIAL

🏨 AVON GORGE

$$ ★★★

SION HILL, CLIFTON
BS8 4LD
TEL 0117-973 8955
FAX 0117-923 8125
www.avongorge-hotel-bristol
.com
Commanding position over-
looking Avon Gorge and
Brunel's famous suspension
bridge. Popular hotel in the
heart of fashionable Clifton.
Well-equipped bedrooms,
many with glorious views;
a choice of bars (one with a
popular terrace), and attractive
restaurant. Prompt, efficient,
friendly service.

ⓘ 75 🅿 25 🔌

🍴 GLASS BOAT

$$$ ❀

WELSH BACK
BS1 4SB
TEL 0117-929 0704
www.glassboat.co.uk
Moored alongside Bristol
Bridge, this converted vessel
has a glass-paneled dining
room. The modern British
menu has Mediterranean
influences, and the kitchen

works to a consistently high
standard. Fixed-price L & D.

🛏 120 🕒 Closed Sun. D,
Mon. L 🔌

CHAGFORD

🏨 GIDLEIGH PARK

🍴 **$$$$$** ★★★ ❀❀❀❀

CHAGFORD
TQ13 8HH
TEL 01647-432367
FAX 01647-432574
www.gidleigh.com
Mock-Tudor house set on
45 acres within Dartmoor
National Park, with rivers,
forests, and peaceful retreats.
The restaurant offers ambi-
tious and outstanding dishes
based on French cuisine, many
using local ingredients. The
wine list is more than a match
for the food. Service is both
friendly and professional. Ten-
nis, fishing, and croquet lawn
available. Fixed-price L & D.

ⓘ 24 🛏 35 🅿 45

CRACKINGTON HAVEN

🏨 TRESMORN FARM

$

CRACKINGTON HAVEN, BUDE
EX23 0NU
TEL 01840-230667 OR
07786-227437
www.lowertresmorn.co.uk
Stay in the gorgeous old
farmhouse or the beautifully
converted barn at Tresmorn
Farm in the Heritage Coast
region of north Cornwall. Tea
and cakes come as part of a
very warm welcome. Recipient
of an AA dinner award.

ⓘ 6 🅿 5

DARTMOUTH

🍴 NEW ANGEL

$$$$ ❀❀❀

2 SOUTH EMBANKMENT
TQ6 9BH
TEL 01803-839425
www.thenewangel.co.uk
Magnificent waterfront views.

Freshness of supplies and a
natural, simple approach are
what distinguish the food. This
is a setup that understands
its materials, but is prepared
occasionally to adventure.
Fixed-price L & D.

🛏 70 🕒 Closed Sun.–Mon.

DUNSTER

🏨 OLD PRIORY COTTAGE

$$

THE OLD PRIORY
TA24 6RY
TEL 01643-821540
www.theoldpriory-dunster
.co.uk
Medieval priory house in a
state of extreme picturesque-
ness, where comfort and
character combine beautifully.
Minimum stay of one week
during April–Oct.

ⓘ 3

FALMOUTH

🏨 ROYAL DUCHY

$$$$ ★★★★ ❀❀

CLIFF RD.
TR11 4NX
TEL 01326-313042
FAX 01326-319420
www.royalduchy.com
Elegant Victorian seafront
hotel just a short walk from
the center of town. Swimming
pool complex contains sauna,
solarium, and spa bath; separate game room. Fresh local
produce on menus.

ⓘ 43 🅿 50 🔌 ❖

🍴 HARBOURSIDE RESTAURANT

$$$ ❀

GREENBANK HOTEL
HARBOURSIDE
TR11 2SR
TEL 01326-312440
www.greenbank-hotel.co.uk
Unrivaled views of Falmouth
harbor from the restaurant,
whose interior achieves a
classic, elegant look. Seafood
figures prominently on the

🏨 Hotel 🍴 Restaurant ⓘ No. of Guest Rooms 🛏 No. of Seats 🅿 Parking 🚇 Tube 🕒 Closed

menu. Bar food.
🔲 60

FOWEY

🏨 **FOWEY HALL**
🍴 **$$$$$ ★★ ✿✿**
HANSON DR.
PL23 1ET
TEL 01726-833866
FAX 01726-834100
www.foweyhallhotel.co.uk
A splendid 1899 mansion looking over the English Channel. Stunning dining room, candlelit at night, with pillars and wood-paneling. Imaginative and accomplished cuisine. Fixed-price D.
ⓘ 36 (8 annex) 🔲 40 🅿 40 ⛱

🍴 **OLD QUAY HOUSE**
$$–$$$ ✿✿
28 FORE ST.
PL23 1AQ
TEL 01726-833302
www.theoldquayhouse.com
The nicest thing at the Old Quay House is to eat on the terrace actually hanging over the gurgling waters of the Fowey Estuary. Inside is also very inviting, with a stylish modern ambience. Locally caught shellfish and whitefish are two star attractions of an eclectic menu.
🔲 38 🕐 Closed L Mon.–Fri. Oct.–May, 1 month in winter

GULWORTHY

🍴 **HORN OF PLENTY**
$$$$ ✿✿
TAVISTOCK, GULWORTHY
PL19 8JD
TEL 01822-832528
www.thehornofplenty.co.uk
Lovely view from the dining room over the Tamar Valley. Excellent canapés, then a dinner that fulfills all expectations. Fixed-price L & D.
🔲 60 🕐 Closed Mon. L, Christmas

HAYTOR VALE

🍴 **ROCK INN**
$$ ✿
TQ13 9XP
TEL 01364-661305
www.rock-inn.co.uk
Charming old Dartmoor inn where the fresh moor air gives an edge to your appetite.
🔲 45

LAMORNA

SOMETHING SPECIAL

🏨 **THE COVE**
$$
NEAR PENZANCE
TR19 6XH
TEL 01736-731411
www.lamornacove.com
Stylish, newly revamped nest of self-catering rooms combines all the advantages of a hotel with the privacy and flexibility of self-catering. Sleep, eat, bask, and swim in the pool, all in a fabulous position high over Lamorna Cove with stunning views down the tree-lined valley toward the sea.
ⓘ 14 🅿 20 ⛱

LANGPORT

🏨 **LYNCH COUNTRY HOUSE**
$$
SOMERTON, SOMERSET
TA11 7PD
TEL 01458-272316
FAX 01458-272590
www.thelynchcountryhouse.co.uk
The house and adjacent Coach House annex offer access to beautifully developed gardens and a lake with black swans.
ⓘ 9

LISKEARD

🏨 **WELL HOUSE**
$$$ ★★ ✿✿✿
ST. KEYNE

PL14 4RN
TEL 01579-342001
FAX 01579-343891
www.wellhouse.co.uk
Charming small hotel in a peaceful valley setting between Liskeard and Looe, offering personal hospitality and service. Afternoon tea with homemade cookies is served on the terrace, which overlooks pretty gardens and hills. Tennis and croquet.
ⓘ 9 🅿 30 ⛱

LOOE

🏨 **COOMBE FARM**
$$
WIDEGATES
PL13 1QN
TEL 01503-240223
FAX 01503-240895
www.coombefarmhotel.co.uk
Set on 10 acres of lawns, meadows, and woodland, this hotel extends a warm welcome to its guests. Game room available. The four-course dinner makes use of local produce whenever possible.
ⓘ 3 🅿 20 ⛱

LYDFORD

🏨 **MOOR VIEW**
$$
VALE DOWN
EX20 4BB
TEL/FAX 01822-820220
Welcoming house on the edge of Dartmoor. The bedrooms all feature family furniture and many thoughtful touches. Home-cooked food. Now has AA dinner award. No children under 12.
ⓘ 4 🅿 15

LYNMOUTH

🏨 **RISING SUN**
$$$ ★★ ✿
HARBOURSIDE
EX35 6EG
TEL 01598-753223

FAX 01598-753480
www.risingsunlynmouth.co.uk
Fourteenth-century inn on
the harborfront of historic
Lynmouth. No children under
eight. Fishing offered.
🛈 14 (5 annex)

LYNTON

🍴 CHOUGH'S NEST
$$
NORTH WALK
EX35 6HJ
TEL 01598-753315
www.choughsnesthotel.co.uk
Spectacular coastal views
accompany your meal here.
Thoroughly cosmopolitan
cooking is the mainstay of
the innovative menu, which is
served in a bright, airy dining
room. Fixed-price D.
🪑 20 🕐 Closed Mon.–Wed.
in winter

MOUSEHOLE

🍴 OLD COASTGUARD
HOTEL
$$$ ❀❀
THE PARADE
TR19 6PR
TEL 01736-731222
www.oldcoastguardhotel.co.uk
Fish prepared in a variety of
different ways is the order of
the day at this relaxing old
inn whose gardens run right
down to the sea. Bar meals.
Fixed-price D.
🪑 50

NEWQUAY

🏨 HOTEL BRISTOL
$$$ ★★★
NARROWCLIFF
TR7 2PQ
TEL 01637-875181
FAX 01637-879347
www.hotelbristol.co.uk
Owner-run hotel with fine
views over the sea. Cocktail
bar and elegant restaurant.
🛈 74 🅿 105 🔄 🌊

PADSTOW

🏨 OLD CUSTOM HOUSE
$$–$$$ ★★★ ❀
SOUTH QUAY
PL28 8BL
TEL 01841-532359
FAX 01841-533372
www.oldcustomhousepad
stow.co.uk
Situated alongside the harbor,
with lovely sea views. Restau-
rant uses locally caught fish.
Real ales and bar meals.
🛈 24 🅿 9 🔄

🍴 SEAFOOD RESTAURANT
$$$$$ ❀❀❀
RIVERSIDE
PL28 8BY
TEL 01841-532700
www.rickstein.com
Rick Stein's TV fame has
attracted people to his seafood
restaurant in Padstow. The
hallmark of the cooking is
tip-top freshness plus simplic-
ity of technique; desserts
are a particular delight, and
the wine list is adventurous.
Fixed-price L. No children
under three.
🪑 104 🔄

PENZANCE

🏨 CHY-AN-MOR
$
15 REGENT TERRACE
TR18 4DW
TEL/FAX 01736-363441
www.chyanmor.co.uk
An elegant Georgian house.
The beautiful and individually
decorated bedrooms vary in
size. No children under ten.
🛈 10 🅿 10 🕐 Closed
Dec.–Jan.

PLYMOUTH

🏨 LEGACY PLYMOUTH
INTERNATIONAL HOTEL
$$$ ★★★
MARSH MILLS
PL6 8NH

PRICES

HOTELS
An indication of the cost of
a double room in the high
season is given by $ signs.

$$$$$	Over $350
$$$$	$250–$350
$$$	$180–$250
$$	$120–$180
$	Under $120

RESTAURANTS
An indication of the cost of
a three-course meal without
drinks is given by $ signs.

$$$$$	Over $80
$$$$	$50–$80
$$$	$35–$50
$$	$20–$35
$	Under $20

TEL 08444-119097
FAX 08444-119098
www.legacy-hotels.co.uk
On the outskirts of the historic
seafaring city of Plymouth, this
stylish hotel is very conveniently
situated for the Devon/Corn-
wall coast and the Dartmoor
countryside.
🛈 140 🅿 100

🍴 TANNERS RESTAURANT
$$
FINEWELL ST.
PL1 2AE
TEL 01752-252001
www.tannersrestaurant.com
An informal restaurant with its
own style, where the prices are
very reasonable and the food
is fresh and homemade.
🪑 28 🕐 Closed Sun.–Mon.

POLPERRO

🏨 TRENDERWAY
$$
PELYNT

🏨 Hotel   🍴 Restaurant   🛈 No. of Guest Rooms   🪑 No. of Seats   🅿 Parking   🚇 Tube   🕐 Closed

PL13 2LY
TEL 01503-272214
FAX 0870-705 9998
Luxurious accommodations in 16th-century farmhouse amid beautiful surroundings. The traditional English breakfasts use only free-range eggs from the farm's own chickens. Recipient of an AA breakfast award. No children.
[i] 8 (2 annex) [P] 8 [⊕] Closed Christmas

ST. IVES

🍴 PORTHMINSTER BEACH RESTAURANT
$$$ ❁
PORTHMINSTER
TR26 2EB
TEL 01736-795352
There is a nautical twist to the decor and a strong maritime flavor to the food in this bright and breezy restaurant set right on the beach.
[▦] 60 [⊕] Closed Mon. in winter

🍴 WAVE RESTAURANT
$$ ❁
17 ST. ANDREWS ST.
TR26 1AH
TEL 01736-796661
www.wave-restaurant.co.uk
If you're eating out in a Cornish fishing town as characterful and sea flavored as St. Ives, you want somewhere just like the Wave. Tucked away in one of the little streets that snakes behind the harbor, this airy modern place offers a varied Mediterranean-influenced menu that's big on locally caught fish and seafood.
[▦] 50 [⊕] Closed Sun., L Mon.–Sat., end Nov.–beginning March

SHEPTON MALLET

🏨 CHARLTON HOUSE
$$$$ ★★★ ❁❁❁
CHARLTON RD.
BA4 4PR
TEL 01749-342008

FAX 01749-346362
www.charltonhouse.com
Sixteenth-century house on pretty grounds, sympathetically restored. Warm, relaxed atmosphere. Imaginative cuisine. Fishing, croquet, archery, clay-pigeon shooting, and hot-air ballooning.
[i] 22 (4 annex) [P] 45 🕸

STAVERTON

🍴 SEA TROUT INN
$$ ❁
STAVERTON
TQ9 6PA
TEL 01803-762274
www.theseatroutinn.com
A fishing theme is evident throughout this good and very busy restaurant and bar. Bar food.
[▦] 35

STON EASTON

🏨 STON EASTON PARK
🍴 $$$$$ ★★★★ ❁❁
STON EASTON
BA3 4DF
TEL 01761-241631
FAX 01761-241377
www.stoneaston.co.uk
Eighteenth-century Palladian mansion on extensive grounds featuring river and lake. Antique pieces and little personal touches in bedrooms. Aperitifs and canapés in the elegant saloon, dinner in the dining room, after-dinner drinks, coffee, and petits fours in the library. Excellent afternoon teas. Tennis, hot-air ballooning, archery, clay-pigeon shooting, croquet, and horseback riding. No children under seven. Bar food. Fixed-price L & D.
[i] 22 (2 annex) [▦] 40 [P] 120

TAUNTON

🍴 THE CASTLE
$$$ ❁❁❁
CASTLE GREEN

TA1 1NF
TEL 01823-272671
www.the-castle-hotel.com
An immediate sense of style throughout, with menus that prove imagination is far from lacking in the kitchen. Carefully sourced local ingredients are used to create the impressive, modern British dishes. Fixed-price L Tues.–Thurs.
[▦] 60 [⊕] Closed Sun.–Mon.

THURLESTONE

🏨 THURLESTONE
$$$$$ ★★★★ ❁
THURLESTONE
TQ7 3NN
TEL 01548-560382
FAX 01548-561069
www.thurlestone.co.uk
Family-owned hotel on beautifully kept gardens and grounds with fine views of the South Devon coast. Golf, tennis, and croquet.
[i] 64 [P] 119 ⬆ 🕸 🏊 🏋

TORQUAY

🏨 GRAND HOTEL
$$$ ❁
SEA FRONT
TQ2 6NT
TEL 01803-296677
FAX 01803-213462
www.grandtorquay.co.uk
A classic Edwardian "white wedding cake" hotel with great sea views and its own swimming pool.
[i] 132 [P] 57 🏊 🏋

TWO BRIDGES

🏨 PRINCE HALL
$$$$ ★★ ❁
TWO BRIDGES
PL20 6SA
TEL 01822-890403
FAX 01822-890676
www.princehall.co.uk
Local ingredients are used regularly on the short, nightly changing menu at this comfortable country-house hotel

in the heart of spectacular Dartmoor National Park. Fishing. No children under ten. Fixed-price D.

🛈 8 🅿 13

VERYAN

🏨 NARE HOTEL
$$$$ ★★★★ ✿
CARNE BEACH
TR2 5PF
TEL 01872-501111
FAX 01872-501856
www.narehotel.com
Unobtrusive country-house atmosphere in seaside setting. Easy access to beach. Choice of restaurants with excellent local seafood. Tennis and windsurfing.

🛈 38 🅿 80 ⬆ ⬇ ⬇ 🔽

WELLINGTON

🏨🍴 BINDON COUNTRY HOUSE
$$$$ ★★★ ✿✿
LANGFORD BUDVILLE,
WELLINGTON
TA21 0RU
TEL 01823-400070
FAX 01823- 400071
www.bindon.com
A wonderful country-house hotel, facing the Blackdown Hills. Each splendid bedroom is named after a battle fought by the Duke of Wellington. The Wellesley Restaurant makes a strong designer statement, and the cooking is full of style with herbs cleverly used. Tennis and croquet available. Fixed-price L & D.

🛈 12 🍴 35 🅿 30 ⬇

WELLS

🏨 BEACONSFIELD FARM
$
EASTON
BA5 1DU
TEL/FAX 01749-870308
www.beaconsfieldfarm.co.uk
Farmhouse set in lovely countryside with a good level

of comfort and hospitality. No children under eight.

🛈 3 🅿 10 🕙 Closed mid-Nov.–March

🍴 GOODFELLOWS
$$ ✿✿
5 SADLER ST.
BA5 2RR
TEL 01749-673866
www.goodfellowswells.co.uk
Out front lie the patisserie and delicatessen—in back, a restaurant that's making a name for itself with its cooking of West Country fish. Adam the chef will sell you fish and suggest how to best cook them, too, if you wish.

🍴 40 🕙 Closed Sun.–Mon., Tues. D, Dec. 25, first 2 weeks of Jan.

WOOLACOMBE

🏨 WATERSMEET
$$$$ ★★★ ✿
MORTEHOE
EX34 7EB
TEL 01271-870333
FAX 01271-870890
www.watersmeethotel.co.uk
Perched above a rocky inlet with sea views from restaurant. Professional and friendly service. Tennis and croquet.

🛈 25 🅿 38 ⬇

■ WALES

ABERYSTWYTH

🍴 CONRAH
$$$ ✿✿
FFOSRHYDYGALED CHANCERY
SY23 4DF
TEL 01970-617941
www.conrah.co.uk
The kitchen rightly favors good regional produce, and the quality of ingredients, cooking, and presentation skills come through in the traditional Welsh and modern International cuisine. Bar food. Fixed-price L & D.

🍴 50

BONTDDU

🏨 BORTHWNOG HALL
$$$
BONTDDU
LL40 2TT
TEL 01341-430271
FAX 01341-430682
http://homepages.enterprise.net/borthwnoghall
Seventeenth-century country house adjoining Garth Gell nature reserve on Mawddach estuary. Superb views toward Cader Idris. Library art gallery contains original watercolors and oils; also pottery and sculpture for sale. Bedrooms are spacious.

🛈 3 🅿 6

BUILTH WELLS

🏨 LLANGOED HALL
$$$$ ✿✿
LLYSWEN (NEAR BRECON)
LD3 0YP
TEL 01874-754525
FAX 01874-754545
www.llangoedhall.co.uk
Perfectly placed for the Hay-on-Wye Festival of Literature and for exploring the wild country of the Black Mountains, this country house hotel is enhanced by antiques and a fine art collection.

🛈 23 🅿 50

CAERNARFON

🏨 SEIONT MANOR
$$$$ ★★★ ✿✿
LLANRUG
LL55 2AQ
TEL 01286-673366
FAX 01286-672840
Snowdon looms just a few miles from this country house on 150 acres of parkland. Hotel cuisine often features regional specialities. Bar food. Fixed-price L & D.

🛈 28 🅿 60 ⬇ 🔽

🏨 Hotel   🍴 Restaurant   🛈 No. of Guest Rooms   🍴 No. of Seats   🅿 Parking   🚇 Tube   🕙 Closed

CAPEL CURIG

🏨 COBDENS

$$ ★★

CAPEL CURIG

LL24 OEE

TEL 01690-720243

FAX 01690-720354

www.cobdens.co.uk

Long-established hotel with lovely views, a famous center for outdoor pursuits in the heart of Snowdonia. Two bars, one with impressive, exposed rock face. Enthusiastic help, advice, and service.

🛏 16 🅿 60

CARDIFF

🏨 ST. DAVID'S HOTEL & SPA

$$$$$ ★★★★★

HAVANNAH ST.

CF10 5SD

TEL 029-2045 4045

FAX 029-2048 7056

www.thestdavidshotel.com

Views over Cardiff Bay outside and a seven-story atrium inside make this a stylish and popular hotel to stay in.

🛏 132 🅿 80 🔲 🟢 🈴 🎖

🍴 WOODS BRASSERIE

$$–$$$ ✿✿

PILOTAGE BUILDING, STUART ST.

CF10 5BW

TEL 029-2049 2400

http://knifeandforkfood .co.uk/woods

Eat outdoors on the patio or indoors looking out of the big windows of this former customs office on the cobbled waterfront. Very French style of cuisine, with something for everyone from chargrilled steak to loin of hake.

🍴 90 🕐 Closed Sun. D (Sept.–May), Dec. 25–26, Jan. 1

🍴 LE GALLOIS-Y-CYMRO

$$ ✿✿✿

6–10 ROMILLY CRESCENT

CF11 9NR

TEL 029-2034 1264

www.legallois-ycymro.com

A stylishly simple and friendly place, Le Gallois-Y-Cymro offers classic French cooking with plenty of modern twists, very strong on fish and on subtle vegetable notes.

🍴 60 🕐 Closed Sun.–Mon., Dec. 25, Jan. 1, 1 week in Aug.

CHEPSTOW

🏨 MARRIOTT ST. PIERRE

$$$$ ★★★★

ST. PIERRE PARK

NP16 6YA

TEL 01291-625261

FAX 01291-629975

www.marriott.co.uk

Hospitable old golf and leisure hotel with own championship golf course and tennis courts. Bedrooms in main house, at lakeside, or in cottage suites.

🛏 148 🅿 430 🈴 🎖

CONWY

🏨 OLD RECTORY COUNTRY HOUSE

$$$$ ★★ ✿✿✿

LLANRWST RD., LLANSANFFRAID GLAN CONWY

LL28 5LF

TEL 01492-580611

FAX 01492-584555

www.oldrectorycountryhouse .co.uk

Peaceful small hotel set in terraced gardens overlooking the Conwy Estuary and the hills of Snowdonia. Family suite available. Bedrooms are individually and characterfully furnished, many with handsomely carved antique beds. No children under five.

🛏 5 (2 annex) 🅿 10

CRICKHOWELL

🍴 BEAR

$$$ ✿

CRICKHOWELL

NP8 1BW

TEL 01873-810408

www.bearhotel.co.uk

Venerable and cozy inn more than six centuries old, full of beams and tankards. Local produce is used to telling effect for both bar and restaurant menus that draw on influences from far and wide. Good selection of wines. Bar food. No children under six.

🍴 70 🅿 38 🕐 Closed Sun. D, L Tues.–Sat.

DOLGELLAU

🏨 PENMAENUCHAF HALL

$$$$ ★★★ ✿

PENMAENPOOL

LL40 1YB

TEL 01341-422129

FAX 01341-422787

www.penhall.co.uk

Impressive country hideaway, dating from 1860, with breathtaking views. Each of the elegant bedrooms is individually styled. The restaurant serves fresh produce, cooked in a modern style. Game room. Fishing. No children under six.

🛏 14 🅿 30

🏨 TYDDYNMAWR FARMHOUSE

$

ISLAWRDREF

LL40 1TL

TEL 01341-422331

www.lokalink.co.uk/dolgel lau/tyddynmawr

Acclaimed 18th-century farmhouse located at the foot of Cader Idris. Home baking and cooking, including hearty farmhouse breakfasts that are most enjoyable. Fishing is available. No children.

🛏 3 🅿 8

GOWER

🏨 THE KING'S HEAD

$

TOWN HOUSE, LLANGENNITH

SA3 1HX

TEL 01792-386212

FAX 01792-386477

www.kingsheadgower.co.uk
This friendly inn—three 17th-century buildings in the village center behind magnificent Rhossili Beach—is perfectly placed for exploring the Gower Peninsula.
🛏3 🅿60

HARLECH

🏨 **HOTEL MAES-Y-NEUADD**
🍴 **$$$$ ★★ ✺✺**
TALSARNAU
LL47 6YA
TEL 01766-780200
FAX 01766-780211
www.neuadd.com
Set on beautiful grounds with views over Snowdonia. Admirable use of fresh local produce—curly kale, laverbread, wild fungi, and much more—with home-baked breads and homegrown fruit and vegetables. Fixed-price D.
🛏12 (4 annex) 🍴65 🅿50

🍴 **CASTLE COTTAGE**
$$$$ ✺
PEN LLECH
LL46 2YL
TEL 01766-780479
**www.castlecottageharlech
.co.uk**
The menu is not large, but it changes every week and features local produce whenever possible. Fixed-price D.
🍴45 🕐Closed L, 3 weeks in Jan.

HAY-ON-WYE

🏨 **SWAN-AT-HAY**
$$$$ ★★★
CHURCH ST.
HR3 5DQ
TEL 01497-821188
FAX 01497-821424
www.swanathay.co.uk
A coaching inn built in 1821, close to the center of this quaint border town. Choice of bars, lounge, and pleasant restaurant. Fishing.
🛏16 (3 annex) 🅿18

🍴 **OLD BLACK LION
HOTEL**
$$$ ✺
26 LION ST.
HR3 5AD
TEL 01497-820841
www.oldblacklion.co.uk
Award-winning local fresh produce and imaginative vegetarian dishes in a nice historic setting.
🍴60

LAUGHARNE

🍴 **CORS**
$$$ ✺✺
NEWBRIDGE RD.
SA33 4SH
TEL 01994-427219
www.the-cors.co.uk
Chef-owner Nick Priestland displays his talent for abstract painting and his gift for gardening, as well as providing a menu with a strong Mediterranean slant. Presentation is all primary colors; flavors are undiluted. The short wine list bubbles with character.
🍴24 🕐Closed Sun.–Wed., Dec. 25

LLANDRILLO

🏨 **TYDDYN LLAN**
🍴 **$$$$ ★★ ✺✺**
LLANDRILLO
LL21 0ST
TEL 01490-440264
FAX 01490-440414
www.tyddynllan.co.uk
Georgian house set on landscaped gardens. Sharp, imaginative cooking. Well-judged dishes with vibrant natural flavors and not too much complication. Bar food. Fixed-price D.
🛏10 🍴40 🅿30 🕐Closed L, Mon.–Thurs.

LLANDUDNO

🏨 **BODYSGALLEN HALL**
$$$$$ ★★★★ ✺✺✺
2 MILES S OF LLANDUDNO

LL30 1RS
TEL 01492-584466
FAX 01492-582519
www.bodysgallen.com
A 17th-century house with fine views over Snowdonia and Conwy Castle. About 200 acres of parkland and formal gardens, mullioned windows, oak paneling, and log fire. Some cottage accommodations and private sitting rooms. Tennis and croquet. No children under eight.
🛏31 (16 annex) 🅿50 🚇📺

SOMETHING SPECIAL

🏨 **LIGHTHOUSE**
$$$
MARINE DR.
LL30 2XD
TEL 01492-876819
**www.lighthouse-llandudno
.co.uk**
Former lighthouse on northern edge of Great Orme, Llandudno's spectacular headland. It was built in 1862 by the Mersey Docks and Harbour

Board and shone a light until 1985. Many original features preserved. Two bedrooms have their own lounge areas; one is the lighthouse's glazed dome. Stunning views; each bedroom equipped with a pair of binoculars. Solid-fuel stove for cold weather.

[i] 3 [P] 6

LLANGAMMARCH WELLS

LAKE COUNTRY HOUSE & SPA
$$$$ ★★★ ✿✿
LLANGAMMARCH WELLS
LD4 4BS
TEL 01591-620202
FAX 01591-620457
www.lakecountryhouse.co.uk
Comfortable and friendly Victorian house in beautiful countryside. Outdoor pursuits include lakeside and river walks, tennis, golf, and fishing.

[i] 30 [P] 72

LLANGEFNI (ISLE OF ANGLESEY)

TRE-YSGAWEN HALL
$$$
CAPEL COCH
LL77 7UR
TEL 01248-750750
FAX 01248-750035
www.treysgawen-hall.co.uk
Georgian mansion on wooded grounds. Drawing room, bar, brasserie, and main restaurant.

[i] 19 (10 annex) [P] 140

LLANGYBI

CWRT BLEDDYN
HOTEL & SPA
$$$–$$$$ ★★★★ ✿✿
LLANGYBI
NP15 1PG
TEL 01633-450521
FAX 01633-450220
www.cwrtbleddyn.co.uk
Victorian building on parkland in Welsh Borders countryside.

Four-posters and carved oak furniture in some bedrooms. Capable cooking, using local ingredients, in the Med Restaurant. Tennis, squash, and a fine leisure complex.

[i] 45 (4 annex) [⛉] 45 [P] 100 [🅰] [🆈]

LLANWDDYN

LAKE VYRNWY
$$$$ ★★★ ✿
LAKE VYRNWY
SY10 0LY
TEL 01691-870692
FAX 01691-870259
www.lakevyrnwy.com
Victorian country house on 26,000 acres of mature woodland above Lake Vyrnwy. Many bedrooms have four-poster beds and balconies; superb lake views. Restaurant and Tavern Bar provide a good variety of meals. Fishing, shooting, and other outdoor pursuits. Hotel holds license for performing civil marriages.

[i] 35 [P] 70

LLYSWEN

LLANGOED HALL
$$$$–$$$$$ ★★★★ ✿✿
LLYSWEN
LD3 0YP
TEL 01874-754525
FAX 01874-754545
Imposing Edwardian country house on Wye Valley parkland, with tennis and fishing. Inside is a splendid balance between comfort and grandeur in day-rooms, corridors, and library. Pretty bedrooms furnished with antiques and smart bathrooms. Welsh menu with a Mediterranean and Provençal twist. No children under eight.

[i] 23 [⛉] 50 [P] 85

MACHYNLLETH

YNYSHIR HALL
$$$$ ✿✿✿
EGLWYSFACH

SY20 8TA
TEL 01654-781209
www.ynyshirhall.co.uk
Creative menus with a real feel for ingredients, scouring the region for what is best and appropriate and, in the kitchen, treating what is served with respect. Now an AA regional food award winner. Service is smooth, cheery, and intelligent. Bar food. Fixed-price L & D. No children under nine.

[⛉] 30

MONMOUTH

CROWN AT WHITEBROOK
$$$ ✿✿
WHITEBROOK
NP25 4TX
TEL 01600-860254
www.crownatwhitebrook.co.uk
Genuine welcome, tranquil atmosphere. Ingredients are from sound Welsh sources and the quality is generally high, with plenty of good ideas. Extensive and very well chosen wine list. Fixed-price L & D. No children under eight.

[⛉] 32 [🕐] Closed Sun. D

NEWCASTLE EMLYN

BRONIWAN
$$
RHYDLEWIS, LLANDYSUL
CEREDIGION
SA44 5PF
TEL 01239-851261
www.broniwan.com
This small organic farm, set among pretty gardens in 45 acres of meadows, woods, and streams, makes a very friendly and welcoming stopover. If you opt to eat dinner here (bring your own wine), the chances are that the beef, vegetables, fruit, and eggs will be the farm's own organic produce.

[i] 2

PRESTEIGNE

🏨 THE OLD VICARAGE
$$

NORTON, RADNORSHIRE,
POWYS
LD8 2EN
TEL 01544 260038
www.oldvicarage-nortonrads
.co.uk
A wonderful old stone-built
house, designed by Victorian
star architect Sir George
Gilbert Scott. Full of comforts
and collectibles.
🛏 3

REYNOLDSTON

🏨 FAIRYHILL
🍴 **$$$$ ★★★ ❀❀**

REYNOLDSTON
SA3 1BS
TEL 01792-390139
FAX 01792-391358
www.fairyhill.net
Eighteenth-century mansion
on 24 acres of wooded
grounds on the Gower Pen-
insula. Warm hospitality. Log
fires, fresh flowers. Imaginative
cuisine featuring Welsh dishes.
Fixed-price L & D. No children
under eight.
🛏 8 🪑 60 🅿 50 🕓 Closed 2
weeks in Jan.

RUTHIN

SOMETHING SPECIAL

🏨 RUTHIN CASTLE
$$$ ★★★ ❀❀

RUTHIN
LL15 2NU
TEL 01824-702664
FAX 01824-705978
www.ruthincastle.co.uk
Characterful early 19th-
century pile with own castle
ruins, which mostly date from
the 13th century, on 30-acre
grounds. The castle withstood
an attack by Welsh rebel leader
Owain Glyndwr in 1400. During the Civil War, it fell to the
Roundhead general Mytton in
1646 after an 11-week siege

and was then dismantled. Paneling, carved ceilings. Medieval
banquets in restored hall.
🛏 58 🅿 200 ❧

ST. DAVID'S

🏨 WARPOOL COURT
$$$$ ★★★ ❀❀

ST. DAVID'S
SA62 6BN
TEL 01437-720300
FAX 01437-720676
www.warpoolcourthotel.com
Former cathedral choir school
overlooking St. Bride's Bay.
Over 3,000 handpainted tiles
on display. Imaginative cuisine.
🛏 25 🅿 100 🔄 🔲

🍴 CWTCH
$$$

22 HIGH ST.
SA62 6SD
TEL 01437-720491
www.cwtchrestaurant.co.uk
A little place that's big on
good local food, a relaxed
atmosphere, and a warm
welcome for family parties.
Open for dinner only.
🪑 50 🕓 Closed Sun.–Mon.
Nov.–March, Dec. 25–26, Jan. 1

SKENFRITH

🍴 BELL AT SKENFRITH
$$$ ❀❀

SKENFRITH
NP7 8UH
TEL 01600-750235
www.skenfrith.co.uk
A welcoming coaching inn by
the bridge and near the castle.
Very friendly, young, local
staff; clean, uncluttered decor;
local produce with a modern
approach. Recipient of an AA
regional food award.
🪑 60 🅿 40 🕓 Closed Tues.

TENBY

🏨 ATLANTIC
$$$ ★★★

THE ESPLANADE

SA70 7DU
TEL/FAX 01834-842881
www.atlantic-hotel.uk.com
Family-run hotel with views
over the sea. Restaurant
menus offer classic French and
English cooking; light meals
served all day in basement
bistro. Fixed-price D.
🛏 42 🅿 30 ❧ 🔄

■ SOUTH MIDLANDS

BIRMINGHAM

🏨 MACDONALD
BURLINGTON
$$$ ★★★★

BURLINGTON ARCADE, 126
NEW ST.
B2 4JQ
TEL 0121-643 9191
FAX 0121-628 5005
www.macdonaldhotels.co.uk
In the heart of the city, this elegant hotel blends together its
original Victorian design with
modern facilities. Imaginative,
carefully prepared cuisine in
the Berlioz Restaurant.
🛏 112 ❧

🍴 AKRAM'S KASHMIRI
RESTAURANT
$$–$$$

1526 PERSHORE RD., STIRCHLEY
B30 2NW
TEL 0121-433 4320
www.akrams.biz
A friendly balti establishment
where the food is as authentic
as you'll get in a Birmingham
restaurant (U.K. home of balti
cooking), and the atmosphere
is very welcoming.
🪑 100

BROADWAY

🏨 BARCELO THE LYGON
🍴 ARMS
$$$$$ ★★★★ ❀❀

HIGH ST.
WR12 7DU
TEL 01386-852255
FAX 01386-858611

www.barcelo-hotels.co.uk
Sixteenth-century inn around courtyard. Log fires, wood paneling. Great Hall restaurant has heraldic panels and Minstrels' Gallery; Goblets Restaurant is less formal. Fixed-price L & D.

🛈 65 🛏 77 🅿 200 🎦 🏋️

🍴 BUCKLAND MANOR
$$$$
BUCKLAND
WR12 7LY
TEL 01386-852626
www.bucklandmanor.co.uk
Medieval, honey-colored stone building set in lovely gardens. Country-house cooking with pleasant variations. Seasonal vegetables, herbs, fruit from manor's garden. Remarkable wine list.

🛏 40

BURFORD

🏨 BURFORD HOUSE
$$$
99 HIGH ST.
OX18 4QA
TEL 01993-823151
FAX 01993-823240
www.burford-house.co.uk
Hotel with enclosed garden in the center of Burford. Four-poster beds, bathrooms with old-fashioned tubs. Lunch, or tea with a tempting array of homemade cakes.

🛈 7

CHELTENHAM

🏨 CLEEVE HILL
$$$
CLEEVE HILL
GL52 3PR
TEL 01242-672052
FAX 01242-679969
www.cleevehill-hotel.co.uk
In a commanding position looking over the Severn Valley to the Malvern Hills beyond. Friendly and attentive service from enthusiastic staff. The modern bedrooms, bar, and spacious lounge are furnished

to a high standard. No children under six.

🛈 10 🅿 10

🍴 LE CHAMPIGNON SAUVAGE
$$$$ ❉❉❉❉
24–26 SUFFOLK RD.
GL50 2AQ
TEL/FAX 01242-573449
www.lechampignonsauvage .co.uk
Exceptional food in an unassuming atmosphere. This is a restaurant where people enjoy eating civilized French cooking. Fixed-price L & D.

🛏 48 🕐 Closed Sun.–Mon., 10 days at Christmas, 3 weeks in June 🆒

CHIPPING CAMDEN

🏨 COTSWOLD HOUSE
$$$$ ★★★ ❉❉
THE SQUARE
GL55 6AN
TEL 01386-840330
FAX 01386-840310
www.cotswoldhouse.com
Seventeenth-century hotel in the center of this typical Cotswolds town. The relaxed Hicks Brasserie is open all day; Garden Room Restaurant is more formal.

🛈 29 🅿 28 🏋️

CHURCH ENSTONE

🍴 CROWN INN
$$ ❉
MILL LN.
OX7 4NN
TEL 01608-677262
A real Oxfordshire village local made of Cotswold stone and serving good, solid pub fare.

🛏 42 🅿 8 🕐 Closed Sun. D

CIRENCESTER

🏨 HARE AND HOUNDS
$$ ❉
FOSSE-CROSSE, CHEDWORTH
GL54 4NN

TEL 01285-720288
www.hareandhoundsinn.com
The Hare and Hounds, a traditional, cozy, golden stone inn, is a well-known rendezvous for walkers, riders, and motorists out to make the best of this glorious part of the Cotswolds.

🛈 10 🅿 40

CLAVERDON

🏨 ARDENCOTE MANOR HOTEL COUNTRY CLUB & SPA
$$$$ ★★★ ❉
LYE GREEN RD.
CV35 8LS
TEL 01926-843111
FAX 01926-842646
www.ardencote.com
Small hotel with good facilities. Bedrooms are decorated with pretty fabrics. Formal dining in the Oak Room; informal snacks and meals in members' bar and at lakeside. Tennis, golf, and fishing.

🛈 110 🅿 150 🎦 🏋️

GREAT MILTON

SOMETHING SPECIAL

🏨🍴 LE MANOIR AUX QUAT' SAISONS
$$$$$ ★★★★ ❉❉❉❉❉
CHURCH RD.
OX44 7PD
TEL 01844-278881
FAX 01844-278847
www.manoir.com
Raymond Blanc's mellow stone 15th-century manor house in immaculately maintained gardens with famous and very busy restaurant. Beautifully appointed bedrooms and suites, some with their own private terrace garden. Outstanding cuisine is enhanced during summer by herbs and vegetables grown in the walled kitchen garden. Croquet lawn. Fixed-price L & D.

🛈 32 🛏 120 🅿 60

🛗 Elevator ❄️ Air-conditioning 🎦 Indoor Pool 🏊 Outdoor Pool 🏋️ Health Club

LEAMINGTON SPA

🏨 MALLORY COURT
🍴 $$$$$ ★★★ ✿✿✿
HARBURY LN., BISHOP'S TACH-
BROOK
CV33 9QB
TEL 01926-330214
FAX 01926-451714
www.mallory.co.uk
English country house with
friendly and attentive service.
Wood-paneled restaurant
offers light, innovative cuisine.
Homemade canapés, breads,
and petits fours; fresh veg-
etables and herbs from the
garden. Tennis and croquet.
Fixed-price L & D. No children
under nine.
🛏 29 🍴 50 🅿 100 ⊠
🕐 Restaurant closed Tues. L

LEOMINSTER

🏨 LOWER BACHE HOUSE
$$
KIMBOLTON
HR6 0ER
TEL 01568-750304
A rustic gem, timber framed
and in cheery red brick, this
award-winning, character-
ful old farmhouse with its
far-flung views is not only
comfortable and welcom-
ing but also boasts its own
extensive nature reserve and a
butterfly house to boot.
🛏 3

MALVERN WELLS

🏨 COTTAGE IN THE WOOD
$$$–$$$$ ★★★ ✿✿
HOLYWELL RD.
WR14 4LG
TEL 01684-588860
FAX 01684-560662
www.cottageinthewood.co.uk
Former haunt of composer
Sir Edward Elgar. There are
magnificent views from the
Malvern Hills. Talented and
innovative chef.
🛏 30 🅿 40

MARLOW-ON-THAMES

🏨 DANESFIELD HOUSE
$$$$–$$$$$
HENLEY RD.
SL7 2EY
TEL 01628-891010
FAX 01628-890408
www.danesfieldhouse.co.uk
Up there in all senses, this
great white country house
looks down across terraced
gardens and impressive park-
land to a vista of the River
Thames in one of its most
picturesque aspects. Luxurious
facilities (you can arrive in a
chauffeur-driven Rolls-Royce
by arrangement) are twinned
with genuine warmth of
service, all in an opulent late
Victorian mansion.
🛏 84 🅿 100 ⊠ 📺

OUNDLE

SOMETHING SPECIAL

🏨 TALBOT
$$ ★★★
NEW ST.
PE8 4EA
TEL 01832-273621
FAX 01832-274545
www.thetalbot-oundle.com
Hospitable 17th-century hotel,
partly built using material from
the ruins of nearby Fothering-
hay Castle where Mary, Queen
of Scots, was imprisoned and
executed. A painting in the
bar of the hotel shows her
descending a staircase, surrounded by solemn courtiers
and wardens and followed by
weeping women. Spacious,
attractive bedrooms; many of
which have exposed beams.
The cozy bar and lounge are in
keeping with the hotel's Old
World charm.
🛏 39 🅿 50

OXFORD

🏨 MACDONALD
🍴 RANDOLPH HOTEL
$$$$ ★★★★ ✿✿
BEAUMONT ST.
OX1 2LN
TEL 01865-256400
FAX 01865-792133
www.randolph-hotel.com
Fine landmark Victorian hotel
across from the Ashmolean
Museum. Afternoon teas in
the drawing room. Formal
dining in the restaurant.
🛏 150 🍴 60 🅿 64 ⊟

🏨 OLD PARSONAGE
$$$$ ✿
1 BANBURY RD.
OX2 6NN
TEL 01865-310210
FAX 01865-311262
www.oldparsonage-hotel
.co.uk
A handsome old house full of
character, conveniently placed
not far from the city centre

🏨 Hotel   🍴 Restaurant   🛏 No. of Guest Rooms   🍴 No. of Seats   🅿 Parking   📺 Tube   🕐 Closed and university.

ⓘ 30 P 14

⊞ MERCURE EASTGATE TOWNHOUSE HOTEL

$$$ ★★★ ✿

73 HIGH ST.

OX1 4BE

TEL 01865-248332

FAX 01865-794163

www.mercure.com

A former coaching inn, this smart and friendly hotel is just opposite Magdalene College in the center of town.

ⓘ 63 P 40

⊞ GABLES

$

6 CUMNOR HILL

OX2 9HA

TEL 01865-862153

FAX 01865-864054

www.gablesguesthouse.co.uk

Charming Victorian house with a conservatory and a large garden in the rear. Warm, friendly welcome. Awarded AA Landlady of the Year.

ⓘ 6 P 6 🕒 Closed Jan.–Feb.

🍴 GEE'S RESTAURANT

$$$ ✿

61 BANBURY RD.

OX2 6PE

TEL 01865-553540

www.gees-restaurant.co.uk

The food is great, the service pleasant, and the company cosmopolitan, but Gee's is really all about the ambience, the clear light pouring in on diners in this lovely Victorian conservatory.

🪑 85 🕒 Closed Dec. 25

PAINSWICK

⊞ BEAR OF RODBOROUGH

🍴 **$$$**

RODBOROUGH COMMON

GL5 5DE

TEL 01453-878522

FAX 01453-872523

This lovely old coaching inn with its stone gables stands on Rodborough Common high above the surrounding valleys. Good eating in the Box Tree Restaurant; good cheer in the friendly public bar.

ⓘ 46 P 70

SOLIHULL

🍴 NUTHURST GRANGE

$$$$$ ✿✿

NUTHURST GRANGE LN., HOCK-LEY HEATH

B94 5NL

TEL 01564-783972

FAX 01564-783919

www.nuthurst-grange.co.uk

Surrounded by landscaped gardens and woodlands, this elegant dining room serves modern British cuisine. Varied and interesting menus change seasonally. Fixed-price L & D. Accommodations also available.

🪑 60 P 80

STRATFORD-UPON-AVON

⊞ BILLESLEY MANOR

$$$$$ ★★★★ ✿✿

BILLESLEY, ALCESTER

B49 6NF

TEL 01789-279955

FAX 01789-764145

www.barcelo-hotels.co.uk

Sixteenth-century manor house on peaceful grounds, which include a topiary garden. Many original features such as oak paneling and magnificent fireplaces. Interesting, carefully prepared menus. Tennis and croquet.

ⓘ 72 P 100 🌊 🔽

⊞ MERCURE SHAKESPEARE

$$$$$ ★★★★ ✿✿

CHAPEL ST.

CV37 6ER

TEL 01789-294997

FAX 01789-415411

www.mercure.com

Charming gabled central hotel, with a profusion of exposed beams, creaking staircases, and wood fires. Restaurant menus or courtyard bistro.

ⓘ 74 P 34 🔼

⊞ MACDONALD ALVESTON MANOR

$$$$ ★★★★ ✿

CLOPTON BRIDGE

CV37 7HP

TEL 0844-879 9138

FAX 01789-414095

www.macdonaldhotels.co.uk

Warm brick-and-timber facade, gable ends, and well-tended grounds grace a striking building that dates to the 16th century. The kitchen is up-to-date with its ideas.

ⓘ 114 P 200

SOMETHING SPECIAL

⊞ FOX AND GOOSE INN

🍴 **$$$ ✿**

ARMSCOTE

CV37 8DD

TEL/FAX 01608-682293

www.foxandgoosearmscote.co.uk

The rooms in this creeper-hung 17th-century village inn are named (and painted!) to reflect Clue ("Cluedo" in Great Britain) characters—mustard, plum, scarlet, peacock—and there's definitely an off-the-wall, cheerful atmosphere here. Trencher-persons will enjoy the mighty helpings of country food, and there's a cozy old-fashioned bar to spot the murderer in!

ⓘ 4 🪑 45 P 20 🕒 Closed Dec. 25

SUTTON COLDFIELD

⊞ NEW HALL

🍴 **$$$ ★★★★ ✿✿**

WALMLEY RD.

B76 1QX

TEL 0121-378 2442

FAX 0121-378 4637

www.e-travelguide.info/newhall

Reputedly the oldest surviving moated manor house in

England. The lovely grounds include a walled rose garden and a yew tree walk. Rooms retain many original features and have delightful decor. High-quality, imaginative cuisine. Golf, fishing, and croquet. Fixed-price D.

🏨 60 🛏 60 🅿 80

TETBURY

🏨 SNOOTY FOX
$$$ ★★★ ✿
MARKET PL.
GL8 8DD
TEL 01666-502436
FAX 01666-503479
www.snooty-fox.co.uk
Sixteenth-century Cotswold stone inn; warm and friendly staff. Restaurant with ornately carved wall paneling and impressive ceiling.

🏨 12

THAME

🏨 SPREAD EAGLE HOTEL
$$
CORNMARKET
OX9 2BW
TEL 01844-213661
FAX 01844-261380
www.spreadeaglethame.co.uk
Traditional coaching inn with plenty of character, full of slanting floorboards and odd creaky corners. Ask for one of the refurbished rooms—the hotel is undergoing long-drawn-out renovations.

🏨 35

TOWCESTER

🍴 VINE HOUSE
$$$ ✿✿
100 HIGH ST., PAULERSPURY
NN12 7NA
TEL 01327-811267
www.vinehousehotel.com
Relaxing country cottage restaurant. Menu changes daily; repertoire is seasonal, style modern British. Fixed-price L.

🛏 26 🕓 Closed Mon. L, Sun.

WALLINGFORD

🍴 BEETLE AND WEDGE
$$$$
FERRY LN., MOULSFORD
OX10 9JF
TEL 01491-651381
www.beetleandwedge.co.uk
This award-winning Thames-side restaurant has literary links (former home of Jerome K. Jerome, author of the classic Thames farce *Three Men in a Boat*), river views, and fine cooking of tip-top freshness on a daily-changing menu that follows the seasons.

🛏 25 (dining room), 60 (boathouse)

WARWICK

🏨 WROXALL ABBEY ESTATE
$$–$$$$$
BIRMINGHAM RD.
CV35 7NB
TEL 01926-484470
FAX 01926-485206
www.wroxall.com
Superb parkland location, magnificent redbrick mansion, and a wide choice of restaurants and bars.

🏨 70 ☎ 🖥

WHITNEY-ON-WYE

🏨 RHYDSPENCE INN
$$ ★★
WHITNEY-ON-WYE
HR3 6EU
TEL 01497-831262
FAX 01497-831751
www.rhydspence-inn.co.uk
A 14th-century inn on the boundary of England and Wales. Attractive restaurant; two quaint bars with low-beamed ceilings and log fires.

🏨 7 🅿 30 🕓 Closed 2 weeks in Jan.

WISHAW

🏨 MOXHULL HALL
$$
HOLY LN.
B76 9PE
TEL 0121-329 2056
FAX 0121-311 1980
www.moxhullhall.co.uk
A handsome Victorian building set in very well-kept gardens, with a nice informal atmosphere.

🏨 18

■ EAST ANGLIA & LINCOLNSHIRE

BLAKENEY

🏨 MORSTON HALL
🍴 **$$$$ ★★★ ✿✿✿**
MORSTON
NR25 7AA
TEL 01263-741041
FAX 01263-740419
www.morstonhall.com
Seventeenth-century house in small village on beautiful and wildlife-rich north Norfolk coast. Conservatory overlooks pretty gardens. Restaurant is full of fresh flowers and paintings. Fixed-price, four-course menu (no choice until dessert) is both well-balanced and skillfully executed; superb produce, wine list, and presentation.

🏨 6 🅿 40 🕓 Closed L (except Sun.)

BURNHAM MARKET

🏨 HOSTE ARMS
$$$ ★★ ✿✿
THE GREEN
PE31 8HD
TEL 01328-738777
FAX 01328-730103
www.hostearms.co.uk
Pub, restaurant, and hotel that's upscale and stylish in appearance, yet down-to-earth and unpretentious. Art exhibitions, a splendid atmosphere,

in addition to excellent cooking that features local fish.

(i) 61 (6 annex) **P** 60 **S**

BURY ST. EDMUNDS

CHANTRY
$$

8 SPARHAWK ST.
IP33 1RY
TEL 01284-767427
FAX 01284-760946
www.chantryhotel.com
Splendid Georgian house standing in the site of a former 12th-century Chantry Chapel. Warm hospitality and friendly service.

(i) 13 (3 annex) **P** 16

CAMBRIDGE

HOTEL DU VIN
$$$$ ✿

15–19 TRUMPINGTON ST.
CB2 1QA
TEL 01223-227330
FAX 01223-227331
www.hotelduvin.com
Superb hotel with lots of attention to guest comfort—library, wine room, powerful showers in the bathrooms, and more.

(i) 41 **P** 12 ⬆ ⬛ ▼

ARUNDEL HOUSE
$$–$$$ ★★

CHESTERTON RD.
CB4 3AN
TEL 01223-367701
FAX 01223-367721
www.arundelhousehotels
.co.uk
Town-house hotel close to River Cam and Jesus Green parkland. Victorian conservatory for meals all day; restaurant serves interesting and varied dishes. Attractively decorated modern bedrooms.

(i) 103 (22 annex) **P** 70
⊕ Closed Dec. 25–26

MIDSUMMER HOUSE
$$$$ ✿✿✿✿

MIDSUMMER COMMON

CB4 1HA
TEL 01223-369299
www.midsummerhouse.co.uk
A bright and airy conservatory is the main focus of this restaurant that goes from strength to strength. Clever use of color and style reflected in the seasonal menu. Earthy, robust ingredients are refined to great effect. Fixed-price L & D.

⊞ 65 ⊕ Closed Sun.–Mon., Tues.–Wed. L, 2 weeks Christmas, Easter, 2 weeks Aug.–Sept.

CASTLE ACRE

OSTRICH INN
$$

STOCKS GREEN, KINGS LYNN
PE32 2AE
TEL 01760-755398
www.ostrichcastleacre.com
Gorgeous old village inn, bursting with warmth and character, full of beams and brickwork, with its comfortable rooms in an annex. Recipient of an AA dinner award.

(i) 6 **P** 30

COLCHESTER

OLD MANSE
$

15 ROMAN RD.
CO1 1UR
TEL 01206 545154
FAX 01206 545153
www.theoldmanse.uk.com
Family run bed-and-breakfast situated close to the town center and Norman castle. Historic Roman wall running along bottom of the garden. Warm hospitality. No children under six.

(i) 3 **P** 1 ⊕ Closed Dec. 23–31

DEDHAM

SOMETHING SPECIAL

MAISON TALBOOTH
$$$$ ★★★ ✿✿

STRATFORD RD., DEDHAM

CO7 6HN
TEL 01206-322367
FAX 01206-322752
www.milsomhotels.com/
maisontalbooth
Overlooking tranquil Dedham Vale, this pretty Georgian hotel gives a warm welcome. Stylish bedrooms equipped with thoughtful touches. Le Talbooth Restaurant is a little under a mile away from the Maison Talbooth. The hotel has a courtesy car for diners, but in fine weather most guests enjoy the 15-minute stroll to and from their dining place on the banks of the River Stour. The restaurant—the 16th-century weaver's cottage and toll house overlooking the river that John Constable featured in his famous landscapes—has good cooking balanced between traditional and modern.

(i) 10 **⊞** 75 **P** 20

DISS

SOMETHING SPECIAL

FOX AND GOOSE INN
$$$ ✿✿

FRESSINGFIELD
IP21 5PB
TEL 01379-586247
www.foxandgoose.net
The Fox and Goose was built in Tudor times, say its deeds, "for the more reverence of God, in avoiding eating and drinking necessary to the profits of the church." Not an easy intention to interpret; possibly the idea was to prevent the locals from eating in church. The parish church still owns the inn and benefits from its rents. A place of great character with bare boards, brickwork, oak beams, log fires, and a lovely view of the church. Good solid cooking. Bar meals. Fixed-price L & D.

⊞ 70 ⊕ Closed Mon., Dec. 27–30, 2 weeks in Jan.

⬆ Elevator   **S** Air-conditioning   ⬛ Indoor Pool   ⬛ Outdoor Pool   ▼ Health Club

ELY

🏨 LAMB HOTEL
$$$ ★★★ ✲
2 LYNN RD.
CB7 4EJ
TEL 01353-663574
FAX 01353-662023
www.thelamb-ely.com
Privately owned and personally managed 15th-century inn. Modern British cooking in the Octagon Restaurant.
🛏 32 ⊞ 40 🅿 20

🍴 ANCHOR INN
$$ ✲
SUTTON GAULT, SUTTON
CB6 2BD
TEL 01353-778537
www.anchor-inn-restaurant.co.uk
This clean and friendly riverside inn is notable for its well-cooked food and cheerful staff—a little treasure in the back of beyond.
⊞ 70 🅿 16

GRIMSTON

🏨 CONGHAM HALL
$$$$–$$$$$ ★★★ ✲✲
LYNN RD.
PE32 1AH
TEL 01485-600250
FAX 01485-601191
www.conghamhallhotel.co.uk
Georgian manor house on extensive grounds, which include a herb garden, walled flower garden, cricket ground, and tennis courts. The Orangery Restaurant overlooks the garden. Appealing dishes feature produce from the garden and focus on Mediterranean and North European flavor combinations. No children under seven.
🛏 14 🅿 50

HARWICH

🏨 PIER AT HARWICH
🍴 $$$ ★★★ ✲✲
THE QUAY

CO12 3HH
TEL 01255-241212
FAX 01255-551922
www.the-pier-hotel.co.uk
Excellent small harborfront hotel. Renowned for its cooking, specializing in seafood: choose from the informal, family oriented Ha'penny Pier—try the delicious fish-and-chips—or more serious dining in the Pier at Harwich Restaurant, which overlooks the quay and harbor and comes complete with ship's wheel and bell, lots of shipping prints, and maritime murals. Fixed-price L & D.
🛏 14 (7 annex) ⊞ 80 🅿 10

HINTLESHAM

🏨 HINTLESHAM HALL
🍴 $$$–$$$$$ ★★★★ ✲✲
HINTLESHAM
IP8 3NS
TEL 01473-652334/652268
FAX 01473-652463
www.hintleshamhall.co.uk
Tudor country house with magnificent Georgian facade. Both the pine-paneled parlor and the Salon restaurant—a magnificent high-ceilinged room that oozes luxury—offer menus that follow the seasons and include razor-sharp cooking. Noted for classical cuisine. Golf, tennis, riding, clay-pigeon and game shooting.
🛏 33 ⊞ 60 🅿 100 🕐 Closed Sat. L 🚇 🔳

HOLKHAM

🍴 VICTORIA AT HOLKHAM
$$$ ✲✲
PARK RD.
NR23 1RG
TEL 01328-711008
Meat and game from the Holkham Estate, fish from the nearby sea, and a weird but welcoming British colonial decor.
⊞ 80 🅿 50

LAVENHAM

🏨 SWAN
$$$$ ★★★★ ✲✲
HIGH ST.
CO10 9QA
TEL 01787-247477
FAX 01787-248286
www.theswanatlavenham.co.uk
Delightful half-timbered hotel in quintessentially picturesque English town. Minstrels' gallery, wood fires, and beautiful courtyard gardens add to the atmosphere and enhance the enjoyment of the fresh, seasonal cooking. Bar food.
🛏 51 🅿 60

LINCOLN

🏨 WHITE HART
$$ ★★★★
BAILGATE
LN1 3AR
TEL 01522-526222
FAX 01522-531798

🏨 Hotel 🍴 Restaurant 🛏 No. of Guest Rooms ⊞ No. of Seats 🅿 Parking 🚇 Tube 🕐 Closed

www.whitehart-lincoln.co.uk
In a delightful central location
between the castle and the
cathedral with good views of
the city. Informal eating in the
Grille; quietly elegant dining
room.

ⓘ 50 🅿 20 ⊟

🍴 THE OLD BAKERY
$$$ ❀❀
26–28 BURTON RD.
LN1 3LB
TEL 01522-576057
www.theold-bakery.co.uk
Wonderful cooking based on
local produce in this nicely
refurbished restaurant, once
a bakery (hence the ovens in
the walls!).

🍴 85 ⊕ Closed Mon., Dec.
25, Jan. 1

NORWICH

🏨 MARRIOTT SPROWSTON MANOR HOTEL & COUNTRY CLUB
$$$ ★★★★ ❀❀
SPROWSTON PARK, WROXHAM
RD., SPROWSTON
NR7 8RP
TEL 01603-410871
FAX 01603-423911
www.marriott.co.uk
Nineteenth-century manor
house on ten acres of parkland
on outskirts of city. Modern
European cooking and veg-
etarian dishes in Manor Res-
taurant. Family and four-poster
rooms. Health spa and golf.

ⓘ 94 🅿 150 ⊟ 🖥 🖳

🍴 ST. GILES
$$$ ❀❀
ST. GILES HOUSE HOTEL,
41–45 ST. GILES ST.
NR2 1JR
TEL 01603-275180/275182
www.stgileshotel.com
Right in the heart of medieval
Norwich, this beautiful town-
house restaurant specializes
in a bistro-style ambience,

keeping ingredients as local as
possible and the cooking clean
and simple.

🍴 50

🍴 BRUMMELS SEAFOOD
$$$$ ❀❀
7 MAGDALEN ST.
NR3 1LE
TEL 01603-625555
The menu here is mostly fish,
and wholly delicious.

🍴 30

SOUTHWOLD

SOMETHING SPECIAL

🏨 SWAN
$$$–$$$$ ★★★ ❀❀
MARKET PL., SOUTHWOLD
IP18 6EG
TEL 01502-722186
FAX 01502-724800
www.adnams.co.uk/
stay-with-us/the-swan
Handsome old hotel on South-
wold's marketplace. Some of
the bedrooms surround an old
bowling green. The restaurant
features appetizing, imagina-
tive cooking and boasts an
excellent wine list. The Swan
backs onto the Sole Bay Brew-
ery of Adnams. Adnams bitter
is justly famed as one of the
tastiest beers in Britain.

ⓘ 42 (17 annex) 🅿 35 ⊟

STAMFORD

🏨 GARDEN HOUSE
$$$ ★★★
ST. MARTIN'S
PE9 2LP
TEL 01780-763359
FAX 01780-763339
www.gardenhousehotel.com
Charming 18th-century house.
Friendly service and good,
varied menus.

ⓘ 20 🅿 30 ⊕ Closed Dec.
26–30, restricted Jan. 1–12

STOKE-BY-NAYLAND

🏨 CROWN INN
$$$ ❀❀
CO6 4SE
TEL 01206-262001/262346
FAX 01206-264026
www.crowninn.net
This hotel and restaurant
does pretty Stoke-by-Nayland
justice. Decorated in restful
colors, light and airy, with a
good varied menu and plenty
of locals to leaven the outsid-
ers, the Crown is a delight.

ⓘ 11 🅿 41

SUDBURY

🏨 BLACK LION
🍴 **$$$**
CHURCH WALK, THE GREEN,
LONG MELFORD
CO10 9DN
TEL 01787-312356
FAX 01787-374557
www.blacklionhotel.net
Individually furnished rooms
and an excellent restaurant
in a Tudor hotel on the green
of this village famous for its
antique shops.

ⓘ 10 🍴 50 🅿 10

WINTERINGHAM

🏨 WINTERINGHAM
🍴 FIELDS
$$$$$ ★★★★★ ❀❀
DN15 9PF
TEL 01724-733096
FAX 01724-733898
www.winteringhamfields.com
An oasis of comfort, good
food, and hospitality. Quality
is impeccable, much of it from
the walled garden. Guests
from Europe fly in just to dine
here. Cooking style is based on
traditional methods, applied
with a light touch and a modern twist. Fixed-price L & D.
No children under eight.

🍴 60 ⓘ 11 (6 annex) 🅿 17
⊕ Closed 2 weeks at Christmas, 2 weeks in Aug.

⊟ Elevator 🔆 Air-conditioning 🏊 Indoor Pool 🏊 Outdoor Pool 🖳 Health Club

■ NORTH MIDLANDS

ACTON TRUSSELL

🍴 MOAT HOUSE
$$ ●●
ACTON TRUSSELL
ST17 0RJ
TEL 01785-712217
www.moathouse.co.uk
Restored 17th-century
timbered building overlooking
canal. Busy pub-restaurant
offering consistently high stan-
dards of cooking and efficient
service. Fixed-price L.
🔼 120 🕓 Closed Dec. 25–26,
all Jan. 🅲

ASHBOURNE

🏨 BENTLEY BROOK INN
$$
FENNY BENTLEY
DE6 1LF
TEL 01335-350278
FAX 01335-350422
www.bentleybrookinn.co.uk
This family-friendly half-
timbered inn is set in an
excellent location for visiting
Chatsworth House and Alton
Towers, walking in Dovedale
and the White Peak district,
and cycling on the Tissington
Trail. Children can let off steam
in the well-kept gardens—
there's a mini-adventure
playground suitable for tykes.
Bedrooms are individually furnished. Cooking is unfussy and
good, using local suppliers and
plenty of organic produce.
🛏 11

SOMETHING SPECIAL

🍴 THE DINING ROOM
$$$$$ ●●
33 ST. JOHN ST.
DE6 1GP
TEL 01335-300666
www.thediningroomash
bourne.co.uk
The Dining Room has just six
tables. But who needs anything larger or more opulent?
Sit back in this gorgeous Tudor

building and tuck into superbly
cooked, fresh produce that's
been raised, picked, or gathered locally. A modest gem.
🔼 16 🕓 Closed L, Sun.–Mon.,
1 week in March, 1 week in
Sept., 2 weeks in Dec.

🍴 IZAAK WALTON
$$$ ●●
DOVEDALE, ASHBOURNE
DE6 2AY
TEL 01335-350555
www.izaakwaltonhotel.com
Ideally placed as a base for
walks in Dovedale, one of the
Peak District's classic beauty
spots where the shallow
River Dove rushes through
a limestone gorge under
weirdly shaped and named
pinnacles of rock. Bar meals
or restaurant. Fishing on river.
Fixed-price L & D.
🔼 100 🅿 80

BAKEWELL

🏨 HASSOP HALL
$$$ ★★★
HASSOP
DE45 1NS
TEL 01629-640488
FAX 01629-640577
www.hassophallhotel.co.uk
Fine historic house, family run.
Walks in gardens and woods,
and tennis. Bright dining room.
🛏 13 🅿 80 🕓 Closed Sun. D,
Dec. 24–25 🅲

🍴 THE PEACOCK AT ROWSLEY
$$$$$ ●●
BAKEWELL RD.
DE4 2EB
TEL 01629-733518
www.thepeacockatrowsley.com
A beautiful, creeper-hung, and
gabled exterior sets the mood
of gracious living; the modern
decor and daring mix of flavor
and textures in the cooking
provide a pleasurable jolt.
🔼 40 🕓 Closed Dec. 24–26

🍴 FISCHER'S BASLOW HALL
$$$$ ★★★ ●●●●
BASLOW HALL, CALVER RD.
DE45 1RR
TEL 01246-583259
www.fischers-baslowhall.co.uk
This Derbyshire manor house
exudes warmth and comfort.
The cooking is worth traveling
for, but it is not in the mold of
country restaurants; innovative
without being outlandish.
Fixed-price L & D.
🔼 40 🕓 Closed Mon. L,
Sun. D

BUXTON

🏨 BEST WESTERN LEE WOOD
$$$ ★★★ ●
THE PARK
SK17 6TQ
TEL 01298-23002
FAX 01298-23228
www.leewoodhotel.co.uk
Friendly Georgian hotel
with two bars, lounge, and
conservatory restaurant. An
extensive menu with a wide
choice of vegetarian dishes.
Fixed-price D.
🛏 39 (5 annex) 🅿 50 🅲

🏨 GRENDON GUEST HOUSE
$$
BISHOPS LN.
SK17 6UN
TEL 01298-78831
FAX 01298-79257
www.grendonguesthouse
.co.uk
Edwardian award-winning
guesthouse, set in immaculate
grounds with stunning country
views. Short walk from town
center.
🛏 5 🅿 8 🕓 Closed Jan. 3–20

CHESTER

🏨 CHESTER GROSVENOR
🍴 **$$$$$** ★★★★★ ●●●●
EASTGATE

🏨 Hotel   🍴 Restaurant   🛏 No. of Guest Rooms   🔼 No. of Seats   🅿 Parking   🚇 Tube   🕓 Closed

CH1 1LT
TEL 01244-324024
FAX 01244-313246
www.chestergrosvenor.co.uk
Inside the Roman walls of the
city. Lots of polished wood,
silver, and oversized glasses in
the formal Arkle Restaurant.
Experienced and discreetly
professional tuxedoed staff.
Good ingredients, fancy
desserts, lots of extras, tremendous wine list. Fixed-price
L & D.
🛈 85 🍴 45 🕐 Closed Dec.
25–26 🛗 ❄️ 🏋️

CHURCH STRETTON

🏨 MYND HOUSE
$$ ★★
LITTLE STRETTON
SY6 6RB
TEL 01694-722212
FAX 01694-724180
www.myndhouse.com
A Visit England–accredited,
friendly, Edwardian-style hotel.
Cooking includes regional spe-
cialties using local ingredients.
No children under ten.
🛈 7 🅿 8

GRINDLEFORD

🏨 THE MAYNARD
$$$ ★★★ ❀❀
MAIN RD.
S32 2HE
TEL 01433-630321
FAX 01433-630445
www.themaynard.co.uk
Handsome old hotel with fine
views of Peak District hills and
dales. Visitors' lounge, lounge
bar, cocktail bar, and restaurant
overlooking gardens.
🛈 10 🅿 80

HOPE

🏨 UNDERLEIGH HOUSE
$$
OFF EDALE RD.
S33 6RF
TEL 01433-621372

FAX 01433-621324
www.underleighhouse.co.uk
Sympathetic barn conversion
with award-winning garden.
Freshly prepared menu. No
children under 12. Recipient of
an AA breakfast award.
🛈 6 🅿 6

LUDLOW

🏨 OVERTON GRANGE
$$$ ★★★ ❀❀
OLD HEREFORD RD.
SY8 4AD
TEL 01584-873500
FAX 01584-873524
www.overtongrangehotel.com
Edwardian house with views
across the Shropshire hills.
Wood-paneled restaurant;
fresh ingredients.
🛈 14 🅿 45

🏨 NUMBER TWENTY-EIGHT
$$
28 LOWER BROAD ST.
SY8 1PQ
TEL 01584-875466
FAX 01584-876860
Combination of three separate
houses, all with original
features and quality period
furnishings. Warm welcome.
🛈 2

🍴 LA BECASSE
$$$$$ ❀❀❀
17 CORVE ST.
SY8 1DA
TEL 01584-872325
www.labecasse.co.uk
A nice cozy nest of rooms. The
cooking is classic French with a
modern flair.
🍴 40 🕐 Closed Mon., Tues. L,
Sun. D, Christmas, New Year

🍴 MR. UNDERHILL'S
$$$$$ ❀❀
DINHAM WEIR
SY8 1EH
TEL 01584-874431
www.mr-underhills.co.uk
A wonderful place to eat, right

on the banks of the beautiful
Teme. The rush of the river
lends a pleasantly timeless
atmosphere as you sip your
wine and prepare to tackle
whatever is on the no-choice
menu for that day—local duck
or venison, perhaps, or some
fresh fish out of the water.
🍴 30 🕐 Closed Mon.–Tues.,
1 week in Jan., 1 week in July

MELTON MOWBRAY

🏨 STAPLEFORD PARK
🍴 $$$$$ ★★★★ ❀❀
STAPLEFORD
LE14 2EF
TEL 01572-787000
FAX 01572-787651
www.staplefordpark.com
Stately home on 500 acres of
woods and parkland; fishing
lake, stables, church, and
Capability Brown gardens. Ten-
nis, riding, shooting, falconry,
off-road driving. Elegant
dining room with 17th-century
carvings by Grinling Gibbons.
Quality and skill are evident
throughout the menu. Bar
food. Fixed-price D. No
children under nine.
🛈 55 (7 annex) 🍴 45 🅿 120
🛗 ❄️ 🏋️

MUCH WENLOCK

🍴 RAVEN
$$$ ❀❀
30 BARROW ST.
TF13 6EN
TEL 01952-727251
www.ravenhotel.com
Characterful inn with original
features, courtyard, kitchen
herb garden, and a deter-
mined effort to provide good
contemporary cooking. Bar
food. Fixed-price L.
🍴 40 🕐 Closed Dec. 25

NOTTINGHAM

🏨 COCKLIFFE COUNTRY HOUSE
$$$ ❀

BURNTSTUMP COUNTRY PARK,
BURNTSTUMP HILL
NG5 8PQ
TEL 0115-968 0179
www.cockliffehouse.co.uk
Set in beautiful grounds, this
country-house hotel offers you
peace and seclusion.
🛏 11

🍴 HART'S
$$$ ◆◆
STANDARD HILL, PARK ROW
NG1 6FN
TEL 0115-988 1900
www.hartsnottingham.co.uk
In a quiet location and featur-
ing unfussy but stylish cooking,
this restaurant has a modern
atmosphere. The seating is
arranged around intimate
booth-style tables.
🪑 80 🕐 Closed Jan. 1

OAKAMOOR

🏨 CROWTREES FARM
$
EAVES LN., STOKE-ON-TRENT
ST10 3DY
TEL 01538-702260
www.crowtreesfarm.co.uk
Perfectly placed for visits to
Alton Towers theme park,
this welcoming working farm
is child friendly, with sheep,
goats, and farmhouse cats.
🛏 3 🅿 6 🕐 Closed Christmas
week

ORTHWICH

🏨 🍴 NUNSMERE HALL
$$$$ ★★★★★★ ◆◆
TARPORLEY RD., OAKMERE
CW8 2ES
TEL 01606-889100
FAX 01606-889055
www.primahotels.co.uk/
nunsmere
Immaculate country-house
hotel, with a careful and atten-
tive version of tasty modern
cooking. Friendly and profes-
sional staff. Fixed-price L.
🛏 36 🪑 60 🅿 80 🚻

RUTLAND

🍴 HAMBLETON HALL
$$$$$ ◆◆◆◆
HAMBLETON, OAKHAM
LE15 8TH
TEL 01572-756991
www.hambletonhall.com
Archetypal country-house
hotel. Clubby bar, drawing
room with stunning views
over the lake, and opulent res-
taurant complete with silk wall
coverings. Mature, restrained,
and assured cooking, full of
flavor, often utilizing fresh local
produce. Fresh meats on the
menu include duck, lamb, rab-
bit, and pigeon. Staff is superb
and offers really skilled service.
Fixed-price L & D.
🪑 60

SHEFFIELD

🍴 RAFTERS
$$$ ◆◆
220 OAKBROOK RD., NETHER-
GREEN
S11 7ED
TEL 0114-230 4819
www.raftersrestaurant.co.uk
A friendly suburban restaurant
with an unpretentious modern
atmosphere. The menu
changes every 6–8 weeks as
seasonal produce becomes
available.
🪑 38 🅿 15 🕐 Closed L,
Sun., Tues., Dec. 25–26, 1 week
in Jan., 2 weeks in Aug.

SHREWSBURY

🏨 MERCURE
ALBRIGHTON HALL
$$$ ★★★★
ALBRIGHTON
SY4 3AG
TEL 01939-291000
FAX 01939-291123
www.mercure.com
Seventeenth-century country
house on 14 attractive acres
that include an ornamental
lake. Oak-paneled rooms;
some with four-poster beds.

🛏 87 (42 annex) 🅿 300 🚻
🚇 🍴

🍴 ALBRIGHT HUSSEY
$$$ ◆◆
ELLESMERE RD.
SY4 3AF
TEL 01939-290571/290523
www.albrighthussey.co.uk
Black swans swim in the moat
of this timber-framed Tudor
house. Food is served in the
fine beamed restaurant, where
the fixed-price menus supplement a menu that is in the
modern British mold. Bar food.
No children under age four.
🪑 84

🍴 MYTTON AND MERMAID
$$$ ◆◆
ATCHAM
SY5 6QG
TEL 01743-761220
www.myttonandmermaid
.co.uk
You can get a snack, and a very
good one, too, in the bar of
this cheerful old inn on the

River Severn; or you can opt for a menu that's full of solid delights in the informal and welcoming restaurant. Recipient of a regional food award.
🛏 100 🕐 Closed D Dec. 25–26

SOUTHWELL

🏢 OLD VICARAGE
$$$
WESTHORPE
NG25 0NB
TEL 01636-815989
www.vicarageboutiquehotel.co.uk
A delightful boutique hotel for visitors who want a touch of luxury and spoiling. The handsome redbrick former vicarage has been carefully converted, with nice pine floors and an intriguing mixture of modern and classic furnishings, a varied theme that's reflected in the individually appointed rooms.
🛏 8

STAFFORD

🏢 MOAT HOUSE
🍴 **$$$$** ★★★★ ❀❀
LOWER PENKRIDGE RD., ACTON TRUSSELL
ST17 0RJ
TEL 01785-712217
www.moathouse.co.uk
This stylish and comfortable hotel has been created around a handsome old 15th-century house, all great thick chimney stacks and stripy black-and-white timber-framed gables. The hotel lies in a peaceful location on the banks of the restored Staffordshire & Worcestershire Canal. Service is friendly and welcoming; fine dining and good food available in the restaurant.
🛏 41 🅿 200

WORFIELD

🏢 OLD VICARAGE
$$$–$$$$ ★★★ ❀❀❀
WORFIELD, BRIDGNORTH
WV15 5JZ
TEL 01746-716497 OR
0800-096 8010
FAX 01746-716552
www.oldvicarageworfield.com
Delightful hotel in the Shropshire countryside, comfortably furnished and thoughtfully equipped.
🛏 10 (4 annex) 🅿 30

◼ NORTHWEST ENGLAND

ALDERLEY

🍴 ALDERLEY
$$$$ ❀❀❀
ALDERLEY EDGE HOTEL, MACCLESFIELD RD.
SK9 7BJ
TEL 01625-583033
www.cheshire-restaurant.com
Superb cooking in the modern British range, with plenty of imagination. Fantastic local cheese and fancy breads, too.
🛏 80

AMBLESIDE

🏢 LAKES LODGE
$$
LAKE RD.
LA22 9NE
TEL 01539-433240
FAX 01539-431474
www.lakeslodge.co.uk
In a hugely popular tourist destination, here's a straightforward, friendly establishment, an excellent value with a very relaxed atmosphere.
🛏 16

🍴 DRUNKEN DUCK INN
$$$ ❀❀
BARNGATES
LA22 0NG
TEL 01539-436347
www.drunkenduckinn.co.uk
A 400-year-old coaching inn with log fires and wooden beams that offers imaginative modern cooking and beers

from its own brewery.
🛏 42 🅿 40

APPLEBY-IN-WESTMORLAND

🏢 BONGATE HOUSE
$
BONGATE
CA16 6UE
TEL 017683-51245
FAX 017683-51423
www.bongatehouse.co.uk
A friendly welcome and warm hospitality await at this charming guest house. Hearty breakfasts, and dinners by arrangement, served in the dining room. No children under seven.
🛏 8 🅿 10

BLACKPOOL

🏢 BIG BLUE HOTEL
$$
OCEAN BLVD.
FY4 1ND
TEL 0871-222 4000 OR
01253-400045
FAX 01253-400046
www.bigbluehotel.com
Family welcome is the name of the game at this seafront hotel near the Pleasure Beach—family suites feature fun bunk beds for the youngsters.
🛏 157 🎮

BRAMPTON

🏢 FARLAM HALL
$$$$$ ★★★ ❀❀
HALLBANKGATE
CA8 2NG
TEL 016977-46234
FAX 016977-46683
www.farlamhall.co.uk
Family-run country house in landscaped gardens; warm welcome. Elegant dining room for daily changing four-course dinner. No children under five.
🛏 11 (1 annex) 🅿 35

BURY

🏨 BEST WESTERN BOL-HOLT COUNTRY PARK
$$ ❁❁❁
WALSHAW RD.
BL8 1PU
TEL 08457-767676
FAX 0161-762 4100
www.bestwestern.co.uk
This former mill owner's house is peacefully situated in 50 acres of parkland. Choice of lounges; friendly service and modern, comfortable bedrooms.
ⓘ 66 🅿 300 🏊 📺

CARLISLE

🏨 BESSIESTOWN FARM COUNTRY GUESTHOUSE
$$ ★★★★★
CATLOWDY
CA6 5QP
TEL 01228-577219
FAX 01228-577019
www.bessiestown.co.uk
One of the best bed-and-breakfast establishments in Britain—an absolute gem, set in beautiful countryside, with a warm welcome guaranteed.
ⓘ 4 🅿 10 🏊

GRANGE

🏨 BORROWDALE GATES
$$$$ ★★★ ❁❁
GRANGE-IN-BORROWDALE,
KESWICK
CA12 5UQ
TEL 017687-77204
FAX 017687-77254
www.borrowdale-gates.com
Family-run hotel with spectacular views of surrounding fells. Cooking uses local produce.
ⓘ 25 🅿 40 🕒 Closed Jan.

GRANGE-OVER-SANDS

🏨 CLARE HOUSE
🍴 **$$ ★ ❁**
PARK RD.
LA11 7HQ
TEL 015395-33026
FAX 015395-34310
www.clarehousehotel.co.uk
Welcoming family hotel in a smart Victorian house with stunning views over Morecombe Bay. Simple well-cooked food with nice touches. Popular with locals.
ⓘ 19 🛏 32 🕒 Closed Dec.–Mar., restricted Nov. 10–30

KESWICK

SOMETHING SPECIAL

🏨 WHITE MOSS HOUSE
🍴 **$$$ ★ ❁**
RYDAL WATER
LA22 9SE
TEL 015394-35295
www.whitemoss.com
One of the most captivating of country-house hotels, in a lakeland setting. Dinner is served in the quaint dining room and offers a five-course menu in keeping with the atmosphere. Ingredients used in the traditional English dishes are chosen with loyalty to the region and the seasons. William Wordsworth bought White Moss House for his son, Willy. Fixed-price D only. Recipient of breakfast award.
ⓘ 7 (2 annex) 🛏 18 🕒 Closed Sun. L, Dec.–Jan.

🏨 SWINSIDE LODGE
$$–$$$ ❁❁
GRANGE RD., NEWLANDS
CA12 5UE
TEL 017687-72948
www.swinsidelodge-hotel.co.uk
This beautifully situated Georgian country house stands alone, surrounded by open countryside, hills, valleys, and woodlands in one of the most unspoiled areas of Lake District National Park. Many awards for its hospitality and food. No children under 12.
ⓘ 8 🕒 Closed L, Dec. 20–26

🏨 CRAGLANDS GUEST HOUSE
$
PENRITH RD.
CA12 4LJ
TEL 017687-74406
www.craglands-keswick.co.uk
Cozy Victorian house. A five-course dinner is served, to which guests should bring their own wine. No children under eight.
ⓘ 5 🅿 6

LANCASTER

🏨 LANCASTER HOUSE HOTEL
$$$$ ❁
GREEN LN., ELLEL
LA1 4GJ
TEL 01524-844822
FAX 01524-844766
www.elh.co.uk/hotels/lancaster
A modern hotel on the outskirts of town, with log fires in winter.
ⓘ 99 📺 🏊

LANGHO

🏨 NORTHCOTE
$$$$ ★★★★ ❁❁❁❁
NORTHCOTE RD.
BB6 8BE
TEL 01254-240555
FAX 01254-246568
www.northcote.com
A wonderfully comfortable hotel with a kitchen that's receiving rave reviews for its superb interpretation of local Lancashire dishes.
ⓘ 14 🅿 50

LIVERPOOL

SOMETHING SPECIAL

🏨 THISTLE LIVERPOOL
🍴 **$$$**
CHAPEL ST.
L3 9RE
TEL 0151-227 4444
FAX 0151-236 3973

---

www.thistlehotels.com
The architect of the modern Atlantic Tower Thistle came up with a curved shape like the bow of a transatlantic liner, in homage to the maritime heritage of the Liverpool waterfront where the hotel stands. Stateroom Restaurant, Club Car Diner, cocktail bar, Tradewinds Bar.
🛈 226 🅰 🛗

🍴 60 HOPE STREET
$$$ ❉
60 HOPE ST.
L1 9BZ
TEL 0151-707 6060
www.60hopestreet.com
Set in the trendy and buzzing University area between Liverpool's two cathedrals, 60 Hope Street offers both restaurant and bistro-style dining. The decor is simple and clean, and so is the modern European cooking, with plenty of emphasis on the best local produce—meat, poultry, and greens from suppliers up the northwest coast.
🪑 90 🕒 Closed Sun., Mon. L, Bank Holidays

LONGRIDGE

🍴 LONGRIDGE
$$$$ ❉❉❉
104–106 HIGHER RD.
PR3 3SY
TEL 01772-784969
www.heathcotes.co.uk/collection/longridge
A very traditional restaurant with a split-level dining room, heavily draped tables, and a comfortable lounge with deep sofas. Staff is correctly drilled, but the ingrained northern sense of hospitality cuts through. This is among the finest cuisine in Lancashire. Fixed-price L & D.
🪑 60 🕒 Closed Mon.–Tues., Jan. 1

MANCHESTER

🏨 MANCHESTER MARRIOTT VICTORIA AND ALBERT
$$$$ ★★★★
WATER ST.
M3 4JQ
TEL 0161-832 1188
FAX 0161-834 2484
www.marriott.co.uk
An interesting hotel created from former warehouses, with exposed bricks, iron pillars, and wooden beams.
🛈 156 🅿 120 🅰 🛗

NEAR SAWREY

🏨 SAWREY HOUSE
$$$$ ❉❉
NEAR SAWREY AMBLESIDE
LA22 0LF
TEL 01539-436387
FAX 01539-436010
www.sawreyhouse.com
Just along the road from Beatrix Potter's house at Far Sawrey, this charming Victorian country-house hotel stands in beautifully landscaped gardens overlooking Esthwaite Water.
🛈 12 🅿 25 🕒 Closed Jan.

POOLEY BRIDGE

🏨 SHARROW BAY
$$$$ ★★★ ❉❉
SHARROW BAY, HOWTOWN
CA10 2LZ
TEL 017684-86301/86483
FAX 017684-86349
www.vonessenhotels.co.uk
Lakeside country-house hotel with a worldwide reputation. Superb views across Ullswater. Some accommodations in cottages and an Elizabethan farmhouse. Public rooms furnished with bric-a-brac, antiques, and paintings. Anglo-French dishes based around Lakeland produce. Fixed-price L & D. No children under 13.
🛈 24 (16 annex) 🅿 35

🏨 RAMPSBECK
$$$–$$$$ ★★★ ❉❉❉
WATERMILLOCK
(NEAR PENRITH)
CA11 0LP
TEL 017684-86442/86688
FAX 017684-86688
www.rampsbeck.fsnet.co.uk
A wonderful lakeside setting, 18 acres of grounds, warm hospitality, and skillful cooking. They do things in style here. Choice of three menus—vegetarian, table d'hôte, and à la carte. Ingredients are treated with respect, allowing authentic flavors to shine through. Bar food. Fixed-price L & D.
🛈 20 🅿 30 🕒 Closed Jan.

ROMALDKIRK

🏨 ROSE AND CROWN
🍴 $$$ ★★ ❉❉
ROMALDKIRK
DL12 9EB
TEL 01833-650213
FAX 01833-650828
www.rose-and-crown.co.uk
Lovingly nurtured pub at the hub of Romaldkirk village, with a huge stone fireplace, old oak beams, and shuttered windows. In the oak-paneled dining room, the daily four-course dinner menu shows a fondness for North Country produce. The locally produced Cotherstone cheese is excellent. Fixed-price D.
🛈 12 🪑 24 🅿 24 🕒 Closed Dec. 24–26

ROSTHWAITE

🏨 HAZEL BANK COUNTRY HOUSE
$$$ ★★★★★ ❉
ROSTHWAITE
CA12 5XB
TEL 017687-77248
FAX 017687-77373
www.hazelbankhotel.co.uk
Victorian house on four acres of lawns and woodland, with fine views of Borrowdale and surrounding fells. Welcoming

atmosphere; home cooking. No children under 12. Recipient of breakfast award.

ⓘ 8 (1 annex) 🅿 12

🏨 ROYAL OAK INN
$$
ROSTHWAITE
CA12 5XB
TEL 01768-777214/777695
www.royaloakhotel.co.uk
A really delightful small hotel, family-run, very comfortable, friendly, and welcoming. Walkers are especially welcome; the landlord is a mountain rescue man.

ⓘ 12 🅿 15

WINDERMERE

🏨 GILPIN LODGE COUNTRY HOUSE HOTEL
$$$$$ ★★★ ❀❀❀
CROOK RD.
LA23 3NE
TEL 015394-88818
FAX 015394-88058
www.gilpinlodge.co.uk
Exceptionally nice award-winning hotel with an endearing mood of honest friendliness. Flexible light lunch menu. The four-course dinner menu is an ambitious affair providing plenty of choice across the board. Bar food. Fixed-price D. No children under seven.

ⓘ 20 🅿 30

🏨 HOLBECK GHYLL COUNTRY HOUSE
$$$$–$$$$$ ★★★★ ❀❀❀
HOLBECK LN.
LA23 1LU
TEL 015394-32375
FAX 015394-34743
www.holbeckghyll.com
Charming country house. Breathtaking views from terrace restaurant and magnificent oak-paneled dining room, which both offer excellent, imaginative cooking. Fixed-price D.

ⓘ 26 (6 annex) 🅿 30 🍽

■ NORTHEAST ENGLAND

ARNCLIFFE

🏨 FALCON INN
$
ARNCLIFFE
BD23 5QE
TEL 01756-770205
Quite simply, a perfect pub with rooms. Friendly, no-nonsense, jug-to-glass beer dispensing, family run and wholly delightful.

ⓘ 4

ASENBY

🍴 CRAB AND LOBSTER
$$$ ❀❀
DISHFORTH RD.
YO7 3QL
TEL 01845-577286
www.crabandlobster.co.uk
From the outside, the Crab and Lobster looks like a dyed-in-the-wool traditional North Yorkshire thatched pub, but inside, the decor is an extravagant clutter of wicker baskets, fishing rods, old slot machines, jockey caps, and crab and lobster pots dangling from the ceiling. The atmosphere fizzes. Fresh fish is the thing to eat here, although the repertoire is a real bonanza of dishes spooned out of the global melting pot. Fixed-price L & D. No children under 12.

🪑 120

BEVERLEY

🏨 TICKTON GRANGE
$$$ ★★★ ❀❀
TICKTON
HU17 9SH
TEL 01964-543666
FAX 01964-542556
www.ticktongrange.co.uk
Georgian house set on four acres of grounds and gardens, with much charm and character. The bedrooms are individually decorated, and

one has a four-poster bed. The resident owners provide friendly service, and there is a restaurant menu.

ⓘ 20 🅿 65 ⊖ Closed Dec. 25–29 🍽

🍴 PIPE AND GLASS INN
$$$ ❀❀
WEST END, SOUTH DALTON
HU17 7PN
TEL 01430-810246
www.pipeandglass.co.uk
Though the name makes it sound like a simple country boozer, the Pipe and Glass is a very classy eatery. The 17th-century inn, whitewashed and red-roofed, is a snug and comfortable place to enjoy locally caught fish and shellfish, backed up by some wickedly delicious puddings—try the chocolate and juniper pudding and you'll be lost forever!

🪑 70 ⊖ Closed Sun., Mon. (except for Bank Holidays)

BLANCHLAND

SOMETHING SPECIAL

🏨 LORD CREWE ARMS

$$$ ★★ ✿

BLANCHLAND
DH8 9SP
TEL 01434-675251
FAX 01434-675337
www.lordcrewehotel.com
Historic hotel in a preserved village. In medieval times, it was the lodging of the Abbot of Blanchland, and it still retains plenty of atmospheric features, including a priest's hole for fugitive clerics in times of persecution and enormous fireplaces to ward off the chill of winter weather here. Flagstone floors, vaulted ceilings, original stonework. Restaurant and crypt bar.

ⓘ 9 (10 annex)

DEWSBURY

🍴 HEALDS HALL

$$$ ✿

LEEDS RD., LIVERSEDGE
WF15 6JA
TEL 01924-409112
www.healdshall.co.uk
A mill owner built this four-square house, and the same no-nonsense air invests the short, traditionally British menu.

🛏 40 🅿 90 🕐 Closed Sat. L, Sun. D

DURHAM

🏨 DURHAM MARRIOTT ROYAL COUNTY

$$$$ ★★★★

OLD ELVET
DH1 3JN
TEL 0191-386 6821
FAX 0191-386 0704
www.marriott.co.uk
Long-established hotel beside the River Wear with views of both the castle and the cathedral. Magnificent carved oak staircase. Informal meals in the brasserie; formal dining in the County Restaurant.

ⓘ 151 🅿 80 ⬍ 🌊 🎔

GRASSINGTON

🏨 GRASSINGTON HOUSE

$$ ★★ ✿✿

5 THE SQUARE
BD23 5AQ
TEL 01756-752406
FAX 01756-752135
www.grassingtonhousehotel.co.uk
A warm and hospitable house right at the heart of the "capital of Wharfedale"; popular bar and restaurant meals. Recipient of an AA breakfast award.

ⓘ 9 🅿 20 🕐 Closed Dec. 25

HARROGATE

🏨 RUDDING PARK

$$$$ ★★★★ ✿✿

FOLLIFOOT
HG3 1JH
TEL 01423-871350
FAX 01423-872286
www.ruddingpark.co.uk
Elegant modern hotel surrounded by a beautifully landscaped park containing a golf course.

ⓘ 84 🅿 150

🏨 HOTEL DU VIN & BISTRO

$$$ ★★★★ ✿✿

PROSPECT PL.
HG1 1LB
TEL 01423-856800
FAX 01423-856801
www.hotelduvin.com
A very smart, modern hotel with a French-style bistro, well placed overlooking the grassy sward of the Stray.

ⓘ 51 🅿 30 ⬍ 🎔

🍴 BOAR'S HEAD

$$$ ✿✿

RIPLEY
HG3 3AY
TEL 01423-771888
www.boarsheadripley.co.uk
The fixed-price menu here is full of invention and vivid modern ideas. Owned by Sir Thomas Ingilby, whose family has lived at the nearby castle for seven centuries. Fixed-price L & D.

🛏 40 🔼

HAWORTH

🍴 WEAVER'S

$$$ ✿

15 WEST LN.
BD22 8DU
TEL 01535-643822
www.weaversmallhotel.co.uk
This likable restaurant near the Brontë Parsonage was originally a cluster of weavers' cottages. Cooking is a mix of homespun northern food and dishes that are in tune with today's gastronomic mood. There's a refreshing lack of pretension about the whole setup, helped along by genuine personal service. Fixed-price D.

🛏 65 🕐 Closed Sun.–Mon., Tues. L, Sat. L 🔼

HELMSLEY

🏨 BLACK SWAN

$$$$ ★★★ ✿✿

MARKET PL.
YO62 5BJ
TEL 01439-770466
FAX 01439-770174
www.blackswan-helmsley.co.uk
Characterful hotel made up of a Tudor rectory, an Elizabethan inn, and a Georgian house, overlooking the market square.

ⓘ 45 🅿 50

HEXHAM

🏨 PETH HEAD COTTAGE

$

JUNIPER
NE47 0LA
TEL 01434-673286
www.peth-head-cottage.co.uk

You can be sure of a warm welcome here—a very friendly B&B with lots of homey touches. Handy for Hadrian's Wall.

🛈 2 🅿 2

HOLMFIRTH

🏨 **UPPERGATE FARM**
$$
HEPWORTH
HD9 1TG
TEL 01484-681369
www.uppergatefarm.co.uk
A wonderful opportunity to stay in a proper working Pennine farm up in the hills of *Last of the Summer Wine* country.

🛈 2 🅿 6

ILKLEY

🏨 **BEST WESTERN ROMBALDS**
$$ ✿
11 WEST VIEW, WELLS RD.
LS29 9JG
TEL 01943-603201
FAX 01943-816586
www.rombalds.co.uk
A Georgian house full of style and comfort, attractively set on the edge of town.

🛈 15 🅿 28 🕓 Closed Jan. 1

LASTINGHAM

SOMETHING SPECIAL

🏨 **LASTINGHAM GRANGE**
$$$$ ★★★
LASTINGHAM
YO62 6TH
TEL 01751-417345/417402
FAX 01751-417358
www.lastinghamgrange.com
Traditional Yorkshire hospitality in a family-run 17th-century farmhouse. Good home cooking; sunken rose garden. At nearby St. Mary's Church with its tiny, ancient crypt, stone carvings date back to the Dark Ages. During the 18th century, the crypt was used for cockfights and for parties hosted

by curate Jeremiah Carter, at which he played the fiddle.

🛈 12 🅿 32 🕓 Closed in winter

LEEDS

🍴 **ANTHONY'S RESTAURANT**
$$$$ ✿✿✿
19 BOAR LN.
LS1 6EA
TEL 0113-245 5922
www.anthonysrestaurant.co.uk
If you enjoy the ultramodern style of cooking—with intense bursts of widely differing flavors and colors on one plate, letting fish, meat, and vegetables talk to each other—this chic place will delight you.

🍴 40 🕓 Closed Sun.–Mon.

🍴 **FOURTH FLOOR CAFE AT HARVEY NICHOLS**
$$
107–111 BRIGGATT
LS1 6AZ
TEL 0113-204 8000
www.harveynichols.com
This minimalist and friendly café is in the Harvey Nichols department store—very handy after you've shopped till you've dropped.

🍴 80 🕓 Closed Sun.–Wed. D, Dec. 25

MORPETH

🏨 **MACDONALD LINDEN**
🍴 **HALL**
$$–$$$$$ ✿✿
LONGHORSLEY
NE65 8XF
TEL 01670-500000
www.macdonaldhotels.co.uk/lindenhall
Linden Hall, a famed golf retreat, looks grand and formal, and that's the style of dining in its classy Dobson Restaurant. No children under ten.

🛈 50 🅿 260

NEWCASTLE

🏨 **VERMONT**
$$$ ★★★★ ✿
CASTLE GARTH
NE1 1RQ
TEL 0191-2331010
FAX 0191-2331234
www.vermont-hotel.com
Former county hall next to the castle; fine views across River Tyne. Choice of bars and restaurants; live music offered in the evening.

🛈 101 🅿 100 🍴 🚇

🍴 **JESMOND DENE HOUSE**
$$$ ✿✿✿
NEWCASTLE UPON TYNE
NE2 2EY
TEL 0191-212 3000
www.jesmonddenehouse.co.uk
A gorgeous Georgian house in landscaped grounds near the city, and a restaurant that makes the most of locally reared meat and locally caught fish and shellfish. Fantastic, elaborate puddings. Recipient of an AA regional food award.

🍴 60

RIPON

🏨 **BEST WESTERN RIPON SPA**
$$ ★★★
PARK ST.
HG4 2BU
TEL 01765-602172
FAX 01765-690770
www.riponspa.com
Traditional service, in modern surroundings; lovely grounds, including croquet lawns. Turf Bar, restaurant.

🛈 40 🅿 60 🍴

SEAHAM

🏨 **SEAHAM HALL**
$$$$ ★★★★ ✿✿
LORD BYRON'S WALK
SR7 7AG
TEL 0191-5161400
FAX 0191-5161410

🏨 Hotel   🍴 Restaurant   🛈 No. of Guest Rooms   🍴 No. of Seats   🅿 Parking   🚇 Tube   🕓 Closed

www.seaham-hall.com
Lord Byron spent his honeymoon in this imposing house on the Durham coast, now a highly acclaimed hotel that cleverly marries old-world dignity and comfort to classy modern conveniences. Dine in style in the Ozone Restaurant with the very best of Thai-infused cooking.

🛈 19 🅿 122 🏊 🏋

SKIPTON

🏨 **DEVONSHIRE ARMS**
🍴 **COUNTRY HOUSE**
$$$$–$$$$$ ★★★★
✿✿✿✿
BOLTON ABBEY
BD23 6AJ
TEL 01756-710441
FAX 01756-710564
www.thedevonshirearms.co.uk
Hotel owned by the Duke and Duchess of Devonshire and decorated with many of their pieces of furniture and art. The Burlington Restaurant uses local produce. Bar food at lunchtime. Tennis, fishing, laser-pigeon shooting, and falconry. Fixed-price D.

🛈 41 🍴 80 🅿 150 🏊 🏋

WHITBY

🏨 **THE SEACLIFFE**
$$
12 NORTH PROMENADE
YO21 3JX
TEL/FAX 01947-603139
www.seacliffehotel.com
Cliff-top hotel with fine sea views. Family suite. Patio catches the sun.

🛈 19

YORK

🏨 **MIDDLETHORPE HALL**
$$$$–$$$$$ ★★★★ ✿✿
BISHOPTHORPE RD.
YO23 2GB
TEL 01904-641241
FAX 01904-620176
www.middlethorpe.com

Magnificent country house less than 2 miles from the center of York. Peaceful walks in the restored gardens. Fine paintings, furniture, and antiques. Gourmet and daily menus; vegetarian alternatives. No children under eight. Fixed-price L & D.

🛈 30 🅿 70 ♿ 🏊 🏋

🏨 **THE GRANGE**
$$$ ★★★★ ✿✿
1 CLIFTON
YO30 6AA
TEL 01904-644744
FAX 01904-612453
www.grangehotel.co.uk
A very friendly and immaculately kept Georgian house just a few minutes' stroll from the center of York. You can dine in style or enjoy a more informal brasserie meal.

🛈 30 🅿 26

🍴 **MELTON'S**
$$$ ✿
7 SCARCROFT RD.
YO23 1ND
TEL 01904-634341
www.meltonsrestaurant.co.uk
Restaurant in a converted shop with a bright, cheery face. Value for money with plenty of flexible deals. Vegetarians handsomely provided for. Fixed-price L & D.

🍴 30 🕐 Closed Sun.–Mon., Dec. 23–Jan. 9

■ SCOTTISH LOWLANDS

ABERFOYLE

🏨 **MACDONALD FOREST HILLS**
$$$ ★★★★ ✿
KINLOCHARD
FK8 3TL
TEL 0844-879 9057 OR
01877-389500
FAX 01877-387307
www.foresthills-hotel.co.uk
Popular and friendly hotel with a choice of lounges and

comfortable bedrooms. Some rooms have loch views. Formal dining in the Garden Restaurant, or try Bonspiel for a more informal atmosphere. Tennis, fishing, and squash.

🛈 56 🅿 80 🏊 🏋

ANSTRUTHER

🍴 **CELLAR**
$$$ ✿✿✿
24 EAST GREEN
KY10 3AA
TEL 01333-310378
A restaurant full of character and completely devoid of pretentiousness. Seafood is the main theme; what is offered is totally dependent on the catch from the local fishing boats. Fixed-price D.

🍴 30 🕐 Closed Sun.–Mon., Tues. L, Dec. 25

BALLOCH

🍴 **MARTIN WISHART AT LOCH LOMOND**
$$$$$ ✿✿✿
CAMERON HOUSE ON
LOCH LOMOND
G83 8QZ
TEL 01389-722504
www.martin-wishart.co.uk
In a beautiful setting on the banks of Loch Lomond, this is star Edinburgh chef Martin Wishart's "in-the-sticks" off-shoot, offering superb cooking in a thoroughly modern style that doesn't lose sight of the cardinal virtues of flavor and texture. The six-course tasting menu is good value, dipping into the extensive repertoire of Wishart's Loch Lomond team.

🍴 40 🕐 Closed Mon.–Tues., Wed.–Fri. L, Dec. 25–26, Jan. 1

CUPAR

🍴 **OSTLERS CLOSE**
$$$ ✿✿
BONNYGATE
KY15 4BU
TEL 01334-655574

www.ostlersclose.co.uk
This restaurant has a well-deserved, loyal following of local people who appreciate good Scottish cooking that is modern without being trendy. The quality of the ingredients is paramount.
🔳 28 🕓 Closed Sun.–Mon., Tues.–Fri. L, Dec. 25, 2 weeks in Oct.

🍴 PEAT INN
$$$ ❖❖❖
CUPAR
KY15 5LH
TEL 01334-840206
www.thepeatinn.co.uk
The kitchen at this charming small restaurant in rural Fife has an enviable reputation. Consistency is the hallmark, ingredients are of irreproachable quality, and the accomplished cooking speaks for itself. Fixed-price L & D.
🔳 48 🕓 Closed Sun.–Mon., Dec. 25, Jan. 1

DUMFRIES

🏨 CHIPPERKYLE
$$
KIRKPATRICK DURHAM,
CASTLE DOUGLAS
DG7 3EY
TEL 01556-650223
www.chipperkyle.co.uk
This delightful and comfortable country retreat, an 18th-century "Laird's house" of great character, is set within 200 acres and is full of family atmosphere—a fine place to relax and feel at home among books, pets, and fabulous views. The owners have an encyclopedic knowledge of what to do and where to go in the locality.
ⓘ 2 🕓 Closed Christmas

EDINBURGH

🏨 SHERATON GRAND
🍴 HOTEL & SPA
$$$$$ ★★★★★

1 FESTIVAL SQUARE
EH3 9SR
TEL 0131-229 9131
FAX 0131-228 4510
www.starwoodhotels.com/sheraton
The hotel's own tartan adorns the Grill Room of this imposing, purpose-built hotel, whose skilled cooking is classical French. Buffet-style menu in the Terrace restaurant. Fixed-price L.
ⓘ 260 🔳 Grill Room 40, Terrace 100 🅿 122 🔄 🔆 📶 🔽

🏨 THE BALMORAL
$$$$–$$$$$ ★★★★★ ❖❖❖
1 PRINCES ST.
EH2 2EQ
TEL 0131-556 2414
FAX 0131-557 3747
www.thebalmoralhotel.com
Elegant Edwardian luxury hotel. Afternoon tea in the Palm Court; club ambience in Lobby Bar; lively atmosphere in NB's Bar. Brasserie menu, or serious dining and polished service in Restaurant No. 1 Princes Street.
ⓘ 186 🅿 100 🔆 🔄 📶 🔽

🏨 THE BONHAM
$$$$–$$$$$ ★★★★ ❖❖
35 DRUMSHEUGH GARDENS
EH3 7RN
TEL 0131-274 7400
FAX 0131-274 7405
www.thebonham.com
One of the classiest and most comfortable hotels in Edinburgh, a lovely Victorian house equipped with all modern conveniences. A real getaway gem for those in the know.
ⓘ 48 🅿 20

🏨 CHANNINGS
$$$$ ★★★★ ❖
SOUTH LEARMONTH GARDENS
EH4 1EZ
TEL 0131-315 2226/274 7401
FAX 0131-332 9631
www.channings.co.uk
Edwardian town-house hotel

with clublike feel. Imaginative modern menu in the conservatory restaurant.
ⓘ 41 🔄

🏨 GEORGE
$$$$ ★★★★
19–21 GEORGE ST.
EH2 2PB
TEL 0131-225 1251
FAX 0131-226 5644
Centrally located hotel with magnificent classical facade, marble-floored foyer with Corinthian pillars, a popular clubby bar, and a choice of eating options; eating and drinking in the award-winning Tempus Bar and Restaurant.
ⓘ 195 🅿 24 🔄 🔽 Nearby

🏨 NORTON HOUSE
$$$$ ★★★★ ❖❖❖
INGLISTON
EH28 8LX
TEL 0131-333 1275
FAX 0131-333 5305
www.handpickedhotels.co.uk

🏨 Hotel 🍴 Restaurant ⓘ No. of Guest Rooms 🔳 No. of Seats 🅿 Parking 📶 Tube 🕓 Closed

A fine handsome Scottish baronial house in its own parkland, very convenient to the airport.

ⓘ 83 ℗ 200

🏨 MALMAISON
$$$ ★★★ ❀
1 TOWER PLACE
EH6 7DB
TEL 0131-468 5000
FAX 0131-468 5002
www.malmaison-edinburgh.com
Stylish hotel conversion from former Seaman's Mission in rejuvenated Leith harbor area. Understated bedrooms offer minibar and stereo system. Scottish food in the brasserie.

ⓘ 100 ℗ 50 🔄 🐚

🏨 SANDAIG GUEST HOUSE
$$
5 HERMITAGE PLACE LEITH LINKS
EH6 8AA
TEL 0131-554 7357
FAX 0131-467 6389
www.sandaigguesthouse.co.uk
A family-run guest house occupying two mid-terraced Victorian villas. It overlooks historic Leith Links park.

ⓘ 9

🏨 LAURISTON PARK
$
6 LAURISTON PARK
EH3 9JA
TEL 0131-228 5557
This is an elegant yet very welcoming town house in a convenient location close to the city center.

ⓘ 6

🍴 SANTINI
$$$$
8 CONFERENCE SQUARE
EH3 8AN
TEL 0131-221 7788
Italian with dash and panache, either in the bright and buzzy bistro or in the more traditional restaurant.

🍴 100 🕐 Closed Sat. L, Sun.

🍴 THE SCOTSMAN
$$$$ ❀
20 NORTH BRIDGE
EH1 1YT
TEL 0131-556 5565
www.thescotsmanhotel.co.uk
You can dine two ways at the Scotsman—either informally in the North Bridge Brasserie or putting on the style in Vermilion Restaurant where the ghosts of a thousand old newspapermen (the hotel was once head office of the *Scotsman* newspaper) gaze approvingly on. No children under 12.

🍴 32 🕐 Closed L

🍴 IGGS
$$$ ❀
15 JEFFREY ST.
EH1 1DR
TEL 0131-557 8184
www.iggs.co.uk
Latin personality is stamped on this popular addition to the Edinburgh scene, and the menus offer an intriguing blend of Spanish and Scottish dishes based around regional produce. Fixed-price L.

🍴 80 🅢

🍴 ATRIUM
$$–$$$ ❀❀
10 CAMBRIDGE ST.
EH1 2ED
TEL 0131-228 8882
www.atriumrestaurant.co.uk
The bullish face of cooking in Edinburgh. The decor is sharp; the approach is casual, cosmopolitan, and friendly. Dazzling modern cuisine that's sure to tingle the senses.

🍴 70 🕐 Closed Sat. L, Sun., Dec. 25–26, Jan. 1–2 🅢

FALKLAND

🏨 LADYWELL HOUSE
$$
FIFE, FALKLAND
KY15 7DE
TEL 01337-858414
www.ladywellhousefife.co.uk

Located on the outskirts of a beautifully preserved village, this big old manse house—once owned by Princess Diana's mother—is a relaxed and very enjoyable hideaway.

ⓘ 6

GALASHIELS

🏨 KINGSKNOWES
$$$ ★★★
SELKIRK RD.
TD1 3HY
TEL 01896-758375
FAX 01896-750377
www.kingsknowes.co.uk
Victorian turreted mansion set on own grounds near the River Tweed, now a family-run hotel. Tennis. Bar meals and restaurant.

ⓘ 12 ℗ 65

GLASGOW

🏨 HOTEL DU VIN AT ONE DEVONSHIRE GARDENS
$$$$ ★★★★ ❀❀❀
1 DEVONSHIRE GARDENS
G12 0UX
TEL 0141-339 2001
FAX 0141-337 1663
www.onedevonshiregardens.com
Very individualistic hotel in three adjoining row houses. Bedrooms have bold, striking decor, sumptuous fabrics, subdued lighting, luxurious bathrooms, music systems, and a supply of CDs. In one house, stylish lounge and bar; in another, elegant cocktail lounge. Consistently high standard of cooking, seasonally changing menus. Attentive service. Fixed-price L. Dinner reservations are required.

ⓘ 48 ℗ 12 🐚

SOMETHING SPECIAL

🏨 MALMAISON
$$$ ★★★ ❀
278 WEST GEORGE ST.
G2 4LL
TEL 0141-572 1000

🔄 Elevator   🅢 Air-conditioning   🏊 Indoor Pool   🏊 Outdoor Pool   🐚 Health Club

FAX 0141-572 1002
www.malmaison.com
Contemporary hotel conversion with stylish rooms. The vaulted crypt and the ecclesiastical pillars and arches of the interior are clues to the hotel's former incarnation—as an Episcopal church. All-day Café Mal; upbeat cuisine in brasserie. Exceptionally friendly, as well as helpful staff.

[i] 72 🔄 🍴

🏨 MARKS HOTEL
🍴 $$
110 BATH ST.
G2 2EN
TEL 0141-353 0800
FAX 0141-353 0900
www.markshotels.com
A friendly boutique hotel (including some superb scenic duplex suites) convenient for Glasgow's theaters and city center.

[i] 103 🔄 🍴

🍴 UBIQUITOUS CHIP
$$ ◑◑
12 ASHTON LN.
G12 8SJ
TEL 0141-3345007
www.ubiquitouschip.co.uk
Simple city suburb diner with stone floors, lots of greenery, and a lively, informal atmosphere. Offers a short, appealing bistro menu.

🔲 200

GULLANE

🍴 GREY WALLS HOTEL
$$$–$$$$ ◑◑
MUIRFIELD
EH31 2EG
TEL 01620-842144
www.greywalls.co.uk
Fresh ingredients, skillful cooking, and a splendid wine list, all to be enjoyed in a Lutyens-designed house, overlooking Gertrude Jekyll–designed gardens and the celebrated Muirfield golf course.

🔲 45 [P] 60 ⊕ Closed Mon.–Tues. Jan.–March

HADDINGTON

🏨 MAITLANDFIELD COUNTRY HOUSE
$$ ★★★
24 SIDEGATE, EAST LOTHIAN
EH41 4BZ
TEL 01620-826513
FAX 01620-826713
www.maitlandfieldhouse.co.uk
Secluded in its gardens but very convenient to main routes to Edinburgh, this friendly hotel lies at the feet of the beautiful Lammermuir Hills.

[i] 25 [P] 80

JEDBURGH

🏨 THE SPINNEY
$
LANGLEE
TD8 6PB
TEL 01835-863525
FAX 01835-864883
www.thespinney-jedburgh.co.uk
Attractively furnished converted cottage. Two lodges on grounds also available for B&B rental.

[i] 3 (2 annex) [P] 8 ⊕ Closed Dec.–Feb.

KELSO

🏨 ROXBURGHE HOTEL &
🍴 GOLF COURSE
$$$$ ★★★ ◑
HEITON
TD5 8JZ
TEL 01573-450331
FAX 01573-450611
www.roxburghe.net
Bonnie Prince Charlie planted a white rose bush here in 1745. The cooking is well worth a detour. Using the best local ingredients, the kitchen produces sound modern British dishes. Fixed-price D. Golf, fishing, and tennis.

[i] 25 (6 annex) 🔲 35 [P] 150

LANGBANK

🏨 BEST WESTERN GLEDDOCH HOUSE
$$$$ ★★★★
LANGBANK
PA14 6YE
TEL 01475-540711
FAX 01475-540201
www.oxfordhotelsandinns.com
Set on a 360-acre estate high above the River Clyde with spectacular views across to Ben Lomond, this historic house offers an ambitious modern menu. Fixed-price L & D. Golf, fishing, and clay-pigeon shooting.

[i] 75 [P] 200

LINLITHGOW

🍴 CHAMPANY INN
$$$$ ◑◑
NEAR LINLITHGOW
EH49 7LU
TEL 01506-834532
www.champany.com
Housed in an old mill that dates from the time of Mary, Queen of Scots, this plush circular restaurant offers good cooking of local supplies. Vast wine list. Fixed-price L. No children under eight.

🔲 50 ⊕ Closed Sat. L, Sun., Dec. 24–26

MELROSE

🏨 BURTS
$$$ ★★ ◑◑
THE SQUARE
TD6 9PL
TEL 01896-822285
FAX 01896-822870
www.burtshotel.co.uk
Long-established, family-run hotel on market square. Elegantly decorated restaurant takes fishing and shooting as its theme, with old rods, flies, and prints dotted around the room. The kitchen handles Scottish ingredients effectively for a modern menu that pulls together many strands and

influences. Lounge bar meals. Fixed-price L & D.

(i) 50 **P** 40 **(·)** Closed Dec. 24–26

MOFFAT

🏨 WELL VIEW
$$–$$$ ✿✿

BALLPLAY RD.
DG10 9JU
TEL 01683-220184
FAX 01683-220088
www.wellview.co.uk
Small Victorian house, immaculately maintained; friendly, cozy atmosphere. Six-course dinner in a light, contemporary style—flavors, not fussiness. Recipient of RAC Gold Ribbon award.

(i) 3 **P** 8 **(·)** Closed 10 days in Mar., 2 weeks in Oct.

NEWTON STEWART

🏨 KIRROUGHTREE HOUSE
$$$–$$$$ ★★★ ✿

NEWTON STEWART
DG8 6AN
TEL 01671-402141
FAX 01671-402425
www.mcmillanhotels.co.uk/kirroughtree-house-hotel
Seventeenth-century mansion in landscaped gardens and woodland; tennis. Relaxed, friendly staff. Imaginative cooking with local produce. No children under ten. Fixed-price L & D.

(i) 17 **P** 50

NORTH BERWICK

🏨 MACDONALD MARINE HOTEL & SPA
$$$$ ✿✿

CROMWELL RD.
EH39 4LZ
TEL 0870-400 8129
FAX: 01620-894480
www.macdonaldhotels.co.uk
A fine large seaside-style hotel overlooking North Berwick golf course and the Firth of Forth.

(i) 83 **⚑** **⊠**

ST. ANDREWS

🏨 🍴 OLD COURSE HOTEL, GOLF RESORT, & SPA
$$$$$ ★★★★★ ✿✿✿

ST. ANDREWS
KY16 9SP
TEL 01334-474371
FAX 01334-477668
www.oldcoursehotel.kohler.com
Internationally renowned hotel overlooking the world-famous golf course. Magnificent flower displays in lobby. Friendly staff. Informal summertime dining in conservatory. Rooftop Road Hole Grill provides spectacular views of the course, West Sands, and the town.

(i) 144 **⊞** 125 **P** 150 **⊟** **☎** **⊠**

🏨 GLENDERRAN GUEST HOUSE
$$

9 MURRAY PARK
KY16 9AW
TEL 01334-477951
www.glenderran.com
A characterful B&B, well placed for the seaside and the golf courses. Aircraft buffs will be fascinated by the aeronautical pictures and collections lovingly displayed around the house. No children under 12.

(i) 5

ST. FILLANS

🏨 🍴 FOUR SEASONS HOTEL
$$$$ ★★★ ✿✿

LOCH EARN, CRIEFF
PH6 2NF
TEL 01764-685333
www.thefourseasonshotel.co.uk
From Scottish coast seafood to local game harvested in the hills and glens around beautiful Loch Earn, the Four Seasons—beautifully set on the shores of the loch—offers some of the most enjoyable dining in mid-Scotland.

(i) 12 (plus 6 chalets, 1 apartment) **⊞** 60

STIRLING

🏨 BARCELO STIRLING HIGHLAND HOTEL
$$$$ ★★★★

SPITTAL ST.
FK8 1DU
TEL 01786-272727
FAX 01786-272829
www.barcelo-hotels.co.uk
Imaginative conversion of old school with superb city views. School features retained. Scholars Restaurant. Squash courts.

(i) 94 **P** 96 **⊟** **☎** **⊠**

🏨 WESTLANDS HOTEL
$

DOUNE RD., DUNBLANE
FK15 9HT
TEL/FAX 01786-822118
www.westlandshoteldunblane.co.uk
A fine Edwardian, turreted and creeper-hung, family-run and friendly. Dine in or out-of-doors. The hotel can arrange sports and activities from shooting to golf.

(i) 5

STRANRAER

🏨 GLENAPP CASTLE
$$$$$ ★★★★★ ✿✿✿

BALLANTRAE
KA26 0NZ
TEL 01465-831212
FAX 01465-831000
www.glenappcastle.com
A beautifully restored, grand Scottish baronial castle in a fine location looking out to the Isle of Arran. Antiques in the bedrooms, classic furnishings, and stylishly presented, locally sourced food.

(i) 17 **(·)** Closed 2 months in winter (dates vary)

⊟ Elevator **S** Air-conditioning **☎** Indoor Pool **⊠** Outdoor Pool **⚑** Health Club

TROON

🏨 LOCHGREEN HOUSE
🍴 $$$$ ★★★★ ❀❀❀
MONKTONHILL RD., SOUTH-
WOOD
KA10 7EN
TEL 01292-313343
FAX 01292-318661
www.costley-hotels.co.uk/
lochgreen
This is one of Scotland's best
hotels, offering an appealing
blend of the stylish and the
warmly welcoming, with
attentive and friendly staff and
a chef who knows all about
local and seasonal ingredients.
🛏 40 🅿 50

TURNBERRY

🏨 WESTIN TURNBERRY
$$$$$ ★★★★★ ❀❀
TURNBERRY
KA26 9LT
TEL 01655-331000
FAX 01655-331706
www.turnberry.co.uk
Famous hotel set on over
800 acres of stunning countryside; spectacular views of the
Firth of Clyde. The Ailsa golf
course is considered one of
the best in the world. Spa for
health and beauty treatments;
65-foot pool. The Ailsa Lounge
is very welcoming, and in
addition to the elegant 1906
Restaurant, there is the new
fine-dining James Miller Room
and chef's table.
🛏 219 🅿 200 🕐 Closed Dec.
12–27 🔁 🚇 🔲

■ HIGHLANDS & ISLANDS

ABERDEEN

🏨 MARCLIFFE HOTEL AND SPA
$$$$ ★★★★ ❀
NORTH DEESIDE RD.
AB15 9YA
TEL 01224-861000

FAX 01224-868860
www.marcliffe.com
Set on 8 acres of mature
grounds. Informal Drawing
Room restaurant; formal
Conservatory Restaurant.
Scottish cuisine. Snooker and
croquet lawn.
🛏 42 🅿 200 🔁

🏨 BIMINI GUEST HOUSE
$
69 CONSTITUTION ST.
AB24 5ET
TEL 01224-646912
www.bimini.co.uk
A peaceful little stopover,
convenient both for the beach
and the city attractions, Bimini
Guest House is built of the
local Aberdeen granite—it
sparkles most attractively in
the sunshine!
🛏 8 🅿 7

🍴 SILVER DARLING
$$$$ ❀❀
POCRA QUAY, NORTH PIER
AB11 5DQ
TEL 01224-576229
www.silverdarling.co.uk
Fish, fish, fish at this wonderful
restaurant (titled after the traditional fisherman's name for the
herring), situated in the old custom house with a tremendous
view out over Aberdeen harbor.
Salmon, sea bass, scallops,
crab-and-prawn gateau, oysters,
anchovies, mullet, shrimp . . .
and much more.
🪑 80 🕐 Closed Sun., Sat. L,
Christmas–New Year's

AUCHTERARDER

🏨 GLENEAGLES
🍴 $$$$$ ★★★★★ ❀❀❀❀
AUCHTERARDER
PH3 1NF
TEL 01764-662231
FAX 01764-662134
www.gleneagles.com
Renowned Edwardian luxury
hotel in beautiful countryside,
surrounded by its own golf

courses and extensive grounds.
Afternoon tea and cocktails
in drawing room. Formal but
friendly service and piano
music in Strathearn Restaurant; modern Scottish cooking.
Many other dining options.
Outstanding range of sporting
activities. Fixed-price D.
🛏 232 🛏 240 🅿 277 🔁
🚇 🔲

BALLACHULISH

🏨 CRAIGLINNHE HOUSE
🍴 $$$ ❀❀
LETTERMORE
PH49 4JD
TEL 01855-811270
www.craiglinnhe.co.uk
The hills of Ardgour and lovely
Loch Linnhe are the setting
for this Victorian house and
gardens. The hotel has been
tastefully refurbished, the
situation is extremely relaxing
(otters and seals on your doorstep), and you couldn't ask for
friendlier or more welcoming

🏨 Hotel 🍴 Restaurant 🛏 No. of Guest Rooms 🪑 No. of Seats 🅿 Parking 🚇 Tube 🕐 Closed

hosts than David (superb chef) and Beverley Hughes.
[i] 5

BALLATER

DARROCH LEARG
$$$$ ★★★ ❀❀❀
BRAEMAR RD.
AB35 5UX
TEL 013397-55443
FAX 013397-55252
www.darrochlearg.co.uk
Friendly, family-run country house with panoramic views across the Dee Valley toward the Grampian Mountains from both the dining room and conservatory. Dinner menus are short and to the point, with highly accomplished cooking from start to finish. Children welcome, and have their own special menu. Fixed-price D.
[i] 13 (5 annex) [P] 25
[clock] Restaurant closed Christmas, all Jan. (excluding Jan. 1)

GREEN INN
$
9 VICTORIA RD.
AB35 5QQ
TEL 01339-755701
www.green-inn.com
This is exactly what Ballater has been waiting for—a friendly, reasonably priced restaurant with rooms. Relax by the wood-burning stove in the conservatory or in the lounge bar; dine on fresh local crab, scallops, venison, beef fillet; then stay over if you can't bear to tear yourself away.
[i] 3

BLAIRGOWRIE

KINLOCH HOUSE
$$$$$ ★★★ ❀❀❀
BLAIRGOWRIE
PH10 6SG
TEL 01250-884237
FAX 01250-884333
www.kinlochhouse.com
Set on 25 acres of wooded grounds, this country house

offers personal hospitality and service. Good Scottish fruit and vegetables are grown in the hotel's own gardens. Imaginative cooking with a particularly light touch; ingredients are of a high standard, textures and flavors come through clearly. Fixed-price D.
[i] 20 [bed] 55 [P] 40 [clock] Closed Christmas

GILMORE HOUSE
$
PERTH RD.
PH10 6EJ
TEL 01250-872791
www.gilmorehouse.co.uk
A warm house, both in itself and in the welcome. Big airy rooms, beautifully furnished; a nice relaxed atmosphere; and mighty Scottish breakfasts to set you up for the day.
[i] 3

BRAEMAR

INVERCAULD ARMS
$$$ ★★★
BRAEMAR
AB35 5YR
TEL 013397-41605
FAX 013397-41428
This traditional Victorian Highland hotel set amidst spectacular scenery is justly popular for its attentive and friendly staff.
[i] 68 [P] 80

CRAIGELLACHIE

CRAIGELLACHIE
$$$ ★★★ ❀
CRAIGELLACHIE
AB38 9SR
TEL 01340-881204
FAX 01340-881253
www.oxfordhotelsandinns.com
Craigellachie has been attracting visitors from all over the world to this lovely part of Speyside since 1893. It is an impressive Victorian hotel complete with sitting rooms,

drawing room, and library. There is a famously broad range of malt whiskies available in the Quaich Bar. Three dining areas; local ingredients are used in cooking.
[i] 26 [P] 50

DORNOCH

DORNOCH CASTLE
$$ ★★★ ❀
CASTLE ST.
IV25 3SD
TEL 01862-810216
FAX 01862-810981
www.dornochcastlehotel.com
Dating back to the 16th century, this friendly family-run hotel was once the palace of the bishops of Caithness. Enjoy the comfortable lounge overlooking the gardens, the cocktail bar, and a choice of dining options.
[i] 21 [P] 16

2 QUAIL ROOMS
$$
CASTLE ST.
IV25 3SN
TEL 01862-811811
www.2quail.com
Smart and stylish, but also very homey (there's definitely a tartan influence!), this friendly B&B extends a reassuringly warm welcome. No children under eight.
[i] 3

DUNKELD

ATHOLL ARMS HOTEL
$$
BRIDGEHEAD
PH8 0AQ
TEL 01350-727219
FAX 01350-727991
www.athollarmshotel.com
This imposing hotel on the River Tay offers a traditional warm welcome (solid furnishings, log fires, a cheerful bar where you can eat, and the aptly named Riverview Restaurant). Conveniently located in

the center of town.

ℹ️ 17

ERISKAY

🏨 **ISLE OF ERISKA**
🍴 **$$$$$ ★★★★ ❀❀❀**
ERISKAY
PA37 1SD
TEL 01631-720371
FAX 01631-720531
www.eriska-hotel.co.uk
This granite and sandstone baronial mansion stands in splendid isolation on its own picturesque island (which has vehicular access to the mainland). Dinners here feature a daily roast, as well as a selection of fish and seafood. Fixed-price D.

ℹ️ 23 🛏️ 40 🅿️ 40 ⊕ Closed Jan. 🔁 🔻

FORT WILLIAM

🏨 **INVERLOCHY**
🍴 **CASTLE**
$$$$$ ★★★★★ ❀❀❀
TORLUNDY
PH33 6SN
TEL 01397-702177
FAX 01397-702953
www.inverlochycastlehotel.com
Victorian pile beneath Ben Nevis on 500 acres of grounds; superb display of rhododendrons. Tennis and fishing. Don't confuse the 19th-century Inverlochy Castle with the square, turreted ruins nearby. These belong to Old Inverlochy Castle, a 13th-century stronghold where at least three battles were fought. Great Hall with frescoed ceiling and crystal chandeliers. Two dining rooms; cooking shows traditional skills and modern ideas, using good local ingredients. Fixed-price L & D.

ℹ️ 17 🛏️ 34 🅿️ 18

INVERNESS

SOMETHING SPECIAL

🏨 **CULLODEN HOUSE**
$$$$$ ★★★★ ❀❀
CULLODEN
IV2 7BZ
TEL 01463-790461
FAX 01463-792181
www.cullodenhouse.co.uk
Historic Adam-style Georgian mansion on 40 acres of wooded grounds and parkland. Bonnie Prince Charlie's army of Highland clansmen spent the night of April 15, 1746, sleeping on the ground in the parks here. Next morning they marched out to be cut to pieces by the English dragoons on Drummossie Moor, the bloody end to the second Jacobite Rebellion. Marble fireplaces, ornate plasterwork, chandeliers. Period suites, master rooms, contemporary bedrooms. Daily changing five-course menu. Tennis, croquet, boules, and badminton.

ℹ️ 23 (5 annex) 🅿️ 50

ISLE OF ARRAN

🏨 **KILMICHAEL**
$$$ ★★★ ❀❀
GLEN CLOY, BRODICK
KA27 8BY
TEL 01770-302219
FAX 01770-302068
www.kilmichael.com
This is a friendly house with a welcoming atmosphere. The accommodations are furnished with a selection of fresh flowers, books, and a variety of items collected from around the world. Modern European cooking. No children under 12.

ℹ️ 5 (3 annex) 🅿️ 12 ⊕ Closed Dec. 25

ISLE OF SKYE

🏨 **KINLOCH LODGE**
$$$$ ★★★ ❀❀❀
SLEAT

IV43 8QY
TEL 01471-833214
FAX 01471-833277
www.kinloch-lodge.co.uk
The mood inside Lord and Lady Macdonald's converted 300-year-old Michelin-starred lodge is one of a family home. Drawing rooms have log fires and comfortable sofas; family portraits and photographs are displayed throughout. Dinner is a fixed-price affair running to four courses, and dishes are based resolutely on what the local region can provide.

ℹ️ 9 (5 annex)

🏨 **CUILLIN HILLS**
$$$ ★★★ ❀❀
PORTREE
IV51 9QU
TEL 01478-612003
FAX 01478-613092
www.cullinhills-hotel-skye.co.uk
Superb views over Portree Bay to the Cuillin Hills. Highland specialties served in restaurant.

ℹ️ 21 (9 annex) 🅿️ 56

🏨 **SHOREFIELD HOUSE**
$–$$ ★★★★
PORTREE
IV51 9PW
TEL 01470-582444
www.shorefield.com
Overlooking Edinbane Loch, Shorefield House welcomes children (they have their own play area) and disabled guests, and caters enthusiastically for walkers and outdoor types. Recipient of an AA breakfast award.

ℹ️ 5 🅿️ 10 ⊕ Closed Nov.–mid-March

SOMETHING SPECIAL

🏨 **THREE CHIMNEYS**
🍴 **$$$$ ★★★★★ ❀❀❀**
COLBOST
IV55 8ZT
TEL 01470-511258
www.threechimneys.co.uk
A 100-year-old crofter's cottage a stone's throw from the sea. You can eat virtually

---

🏨 Hotel   🍴 Restaurant   ℹ️ No. of Guest Rooms   🛏️ No. of Seats   🅿️ Parking   🚇 Tube   ⊕ Closed

any time of day, although the greatest pleasures are reserved for the evening. Fresh seafood is the star attraction. Recipient of AA regional food award.
🛈 6 ⊞ 30 ⏱ Closed Sun. L, Jan.

JOHN O'GROATS

🏨 CREAG-NA-MARA
$
EAST MEY
KW14 8XL
TEL 01847-851850
www.creagnamara.co.uk
Only 5 miles west of John O'Groats, hospitable Creag-Na-Mara commands stunning views over the Pentland Firth and the Isle of Stroma. No children under three.
🛈 4

KINGUSSIE

🏨 THE CROSS AT
🍽 KINGUSSIE
$$$$ ★★ ❀❀❀
TWEED MILL BRAE, ARDBROIL-ACH RD.
PH21 1LB
TEL 01540-661166
FAX 01540-661080
www.thecross.co.uk
Converted tweed mill run as a friendly restaurant-with-rooms offering lovely accommo-dations. Superbly comfortable beds and many thoughtful touches. Menu features local ingredients. Fixed-price D. No children under 12.
🛈 9 ⊞ 28 ⏱ Closed Mon.–Tues. & some time in winter (dates vary)

🏨 SCOT HOUSE
$$ ★★ ❀
NEWTONMORE RD.
PH21 1HE
TEL 01540-661351
FAX 01540-661111
www.scothouse.com
Small family-run hotel; genu-ine warmth of welcome. Fresh

local produce in restaurant.
🛈 9 ᴘ 30

KYLESKU

🏨 KYLESKU
$$
KYLESKU
IV27 4HW
TEL 01971-502231/502200
FAX 01971-502313
www.kyleskuhotel.co.uk
Pleasant small waterside hotel with good reputation for very fresh seafood. Fishing.
🛈 7 (1 annex) ᴘ 50
⏱ Closed some time in winter (dates vary)

MULL

🏨 WESTERN ISLES
$$$–$$$$ ★★★
TOBERMORY
PA75 6PR
TEL 01688-302012
FAX 01688-302297
www.westernisleshotel.co.uk
Victorian hotel high above the pier, with picture-postcard view of bay, sea, and hills. Con-servatory bar. Eastern cuisine in Spices Restaurant; more traditional main dining room.
🛈 28 ᴘ 20

ORKNEY ISLANDS

🏨 AYRE HOTEL
$$$ ★★★
AYRE RD., KIRKWALL
KW15 1QX
TEL 01856-873001
FAX 01856-876289
www.ayrehotel.co.uk
This welcoming hotel over-looks Kirkwall's harbor, jump-ing-off point for the northern Orkney Islands, and is only a few minutes' walk from the charming and historic center of town. Modern rooms and accommodating staff make for a comfortable and pleasant stay at the only four-star hotel on Mainland Orkney. Also houses a restaurant and a

popular local bar. Surcharge for rooms with a sea view.
🛈 33 ᴘ 18 ⏱ Closed Dec. 25, Jan. 1

🍽 CREEL
$$$ ❀❀
FRONT RD., ST. MARGARET'S HOPE
KW17 2SL
TEL 01856-831311
www.thecreel.co.uk
Situated in the center of the village right beside the bay, Creel Restaurant has a sound reputation with visitors and islanders alike. The menu's focus is on fresh Orkney produce. Advance reservations are always advisable.
⊞ 20 ⏱ Closed Mon.–Tues., L, mid-Oct.–April

PORT APPIN

🏨 THE AIRDS
🍽 $$$$$ ★★★★ ❀❀❀
PORT APPIN
PA38 4DF
TEL 01631-730236
FAX 01631-730535
www.airds-hotel.com
The scenery is stunning with views across Loch Linnhe, scattered with islands, to the Morvern mountains beyond. Skillful cooking that shows lots of creativity and finesse. Superb wine list. Fixed-price D.
🛈 12 ⊞ 36 ᴘ 15

Shopping

In the main cities and towns, shops usually open at 8:30 or 9 a.m., and many now stay open until 6 p.m. or later (supermarkets until 8 p.m. or later, some on Sundays, too). In the smaller and sleepier provincial towns and in many villages, you will find some stores close at 1 p.m. on Wednesday or Thursday. Over the past 20 years, national chain stores and supermarkets have posed an increasing threat to traditional family-run stores. The stores recommended here still retain their local or individual character.

■ LONDON

Books
Foyles, 113–119 Charing Cross Rd, tel 020-7437 5660
Waterstone's Booksellers, 203–206 Piccadilly, tel 0843-290 8549

Designer Clothing
Harvey Nichols London, 109–125 Knightsbridge, tel 020-7235 5000
Paul Smith, 43–46 Floral St., Covent Garden, tel 020-7379 7133. British designer clothing for men.

Food & Drink
Berry Bros. & Rudd, 3 St. James's St., tel 0800-280 2440. Wine merchant.
Fortnum & Mason, 181 Piccadilly, tel 020-7734 8040. Fabulous chocolates to luxurious hampers.
Harrods, 87–135 Brompton Rd., Knightsbridge, tel 020-7730 1234. Lavish food halls.
Neal's Yard Dairy, 17 Shorts Gardens, Covent Garden, tel 020-7240 5700. The finest British and Irish cheeses.

Markets
Camden Lock. Daily. London's busiest market, with a carnival-like atmosphere and everything from street fashion to second-hand clothes.
Greenwich (College Approach). Daily; Thurs., antiques; Fri.–Sun., arts and crafts. A more sedate feel but still full of local character.
Petticoat Lane (Middlesex St.). Sun.–Fri. A traditional East End street market over a mile long.
Portobello Road. Mon.–Sat.,

closed Thurs. p.m. London's best known market attracts many visitors to the associated souvenir stalls.

Traditional Clothing
Church's Shoes, 108–110 Jermyn St., tel 020-7930 8210. Handmade gentlemen's shoes.
Burberrys, 18–22 Haymarket, tel 020-7930 3343
Gieves & Hawkes, 1 Savile Row, tel 020-7434 2001. One of the best known gentlemen's outfitters of high-quality tailor-made clothing on world-famous Savile Row.
Thomas Pink, 85 Jermyn St., tel 020-7930 6364. Fine shirts.

■ SOUTH COUNTRY

Clothing
Classic clothing is available in many South Country towns, where smaller stores still cater to country gentlefolk. Try:
County Clothes, 19 St. Margarets St., Canterbury, tel 01227-765294. Menswear.
Gieves, 1–2 The Square, Winchester, Hampshire, tel 01962-852096. Menswear.

Tea
Whittards of Chelsea, 27 Market Pl., St. Albans, tel 01727-899947. Specialist teas and coffees.

■ WEST COUNTRY

Art/Design
Tate Gallery St. Ives, Porthmeor Beach, St. Ives, tel 01736-796226

Cider
Burrow Hill Cider, Pass Vale Farm, Burrow Hill, Kingsbury Episcopi, Martock, tel 01460-240782

Crafts
Highgrove Shop, 10 Long St., Tetbury, Glocestershire, tel 01666-505666. Fine cheeses.

Glass
Bristol Blue Glass Factory Showroom and Shop, Unit 05, St. Catherine's, Bedminster, Bristol, tel 01179-636900

■ WALES

Pottery
Portmeirion Pottery Seconds Warehouse, Portmeirion Village, Gwynedd, tel 01766-772326. Seconds of distinctive pottery.

Slate
Llechwedd Slate Caverns, Blaenau Ffestiniog, Gwynedd, tel 01766-830306. For clocks, house nameplates, place mats, and other Welsh slate products.

■ SOUTH MIDLANDS

Ethnic Fabrics
Shops selling exquisite ethnic fabrics are often found in towns with large Asian communities.
Saree Mandir, 117–129 Belgrave Rd., Leicester, tel 0116-266 8144. This shop selling beautiful fabrics is the largest East Asian fabric shop in the world outside India.

Jewelry

Hundreds of jewelry workshops in **Birmingham's Jewellery Quarter** produce much of Britain's finest handcrafted jewelry. For more information, visit the Museum of the Jewellery Quarter, 77–79 Vyse St., tel 0121-554 3598.

Markets

Birmingham: Tues., Thurs.–Sat.
Coventry: Mon.–Sat.
Hereford: Wed., Sat.
Leicester: Mon.–Sat.
Moreton-in-Marsh: Tues.
Northampton: Tues.–Sat.
Oxford: Mon.–Sat.
Worcester: Mon.–Sat.

◼ EAST ANGLIA & LINCOLNSHIRE

Mustard

The Mustard Shop, 15 Royal Arcade, Norwich, tel 01603-627889. Norwich is synonymous with fine mustard.

◼ NORTH MIDLANDS

Beer

Burton-upon-Trent is the center of the British brewing industry. As well as at many fine pubs in town, you can buy bottled ale at: **The National Brewery Centre,** Horninglow St., Burton-upon-Trent, Staffordshire, tel 01283-532880

Pottery

Many factory shops in the Potteries sell famous brands manufactured in the area.
Spode Factory Shop, London Rd., Stoke-on-Trent, tel 01782-411756
Waterford Wedgwood Factory Shop, King St., Fenton, Stoke-on-Trent, tel 01782-316161

◼ NORTHWEST ENGLAND

Markets

Ashton-under-Lyne: Mon.–Sat.
Blackburn: Wed., Fri., Sat.
Carlisle: Mon.–Sat.
Chester: Mon.–Sat.
Clitheroe: Tues., Thurs.–Sat.
Kendal: Wed., Sat.
Lancaster: Wed., Sat.
Rawtenstall: Thurs., Sat.

Outdoor Clothing

George Fisher, 2 Borrowdale Rd., Keswick, tel 01768-772178. The most famous of specialist shops selling outdoorwear in the small Lake District town of Keswick.

Pottery

Wetheriggs Country Pottery, Clifton Dykes, Penrith, tel 01768-892733. Traditional earthenware pottery produced in restored Victorian steam pottery.

◼ NORTHEAST ENGLAND

Cheese

Wensleydale cheese is a crumbly, white, hard cheese produced in the Yorkshire dale of the same name.
Wensleydale Dairy Products, Visitor Centre, Gayle Ln., Hawes, tel 01969-667664

Jewelry & Design

West Yorkshire has produced many fine craftspeople and is still a center of design.
Crafts and Design Shop, City Art Gallery, The Headrow, Leeds, tel 0113-247 8241

Markets

Bradford: Mon.–Sat.
Darlington: Mon.–Sat.
Doncaster: Mon.–Sat.
Durham: Tues., Fri.–Sat.
Halifax: Fri.
Hexham: Tues.

Huddersfield: Mon.
Hull: Tues., Fri.–Sat.
Leeds: Tues., Fri.–Sat.
Sheffield: Mon.–Wed., Fri.–Sat.
Wakefield: Mon., Fri.–Sat.

Tea

Betty's of Harrogate, 1 Parliament St., Harrogate, tel 01423-877300. Tea is sold here by the ounce, or drink it in their world-famous tearooms.

◼ SCOTTISH LOWLANDS

Farmers Markets

Edinburgh: Sat.
Glasgow: Sat.
Peebles: 2nd Sat. of month
St. Andrews: 1st Sat. of month

Kilts

Hector Russell Kiltmakers, 95 Princes St., Edinburgh, tel 0131-225 3315.
Kirk Wynd Highland House, 149a Market St., St. Andrews Fife, tel 01334-473268

Woolens

Edinburgh Woollen Mill, 139 Princes St., Edinburgh, tel 01312-263840. Traditional knitwear.

◼ HIGHLANDS & ISLANDS

Traditional Music

Ceilidh Place, 14 W. Argyle St., Ullapool, tel 01854-612103
Celtic Chords, 8 Barclay St., Stonehaven, tel 01569-763913

Whisky

Among the distilleries open to the public are:
Dalwhinnie Distillery Visitor Centre, Dalwhinnie, tel 01540-672219
Glenfiddich Distillery, Dufftown, Keith, tel 01340-820373

Entertainment

In the smaller towns, nightlife tends to be concentrated in the pub or restaurant, with perhaps a more or less mediocre nightclub or provincial theater. The biggest centers offer a huge number of pubs, clubs, theaters, bars, and halls to choose from. Major cities publish their own listings magazines with reviews, comment, and full details of what's on. These are available from newsdealers, bookstores, and visitor centers. Following is a selection of some of the main theaters and concert venues.

■ LONDON

Concert Halls
Royal Albert Hall, Kensington Gore SW7, tel 020-7589 8212, tube: South Kensington, High Street Kensington. London's circular concert hall, venue for the Promenade Concerts.
Royal Festival Hall, Belvedere Rd. SE1, tel 020-7960 4200, tube: Waterloo, Embankment. Designed for the 1951 Festival of Britain.

Opera
Royal Opera House, Covent Garden WC2E, tel 020-7304 4000, tube: Covent Garden. Britain's premier ballet and opera venue.

Theaters
National Theatre, South Bank SE1, tel 020-7452 3000, tube: Embankment, Waterloo. Three theaters offering classic to experimental pieces.
Shakespeare's Globe Theatre, New Globe Walk, Bankside, Southwark, SE1, tel 020-7902 1400, tube: London Bridge, Mansion House. Outdoor Elizabethan plays May through September.

■ HOME COUNTIES
Theatre Royal, Thames St., Windsor, tel 01753-853888. Mainstream drama.

■ SOUTH COUNTRY
Theaters
Chichester Festival Theatre, Oaklands Park, Chichester, tel 01243-781312. Venue for a summer performing-arts festival.
Salisbury Playhouse, Malthouse Lane, Salisbury, tel 01722-320333.

Drama, musicals, opera, ballet.
Theatre Royal, New Road, Brighton, Tel 01273-328488. Drama, musicals, opera, ballet.

■ WEST COUNTRY
Theatre Royal, Sawclose, Bath, tel 01225-448844. One of Britain's oldest and most beautiful theaters.
Theatre Royal, King St., Bristol, tel 01179-493993. The country's oldest theater.

■ WALES
Opera
Welsh National Opera, tel 029-2063 5000. Superb Welsh singing voices.

Theater
Sherman Theatre, Senghennydd Rd., Cardiff, tel 02920-646900. Unconventional and challenging productions.

■ SOUTH MIDLANDS
Symphony Hall, Intl. Conference Centre, Broad St., Birmingham, tel 0121-780 3333. Concerts by the City of Birmingham Symphony Orchestra.

Theaters
Oxford Playhouse, Beaumont St., Oxford, tel 01865-305305. Drama, dance, music, and opera presented within a Georgian building.
Royal Shakespeare Theatre, Stratford-upon-Avon, tel 01789-403409. Home to the Royal Shakespeare Company.

■ NORTHWEST ENGLAND
Concert Halls
Bridgewater Hall, near G-Mex Centre, Manchester, tel 0161-907 9000. Home of the Hallé Orchestra.
Philharmonic Hall, Hope St., Liverpool, tel 0151-709 2895. Home of the Royal Liverpool Philharmonic Orchestra.

Theaters
Empire Theatre, Lime St., Liverpool, tel 0151-702 7320. Hosts major touring companies: ballet, opera, drama, musicals, and concerts.
Royal Exchange, St. Ann's Sq., Manchester, tel 0161-833 9833. Stages a wide range of plays.

■ NORTHEAST ENGLAND
Theatre Royal, Grey St., Newcastle upon Tyne, tel 0191-232 0997. Seasonal performances by the Royal Shakespeare Company.

■ SCOTTISH LOWLANDS
Concert Hall
Glasgow Royal Concert Hall, 2 Sauchiehall St., Glasgow, tel 0141-353 8000. Home of the Royal Scottish National Orchestra.

Theaters
Citizens Theatre, 119 Gorbals St., Glasgow, tel 0141-429 0022. One of the most respected theaters in Britain; adventurous productions.
Edinburgh Playhouse, 18–22 Greenside Place, Edinburgh, tel 0161-385 1025. Big shows.

INDEX

ILLUSTRATIONS CREDITS

National Geographic
TRAVELER
Great Britain

Published by the National Geographic Society
John M. Fahey, Jr., *Chairman of the Board and Chief Executive Officer*
Timothy T. Kelly, *President*
Declan Moore, *Executive Vice President; President, Publishing*
Melina Gerosa Bellows, *Executive Vice President; Chief Creative Officer, Books, Kids, and Family*

Prepared by the Book Division
Barbara Brownell Grogan, *Vice President and Editor in Chief*
Jonathan Halling, *Design Director, Books and Children's Publishing*
Marianne R. Koszorus, *Director of Design*
Barbara Noe, *Senior Editor*
Carl Mehler, *Director of Maps*
R. Gary Colbert, *Production Director*
Jennifer A. Thornton, *Managing Editor*
Meredith C. Wilcox, *Administrative Director, Illustrations*

Staff for This Book
Jane Sunderland, *Project Editor*
Kay Kobor Hankins, *Art Director*
Linda Makarov, *Designer*
Kevin Eans, Meredith Wilcox, *Illustrations Editors*
Michael McNey and Mapping Specialists, *Map Production*
Rachael Jackson, Larry Porges, *Contributors*
Connie Binder, *Indexer*

Manufacturing and Quality Management
Christopher A. Liedel, *Chief Financial Officer*
Phillip L. Schlosser, *Senior Vice President*
Chris Brown, *Technical Director*
Nicole Elliott, *Manager*
Rachel Faulise, *Manager*
Robert L. Barr, *Manager*

National Geographic Traveler: Great Britain (Third Edition)
ISBN: 978-1-4262-0820-1

First edition: Edited and designed by AA Publishing (a trading name of Automobile Association Developments Limited, whose registered office is Norfolk House, Priestley Road, Basingstoke, Hampshire, England RG24 9NY. Registered number: 1878835).

Cutaway illustrations drawn by Maltings Partnership, Derby, England

Printed in China
11/TS/1

The National Geographic Society is one of the world's largest nonprofit scientific and educational organizations. Founded in 1888 to "increase and diffuse geographic knowledge," the Society works to inspire people to care about the planet. National Geographic reflects the world through its magazines, television programs, films, music and radio, books, DVDs, maps, exhibitions, live events, school publishing programs, interactive media and merchandise. *National Geographic* magazine, the Society's official journal, published in English and 33 local-language editions, is read by more than 40 million people each month. The National Geographic Channel reaches 370 million households in 34 languages in 168 countries. National Geographic Digital Media receives more than 15 million visitors a month. National Geographic has funded more than 9,600 scientific research, conservation and exploration projects and supports an education program promoting geography literacy. For more information, visit www.nationalgeographic.com.

For more information, please call 1-800-NGS LINE (647-5463) or write to the following address:

National Geographic Society
1145 17th Street N.W.
Washington, D.C. 20036-4688 U.S.A.

For information about special discounts for bulk purchases, please contact National Geographic Books Special Sales: ngspecsales@ngs.org

For rights or permissions inquiries, please contact National Geographic Books Subsidiary Rights: ngbookrights@ngs.org

The Library of Congress has cataloged the first edition as follows:
Library of Congress Cataloging-in-Publication Data
National Geographic Traveler. Great Britain.
   p. cm.
  Includes index.
  ISBN 0-7922-7425-3 (alk. paper)
  1. Great Britain—Guidebooks. I. National Geographic Society (U.S.) 11. Title: Great Britain.
DA650.N29 1999
914.104'859—dc21
                       99-11700
                       CIP

The information in this book has been carefully checked and to the best of our knowledge is accurate. However, details are subject to change, and the National Geographic Society cannot be responsible for such changes, or for errors or omissions. Assessments of sites, hotels, and restaurants are based on the author's subjective opinions, which do not necessarily reflect the publisher's opinion.

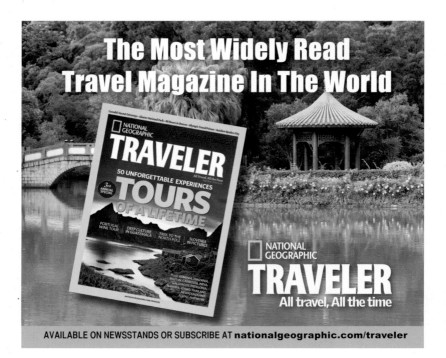